The Ryukyu Islands

James A. Millward, *Series Editor*

The Silk Roads series is made possible by the generous support of the Henry Luce Foundation's Asia Program. Founded in 1936, the Luce Foundation is a not-for-profit philanthropic organization devoted to promoting innovation in academic, policy, religious, and art communities. The Asia Program aims to foster cultural and intellectual exchange between the United States and the countries of East and Southeast Asia and to create scholarly and public resources for improved understanding of Asia in the United States.

A Chinese Rebel Beyond the Great Wall: The Cultural Revolution and Ethnic Pogrom in Inner Mongolia
T. J. Cheng, Uradyn E. Bulag, and Mark Selden   PUBLISHED 2023

Gifts in the Age of Empire: Ottoman-Safavid Cultural Exchange, 1500–1639
Sinem Arcak Casale   PUBLISHED 2023

Daemons Are Forever: Contacts and Exchanges in the Eurasian Pandemonium
David Gordon White   PUBLISHED 2021

The Compensations of Plunder: How China Lost Its Treasures
Justin M. Jacobs   PUBLISHED 2020

Geocultural Power: China's Quest to Revive the Silk Roads for the Twenty-First Century
Tim Winter   PUBLISHED 2019

∴

The Ryukyu Islands

∵

A NEW HISTORY FROM THE
STONE AGE TO THE PRESENT

Gregory Smits

THE UNIVERSITY OF CHICAGO PRESS
CHICAGO AND LONDON

The University of Chicago Press, Chicago 60637
The University of Chicago Press, Ltd., London
© 2025 by The University of Chicago
All rights reserved. No part of this book may be used or reproduced in any
manner whatsoever without written permission, except in the case of brief
quotations in critical articles and reviews. For more information, contact the
University of Chicago Press, 1427 E. 60th St., Chicago, IL 60637.
Published 2025
Printed in the United States of America

34 33 32 31 30 29 28 27 26 25   1 2 3 4 5

ISBN-13: 978-0-226-84319-3 (cloth)
ISBN-13: 978-0-226-84321-6 (paper)
ISBN-13: 978-0-226-84320-9 (e-book)
DOI: https://doi.org/10.7208/chicago/9780226843209.001.0001

Library of Congress Cataloging-in-Publication Data

Names: Smits, Gregory, 1960– author
Title: The Ryukyu Islands : a new history from the Stone Age to the
     present / Gregory Smits.
Other titles: Silk roads (Chicago, Ill.)
Description: Chicago : The University of Chicago Press, 2025. |
     Series: Silk roads | Includes bibliographical references and index.
Identifiers: LCCN 2025018547 | ISBN 9780226843193 cloth |
     ISBN 9780226843216 paperback | ISBN 9780226843209 ebook
Subjects: LCSH: Ryukyu Islands—History | Ryukyu Islands—Civilization—
     Chinese influences | Ryukyu Islands—Civilization—Japanese influences |
     Ryukyu Islands—Civilization—Korean influences
Classification: LCC DS895.R95 S646 2025 |
     DDC 952/.29—dc23/eng/20250729
LC record available at https://lccn.loc.gov/2025018547

♾ This paper meets the requirements of ANSI/NISO Z39.48-1992
(Permanence of Paper).

Authorized Representative for EU General Product Safety Regulation (GPSR)
queries: **Easy Access System Europe**—Mustamäe tee 50,
10621 Tallinn, Estonia, gpsr.requests@easproject.com
Any other queries: https://press.uchicago.edu/press/contact.html

For my wife, Akiko

Contents

Part Four

Naming Conventions

Names of people, places, titles, institutions, and so forth in the Ryukyu Islands typically have multiple possible forms and pronunciations. Although some activists insist that a certain pronunciation is correct, such assertions are problematic for a variety of reasons. In this book, as in all my previous writing on the Ryukyu Islands, I usually follow the pronunciations most commonly used in the Japanese-language academic literature unless there is a good reason not to do so in a particular case. Occasionally, primary sources give no indication of the pronunciation of a name other than the Chinese characters for it. In those rare cases, I use my best judgment to come up with a spelling.

In these pages, I use what I regard as the most common or conventional pronunciation for Ryukyuan terms, listing alternatives in parentheses if appropriate. If necessary for clarity, I employ the abbreviations *J., Ch., K.,* and *O.* for *Japanese, Chinese, Korean,* and *Okinawan,* respectively. Except for the most common place-names and the names of dynasties, all Chinese names and terms include (modern) tone marks along with Pinyin spelling. Korean words appear in the Revised Romanization system.

Premodern dates more specific than the year appear as "[Gregorian year].[lunar month].[day]." Therefore 1609.4.2 means "second day of the fourth lunar month, 1609," not "April 2." From approximately the 1880s, local dates accord with the Gregorian calendar.

The titles of Chinese government posts and officials follow those in Charles O. Hucker, *A Dictionary of Official Titles in Imperial China* (1985).

Introduction

The Ryukyu Islands is a history of the Ryukyu Islands from approximately thirty-five thousand years ago to the twenty-first century. Its content combines summaries of work that I have discussed elsewhere in greater detail with new research based mainly on primary sources and Japanese-language scholarship. The book is a critical reappraisal of the history of this region based on nearly forty years of study and research.

Although a general history, *The Ryukyu Islands* is likely to make significant demands on the attention of many readers. I would perhaps characterize it as a graduate-level textbook at its core. Two broad goals are to present an academically sound, up-to-date version of Ryukyuan history ca. 2024 and to provide a bibliography sufficient to facilitate more detailed study and research by interested readers. It is my hope that motivated undergraduates, scholars of East Asia, and motivated general readers with an interest in the topic will also benefit from *The Ryukyu Islands*.

Academic history can function as a database of human possibilities, a protocol for thinking about and describing important human interactions, and a lens through which to study social change. The Ryukyu Islands functioned as conduits through which people, culture, and technology spread among Korea, China, and Japan, and they were home to a succession of different societies. This book is not only a new history of the Ryukyu Islands themselves. It also sheds important light on the East China Sea region and topics in world history such as migration, agriculture, trade networks, identity formation, and more.

Actual human societies are complex and nuanced. Nevertheless, journalists and scholars focused on recent or contemporary matters often deploy highly simplified or idealized versions of the past in the service of social, identitarian, or political agendas. The Ryukyu Islands have been subject to this process since approximately 1650, the date of Ryukyu's first official history. In today's diverse and unfiltered media environment, all manner of historical Ryukyus proliferate. There is much that we do not know about the past of the Ryukyu Islands, and there are reasonable differences in interpretation between scholars, especially across different academic disciplines. The vast majority of popular and journalistic writing dealing with the Ryukyus invoke the islands' history, often in ways that are poorly informed or demonstrably incorrect. Even within the scholarly community of East Asianists, dated or superficial understandings of the Ryukyu Islands are common. My hope, of course, is that this book will contribute to more complex and nuanced understanding of the Ryukyuan past among scholars, motivated general readers, and perhaps some corners of journalism.

Common Misconceptions about Ryukyuan History and Major Arguments of This Book

Here I foreground some of this book's arguments by way of reacting to common misconceptions about the Ryukyuan past. In the paragraphs that follow, I state the misconceptions and briefly counter with the relevant arguments in this book. Subsequent chapters will, of course, expand on each of these points. I readily acknowledge that some of these misconceptions contain a grain of truth, the details of which become apparent in later chapters.

1. *The modern population of the Ryukyu Islands, people we could reasonably call "Ryukyuans," are descendants of a single, unbroken line of settlers who have resided in the islands since the Stone Age.* People lived in the Ryukyu Islands as far back as thirty-five thousand years ago. These Stone Age people, however, were not the ancestors of the islands' modern inhabitants. There were several breaks and discontinuities in the peopling of the islands, and the modern population descends mainly from waves of settlers from Japan who arrived during the eleventh and twelfth centuries. These settlers replaced an indigenous Jōmon population (hunter-gatherers) and brought Japonic languages and culture.

2. *The historical Ryukyu Islands constituted a natural, unified political community.* A strong central state centered at Shuri (overlooking Naha on the island of Okinawa) developed during the early decades of the sixteenth century. This state conquered most of the other Ryukyu Islands by military force and extracted taxes from them. At several points throughout the sixteenth century, forces from Shuri reconquered certain areas. In short, the

resulting "Ryukyu Kingdom" based in Shuri was a maritime empire. In this context, it is important to note that the island of Okinawa does not stand in for the Ryukyu Islands as a whole.

3. *Throughout most of their history, the Ryukyu Islands were isolated.* At certain points in the very distant past, the southern Ryukyu Islands appear to have been isolated. Otherwise, however, the seas around the islands connected them with the rest of the East China Sea region. From the eleventh to the sixteenth centuries, and to some extent during the sixteenth century, the Ryukyu Islands functioned as a frontier region, mainly but not exclusively of Japan. They did not become significantly isolated until approximately the 1620s, when shogunal policies and those of Satsuma closed Okinawa and the southern Ryukyu Islands off from the rest of Japan. DNA evidence indicates that genetic diversity in the Ryukyu Islands is similar to that in the mainland of Japan and other parts of East Asia, indicating that the Ryukyu Islands did not undergo long periods of isolation.

4. *Ryukyuan culture and history started in Okinawa.* The oldest extant human remains in all the Japanese islands were found in Okinawa. However, the history of Japonic Ryukyu did not begin in Okinawa. The geographic location from which people and culture from Japan moved into the Ryukyu Islands, starting in the eleventh century, was the northern island of Kikaijima. Eventually, the island of Okinawa came to dominate the rest of the islands. The narrative in the first official history, Shō Shōken's *Reflections on Chūzan* (1650), located Okinawa as the origin of Ryukyuan history and culture. Since the 1980s, however, archaeological evidence has undermined that narrative and many other points found in the official histories and many modern survey histories.

5. *Ryukyuan culture is, to a large extent, a blend of Chinese and Japanese elements.* Classical Ryukyuan culture from the period spanning roughly the twelfth through the sixteenth centuries came mainly from Japan but included a substantial Korean component. Stone-walled fortresses (*gusuku*) and sacred groves (*utaki*), for example, were of Korean origin. Therefore, the foundations of Ryukyuan culture are Japonic with some Korean elements in the mix. During the seventeenth century, some elite Ryukyuans began seriously to undertake the study of Chinese high culture in connection with government incentives to promote competence in Chinese

learning. Because of trade with China via the port of Naha, a few forms of popular culture from southeast China such as turtle-shaped tombs found their way into parts of the Ryukyu Islands. For the most part, however, Chinese culture was the preserve of a small number of Ryukyuan elites. Moreover, very few Chinese people ever settled into the Ryukyu Islands.

6. *Participation in the Chinese tributary system during the Ming and Qing dynasties meant that the Ryukyu Islands were Chinese territory.* Dozens of large and small countries participated in tributary relations with the Ming and/or Qing dynasties of China. The main reason was that doing so was economically profitable for the participants. Moreover, many monarchs of participating states used formal relations with the Chinese court to bolster their domestic prestige. In terms of size and frequency of embassies, Korea was the most vigorous participant in tribute trade. Okinawa was second. Participation in tribute relations with the Ming or Qing courts entailed ritual recognition of Chinese cultural superiority. It did not entail political subordination. At no time in the past were the Ryukyu Islands ever Chinese territory. Indeed, if past participation in tributary relations meant that a place was Chinese territory, Korea, Thailand, Vietnam, various parts of Central and Southeast Asia, and even Japan (insofar as some of the Ashikaga shoguns accepted and used the title *king of Japan*) would qualify as Chinese territory. Modern and contemporary claims by China that the Ryukyu Islands are or should be Chinese territory reflect China's contemporary economic and military power, not past historical reality.

7. *Prior to 1879, the Ryukyu Islands were an independent kingdom.* This claim is partially accurate. Shō Shin launched a series of military campaigns to conquer the island of Okinawa and most of the other Ryukyu Islands. The largest of these wars was the conquest of most of the Yaeyama Islands in 1500. By roughly 1530, a maritime empire, based at Shuri, had emerged. The Shuri Empire—more commonly known today as *the Ryukyu Kingdom*—was independent. That independence was short-lived. By the 1570s, the Shimazu lords of Satsuma began aggressively to assert hegemony over the Ryukyu Islands, requiring, among other things, that Shuri send embassies and gifts whenever a new Shimazu lord came to power in Kagoshima. Toyotomi Hideyoshi regarded the Ryukyu Islands as his possession, required them to contribute to his military campaign in Korea, and briefly gave them to his retainer, Kamei Korenori. In 1609, Ryukyu and Satsuma fought a brief war. Satsuma won decisively, and, from that point on, the Ryukyu Islands

became the territory of Satsuma. Depending on the definition of *independent*, the independent Ryukyu Kingdom existed from approximately 1530 to the 1570s or 1609. Thereafter, although a subset of the Ryukyu Islands posed as an independent kingdom to maintain relations with China, all the islands were in the possession of the Shimazu lords of Satsuma in Japan. The creation of Okinawa Prefecture in 1879 did not represent the annexation of an independent kingdom.

8. *The Ryukyu Kingdom developed independently of Japan.* The various iterations of the Ryukyu Kingdom developed in ways that were distinct from the main trajectory of Japanese history, mainly because of the physical environment. After the eleventh century, most of the people who settled in the Ryukyu Islands came from Japan, and the islands functioned as a frontier region of Japan. The local warlords who controlled the major harbors did business with entities in Japan, and there was a constant flow of people and goods between the Ryukyu Islands and the main Japanese islands until approximately the 1630s. During the early modern era, silver coins from Satsuma financed Ryukyu's tribute trade with China. The Ryukyu Islands were inextricably connected with Japan throughout most of their history.

9. *The Ryukyu Kingdom was a benevolent organization, and the Ryukyu Islands were a rare example in world history of a pacifist society without wars, weapons, or punitive coercion.* The myth of Ryukyuan pacifism is of European origin, part of a desire after the Napoleonic Wars to find some part of the world free from the scourge of warfare. The Ryukyu Islands were sufficiently obscure at the time that the myth of Ryukyuan pacifism could seem plausible to anyone unable to read the kingdom's official histories. Between approximately the thirteenth century and the early sixteenth, the islands were home to *wakō* (traders and raiders from parts of Japan and Korea), and these groups fought frequently for economic gain. Warfare during the period from the 1370s through the 1420s was especially intense, and several powers based at Shuri waged wars of conquest throughout the fifteenth century and the early sixteenth. Shuri extracted heavy taxes from the other Ryukyu Islands. Particularly severe were the extractions from the southern Ryukyu Islands from about 1650 on, which caused severe hardship to the people living there. Like other states and empires, the government at Shuri sought first and foremost to keep itself solvent and in power.

It is also important to bear in mind that, in islands other than Okinawa, the term *Ryukyu Kingdom* rarely has positive connotations. Historically, the kingdom was an oppressive, conquering force. The prefectural government today promotes a colorful, benevolent kingdom to attract tourists, but the historical memory of the kingdom in islands like Amami-Ōshima or Yonaguni is not positive.

10. *Most residents of the Ryukyu Islands opposed formal incorporation into Japan during the 1870s and 1880s.* By the time the government in Tokyo officially abolished the kingdom and established Okinawa Prefecture, it had become a failed state, at least with respect to its economic foundation. So severe was the tax burden that many ordinary people had come to resemble indentured servants. By 1879, the royal government had lost whatever popular support it might once have had. Government officials, however, protested the change vigorously, albeit passively. These officials refused to stay in their jobs until Japanese officials ensured that they would continue to receive salaries and other customary benefits. The losers in this arrangement were the ordinary people, especially in the southern Ryukyu Islands.

11. *The Ryukyu Islands were a colony of Japan.* When the government in Tokyo decisively moved to create Okinawa Prefecture in 1879, it deployed rhetoric about liberating the islanders from an oppressive regime. Oppressive it was, but Tokyo ended up extending the de facto oppression by keeping many of the kingdom's institutions of governance and taxation in place until 1903. Tokyo's overall goal, however, was for Okinawa Prefecture to function just like any other prefecture, and the residents of Okinawa Prefecture all became Japanese citizens. In practice, assimilation of the former kingdom was a difficult, painful process that required several decades to accomplish. Arguably, Tokyo treated Okinawa Prefecture poorly from the 1880s into the twentieth century, causing many scholars to liken the prefecture to a colony. Nevertheless, there was a fundamental difference between Okinawa Prefecture and the territories of Japan's colonial empire such as Taiwan or Korea.

12. *Many or most contemporary residents of the Ryukyu Islands are conflicted about their identity.* Most of the residents of Okinawa Prefecture and the other Ryukyu Islands located in Kagoshima Prefecture unproblematically regard themselves as Japanese and could not imagine any other national identity for themselves. Many of these people also embrace one or more local identities, a phenomenon common throughout Japan and much of the rest of the world. Intellectuals occasionally talk of Okinawan or Ryukyuan

independence, but what they often mean is a greater degree of regional autonomy. Survey data consistently show that, while only a tiny number of residents of Okinawa Prefecture advocate for independence from Japan, a plurality or a majority favor greater local autonomy vis-à-vis the central government. Moreover, a majority of residents regard mainland discrimination against Okinawa Prefecture to be a real phenomenon. However, complaints about rigid government bureaucracy or discrimination do not mean that most people in Okinawa Prefecture are confused about or frequently ruminate about their identity.

The Importance of Location

The Ryukyu Islands are poorly endowed with the kind of natural resources that typically made land valuable. Most of their soil is poorly suited to cereal-grain agriculture, sources of fresh water are problematic in many areas, and valuable minerals are rare. Iron is found in Kikaijima and Kumejima in the form of iron sand, but those resources were insufficient to meet the demand for weapons, agricultural tools, and other iron products. Why, therefore, did waves of Japanese migrants come to the islands starting in the eleventh century? Initially, they came to trade in valuable marine products such as the turbo shells used for making mother-of-pearl. Soon thereafter, many of the anchorages in the Ryukyu Islands became bases for groups of mariners who engaged in trading and raiding.

Although valuable marine products are found in many parts of the Ryukyu Islands, ultimately it was the islands' location that proved especially valuable. In premodern times, they were located within relatively easy sailing distance of China, Korea, and Japan. However, they were at the same time far enough removed from these places that, at least until the war of 1609, they were not vulnerable to encroachment by military forces of established states in the region. The many anchorages and limestone caves in the islands further added to their value as bases for *wakō*. The term *wakō* is commonly translated as "Japanese pirates," but that appellation describes only part of *wakō* composition and activities. Prior to the sixteenth century, most *wakō* were a mix of Japanese and Koreans (with Chinese replacing Koreans throughout the sixteenth century). While they often engaged in piratical activities such as marauding, smuggling, and human trafficking, they also functioned as merchants and agents of technology transfer. The Ryukyu Islands were an ideal location for *wakō*, and, during the fourteenth and fifteenth centuries, the port of Naha was a major hub of human trafficking.

In the modern era, the islands' strategic location contributed to the tragedies of the Battle of Okinawa and subsequent US occupation. Today, the islands are home to multiple Japanese Self-Defense Force and US military bases. Geopolitically, these bases function mainly to counter Chinese military power. Domestically, they are and long have been controversial.

Three Different Ryukyu Kingdoms

It is commonplace in discussions of Ryukyuan or Okinawan history to deploy the term *Ryukyu Kingdom* (J. *Ryūkyū ōkoku*), but there are two problems with it. First, its meaning is not obvious. More important, historically it does not always refer to the same basic entity. There were three different Ryukyu Kingdoms:

Kingdom 1: 1372–ca. 1500, a kingdom or multiple kingdoms for trade purposes
Kingdom 2: ca. 1500–1609, the Ryukyu or Shuri Empire
Kingdom 3: 1609–1879, a dependency of Satsuma that posed as an independent state

Kingdoms 1 and 3 were to a substantial degree theatrical states. In the context of all the kingdoms, it is important to bear in mind that the term *Ryukyu Kingdom* (and similar terms) was of Chinese origin. For the most part, Japanese and Ryukyuans used an entirely different set of terminology in describing both the Ryukyu Islands as geopolitical entities and the social positions occupied by elite Okinawans, including kings. Subsequent chapters examine these kingdoms in detail. What follows here is a brief summary.

KINGDOM 1: 1372–CA. 1500, KINGDOM(S) FOR TRADE PURPOSES

Multiple kings emerged in Okinawa during this era, with four de facto kings operating simultaneously during the last decade of the fourteenth century (one under the Sanhoku banner, one under the Chūzan banner, and two under the Sannan banner). The kings of this era were trade kings, and their Chinese title, *wáng*, was mainly a license to participate in the tribute trade with China. This participation also included substantial legal private trade for those who undertook the voyages to China. The Chinese title *king* also permitted properly credentialed Okinawans to trade with the Goryeo court in Korea. Japanese traders and *wakō* based in Kyushu or Tsushima often attempted to trade with the Korean court by posing as envoys of one or another Okinawan trade king.

It is not entirely clear whether all the kings of this era even actually existed. As we will see in more detail below, they functioned mainly as *names* under which official trade took place. That is why it was relatively easy for people outside the Ryukyu Islands to pose as envoys from one or another Okinawan trade king. Importantly, these kings did not control even the entire island of Okinawa, much less the other Ryukyu Islands. Their political control was typically limited to the port of Naha and the surrounding area. During the time of the first Shō dynasty in Okinawa (from some point in the 1420s to 1469), there was only one trade king at a time.

Kingdom 1 came about because of the antipiracy policies of the newly created Ming dynasty. The Ming court granted generous trade terms to local powers based at Okinawan harbors to entice them into formal tribute trade. These kings were leaders of trading-and-raiding groups. They were not the heads of centralized bureaucratic states. Some of them, especially Shō Taikyū, expanded their portfolio of trade harbors through conquest. Nevertheless, all the kings of the fourteenth and fifteenth centuries functioned predominantly as names under which official trade took place. Therefore, the Ryukyu Kingdom of this era was mainly a kingdom on paper, that is, a kingdom for trade purposes. It was not a kingdom in the usual sense of a bureaucratic state headed by a monarch.

KINGDOM 2: CA. 1500–1609, THE RYUKYU OR SHURI EMPIRE

Soon after Shō Shin consolidated his power in the late 1490s, he and his military forces burst forth in a series of conquests, starting with an amphibious assault on Ishigaki and other southern Ryukyu Islands in 1500. By the end of the 1530s, Shuri's military forces had conquered—and in some cases reconquered—all the northern and southern Ryukyu Islands. For the first time, all the islands were under the control—at least nominally—of the royal court in Shuri, which also controlled the island of Okinawa.

The royal court extracted taxes from this territory, and, with the help of Buddhist priests from Japan, it created a series of official state rituals. Kings Shō Shin and Shō Sei also established a formal hierarchy of female religious officials, many of whom were involved in carrying out the newly created rituals of state. Similarly, a formal hierarchy of male officials developed during approximately the 1530s through the 1550s, and Shuri sent out agents to reside in and administer the other Ryukyu Islands. Monument and temple construction was widespread during the first half of the sixteenth century,

TABLE I.1. List of official reigns of kings, trade kings, and quasi kings

Shunten line (舜天王統)		Second Shō dynasty (第二尚氏)	
Shunten (舜天)	1187–1237	Kanemaru (金丸)/	1470–76
Shunbajunki (舜馬順熙)	1238–48	Shō En (尚円)	
Gihon (義本)	1249–59	Shō Sen'i (尚宣威)	1477
Eiso line (英祖王統)		Shō Shin (尚真)	1477–1526
Eiso (英祖)	1260–99	Shō Sei (尚清)	1527–55
Taisei (大成)	1300–1308	Shō Gen (尚元)	1556–72
Eiji (英慈)	1309–13	Shō Ei (尚永)	1573–88
Tamagusuku (玉城)	1314–36	Shō Nei (尚寧)	1589–1620
Sei'i (西威)	1337–49	Shō Hō (尚豊)	1621–40
Satto line (察度王統)		Shō Ken (尚賢)	1641–47
Satto (察度)	1350–95	Shō Shitsu (尚質)	1648–68
Bunei (武寧)	1396–1405	Shō Tei (尚貞)	1669–1709
Sannan kings (山南王系)		Shō Eki (尚益)	1710–12
Shōsatto (承察度)	1380?–96?	Shō Kei (尚敬)	1713–51
[Royal uncle] Ōeiji[shi]	1388–1402?	Shō Boku (尚穆)	1752–94
(汪英紫[氏])		Shō On (尚温)	1795–1802
[Royal brother, king] Ōōso	ca. 1404–14/15	Shō Sei (尚成)	1803
(汪應[応]祖)		Shō Kō (尚灝)	1804–34
Tarumi (or Taromai) (他魯毎)	1415?–29	Shō Iku (尚育)	1835–47
Sanhoku kings (山北王系)		Shō Tai (尚泰)	1848–79
Haniji (怕尼芝)	1322?–95?		
Bin (珉)	1396?–1400?		
Han'anchi (攀安知)	1401–16		
First Shō dynasty (第一尚氏)			
Shō Shishō (尚思紹)	1406–21		
Shō Hashi (尚巴志)	1422–39		
Shō Chū (尚忠)	1440–44		
Shō Shitatsu (尚思達)	1445–49		
Shō Kinpuku (尚金福)	1450–53		
Shō Taikyū (尚泰久)	1454–60		
Shō Toku (尚徳)	1461–69		

Source: *Genealogy of Chūzan* and Ming records (for Sannan and Sanhoku kings).

and Shuri's military forces became well organized. For the first time, written documents came into use for domestic governance. These documents included writs of appointment for local officials and tax records.

Within several decades of taking the throne, Shō Shin and his allies had made Shuri the strong capital of a centralized state. This state ruled over a maritime empire that included all the Ryukyu Islands. Kingdom 2 was a *kingdom* in every sense of the word, and it also was an empire insofar as it conquered far-flung territories and subjected them to regular resource extraction. Part 2 of this book is about kingdom 2, which lasted roughly a century.

KINGDOM 3: 1609–1879, DEPENDENCY OF SATSUMA WHILE POSING AS INDEPENDENT

Kingdom 3 is the topic of part 3 of this book. The main turning point was the 1609 war between Shuri's empire and the powerful Japanese domain of Satsuma. Despite some fierce fighting in Tokunoshima and in the Shuri-Naha area, Satsuma won the war quickly and decisively. One result was that all the Ryukyu Islands became the possession of the Shimazu lords of Satsuma. The domain government of Satsuma directly administered the northern Ryukyu Islands, whereas Okinawa and the southern Ryukyu Islands remained under Shuri's administration. The main reason for this arrangement was to allow the tribute trade with China to continue, and much of this trade became financed by merchants and officials from Satsuma. Both Ryukyuan and Satsuma officials went to great lengths to hide the true nature of Ryukyuan dependency on Satsuma from Chinese eyes, thereby creating a fascinatingly complex theatrical state. The economic basis of kingdom 3 was agriculture, not trade. During the nineteenth century, agriculture came under severe strain, to the point of collapse in some areas.

Table I.1 provides a chronological list of kings, trade kings, and quasi kings.

Geographical Naming Conventions

Nomenclature connected with the Ryukyu Islands is confusing. Moreover, key nomenclature has changed over time. For example, the term *Ryukyu* (J. *Ryūkyū*) today typically refers to some or all the Ryukyu Islands. Until approximately the 1880s, however, in Japanese usage it meant the island of Okinawa. Moreover, in old documents, the equivalent term in Chinese, *Liúqiú*, sometimes referred to Taiwan.

Let us start in the present. Today, the Ryukyu Islands are most commonly called *Nansei shotō* (Southwest islands, 南西諸島) in Japanese. The term

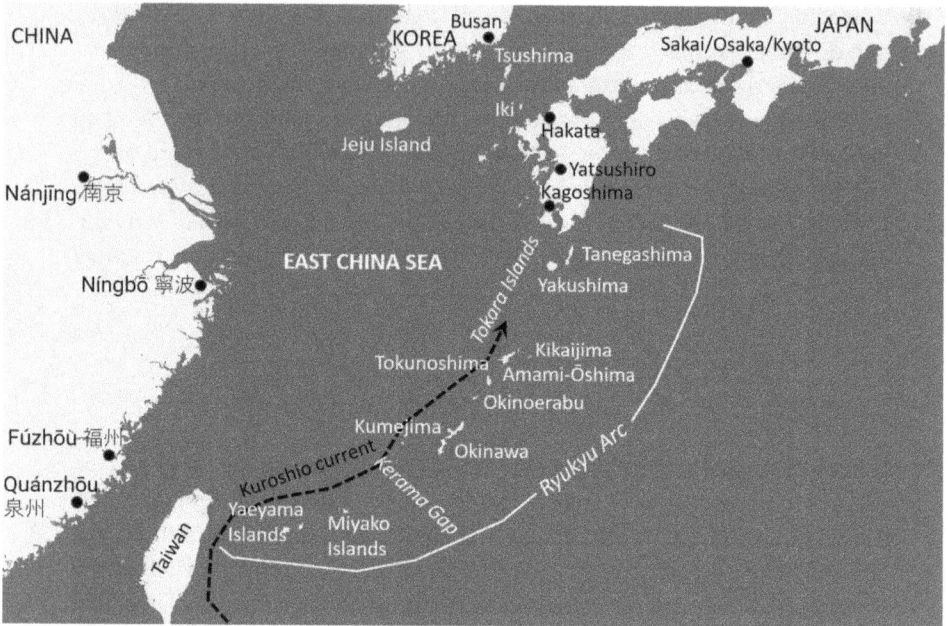

FIGURE I.1. The East China Sea region

Ryūkyū rettō (琉球列島) is also fairly common, and the term *Ryukyu-ko* (Ryukyu Arc, 琉球弧) puts an emphasis on the geology of the region. The Ryukyu Arc includes islands like Tanegashima and Yakushima that were never part of any political unit that included the Ryukyu Islands (fig. I.1). That said, the precise northern ending point of the Ryukyu Islands is uncertain in casual usage.

Generally, the small islands just north of Amami-Ōshima, which include Nakashima and Suwanosejima, are known as the Tokara Islands (*Tokara rettō*, トカラ列島 or 吐噶喇列島). Culturally, these islands have much in common with the northern Ryukyu Islands. In premodern times, they often appeared in maps under their Korean name, *Wasa*, or in its Japonic pronunciation, *Gaja* (臥蛇 and other characters). In premodern texts, the term *Gaja* typically meant the Tokara Islands, not just the tiny island of Gajajima (臥蛇島), which today is uninhabited. Another common term for these islands in premodern texts and maps was *Shichitō* (七島, lit. "seven islands"). The islands around them—Yakushima, Tanegashima, and smaller islands— are called the *Satsunan Islands* (*Satsunan shotō*, 薩南諸島).

In premodern times, the northern Ryukyu Islands, the Tokara Islands, and the Satsunan Islands collectively were often called *Michinoshima* (道之島), which literally means "islands constituting a road." It was possible to sail between Kyushu and Okinawa through this road of islands in good weather with one island visible from the stern and an upcoming island visible from the bow. This relative ease of navigation is one reason for frequent travel and exchanges between the Ryukyu Islands and the main Japanese islands (fig. I.2).

The Ryukyu Islands are a very long chain. I use the term *northern Ryukyu Islands* to indicate Amami-Ōshima, Kikaijima, Tokunoshima, Okinoerabu, and nearby small islands. In Japanese, these islands are often called the *Amami Islands* (*Amami shotō*, 奄美諸島). The term *central Ryukyu Islands* refers to Okinawa, Kumejima, and nearby small islands. The term *southern Ryukyu Islands* indicates the Miyako Islands, which are centered on Miyakojima, and the Yaeyama Islands, including Ishigaki, Iriomote, Hateruma,

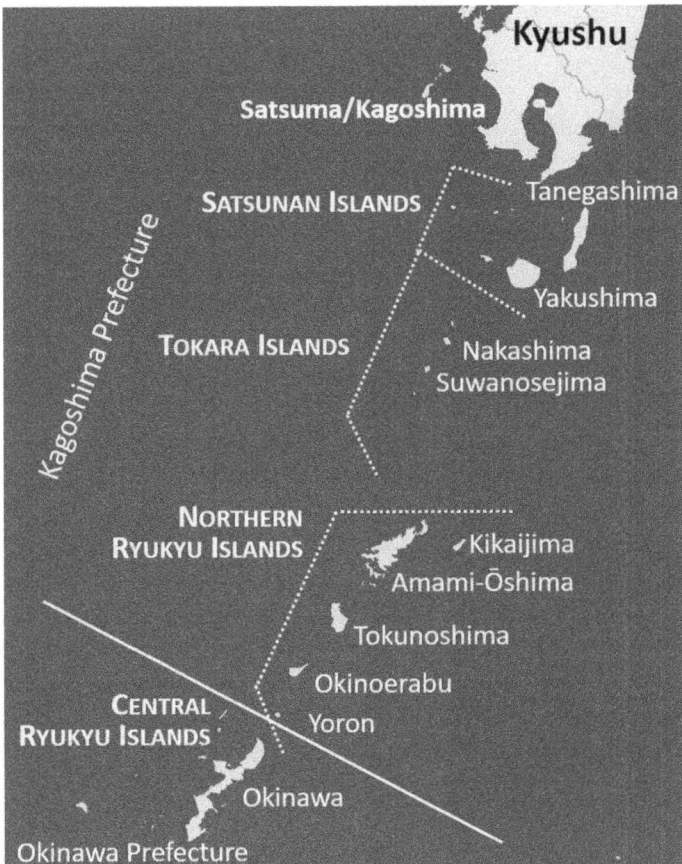

FIGURE I.2. The Satsunan Islands, the Tokara Islands, and the northern Ryukyu Islands

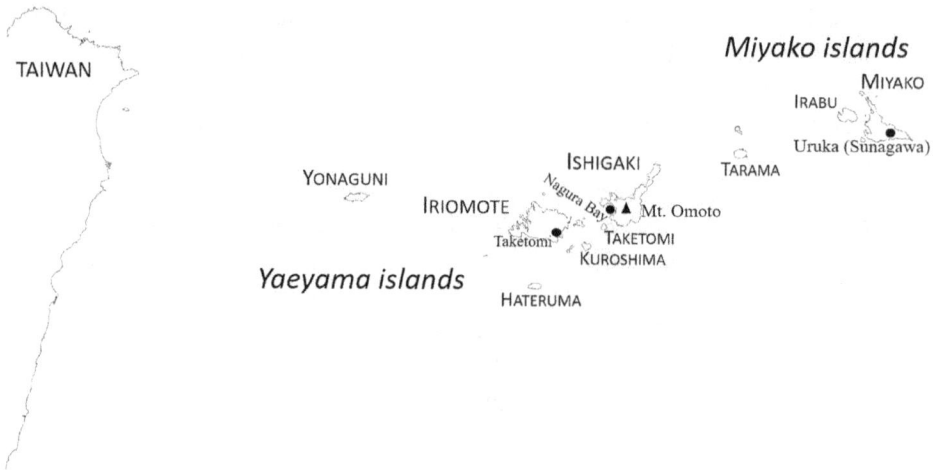

FIGURE I.3. The southern Ryukyu Islands

Yonaguni, and nearby small islands. In Japanese, the southern Ryukyu Islands are most commonly known collectively as *Sakishima* (先島) or sometimes *Ryōsakishima* (両先島) (see fig. I.3).

The term *Ryukyu Kingdom* is very common today in Western languages and Japanese. It was not typically used in premodern times, and, as briefly noted above, today it carries positive connotations only on Okinawa. A common premodern title for the king was *Ryūkyūkoku Chūzan ō* (琉球国中山王), but there were many other ways to refer to him. The term *king* is problematic in the context of Ryukyu's premodern past. It corresponds to the Chinese title *wáng* in connection with tributary relations and trade. *King* was never used natively in Okinawa, and the usual premodern Japanese term for such a person was *Ryūkyūkoku yononushi* (ruler of Ryukyu, 琉球国世の主). For reasons I have explained in detail elsewhere, the terms *king* and *kingdom* employed in connection with the premodern Ryukyu Islands are problematic and overused (see Smits 2024, 13–14, 30, 194–95, 201, 275 n. 18). As I have also argued elsewhere, the entity commonly called the *Ryukyu Kingdom* today was actually a maritime empire, and the terms *Ryukyu Empire* or *Shuri Empire* would therefore be more accurate (see Smits 2019, 161–92).

The term *Chūzan* can be confusing. According to the story in Ryukyu's official histories, from roughly the 1330s to the 1420s three territorial states existed on the island of Okinawa. This book casts doubt on that claim. Conventionally, however, Chūzan was the area of Okinawa that includes Urasoe, Shuri, Naha, and some adjacent territory. *Sanhoku* (山北)—or *Hokuzan*—refers to northern Okinawa and is roughly synonymous with the term *Kunigami* (国頭). Likewise, *Sannan* (山南)—or *Nanzan*—refers to the south of Okinawa below Naha and roughly corresponds to *Shimajiri* (島尻). Collectively, these three purported territorial states are called *Sanzan* (lit. "three mountains," 三山). However, in many contexts, especially after the 1420s in official documents, *Chūzan* often stood for the whole of Okinawa or even the entire Ryukyu Islands.

In these pages, and in my other recent books, I use *Ryukyu* as a relatively loose term of convenience. In my usage, it typically refers to the territory of Shuri's empire or the Ryukyu Islands as a whole. In Japanese and Chinese texts prior to approximately 1880, however, it always meant the island of Okinawa. In premodern Japanese documents, *Hon-Ryūkyū* (Main Ryukyu, 本琉球) or *Dai Ryūkyū* (Great Ryukyu, 大琉球) meant the island of Okinawa. Amami-Ōshima was sometimes called *Shō-Ryūkyū* (Small Ryukyu, 小琉球). In a Chinese context, *Small Ryukyu* often indicted Taiwan to distinguish it from Great Ryukyu (Okinawa). In today's Taiwan, commercial flights to Naha are flights to "Liúqiú" (Ryukyu).

In the Japanese court from the eighth century through the tenth, nomenclature involving the Ryukyu Islands was especially varied and complex (see Smits 2024, 80–83, 277 n. 7). The name *Okinawa*, referring to that island, dates back to this era, although it was written with a wide variety of Chinese characters. One common form was 悪鬼納, the first two characters of which mean literally "evil demon." During Japan's Heian Era, the island of Okinawa was often portrayed as home to cannibals.

As noted above, one problem with the term *Ryukyu Kingdom* is that it can refer to three different historical entities. As a term indicating political territory under the rule of a central state based at Shuri, *Ryukyu* as I use it would mean all the Ryukyu Islands from about 1520 or 1530 to 1609. Soon after 1609, the northern Ryukyu Islands were removed from Shuri's control and directly administered by Kagoshima, which is why they are part of Kagoshima Prefecture today. Therefore, from approximately 1609–1879, "Ryukyu" (i.e., Shuri's empire), as I use it here, indicates the central and southern Ryukyu Islands.

In older Anglo-European written works, *Ryukyu* often appears as *Lew Chew, Loo Choo*, or some other variant. Today, it is common for *Okinawa* to stand for all the islands of Okinawa Prefecture or even all the Ryukyu Islands. In these pages, however, it consistently refers only to the island of Okinawa in premodern contexts and either Okinawa Prefecture or the island of Okinawa in modern contexts. Each of the Ryukyu Islands has a distinctive history, and, as noted above, they did not constitute a natural political community. It is important, therefore, not to conflate all the Ryukyu Islands under the name *Okinawa*.

Historical Eras and Time Periods

We are currently undergoing a shift in the periodization of early Ryukyuan history because of new archaeological discoveries and an ongoing reinterpretation based on those discoveries. Offered below is a relatively simple periodization scheme, one that includes some traditional time periods/dates with modifications based on my ongoing research:

Prehistory (ca. thirty-five thousand years ago to the ninth century)
The Shell Mound/Shell Trade Era (ca. the ninth to the eleventh centuries)
The Early Gusuku Era (ca. the eleventh to the twelfth centuries)
The Later/Large Gusuku Era (the thirteenth to the fifteenth centuries)
    the Three Principalities (Sanzan [三山]) Era (1314–1420s)
    the Kingdom for Trade Purposes Era (1372–ca. 1500)
The Shuri Empire (ca. 1500–1620s); the Reduced Empire (1620s–1879)
    the wars of the early sixteenth century
    the 1609 War with Satsuma
The early modern era (ca. 1620s–1880)
The End of the Kingdom (*Ryūkyū shobun*) Era (ca. 1869–95)
Okinawa Prefecture (1879–1945); the preservation of old institutions
    (*kyūkan-onzon*) period (1879–ca. 1903)
The period of US occupation and rule (1945–72)
Okinawa Prefecture (1972–)

This relatively simple periodization will be sufficient for most of my purposes. However, occasionally I will need to make reference to more detailed chronologies. Table I.2 is a comparative chronology of the Ryukyu Islands and other parts of the East China Sea region. Refer back to it as needed.

Linguistic Geography

All Ryukyuan languages are part of the Japonic family. To say that languages belong to a family means that at one time—typically very long ago—they were the same language. For example, English, West Frisian (the closest living language to English), Dutch, German, Norwegian, and others are members of the Germanic family. French, Italian, Romanian, Spanish, and Portuguese are Romance languages (i.e., "Rome languages"), all derived from Latin.

FIGURE I.4. The Japonic languages and dialects

What is the difference between a language and a dialect? There is no clear or obvious dividing line. For example, are English and Scots (Germanic Scots, not Scots Gaelic) different dialects or different languages? If speakers of each were to meet and make an effort to speak slowly and clearly, they could communicate over a wide range. Therefore, most people classify English and Scots as dialects, not different languages. If speakers of English and West Frisian (spoken in Friesland, a province of the Netherlands) were to do the same thing, they would generally not be able to communicate even though their languages are very closely related. Simple phrases like *cup of coffee* (*kopke kofje*) might be understood but not full, complex sentences. Therefore, English and West Frisian are different languages within the Germanic family.

Figure I.4 maps out the Japonic language family. Notice that most of the different entities are classified as dialects. Many of these dialects are at least as far apart as are English and Scots and some farther. Somebody speaking full Tōhoku dialect, for example, or full Satsuma dialect (any of the several Satsuma dialects) would probably not be understood in Tokyo. Web searches can provide interesting audio examples of the various Japanese dialects and Japonic languages.

TABLE 1.2. Comparative time periods in Okinawa, the Southern Ryukyu Islands, Japan, Korea, and China

Approximate dates	Okinawa and vicinity	Southern Ryukyu Islands	Japan	Korea	China
Up to 8000 BCE	Paleolithic	Paleolithic	Early Jōmon (from ca. 12,000 BCE)	Paleolithic	Pre-Han
7000 BCE					
5000 BCE			Jōmon (to ca. 300 BCE), overlap with Yayoi		
3000 BCE		Early Neolithic/Shimotabaru (ca. 2500–1500 BCE)			
2000 BCE		Uninhabited (ca. 1500–800 BCE)			
1000 BCE	Early Shell Mound Era (ca. 7000–300 BCE) Trade in shells etc. (ca. 600 BCE–CE 1300)		Yayoi (ca. 1000 BCE–CE 300)		
300 BCE	Late Shell Mound Era (ca. 300 BCE–ca. 1050 CE)	Late Neolithic (ca. 800 BCE–1100 CE), no pottery		Ancient	
1 CE					Han (202 BCE–220 CE)
300 CE				Three Kingdoms: Goguryeo, Baekje, Silla (57 BCE–935 CE)	
550 CE			Kofun (to 538)		Sui and Tang (581–907)
700 CE			Asuka and Nara (538–784)		
800 CE			Heian (794–1185)		
1000 CE	Early Gusuku Era (ca. 1000–1250)	Suku (Gusuku) Era (ca. 1100–1500)		Goryeo (918–1392)	Northern and southern Song (960–1279)
1200 CE					
1300 CE	Later Gusuku Era (1250–1420s)		Kamakura and Muromachi (1192–1573) Northern and southern courts (ca. 1335–92 and later flare-ups)		Yuan (1271–1368)
1400 CE	Sanzan Era (ca. 1370s–1420s) and first Shō dynasty				
1450 CE				Joseon (1392–1897)	Ming (1368–1644)
1500 CE	Kingdom and empire (centralized state by ca. 1530)	Invasion of Yaeyama (1500), incorporation into Shuri Empire (ca. 1500–1520)			

1600 CE	Early modern era (control by Satsuma) Okinawa Prefecture (1879), land reform (1903), economic recession (1920s), Battle of Okinawa (1945)	Okinawa Prefecture (1879), land reform (1903), economic recession (1920s), malaria outbreaks and starvation (1945)	Edo (1603–1868)		Qing (1644–1911)
1700 CE					
1800 CE					
1900–1945 CE			Meiji (1868–1912) Taishō (1912–26) Shōwa (1926–89)		
1945–72 CE	US control of the Ryukyus, popular reversion movements, beginning of tourism	US control of the Ryukyus, popular reversion movements	Shōwa (1926–89), era of high growth (1960s–1980s)	Korean War (1950–53)	People's Republic of China (1949–)
1972– CE	Reestablishment of Okinawa Prefecture, military base problems, tourism	Reestablishment of Okinawa Prefecture	Shōwa (1926–89) Heisei (1989–2019) Reiwa (2019–)		

The Ryukyuan languages are closely related to Japanese and to each other, but they are mutually unintelligible. How many Ryukyuan languages are there? The chart shows seven, but some linguists would list more. In Okinawa, the Nakijin speech of northern Okinawa differs so much from southern Okinawan dialects that it would have been difficult or impossible to understand in Shuri or Naha, a point attested in some early modern documents.

When did the speech of the Ryukyu Islands and that of mainland Japan begin to diverge significantly? Analysis of the folk and religious songs in the *Omoro sōshi* collection (discussed below in greater detail) indicates a large overlap in vocabulary with Muromachi Era (1336–1573) Japanese. During diplomatic negotiations in 1570 between Ryukyuan envoys (a Buddhist priest and a government official) and officials in Satsuma (Kagoshima), the latter complained that it was very difficult (but not impossible) to understand the Ryukyuan envoys. Sailors from the Ryukyuan ship's crew served as interpreters. This suggests that, by 1570, the Shuri variety of Ryukyuan speech was becoming a different language from the variety of Japanese spoken in Kagoshima.

Interestingly, in the 1570 example, social elites had difficulty communicating, whereas at least some of the sailors were much better practiced in the region's dialects. That makes sense given their trade. Into the early seventeenth century, there are several documented cases of people from different parts of mainland of Japan residing in Okinawa for long periods or relocating there permanently, including one of a Ryukyuan official becoming a military officer in mainland Japan and participating in the siege of Osaka Castle in 1614. At that time, therefore, cultural and linguistic traditions in the Ryukyu Islands were not so different from those in mainland Japan as to be an impediment to migration and easy assimilation. After the 1630s, however, the Ryukyu Islands became relatively more isolated. Among other things, this situation accelerated the development of Ryukyuan languages on paths separate from those of mainland Japanese languages and dialects.

Although the various Ryukyuan languages are close relatives and share many similarities, prior to modern forms of education in the twentieth century, a person from Amami-Ōshima would not have been able to converse with an Okinawan, and an Okinawan would not have been able to converse with someone from Miyako. Today, standard Japanese is the common language of the Ryukyu Islands as well as all Japan. This situation is hastening the demise of many local languages and dialects, but a common language is undeniably beneficial for modern societies.

China and the East China Sea Region

As the region's wealthiest and most powerful country, China played a crucial role in the formation of Ryukyu as a political entity. It was a source of *wealth* for the islands and many other places. Nevertheless, it was *not* a major source of *people*. As we will see, people came to the Ryukyu Islands from a variety of places. However, except for a small community of Chinese merchant-officials near Naha and some later Mongol and Alan refugees from the Yuan dynasty, China was not one of them.

Similarly, China was not a major source of culture for the Ryukyu Islands until the late seventeenth century. Even then, it was a source of culture mainly for a subset of Okinawan elites. Owing to its size and wealth, China influenced early Ryukyuan politics, much as it influenced the politics of most other states surrounding it. That said, however, at no point in the past were any of the Ryukyu Islands Chinese territory, politically or culturally. This point is important to bear in mind in light of the challenges that Japan generally and the Ryukyu Islands in particular face today from an increasingly aggressive Chinese posture vis-à-vis the islands.

From the earliest known human presence in the Ryukyu Islands (roughly thirty to thirty-five thousand years ago) until about the 1620s, most of the Ryukyu Islands were not isolated. Therefore, they cannot be understood through time without reference to other places in the region. For the most part, these other places were maritime societies in and around the East China Sea. This region includes coastal areas of China, Japan, and Korea and major islands such as Jeju, Tsushima, and Iki (fig. I.5).

Structure of the Book

This book consists of twenty chapters, starting with a broad overview of Ryukyuan history and historiography. The remaining chapters are divided into four sections covering, respectively, prestate societies, the development and transformation of the Shuri Empire, the mature theatrical kingdom and its collapse, and the modern era.

The bibliography is a tool for further research. It includes all the material that I quote or cite directly plus material potentially useful for researchers. It includes a selection of major primary sources, a selection of useful internet resources, and a large but not comprehensive selection of the major secondary literature in Japanese and English. Missing from it

Korea

China

Japan

Ryukyu Islands

Island SE Asia

Maritime Silk Road

Major and Derivative

Flows of People, Goods,

Technology & Culture

through the Ryukyu Islands

FIGURE I.5. Major flows of people, goods, technology, and
culture throughout the East China Sea region and beyond

are secondary sources in Chinese and other languages. As of this writing,
Japanese-language scholarship is the main foundation for our understanding of Ryukyuan history, but Chinese scholarship on this topic is growing.
Material in English dealing with the Ryukyu Islands is vast, spread out over
a wide range of publications and highly variable in quality. The items in the
bibliography represent only a fraction of this material.

It is, of course, impossible to cover all Ryukyuan history in a single volume. Moreover, the practical demands of publishing impose a maximum
word limit on this project. I have published extensively on Ryukyu history,
covering time periods from prehistory through the early twentieth century.
Some of the contents of this book—especially the premodern material—are

revised condensations of previously published work. In the interest of brevity and readability, I have kept citations to a minimum and have left out some topics. I cite only direct quotations and some of the most innovative ideas. Brief introductions to each section identify the most important sources for the major ideas and arguments of those chapters. All translations into English from other languages are mine unless otherwise indicated.

CHAPTER ONE

A Broad Overview of Ryukyuan
History and Historiography

Shō Shōken's 1650 *Reflections on Chūzan* (*Chūzan seikan*) was the first official history sponsored by the royal court at Shuri and the first history of the Ryukyu Islands in any context. Subsequent official histories were two versions of *Genealogy of Chūzan* (*Chūzan seifu*, 1701, 1725) and *Kyūyō* (1745 and updated thereafter). Although these works all differ in terms of style, language, and content, they share some broad commonalities. They all place the island of Okinawa and the Shuri-Naha region at the center of Ryukyuan history, they arrange Ryukyuan history around royal reigns, and they place the formation of a centralized state much farther back into the past than contemporary evidence warrants. Moreover, they all reflect classical Chinese historiography, according to the standards of which the moral status of rulers is the main driver of history. Although modern historians rarely interpret history as a morality play, almost all have accepted the basic framing found in the official histories—problematically so, I have argued. Today, the official histories are regarded as primary sources even though in their own time they were secondary sources (based mainly on legends) for material prior to the sixteenth century.

The earliest generation of modern historians includes Majikina Ankō (1875–1933), Iha Fuyū (1876–1947), Higashionna Kanjun (1882–1963), Higa Shunchō (1883–1977), and Nakahara Zenchū (1890–1964). These scholars disagreed regarding specific facts such as whether Shunten was Okinawa's first king and whether he was the son of Minamoto Tametomo. They also differed in the way they organized Ryukyuan history and the types of sources they privileged. Nevertheless, all of them were influenced by the framing found in the official histories. More important, all of them regarded Ryukyuan history and the Ryukyuan people as offshoots of mainland Japanese history and the mainland Japanese. While acknowledging some influence of the physical environment on the islands' historical development, they tended to interpret Ryukyuan history as a late-developing microcosm of Japanese history. Therefore, in *Early Ryukyuan History: A New Model*

(2024), I characterize the dominant framework of Ryukyuan history between approximately the 1920s and the 1970s as *the ancient branch model*.

In connection with the 1945 Battle of Okinawa and its immediate aftermath, US research and information services compiled an English-language history of the region published under the title *The Okinawans of the Loo Choo Islands: A Japanese Minority Group* (Okinawa kenritsu toshokan shiryō henshūshitsu 1996, 1–148). This material became the basis for George H. Kerr's *Okinawa: The History of an Island People* (1958/2000), which has been and continues to be immensely influential in Anglophone circles. Both books supported US occupation authorities' policy of accentuating real or imagined differences between Ryukyuans or Okinawans and mainland Japanese. Kerr, especially, stressed Okinawan (Ryukyuan) exceptionalism in various forms. Perhaps most influential was his portrayal of the Ryukyu Islands as a pacifist paradise, a notion that remains prominent in journalistic circles and among some political activists.

By 1980, Okinawa and the southern Ryukyu Islands were firmly back within the Japanese state. Therefore, the need to counter US policy by emphasizing the close connections between the Ryukyu Islands and the Japanese mainland was no longer urgent. With Takara Kurayoshi leading the way, a new generation of university-trained historians began establishing a very different framework for Ryukyuan history. Stressing the distinctiveness of the Ryukyu Kingdom, they emphasized internal development, and I have called their approach *the internal development model*. While acknowledging that the people of the Ryukyu Islands came from Japan, these historians typically minimized the role of Japan in early Ryukyuan history. Instead, it was the island people themselves who toiled to create an impressive, distinctive kingdom. For these historians, Ryukyuan history was not a late-developing small-scale version of mainland Japanese history. It was a unique development. There were many differences in emphasis and interpretation among this generation of historians, but their general approach was new and exciting.

Neither the ancient branch model historians, nor Kerr and the US research and information services, nor the early internal development model historians had access to significant archaeological findings. Even as important archaeological discoveries and data accumulated during the 1980s and 1990s, few historians engaged it. Documentary sources for early Ryukyuan history are extremely rare (fig. 1.1). Therefore, nearly all these historians wrote speculatively about the ancient past, often repeating parts of the narrative found in the official histories. While the ancient branch model historians tended frankly to acknowledge the role of warfare in driving Ryukyuan

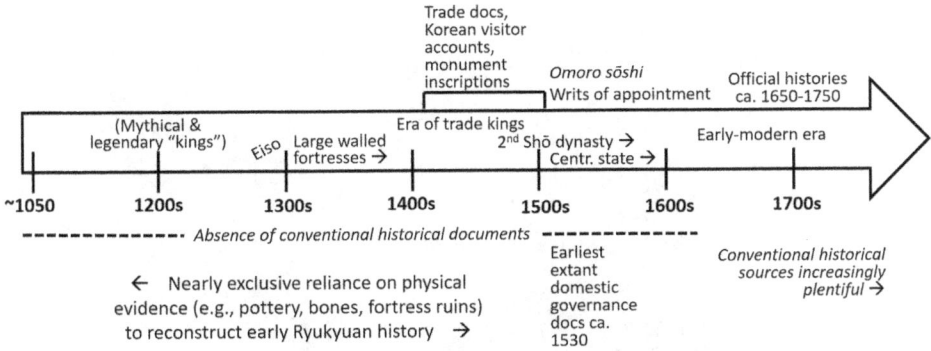

FIGURE 1.1. Major sources for Ryukyuan prehistory and early history

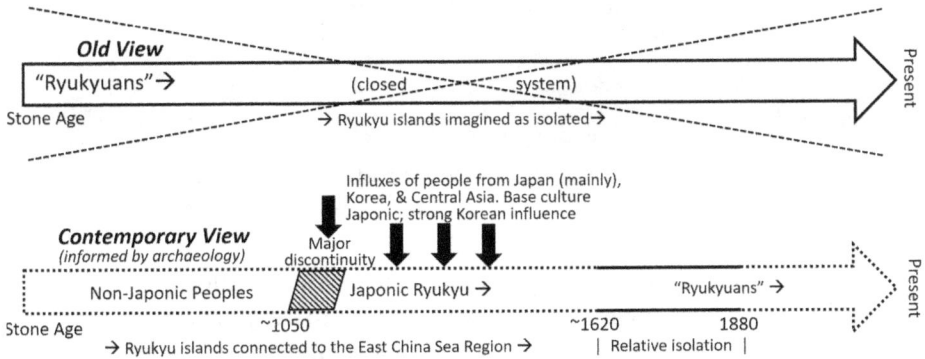

FIGURE 1.2. The older view of a single, continuous evolution of the residents of the Ryukyu Islands within a closed system contrasted with the contemporary understanding of a major discontinuity in the islands' population in the context of active exchanges with other parts of the East China Sea region

history, the internal development model historians, and Kerr even more so, minimized the role of warfare.

A tendency shared by all these historians was the assumption that the modern population of the Ryukyu Islands was the product of a single, unbroken line extending far back in time—either before the Common Era or as long ago as the Stone Age (ca. 20,000 BP–800 CE in Ryukyu). This view is still widespread even though archaeological, DNA, and other evidence clearly indicates a major discontinuity in the population during the eleventh and twelfth centuries. At that time, immigrants arriving mainly from Japan replaced the dwindling indigenous population of Jōmon people (fig. 1.2).

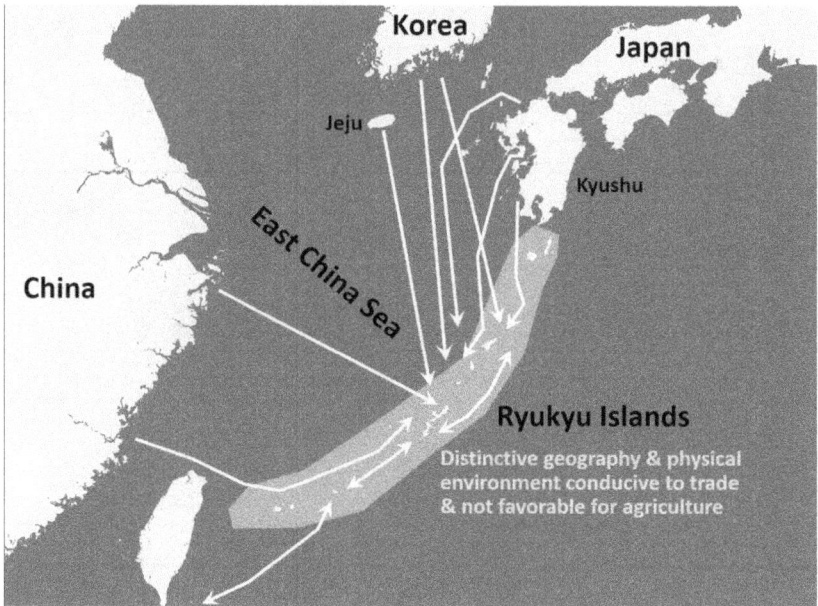

FIGURE 1.3. Illustration of my external agents model of early Ryukyuan history

Advances in archaeology have undermined the foundational premises of the internal development model with respect to early history. In *Early Ryukyuan History* (2024), I call for a new model for Ryukyu's ancient past, one based mainly on archaeology. I call it *the external agents model* because, until approximately the early sixteenth century, outsiders drove Ryukyuan history (fig. 1.3). By *outsiders* I mean people who arrived in the Ryukyu Islands from elsewhere in the East China Sea region. This new framework informs much of part 1 (chaps. 2–7) of this book.

Prestate Societies, ca. 35,000 BP–1490

A strong centralized state developed in the Ryukyu Islands from approximately the late 1490s through about 1530. What was the situation during the centuries and millennia prior to the emergence of this centralized state? Three excavations—in 1968, 1970, and 1974—from a limestone fissure in Minatogawa in southern Okinawa yielded skeletal remains approximately twenty thousand years old. Experts have put together two male and two female skeletons from these remains. We cannot draw conclusions about the nature of the human population from which these remains came because there were no assemblages of artifacts excavated along with the bones. Nevertheless, until recently many scholars and journalists assumed that the modern population of Okinawa descended from these Stone Age Minatogawa people.

From the 1990s on, many other human remains have been excavated, their age ranging temporally from the Paleolithic (Old Stone Age) period (ending ca. 8000 BCE) through the early modern era. Some of these remains have yielded valuable DNA evidence. As of this writing, it appears that all or most of the inhabitants of the Ryukyu Islands before approximately the eleventh century CE were Jōmon people. Many scholars have argued that the ancient, prehistoric people of the southern Ryukyu Islands were Austronesians, closely related to the indigenous people of Taiwan. It is possible that some Austronesian people did dwell in the Ryukyu Islands prior to the Gusuku Era, although we cannot be certain. Austronesian culture existed in the Ryukyu Islands, but it may have arrived there via trade or some other means of diffusion.

We know very little about the Paleolithic peoples whose remains have been unearthed at different sites. On the island of Okinawa, trade in seashells and other marine products started around 600 BCE and continued in some form until about 1300 CE. By roughly 1000 CE the population of Okinawa had dwindled. A century or so later, northern immigrants, mainly from Japan, began to swamp this dwindling population of Jōmon people. By about 1200 or 1300 (depending on the location), the population and culture of the Ryukyu Islands had changed from Jōmon to Japonic.

It does not appear that the southern Ryukyu Islands were in communication with Okinawa and points north until around 1100 CE or slightly later. The Shimotabaru Era in the southern Ryukyu Islands lasted from about 2500 to 1500 BCE, and the Shimotabaru people produced simple pottery. They were followed by a gap of roughly seven centuries during which the human population of the southern Ryukyu Islands either died off or left. Humans returned to the islands around 800 BCE, but they neither produced nor possessed pottery until the arrival of people from Japan. In other words, ca. 1050–1150 CE, all the Ryukyu Islands possessed a common material culture for the first time, a culture that spread along with the Japonic people.

These Japonic migrants came to pursue trade in southern islands products, many of which were in high demand in the Japanese mainland. With their arrival, the Ryukyu Islands became a frontier region mainly but not exclusively of Japan. Over the centuries, groups of traders, raiders, refugees, and others came into the Ryukyu Islands from Korea and the Korean island of Jeju. As the Yuan dynasty collapsed, Mongol and Alan refugees from coastal China made their way to northern Okinawa. The ancient

Ryukyu Islands functioned as conduits for people, goods, and technologies throughout the East China Sea region.

The Gusuku Era is named for the fortresses (*gusuku, suku*, and other terms) built throughout the Ryukyu Islands. There are hundreds of *gusuku*, many of which feature stone walls. By the fourteenth century, the political geography of the Ryukyu Islands consisted of harbor-fortress units occupied by groups maritime traders and raiders. Leaders of these trading-and-raiding groups are known as *aji*. Harbor-fortress pairs functioned as nodes of larger trading networks that often extended throughout the Ryukyu Islands, as far north as Japan and Korea, and as far south as coastal southeast China. Moreover, some groups of traders in the southern Ryukyu Islands sailed as far as Southeast Asia.

Agriculture emerged in the Ryukyu Islands at the start of the Gusuku Era and even earlier in a few places. Poor soil quality, mountainous landscapes, and other environmental constraints put limits on potential productivity. During the Gusuku Era, agriculture contributed to the food supply, but it did not generate surpluses sufficient to drive state formation. Maritime activity generated wealth, drove social change, and became the basis of state formation.

During the fourteenth and fifteenth centuries, regional trade and piratical activity increased. The Ryukyu Islands became the abode of *wakō* powers, and these powers competed for profits. Large stone-walled fortresses developed near some of the major harbors such as Naha, Nakagusuku, and Katsuren. By approximately the 1350s, and earlier in the southern Ryukyu Islands, powers based in Ryukyu harbors began trading directly with counterparts in China, transmitting goods between China, Korea, and Japan. Soon after the 1368 establishment of the Ming dynasty in China, private trade between groups in the Ryukyu Islands and Chinese merchants was made illegal but continued nevertheless.

In the late 1370s, the newly minted Ming dynasty offered lucrative terms to those Ryukyuan powers willing to trade with Chinese merchants via what today we call *the tribute system*. The basic idea was to make legitimate tribute trade so profitable for Ryukyuan powers that they would choose it over raiding and illicit trade. Moreover, specifically in the case of Okinawa and the deepwater port of Naha, bringing Ryukyuan powers into the Ming tribute trade became a way for favored Chinese merchants legally to evade the Maritime Prohibitions (Ch. *hǎijìn*) imposed by the dynasty on international trade. Ming officials and merchants gave Chinese ships to select Ryukyuan powers so that they could use them to conduct tribute trade. Because these ships were ostensibly Ryukyuan, they were able to trade in places like Southeast Asia and then bring those goods into Chinese ports under the umbrella of

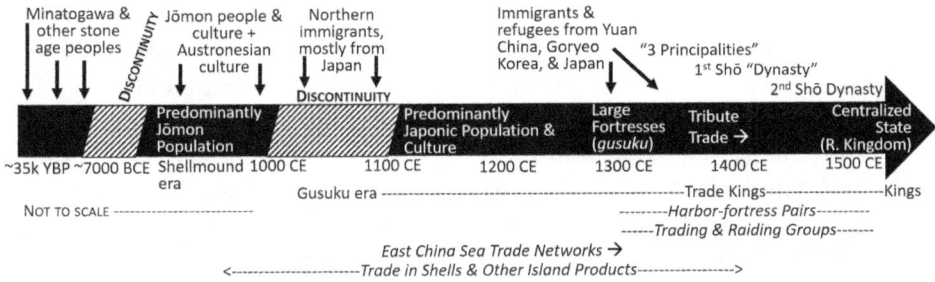

FIGURE 1.4. Major eras, discontinuities, and geopolitical developments up to the emergence of a centralized state during the early decades of the sixteenth century

the tribute trade. From about 1380 into the early sixteenth century, the port of Naha functioned much like a de facto shipping company whose main customer was the Ming dynasty and select Chinese merchants.

This tribute trade could be highly profitable. Technically, only people holding the Chinese title *wáng* could directly participate. *Wáng* is always translated as *king*, but the English word is misleading. Multiple kings sprung up in Okinawa after about 1380, but they were not the heads of bureaucratic governments. Instead, they were people or groups who held licenses to trade officially with China. They were kings for trade purposes, so I call them *trade kings*.

Chinese documents from around 1380 list a king of Sanhoku in the north, a king of Chūzan near Naha, and two royal lines in Sannan, somewhere in the south of Okinawa, also near Naha. There were four lines of trade kings, at least according to official documents, and the actual situation was even more complex. Tribute trade profits powered warfare in Okinawa as different powers sought to gain better purchases on the trade. Traditionally, the period from about the 1370s through the 1420s is known as the Three Principalities Era, but many more than three local powers participated in the trade and warfare of the era. By 1429, only one trade king remained in Okinawa, Shō Hashi.

Shō Hashi and his group, the Samekawa, were recent arrivals from the Yatsushiro area of Kyushu. Shō Hashi did not rule over the island of Okinawa, but his was the sole name under which the tribute trade with China took place. Okinawa and the other Ryukyu Islands still consisted of warlords at harbor-fortress units linked into maritime trade networks. Several trade kings followed Shō Hashi, some of whom seized control of the tribute trade by force. Although these trade kings were not all biological relatives, the official histories portrayed them as "the first Shō dynasty." It lasted until 1469 (fig. 1.4).

In addition to archaeological evidence and official Chinese and Korean records connected with trade, an important source for our knowledge about these early centuries of Ryukyuan history is a collection of songs called *Omoro sōshi*. The first volume of this collection, produced in the early 1530s, affords glimpses of life in the Ryukyu Islands during the Later Gusuku Era. These songs depict mariners engaging in warfare, celebrations, drinking wine, praising various maritime deities, and celebrating the power and wealth of various harbor-fortress units. *Omoro* songs typically depict wealth and power in sonic terms. Powerful *aji* such as the lords of fortresses like Katsuren are portrayed as "resounding" over a wide area. Indeed, some Okinawan *aji* were depicted as being so powerful that their power resounded and reverberated as far as the Japanese mainland.

Development and Transformation of the Shuri Empire, 1490–1630

Around 1470, a new group took control of the tribute trade at Naha and established a genuine dynasty of rulers, the second Shō dynasty. Its founder was Kanemaru, a seafarer who became the trade king Shō En. His death in 1476 precipitated an intragroup power struggle and the elevation of the twelve-year-old Shō Shin to the throne in 1477. Shō Shin eventually emerged as a militarily powerful ruler who gained control over all or most of the island of Okinawa. In 1500, he launched a massive invasion of the Yaeyama Islands. By the time of his death in 1527, he had forged a strong centralized state based at Shuri. This state was also a far-flung maritime empire consisting of all the Ryukyu Islands.

The next king, Shō Sei, continued the consolidation process, creating new state rituals, refining a new hierarchy of state religious officials, creating elements of a state ideology, bolstering the military infrastructure in and around the port of Naha, and reconquering parts of the northern Ryukyu Islands that had tried to break away from Shuri's control. The decade of the 1530s marks the approximate peak of Ryukyuan wealth and power. By the 1540s the wealth of the newly created kingdom had begun to decline. One reason was that the Ming dynasty began to relax the Maritime Prohibitions and therefore had less need for Ryukyuan shipping. Moreover, the Shuri Empire had become a legitimate state in the region, and it opposed piracy. The Ming dynasty therefore had little incentive to continue extending generous tribute trade terms to Okinawan powers.

The succession of kings in Okinawa during the sixteenth century was fraught with tension. By the 1550s, Ryukyu had come under strong pressure from the Japanese domain of Satsuma to cooperate in regulating trade in the port of Naha. In Shuri, some kings favored cooperation with Satsuma, and others resisted it. Shō Nei, from a collateral branch of the royal family, caused considerable turmoil when he came to the throne in 1587. After some prevarication, he eventually adopted a position of refusing to cooperate even minimally with any Japanese entity. This rigid position eventually led to war with Satsuma in 1609.

Although Ryukyuan military forces and infrastructure appeared strong on the surface, Shuri's armies lacked modern equipment and recent experience in large-scale warfare. Moreover, Ryukyuan officials under Shō Nei were deeply divided. Despite some fierce Ryukyuan resistance on the island of Tokunoshima and in the port of Naha, Satsuma's victory was swift and decisive. One result of the war was that the Ryukyu Islands became substantially cut off from Japan. Another was that all the Ryukyu Islands became the territory of Satsuma. Satsuma directly administered the northern Ryukyu Islands, but Shuri continued to administer Okinawa and the southern Ryukyu Islands. The main reason for this arrangement was to continue tributary relations with China. Throughout much of the early modern era, Satsuma underwrote many of the costs of Shuri's participation in the tribute trade.

During the seventeenth century and beyond, the Ryukyu Kingdom was subordinate to and dependent on the domain of Satsuma. It was not an independent country, but it posed as such vis-à-vis China and the larger world.

The Mature Theatrical Kingdom and Its Collapse, 1630–1880

After 1609, the king and royal officials quickly realized that the only thing preventing Satsuma from simply annexing all the Ryukyu Islands outright was their formal connection with China. Shuri therefore devoted significant resources to upping its game with China. The royal government arranged for the best and brightest of elite Okinawans to settle in Kumemura, the Chinese enclave in Naha, take Chinese surnames, devote themselves to mastering Chinese high culture, and serve as diplomats. Thus began the process whereby some Okinawan elites became highly proficient in Chinese culture.

Cooperating with Satsuma, the royal court also put into place elaborate measures to hide Ryukyu's connections to Satsuma from Chinese eyes. The Ryukyu of this era was a theatrical state, playing the role of an independent kingdom. Moreover, some elite Ryukyuans actively sought literally to perform Ryukyu via a new dramatic genre, *kumiodori*. Modeled on Japanese stage drama, *kumiodori* took real or imagined incidents from Ryukyuan history that both presented dilemmas to the characters involved and highlighted moral virtues. Visiting Chinese envoys were treated to *kumiodori* performances and commented favorably on them in their reports.

That Shuri's empire began to function as a theatrical state does not mean that the state was somehow unreal. It continued to exercise powers such as policing and law enforcement, taxation, and infrastructure maintenance. It maintained military capabilities to support the defense of tribute embassies to China. Shuri's demands for tax revenue profoundly shaped the lives of ordinary people in Okinawa and in other islands.

The two most prominent leaders after the war were Shō Shōken (1617–75) and Sai On (1682–1762). Although not kings, these high-ranking officials initiated a series of reforms of government and society. Shō Shōken revised many of the government's internal operating procedures. Sai On's reforms were more thoroughgoing, although not all of them were successful. He tried to increase agricultural efficiency, with mixed results, and created an effective system for the cultivation and preservation of forest resources. On balance, Sai On was able to bring about greater agricultural efficiency, albeit at considerable social cost. His efforts extended temporarily the viability of Ryukyu as an agricultural society.

The Ryukyu Islands are ideally situated for regional trade, but they are poorly suited to cereal-grain agriculture because of poor soil, minimal water infrastructure, malaria, typhoons, and saltwater intrusion. Trade declined during the sixteenth century and was greatly curtailed after the 1609 war. From the seventeenth century on, therefore, agriculture became the main economic activity in the Ryukyu Islands. Most of the grain produced went to Shuri as tax payments, and the population became increasingly reliant on sweet potatoes as their staple food. Starting in the late eighteenth century, natural disasters and declining agricultural production set the stage for economic collapse. By the time the kingdom formally came to an end in 1879, the majority of its people were impoverished, and Shuri enjoyed no popular support among Ryukyu's peasants.

During the seventeenth century, the histories of the northern Ryukyu Islands began to diverge from those of Okinawa and the southern Ryukyu Islands. In the north, becoming a formal part of Satsuma initially caused few changes in the lives of ordinary people. This situation began to change with the introduction of sugarcane. Sugar production had great potential for profit, and Satsuma's government in Kagoshima was always in need of funds. Eventually, Kagoshima made the northern Ryukyu Islands into a vast sugar plantation, with the peasantry forced to grow and harvest sugarcane under increasingly oppressive conditions.

In the southern Ryukyu Islands, the situation was similar. Shuri levied heavy taxes in the form of grain and cloth on the populations of the Miyako and Yaeyama island groups. Penalties were potentially severe for those unable to pay taxes in full, and abuses by government officials were rampant. The suffering under Shuri's crushing tax extractions during the early modern era remains a profound part of the folk memory in the southern Ryukyu Islands to this day. Sadly for the residents of those islands, the kingdom's tax system was not fully abolished until 1903. George Kerr's *Okinawa* (1958/2000) portrays Shuri's government as a moderate or even benevolent entity. Such a portrayal can be rendered plausible only by focusing exclusively on the urban elite and ignoring the suffering of the vast majority of the ordinary inhabitants of the Ryukyu Islands.

In the major urban areas of the Shuri-Naha area, scholarship, literature, and the arts flourished in elite circles. In addition to *kumiodori*, many members of the Kumemura elite produced Chinese poetry and cultivated certain aspects of Confucian culture and rituals. Nearby in Shuri, Japanese literature and culture flourished among elites. Some of this literary culture was critical of society and the state. When Heshikiya Chōbin (1700–1734) and other members of his literary circle attempted to undermine Sai On, they were all arrested and executed, with surviving family members banished to remote locations. The government in Shuri tolerated literary work vaguely critical of society, but it did not tolerate direct challenges to its rule.

Toward the end of the eighteenth century and into the early nineteenth, the royal court at Shuri reached its mature form. The government consisted of a relatively complex bureaucracy, one developed mostly in an ad hoc manner. The court promulgated and revised comprehensive law codes and created a basic school system for the Shuri-Naha urban area. This system culminated in a national academy and the principle that government officials should be selected on the basis of merit. However, the problems with agriculture mentioned previously prevented the new school system from having much of an effect.

By the 1840s, agricultural productivity began to decline extensively. Poverty spread, and royal government revenue fell. Much of the 1860s saw severe inflation. In the meantime, economic and other forms of unrest were beginning to manifest themselves in the Japanese mainland. One result was the creation of a new government in 1868, ostensibly headed by the Meiji emperor. The newly minted Meiji state faced a series of domestic and foreign challenges and was chronically short of revenue. One urgent order of business was to protect Japan from imperialist encroachment, and one part of this process was the clarification of Japan's northern and southern boundaries.

The Ryukyu Islands had been Japanese territory in a formal sense since 1609, and they had functioned as a frontier region of Japan for centuries prior to that. The post-1609 arrangement was convoluted. First, the islands were the territory of Satsuma, not under the direct control of Edo/Tokyo. Second, Okinawa and the southern Ryukyu Islands had been performing the role of an independent state. This posturing took place vis-à-vis not only China but also other countries. Indeed, the royal court signed simple treaties with the United States, Britian, and France. In the early modern era, theatrical states like Ryukyu were viable within the prevailing norms of East Asia. However, in an era dominated by Western notions of sovereignty, Ryukyu's theatrical state was no longer feasible.

In the early 1870s, officials in Tokyo debated the best strategy for dealing with the Ryukyu Islands. A majority view understood that the strategic position of the islands made it imperative that the government in Tokyo formally and publicly incorporate them into its territory. Not surprisingly, the king and his officials resisted the change to whatever degree they could—mainly by obfuscation and repeatedly petitioning Tokyo to continue the present system. In 1879, Tokyo announced the end of the kingdom and the establishment of Okinawa Prefecture in its place.

The Modern Era, 1880–2024

One of Tokyo's arguments for abolishing the kingdom was that the royal government was an oppressive force and that the people of the islands would benefit from a modern form of government. There was merit to this argument. However, the actual governance of Okinawa Prefecture during the final decades of the nineteenth century indicates that the welfare of the people was not a high priority for Tokyo. Immediately after the kingdom's abolition in 1879, Tokyo's representatives ordered former royal officials to continue performing their duties. Initially, they refused. Despite the high-principled rhetoric, these officials were concerned with maintaining their wealth, power, and traditional privileges. Once Tokyo agreed to preserve traditional governing practices, albeit for a limited time, most former officials willingly cooperated.

This expedient policy of preserving government and tax practices from the days of the kingdom is known as *kyūkan-onzon*, often translated rather literally as "preserving old customs." The late 1870s and the 1880s were a time of especially strong interest in and disputes over culture within urban areas of Japan, the so-called era of civilization and enlightenment (*bunmei kaika*). In Okinawa Prefecture, especially among urban residents, matters of culture became an obsession. Cultural tension and debate over what it meant to be Okinawan (or Ryukyuan) and what it meant to be Japanese were a prominent part of life in Okinawa Prefecture throughout the nineteenth century and well into the twentieth. It is important to keep in mind that Japan as a whole was undergoing a profound, often jarring transition at this time. The peculiar circumstances of Okinawa Prefecture, its poverty, and the degree of cultural differences between Okinawa and other parts of Japan tended to amplify the difficulties inherent in this transition.

Schools and other institutions in the newly minted prefecture inculcated two simultaneous identities, both of which were new for most people. One the one hand, the prefecture's residents were told that they were Ryukyuan or Okinawan. Although Ryukyuan elites had been conscious of a Ryukyuan identity since the late seventeenth century, Ryukyu or Okinawa was an abstraction for ordinary people, who typically identified with their village or, at the broadest, their district. At the same time that ordinary people became Ryukyuans, they also became Japanese. Moreover, the official rhetoric and policies put these identities into opposition.

Not surprisingly, such an environment was rife with debate, confusion, and mixed messages. Several Okinawans who received high-powered educations in mainland schools became public intellectuals, the most prominent among them being Iha Fuyū and Ōta Chōfu (1865–1933). These intellectuals attempted to create and reconcile Okinawan/Ryukyuan, Japanese, and modern identities. They also advocated schemes for reducing the prefecture's poverty. The blunt force of economic reality often thwarted idealistic programs advocated by public intellectuals.

Sugar became a valuable commodity during the eighteenth century, and, eventually, as much as 60 percent of tax revenue from within Okinawa came from village-level sugar production. Sugar was a royal monopoly that benefited select merchants and officials in Okinawa and Kagoshima. During the modern era the cultivation of sugarcane and the production of sugar became the prefecture's main industry. It was potentially lucrative, but there were several variables affecting profits, including relative efficiencies, scale, regional competitors, and fluctuating market prices. During the years of World War I and shortly thereafter, world sugar prices were high, and Okinawa's economy was in relatively good shape. Those prices peaked in early 1920, then collapsed and remained low. Moreover, Japan's economy went into recession during the mid-1920s. These developments in the context of Okinawa's heavy dependence on sugar resulted in severe poverty and food shortages that came to be called *the sago palm hell* (*sotetsu jigoku*). The name suggests that some islanders were driven by desperation to eat the fruit of the sago palm (*Cycas revoluta*), which was unpalatable and even poisonous if not carefully prepared.

The era of the sago palm hell lasted from the early 1920s into the 1930s. Among its local effects was a vast increase in emigration from Okinawa Prefecture to major cities in mainland Japan, to Taiwan and other Japanese colonies, and to foreign countries such as the United States (especially Hawaii) and Brazil. Although some emigration had taken place prior to the 1920s, the worldwide Okinawan diaspora is largely the result of the subsequent economic depression. The situation resulted in the partial modernization of agriculture in Okinawa Prefecture, including the introduction of new varieties of rice and sweet potatoes. Economic difficulties also affected public intellectual and policy discourse. A discouraged Iha Fuyū, for example, turned from contemporary activism to technical scholarship in the fields of linguistics and history. His vast academic output from this era set the stage for subsequent work in Ryukyuan history.

During the 1930s, as Okinawa Prefecture slowly recovered economically, a generation of prominent literary figures emerged, including the poets Iba Nantetsu (伊波南哲, 1902–76) and Yamanokuchi Baku (山之口貘, 1903–63 [Yamaguchi Jūsaburō (山口重三郎)]) and the novelist Kushi Fusako (久志芙沙子, 1903–86). Rooted in both local and mainstream Japanese culture, these writers drew on local traditions and the interplay of layered identities to produce outstanding poetry, novels, and other literature.

Japan increasingly shifted to a war footing. By 1939, Japanese armies were bogged down in an unwinnable "incident" (read full-scale war) in China. Circumstances connected with Tokyo's attempts to subdue China eventually led to war with the United States and the United Kingdom at the end of 1941. Other than hoping for an early negotiated settlement to the war, Japan's planners lacked a coherent strategy for winning or ending the conflict. In this context, the strategically important position of the Ryukyu Islands set the stage for disaster for the people of Okinawa and several other islands.

The main Battle of Okinawa began on April 1, 1945. Nearly three months later, when the battle wound down, the civilian population was devastated. Nearly all the urban areas of southern Okinawa were reduced to rubble, and vast numbers of Okinawan survivors were homeless. Soon after the end of the war in August, former residents of Okinawa Prefecture who had been working in Japan's colonies began returning to a war-ravaged land. The US military established camps for civilian survivors and returnees and began to rebuild basic infrastructure. Eventually, the camps emptied, and a rudimentary civil government began operation. Okinawa Prefecture was not reestablished until 1972.

Okinawa and the southern Ryukyu Islands were under US military occupation between the summer of 1945 and May 1972. During that time, the specific details of government and civil administration frequently changed. While there were some early material benefits to US rule, most Okinawans quickly tired of life under foreign occupation. By the end of the 1950s, the Okinawan public coalesced around the demand for reversion to Japanese sovereignty. During the 1960s, the reversion movement often manifested itself in mass protests.

The re-creation of Okinawa Prefecture in 1972 was a relatively subdued event because it failed to resolve the major problem in the minds of many Okinawans: the continued presence of US military bases. That continues to this day, and Japanese military forces have recently moved into the Ryukyu Islands in greater numbers to counter Chinese military buildup in the region.

Starting in the 1950s, tourism developed in Okinawa and expanded steadily thereafter. Initially, it focused on war-related memorials and battle sites. Given the semitropical climate of the Ryukyu Islands, general recreational tourism expanded from the 1970s on. Okinawa and other Ryukyu Islands became a domestic alternative to Hawaii and began to attract visitors from other locations in Asia. With the reconstruction of Shuri Castle, which had been destroyed in 1945, Okinawan tourism began to promote a colorful and highly idealized Ryukyu Kingdom to attract visitors. Today, tourism is the foundation of the prefecture's economy, and agriculture occupies a secondary or tertiary position.

Despite some portrayals in Anglophone media and the voices of a tiny number of activists in Okinawa, Hawaii, and elsewhere, the vast majority of the prefecture's residents readily embrace Japanese identity—as they have for several generations. Surveys consistently show that only 2–4 percent of respondents indicate a preference for independence from Japan. However, a much larger number of respondents want greater autonomy for the prefecture vis-à-vis heavy-handed central government bureaucracies. Moreover, many prefectural residents regard the disproportionate presence of military bases—especially the US presence—as a de facto form of discrimination on the part of mainland residents.

In terms of per capita income and other measures, Okinawa remains Japan's poorest prefecture, although living standards have risen steadily since the 1970s. Moving into the future, many challenges remain, including economic diversification and environmental degradation. The broader geopolitics of the region are relatively tense. Although in surveys the majority of residents of Okinawa Prefecture report a distrust for China, there is less agreement about the ideal response to geopolitical tensions. Many residents support Japan's expansion of military bases in the islands, but others argue that these facilities make the islands more of a target. The large US military presence remains a source of tension, especially the construction of a marine air base at Henoko in northern Okinawa.

PART ONE

PRESTATE SOCIETIES, 35,000 BP–1490

Between the late 1490s and roughly 1530, a state centered at Shuri came to control all the Ryukyu Islands. Developments prior to this time within the Ryukyu Islands are poorly understood outside a small circle of academic specialists. The chapters in this section explain, insofar as possible, who lived in which parts of the Ryukyu Islands, the nature of early societies in the islands, the Japonic transformation of the islands starting in the eleventh century, and the rise of local trading-and-raiding powers based at harbor-fortress units. A final chapter examines some iconic manifestations of classical Ryukyuan culture, several of which are of Korean origin.

Some Japanese, Chinese, and Korean primary sources that shed limited light on the fourteenth and fifteenth centuries. They appear in the bibliography as *Goryeo History* (2005), Harada (2004), *Joseon Veritable Royal Records* (2005, n.d.), *Ming Veritable Records* (2001–6), *Rekidai hōan* (1994–2022), Sin (1471/1991), and *Suíshū "Liúqiúguó"* (636). The most important domestically produced source for understanding the situation within the Ryukyu Islands is the song collection *Omoro sōshi*. For the most part, however, our understanding of this era comes from the physical evidence unearthed by archaeologists. Physical anthropology (especially DNA evidence), cultural anthropology, and historical linguistics are important supporting disciplines.

I have written extensively about most of the topics in this section. Especially important are the books *Maritime Ryukyu, 1050–1650* (Smits 2019) and *Early Ryukyuan History: A New Model* (Smits 2024). They detail the evidence for all my arguments, the sources for that evidence, and the scholars on whose work I rely. These books—especially *Early Ryukyuan History*—provide extensive citations to archaeological field reports. Because new work in archaeology appears frequently, interested readers should make use of the Comprehensive Database of Archaeological Site Reports in Japan to keep abreast of new developments. Those seeking an overview of the relevant archaeology in English should start with Pearson (2013) and the work of Mark Hudson.

The following works by other scholars are of particular importance for informing my understanding: Akamine (1988), Asato (2010), Doi (1998, 2018), Eguchi (2006), Fuku (2008, 2013), Hudson (2020, 2022a, 2022b), Ikeda (2012, 2019), Ikuta (1984a, 1992), Inamura (1957), Jaroz et al. (2022), Kinoshita (1996, 2003), Korea Fortress Academy (2007), Kurima (2013), Mamiya (2014), Murai (2019), Naka (1992), Ōhama (2008), Okamoto (2008, 2010), Okaya (2019), Pearson (2013), Pellard (2015), Robbeets et al. (2021), Robinson (1997, 2000a, 2000b, 2001), Seto (2019), Shimoji (2008), Shinzato Akito (2018), Shinzato Takayuki (2010, 2018), Takahashi (2008), Takamiya (2005, 2018), Takanashi (2008, 2015), Tanaka (2012), Tanigawa (2007, 2008), Tanigawa and Orikuchi (2012), Tōma (2012), Uema (2018), Uezato and Yamamoto (2019), Yamazato (2012), Yano (2014), Yoshinari (2008, 2018, 2020), Yoshinari and Fuku (2006, 2007), and Yoshinari, Takanashi, and Ikeda (2015).

Among the major books in English, the relevant portions of Akamine (2017) and Kerr (1958/2000) are not reliable guides for this era. For more details about the major Anglophone books and their approaches to early Ryukyuan history, see Smits (2024, 47–51).

Most modern and contemporary Japanese accounts dealing with this era—often in the context of survey histories—rely to a problematic degree on the narrative in the official histories. It is important to bear in mind that Ryukyu's official histories were secondary sources at the time of their creation. They reflect the values, outlook, and issues of the seventeenth and eighteenth centuries, and their coverage of events before the sixteenth century is based mainly on legends. Legends often do encode past events, but they are not an ideal source. *Maritime Ryukyu* was in part an attempt to write a history of early Ryukyu without relying on the official histories for material before the sixteenth century. *Early Ryukyuan History* continues that project, although there I make slightly greater use of the official histories, sometimes reading them against the grain for clues.

[CHAPTER TWO]

First Peoples

The Earliest Inhabitants of the Ryukyu Islands

Who were the first people to dwell in the Ryukyu Islands? Ultimately, we cannot say. Modern humans (*Homo sapiens sapiens*) left Africa roughly seventy thousand years ago and gradually spread out across the globe, reaching East Asia about forty-five thousand years ago. Prehistoric people were highly mobile. As the genetic anthropologist David Reich points out: "Human history is full of dead ends, and we should not expect the people who lived in any one place in the past to be the direct ancestors of those who live there today" (2018, 90). This point applies to the Ryukyu Islands.

Before the early 1980s, the physical evidence for prehistoric human settlements in the Ryukyu Islands was so sparse that there was ample room for pure speculation. The first generation of modern scholars of the Ryukyu Islands typically imagined a group of people called *Ryukyuans* (or *southern islanders* or other terms) to have existed as a singular ethnic group for as long as people lived in the Ryukyu Islands. We now know that this view is inaccurate. Different groups of people came into different parts of the Ryukyu Islands at different times, and many of them left or died out. The modern population of the islands derives mainly from waves of migrants who arrived during the eleventh and twelfth centuries.

This chapter establishes a foundation for the study of Ryukyuan history and culture by surveying the peoples of the Ryukyu Islands prior to the massive migrations from the north during the Early Gusuku Era. In other words, it examines the pre-Japonic Ryukyu Islands.

Earliest Human Remains

In 1968, the oldest human remains in all the Japanese islands were discovered in a cave in Naha, Okinawa. They were two fossilized pieces of leg bone, roughly thirty-two to thirty-six thousand years old, from a girl of about eight or nine years of age. Obviously, this girl had parents, so she was not the oldest human inhabitant of the Ryukyu Islands (unless she washed ashore, but other bones have been found in the cave). What sort of person was she? From where did she and her group come? For how long did they dwell in Okinawa? We do not know.

In 2003 and 2024, archaeologists discovered hearth remains and fire traces made by humans at the Futenma-gū (Futenma Shrine) cave site in central Okinawa. The charcoal layer is over thirty thousand years old. In 2024, bones were discovered at the site. As of this writing, excavation of the site and analysis of the findings are in the early stages, and work will probably continue for years.

Between 1974 and 1989, bone fragments were excavated from the Pinza-Abu cave site in Miyako Island, enabling the reconstruction of part of a skull. The remains are about thirty thousand years old, but otherwise we lack concrete knowledge of the Pinza-Abu caveman's life or origins.

The next discovery of Stone Age remains came along about fourteen years later. In 1982, Suzuki Hisashi of Tokyo University and his team announced the results of excavations in a limestone quarry in Minatogawa, south of Naha. They had found a large quantity of human bones in a vertical fissure along with a variety of animal bones and other ancient refuse. They managed to construct four nearly complete skeletons, two male, two female, with a few bones left over. Dating of these human remains indicated that they were roughly twenty to twenty-two thousand years old. Scholars debate the role of these Minatogawa people. Were they a very early precursor of the Jōmon people who eventually dwelled throughout the Japanese islands? Were they Melanesian or Austronesian people from Southeast Asia? Or were they members of some other human population? In the 1980s, some people speculated that the modern populations of Okinawa or other Ryukyu Islands were direct descendants of Minatogawa people. The massive accumulation of archaeological and other data since then has ruled out this possibility.

In 2007, human remains were discovered in a limestone cave in Ishigaki Island. Subsequently the Shiraho Saonetabaru cave ruins have yielded over one thousand fragments of human remains, several of which have been dated to approximately twenty to twenty-four thousand years ago. This site appears to have been a graveyard, but, as with the other Paleolithic remains mentioned above, the origins and lifestyles of these people are unknown. It is important to emphasize that there is no evidence that any of the Paleolithic people discovered in the Ryukyu Islands are ancestors of present populations.

Although it may be interesting to speculate about human remains far in the past, bones and bone fragments alone are unlikely to reveal even a rough picture of life in the Ryukyu Islands twenty or thirty thousand years ago. For that we need a wider array of physical evidence such as pottery, tools, and other objects connected with human settlements.

Earliest Human Communities

The dates for the end of the Paleolithic and the start of the Neolithic (New Stone Age) differ from place to place, but, to keep things simple, we can say that, as noted above, the break occurred ca. 8,000 BCE (roughly ten thousand years ago). The oldest known human settlements in the Ryukyu Islands are Neolithic. They date to about 7000 BCE in the central and northern Ryukyu Islands and 2,500 BCE in the southern Ryukyu Islands.

Archaeologists have excavated large shell mounds (also called *shell middens*) in the central and northern Ryukyu Islands, the physical remains of hunter-gatherer communities. They include many shells, some discarded after the living part had been eaten, and some used as trade goods or fashioned into tools. In the early centuries of the Shell Mound Era, it is likely that communities subsisted by hunting, gathering, fishing, and local trade.

Who were these shell mound people? Genetic evidence and artifacts indicate that, in the main, they were descendants of Jōmon people who arrived in the Ryukyu Islands from Kyushu (fig. 2.1). (*Jōmon* refers to an era, a culture, and a biological human population. It is important to note that biology [genetics] and culture are independent of each other and that all humans are capable, especially at a young age, of habituating to any culture.) The name *Jōmon* literally means "rope pattern" and refers to a distinctive type of pottery. Jōmon culture flourished from about 14,000 BCE to 1000 BCE, fading out around 300 BCE in the Japanese mainland.[1] Jōmon pottery has been excavated in the central and northern Ryukyu Islands. Some of it probably arrived there along with the people who produced it, and some of it was probably the result of trade.

Like *Jōmon*, the term *Yayoi* refers to an era (1000 BCE–300 CE, according to recent estimates), a culture, and a human population. In the main Japanese islands, Jōmon and Yayoi people and culture coexisted for several centuries. Yayoi people came into the Japanese islands from the Korean Peninsula via northwest Kyushu. They brought with them material culture (e.g., pottery) and nonmaterial culture (e.g., language, agricultural know-how), both of which had a large impact on the prehistory of the Japanese islands. Importantly, Yayoi people were farmers. Although many Jōmon groups cultivated edible plants, Yayoi people brought full-scale agriculture into the Japanese islands. Agricultural surpluses led to state formation in

FIGURE 2.1. Major Paleolithic sites, the approximate range of
Neolithic peoples, and the approximate range of the Jōmon
people given current archaeological and DNA evidence

the main Japanese islands. This point is important because, as we will see, it
contrasts with the situation in the Ryukyu Islands.

It is possible that small groups of Yayoi people resided in the northern
Ryukyu Islands in connection with the shell trade (discussed below). However, the main infusion of Yayoi-descended people (whom I call *Japonic*)
into the Ryukyu Islands took place much later, during the eleventh and
twelfth centuries, at the start of the Gusuku Era.

Early Shell Trade

Seashells were valuable products in ancient Japan. Living shells can be a
source of food, and the shells themselves can be made into tools, decorative
objects, and jewelry. By about 600 BCE, a vigorous trade in valuable shells
had developed, centered in western Kyushu. From there, a "shell road" (*kai
no michi*) extended to the northern and central Ryukyu Islands, as far south

as Okinawa. The shell road extended north as well, encompassing much of western Japan. It was not the case that a single merchant or a single team of merchants transported shells over such long distances. Instead, the shell road consisted of relay collection, transportation, manufacturing, and commerce. Groups of people in the Ryukyu Islands gathered shells, and other groups transported them toward Kyushu. Much of the manufacturing of bracelets took place in Kyushu. From there, shell products made their way into the rest of the Japanese islands. Shown in figure 2.2 is a basic diagram of the shell road and the shell trade. Notice that much of the shell road corresponds to a region called *Michinoshima*, the islands of the Ryukyu Arc between which travel by boat was relatively easy.

Trade in seashells and their products linked the ancient Ryukyu Islands into a network of exchange. Maritime bands traveled between Kyushu and the central and northern Ryukyu Islands to obtain shells. In places like the

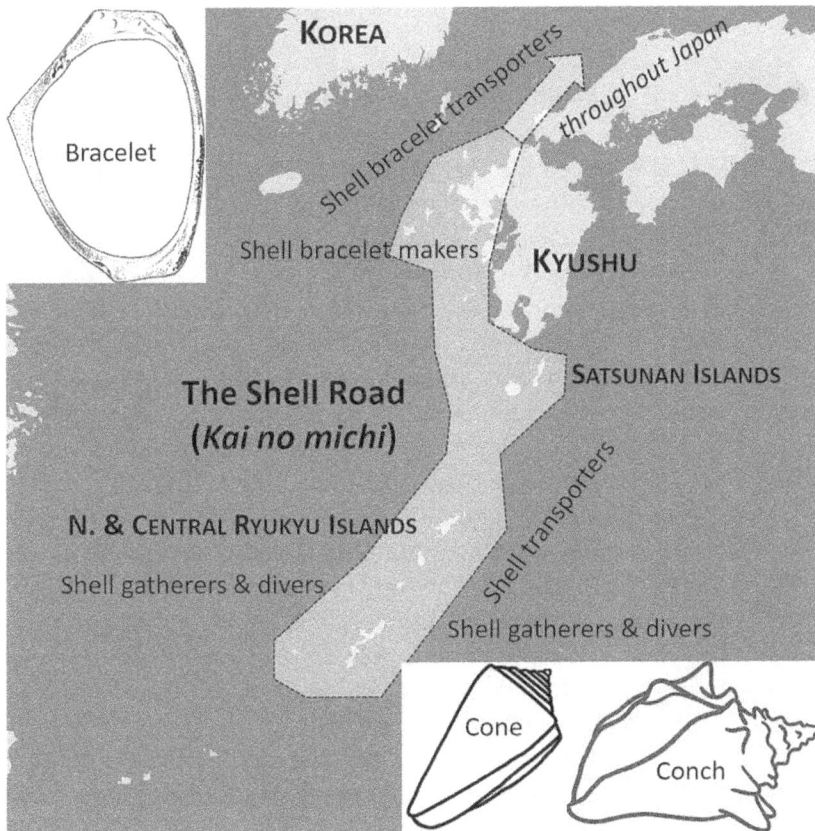

FIGURE 2.2. The shell road and shell trade during the Shell Mound Era

Takahashi site in Minami–Satsuma City (southern Kyushu), the shells were made into bracelets and moved north along the coast of western Kyushu. The maritime distribution route continued along the coast of western Honshu to Tsugaru Bay in Aomori and across to Hokkaidō.

Bracelets began to be made from copper or other materials late in the Yayoi Era, but other uses for shells developed. Cone shells, for example, became widely used for the manufacture of horse ornaments, which were consumed all over Japan during the sixth and seventh centuries CE. The cone and conch shells from Ryukyu did not stop at Kyushu or other parts of Japan. They were intermittently imported to Korea and have been excavated at tomb sites there, as have mother-of-pearl objects made from Ryukyuan turbo shells. The majority of these shells probably arrived in Korea via Kyushu, with sea peoples from the coasts of Higo (Kumamoto) and Satsuma (Kagoshima) working as intermediaries. It is also possible that Korean merchants purchased the shells directly from central or northern Ryukyu Island locations.

The Southern Ryukyu Islands

The earliest known Neolithic settlement sites in the Yaeyama Islands date to approximately forty-two to forty-five hundred years ago. This early Neolithic population persisted until about thirty-five hundred years ago, and it produced simple pottery. About thirty-five hundred years ago, the population that produced this pottery either died out or moved out of the southern Ryukyu Islands, which subsequently lacked permanent human inhabitants for about seven hundred years. Humans returned to the Yaeyama Islands starting around twenty-eight hundred years ago. This late Neolithic phase was characterized by a lack of pottery (the Nonceramic Period). It was also characterized by shell and stone adzes. Adzes are handheld tools for cutting and shaping. It is likely that one use for these tools was to carve out large trees to make dug-out boats capable of sailing between islands.

The traditional narrative in many Japanese-language survey histories is that the people living in the southern Ryukyu Islands were Austronesians, related to the indigenous people of Taiwan. Indeed, Austronesian culture was widespread in the Ryukyu Islands, especially the southern Ryukyu Islands. However, culture can be transmitted independently of migration. In the case of the southern Ryukyu Islands, it now seems unlikely that large numbers of Austronesians lived there in prehistory. Recent full-genome DNA research has found that most or possibly all the residents of the Miyako

Islands were genetically Jōmon. We still do not have good DNA data for the Yaeyama Islands, but it is likely that they too were settled by Jōmon people. Therefore, most or all of the people dwelling in the southern Ryukyu Islands before the eleventh and twelfth centuries were Jōmon. However, their material culture consisted of a mix of Jōmon and Austronesian elements. We do not know what language or languages they spoke, but it is highly unlikely that Japonic languages were spoken widely in the Ryukyu Islands until the eleventh century.

Trade is the likely reason for the Austronesian culture, and it is possible that it resulted in a few Austronesian people residing in the Ryukyu Islands. In general, Austronesian peoples were excellent seafarers. Contemporary Austronesian peoples and cultures range from the Hawaiian Islands, to New Zealand, to Madagascar off the coast of Africa. Island Southeast Asia (Indonesia, the Philippines, etc.) is Austronesian in terms of base culture, as are the indigenous peoples of Taiwan. In addition to the Ryukyu Islands, it is likely that Austronesian culture reached as far as southern Kyushu in Japan and even parts of the west coasts of the Americas.

Writing in the early 1960s, the anthropologist William P. Lebra noted a variety of cultural practices in the island of Okinawa with likely southern roots:

> A few of the specific traits shared by Okinawa and Taiwan are sibling creator deities, dugout canoes (without outriggers), tattooing, red fingernail coloring, postnatal "roasting" of mother and child, fermentation of ceremonial wine by chewing grain, banana cloth, ikat textiles, special houses for young unmarried adults, cockfighting, and bullfighting. Some of these are rare or moribund on Okinawa today but can be readily recalled by older informants.
>
> ... It is not my intention to argue here for an Indonesian substratum in Okinawa but merely to indicate that the instances of shared traits are too numerous to be ignored and that these suggest lengthy contiguity and mutual influence. (Lebra 1966/1985, 11)

When did Austronesian culture arrive in the Ryukyu Islands? We cannot say with certainty. One possibility is that it arrived after the prehistoric era covered in this chapter. In the early fourteenth century or earlier, seafarers from the southern Ryukyu Islands—especially Miyako—began sailing to Southeast Asia and China to trade. Noting that we cannot be certain precisely when or how Austronesian culture entered the Ryukyu Islands, here are a few specific aspects of it, starting with food cultivation.

PLANT CULTIVATION, RED RICE,
AND TREADING CULTIVATION

Before the eleventh century, the people dwelling in the Ryukyu Islands lived in hunting-and-gathering societies. They did not practice agriculture, or systematic, large-scale farming, per se. They did, however, engage in the small-scale cultivation of useful plants. Most hunter-gatherer societies cultivated certain plants to supplement their food supply.

It is likely that people in the Ryukyu Islands cultivated tubers before the Gusuku Era. Tubers require no equipment or infrastructure, and they are not strongly seasonal crops. The most common term for them in Japanese is *daijo*,[2] and they can be cultivated year-round and harvested as needed. It is likely that *daijo* had been cultivated well before Koreans shipwrecked in the Ryukyu Islands wrote about them in 1477. For example, the pottery of the Shimotabaru shell mound was accompanied by cooking stones, indicating the use of earth ovens used to cook tubers. Therefore, it is possible that tuber cultivation had taken place in the Ryukyu Islands since the Later Jōmon Era. DNA analysis also indicates that tubers entered the Ryukyu Islands from Southeast Asia via Taiwan.

Taro cultivation spread north as far as the Tokara and Satsunan Islands. A wild tropical taro (*Colocasia esculenta* var. *aquatilis*), known as *fee-muji* in northern Okinawa, is of Southeast Asian origin. This tuber is also found in Tanegashima. In both places, it grows on waste ground or among refuse (i.e., in ruderal habitats), not in the natural habitat. Therefore, it is most likely that wild taro from Southeast Asia entered the central and northern Ryukyu Islands via human contact.

Each year red rice (*akagome* or *akamai*) is planted in two plots of the Hōman Shrine in southern Tanegashima. In the past, red rice was planted all over Tanegashima in both wet and dry fields. The red rice of Tanegashima is a southern rice cultivar, similar morphologically, ecologically (e.g., growing in wet or dry fields), and genetically to a variety of red rice called *bulu* in Indonesia. Before the 1930s, red rice was also cultivated extensively in Okinawa. Around 1917, an agricultural survey of rice from different regions in Okinawa plus Miyako and Yaeyama indicated that most varieties resembled red *bulu* rice. There is a chemically distinctive subtype of red rice in Yonaguni that is identical to a variety of rice found in Indonesia. The red rice of Tanegashima and elsewhere in the Ryukyu Arc is an Austronesian cultivar, ultimately of Southeast Asian origin.

The distribution of red rice substantially overlaps the distribution of a distinctive method of cultivating rice. Called *tōkō* in modern Japanese and something different in each locality, this method involves using oxen in most cases but sometimes horses to trample back and forth across dry fields to prepare them for seeding or transplanting. It is found throughout most of the western part of the Austronesian world and throughout the Ryukyu Islands. Korean observers in 1477 recorded oxen being used to trample the soil prior to sowing rice seeds in Yonaguni and Miyako. Red rice and treading cultivation indicate the presence of Austronesian culture and possibly some Austronesian people throughout the Ryukyu Arc.

SOUTHERN MYTHOLOGY

In mythology from Miyako and Yaeyama, deities sometimes emerged from the ground. For example, in a tale from Shiraho in Ishigaki, the solar deity ordered the deity Aman to create an island and people. Aman piled up stone and dirt in the sea to create the island. To seed it with humans, Aman placed a hermit crab on the island, which dug a hole. A man and woman were born from this hole and populated the island. Of Austronesian origin, this motif and variations of it are found as far north as southern Kyushu and Jeju Island in Korea. Its distribution includes Southeast Asia, Taiwan (among several aboriginal groups), Yaeyama, Miyako, southern Kyushu, and Jeju Island. It is also found in Okinawa, but in slightly different form.

In the creation tale from Shiraho, ancestral humans came forth from a hole in the ground dug by a hermit crab. That humans came from a hermit crab is perhaps the most pervasive Austronesian myth in the Ryukyu Islands. The word *aman-yo* (locally, *aman-yū*) is found in all Ryukyuan languages. It means "long ago" (J. *ōmukashi*), but literally it means "age of the hermit crab." Variations of creation myths involving terrestrial hermit crabs are common in Austronesian societies of island Southeast Asia. In Ryukyuan languages and dialects, the term *aman*, or variations of it such as *amamu*, means "hermit crab." In the former Ryukyuan custom of women having their hands and arms tattooed (*hajichi*), one pattern for the left arm was that of a hermit crab. According to an informant in Okinoerabu (ca. 1960), the reason for this tattoo is that humans are all descendants of Amamu, that is, a primordial hermit crab.

The creation tale from Shiraho involves two deities, Aman and a solar deity, and the solar deity is superior. This solar deity element is *not* Austronesian. It comes from the north, that is, from the Japanese islands. By the time local myths and legends were written down, the Ryukyu Islands had become thoroughly Japonic in terms of culture. Nevertheless, here and there, remnants of Austronesian culture have been preserved.

Southern Islands Products

During the Gusuku Era, especially during the thirteenth and fourteenth centuries, trading and raiding became the predominant economic activities in the Ryukyu Islands. It was the *location* of the islands—close to China, Korea, and Japan but outside government reach—that became the main economic asset. Plentiful harbors further contributed to an economy based on maritime exchanges.

As we have seen, the Ryukyu Islands were also a source of several valuable natural products, especially seashells. Valuable shells included cone, conch, turbo shells, and giant trumpet shells. Turbo shells, also called *turban shells*, were especially valuable. They were a source of mother-of-pearl inlay, and worldwide distribution of turbo shells is limited to the Ryukyu Islands, the Philippines, and some islands near India. Giant trumpet shells were in demand for use in the mantic arts (sorcery, magic, etc.) from the Yayoi Era on. By themselves, or with modification, seashells could function as fishing or household equipment: illumination plates, food-serving utensils, washbasins, water bowls for livestock, incense burners, vessels for boiling water, radish scrapers, ladles, tools for threading ramie, and pot cleaners and polishers. They also functioned as talismanic objects, weasel repellents (in chicken coops), and decorative objects or the raw material for mother-of-pearl.

Several varieties of tropical and semitropical bishopwood known as *akagi* (*Bischofia javanica*) were prized in Japan. According to tenth-century documents, bishopwood was shipped to Dazaifu from the southern islands each year.[3] From there, bishopwood logs went to the court in Kyoto, where government offices used the cores for bound volumes of royal proclamations. The wood was also used in sutra scrolls, sword hilts, and probably in the making of zithers (*koto*) and other musical instruments.

Other southern island products were palm fronds (J. *biro* or *binro*, O. *kuba*), sea turtles (*taimai*), and later, during the Gusuku Era, sulfur and horses. The range of palm fronds (*Livistona chinensis*) extends to southern parts of the Japanese mainland. According to the ancient text *Engishiki*, palm frond fans were used in the imperial kitchen to circulate the air. They were also used to decorate oxcarts of the nobility and in other ways. In general, palm fronds were an elite item, limited to emperors and high nobles. The seed kernels of the palm trees were used as medicine.

Taimai is a type of tropical sea turtle, especially numerous in the Yaeyama Islands. Its meat is not prized, but its shell and scales were used for crafts. Other southern island products included sea cucumbers, dugongs, animal hide, ramie, banana fiber cloth (*bashōfu*), shark fins, pearls, and medicinal plants. In short, the Ryukyu Islands were a source of products prized in Japan, especially among court nobles, and in Korea and China. Trade activities might involve relaying valuable raw materials from parts of the East China Sea region via the Ryukyu Islands in exchange for finished products such as pottery, tools, or alcoholic beverages.

THE JAPANESE COURT AND THE SOUTHERN ISLANDS ROUTE TO CHINA

In 633, Japanese forces suffered a major defeat at the Battle of Baekgang (J. Hakusonkō) on the Korean Peninsula. As a result, the imperial the court began sending embassies to China (*kentōshi*) as part of an effort to absorb as much advanced technology as possible. Because of strained relations with the Korean state of Silla, the northern route to China via Korea was no longer viable. The eighth through the twelfth embassies (702–52) used the southern islands route (*nantōro*). Having become aware of the Ryukyu Islands, the Japanese court sought bishopwood, palm fronds, and shells from them, typically portrayed as tribute in official documents.

From as early as the seventh century, a southern island route to China via the Satsunan and Ryukyu Islands was known in Japan (fig. 2.3). In 677,

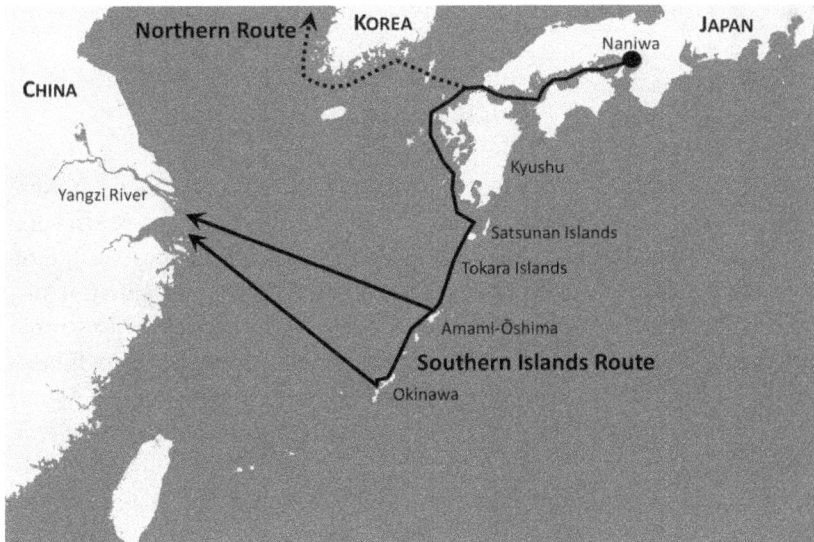

FIGURE 2.3. The southern islands route taken by Japanese embassies to China, ca. 702–52

visitors from Tanegashima lodged at the Asuka temple in Nara. According to a 682 entry in the official history *Chronicles of Japan* (*Nihon shoki* or *Nihongi*, 720), people from the islands of Tanegashima, Yakushima, and Amami-Ōshima each received gifts from the court. During Empress Suiko's reign (592–628), all people south of Kyushu were called *Yaku people* (named for the island of Yakushima). However, from the 670s, the individual southern islands gradually become distinguished from each other in official documents.

In 707, the court dispatched an envoy to Dazaifu, where people from the southern islands who had come to present tribute (i.e., had come to trade) received gifts and formal rank. In 715, a total of seventy-seven people from Amami, Ishigaki, Kumi (either Kumejima or Kome on Iriomote), Amami-Ōshima, Yakushima, and Tokunoshima plus *emishi* (indigenous people from Mutsu and Dewa in the far north of Honshu) assembled at the imperial court, all of whom presented tribute. No Okinawans are mentioned. At least in the eyes of the Japanese court, Okinawa was not a major participant in southern island exchanges during the eighth century. In 735, Dazaifu dispatched officials to the southern islands to set up placards, but over the years they rotted away. In 754, a group was sent to restore them. On each placard was written the name of the island, an indication of where a ship could dock, water conditions, and the distance to the next island. From context we know that there was also such a marker in Okinawa even though Okinawa was not represented by those presenting tribute to the court during this era.

Population Crash

The people inhabiting the Ryukyu Islands before the Gusuku Era were entirely or mostly Jōmon in terms of genetic makeup. In the central and northern Ryukyu Islands, the material culture of these people was Jōmon with some Austronesian elements. In the southern Ryukyu Islands, the Austronesian cultural influence was greater. It is possible that some Austronesian people lived in the Ryukyu Islands before the Gusuku Era even though the majority of the population was Jōmon. Let us call these Jōmon people *the indigenous population* even though they were not the original inhabitants of the Ryukyu Islands. Starting around 400 or 500 and continuing into the eleventh century, these indigenous populations in the Ryukyu Islands declined.

Figure 2.4, based on work by Takamiya Hiroto, uses the number of archaeological sites as a rough proxy for population. There was a significant

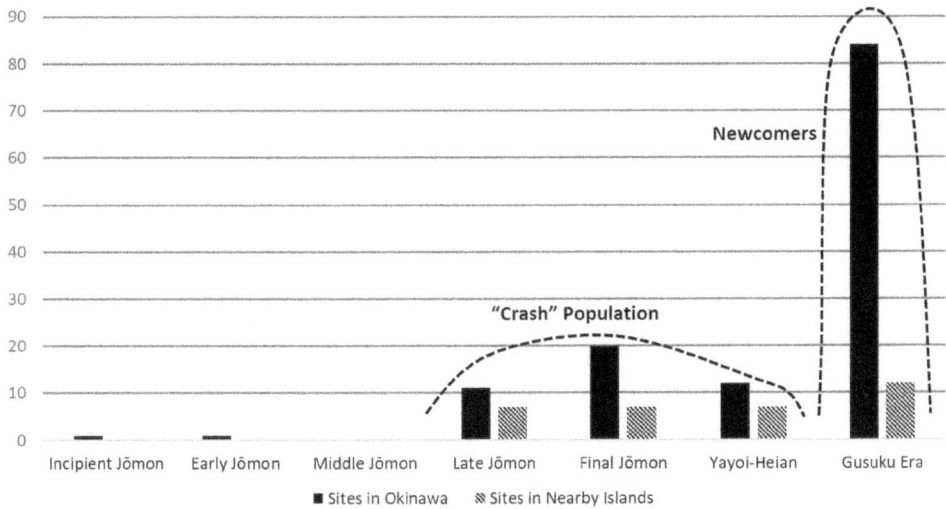

FIGURE 2.4. An illustration of the crash of the indigenous population during the late Shell Mound Era and their replacement with newcomers from Japan, measured by number of sites (data from Takamiya [2005, 189])

population increase during the Later Jōmon Era, with the indigenous population reaching a peak at the end of the Jōmon Era, possibly supported in part by the practice of limited cultivation of plants and animals. From the Yayoi to the Heian Periods, however, and despite trade with Kyushu, or perhaps in part because of it, the indigenous population came under stress and began to crash. In the Ryukyuan case, the result was a replacement of the indigenous population by northern migrants, mostly from the Japanese islands. The relatively small indigenous population either died out or was absorbed by the waves of migrants from Japan. It is to those northern migrants that I turn next.

Origins of Japonic Ryukyu

The Early Gusuku Era, circa 1050–1250

None of the peoples discussed in the previous chapter became the basis of the modern population of the Ryukyu Islands. This chapter, based mainly on physical evidence, identifies the Japonic roots of the modern population of the Ryukyu Islands. Recall the important point that prehistoric populations tended to move over vast distances and that dead ends (one population dying out or being replaced by another) were common. The crucial change that created Japonic Ryukyu was the replacement of the Jōmon population by waves of immigrants from the north. The vast majority of these immigrants came from the Japanese islands, but some of them came from the Korean Peninsula. Recall that the indigenous Jōmon population had been declining for several centuries. Between about 1050 and 1150 in the northern Ryukyu Islands, and about a century later in the southern Ryukyu Islands, Japonic newcomers replaced the Shell Mound Era population. This chapter examines that process from several perspectives.

Starting in the eleventh century and proceeding rapidly, the indigenous, pre–Gusuku Era population disappeared. Some aspects of their culture remained, but the people were absorbed into the new population. This new population resembled mainland Japanese physically and culturally. The physical anthropologist Doi Naomi, among many others, points out not only that the Gusuku Era was a time of cultural change but also that it marked a major change in human morphology. The present-day population of the Ryukyu Islands can trace a continuous connection back as far as the Gusuku Era.

The historian Kurima Yasuo (2013) has identified six technological and cultural characteristics of the Gusuku Era. First is the emergence of power holders (often called *aji*) and their fortresses (*gusuku*). Second is the emergence of agriculture, indicated by excavated carbonized grain and bone fragments from livestock. Third is the presence throughout the Ryukyu Islands of soapstone cauldrons (i.e., pots) manufactured mainly in the Nishisonogi Peninsula near Nagasaki and gray stoneware, *kamuiyaki*, manufactured in Korean-style kilns on the nearby island of Tokunoshima and modeled after Korean Goryeo pottery. Fourth is widespread trade, indicated by an abundance of Chinese trade ceramics and items like metal tools, coins, and jewels. Fifth is the use of metal tools. Sixth is the inclusion of the southern Ryukyu Islands as well as the central and northern Ryukyu Islands in a single zone of material culture. Here and in the next chapter I examine these characteristics as well as changes in human populations.

The Official Histories and *Omoro sōshi*

During the seventeenth century, Ryukyu's royal court became concerned with formally presenting the Ryukyuan past to the broader East Asian world. This concern manifested itself as several works of history collectively known as *the official histories*. These histories were biased in several respects. For example, they claim that a centralized state existed several centuries before it actually did, and they portray Ryukyu's past as more orderly than it was.

The official histories reflect the circumstances, ideas, and values of their own time period, roughly 1650–1750. In general, they do not accurately portray the circumstances of the early Ryukyu Islands. Nevertheless, if read cautiously and against the grain, they can reveal useful hints about early Ryukyu. The following is a list of the official histories, plus *Origins of Ryukyu*, an official compilation that focuses on culture:

Reflections on Chūzan (*Chūzan seikan*), 1650
Sai Taku Genealogy of Chūzan (*Chūzan seifu Sai Taku bon*), 1701
Origins of Ryukyu (*Ryūkyūkoku yuraiki*), 1713
Sai On Genealogy of Chūzan (*Chūzan seifu Sai On bon*), 1725
Kyūyō (Beautiful Ryukyu), 1743–45, with updates into the 1880s

Refer to this list in this and later chapters.

Another very important document is *Omoro sōshi*, often called "the Omoro." It is a collection of 1,553 songs (*omoro*), 1,144 of which are unique (409 are repeated). Buddhist priests in the Shuri area created the first volume in the 1530s, writing down the songs in Japanese *kana* script. The second volume appeared in 1613, and the remaining twenty volumes appeared in 1623. However, the version of the text that we have today was reconstructed from fragments following a Shuri Castle fire in 1710 that destroyed the master text.

Northern Orientations

In somewhat different ways, and with differing emphasis, the official histories start the history of the Ryukyu Islands by invoking aspects of royal mythology that had developed by the seventeenth century. In this mythology, deities from the north created the islands. The main focus in this story is the island of Okinawa. The official histories all assume that Ryukyuan history started in Okinawa, although we will see below that this claim is inaccurate.

Looking at the account found in *Reflections on Chūzan*, the deity Amamiku came to Okinawa from the north and created a series of sacred groves there. In order, they were Asumori in Hedo (1), Kanahiyabu in Nakijin (2), Chinen mori (3), Seifaa utaki (4), Yabusatsu utaki (5), Tamagusuku utaki (6), Kudaka kobau mori (7), and the pair Shuri mori/Madama mori (8). (The terms *mori* and *utaki* can be translated as *grove* or *sacred grove*.) The map in figure 3.1 lists these groves in order from one to eight. Is there a pattern to this sequence?

Notice that the overall direction is from north to southeast, then to the southwest, culminating in Shuri, the capital of Ryukyu at the time *Reflections on Chūzan* was written. Notice also the large concentration of groves in southern Okinawa as well as Kudaka kobau mori on nearby Kudakajima, an island that acquired great religious significance during the sixteenth century. Overall, the sequence of divine sacred grove creation reflects a north-to-south flow and a concentration in southern Okinawa, by far the most populous area of the island.

Broadening the horizon beyond the island of Okinawa, notice the Amami component in the name of the deity. It refers to the northern Ryukyu Islands. In the Kasari Peninsula of Amami-Ōshima, there is a mountain, Amami-dake, where, according to legend, Amamikyo descended from the heavens. The northern Ryukyu Islands abound with present or past placenames containing the term *Amami*.

We can find many northern frames of reference in the oldest historical documents. For example, in 1458, Shō Taikyū, a powerful trade king, commissioned the Sea Bridge to the Many Countries Bell (Bankoku shinryō no kane) after success in a series of wars. Its inscription is in classical Chinese, and it begins: "The country of Ryukyu is located favorably in the southern seas. It has gathered the excellence of the Korean kingdoms. It is a supplementary vehicle to the Great Ming. It is to Japan as teeth are to lips" (Smits 2024, 60). According to the inscription, Ryukyu has received the excellence or superiority of Korea, and, indeed, there was extensive early

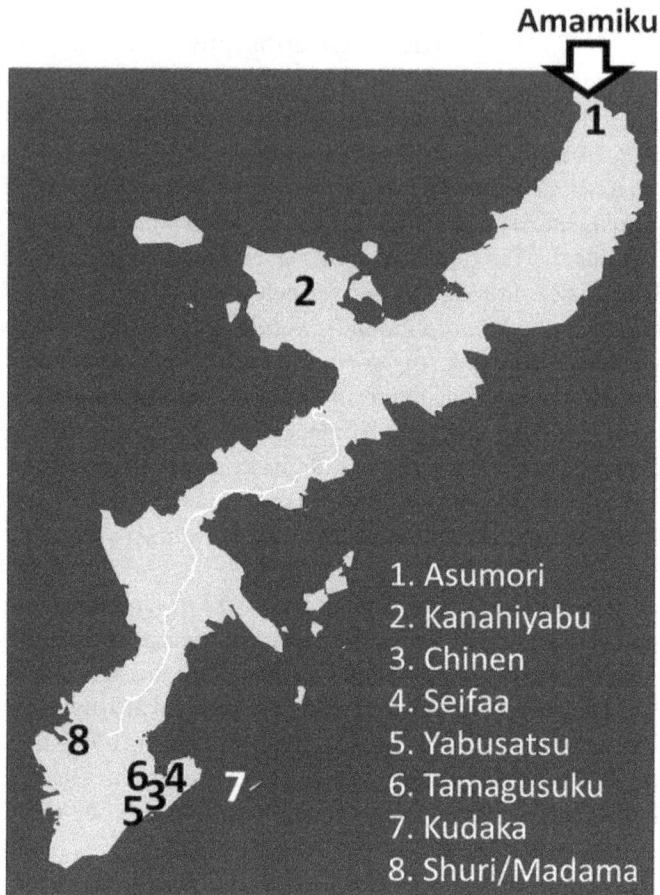

FIGURE 3.1. Location and temporal sequence of sacred groves purportedly created by the deity Amamiku in *Reflections on Chūzan* (1650)

Korean cultural and technological influence on the Ryukyu Islands. By contrast, Ryukyu's relationship with Ming China is described in functional terms. In the 1450s, Okinawa's port of Naha operated much like a shipping company, with the Ming dynasty as its largest client. Finally, as a fundamentally Japonic society with extensive ties to the Japanese islands, Ryukyu would indeed have been as close to Japan as teeth are to lips. The Ryukyu of this inscription has received superior culture and technology from Korea, maintains a good working relationship with China, and is culturally and ethnically akin to Japan. However, what may be the most significant term in this passage is easy to overlook: *southern seas*. The expression speaks to a *northern* frame of reference that pervades early Ryukyuan history.

Next, consider the use of snow as a metaphor in the *Omoro*. One *omoro* praises the rice grown in Sashiki as being "as white as snow" (*Omoro sōshi*, 19-1287),[1] and several others praise top-quality rice as "snow" (*Omoro sōshi*, 12-672–73, 22-1511). The Yonaha and Yonabaru beaches are each called "snow beach" because of their white sand (*Omoro sōshi*, 1-39, 3-100). White horses are "the color of snow" or otherwise likened to snow (*Omoro sōshi*, 10-541, 583). A deity of a sacred grove in Kumejima is called "Venerable snow" (*Omoro sōshi*, 13-955). Another *omoro* speaks of snow falling in the first lunar month (*Omoro sōshi*, 14-1000). However, in the semitropical Ryukyu Islands, snow never accumulates, not even on the highest mountains, and even a few passing flakes are extremely rare. Denizens of the islands would have had no experience with or concept of snow unless they sailed to colder climates. These snow references would have made sense only to people whose roots were in places like Japan or Korea.

On the basis of what we have seen from written sources, we could draw a conclusion that people and culture came into the Ryukyu Islands mainly from northern locations such as Japan or Korea and that they moved through the Ryukyu Islands in a north-to-south flow. A variety of anthropological, archaeological, morphological, and genetic data also bear out this scenario.

In the Beginning There Was Kikaijima

Thinking in terms of geography, and taking into account what we have seen so far, where did the Gusuku Era in the Ryukyu Islands begin? A look at the map of the region would suggest that it was not Okinawa, which is in the center of the Ryukyu chain. Indeed, Japonic Ryukyu began in the northernmost Ryukyu Islands and spread south from there.

Kikaijima is a low island but not uniformly flat. It tends to slope down toward Amami-Ōshima to the west. Along much of the east side, there is a steep cliff or drop-off to the sea. The Gusuku site group remains ("Gusuku" hereafter) sit on a plateau about halfway between sea level and the highest point on the island (fig. 3.2). At approximately 130,000 square meters, Gusuku is the largest archaeological site in the Ryukyu Islands. Kikaijima was the location of advanced technology, great wealth, and potential power. The history of Japonic Ryukyu started there.

We know from pottery distribution, funeral customs, and other evidence that the residents of Gusuku came from outside the Ryukyu Islands. Among their many imported goods were containers from Japan, Korea, and China. The one abundant variety of local container pottery was *kamuiyaki*.

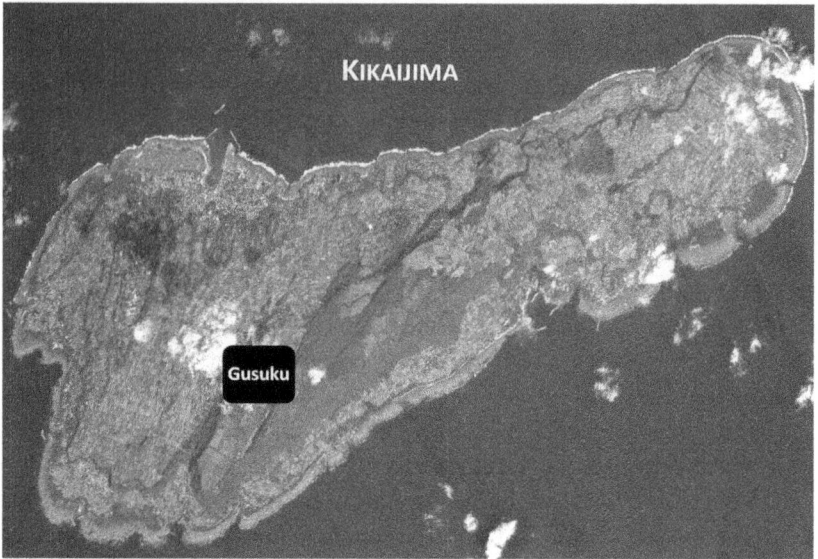

FIGURE 3.2. Location of the Gusuku site group in Kikaijima (Wikimedia Commons, Image Science and Analysis Laboratory, NASA–Johnson Space Center)

Pottery excavated at Gusuku includes large quantities of Japanese-made ware, soapstone cauldrons, and high-quality imported wares from China and Korea. Although the soapstone cauldrons were manufactured in Nagasaki, they probably came from Song Chinese merchants residing in Hakata (present-day Fukuoka, northwest Kyushu). Gusuku maintained close connections with Hakata. Prior to Gusuku's discovery and excavation in the twenty-first century, the presence of Korean ceramics in the Ryukyu Islands was thought to have been the result of trade during the fourteenth century. We now know that these Korean wares were present in quantity as early as the eleventh century. The traders at Gusuku were connected directly or indirectly with every country bordering the East China Sea.

Many round iron furnaces were discovered in the Gusuku sites, and the furnaces and the technology they employed probably came from Bōnotsu in the southern Satsuma Peninsula. At these furnaces, old iron goods and iron sand was melted down to make new tools and other items. Over one hundred sunken-pillar structures have been identified in Gusuku, many very large. The majority are thought to have been built during late eleventh century and the twelfth century, the peak period of Gusuku's prosperity.

Kikaijima does not have significant forests. Therefore, the lumber for the Gusuku buildings had to be imported, almost certainly from nearby Amami-Ōshima. Nearly all the ninth- and tenth-century shell-trade sites in Amami-Ōshima are in the Kasari Peninsula, just across from Kikaijima, and it is likely that Kikaijima and this part of Amami-Ōshima were part of the same geopolitical unit. This unit might also have included other territory in the northern Ryukyu Islands such as the *kamuiyaki* kiln sites. Amami-Ōshima was a source of valuable raw materials. Eighty-five percent of Amami-Ōshima is forests. Its natural resources include manganese, copper, gold, silver, and coal, and mining continued on the island into the early twentieth century. The Kasari Peninsula also includes the largest area of land suitable for agriculture on Amami-Ōshima (fig. 3.3).

A simple periodization scheme for Gusuku will serve our purposes:

Phase 1, the ninth century through the early eleventh
Phase 2, the mid-eleventh century through the twelfth century
Phase 3, the thirteenth century through early fifteenth

Phase 2 was the peak of Gusuku's prosperity and saw a rapid population increase. During this time, Gusuku resembled a medieval Japanese city like Hakata or Kamakura, albeit on a smaller scale.

During phase 2, Kikaijima broke or drifted away from Dazaifu control and began to flourish as an international commerce hub. It exerted great influence over Ryukyu-wide trade networks and was a branch hub for Japanese-Chinese trade. Chinese-made ceramics spread from northwest Kyushu south. It is unlikely at this time that Chinese merchants visited any

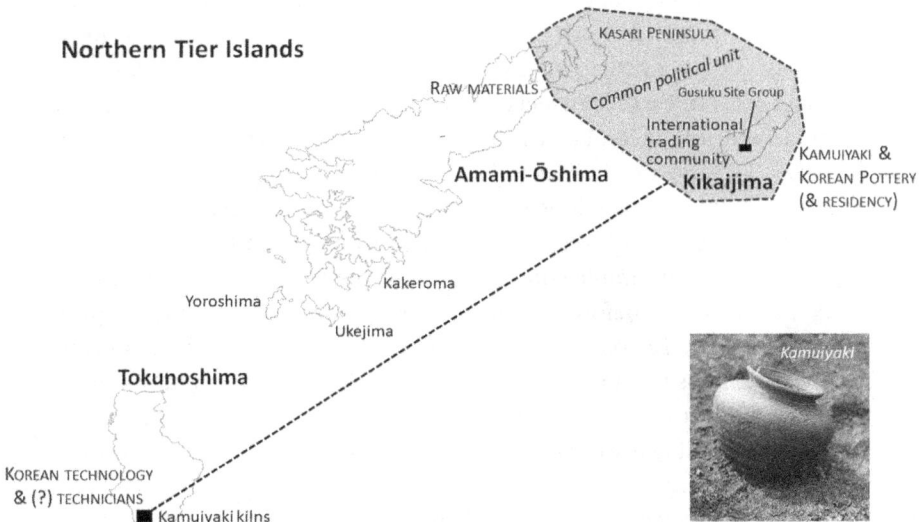

FIGURE 3.3. Key locations in the northernmost Ryukyu Islands during the Gusuku Era

of the Ryukyu Islands directly or that there was a direct south-to-north Chinese trade route via the islands. The likely scenario is that people from Korea came to Kikaijima for trade and developed a community there where they created *kamuiyaki*. The vast majority of excavated *kamuiyaki* has been found in Tokunoshima and Kikaijima, with relatively little found in the southern Ryukyu Islands. Further evidence for the presence of Korean traders in the northern Ryukyu Islands is that blue ware bowls made from kilns in Jeollanam (South Jeolla) Province and Goryeo earthenware have been excavated at Gusuku. These items were meant for daily use and, thus, not trade ware, a strong indication of Korean residency.

In other words, the trading and manufacturing operation based in Kikaijima also encompassed the northern Ryukyu Islands of Amami-Ōshima and Tokunoshima. I call these three—Kikaijima, Amami-Ōshima, and Tokunoshima—*the northern tier islands* (fig. 3.3). Those who resided at Gusuku came mainly from Japan and Korea. Because of close ties to the port of Hakata, Gusuku imported goods from Japan, Korea, and China. The Chinese goods came from Chinese merchants who resided in Hakata. What did the merchants in Gusuku use to pay for these imports? They collected valuable southern island products, especially turbo shells, which were widely available in the Kasari Peninsula of Amami-Ōshima.

Migration into the Ryukyu Islands

We have no written records from the people who settled into the Ryukyu Islands during the eleventh century or even during much later periods. Therefore, we must turn to physical evidence such as skeletal remains, pottery, and other unearthed objects to draw conclusions about them. The hot, humid climate of the Ryukyu Islands is not conducive to preserving human remains. Nevertheless, in recent years, physical anthropologists have had access to an increasingly larger sample size of remains. Skeletal analysis, which can include DNA analysis, is highly technical, but the results so far point to a relatively simple conclusion. Most skeletal remains found in the Ryukyu Islands from before the Gusuku Era resemble non-Japonic peoples. From the Gusuku Era on, skeletal morphology closely resembles mainland Japanese remains for similar time periods. Shell Mound Era skulls tend to be shorter and rounder; those from the Gusuku Era feature an elongated face and protruding lower jaw. The crucial period of major change was the Early Gusuku Era.

When the Urasoe yōdore mausoleum was excavated (1996–2004), remains belonging to approximately 156 skeletons were recovered, but the bones and bone fragments were mixed and dispersed. The Eiso #2 tomb within the mausoleum contained well-preserved bones and fragments, and the excavation team put them together in the manner of a jigsaw puzzle. The reconstructed skull was entirely unlike prehistoric skulls. It was elongated, with a flat face, and displayed characteristics typical of skulls from mainland Japan during the Kamakura and Muromachi Eras. Indeed, all remains that can reliably be dated from the Gusuku Era indicate migration from the Japanese islands into the Ryukyu Islands starting in the eleventh century.

The pottery record indicates a similar process. We can speak broadly of "group A" pottery and "group B" pottery. Group A items are typical of the Shell Mound Era. They feel sandy, contain grains of sand in the base soil, are red or contain red clay, and the surface flakes off when touched. Group B pottery pieces feature gray minerals, phlogopite (magnesium mica), and talc or other minerals mixed into the base soil. Compared with group A, group B items are thicker, darker in color, and smooth to the touch. In this way, fragments lacking any design or indication of pot shape can still be assigned to one or the other group.

Gusuku in Kikaijima was the main source of the group B pottery discussed above. *Kamuiyaki*, white porcelain, and soapstone cauldrons were the main components of a container package that spread south through the Ryukyu Islands. The components of this package are found most abundantly at Gusuku, again identifying Kikaijima as the place of origin within the Ryukyu Islands of Early Gusuku Era human populations and material culture.

Kamuiyaki was a particularly important variety of group B pottery. It was manufactured in Tokunoshima from the eleventh century until the early fourteenth. The most likely scenario is that people from or passing through Kikaijima brought *kamuiyaki* with them as they migrated. Given that it was distributed mainly in the Ryukyu Islands, *kamuiyaki* was produced not as a trade good, but to supply the northern migrants moving south with daily life products.

During the eleventh and twelfth centuries, there was a significant group B pottery gradient. The largest quantity is found in the northern Ryukyu Islands, a large but lesser quantity in Okinawa, and much less in the southern Ryukyu Islands. After the twelfth century, the movement of people and goods became more complex, but during the early phase of the Gusuku Era, the spread of new people and culture was a simple flow from north to south, with Kikaijima and other northern Ryukyu Islands serving as staging areas for migration south.

All indications are that the main motivating force for this migration south was economic. The demand for southern island products remained high. Demand for turbo shells, especially, increased sharply during the eleventh and twelfth centuries, and the Ryukyu Islands were the only practical source for them in the region. Mother-of-pearl had diffused into elite society in Japan and elsewhere in East Asia, and the demand for it, and therefore for turbo shells, remained strong into the fourteenth century.

The high regional demand for southern island products created a new trade network extending to the Yaeyama Islands. Kikaijima was the administrative center of this network. The northern tier islands provided much of the material, technology, and personnel. It is important to bear in mind that, during the Gusuku Era, the Ryukyu Islands were not a self-contained geopolitical entity, and they were not isolated within the East China Sea region. Let us now zoom out to see how the Ryukyu Islands of the eleventh and twelfth centuries fit into the broader regional trade patterns.

Trade within the East China Sea Region

Fujiwara-no-Akihira (989–1066) wrote *Shin-sarugaku ki* (New account of *sarugaku* drama) in the 1050s. It describes a merchant called Hachirō-no-mahito. Though he is a fictional character, his trading activities as described were typical of merchants during that time period. Hachirō-no-mahito conducted business across a wide area from northern Honshu to "Kikaigashima" (Kikaijima or somewhere in the Satsunan Islands). The list of the Japanese goods that he traded includes gold, silver, copper, sulfur, quartz, amber, silk, cloth, thread, brocade, several types of cloth, pearls, and turbo shells. Of these items, those most desired by Song Chinese merchants were gold, silver, copper, sulfur, pearls, and turbo shells. It was merchants like Hachirō-no-mahito who connected ports in Japan, the Ryukyu Islands, and elsewhere in the region.

By the tenth or eleventh century, the outer ring of the East China Sea had become a collection of maritime networks through which people, goods, and technology flowed. A hub-and-spoke model is useful for illustrating exchanges within the region. Figure 3.4 shows two hubs and the spokes radiating from each. This image focuses on the Ryukyu Islands, thus rendering several major Chinese ports as the ends of spokes. If we were to shift the focus to southern China, then the configuration would be different, and these Chinese spokes would become hubs, with spokes radiating out across the sea and across the Eurasian continent.

For my purposes, the two Early Gusuku Era hubs were Hakata and the northern tier islands. Spokes extended from the northern Ryukyu Islands hub to the rest of the Ryukyu Islands. Spokes also connected the northern

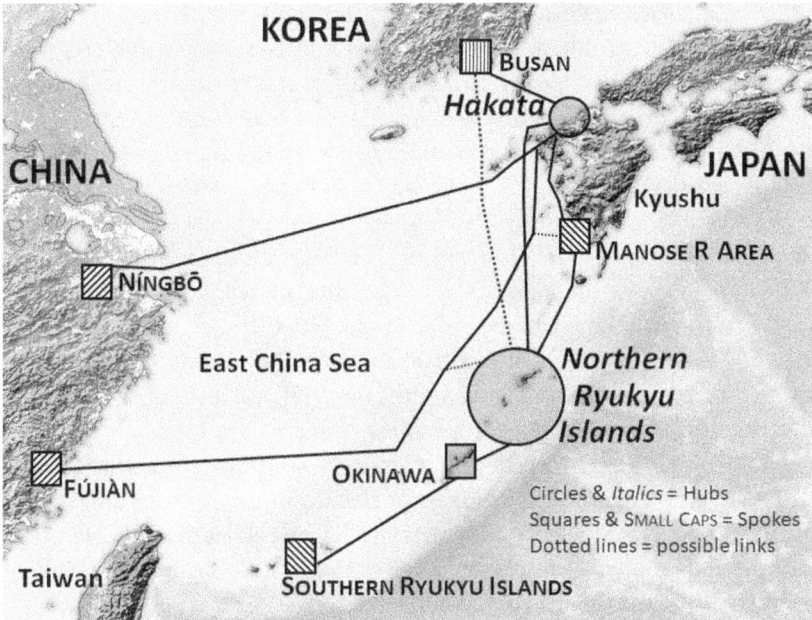

KOREA
BUSAN
Hakata
JAPAN
Kyushu
CHINA
MANOSE R AREA
NÍNGBŌ
East China Sea
Northern
Ryukyu
Islands
FÚJIÀN
OKINAWA
Circles & *Italics* = Hubs
Squares & SMALL CAPS = Spokes
Dotted lines = possible links
Taiwan
SOUTHERN RYUKYU ISLANDS

FIGURE 3.4. A hub-and-spoke model of regional trade during the Early Gusuku Era

Ryukyu Islands with Hakata in northwest Kyushu via the coastal waters of western Kyushu. The northern Ryukyu Islands were also linked directly with a region in the southern part of the Satsuma Peninsula near the mouth of the Manose River (Minami–Satsuma City today).

The port of Hakata rose to prominence during the mid- to late eleventh century as Gusuku began to flourish and Dazaifu began to fade. The ascendancy of Hakata in the eleventh century marked the onset of a period when Japanese and other maritime traders became especially active. Chinese merchants set up shop in Hakata, which eventually became home to a vast Chinese merchant district. Major imports from China were incense, brocade, copper coins, writing tools, books, sugar, sappanwood, and porcelain. The major exports sent from Japan to China, often via Hakata, were gold or silver, sulfur, mercury, pearls, lumber, fine jewelry and crafts, and weapons. Of these items, lumber and sulfur were especially prominent in terms of volume.

Turning to specific spokes, one connected Hakata and southern Korea. Since ancient times, northwest Kyushu served as the major point of contact between Japan and the Korean Peninsula. In *Goryeo History* (*Goryeosa*, 1451), we find the following items brought by Japanese traders to Korea during the second half of the eleventh century: mother-of-pearl inlaid saddles, swords, *suzuribako* (brush and ink writing sets), mirror boxes, combs, desks, illustrated folding screens, incense burners, arrow quivers, mercury, mother-of-pearl, pearls, livestock, sulfur, and turbo and conch shells. Southern island products like conch and turbo shells typically shipped to Korea from Hakata. Korean ceramics have been excavated in large quantities from sites in or near Hakata, but they become much less common moving farther south within Kyushu. As the pace of East China Sea trade increased during the eleventh century, Hakata, via the islands of Iki and Tsushima, became the major conduit for goods flowing between the Korean Peninsula and the Japanese mainland.

Another set of spokes linked Hakata with the trading ports of Song China. During the eleventh and twelfth centuries, the journey from Hakata to the Chinese port of Níngbō became as short as one week. Underwater excavations have recovered many anchor stones from Chinese ships and Chinese trade ceramics from Maegata Harbor in the Gotō Islands of Nagasaki Prefecture. It is now clear that this harbor was a pivotal anchorage along a trade route that ran directly across the East China Sea from Níngbō to the Gotō Islands and then north to Hakata.

In addition to this relatively direct but somewhat more dangerous route, there was the southern islands route between China and Japan discussed previously. Early in the Gusuku Era, this route ran from ports in southern China across to Okinawa, north along the Ryukyu Arc, then along western Kyushu to Hakata. Large quantities of Chinese ceramics from a ship bound for Hakata have been excavated from the seafloor off Uken in Amami-Ōshima, along with two anchor stones from Chinese ships. They date from the twelfth to the thirteenth century.

Consider exchanges between the two hubs. Early in the Gusuku Era, Hakata was the main gateway into Japan for Chinese people and products. It was also the main conduit for Chinese and Korean products coming into the Ryukyu Islands. Soapstone cauldrons arrived in the Ryukyu Islands via the Hakata–northern Ryukyu Islands link.

From the late twelfth century to the mid-thirteenth, the quantity of Chinese ceramics passing through Kyushu reached its peak. Ryukyuan sites reflect this situation, with an increase in both the number of sites containing imported kitchenware and the number of shards. The shard count increased significantly in Okinawa and the southern Ryukyu Islands but decreased in absolute and relative terms in the northern Ryukyu Islands. This shift is one indication that, from the end of the twelfth century, Okinawa had begun replacing the northern islands as the center of economic activity within the Ryukyu chain.

Soapstone cauldrons tell a similar story. The Ryukyu Islands contain the third largest concentration of soapstone cauldron fragments. The vast majority of these fragments have been found at Gusuku and very few in the southern Ryukyu Islands. This pattern suggests a multitiered delivery system. The main conduit was Hakata to Gusuku, and a secondary distribution zone was from Gusuku south to the other Ryukyu Islands. Because soapstone cauldrons spread at the same time and in the same pattern as did Chinese trade ceramics, it is possible that Chinese merchants in Hakata or their agents sent stoneware to Gusuku in exchange for southern island products.

A close look at imported pottery distribution shows that, until the end of the twelfth century, all the Ryukyu Islands moved in step with Gusuku and the northern tier islands. From the thirteenth century on, however, trade routes became more complex. One or more alternative routes may have developed to bring Chinese goods into the Ryukyu Islands, offsetting the decline of the Hakata–northern tier islands spoke. Okinawa was beginning to break away from Gusuku, and communities in Okinawa appear to have found alternative sources for Chinese ceramics. The Hakata–northern tier islands link was a vigorous trading conduit during the eleventh century and most of the twelfth. Thereafter, it declined.

Archaeological excavations near the mouth of the Manose River in the southern Satsuma Peninsula indicate that this area was an active trading center during the eleventh and twelfth centuries. Mottaimatsu is the most prominent site in that area. Of the pottery excavated there, container vessels are most prominent, which is a sign of trade. Excavations revealed five sunken-pillar buildings, a dug-out building, and two earth pit graves. Among these remains were found imported foreign pottery, pottery from every region of Japan, soapstone cauldrons, grindstones, inkstones, and iron goods. Of the excavated fragments, about half came from local pottery. Chinese blue ware constituted 17 percent, Chinese white ware 11 percent, and Chinese containers 11 percent. Pottery from other parts of Japan constituted 12 percent.

The composition of imported trade pottery at the Manose River area matches the items that would have been found in a Chinese cargo ship's hold, and the port at the old mouth of the river was a suitable anchorage for Chinese ships. The presence of a significant quantity of Chinese porcelain in the lower Manose River area indicates a connection with Hakata and the likely possibility that Chinese ships bound for Hakata sometimes anchored there. The presence of *kamuiyaki* and turbo shells—rare elsewhere in Kyushu—indicates that a regional spoke extended from the northern Ryukyu Islands to the Manose River area.

Turning to the island of Okinawa, Early Gusuku Era communities are found mainly along the central and southern portions of the west coast. Unlike Shell Mound Era communities, these newer settlements featured standardized buildings and pit tombs for the reburial of cremated bones as well as typical Gusuku Era pottery. These features had much in common with Kikaijima. The island of Okinawa was closely connected with both the northern and the southern Ryukyu Islands at this time.

The Gusuku Era did not begin until the early twelfth century in the southern Ryukyu Islands, another indication of a north-to-south movement of people and culture. All but one of the seven known early settlements on the island of Miyako are located along its northeast coast. At these locations, dark-brown glazed ware and *kamuiyaki* from Tokunoshima are found in much greater quantities than are Chinese goods. In other words, the majority of goods excavated in Miyako from the twelfth and the thirteenth centuries arrived there from Okinawa and from Japanese merchants. Indeed, the communities themselves were probably founded by people who came to Miyako from Okinawa and/or the Japanese mainland. These were groups of mariners who founded communities that persisted until the fourteenth or fifteenth centuries. The twelfth- and thirteenth-century population of Miyako was relatively small, but it grew rapidly during the fourteenth century.

In the Yaeyama Islands between the eleventh and the thirteenth centuries, trade was conducted by groups from Japan traveling south. Products included soapstone cauldrons and Chinese white ware and eating utensils. Later, more varieties of white ware, several varieties of blue ware, dark-brown glazed storage pots, and a variety of beads and jewels came into the area. Other excavated goods include stone ovens, broad fibrous leaves (banana and others), *kamuiyaki*, and other large storage containers. These items reflect an important change in material culture for a region that had previously been without any pottery. In addition to pottery, iron tools appeared in the southern Ryukyu Islands around this time. Valves for small-scale earth bellows have been found in Ishigaki, in Hateruma, in Taketomi Island, and at other locations dating from the eleventh through the thirteenth century. Valves from large stone bellows have been found in Ishigaki, in Iriomote, in Yonaguni, and in Hateruma. In other words, during the twelfth and the thirteenth centuries, blacksmith facilities spread throughout the southern Ryukyu Islands.

Maritime routes connected Busan in southern Korea, Hakata, and the Ryukyu Islands. As noted previously, it is almost certain that Koreans resided in Gusuku. Excavations indicate iron manufacture during the eleventh and twelfth centuries in Kikaijima, and the furnaces used technology imported from the Korean Peninsula. Given the vast amount of pottery production in Tokunoshima and the use of Korean technology, it is likely that Korean technicians resided on the island. There was extensive Korean technical and cultural influence on the northern Ryukyu Islands during the Early Gusuku Era. The extent to which that influence reflected movements of Korean people into the Ryukyu Islands is less clear, although at least some presence is almost certain.

Expanding Trade and Warfare

The Later Gusuku Era

During the Gusuku Era, the Ryukyu Islands became a frontier region of Japan. Although poorly suited to agriculture, the islands were ideal for obtaining valuable marine resources. More important, the many harbors and anchorages were ideal for maritime trade. Sailors based in the islands picked up products in one location in the East China Sea region and transported them to another part for sale at a profit. Similarly, before the sixteenth century, the Ryukyu Islands were an ideal location for piratical activities such as smuggling, marauding, and human trafficking. First, there was no central government that might suppress such activities. Second, Ryukyuan harbors put pirates within raiding range of China, Japan, and Korea (via western Kyushu). Additionally, Ryukyuan harbors were beyond the range of naval forces from the region's major states. During the Gusuku Era, both trade and piracy increased. The same groups often practiced both trade and piracy, depending on the circumstances.

The island of Okinawa was a relative backwater at the start of the Gusuku Era. However, during the thirteenth century, Okinawa became ever more populous, and its harbors became bases for trade. By the fourteenth century, it was the most prominent of the Ryukyu Islands. As we have seen, the Gusuku Era is named for the hundreds of fortresses built throughout the Ryukyu Islands. Initially, these fortresses were small, but their size increased over time. By the start of the fourteenth century, large stone-walled fortresses began to appear in Okinawa. Many of them are called *castles* in the modern era, although not always consistently. For example, the names *Nakagusuku gusuku*, *Nakagusuku Fortress*, and *Nakagusuku Castle* refer to the same structure.

Excavations at medium and large fortress sites typically turn up armor and weapons fragments. Archaeologists have noted a steady increase in the quantity of arrowheads excavated from such sites from the thirteenth century on, reaching a peak in the early fifteenth century. These arrowheads are one indicator of the increasing frequency of warfare. The lucrative trade at harbors in Okinawa and the other Ryukyu Islands was conducive both to cooperation between trading groups and to violent struggle.

As I have discussed at length in *Maritime Ryukyu* (2019), the late thirteenth century through the early fifteenth was a time when *wakō* groups were the main drivers of the region's maritime history. *Wakō* found their way into the Ryukyu Islands in part because of economic opportunity and in part because of political and military convulsions around the East China Sea region. Relevant regional geopolitical disturbances include the following:

1. The Sambyeolcho Rebellion in mainland Korea and Jeju Island, 1270–73
2. The collapse of the southern Song dynasty in 1279
3. The breakup of the Yuan dynasty during the 1350s and 1360s
4. The tumultuous final decades of the Goryeo dynasty in Korea, ca. 1350–92
5. The struggle between the northern and the southern courts in Japan, ca. 1335–92

The collapse of the Song dynasty and its replacement by the Mongol Yuan dynasty encouraged direct trade between parts of the Ryukyu Islands and southern China. The other four events drove people into the Ryukyu Islands.

Wakō

The term *wakō* (K. *waegu*) is of Korean origin, appearing first in the Gwanggaeto Stele of 414 and, more relevantly for our purposes, in *Goryeo History* in an entry dated 1223. The common translation, *Japanese pirates*, is misleading. Although many *wakō* were based in Japan, many were not Japanese. During the time period covered in this chapter, most *wakō* were either Japanese, Korean, or of mixed Japanese and Korean ancestry. In addition to the Ryukyu Islands, *wakō* bases were located in Japanese harbors, especially in western Kyushu, Iki, and Tsushima.

Wakō of this era often engaged in piratical activities such as marauding, human trafficking, and smuggling. They were dangerous and often destructive. Depending on circumstances, they also engaged in ordinary trade, thereby dispersing goods, culture, and technology throughout the East China Sea region. *Wakō* groups sometimes also facilitated diplomacy or functioned as hired security, often vis-à-vis other *wakō* groups. They maintained horse pastures in several locations, in part to provide for their own cavalry and in part for sale at a profit. The dividing line between maritime merchants, who operated with armed crews, and *wakō*, who often functioned as maritime merchants, was often unclear. This point would apply to pirates in many parts of the world, who often moved back and forth between legitimate enterprises and piratical activities. Like pirates the world over, *wakō* mainly pursued profit. They switched modes accordingly, sometimes marauding, sometimes smuggling, sometimes acting like conventional merchants, and sometimes engaging in other pursuits—even fishing or agriculture—if conditions were favorable. Buying them off became the preferred approach of China's Ming dynasty.

Attacks by *wakō* on coastal areas of southern Korea were especially common during the fourteenth century. Marauding in coastal China was somewhat less frequent, but *wakō* became a major concern for the Ming dynasty. In their raids, they carried off food, livestock, other valuables, people, and even boats and ships. Captives were especially valuable. Many were sold into servitude, typically for limited periods of time. Brokers from Korea sought to repatriate victims of *wakō* raids, and Korean captives were also valuable diplomatically. Nearly every voyage to Korea authorized by Okinawan trade kings included Koreans to be repatriated, a certain indication of close ties between *wakō* groups and the trade kings. In this context, the port of Naha functioned as a regional center for human trafficking. Koreans captured by one *wakō* group, for example, might end up in Naha. From Naha, another *wakō* group might profit from sending them back to Korea.

On the basis mainly of the archaeological record, we know that the overall pace of economic activity and warfare within the Ryukyu Islands corresponded closely with an upsurge in *wakō* activity in the East China Sea region. Moreover, during the thirteenth and fourteenth centuries, legends derived from Japan's Genpei Wars (1180–85) spread throughout the Ryukyu Islands. Most prominent among these was that of Minamoto Tametomo (1139–70), a legend so important that chapter 16 is devoted to it.

Okinawa was an especially favored by *wakō* groups because of its location and its anchorages. It was connected with Japan, Korea, and northern China via relatively easy island hopping and coastal sailing. For larger ships with skilled crews, the wealthy areas of the lower Yangzi River and coastal southern China were approximately one week's voyage away with decent weather. It is also important to note that, during the Yuan dynasty and continuing into the Ming dynasty, the demand for sulfur in China increased as gunpowder weapons proliferated. *Wakō* groups were closely connected with the sulfur trade. The source of most of the sulfur sent to China was western Kyushu, the Satsunan Islands, and the small the island of Iōtorishima just west of Tokunoshima.

In the context of the Later Gusuku Era, it is common to speak of local warlords (*aji*), and, from the 1370s on, kings (i.e., trade kings). Many of these people were also *wakō* or worked closely with *wakō* groups. Almost every official voyage from Naha to Korea included repatriated captives. Moreover, no official voyages during this time were attacked by *wakō* (this situation changed during the early modern era). These facts indicate that Ryukyuan powers worked closely with the *wakō* who supplied these captives. This and subsequent chapters will provide additional insights into that situation.

Iron Tools

Settlements in the Ryukyu Islands developed origin tales. Islandwide origin tales also developed during the fifteenth and sixteenth centuries. Origin stories for local warlords and priestesses (*noro*) come in several motifs. In all of them, maritime warlords and priestesses arrive in island communities from the outside, either vertically (from the heavens) or horizontally (from across the sea). In the latter case, the legendary founders of communities typically arrived from "Yamato" (mainland Japan).

The earliest iterations of origin tales had nothing to say about kings. Origin tales of kings were later, early modern adaptations of the origin tales of maritime warlords and priestesses. In the legendary royal biographies found in the official histories, Shunten, Satto, Shō Hashi, and Shō En (Kanemaru) managed, after considerable adversity, to gain the throne. Their success was due in large part to iron and to assistance from blacksmiths. Satto, Shō Hashi, and Shō En were all outsiders who came into Okinawa from points north. Iron obtained from Japanese ships is a key part of their stories. In royal biographies, obtaining iron from Japan indicates someone who came into the Ryukyu Islands from the Japanese islands.

Tales of blacksmiths and iron in connection with figures like Satto coincide with the start of large fortress construction. Iron tools would almost certainly have been necessary for building these structures. *Omoro sōshi*, 17-1204, tells of Nakijin's Serikaku priestess making a stone wall using a hammer-like tool called a *hetsu*. The song employs the paired term *ishihetsu-kanahetsu*. The first part of the pair, *ishihetsu*, indicates a stone hammer. *Kanahetsu* could mean either a metal hammer or a strong hammer. Similarly, *Omoro sōshi*, 20-1348, tells of the stonemason Machiyayo working in southern Okinawa with a stone/metal axe. The pairing of stone and iron tools for cutting stone occurs in three other *omoro* (*Omoro sōshi*, 9-496, 10-527, 10-538). Iron and blacksmiths figure prominently in Ryukyuan legends because iron was chronically in short supply. Stone tools were not as efficient as their iron counterparts. However, in an environment of cheap, plentiful labor, they could be economically viable.

The Slave Trade and Human Trafficking

During the fourteenth and fifteenth centuries, Naha was a regional center for human trafficking. Large fortress construction required quarrying stone, hauling it up to construction sites atop elevated terrain, and building high stone walls with simple tools. Given the prevalence of unfree labor in the region and *wakō* activity in Okinawa, unfree labor must have contributed to building Okinawa's large fortresses and other infrastructure. Many documents mention human trafficking, and the example offered below is a rare example of a detailed account.

A 1453 entry in *Joseon Veritable Royal Records* (the official records of the Joseon court in Korea) is a lengthy account featuring Dōan, a Japanese Buddhist priest from Hakata serving as an envoy for the Okinawan trade king. Dōan explained to a Korean official that, in 1450, four Koreans drifted into the "Wasa Islands" (Korean for the Tokara Islands). He stated that half the islands belonged to Ryukyu and half to Satsuma. However, it was not the case that there was a territorial boundary line running through the islands. Instead, Dōan's statement indicated that the Tokara Islands as a whole were a border region where Ryukyuan powers and the power of Satsuma overlapped. The Tokara Islands had no overlord. They functioned as a maritime commons in which the business of buying and selling people took place (fig. 4.1).

Dōan explained that, from the Tokara Islands, two of the shipwrecked Koreans went to "people from Satsuma." The other two, Mannyeon and Jeonglu, were brought to Kasari in Amami-Ōshima, just across from Kikaijima. After about ten days, an agent arrived from "Ryukyu" (Okinawa) and purchased Mannyeon, using fine cloth as payment. The agent brought Mannyeon to Okinawa and delivered him to the trade king in Shuri, Shō Kinpuku. There, Mannyeon and two others were assigned to learn how to use a "torch" (the precise meaning of which is unclear).

One day Mannyeon observed one of the other slaves stealing ramie from a storehouse, and he reported the theft. Impressed, the king put him in charge of watching over a royal storehouse. After three months, another Okinawan agent—an agent for someone other than the Shuri king, who was unaware of Mannyeon's arrival in Okinawa—went to Kasari and purchased Jeonglu with copper cash. Eventually, Mannyeon found out that Jeonglu was in Okinawa, and the king told him to go to the house where Jeonglu

FIGURE 4.1. The Tokara Islands as a maritime commons
between Satsuma and the Ryukyu Islands

was residing and exchange another slave for him. Mannyeon and Jeonglu
worked for the king for three years, after which time he sent them back to
Korea with Dōan. He told Dōan that, if Korean officials are pleased with the
return of Mannyeon and Jeonglu, the Shuri king had other Koreans who
could be returned as well.

The case of the four Koreans illuminates some important details about
human-trafficking networks. First, agents of the Shuri king and other Okinawan agents actively procured Koreans in the northern Ryukyu Islands.
The passage also notes that Okinawan military forces were active in the area
and that the king's brother was preparing to attack Kikaijima. Nevertheless, it is unclear whether the Kasari Peninsula of Amami-Ōshima was under
Shuri's firm control at this time. The passage also indicates that slaves were
often exchanged. A new one coming into the king's service would free an
existing one to be repatriated.

The powerful Okinawan lord Gosamaru (d. 1458), who eventually resided in Nakagusuku Fortress, previously built Zakimi Fortress. According to an early modern biography, the people who built Zakimi included

laborers brought in from places like Kikaijima and Amami-Ōshima. Unfortunately, we have no further details. Nakagusuku and Katsuren Fortresses maintained close ties with the northern Ryukyu Islands and, in the case of Katsuren at least, also with Korea.

Among Koreans who found themselves in Naha or other parts of the Ryukyu Islands against their will, Mannyeon and Jeonglu ended up in relatively good circumstances. They may well have suffered privation, including poor compensation for their labor. Nevertheless, because Mannyeon oversaw a storehouse, his situation was much better than, for example, that of a laborer quarrying, hauling, or cutting rocks to make the steep walls of a fortress. As of this writing, a detailed understanding of unfree labor in the early Ryukyu Islands still eludes us.

Hub-and-Spoke Changes

Looking at the northern, central, and southern Ryukyu Islands as three distinct groups, the general pattern of vigorous activity in Okinawa and the southern Ryukyu Islands from the late thirteenth century to the early fifteenth emerges. For part of this time, the northern Ryukyu Islands became more closely connected with Satsuma in southern Kyushu and less closely tied to the other Ryukyu Islands. However, during the early fifteenth century, the northern islands again became closely connected with Okinawa.

Archaeologists have noted a substantial increase in the presence of Chinese ceramics from the mid-fourteenth century on, in both Okinawa and the southern Ryukyu Islands. Did this increase mean that local powers had started trading directly with their Chinese counterparts? Or were the ceramics still coming from Hakata as before? Or was it a combination of both? We know that by about 1350 there was direct trade between Chinese merchants and the port of Naha in Okinawa. It is unclear at what point prior to 1350 this trade started. In the southern Ryukyu Islands, direct trade between seafarers based at the island of Miyako and locations in southern China and Southeast Asia was under way by the early fourteenth century, as explained in more detail below.

The hub-and-spoke model for the Later Gusuku Era became more complex than the one illustrating the Early Gusuku Era situation. By the mid-fourteenth century, both Okinawa and the southern Ryukyu Islands had become hubs (fig. 4.2). Moreover, major political and military events in the region all had important implications for the Ryukyu Islands. The following paragraphs examine different parts of the region.

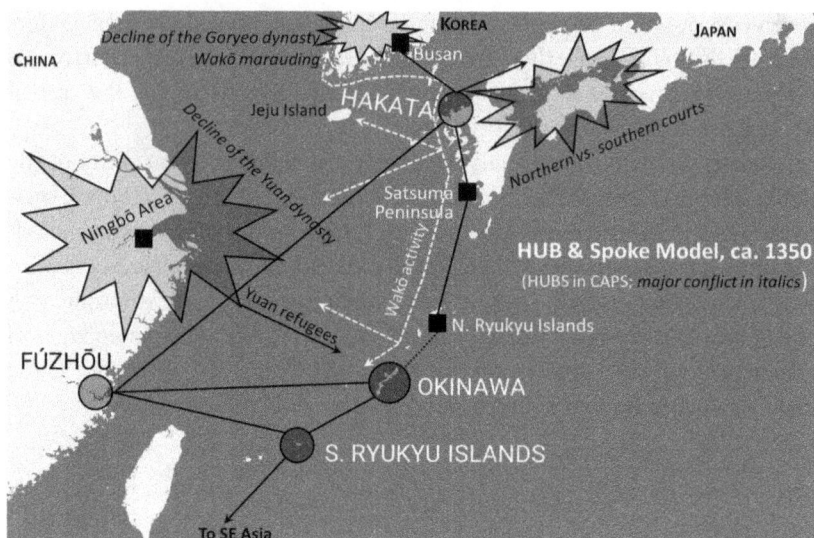

FIGURE 4.2. An updated iteration of the hub-and-spoke model of regional
trade reflecting conditions ca. 1350, including major regional conflicts

For much of the fourteenth century, the northern Ryukyu Islands became more closely linked with powers in Satsuma than with Okinawa and
the southern Ryukyu Islands. A 1306 document, *Chikama monjo*, describes
the property of Chikama Tokiie, in Kawanabe-gun, Satsuma. The northern Ryukyu Islands were part of Chikama's holdings, and he distributed
them to various members of his family. A half map of Japan surrounded
by a dragon from the early fourteenth century confirms this situation. Beyond the dragon is territory labeled "Ryūkyū-koku Ushima [Okinawa] . . .
Amemi [Amami], private territory." During the early fourteenth century,
the northern Ryukyu Islands were the territory of the Chikama family.
Late in the century, they became more closely attached to the rest of the
Ryukyu Islands via trade networks. The deterioration of China's Yuan dynasty, which stared in the 1340s, made the voyage from Hakata to the port
of Níngbō in China increasingly perilous. Therefore, more ships began using the southern islands route from Hakata to Fúzhōu via western Kyushu
and the Ryukyu Islands. Maritime traffic thereby reconnected the northern
Ryukyu Islands to Okinawa and points south during the latter half of the
fourteenth century.

The southern Ryukyu Islands became more populous and active throughout the fourteenth century, especially the island of Miyako. At some point
during the late thirteenth century or the early fourteenth, traders residing in Miyako began to deal directly with entities in China and beyond.

According to Chinese records, fourteen Mìyágǔ (Miyako) people on their way to conduct trade in Southeast Asia were caught in a storm, blown into China, and returned to their country in 1317. The account of their rescue and repatriation reveals that people from Bora in eastern Miyako had been sailing to Southeast Asia to trade. Excavations at the Boranomotojima site in Miyako unearthed pottery from Vietnam and Southeast Asian locations as well as from China. In coastal southern China, there were people who could communicate with these Bora sailors, indicating direct contact with China as well. If direct trade between Miyako, China, and Southeast Asia was in place by 1317, it must have been occurring for some time previously, although we cannot say precisely when given the current evidence.

The fourteenth and fifteenth centuries were a time when Chinese wares rapidly increased in quantity everywhere in Miyako. The most likely scenario is that most of these wares came from direct trade with merchants in China, especially after the establishment of the Ming dynasty in 1368. Technically, such trade would have been illegal. In 1390, for the first time, pepper and sappanwood (*Biancaea sappan*) were listed as items that Chūzan (an entity in Okinawa) presented to China's Ming court as tribute (de facto trade goods). Contact with the southern Ryukyu Islands put Chūzan in possession of those valuable items, which came from tropical Asia. Moreover, these two products were listed in the items Chūzan sent to Korea in 1389 along with Koreans who had been captured by pirates. The story in the official histories of Miyako presenting tribute to Chūzan in 1390 actually reflects Okinawan traders obtaining pepper and sappanwood via trade with Miyako sailors, who obtained the items in Southeast Asia.

During the 1370s, the Ming court banned private international trade, but a flood of Chinese ceramics came into all parts of the southern Ryukyu Islands starting around this time. Chinese goods poured into the southern Ryukyu Islands in relatively larger quantities than they came into Okinawa or the Japanese mainland. Items exchanged for Chinese goods included maritime products such as seashells and turtle shells. In addition, local residents traded sea cucumbers, shark fins, dugongs, cowhide, ramie, banana fiber cloth, and medicinal plants. Nagura Bay on the west side of Ishigaki Island was a major site for this trade. Several thousand pieces of fifteenth- and sixteenth-century white ware and blue ware from a sunken Chinese ship have been excavated from the bottom of the bay at the Nagura Shitadaru Seafloor Site, indicating the large scale of private (illegal) trade. Because tribute trade ships sailing to Fúzhōu from Okinawa would occasionally have put in at local ports, the private trade in the region would almost certainly have been known to both Shuri and Chinese authorities.

In relative terms, the period from the late fourteenth century through the fifteenth century was the time of maximum maritime activity in the southern Ryukyu Islands, and much of this activity was illegal in the eyes of the Ming court. A 1452 order from the Chinese Ministry of Justice to residents of coastal Fúzhōu, in the context of a local uprising, is revealing. Among other things, the order prohibited contacting Ryukyuans by ship and serving as guides for pirates. In this document, pirates and Ryukyuans were synonymous. The surge in the trade between the southern Ryukyu Islands and southern China may have encouraged Shuri's 1500 (and later) invasions of the Yaeyama Islands.

Yuan Dynasty Breakup and Refugees in Northern Okinawa

The Mongol Yuan dynasty began to deteriorate in the 1340s after a revolt by Fāng Guózhēn established a separatist area based in Táizhōu (near Níngbō). Fāng's supporters included pirates, and their activities destabilized the Níngbō-to-Hakata route, increasing maritime traffic through the Ryukyu Islands. The Red Turban Revolts of 1351 and 1368 further weakened the Yuan dynasty. After the establishment of the Ming dynasty in 1368, remnants of the military forces of coastal rebels like Fāng remained active as brigands. Farther inland, fighting continued against various Mongol powers in the north.

In 1305, the Korean island of Jeju came under the nominal control of the Goryeo court, but it was never fully conquered. Mongols moved into Jeju as part of a project to raise horses, and they intermarried with local people. When *wakō* fled to Jeju in 1367 under pressure from Goryeo forces, the Mongols fought alongside them. In 1372, when Jeju came under *wakō* attack, local people did not help efforts to suppress them. The key point is that Mongol remnants in Jeju were closely connected with *wakō*, and they were active during the last half of the fourteenth century. With this point in mind, let us turn to northern Okinawa.

The linguist and historian Uema Atsushi argues that, during the late fourteenth century, refugees from the Yuan dynasty took up residence in Nakijin (Uema 2018). Many of these refugees consisted of ethnic Alans who had served the Yuan court. Moreover, Han'anchi, the lord of Nakijin Castle, came from these people. Uema's evidence is extensive, and the paragraphs below offer a highly abbreviated summary of it.

Alans were widely distributed across the Eurasian continent. In the mid-thirteenth century, a group of Alans adopted Greek Orthodoxy and began using Greek script when writing their language. When Kublai Khan assembled an army composed of units from Central Asia, an Alan cavalry unit served as an advance guard. Later, when invading the lower Yangzi delta, Kublai deployed Alan cavalry as part of his forces. One record from 1330 indicates a Christian force on the outskirts of Yángzhōu, near Nánjīng. It is plausible that an Alan squadron had been posted there to guard recently pacified southern Song territory.

Alan-specific items excavated from Nakijin include left-turning, Greco-Roman-style grooved portable stone grain mills. (Stone mills for grinding grain in East Asia were right-turning mills.) The Nakijin mills are small, commensurate with cavalry use, and predated grain mills in Japan by about two centuries. Excavated items associated with the mantic arts include white ceramic bowls stamped with swastikas to form a convex impression. In Mongolian culture, swastikas were amulets that protected horses (among other functions).

Han'anchi ruled Nakijin from about 1401 to 1406, and the story of his military demise in *Sai On Genealogy of Chūzan* has him carving a cross in the sacred stone of Kanahiyabu before killing himself. Items excavated from the center of Nakijin Castle included two solid body blue ware bowls with Greek-style crosses stamped into them and a blue flower bowl decorated with a Greek cross on the bottom of it. Given that the Ryukyu Islands were a frontier region of Japan by this time, Han'anchi and his group may have included the earliest Christians in the greater Japan region.

Military gear excavated from Nakijin includes portable rasps similar to those used by Mongolian cavalry, flat and chisel-headed arrowheads, and small swords and daggers. The triangular flat arrowheads and bone arrowheads from Nakijin resemble those used by the Mongol cavalry. Excavated small swords are of the same design as those used by peoples of the Eurasian plains. Nard is a Persian game similar to backgammon. Nard dice and stone playing pieces were excavated at Nakijin.

Why and how did these Mongols and Alans end up in northern Okinawa? During both the Song and the Yuan dynasties, Persian, Arab, Jewish, and Armenian merchants resided in the Jiāngnán trading cities (the area near the mouth of the Yangzi River) and formed foreign enclaves along the coast. During the breakup of the Yuan court and the start of the Ming, forces rebelling against the Yuan expelled these enclaves as part of a general anti-foreign sentiment. Uema (2018) argues that the distinctive Alan and Mongol items found at Nakijin were not the result of trade but left behind by refugees from the collapsing Yuan dynasty crossing over to northern Okinawa. The Alan served the Yuan court as cavalry and frontline soldiers, but they were not the only foreign force. Those who ended up in Nakijin from the continent probably constituted a broad spectrum of Mongol remnants.

Note also the situation in Jeju Island described above whereby anti-Ming Mongol remnants aligned with *wakō*. The same thing may have happened in northern Okinawa.

Okinawa-Based China Trade

Survey histories often imply or assume that direct trade between entities in Okinawa and in China did not occur until the start of formal tribute relations with the Ming dynasty in the 1370s. However, direct trade between local Ryukyuan powers and Chinese entities became well established during the Yuan Era. Horses and sulfur were tribute goods from the very beginning of the Ming tribute trade, and Chinese agents came to Okinawa to buy horses in 1376. Given these dates, trade in horses and sulfur must have been established at some point prior to the start of the Ming dynasty. Official records indicate the same conclusion. An entry dated 1411 in *Ming Veritable Records* notes that the Chinese head envoy, Chéng Fù (Tei Fuku), had served the Okinawan king Satto diligently for more than forty years. This year, the entry states, Chéng is eighty-one, and he has asked permission to return to China. According to official sources, Satto died around 1395. If so, then Chéng Fù had been in Okinawa during the 1350s.

The powerful Katsuren Fortress on Okinawa's east coast did not accumulate much Chinese pottery before the mid-fourteenth century, nor did it formally participate in the tribute trade with Ming China. Nevertheless, from the mid-fourteenth century on, the quality and quantity of Katsuren's Chinese pottery increased greatly. The rapid growth in wealth of Katsuren could have been the result only of private trade with merchants in China.

Regional Disruptions

During the fourteenth century, Okinawan harbors filled up with powerful maritime traders, many of whom were *wakō*. They functioned as pirates, smugglers, or merchants, depending on the circumstances. Political and social dislocation contributed much to this *wakō* presence. Consider the year 1350. The Yuan dynasty in China was beginning to break up. Japan was in the midst of a civil war between the northern and the southern courts. Strife in Korea was also intensifying (fig. 4.2). One likely effect of conflict in Korea was the arrival in Urasoe, Okinawa, of Satto, or more likely a group using that name. Another likely effect of regional strife was the port of Naha becoming a major center for human trafficking.

Recall that unrest in China caused the southern islands route from Hakata to China to become active, thus increasing the volume of shipping passing through the Ryukyu Islands from the 1340s on. Conditions in Korea, Japan, and China all had direct and indirect impacts on the islands. Okinawa became an appealing location for maritime groups from all over the East China Sea region as the major states underwent violent political transitions. Moreover, for complex reasons that I have explained elsewhere, concentrating *wakō* in the Ryukyu Islands became official Ming policy during the 1370s (see Smits 2019, 64–66).

This situation set the stage for several decades of intense warfare within Okinawa. The official histories later portrayed this warfare relatively simply—as a military struggle between the armies of three small kingdoms. In fact, as we will see, the struggle was more complex than a three-way battle.

The Ryukyu Islands as a Barbarian Zone

This chapter describes major changes in the Ryukyu Islands that took place during the fourteenth century or thereabouts. Political disruptions around the East China Sea region caused dislocations of people, trade routes, and trade dynamics. These dislocations resulted in an increase in *wakō* activity and in new groups of people of diverse ethnic backgrounds coming into the Ryukyu Islands, some willingly, and others as a result of human trafficking. The most striking physical manifestation of this situation was the creation of large fortresses. Well before the start of formal tribute trade in the 1370s, entities in Okinawa and the southern Ryukyu Islands began trading directly with China. They traded local products plus items acquired in or from Japan, Korea, and Southeast Asia.

Zooming out to consider the big picture, the major discontinuity in the history of the Ryukyu Islands was the replacement of the previous indigenous populations and cultures by northern migrants, mostly from Japan, starting in the eleventh century. Thus began Japonic Ryukyu, a group of societies based on trade and supplemented by agriculture whose people spoke Japonic languages. The fourteenth century—or more precisely what might be considered the long fourteenth century—was a time of major transition within the broad framework of Japonic Ryukyu as the entire East China Sea region experienced political turmoil. This turmoil sent refugees and others into the Ryukyu Islands. New powers emerged there, and the competition for profit became more violent and intense.

Another big-picture point to consider is that, from the Stone Age until about the 1620s or the 1630s, most of the Ryukyu Islands were not isolated.

Their location and the presence of valuable marine products ensured some degree of movement of people and goods prior to the Gusuku Era. During the Gusuku Era, the frequency of movement of people into, out of, and between the Ryukyu Islands intensified. In general, this movement was north to south. However, as the case of the Mongol refugees in Nakijin illustrates, the Ryukyu Islands functioned as a de facto frontier region not only vis-à-vis Japan but with respect to the entire East China Sea region. In chapter 7 below, I examine the strong influence of Korean culture and technology in the Ryukyu Islands.

The major states of the East China Sea region were all agricultural societies. By contrast, the early Ryukyu Islands were based mainly on trade, not agricultural surpluses. Furthermore, until about 1530, the islands were not part of a single state. With a focus on ancient Mesopotamia, James C. Scott has examined the interaction between states and the groups states typically labeled *barbarians*, that is, the nonstate peoples beyond their borders. This interaction might take many forms depending on the circumstances, sometimes relatively peaceful trading, sometimes violent raiding. Ultimately, early states depended on the nonagricultural people outside their borders to provide them with essential goods and services. According to Scott, the heyday of such barbarian groups (he attaches no pejorative sense to *barbarian*) around the world lasted into the sixteenth century (Scott 2017).

The prestate Ryukyu Islands constituted such a barbarian zone. Sailors based in the islands conducted widespread commerce, facilitating the movement of people, goods, culture, and technologies between the Korean Peninsula, the Japanese islands, southern China, and island Southeast Asia. These same sailors, however, were also capable of seizing people and goods by force and inflicting significant violence on the region's coasts.

Within the frontier region that was the Ryukyu Islands, when did a distinct ethnic group that we could reasonably call *Ryukyuans* emerge? This question is complex, but, as of approximately 1400, such an ethnic group had yet to emerge. In other words, there is no evidence that people living anywhere in the Ryukyu Islands regarded themselves as Ryukyuans (or anything else) at that time. We have seen one example of a fifteenth-century Chinese document referring to the inhabitants of the southern Ryukyu Islands as *Ryukyuans*, but the term indicated pirates or potential pirates, not a distinct cultural or ethnic group. There are several likely reasons for the absence of ethnogenesis ca. 1400. One is that there was no centralized state. The existence of a centralized state does not in itself cause ethnogenesis, but it can set the stage for it. I examine the creation of a state and the emergence of ethnogenesis in parts 2 and 3 below.

[CHAPTER FIVE]

The Early Theatrical Kingdom and the Three Principalities Era in Okinawa

Nearly every modern survey history of Ryukyu contains a similar narrative about the period from the early fourteenth century to ca. 1429. Simply stated, the island of Okinawa consisted of three small kingdoms or principalities, arrayed from north to south. These principalities were confederations of local warlords. Each was a complete state, with a monarch, military forces, a diplomatic corps, and a bureaucracy. Moreover, agriculture was the basis of the economies of all three states. Sometimes these little states cooperated and sometimes they competed or went to war with each other. Eventually, Shō Hashi of Chūzan, originally of Sannan, waged war against the other principalities and, in 1429 or thereabouts, united all Okinawa under his rule.

This narrative, derived from the official histories, is inaccurate in almost every way. For example, *Reflections on Chūzan* states that Shō Hashi conquered the other two principalities to end the suffering of the common people. It then claims that Hashi notified China's Ming court of unification in 1423. However, no such notification ever took place. Ryukyu's official histories are not even in agreement about when the principalities were united, with *Reflections* claiming that the process was completed in 1422 and the 1725 version of *Genealogy of Chūzan* putting the year at 1429. Similarly, the start of the Three Principalities Era is unclear. Both *Reflections* and *Genealogy* indicate only that it began at an unspecified time during the reign of Tamagusuku (r. 1314–36). In sum, there is no strong evidence to support the standard narrative about the three principalities, and much evidence calls it into question.

The historian Ikuta Shigeru has advanced a strong argument that these three little kingdoms did not exist except on paper (Ikuta 1984a, 1992). Most modern historians and other scholars, however, have been unwilling to contradict the official histories in any substantial way. Taking an interdisciplinary approach, and drawing on a variety of insights from Japanese scholarship, this chapter presents a new and original account of the political history of Okinawa during the Three Principalities Era. For it to make sense, we need to examine some fundamental concepts and assumptions, starting with the idea of kings.

What Did *King* Mean?

The word *king* can be misleading because it did always not mean the same thing across periods, languages, and places. Consider a recent definition from *Merriam-Webster*:

> a: a male monarch of a major territorial unit
>   *especially*: one whose position is hereditary and who rules for life
> b: a paramount chief[1]

King is, of course, an English word, but, in the case of fourteenth- and fifteenth-century Okinawa, the relevant term is the Chinese title *wáng*.[2] More specifically, the rank of Okinawan *wáng* was *jùnwáng* (郡王). In late imperial China, sons of imperial princes often held *jùnwáng* status. When applied to foreign rulers or powerholders, *jùnwáng* (and other *wáng* gradations) typically conferred trade privileges. Now consider this short, dictionary-like definition of *wáng* from the standpoint of China's Ming dynasty:

> a: a license to trade with the Chinese court and authorized Chinese merchants
>   *especially*: a foreign ruler who participates in the Ming tribute system according to specified conditions
> b: a locally prominent foreign ruler of sufficient power and status to be of interest to the Ming court as a potential ally

This definition changed over time. For example, from the 1530s on in Okinawa, in addition to the trade component, the title *wáng* included formal recognition by the Chinese court of a ruler's legitimacy, a process typically called *investiture* (Ch. *cèfēng*, J. *sappō* or *sakuhō* [冊封]). Moreover, the specific conditions or rules by which *wáng* interacted with the Chinese court changed over time and were often different from country to country.

Notice that holding the title *wáng* did not indicate anything about the extent of a holder's territory, wealth, or power, nor did it indicate a specific form of government. The crucial point for our purposes is that people who held that title in Okinawa or groups operating under the auspices of the title were not part of centralized states until the early sixteenth century. The English word *king* implies the existence of a kingdom, and the term *kingdom* implies a centralized, bureaucratic state headed by a monarch. Such a state did develop in the Ryukyu Islands, but not before the sixteenth century.

For additional context, consider Japan. There, in the standard narrative, the Ashikaga shoguns held the Chinese title *kings of Japan*. However, during much of the sixteenth century, the Ōuchi of southwest Honshu and northwest Kyushu possessed the "king of Japan" seal and the know-how to conduct trade with both China and Korea. They also traded with Okinawan trade kings. Ōuchi rulers thereby became fabulously wealthy, and they were "kings in all but name," to reference the title of a book by Thomas Conlon (2024). As we will see, Okinawan trade kings were often the inverse: kings in name only.

Because using the term *wáng* is awkward, in these pages I refer to *kings* whose primary attribute was holding a license to trade with China as trade kings. All the Okinawan kings up to and including Shō En were trade kings. I designate rulers of a centralized bureaucratic state *kings*, dropping the qualifying *trade*. Shō Shin was a transitional figure. He began his long reign as a trade king and ended it as the monarch of a state that ruled, at least nominally, over all the Ryukyu Islands. Shō Shin, in other words, created the entity that we could reasonably call *the Ryukyu Kingdom* and, even more accurately, *the Shuri Empire*.

Holders of the title *wáng* in Okinawa during the fourteenth century and the early fifteenth enjoyed highly favorable conditions. Indeed, even some Okinawans who did not hold the title but simply claimed to be relatives of a trade king sometimes participated in formal trade with China. Moreover, because verification was almost nonexistent before the 1530s, almost any group of sailors based in Okinawa or elsewhere in the region could conduct business with China by using the name of a trade king even if the actual person bearing that title was no longer alive. Until the sixteenth century, the situation with respect to trade kings in Okinawa or people posing as trade kings was fluid and complex. The reason was the prominence of *wakō* in the Ryukyu Islands. The emergence of multiple trade kings in the island of Okinawa was a direct result of the Ming court's long-term policy of taming the region's *wakō*.

The Tribute System and Ming *Wakō* Policy

Like the word *king*, the term *tribute system* can be misleading. For one thing, there was no single system governing the interactions of foreign agents with the Chinese court. The rules and conditions changed over time and were specific to each country or polity. In these pages, I use *tribute system* loosely to describe the dominant approach or style with which China's Ming court interacted with foreign countries or outside groups (*barbarians* as defined in the previous chapter).

In the abstract, this approach was based on the classical notion of *lǐ*, the ritual enactment of social bonds. It was an extension of Chinese social organization to other countries. By presenting tribute to the court, countries and peoples outside the borders of China expressed ritual cultural subordination to the Chinese emperor. This subordination was a facade. The functional purpose of Chinese tribute policy was to make legitimate trade—trade according to rules made by the Chinese court—more profitable for foreign powers than piratical activities. *Wakō* were notorious for raiding and smuggling, but they could be incorporated into the framework of the tribute trade if the price was right.

One aspect of tribute practices involved certain foreign leaders receiving the title *trade king* from the Chinese court, along with formal seals, robes, hats, and other accoutrements. Typically, once every three years these foreign kings sent tribute to the Chinese emperor in the form of useful, prized, or exotic products, often domestically produced. To present this tribute, the kings sent delegations commonly called *tribute embassies*. Embassies consisted of formal envoys and official tribute plus a large entourage of merchants and a large quantity of other merchandise for use in private trade. After formally receiving the tribute goods in a ceremony, the emperor demonstrated his wealth and magnanimity by bestowing gifts on the envoys. These gifts typically were worth more than the tribute the envoys had just presented. Even more profitable was the private trade, which the merchants conducted after the formalities had concluded.

In this context, the title *king* identified groups that participated in the tribute trade. In principle, there was no limit to the number of kings within a territory. In Okinawa, almost as soon as Satto (or the Satto group) took the title *king* in 1372, two other trade kings appeared. The same thing happened in the tiny sultanate of Sulu near the Philippines. When it entered tributary relations with the Ming court, two more kings quickly appeared there. In the case of Okinawa, the situation was even more complex because the Ming court actually recognized two different royal lines doing business under the banner of Sannan. In other words, there were four lines of trade kings plus several more one-off trade kings.

Typically, both the public and the private aspects of the tribute trade were profitable for the elite members of the participating countries, potentially profitable for Chinese merchants, but expensive for the Chinese court.

Therefore, most Ming tributaries were eager to send embassies frequently, but the court imposed limits, most commonly one embassy every three years. In addition to trade, most participating countries were permitted to send a certain number of young men to study in China at Chinese government expense.

Entering into a tributary relationship did not entail political subordination to China. Therefore, tributary states usually could not expect Chinese assistance in times of emergency such as war, natural disasters, or internal rebellions. Occasionally China did intervene, for example, dispatching an army to block Toyotomi Hideyoshi's invasions of Korea in 1592 and 1597 (the Imjin War). In this case, however, the intervention served China's interests and was not altruistic. The court's main interest when it came to tributary states was in regulating trade and reducing military or piratical aggression directed at Chinese territory.

In *Maritime Ryukyu* (2019), I argue at length that concentrating *wakō* in the Ryukyu Islands was official Ming policy. The Ming court made several failed attempts to gain the cooperation of Prince Kaneyoshi (?–1388), the head of Japan's southern court in Kyushu. The original plan was for Kaneyoshi to take the title *king of Japan*, suppressing *wakō* in return for being permitted to trade with China. However, Kaneyoshi was a disappointment. He took full advantage of the trade but made no effort to suppress *wakō*. The Ming court then encouraged *wakō* powers to settle in the Ryukyu Islands, at which point they would be brought into the official tribute trade on generous terms. The short-term plan was, essentially, to pay off *wakō* powers. The long-term plan was for the Ming court gradually to regulate and tame the *wakō* (Smits 2019, 62–66; see also Yoshinari 2020, 176–77). To quote Yoshinari Naoki: "On the stage of Ryukyu the unlawful behavior of *wakō* was fundamentally transformed via the framework of the tribute system" (Yoshinari 2015, 93).

The three principalities in Okinawa functioned as channels whereby a variety of Okinawan powers could participate in the tribute trade. Until well into the fifteenth century, Ryukyuan powers were allowed unlimited tribute shipments, something permitted to no other country or group. The Ming court provided Chinese-made ships (captained by Chinese) for transporting this tribute, and it sent official merchants to Naha to process the relevant paperwork. Ryukyuans operating under the Sannan and Chūzan banners could study at China's National Academy. From the mid-fifteenth century, the Ming court gradually tightened the rules, in part because of Ryukyuan abuses of the system.

One result of the profitability of the tribute trade was almost constant warfare within Okinawa as ambitious local powers sought to control as much of the trade as possible. The most intense period of struggle was approximately 1380–1430. Several events and policies from around the East China Sea region fueled this competition. Most distant was the collapse of the Yuan dynasty. The dynasty did not fully collapse in 1368, however, and the Ming court was at war with Mongol Yuan remnants throughout the Three Principalities Era. The turbulent decline of the Goryeo state in Korea eventually resulted in the rise of the Joseon dynasty in 1392. In the background of the Korean situation was frequent attacks on the Korean coast and even inland areas by *wakō* based in Tsushima, Iki, and western Kyushu. Many of these *wakō* were affiliated with Japan's northern or southern courts.

Civil war had been raging throughout Japan since 1335, and during the 1380s the position of the southern court in Kyushu declined precipitously. Many southern court *wakō* in search of new bases came to the Ryukyu Islands. In the southern Ryukyu Islands, these arrivals became the main players in the warfare connected with the so-called age of heroes (*eiyū jidai*, ca. fifteenth century) in the Miyako and Yaeyama island groups. The age of heroes could more accurately be called *the age of warfare*, and an extensive body of legends developed in connection with these conflicts.

In the midst of this turmoil, Ming policy was to make the tribute trade more profitable than marauding and smuggling for *wakō* based in Okinawa. Before we look at some of the details, we need to pause and examine the political geography of Okinawa and the other Ryukyu Islands. To state the conclusion in advance, the main political unit in the Ryukyu Islands was independent harbor-fortress pairs.

Political Geography

Many survey histories provide "conceptual maps" featuring two arbitrary parallel lines dividing Okinawa into three parts. There is no evidence, however, that any such boundaries ever existed. These maps are also problematic because they give the impression that the three principalities were states consisting of contiguous territory encompassing large tracts of land. A focus on territory in the form of land distorts our view of early Ryukyuan history. Instead of terrestrial boundaries, we should focus instead on maritime networks.

The traditional focus on land results in part from the tendency to view the Ryukyu Islands as a small-scale, late-developing iteration of the history of the Japanese islands. In this mode of thinking, scholars tend to assume that the rise of the three principalities was based on agricultural surpluses. Similarly, the three principalities constituted a natural evolutionary process in state formation, leading to the full-fledged Ryukyu Kingdom. All these ideas are problematic. I examine agriculture in the next section. Here, the task is to survey the political geography of Okinawa during the fourteenth century and the early fifteenth. I do so from three perspectives: the fundamental geopolitical unit, the regional networks into which these units were embedded, and differences between eastern and western Okinawa.

The people modern histories commonly call *aji* (local chieftain, local warlord) did not rule large expanses of land. Instead, they controlled or partially controlled portions of sea-lanes. Their bases were at locations that featured a harbor suitable as anchorage for medium or large ships and a fortress overlooking that harbor. Most of these fortresses were of a type that featured stone walls, but some consisted of earthworks and trenches. Both types of fortresses are called *gusuku* (O. *gushiku*).

In 1350, or even a century later, neither Okinawa nor the Ryukyu Islands as a whole were part of a centralized state. Instead, the Ryukyu Islands were home to dozens or hundreds of local powers based mainly at fortresses overlooking harbors. Figure 5.1 indicates some prominent harbor-fortress units. In all cases, the wealth of these powers came largely from maritime trading and raiding, not from control of extensive land or from agricultural production.

The paragraphs below examine four of these harbor-fortress local powers, all located on the east coast of Okinawa. From north to south they are Katsuren, Nakagusuku, Sashiki (including Nawashiro and Tedokon), and Itokazu (fig. 5.1). We could add many more locations to the list, but these four are representative. My sources for examining them are *Omoro sōshi* songs and archaeology.

Each of these harbor-fortress locations has, according to *Omoro* songs, the following overlapping characteristics:

1. They accumulate or pile up wealth, often acquired from far-flung sources.
2. They pacify and/or rule over a wide area.
3. They possess soldiers and impressive weapons.
4. They possess impressive infrastructure or resources, often connected with water.

Because these four powers were linked with other harbors, a brief look at some of those locations is necessary.

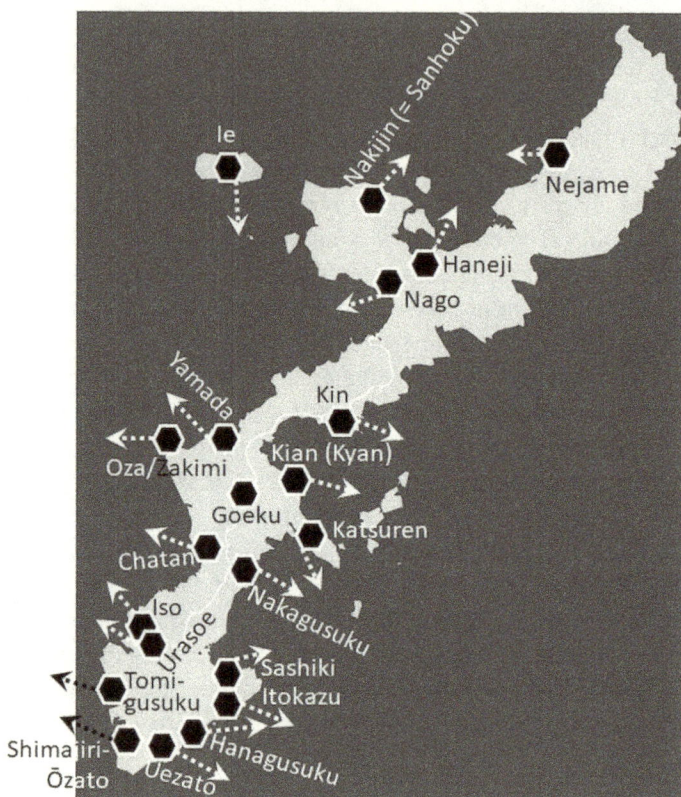

FIGURE 5.1. Locations of several harbor-fortress
units in and around Okinawa, ca. 1400

KATSUREN

"With what might we compare Katsuren," begins one short song. "It compares with Kamakura in Yamato" (*Omoro sōshi*, 16-1145). The city of Kamakura flourished between 1192 and 1333 as the capital of Japan's first military government (*bakufu*). This song praises Katsuren by likening it to Kamakura in its heyday. From the mid-fourteenth century, Katsuren was the scene of a rapid accumulation of wealth. Katsuren Fortress features four walled enclosures with dug-out trenches in strategic locations. The Chinese ceramics excavated from these enclosures indicate active international trade, and some structures in Katsuren feature Korean-style roof tiles.

Katsuren had close ties with the northern Ryukyu Islands, Kyushu, and the Korean Peninsula. The following two songs indicate some of those ties:

The sailors of Katsuren
Are a bridge to Ukejima and Yoroshima
Tokunoshima and Okinoerabu
Are relatives [of]
[Katsuren] sailor Mashifuri.

(*Omoro sōshi*, 13-938)

The sailors of Katsuren
Gain wealth when they sail
[From] Kikaijima and Amami-Ōshima
With which they are connected
[Katsuren] sailor Mashifuri.

(*Omoro sōshi*, 13-939)

Ukejima and Yoroshima—small islands near the southernmost part of Amami-Ōshima—were navigational markers for ships sailing north to Kikaijima. In these songs, Katsuren's power and wealth derived from its maritime connections and ships, not from agriculture.

NAKAGUSUKU

Nakagusuku is located just south of Katsuren along Okinawa's east coast. It was a maritime hub connected to parts of the northern Ryukyu Islands, Japan, and China. One *Omoro* song describes it as follows:

Nakagusuku, the base
The ship Falcon at the base
Pulls in and controls
Tokunoshima and Amami-Ōshima
Resounding base of the territory
Base of the territory wherein lies the ship *Falcon*.

(*Omoro sōshi*, 2-53)

As with Katsuren, the ships of Nakagusuku are connected with territory in Tokunoshima and Amami-Ōshima. Recall that the most prominent lord of Nakagusuku, Gosamaru, appears to have used laborers from the northern Ryukyu Islands to build his previous fortress, Zakimi gusuku.

Nakagusuku Fortress consists of six adjacent stone-walled enclosures arranged northeast to southwest. The core of the fortress consists of three enclosures atop a 150–60-meter-high limestone rise. The east side of the fortress overlooks Nakagusuku Bay and makes use of a cliff to create a defensive wall nearly twenty meters high. The north, south, and west walls feature parapets, troop passageways, and infoldings such that attacking soldiers would face defenders both head-on and on each side. Battlements for firearms helped secure entrances.

The *Omoro* portrays Nakagusuku as a powerful military center:

> Acclaimed Nakagusuku
> Should the southern powers think to come up our way
> And attack
> With [our] metal and stone [weapons]
> We will push them back
> Acclaimed Nakagusuku.

> (*Omoro sōshi*, 2-47)

Okinawan warlords adopted firearms in the early fifteenth century, slightly before their Japanese counterparts did. The early adoption of firearms and advanced military architecture in fortresses like Nakagusuku indicates technology transfer in the context of trade with China and Korea. Stone-walled fortresses like Nakagusuku closely resemble Korean mountain fortresses.

Yagi was a coastal location about two kilometers away that functioned as Nakagusuku's port. One *Omoro* song describes a magnificent folding screen that has arrived at Yagi (*Omoro sōshi*, 2-59), almost certainly a trade item obtained from Japan and ultimately bound for China. The next song describes splendid military gear from Japan:

> Up from Yagi [to Nakagusuku]
> Warrior clothing and armor [from Japan]
> Who should wear such things?
> Rulers and lords
> Should wear such things
> Up from Higa [= Yagi].

> (*Omoro sōshi*, 2-60)

In these songs, Yagi functioned as a port receiving valuable trade items from Japan to be stored at Nakagusuku. The Yagi-Nakagusuku harbor-fortress pair exemplifies the basic geopolitical unit in the Ryukyu Islands during the fourteenth and fifteenth centuries. Territory consisting of contiguous tracts of land was of little or no importance in a society whose economic basis was maritime activities.

SASHIKI

Shō Hashi arrived in Okinawa from western Kyushu with his family group, the Samekawa. The Samekawa were from Sashiki, near Yatsushiro in today's Kumamoto Prefecture, and they named their base in Okinawa after their hometown. Just below Sashiki Fortress was the harbor Yamato banta (Yamato cliffs). In the *Omoro*, Sashiki is often referred to as *Nawashiro*, a likely reference to the Nawa lineage in the Yatsushiro area of Kyushu.

The Sashiki area was one of the few locations in Okinawa where the soil was good for wet rice cultivation. Cultivating wet rice effectively requires considerable know-how, iron tools, and the construction of water-control infrastructure. *Omoro* songs praise the water-control infrastructure at Sashiki and "the admirable man [there] who conquers the many villages" (*Omoro sōshi*, 14-1012–13). Another song refers to the lord of Tedokon (part of Sashiki) as having "opened the route to China" and "resounding throughout Japan" (*Omoro sōshi*, 14-1018). The *Omoro* portrays Sashiki as a powerful geopolitical base connected with distant locations.

Today Sashiki Fortress (Sashiki ui gusuku) is mainly a flattened area atop a 150-meter-high hill overlooking Nakagusuku Bay. There are no stone walls. Sashiki was a trench-and-earthworks fortress of Japanese design consisting of four levels built into a hillside. Its defensive bulwarks were made of piled-up stone and earth. Items excavated from Sashiki include *kamuiyaki*, Chinese trade ceramics, tea items, coins, iron nails, carbonized grain, and iron arrowheads plus other military gear.

According to *Kyūyō*, while based at Sashiki, Shō Hashi drilled cavalry forces. *Omoro sōshi* makes the same point:

> At Nawashiro in Sashiki Castle
> The soldiers are spirited
> They compete to display their power
> At splendid Nawashiro in Sashiki Castle
> The troops shout, "Sare, sare!"
> The troops shout, "Doke, doke!"
> Competing to display their power.

> (*Omoro sōshi*, 19-1297)

Sashiki became a powerful military site under Shō Hashi and helped enable his eventual conquest of the Shuri-Naha area (more about that in the next chapter).

Itokazu Fortress is in the Tamagusuku region of southern Okinawa near Sashiki. The *Omoro* describes it as a splendid fortress that receives envoys from other local powers. The lord of Itokazu commands a splendid military force and rules over a wide area (*Omoro sōshi*, 17-1223–24, 18-1279–80). Itokazu Fortress was excavated between 2006 and 2013. Like many other stone-walled fortresses, it was built atop a limestone ridge during the fourteenth century. The west side makes use of a natural cliff. The east side features a dug-out trench to enhance the protective function of the walls. The north and south sides feature extension towers (*azama*) protruding from the walls to provide cross fire against attackers.

Excavations of Itokazu have recovered large quantities of pottery, including earthenware and *kamuiyaki*. Especially numerous are pieces of Chinese, Korean, and Southeast Asian trade ceramics, indicating that Itokazu was a major center of international trade. Iron goods, weapons, and military gear were also among the items excavated. The extension towers of the fortress closely resemble similar structures in Goryeo mountain fortresses. Itokazu was a large fortress and base of commerce, connected via sea-lanes to areas outside the Ryukyu Islands.

The official histories conceived of political geography in terms of land territory and an agricultural economy. Nearly all modern historians have adopted this problematic framework. *Omoro sōshi* songs and recent archaeology sketch a different picture. Local powers in Okinawa and other Ryukyu Islands were based at units consisting of anchorages with a fortress nearby on higher ground. The orientation of these harbor-fortress units was outward, to sea-lanes and other harbors throughout the East China Sea region.

Regional Networks

All the locations discussed above and many others not examined here dealt directly or indirectly with merchants in China, Japan, and/or Korea. Many were also linked into locations in the northern Ryukyu Islands. These local Okinawan powers functioned much like small hubs in the hub-and-spoke model discussed earlier. During the fourteenth century, although turbo shells and other southern island products remained in high demand, the

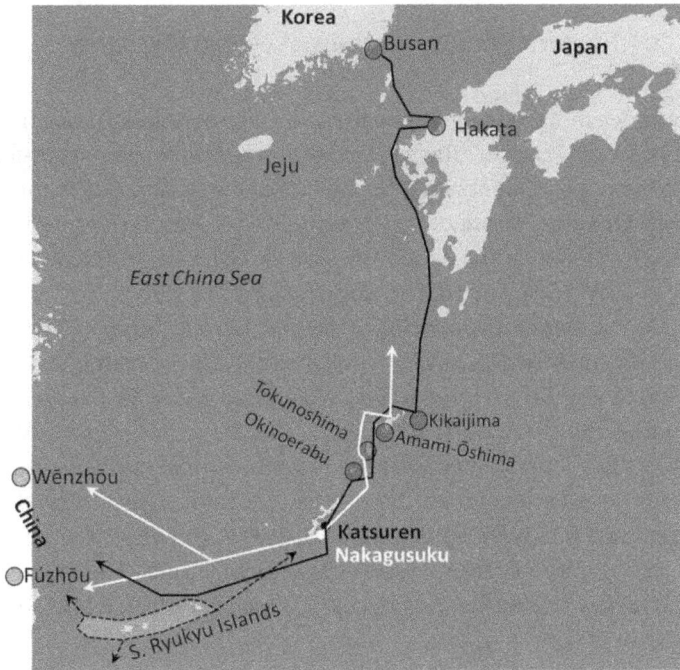

FIGURE 5.2. Illustration of maritime networks connected with the Okinawan power centers of Katsuren and Nakagusuku. Other major power centers were also embedded in extensive regional networks.

focus of trade shifted from local products to relay trade. Okinawa-based trade networks moved goods from Korea and Japan into China, and vice versa. The southern Ryukyu Islands also became a conduit for tropical products from Southeast Asia. Figure 5.2 features only Katsuren and Nakagusuku to illustrate the essential point. Adding in the other harbor-fortress locations in Okinawa and their extended networks would result a thicker and more complex web of maritime connectivity.

This trade was largely unregulated, and each local power was an autonomous entity. These powers cooperated and competed with each other as circumstances changed. Almost as soon as it came to power in 1368, the Ming dynasty attempted to regulate regional trade and control piracy. Okinawa played a major role in that project even though no centralized state existed there in the fourteenth and fifteenth centuries. However, local powers throughout Okinawa and the rest of the Ryukyu Islands continued trading privately with entities in China and elsewhere even after the establishment of the Ming dynasty. In the eyes of Ming officials, much of that trade became illegal from the 1370s on, but it continued nevertheless.

Eastern Okinawa versus Western Okinawa

The examples of harbor-fortress pairs we have seen thus far are from the eastern coast of Okinawa. The west coast was also home to harbor-fortress pairs, the most prominent being Nakijin in the north, Yomitan in the center (including Oza and Zakimi), and Urasoe and Tomigusuku in the south, the latter two located near the deepwater port of Naha. Shuri Castle was built ca. 1405 or 1406 and soon came to dominate the Naha area.

Despite the general similarity of the political geography, there were some significant differences between east and west. For example, east coast harbor-fortress pairs were generally older than those on the west coast. Even though the stone walls at a fortress like Katsuren were constructed during the early fourteenth century, a community had resided at that location since the twelfth century. By contrast, most local powers on the west coast appeared relatively suddenly during the fourteenth century, indicating the arrival of people from outside the Ryukyu Islands. The Samekawa of Sashiki was one such group. Satto's group, which established Urasoe Castle, was another.

The oldest extant map of Okinawa is Korean, appearing in *Account of East Sea Countries* (Sin 1471/1991). One noteworthy feature of the map is that many of its Okinawan place-names are the same as those found in the *Omoro*. In terms of its visual lines and nomenclature, the map divides Okinawa into an eastern section, from Kunigami in the north through Shimajiri in the south, and a western section, centered on the Ryukyu capital (Shuri). Noting that a perception of east-west difference could be found as late as 1471, both the historian Ikuta Shigeru and the archaeologist Seto Tatsuya have argued convincingly that, whatever the three principalities may have been geographically, they did not include the east coast of Okinawa (see Ikuta 1984a, 1992; and Seto 2019). As we will see, it is best to regard the three principalities as brand names or as dummy corporations. Moreover, all the local Okinawan powers who engaged in official trade with China were based on the west coast, and all conducted that trade via the port of Naha, the only port large enough to accommodate the large Chinese ships that carried tribute from Okinawa to China.

Agriculture without Agricultural Societies

Arguably, agriculture has been the most powerful force shaping human societies around the globe since its gradual emergence roughly ten thousand years ago. Indeed, many scholars regard agricultural surpluses as having been required for the emergence of states. Scott A. Johnson is typical in this regard: "Surplus agricultural production was a prerequisite for the existence of every state-level society. No other technology, such as writing, wheels, metallurgy, or beasts of burden, was universal" (Johnson 2017, 11). Agricultural surpluses have been the foundation of most states throughout world history. In the Ryukyu Islands, however, they did not power state formation. The conventional view of social development in world history is that agriculture inevitably led to the development of agricultural societies. These agricultural societies—at least over the long term—generate agricultural surpluses that in turn enable greater social complexity. Typical descriptors of increasing social complexity, from smallest to largest, are *bands*, *villages*, *tribes*, *chiefdoms*, and *states*. Beyond *states*, we could add *empires*. Obviously, states and empires also engage in trade. However, trade is typically regarded as a supplement to a state's agricultural foundation, at least for most premodern societies.

Likewise, most historians of the Ryukyu Islands have assumed that agriculture, which developed early in the Gusuku Era, led to agricultural surpluses and increasing social complexity. In this narrative, locally powerful chiefs or warlords (*aji*) emerged in Okinawa and elsewhere. Confederations or alliances of *aji* coalesced to form the three principalities (roughly, chiefdoms), and, by conquering the other principalities, Shō Hashi created a state. All these assertions—except that agriculture developed early in the Early Gusuku Era—are problematic for different reasons. I examine Shō Hashi in the next chapter. Here, the question is agriculture. Specifically, did agriculture develop beyond the subsistence level in Okinawa, to the point that farmers generated sustained surpluses that drove increasing social complexity? In other words, did Okinawa (or parts of it) become a fully agricultural society (J. *nōkō shakai*) during the Gusuku Era?

One the one hand, yes, agriculture existed in Okinawa from the tenth or the eleventh century on. The development of a fully agricultural society did not, however, follow. Still, agriculture provided a significant supplement to the food supply and was, therefore, crucially important. Recent archaeology has shown that, as the Gusuku Era progressed, the Okinawan diet included a larger percentage of grains than of nuts. Had agriculture become the economic basis of society? Was agricultural production able to generate sustained surpluses year after year? All available evidence indicates that agricultural production was not even sufficient fully to supply food for the population, much less a sustained surplus (fig. 5.3).

Agriculture refers to the systematic cultivation of useful domesticated plants and animals. Of particular importance were cereal grains (e.g., rice,

Increasing social and political complexity: the conventional view

bands → villages → tribes → chiefdoms → states → empires

Hunting & Gathering ┊ *Agriculture* (food source + wealth-to-power generator) → **Ag. Society**

Trade (wealth supplement made possible by ag.) - - ->

Increasing social and political complexity in the early Ryukyu islands

bands → trading posts → harbor-fortress pairs → state & empire

Hunting & Gathering ->⎤
Agriculture ->⎬ (Food sources)
Trading & Raiding - - - - - - - - - - - - - - - - - ->(wealth-to-power generator)⎦

1000s   1600s

Trade Society

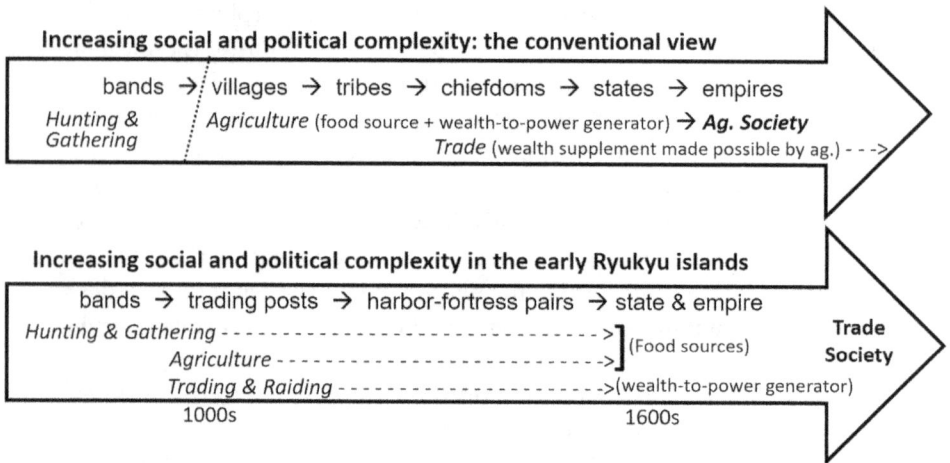

FIGURE 5.3. The Ryukyu Islands as home to trading-and-raiding societies over time contrasted with a conventional understanding of socioeconomic development

wheat, millet, barley) because the extraction of the surplus grain production became the basis of taxation throughout much of the world, including East Asia. We have no evidence that any system of taxation existed prior to the sixteenth century in the Ryukyu Islands. Indeed, there was no state to carry out such a program. The harbor-fortress political units derived their wealth mostly from trading and raiding. Any agricultural production taking place nearby supplemented the food supply.

The main evidence against agricultural surpluses during the Gusuku Era is that, for the most part, the soil of the Ryukyu Islands is poorly suited to cereal-grain agriculture. Today, except for a very few locations in the northern Ryukyu Islands, cereal grains are not cultivated. Instead, sugar, pineapple, and some niche products such as bitter melons (*nigauri*) dominate the relatively small agricultural sector of the economy. There are three main soil types throughout the Ryukyu Islands: *Kunigami-maaji, Shimajiri-maaji,* and *jaagaru.* They differ in terms of structure, composition, drainage characteristics, and microbiome. *Kunigami-maaji* is the most prevalent. It is acidic and can support the growth of certain fruit trees. Overall, it is unsuited to agriculture. *Shimajiri-maaji* is next most prevalent. It can support dry field-grain agriculture under certain conditions, and it requires periodic fertilization. Although doing so is difficult, *Shimajiri-maaji* can be worked with wooden agricultural tools. *Jaagaru* is the least prevalent. It is also the richest in nutrients. However, iron tools are required to work it.

The technical details of the argument that agriculture did not drive state development in the early Ryukyu Islands are complex, and I have presented them in detail elsewhere (see Smits 2024, 137–55). A brief summary is as follows: the soil is poor; typhoons, saltwater intrusion, and other environmental conditions constrained agriculture; archaeologists have found no evidence of the widespread use of iron tools except for small spades and sickles; there was no taxation system; malaria hindered agriculture; and during the early modern era and the early part of the modern era written records indicate very low agricultural productivity. Moreover, even during the early modern era, most peasants cultivated fields with wooden tools, and the only iron tools available were small spades and sickles. It is highly unlikely that agricultural tools and technology were more advanced in, for example, the fourteenth century than in the nineteenth century. Finally, most Chinese investiture envoys commented on the undeveloped state of agriculture in Okinawa.

Several prominent historians have argued that the Ryukyu Islands were not home to agricultural societies during the Gusuku Era or possibly ever.[3] Why, however, do most historians assume that Gusuku Era Okinawa was an agricultural society? One reason is the power of the official histories. The early modern authors of these histories worked under the assumption that all proper societies are agricultural societies. The axiom that agriculture is the basis of society was built into classical Chinese social theory. Modern and contemporary historians typically reject the explicitly Confucian intellectual framework of the official histories. However, many of these historians have taken the official histories as their starting point, assume that the Ryukyu Islands developed like the Japanese mainland, only later, and assume that, once agriculture takes hold in a place, it quickly becomes a full-fledged agricultural society. All these assumptions are problematic. Agricultural surpluses powered social and state development in Japan, Korea, and China. In the Ryukyu Islands, however, trading and raiding set the stage for state development.

The Three Principalities and Ming Maritime Prohibitions

A great deal of warfare took place during the fourteenth and fifteenth centuries, but not over agricultural fields or tracts of land. Instead, it was spurred by competition for superior harbors, trade routes, and access to markets. Particularly important was the lucrative tribute trade with China, which began in the 1370s. Indeed, we can say that the Three Principalities Era began in the 1370s, not earlier, because it was then that an array of different trade kings and their purported relatives began to appear in Chinese records as sponsors of tribute shipments.

What I have been calling *the three principalities* corresponds to the Japanese term *sanzan* (lit. "three mountains"). In this case, *mountain* indicates well-fortified high ground. From north to south, these territories were the following:

Sanhoku (or Hokuzan), northern mountain/castle
Chūzan, central mountain/castle
Sannan (or Nanzan), southern mountain/castle

These names are misleading, as is the term *three principalities*. Sanhoku was connected with territory around Nakijin, in the north. There were no specific boundaries for Chūzan and Sannan. As mentioned previously, it is better to regard these three entities more like brand names than territorial states. Furthermore, it is important to bear in mind that all three were the creation of Chinese merchant-officials in Naha and that their names appeared *only* in official Chinese and Korean records. Moreover, many more than three local powers participated in the trade and warfare of the era.

Consider a few points. First, agriculture was not the main economic activity in Okinawa at this time. Not a single domestically produced document exists from this era other than trade records.[4] *Omoro sōshi* songs are rich in place-names, but no song mentions Sanhoku, Chūzan, Sannan, or anything equivalent. All three principalities conducted trade with China through the port of Naha, and tribute/trade shipments from two and even three often reached China aboard the same ship. Official envoys from Chūzan and Sannan often changed places, representing one principality on one voyage and the other on another. These principalities are mentioned only in trade-related Chinese and Korean records, and these records do not describe any concrete details about the governance, boundaries, or internal organization of the principalities.

Not only were the three principalities more akin to brand names or banners under which trade took place; so were the names of many of the trade kings associated with them. Because phrases like *King —— of [principality name]* occur in Ming records, modern historians have assumed that these kings were actual people. Shō Hashi was definitely a real person, and Shō Shishō and Han'anchi probably were as well. Satto and several others may or may not have been actual people, whereas *Bunei* (K. *Muryeong*) was probably a Korean-sounding name that someone invented. Moreover, some of these trade kings appear to have had remarkably long lives or afterlives, with trade in their names continuing well after their likely deaths. It is best to regard the

SHUNTEN LINE*
Shunten 舜天
1187-1237
Shunbajunki 舜馬順熙
1238-1248
Gihon 義本
1249-1259

EISO LINE 英祖王統
Eiso 英祖
1260-1299
Taisei[†] 大成
1300-1308
Eiji[†] 英慈
1309-1313
Tamagusuku[†] 玉城
1314-1336
Sei'i[†] 西威
1337-1349

SATTO LINE 察度王統
Satto** 察度
1350-1395
Bunei** 武寧
1396-1405
SANNAN KINGS 山南王系

Shōsatto** 承察度
1380?-1396?
[Royal uncle] **Ōeiji[shi]** 汪英紫[氏]
1388-1402?
[Royal brother; king] **Ōōso** 汪應[応]祖
~1404-1414/1415
Tarumi** (or Taromai) 他魯毎
1415?-1429

SANHOKU KINGS 山北王系
Haniji** 怕尼芝
1322?-1395?
Bin** [†] 珉
1396?-1400?
Han'anchi 攀安知
1401-1416

FIRST SHŌ DYNASTY 第一尚氏
Shō Shishō 尚思紹
1406-1421
Shō Hashi 尚巴志
1422-1439

*Mythical/Legendary; **May have existed in name only; [†]Extremely obscure

FIGURE 5.4. Legendary kings and kings (i.e., names under which official trade took place) during the Three Principalities Era. Reigns shown are based on official sources.

names of the principalities *and* the names of the trade kings simply as appellations under which the official tribute trade with China was conducted.

Nearly all the trade kings of the Three Principalities Era have peculiar names, and at least several are generic (fig. 5.4). Many kings have extremely long lifespans, sometimes punctuated by as much as a decade of inactivity before they suddenly reappear—again, only in Chinese or Korean records. Just because a king exists as a name in Chinese records does not necessarily mean that this name corresponded to a single person or to the same person over the course of the period during which that name was in use in documents. Moreover, some kings are so obscure that they may have been entirely fictitious. Importantly, with one possible exception,[5] other than Shō Shishō and Shō Hashi, none of the trade kings of the era are mentioned in the *Omoro*. While not definitive proof, this absence suggests that many of these trade kings may have existed only as names in Chinese and Korean records. We have no record of any of the trade kings during the Three Principalities Era pursuing a domestic agenda that went beyond trade and trade-related warfare. One exception might be Shō Hashi's construction of Shuri Castle around 1405, but even that endeavor was closely connected with local Chinese merchant-officials.

All tribute trade with the Ming dynasty was governed by rules, and those rules were often enforced. For example, tribute embassies had to be sent by a recognized king or crown prince (in the case of a king's recent death). Tribute embassies took place at set times (typically once every three years), and the ships sailed to specified ports. Importantly, most of these rules did not apply to Okinawan powers during the late fourteenth century and the early fifteenth. Chinese officials did not carefully check the legitimacy of Ryukyuans claiming to be kings (they began to do so only in the 1530s). The frequency of tribute shipments was unlimited, and in some years as many as four arrived in China from Okinawa. Although most shipments went to Fúzhōu, Ryukyuan vessels were permitted to use other ports. Moreover, the Ming court provided old Chinese naval ships for use in shipping tribute, and Chinese officers commanded these ships. Some of these ships may also have been funded by favored Chinese merchants. The Ming court eventually placed significant restrictions on the Ryukyuan tribute trade, but, during the Three Principalities Era, Okinawan powers needed only to conform to minimal formalities. Chinese merchant-officials stationed in Naha took care of the paperwork and other formalities.

Tribute trade ships were nominally Ryukyuan, but they were in fact Chinese in terms of manufacture and officers. After departing Naha and arriving in Fúzhōu, they sometimes continued on to Southeast Asia before making their way back to Naha. Thereby, these ostensibly Ryukyuan ships provided a legal (or legal enough) way for favored Chinese merchants to circumvent the Ming dynasty's Maritime Prohibitions. In effect, the Ming court outsourced foreign trade to the port of Naha. Prohibiting it outright, as the Maritime Prohibitions ostensibly did, was unworkable in practice.

The tribute trade at Naha was a way of bringing dangerous *wakō* into the framework of the tribute system and conducting essential foreign trade at the same time. The Ming court pursued a dual policy of taming *wakō* while conducting de facto foreign trade within a system that the Chinese court could control, at least to some degree. The multiple principalities and trade kings probably facilitated the goal of incorporating as many Ryukyu-based *wakō* into the system as possible.

In this context, instead of thinking of the late fourteenth century and the early fifteenth in terms of individual kings governing tiny states, it is more accurate to think in terms of numerous trading-and-raiding groups based at harbors

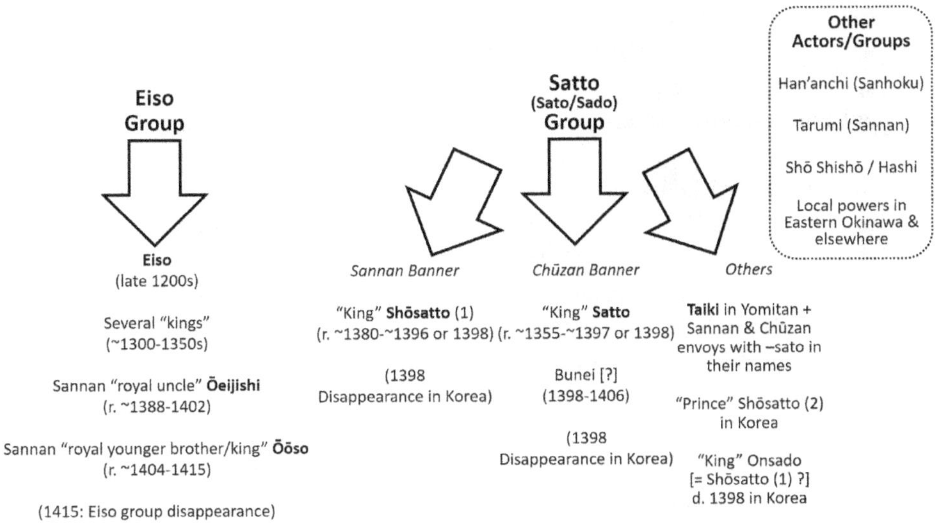
Eiso Group
Eiso
(late 1200s)
Several "kings"
(~1300-1350s)
Sannan "royal uncle" Ōeijishi
(r. ~1388-1402)
Sannan "royal younger brother/king" Ōōso
(r. ~1404-1415)
(1415: Eiso group disappearance)
Satto (Sato/Sado) Group
Sannan Banner
"King" Shōsatto (1)
(r. ~1380-~1396 or 1398)
(1398
Disappearance in Korea)
Chūzan Banner
"King" Satto
(r. ~1355-~1397 or 1398)
Bunei [?]
(1398-1406)
(1398
Disappearance in Korea)
Others
Taiki in Yomitan + Sannan & Chūzan envoys with –sato in their names
"Prince" Shōsatto (2) in Korea
"King" Onsado [= Shōsatto (1) ?] d. 1398 in Korea
Other Actors/Groups
Han'anchi (Sanhoku)
Tarumi (Sannan)
Shō Shishō / Hashi
Local powers in Eastern Okinawa & elsewhere

FIGURE 5.5. Major Okinawa-based trading groups that we can identify during the Three Principalities Era, ca. 1350–1430

and fortresses. Some of these groups conducted trade on their own, which technically was smuggling when such business transpired in China. Many of these groups conducted trade under the names of one or more living or fictitious trade kings. Many such groups have been lost to time, but, by drawing on diverse lines of evidence, it is possible to reconstruct several of them.

Identifiable Groups

Most of the individual actors at this point in Ryukyuan history are obscure. It is possible to identify several groups that operated during the Three Principalities Era, the two most important of which were the Eiso group and the Satto group (fig. 5.5). This section examines groups based in Okinawa. In the next chapter we encounter two groups based in other Ryukyu Islands.

THE EISO GROUP

Eiso was a local warlord in the Urasoe area. The official histories portray him as a king who ruled all Okinawa and even received tribute from some other islands. Recall, however, that *king* was exclusively a Chinese title, essentially a license to conduct tribute trade. Therefore, the application of it to anyone in Okinawa before 1372 is an anachronism. Eiso is mentioned frequently in *Omoro sōshi* songs and on sixteenth-century monuments as well as on the official histories. Consequently, unlike some other early kings appearing in the official histories, he almost certainly existed. These different sources, however, are inconsistent regarding the details of his life.

Although pronounced "Eiso" today, "Iizu" is the most likely pronunciation at the time he lived.[6] In this context, Iizu was a place-name, referring to Iizu Fortress (Iso in modern terms). Although many histories of Ryukyu claim that Eiso was based at Urasoe Castle and buried near the castle in a tomb complex called Urasoe yōdore, both these claims are highly unlikely.[7] Indeed, the walls of Urasoe Castle did not even exist at the time Eiso supposedly reigned. Despite many legends about Eiso and the accounts in the official histories, all we can reliably say is that he was a locally powerful ruler in the Urasoe area during the late thirteenth century.

Descendants of Eiso relocated to Tamagusuku, in southeast Okinawa, most likely in 1314 or soon thereafter. In addition to local legends to that effect, one indication is in the names of Eiso's descendants. According to the official histories, four kings descended from Eiso. All have -*ei* in their names except one, "King Tamagusuku" (r. 1314–36), whose name is a place-name. It was supposedly during Tamagusuku's reign that the unified kingdom of Okinawa broke up into three small states. While such a claim is clearly inaccurate, it probably does reflect warfare that drove the Eiso group out of the Urasoe area and into southeastern Okinawa.

The last of the Eiso group consisted of two de facto trade kings who operated under the Sannan banner. One was Ōeijishi (often called Ōeiji or Ōeishi), who appeared in Chinese records as the uncle of a Sannan king. It would not normally have been appropriate for a royal uncle to send tribute shipments to China, but, as we have seen, the Ming court was flexible with Okinawa at this time. The court provided two official seals to Sannan royalty, one to the Eiso group and the other to those Satto group members who operated under the Sannan banner. In 1403, Ōōso was called "royal younger brother" of the Sannan king in Chinese records, and, in 1404, he appeared in the records as "king." Although Ōeijishi and Ōōso look quite different in their typical Japanese pronunciation, in Chinese they are Wāngyīngzǐshì and Wāngyīngzǔ, respectively. In other words, their names are very similar to each other but very different from those of the other Sannan kings, who were part of the Satto group. Ōōso—and with him the Eiso group—vanished around 1414 or 1415.

THE SATTO GROUP

One interesting and important detail about the names of Ryukyuan kings appearing in Chinese and Korean records is that some of them were generic.

For example, the last trade king of Sannan was Tarumi. The -*mi* part of the name is an honorific, and, in modern Japanese, the name would be Tarō-sama. A similar name in English would be something like "Mr. Bob" or "Mr. Bill." In other words, Tarumi seems more like a name somebody made up to put on a document. Similarly, Satto appears not to have been the name of a specific person but a generic name.

According to the official histories, Satto was born in the village of Jana near Urasoe. In fact, however, the Satto group was closely associated with the Korean Peninsula. The last known surviving members of the group appear to have died in Korea in 1398.[8] "Satto" is the Japanese pronunciation of characters pronounced "Chádù" in Chinese. There is an alternative set of characters for this name, pronounced "Zhādōu" in Chinese and "Sato" in Japanese. There are several hypotheses regarding the origin of this name, but most likely it came from *sado*, a generic Korean term for local officials. The possible origin or meaning of the name is, however, less important than its function. *Satto* was a name in official documents under which trade took place between Okinawans in the Naha and Yomitan areas and the Ming court. This trade took place under the banner of Chūzan, but other members of the Satto group conducted trade under the banner of Sannan.

If Satto was a specific individual, he was most likely the head of a group of seafarers who left the turmoil of late Goryeo Korea and ended up in Urasoe. The Satto group probably arrived during the 1330s or 1340s. The date the official histories state Satto became king of Chūzan, 1355, marks the approximate point at which the Satto group had built up Urasoe Castle and developed a significant maritime trade network. Significantly, the Chinese merchant Chéng Fù came to Okinawa and began assisting Satto and his group in conducting trade with China. Chéng came to Okinawa probably in the 1350s, roughly two decades before the official tribute trade began. As we have seen, trade between entities in Okinawa and China became well established during the latter part of the Yuan dynasty.

Satto had been trading with entities in China since the 1350s, but the Satto group did not initiate any formal trade with Korea until 1389, the year after the Joseon founder Yi Seonggye established himself as the de facto ruler there. Soon after the political tide turned in Korea, the Satto group dispatched an envoy repatriating Koreans who had been captured by *wakō* and bearing gifts of sulfur, sappanwood, black pepper, and twenty shells, probably turtle shells. That Koreans were repatriated indicates *wakō* connections, and the sulfur would have come from Japan or possibly Iōtorishima (west of Tokunoshima). The tropical wood and pepper came from trade with Chinese or Southeast Asian merchants, probably via the southern Ryukyu Islands. The shells were a local commodity. The

Satto group was connected with the entire East China Sea region and even Southeast Asia.

Besides Satto in Urasoe doing business under the Chūzan banner, a "King Shōsatto" did so under the Sannan banner. Interestingly, there was also a Sannan prince of exactly the same name who, according to Korean records, had been residing in Korea. Because scholars have traditionally assumed that names like Satto or Shōsatto refer to specific individuals, they were at a loss to explain convincingly how the same person, Shōsatto, could have been both a king in Okinawa and a prince in Korea. If we regard Shōsatto simply as a name under which the tribute trade with China and Korea took place, the matter makes more sense, especially when we consider the strong ties of the Satto group to Korea.

Several Ryukyuan envoys appear in Ming records with -sato or -satto in their names. One was Sato, an envoy from Satto of Chūzan in 1392. Another, Asato, was an envoy of Satto of Chūzan in 1395. A similarly named envoy also appeared in 1398. After 1398, however, -sato/-satto-named envoys no longer appear in Ming records, another indication of the 1398 demise of the group.

Particularly interesting is someone named Taiki. According to Ming records, Taiki was King Satto's younger brother. Satto dispatched him as an envoy in 1372, on the first official tribute mission, and again in 1376 and 1377. Importantly, Taiki also appears in the *Omoro* as "Taichi":

> Taichi of Oza
> Made trade with China flourish
> This lord is beloved
> The magnificent Taichi!
>
> (*Omoro sōshi*, 15-1117)

> Taichi of Oza
> Set out on the sea
> Gazed on Chinese palaces and returned
> The magnificent Taichi!
>
> (*Omoro sōshi*, 15-1118)

(Oza is a location in Yomitan, on the western coast of central Okinawa.) Here we have a rare overlap between official records and the *Omoro*.

Whether Taiki was actually the younger brother of Satto, as the Ming records state, or simply posed as such does not matter. He was a local strongman based in Yomitan, and he was part of or allied with the Satto group.

Lords of harbor-fortress pairs like Taiki were the main drivers of the tribute trade and trade in general during this time.

Taiki and most others who arrived in China via the tribute trade were conducting legal trade, at least most of the time. Other powers in Okinawa and in other Ryukyu Islands continued trading with Chinese entities even after the Ming dynasty outlawed private foreign trade. Throughout most of the fifteenth century, the Ming court considered the Ryukyu Islands to be the abode of *wakō*. Some of those *wakō* entered the tribute system, eventually became dependent on it, and thereby became less of a threat to China. Others continued to pursue private trade, which in official Chinese eyes was smuggling. They likely also engaged in marauding on occasion.

THE ENIGMATIC BUNEI (MURYEONG)

A mysterious figure called Bunei was, at least on paper, a Chūzan trade king from 1398 to 1406. Once again, we find a peculiar name. As we have seen, "Bunei" is the Japanese pronunciation of what would be "Muryeong" in Korean. The characters were identical to those of King Muryeong of Baekje (r. 462–523). The official histories are very sparse regarding family details. They do not list a queen or any progeny for Bunei, who is described as having been immersed in debauchery throughout a short, miserable reign that ended around 1405 or 1406. There is no place purporting to be Bunei's tomb.

Bunei probably functioned as a facade, a name under which tribute embassies to China were dispatched. Although ostensibly Satto's heir, Bunei probably took over from Satto (or the Satto group) rather than succeeding him as his son—if he existed in the flesh. The appearance of Bunei in documents may reflect someone having created a Korean-sounding name to appear as a plausible successor to Satto. Assuming that Bunei was not one of them, the Satto group vanished in Korea on the death of the mysterious Sannan king Onsado in late 1398. If Bunei (or people operating under that name) was part of the Satto group, then the date of its disappearance would be 1405 or 1406.

The Three Principalities in Chinese Records

Okinawa's three principalities appear to have been mainly the creation of Chinese merchant-officials who resided in Naha at a location later known as Kumemura. Why create three state-like entities on paper? One possible reason is that the arrangement channeled numerous local powers in Okinawa into the tribute trade. In other words, the appearance of three tiny

kingdoms and even more royal lines in Okinawa was a concrete manifestation of the Ming effort to tame *wakō* in the Ryukyu Islands by bringing them
into the tribute trade. It was the job of Chinese merchant-officials residing
in Naha to make this policy work. They supervised the logistics of tribute
shipments and envoys. Importantly, merchant-officials arranged the documentation so that the situation in Okinawa appeared orderly enough to
satisfy officials in China. Undoubtedly, their job was very difficult at times.

Notice that the creation of multiple trade kings and royal relatives, along
with the facades of three little states, was at some level a theatrical process. As long as all participants played their parts reasonably well, everyone could profit. Collectively, the Ryukyu of this era is an early iteration of
a theatrical state. Importantly, however, there does not appear actually to
have been any states at this juncture. A later version of Ryukyu as a theatrical
state, this time taking place within the framework of an actual state, developed during the early modern era.

In this arrangement, it was to everyone's economic advantage for tribute
shipments (de facto trade) to take place frequently. Usually they did, with
as many as three or four tribute-bearing ships per year sailing from Naha
to Fúzhōu.[9] Often Chinese-built ships sailing out of Naha carried tribute
from more than one principality as well as envoys and personnel representing more than one principality. Moreover, in the case of Sannan and
Chūzan, sometimes envoys representing one of them would later represent
the other. This interchangeability makes sense, especially because members
of the Satto group conducted trade under both the Chūzan and the Sannan
banners. Although Sanhoku tribute shipments often shared the same ship
with those of Chūzan or Sannan, their envoys were not interchangeable.
Sanhoku—that is, the Nakijin area—seems to have been an entity unto itself,
most likely because of the presence of Yuan dynasty remnants there.

A detailed look at Chinese records requires technical knowledge beyond
the scope of this general history. However, these records illustrate a few crucially important points that we should survey. The first is warfare. On the one
hand, the Chinese records do not convey a sense that the three principalities
were three small territorial states at war with each other, the portrayal found
in both the official histories and most modern histories. However, evidence
of a more general state of conflict in Okinawa is abundant.

Recall that, with the death of Onsado in Korea in late 1398, the Satto
group vanished.[10] What follows is extraordinary. Chinese records indicate
no tribute or other activity connected with Ryukyu from 1398 to 1403, a gap
of nearly five years. Whatever conflict caused the Satto group to disappear
was so disruptive that it stopped tribute shipments for years. Nothing like
this had happened in the past or would happen again until the aftermath

of Ryukyu's 1609 war with Satsuma. This nearly five-year gap in tribute activity was almost certainly the result of devastating warfare between local Okinawan powers.

Another indication of warfare is more subtle. Assuming the *Bunei* refers to a group conducting trade under that name, which replaced the Satto group, in 1396.[11] Bunei sent tribute to China as Satto's crown prince. Assuming Satto died in 1395, the date given in the official histories, Bunei did not report it at the time of the 1396 tribute embassy. In 1397 and 1398, Bunei sent a total of five tribute embassies under Satto's name. After a lengthy gap, there were two tribute embassies in Satto's name in 1403. It was not until 1404 that Bunei reported Satto's death, most likely about nine years after the fact, possibly more (again, assuming Satto was, indeed, an actual individual). This extended use of Satto's name probably reflects conflict between competing *wakō* groups in Okinawa during these years.

In any case, Bunei's group did not last much longer. In 1406, Bunei sent tribute along with the Sannan king. Then the Bunei group disappeared from the stage entirely. This disappearance occurred soon after an incident in 1406 in which several castrated men arrived from Ryukyu potentially to serve as eunuchs in China, causing an angry response from the emperor. The incident is yet another reflection of ongoing conflict in Okinawa. Han'anchi of Sanhoku also disappeared at about the same time. The demise of the Bunei group and Han'anchi took place in approximately 1406, most likely at the hands of Shō Hashi, and possibly with local Chinese encouragement or assistance.

On the basis of *Ming Veritable Records*, we can identify three likely points of change resulting from conflict in Okinawa. The most prominent is 1398, when the Satto group vanished and tribute ceased for nearly five years. Next is 1406, when both the Bunei group and Han'anchi vanished. In 1415, Tarumi of Sannan, or a group using that name, replaced the Eiso group of trade kings. Because Tarumi made his last appearance in documents in late 1429, the standard narrative concludes that he and the army of Sannan went down to defeat at the hands of Shō Hashi and his Chūzan forces in that year. However, there is no mention in the Ming records of such an event or of the downfall of either Sannan or Sanhoku. Whatever may have happened, after 1429, Shō Hashi was, indeed, the only trade king remaining in Okinawa. I take up his activities in the next chapter.

In addition to discerning periods of especially intense conflict, it is possible to get a rough sense of the number of Okinawans sent to China in each tribute embassy. Specific entries in the Ming records typically list only one or two envoys, followed by "others" or "et cetera." Therefore, we cannot usually know how large of a group typically made the voyage from Naha to Fúzhōu.

In 1403, however, an entry mentions that Satto of Chūzan and the "royal younger brother" of Sannan, Ōōso, sent two envoys and a party of sixty-five.

The official part of the tribute trade was mildly profitable in the sense that Ryukyuan envoys received generous gifts from the Ming court in return for the tribute they sent. However, the main opportunity for profit, for both the Okinawans and the Chinese merchants, was in connection with private trade when the envoys were in China. The larger the entourage accompanying the tribute envoys, the greater the total potential profit. If this party of sixty-five traders was typical of a single tribute voyage, then the number of Ryukyuans directly participating in and potentially profiting from the tribute trade was large.

Apparently, there were some restrictions on private trade because the Chinese Board of Rites weighed in on an incident that arose in connection with a 1404 Sannan tribute embassy. Some members of the Sannan party traveled to purchase ceramics illegally and were caught. In response, the board determined that the matter did not rise to the level of a crime. This incident was an early and mild example of a host of problems that Ryukyuans in China caused during the fifteenth century, including illegal commerce, abuses of official hospitality, disorderly conduct, illicit military activity, arson, and murder (see Smits 2019, 60–61, 67–69, 134–36). The lenient and generous terms the Ming court extended to Okinawan entities was not an indication of endearment. On the contrary, the Ming plan was to entice *wakō* to become reliant on the tribute trade. That large groups of *wakō* from Ryukyu going to China sometimes resulted in criminal behavior or other problems should hardly be surprising.

A New Model of the Three Principalities

What were Okinawa's three principalities? First, they were not principalities or little kingdoms. Instead, they were part of a system devised by Chinese merchant-officials stationed in Naha to implement the Ming dynasty policy of routing *wakō* into the tribute trade. The presence of three banners or brand names that appeared on paper to be small kingdoms facilitated this process. Geographically, the principalities were limited to western and southern Okinawa (fig. 5.6). Most of eastern Okinawa, including powerful harbor-fortress units such as Katsuren and Nakagusuku, appear to have pursued trade on their own during this time. Moreover, Sanhoku was the Nakijin area, not all northern Okinawa.[11]

The Chūzan and Sannan banners did not necessarily delineate trade groups because the Satto group operated under both banners and some

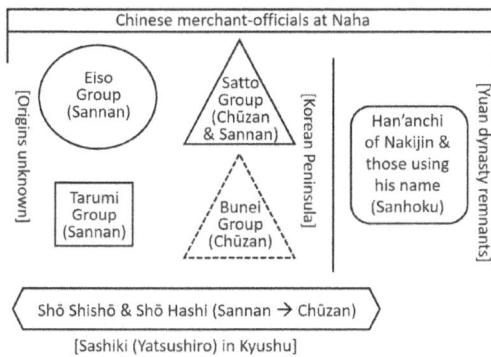

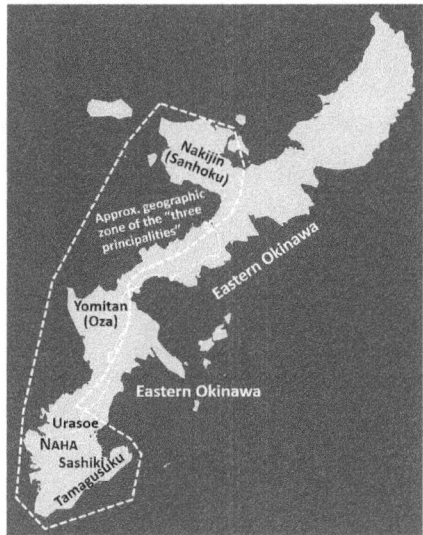

FIGURE 5.6. A new model for the Three Principalities Era and the approximate geographic range within which major trading groups were based, with likely origins in brackets

envoys represented both. Warfare was common during this era, but not in the form of state-sponsored armies fighting for Sanhoku, Chūzan, or Sannan. During the late fourteenth century, there were many more than three major political and military powers in Okinawa. If we consider each group that sponsored tribute embassies as a de facto separate royal line, there were at least six (Satto, Bunei, Eiso, Tarumi, Han'anchi, and Shō Shishō/ Hashi), assuming that Satto and Bunei were different, and leaving out the extremely obscure Haniji and Bin of Sanhoku. Moreover, it is almost certain that other local powers—people like Taiki of Oza in Yomitan—participated in the system under one or another banner and royal name. To add even more complexity, the powers along the east coast of Okinawa do not seem to have been incorporated into the network.

All indications are that Shō Hashi was an effective warrior. After about 1429, his family was the only trade king remaining in Okinawa. From this time, all tribute trade came to be conducted under the Shō name, even though other local powers continued contributing to it. Traditionally, but inaccurately, Shō Hashi is credited with creating a dynasty of kings, the first Shō dynasty, and a state that encompassed all Okinawa. The next chapter examines his era and the transition to the more aptly named second Shō dynasty. I also examine two additional trading groups who operated outside Okinawa.

CHAPTER SIX

The First Shō Dynasty Era

By the end of 1429, Shō Hashi was the only trade king remaining in Okinawa. It was not the case that Shō Hashi *ruled* the island of Okinawa or even most of it. Instead, he controlled the official trade with China, at least nominally. He was king of the tribute trade.

The first person to rule all Okinawa was Shō Shin and then only toward the end of his long reign. Throughout most of the fifteenth century, the general situation described in the previous chapter continued to prevail. Although only one person at a time held the title *king*, all the kings continued to function as trade kings, that is, people under whose auspices tribute trade embassies were dispatched to China. With Shō Taikyū as a possible exception on some points, there is no indication that any of them were literate, ruled over significant tracts of land, or presided over organized bureaucracies that dealt with matters other than trade. For example, we have no evidence of a system of taxation during the fifteenth century, nor are there any extant written documents pertaining to domestic administration.

The trade kings constituting the first Shō dynasty appear in the lineage because their names appeared in official Chinese records as dispatchers of tribute. Did they all exist as individuals? Probably, but Shō Chū, Shō Shitatsu, and Shō Kinpuku are so obscure that we know almost nothing about them. Were all the dynasty's trade kings biological relatives? Almost certainly not, even though the official histories present them as such. If we assume that Chū, Shitatsu, and Kinpuku were all sons of Hashi, as the official histories say, then we might refer to Shō Shishō through Shō Kinpuku as the *Samekawa line* of trade kings. However, it is possible that Shō Kinpuku was not related to his predecessors. Kinpuku's tomb is in a different location from any other members of the Samekawa line, and Kinpuku is associated with Shiro (officially his son) and Furi (officially his younger brother). Warfare involving Shiro and Furi ca. 1453–54 brought an outsider, Shō Taikyū, to the throne. In other words, Kinpuku, Shiro, and Furi may have constituted a distinct group, unrelated to either Hashi or Taikyū.

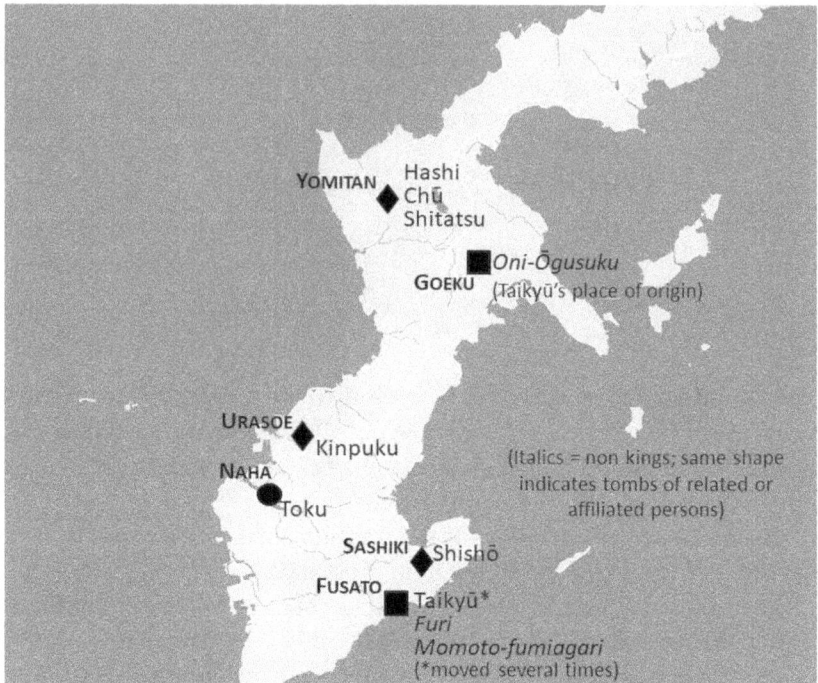

FIGURE 6.1. Dispersed tombs of prominent first Shō dynasty figures

The official histories do not agree on the basic facts of Shō Taikyū's life. According to *Reflections on Chūzan*, for example, he was the brother of Kinpuku. According to the 1725 version of *Genealogy of Chūzan*, he was yet another son of Shō Hashi. However, *Omoro sōshi* identifies him as the son of the local lord of Goeku in central Okinawa. That Taikyū came from Goeku and eventually took the throne is the most plausible scenario.

Similarly, Shō Toku does not appear to have been Shō Taikyū's son or otherwise related to him. The official histories all portray him as evil and warlike, and the 1725 *Genealogy* portrays him as a pirate. It is unlikely that he died a natural death, and, when Kanemaru took the throne as Shō En, he had Shō Toku's wife and child killed. The lineage that Shō En established, the second Shō dynasty, lasted for over four centuries.

With the exception of Shō Nei, who came from a collateral branch of the family, all the kings of the second Shō dynasty are buried in the Tamaudun mausoleum near Shuri. By contrast, the tombs and remains of the kings of the first Shō dynasty as well as prominent family members and allies are widely dispersed and often located far from their place of origin (fig. 6.1). This situation reflects in part hostility or neglect by kings of the second Shō dynasty and in part a lack of biological relatedness among several members of the first Shō dynasty.

What are the origins of the Shō surname? The inaccurate idea that the Ming emperor bestowed it on Shō Hashi comes from *Genealogy of Chūzan*, although the dates and details differ in the two versions of this text. There is no mention of this in any Chinese record, nor was it a custom of Chinese emperors to give out surnames. However, because George Kerr repeated this claim, it has become well established in Anglophone literature (Kerr 1958/2000, 89). Scholars writing in Japanese have come up with a variety of hypotheses for the origin of the Shō name. Whatever its origins, Shō Hashi began using it around 1415 while still technically crown prince. Thereafter, all subsequent kings did so, whether biologically related to their predecessor or not.

Like the Sanzan Era, the fifteenth century was a time of frequent warfare, some of which I examine later in the chapter. Not surprisingly, warfare is a major theme in *Omoro sōshi* songs. As one example, the term *island smashing* (*shima-utchi*)—with *island* here referring to communities—occurs by my count at least once in twenty-eight different songs. Piratical activity comes up in the *Omoro* as well, with one song placing the "king of Okinawa" amid a celebration of a successful raid that has obtained "splendid goods" by "stealth" and "pilfering" (*Omoro sōshi*, 10-546). In another, a local power in the island of Kumejima "grabs the valuable goods of other people's harbors" (*Omoro sōshi*, 11-597).

Model for First Shō Dynasty Okinawa

Shō Hashi's seizure of the entire tribute trade with China was a major accomplishment. Because the volume of trade did not drop off during the 1420s and 1430s, it is almost certain that Hashi continued working with many of the same local powers who had previously contributed to the tribute trade. Although we do not know the details, Hashi emerged as the sole trade king with the support of local Chinese merchant-officials in the wake of the ill-fated eunuch incident of 1406 (discussed in the previous chapter). Most likely the merchant-officials' support for Hashi was part of an effort to control the tribute trade more effectively. Shō Hashi was clearly a capable warrior, and he became lord of the newly built Shuri Castle. Between 1406 and 1421, his father, the enigmatic Shō Shishō, officially functioned as king.[1] Most likely the dominant power at that time was not so much Shō Hashi as the Chinese ministers and advisers who ran the trading operation. By the time Hashi formally became king, he appears to have functioned much like his predecessors, as a name under which the tribute trade took place.

Tribute Trade
Chinese merchant-officials at Naha

<Shō Hashi becomes
sole trade king via
warfare & with
support of Chinese
merchant officials>

Magohachi of Okinoerabu
(allied with Shō Hashi;
provider of horses)

"Samekawa Line"

Shishō / **Hashi**

Chinese "ministers"

Chū
Shitatsu
Kinpuku

<Shiro-Furi war>

Taikyū of Goeku
(1454–60)
<Wars of 1458>

<Warfare in Amami-
Ōshima & Kikaijima>

Toku
(1461–69)

Kanemaru /
Shō En
(1470–76)

2nd Shō Dynasty

"Era of Heroes"
in the southern
Ryukyu islands

In Okinawa

Katsuren-gusuku (1418)
Mochizuki (early 15th c.)
Otomoi in the *Omoro* (15th c.)
Amawari (mid 15th c.)

**The
Tomoi
Group**

Taikyū conquers
Katsuren, 1458

Move from Katsuren peninsulo to Amami-Ōshima after 1458

Tomoi /Otomoi, "Lords
of Ezu in Heda,
Ōshima" (1468-1533)
*(Active in the northern
Ryukyu islands, Korea,
Japan, and China)*

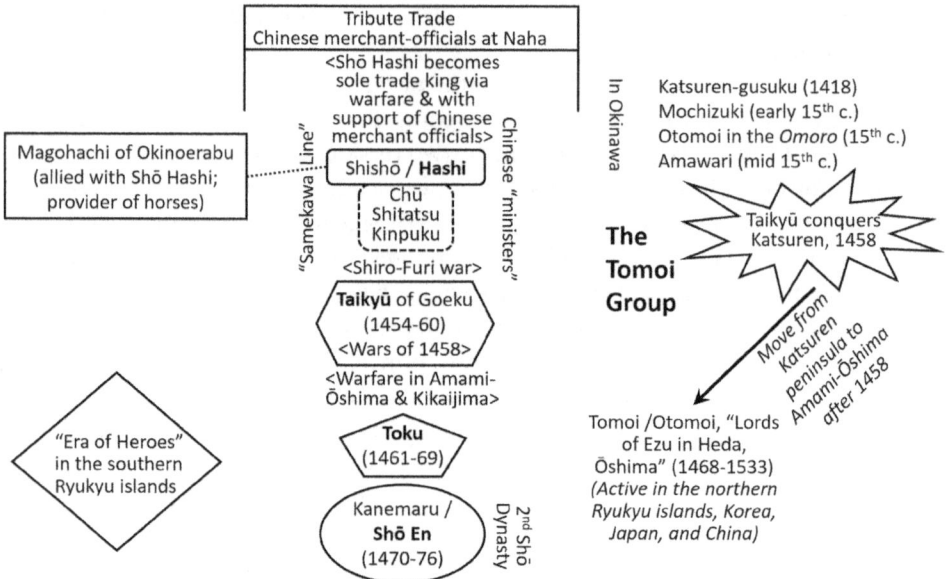

FIGURE 6.2. A new model indicating groups, trade kings,
and powerful individuals during the fifteenth century

The best model for the political geography of Okinawa during the first half of the fifteenth century is a modified version of the one we have seen for the Three Principalities Era. Chūzan had become the only banner under which the tribute trade with China took place, and Chinese merchant-officials became especially powerful during Shō Hashi's reign and for a few years thereafter. Japan's Muromachi *bakufu* was at the peak of its power at the start of the fifteenth century, and trade between Ryukyuan entities and Japanese merchants flourished. Shōgun Ashikaga Yoshimitsu (r. 1368–94, de facto until 1408) established an office to deal with Ryukyuan ships.

Other conditions carried over with little change. Okinawa and the rest of the Ryukyu Islands were home to local rulers based mostly at harbor-fortress units. These local rulers conducted trade and maintained military forces. Other than the replacement of Urasoe Castle with Shuri Castle as the administrative center of the Naha area, little changed in terms of the geo-political landscape examined in the previous chapter. The Ryukyu Islands remained the abode of *wakō*, and the Ming dynasty continued its policy of taming these *wakō* groups via generous tribute trade conditions. *Wakō* powers became especially prominent in the southern Ryukyu Islands during the fifteenth century, and they operated outside the tribute trade.

Figure 6.2 is a model for the era of the first Shō dynasty. The most important kings were Shō Hashi and Shō Taikyū. The Tomoi group at the right
refers to rulers based initially at Katsuren who relocated to the northern
Ryukyu Islands after 1458. There, the Tomoi group pursued trade with Korea until the 1530s. The sections below examine aspects of the diagram in
greater detail.

Shō Hashi

The official narrative of Shō Hashi is that he and his family originated in
the tiny island of Iheya, just north of Okinawa. However, there is strong
evidence that he was born in or near Sashiki in western Kyushu, near Yatsushiro. Contrary to the official narrative, he was not born in Iheya, Okinawa, or any other of the Ryukyu Islands.[2] By claiming Hashi's origins to
have been Iheya Island, the official histories identified Hashi and his group
as outsiders who arrived in Okinawa from the north. As a child, along
with his family and their associates, Hashi migrated to Okinawa. Although
initially arriving in Nakijin, the group eventually settled in southern Okinawa. There, its members built a Japanese-style trench-and-earthworks
fortress that they named Sashiki. In other words, in the late fourteenth
century, there was a Sashiki in Kyushu and a Sashiki (identical characters)
in Okinawa.

Like Satto, Shō Hashi emigrated to Okinawa from elsewhere. Not surprisingly, the official biographies of Shō Hashi and Satto (Jana) are very
similar. According to the plot, both of these figures obtained iron from Japanese ships, used it to make agricultural tools, distributed the tools to the
peasants, and improved their lives. In this way, each became king. In fact,
however, it was not through agriculture that they became powerful. It was
through warfare and trade. Many scholars have noted that one reason for
Shō Hashi's success was that he traded Chinese porcelain and other goods
for weapons from Japan. This point is correct, but weapons—most of Japanese origin or design—have been excavated at most large fortress sites in
the Ryukyu Islands. Shō Hashi was not unique or distinctive in obtaining
weapons from Japan via trade.

Hashi made his mark as a warrior, not as an administrator. His major accomplishment was prevailing in the maelstrom of warfare during the Three
Principalities Era and thereby becoming the sole Okinawan under whose
name the tribute trade with China could proceed. He was also—at least
nominally—the one who built the first version of Shuri Castle.

Magohachi of Okinoerabu

Guraru (or Goran) Magohachi was a *wakō* head based on the island of Okinoerabu. We do not know his death date, but he seems to have been a rough contemporary and close associate of Shō Hashi. Magohachi and his group were traders who specialized in horses, an animal considered valuable throughout the region.

One *Omoro* song describes the ships of the ruler of Okinoerabu functioning as a bridge to other locations. The next song describes the herd of splendid horses at his disposal. The following song invokes the deity of a local sacred grove to protect a large ship anchored in Okinoerabu. We have already seen the next two songs. They describe the ships of Katsuren functioning as a bridge to various northern Ryukyu Islands, including Okinoerabu (*Omoro sōshi*, 13-935–39). *Omoro* songs in close proximity are often related geographically or topically. In this sequence, we see the ruler of Okinoerabu linked to a maritime trade network connected with Katsuren. Notice also the tendency in the *Omoro* to describe powerful coastal castle-harbor combinations as bridges to other islands. Such descriptions highlight the islands' function as maritime conduits.

The Tomoi Group

In Korean records, there are nine instances of someone posing as the younger brother of the Ryukyuan king and calling himself Tomoi or Otomoi. In each case, Tomoi/Otomoi dispatched an envoy and presented tribute to the Korean court, ostensibly on behalf of the Shuri royal court. The dates of each occurrence are 1468, 1470, 1480, 1509, 1519, 1523, 1525, 1527, and 1533. In many of these instances, Tomoi/Otomoi titles himself "Otomoi, Lord of Ezu in Heda, Ōshima, Ryukyu." This Tomoi group was based in Amami-Ōshima, at least loosely. It consisted of a mobile group of seafarers who opposed the Ryukyuan court at Shuri. The origins of the Tomoi group, however, were at Katsuren and a nearby trench-and-earthworks fortress of Ezu.

Recall the *Omoro* songs describing the ships and sailors of Katsuren functioning as a bridge to Amami-Ōshima and Kikaijima. Now consider the following song, which makes a similar point:

> The people of Katsuren take to the sea
> Take to the sea and reap profits
> From Tokunoshima and Amami-Ōshima

And connect to the mainland
Otomoi takes to the sea.

(*Omoro sōshi*, 13-867)

The "mainland" in the fourth line may refer to Japan, Korea, or both places. The final line is especially important. It mentions a specific person like Taiki, someone (or several people using that name) whose name is also found in official sources. The name of this person or group is Tomoi/Otomoi. This song most likely dates to the fifteenth century.

Someone named Amawari ruled Katsuren in 1458 when Shō Taikyū conquered it. We do not know when Amawari became the ruler of Katsuren, but, according to legend, he killed Katsuren's previous lord, Mochizuki. If so, then Mochizuki was a local ruler based in Katsuren sometime in the early fifteenth century.

Tomoi/Otomoi of the late fifteenth century and the early sixteenth posed as the younger brother of the Ryukyuan king. Such posturing vis-à-vis Korea is recorded as early as 1418. In that year, someone calling himself Katsuren or Katsuren-gusuku stated that he was the second son of the king of Chūzan, and he sent an envoy to Korea bearing a letter and a variety of gifts. Based at Katsuren in eastern Okinawa, this person had no genuine family connection to any king. He was conducting trade and diplomacy with Korea under the cover of the tribute trade, claiming to be related to an Okinawan trade king. This 1418 Katsuren may also have been the earliest manifestation of the Tomoi group.

The fortress of Ezu was a Japanese-style trench-and-earthworks fortress located next to Katsuren Fortress. Ezu was the site of a large storehouse that probably functioned as a marketplace (*Omoro sōshi*, 16-1160). *Omoro sōshi*, 16-1163, sings of the close relationship between Katsuren and Ezu. It is likely that the "Hezu" in Otomoi's title refers to Ezu. Moreover, we know from another ancient song that Ezu in Okinawa had connections with Amami-Ōshima.

In the early fifteenth century, Katsuren and its allied fortress of Ezu constituted a wealthy, powerful, politically independent naval and trade base, occupying the Katsuren Peninsula in eastern Okinawa. This base had close ties to the northern Ryukyu Islands, Korea, Japan, and China. The *Omoro* portrays Amawari, its ruler in the 1450s, as a person of immense power and far-reaching influence:

Amawari of Katsuren
With the jeweled ladle

As far as Kyō[to] and Kamakura
Your voice resounds and reverberates
Powerful Amawari.

(*Omoro sōshi*, 16-1134)

With these details in mind, here is a rough lineage of key Katsuren/Ezu personnel: Katsuren-gusuku (1418), Mochizuki (early fifteenth century), Otomoi of the *Omoro* (fifteenth century), Amawari (mid-fifteenth century), and Tomoi/Otomoi, Lords of Ezu in Heda, and Ōshima (1468–1533). In 1458, Shō Taikyū, the king in Shuri, conquered Katsuren. Like all the harbor-fortress pairs thus far examined, Katsuren was part of a larger network. Its conquest by Taikyū was, therefore, not a conquest of the entire network. Most likely, the survivors of what for them was a military disaster in 1458 relocated to Amami-Ōshima, where they continued to pursue trade with Japan and Korea.

These Katsuren remnants in Amami-Ōshima were the Tomoi group. The date of their last recorded activity, 1533, is probably significant. Faced with growing opposition by local powers in Amami-Ōshima, King Shō Sei launched invasions of the island in 1535, fully pacifying it by 1537. In addition to gaining firmer control over Amami-Ōshima, Shō Sei's invasions probably put the Tomoi group out of business.

Shō Taikyū

By conquering several major centers in eastern Okinawa, Shō Taikyū made significant strides in the direction of creating a centralized state, although we cannot know whether that was his goal. Taikyū was a local ruler in Goeku who took the throne in the wake of—and most likely as the result of—warfare that destroyed parts of Shuri Castle. In the official account, based on Chinese records, the dispute was a struggle between the Shō family members Furi and Shiro. We know that serious warfare broke out in 1453, causing damage to Shuri Castle (verified archaeologically), and that Taikyū emerged as king from this struggle. All other details of the conflict are unclear.

One possible scenario is that Shiro and Furi—be they royal family members or something else—went to war in an effort to gain the throne and killed or weakened each other. Then Taikyū of Goeku came in and took over in their stead. Another scenario is that it was a three-way contest from the start. Interestingly, although the official histories state that both Shiro and

Furi died from wounds, according to local legend Furi survived and went into hiding. Furi has a tomb in Fusato (southern Okinawa), but the location of Shiro's remains is unknown.

Recall the close connection between Katsuren Fortress and the nearby fortress of Ezu. According to legend, Furi once dwelled in the latter. After losing out in the war, he went into hiding, and Taikyū sent one of his sons to rule Ezu. Later, Taikyū's daughter, Momotofumiagari, married Amawari of Katsuren. Although the details are obscure, it appears that, from the start of his reign, Taikyū laid the groundwork for connecting himself with Katsuren and, ultimately, conquering it.

There is much that we do not know about Taikyū's conquest of Katsuren. The chapter on Taikyū in *Reflections* is extremely brief. Other than mentioning his formal recognition by the Ming court, it notes that Taikyū was active in establishing Buddhist temples and installing large bells in them. It is almost as if the author of *Reflections* did not want to dwell on this awkward member of the line. Similarly, the 1701 *Genealogy* has little to say about Taikyū but does outline the conquest story.

The basic story is as follows. Amawari of Katsuren convinced Taikyū that Gosamaru of Nakagusuku was plotting against Taikyū. Taikyū ordered Amawari to destroy Gosamaru, which he did. Soon thereafter, Amawari plotted to seize the throne from Taikyū. However, the loyalty of Taikyū's daughter Momotofumiagari and her soon-to-be-new-husband Oni-Ōgusuku saved the day for the king. The 1725 *Genealogy* and *Kyūyō* contain the same story in a more detailed and dramatic version. These official history accounts assume, incorrectly, that Okinawa was united under one king from as far back as Eiso's time. In their pages, therefore, local warfare had to be framed in terms of loyalty or disloyalty to the throne.

The accounts in the official histories resemble classic Japanese war stories, with Gosamaru as the typical tragic hero. The story of Amawari and Gosamaru remains immensely popular today in Okinawa, with intramural school sports teams, for example, competing under the banner of one or the other of these legendary warlords.

By the end of 1458, Taikyū or his allies, such as Oni-Ōgusuku, controlled Goeku, Nakagusuku, Ezu, and Katsuren. It would be fascinating to know exactly how they pulled this off. Prior to Taikyū's reign, to be king of Chūzan meant to be the person under whose name the tribute trade with China and, by extension, official trade with Korea took place. It was a lucrative position, and the kings in Shuri were, therefore, potential targets of ambitious outsiders such as Taikyū. Shō Taikyū's significance was that he added northern trade routes and territory in Okinawa to the royal portfolio (fig. 6.3). He took significant steps in the direction of creating a unified Okinawa and a

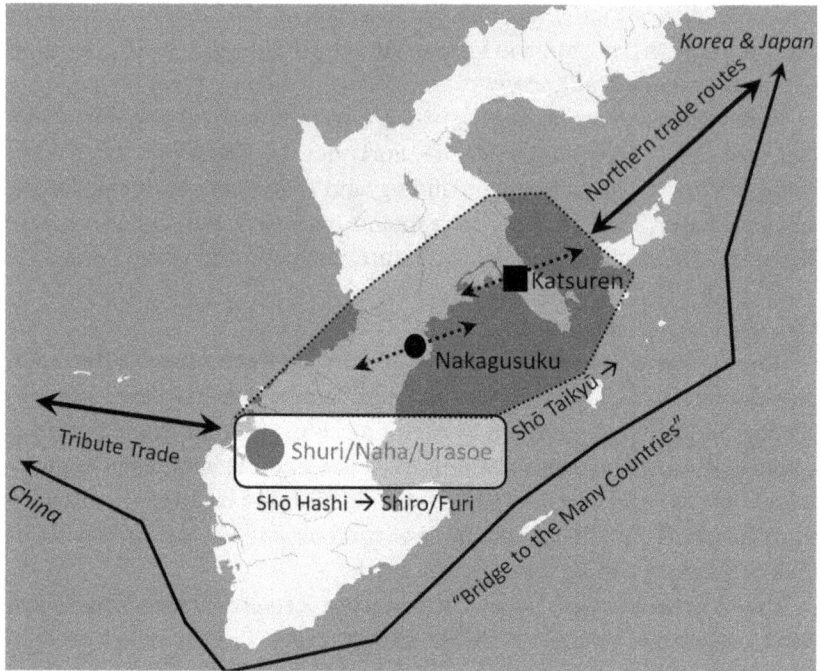

FIGURE 6.3. The expansion of Shuri's trade
network after Shō Taikyū's wars of conquest, 1458

larger empire centered at Shuri, but he died in 1460 in his mid-forties. No
cause of death is stated, but, given that Taikyū's allies went into hiding when
Shō Toku took the throne, his death may not have been natural.

The area later known as Kumemura near Naha Harbor is where the resident Chinese officials were located. Importantly, in 1456, the Korean castaway Ryang Seong noted that all the households there consisted of people
from "my country" (Korea) or from China. In other words, there was a
significant resident Korean presence in Naha Harbor at this time, almost
certainly there to assist with overseas trade. Although Ryang happened
to make this observation during Taikyū's reign, the presence of a resident
Korean population probably extended as far back as Satto's era. With his
conquest of Katsuren, Taikyū wrested control of the two major Okinawan
centers of trade with Korea. After seizing control of at least some of the
northern trade routes previously maintained by Nakagusuku and Katsuren,
Taikyū's Shuri became a center of trade with Korea, China, and Japan, although not yet the exclusive center.

The official histories note that Taikyū was a devout Buddhist who established temples and sponsored the casting of bells for them. He might well

have been devout, but these acts also functioned as symbolic legitimation of his rule. Moreover, he was one of only three Ryukyuan kings who minted coins bearing their divine names. The others were Shō Toku and Shō En (Kanemaru). The minting of coins was of no importance economically. But it did function to bolster the legitimacy of three men who seized the throne by force.

The extensive warfare in and around the Ryukyu Islands deserves a book of its own. Here, I briefly mention that both Shō Taikyū and Shō Toku conducted military operations in the Kasari Peninsula of Amami-Ōshima and sought to conquer Kikaijima. In the official histories, Shō Toku is the one credited with the final conquest of Kikaijima, but it is clear from a variety of sources that military forces connected with Shuri had been attempting to conquer the island since the 1450s. Moreover, Katsuren maintained close ties with Kikaijima. Any campaigns to pacify Kikaijima after 1458 were, therefore, probably attempts to capitalize on Shō Taikyū's conquest of Katsuren.

Shō Toku

Like so many early trade kings, Shō Toku is a mysterious figure. According to *Reflections on Chūzan*, he was either the third son of Taikyū or the seventh. Furthermore, his rule was more violent than those of Jié and Zhòu, a reference to two demonized classical Chinese rulers, the last kings of the Xia and Zhou dynasties. The relatively short chapter on Shō Toku in *Reflections* emphasizes his flawed and violent personality and describes him leading an army of two thousand to conquer Kikaijima. It portrays the violence of the Okinawan force in detail, including the burning of civilian houses and, after their surrender, the killing of the Kikaijima leaders one by one. If one considers only this passage, it would appear that the conquest of Kikaijima was extremely violent and costly in terms of lives and good relations. In this context, *Reflections* seeks to make a scapegoat of the allegedly depraved king.

Interestingly, the 1701 *Genealogy* presents a more compact, clinical account of the conquest. It states that, after returning from the campaign, Shō Toku grew ever more depraved and killed blameless people capriciously. We are told in what is perhaps a reference to Taikyū's allies that good ministers hid in the forests and mountains, a common classical Chinese trope used in connection with evil rulers. The 1725 version of *Genealogy* includes details about Toku's behavior during the conquest of Kikai that are *wakō* specific. These details include shooting a bird out of the sky as a good omen, the miracle of a large temple bell floating on the waves, and the establishment of a shrine to Hachiman on his return.

Probably in the 1930s, Orita Noboru, a former mayor of Kikai Village, wrote down lore about the battle that had been passed down orally in Kikaijima. His account resonates with the description found in *Reflections*. According to Orita, the island's beaches and cliffs were well defended. One tactic was to deploy straw dummies at which the invaders shot arrows. The defenders then took those arrows and shot them back at the invaders. Moreover, the defenders hid themselves in the shadows of boulders to surprise the attackers. When at last the attackers overwhelmed the defenders at Araki beach and came ashore, the carnage was immense on both sides (Takeuchi 1933/1960, 80–81). It is impossible to verify any of these details. The point is that, even into the twentieth century, Shō Toku's conquest of Kikaijima lingered in local folk memory as an especially terrible event.

There is no cause listed for Shō Toku's death after a reign of about eight years. The official histories note that his surviving family members were slaughtered while hiding in one of Shuri Castle's sacred groves. This area of the castle later became known as Kundagusuku, and the remains became the focus of a popular cult around the power of royal bones, possibly a version of older Korean bone cults. According to one legend, a coup took place while Shō Toku was away visiting the island of Kudakajima. Hearing of the coup on the way back, Toku threw himself into the sea to drown. We cannot verify the legend, but it is certainly possible that Shō Toku did not die naturally.

There are few sources about Shō Toku other than official trade records and the official histories. He appears to have indeed been a *wakō* whose group managed to seize power from Shō Taikyū and enjoy the benefits of the tribute trade for a while. It is also likely that he engaged in warfare in Kikaijima, although the precise cause and larger context remain unclear. In general, however, his reign is a blank space. It is likely that a backlash from remnants of Taikyū's group led to the violent end of Toku's group and the coming to the throne of yet another outsider, Kanemaru (sometimes pronounced "Kanamaru" or "Kanimaru"), traditionally regarded as an associate of Taikyū.

Heroes of the Southern Ryukyu Islands

Contemporary Japanese writing about the Three Principalities Era, especially pieces geared toward popular audiences, often refers to kings and other combatants as *heroes* (*eiyū*). Likewise, in the southern Ryukyu

Islands, the fifteenth century is often known as *the era of heroes*. In this case, the heroes were locally powerful people who often waged war against each other. As Inamura Kenpu demonstrated, most or all of these local powers were *wakō* groups (Inamura 1957).

With the harbor-fortress-based political geography of the Ryukyu Islands in mind, it is possible that Nakasone, the most powerful figure in the island of Miyako and briefly an ally of Shuri, controlled parts of the Yaeyama island of Iriomote prior to 1500. The economic dynamic was that Miyako was a center for trade, but, as a low-lying island, it lacked timber. The nearest timber suitable for shipbuilding was in Iriomote, Kuroshima, and other locations in the Yaeyama Islands. Therefore, powers in Miyako obtained lumber or actual ships (*komibune* were ships built in Komi, Iriomote) from Yaeyama. Our sources for this era are songs, legends, and various collections of origin tales (*yuraiki*) written during the early modern era. These diverse sources are not in agreement. Nevertheless, the general impression given of life in the southern Ryukyu Islands during the fifteenth century is that of local warlords competing for resources. Moreover, Miyako appears to have been the most powerful location.

We have seen that people based at Bora (today's Boranomotojima) in Miyako traded with entities in China and Southeast Asia. The popular modern image of Ryukyuans boldly sailing to Southeast Asia to trade probably applies mainly to parts of the southern Ryukyu Islands and to the era before 1500. This trade took place in Japanese-style Uruka ships (named after the Uruka [Sunagawa] region of Miyako) and other vessels built in the southern Ryukyu Islands. By contrast, Shuri's tribute trade took place in Chinese ships with Chinese captains and officers.

During the fourteenth century, Chinese ceramics began to accumulate at several sites in Miyako. During the fifteenth century, nearly every harbor or settlement in the southern Ryukyu Islands saw a vast increase in Chinese trade goods. Significantly, the origin of many of the fifteenth-century Chinese ceramics in the southern Ryukyu Islands was southern China. Clearly, some Chinese vessels sailed to the southern Ryukyu Islands, and some southern Ryukyuan vessels sailed to the Fúzhōu area of the Chinese coast.

There are three key points to bear in mind about the southern Ryukyu Islands during the fifteenth century. First, they were not under the control of Shuri until the sixteenth century.[3] The official histories imply that the southern Ryukyu Islands had been subordinate to Shuri before a "revolt" in 1500. However, that implication is part of the general trend in those histories to push state and empire formation back far earlier in time than the evidence available today warrants. Second, we have indirect evidence of trade between Miyako and Naha as early as the 1380s, although a relationship of political subordination was not involved. There is good evidence for trade between Miyako, China, and Southeast Asia from the early fourteenth century. The southern Ryukyu Islands became a significant source of tropical products that powers in the Naha area used not only in the tribute trade but also in trade with Korea and Japan. Finally, the scale of what was from the Ming court's point of view illegal trade with China in this region during the fifteenth century was vast. Although many details and motivations connected with the military campaigns in the southern Ryukyu Islands between 1500 and the 1520s remain obscure, it is likely that the Ming court looked favorably on Shuri's conquest of the region.

KANEMARU AND THE KAWARA *WAKŌ*:
ORIGINS OF THE SECOND SHŌ DYNASTY

According to the official histories, Kanemaru, a former official of Shō Taikyū, became king almost against his will. In the tale, after Shō Toku's death in 1469, a vague group of officials met and decided to offer the throne to Kanemaru. At the time, he was hiding in Uchima in central Okinawa. Supposedly, he declined twice before finally accepting.

In the *Omoro*, Kanemaru appears under that name and as Onisanko. As king, he is known as Shō En. We have seen that the founders of the first Shō dynasty came from Sashiki in Kyushu, near Yatsushiro. Kanemaru was also an outsider from the north, but tracing his roots has proved to be more difficult. One problem is that we have no idea who his father was. Nevertheless, by bringing several lines of evidence together, it is possible to draw some conclusions about the likely approximate geographic origins of the second Shō dynasty.

First some background. Throughout the Ryukyu and Tokara Islands, and extending as far north as Hakata, we find place-names that were closely associated with *wakō*. In *Maritime Ryukyu* (2019), the general term I use for them is *Gaara group names*. Examples include Gara, Gaara, Goriya, Guraru, and Gura. Their original meaning is "head," as in the leader or chief of a group. Importantly, Kawara is one of the Gaara group names, and the term *honkawara* means "main or big leader." Groups with the Kawara name settled mainly in Kumejima, an island to the west of Naha, and in the southern Ryukyu Islands.

Next, there were close connections between key institutions and religious officials of the early second Shō dynasty and the island of Kumejima. Elements of the *hiki* system,[4] for example, probably originated in Kumejima. The *kikoe-ōgimi* (high priestess, O. *chifuijin-ganashii*), several Nakijin priestesses, and the *kimihae* (O. *chinpei* or *chinbei*) priestess of Kumejima were all closely connected with each other. Kumejima, also known as Kaneshima (metal island) in the *Omoro*, was a valuable source of iron. Furnaces on the island produced iron from iron sand, and parts of the island itself were natural fortresses, ideally situated for control of sea-lanes between the Ryukyu Islands and China.

Several of the deities of sacred groves in the southern Ryukyu Islands came from Kumejima, an indication of the movement of people. Especially important is the legend of the three sister deities of Kumejima. According to the basic plot, the sisters came from Japan and resided for a while at Kumejima. Later, one of them went to Okinawa and resided at the Benten (Benzaiten) grove in Shuri (becoming the deity of the high priestess), one remained in Kumejima as *kimihae,* and another moved to Ishigaki to reside at Mt. Omoto.

Kumejima was a powerful and prosperous place, closely connected with China, Japan, and the rest of the Ryukyu Islands. Consider this example from the *Omoro*:

> Gushikawa Castle [in Kumejima]
> Is magnificently built
> . . . .
> The fortress that accumulates
> Wine and treasure from Chinese ships
> Is magnificently built
> The fortress that accumulates
> Wine and treasure from Japanese ships.
>
> (*Omoro sōshi,* 11-852)

In addition to being valuable territory in its own right, Kumejima was a nexus. It possessed a commanding view of sea-lanes connecting Japan, China, Naha-Shuri, and the southern Ryukyu Islands. It was also interconnected with the Tokara Islands, Nakijin in northern Okinawa, and Mt. Omoto in Ishigaki.

In addition to the three sisters, there is another migratory deity or set of deities that sheds light on Kanemaru's origins. A female deity in the Tokara Islands known as Sashikasa became Sasukasa in the Ryukyu Islands. Sasukasa, a military deity, is closely related to the storm deity Aoriyae of Nakijin. In Kumejima, Sasukasa and Aoriyae are a single deity called Sasukasa-aoriyae. Using the distribution of these deities as a proxy for the movement of people, one can postulate the scenario that the Tokara Sashikasa migrated to Kumejima and became Sasukasa-aoriyae. Later, this

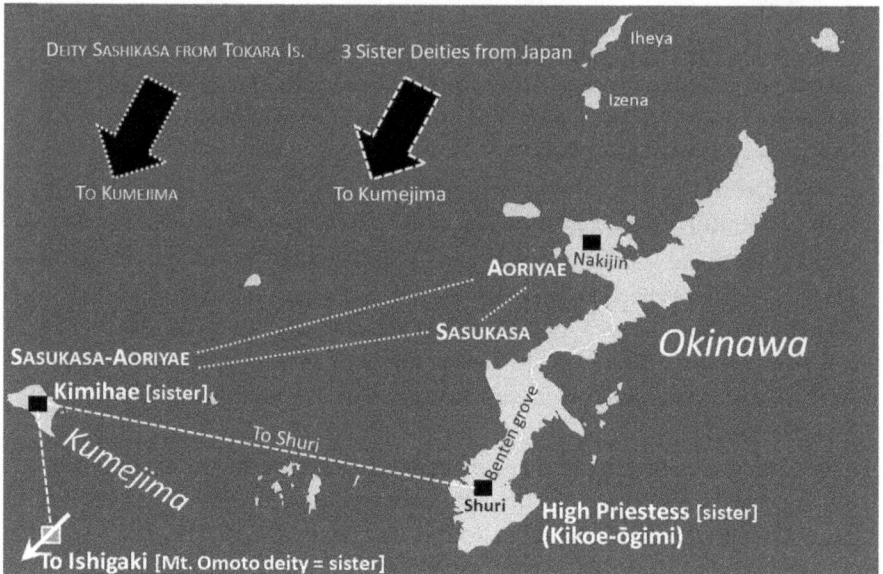

FIGURE 6.4. Legendary and religious links between Kumejima, Nakijin, Shuri, and Ishigaki in connection with Kanemaru and the second Shō dynasty

paired deity traveled to Nakijin and elsewhere in northern Okinawa, where it became two separate deities (Sasukasa and Aoriyae are known separately in the *Omoro*). A second possible scenario is that the Tokara Sashikasa went first to Nakijin and then later to Kumejima (fig. 6.4).

The official histories make the improbable claim that Kanemaru was born in the tiny island of Izena, just north of Okinawa. Similar to the claim that Shō Hashi was born in Iheya, the point seems to be that both men came into Okinawa from the north. The initial homeland of the second Shō dynasty in Okinawa appears to have been Nakijin. This conclusion is based mainly on passages from the *Omoro sōshi*. Consider an example of Kanemaru's northern Okinawan roots:[5]

> In Kunikasa [in Kunigami, northern Okinawa]
> The priestess is revered
> The conquering
> Lord is celebrated
> In Yakabi grove [in Kunigami, northern Okinawa]
> Kanemaru is revered.

> (*Omoro sōshi*, 13-927)

The *Omoro* also links Kanemaru with Kumejima:

> Chiefs of Kadekawa [in Kumejima]
> Kanemaru of the north
> Heralds the future [political] order
> Shō Shin is here
> The wind now blowing from the north
> Is Kanemaru of the north
> The wind now blowing from the north
> Is Kanemaru of the north.

(Omoro sōshi, 11-618)

Kanemaru's precise location in "the north" is unclear. The phrase might refer to northern Okinawa, somewhere farther north, or both. The image of a wind blowing from the north ushering in a new political order fits with the nature of the local deities. Both the Aoriyae and the Sasukasa deities typically manifest their power as wind and storms. The reference to Shō Shin in this song may indicate that it was composed after his conquest of Kumejima, which is traditionally dated to 1506.

Given this large quantity of interconnected cultural data, and in light of the *Omoro* songs, the following description of Kanemaru's origins is plausible. First, like the three sister deities, Kanemaru came from Japan. We cannot say where, but, given his *wakō* roots, western Kyushu is a likely possibility. Kanemaru and his group came south, through the Tokara Islands and some of the northern Ryukyu Islands. At this point there are two possible scenarios. The first scenario is that the entire group may have sailed first to Kumejima and later split into subgroups, one settling in Nakijin and eventually Shuri, the other in Ishigaki and possibly other locations in the southern Ryukyu Islands. That pattern would fit the three sister deities narrative. The second scenario is that, from the start, part of the group settled in Nakijin and part in Kumejima. Later, some of the group migrated to Ishigaki and possibly other locations in the southern Ryukyu Islands. Significantly, according to legend several blacksmith deities in the islands of Miyako and Irabu arrived there from Kumejima. In either case, early kings of the second Shō dynasty had close ties to Kumejima.

In *Kyūyō* and other accounts of Shuri's 1500 invasion of Ishigaki, a priestess led troops along with a general. Typically, Ryukyuan priestesses participated in military battles by cursing the enemy in the course of a choreographed dance and marshaling the power of the deities. In this case, the priestess was Kumejima's *kimihae*. When the defenders of

Ishigaki saw the sister priestess of Ishigaki's Mt. Omoto deity in the vanguard of the invading forces, they allegedly lost the will to fight. The *Kyūyō* passage, of course, presents Shuri's victory as a natural restoration of the proper order of things. Most official sources portray the 1500 invasion of Ishigaki as a response to a rebellion, the "Honkawara revolt," led by Oyake Akahachi. Incidentally, Akahachi has been and remains a hero in Ishigaki to this day.

Soon after conquering Ishigaki, the Okinawan forces invaded Kumejima, another Kawara location. Naturally, the official sources have nothing to say about *kimihae* in this context. I revisit the wars of conquest that Shō Shin and Shō Sei waged in a later chapter.

Summary

Many narratives of early Ryukyuan history list 1429 as the date when a centralized state emerged. The reason is that, according to the 1725 version of *Genealogy of Chūzan*, Shō Hashi conquered Sannan in 1429 and, therefore, became king of all Okinawa. A better description, however, is that he became the king of the tribute trade with China. There is no indication that he controlled any territory outside the Shuri-Naha area. Moreover, it is not clear that he was even in full control of the tribute trade because he was surrounded by Chinese trade officials. It is quite likely that, from 1406 on, Shō Shishō and Shō Hashi functioned mainly as names under which tribute shipments took place.

By midcentury, the prominence of Chinese trade officials faded, and a new and powerful warlord, Shō Taikyū, burst onto the scene. By conquering the powerful east coast trade hubs of Nakagusuku and Katsuren, Taikyū was a transitional figure between trade kings and kings who ruled over centralized bureaucratic states. He did not control all Okinawa, but his conquests added northern trade routes to the royal portfolio.

Taikyū is famous for inscribing a Buddhist-style bell in 1458, just after his conquests. The bell, Bankoku shinryō no kane, is usually translated as Sea Bridge to the Many Countries Bell. Although it was a direct result of warfare, ironically, some modern Okinawans cite the bell as evidence for a long history of pacifism in the Ryukyu Islands. Recall that the inscription states that Ryukyu has gathered together the excellence of Korea, provides shipping for the Ming dynasty, and is as close to Japan as teeth are to lips. Taikyū's conquests made it possible for Okinawan kings to envision themselves as regional maritime powers with far-reaching connections. Before Taikyū's conquests, such a bell inscription would not have been plausible.

Taikyū's conquests of Nakagusuku and Katsuren led to further warfare, this time over control of northern Amami-Ōshima (the Kasari Peninsula) and Kikaijima. Shō Toku took over Taikyū's operation and appears eventually to have succeeded in conquering Kikaijima. The precise timing of Shuri's conquest of Amami-Ōshima is less clear. There were several rounds of warfare between Shuri and Amami-Ōshima in the 1530s in which Shuri appears, eventually, to have been victorious. To the south, between 1500 and the 1520s, Shuri's military forces, working in concert with local allies, conquered the major southern Ryukyu Islands.

CHAPTER SEVEN

Classical Ryukyuan Culture

Classical Ryukyuan culture has two main sources, Japan and Korea. The Japanese cultural influences are fairly obvious. All Ryukyuan languages, for example, are Japonic. A major source for our understanding of Ryukyuan languages is *Omoro sōshi*. Thus far, I have used the *Omoro* as primary source. In this chapter, I examine it as a work of literature. The Korean cultural influences *should* be obvious in the sense that manifestations of them—most prominently sacred groves and stone-walled fortresses—are prominent features of the geocultural landscape of the Ryukyu Islands. However, outside a few specialists, the Korean origins of early Ryukyuan culture are not widely known. Let us take a closer look, starting with sacred groves.

Sacred Groves

Sacred groves, known as *utaki, uganjo,* and other terms, are an iconic feature of Ryukyuan culture. Consider the image in figure 7.1, which is one of the three sacred spaces (J. *ibe*, O. *ibi*) in the Baten grove in southern Okinawa. This grove is associated with Shō Hashi's Samekawa group. Sacred groves typically feature stones or a tree as their sacred space, typically situated among thick vegetation.

The Yabusatsu grove at Hyakuna beach in southeast Okinawa is, according to *Reflections on Chūzan* (chap. 3), one of groves the creator deity Amamiku established on Okinawa. It is a typical sacred grove, consisting of a thick, tangled growth of trees and other vegetation. It contains no shrine buildings or other formal structures. A thick canopy of vegetation encloses two sacred spaces consisting of rocks. The grove sits atop a sixty-meter-high hill whose slope was once used for open-air burials. Today, the Yabusatsu grove is overgrown and difficult to access.

Sacred groves in the Ryukyu Islands typically enshrine unique deities, and these deities can be divided into two potentially overlapping categories:

founders of communities and deities who arrived from across the sea. The majority of groves on the island of Okinawa are of the community founder type, although Yabusatsu and the others attributed to Amamiku are of the sea deity type. In the southern Ryukyu Islands, and on the various small islands near Okinawa, groves enshrining deities who arrived from across the sea are relatively more common.

Sacred groves are unrelated to mainstream Japanese Shinto shrines. Groves have no torii gateways (with a few exceptions),[1] coin boxes, guardian lion dogs (*komainu*), or other typical features of Shinto shrines. Importantly, women customarily perform formal rites at sacred groves, whereas Shinto priests are men. Sacred groves often include grave sites, something not found at Shinto shrines. There are tens of thousands of Shinto shrines around Japan enshrining the same deity, for example, Hachiman or Inari. By contrast, it is extremely rare for different sacred groves to venerate the same deity.

Although forming the bedrock of native Ryukyuan religion, sacred groves are not unique to the Ryukyu Islands. South of the islands, in places like Taiwan or the Philippines whose classical culture was Austronesian, we do not find anything resembling sacred groves. By contrast, there are many sacred

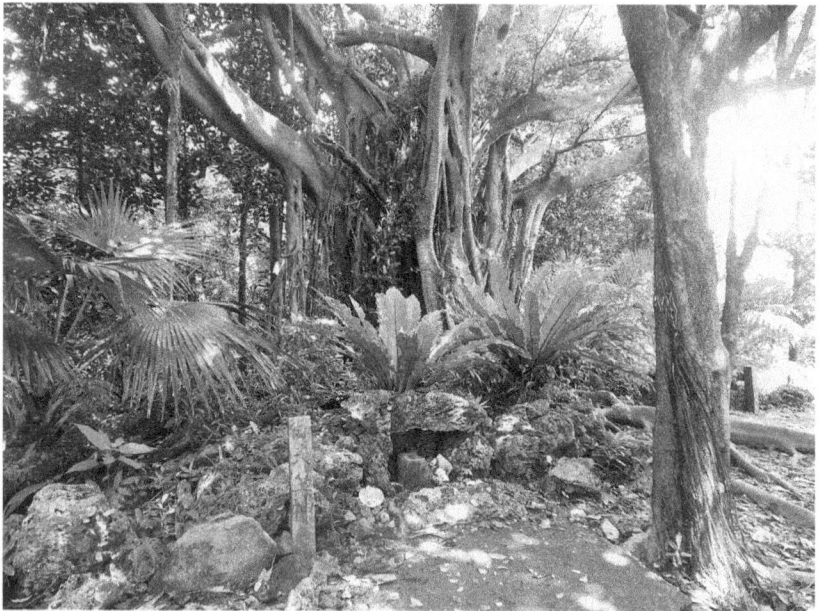

FIGURE 7.1. A sacred space (*ibe*) in the Baten grove in Sashiki, Nanjō City, Okinawa (photograph by the author)

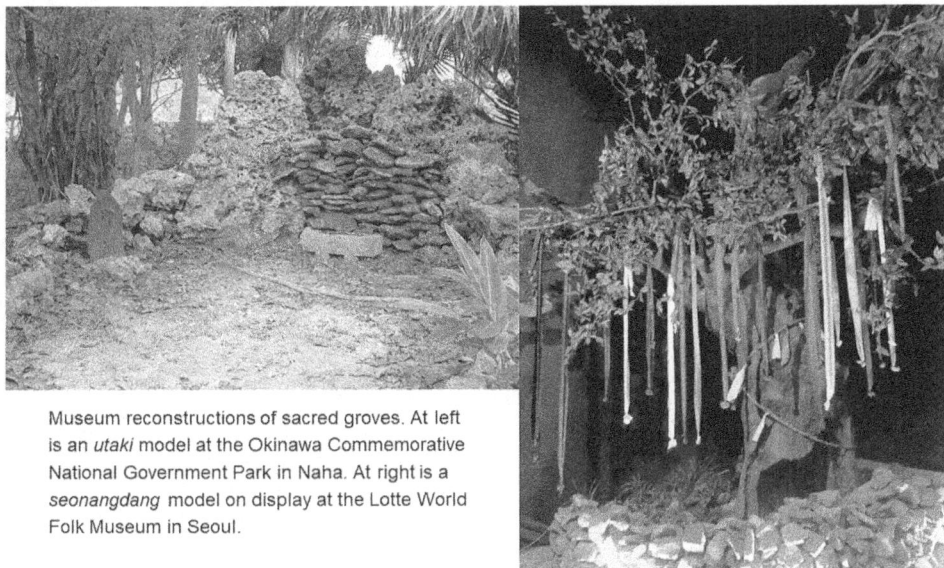

Museum reconstructions of sacred groves. At left is an *utaki* model at the Okinawa Commemorative National Government Park in Naha. At right is a *seonangdang* model on display at the Lotte World Folk Museum in Seoul.

FIGURE 7.2. Sacred grove depictions in Okinawa (*left*) and Korea (*right*) (*left*, Wikipedia, Turlington, CC BY-SA 3.0; *right*, Wikimedia Commons, Ethan Doyle White, CC BY-SA 4.0)

groves to the north. To state my conclusion in advance, following the work of Okaya Kōji (2019) and others, the ultimate ancestor of Ryukyuan groves is a type of sacred grove in Korea known as *dang*. Found throughout the Korean Peninsula, *dang* are especially numerous on the island of Jeju. Figure 7.2 shows a typical sacred grove from Okinawa next to one from Korea.

Distribution of Sacred Groves

The distribution of sacred groves maps out a zone of culture and sea-lanes linking the Korean Peninsula, the Japanese islands, and the Ryukyu Islands. Sacred groves are not the only example of common culture within this zone, and the main disseminators of this common culture were mariners.[2] The worship of local deities or other divine forces at sacred groves can be found throughout coastal areas of western Honshu from Wakasa Bay in Fukui Prefecture south. (Groves are also found around Lake Biwa and at a few other Kansai area locations.) Their distribution continues south through western Kyushu and all the way through the Ryukyu Islands. Importantly, sacred groves are also found in Jeju Island and mainland southern Korea. I call this region *the sacred grove zone* (fig. 7.3).

FIGURE 7.3. The sacred grove zone

The groves are known by a variety names, but they share many fundamental characteristics, including a strict deity, prohibitions against cutting vegetation, restricted entry, the presence of grave sites, the presence of sacred stones or trees, a simple stone wall or fence enclosure, and women as the main performers of rites. Many groves are located on high ground, and the deity is often the spirit of the human who founded a nearby local community or was otherwise closely associated with the area. Leaving out western Honshu, I now briefly survey sacred groves in different locations around the zone.

IKI AND TSUSHIMA

The islands of Tsushima and Iki were conduits between the Japanese islands and the Korean Peninsula. They functioned as maritime stepping stones between ports such as Hakata and Busan. In Iki, a type of sacred grove known as *yabusa* or *yabosa* (and other variants) is especially prevalent. *Yabusa* sites are also found in Tsushima and throughout the western coast of Kyushu. There is a *yabusa* site at Shomi in Izena Island, just north of Okinawa, and the Yabusatsu grove in Okinawa mentioned above is another example.

Another type of grove found in Tsushima is called *tendō-chi* (other names containing *tendō* are also employed). *Tendō* groves consist of densely overgrown forest. Cutting trees or branches in them is prohibited, as is the entry of unauthorized people. In addition to *yabusa* and *tendō* sites, another variety of sacred grove, known as *shigechi* (or *shige*), is widespread in Tsushima.[3] *Shigechi* sites were off-limits to most people, and, originally, they contained no buildings. Like many other sacred groves in the region, they often feature sacred trees. Although bearing different names, *tendō* and *shigechi* sites are nearly the same.

WESTERN KYUSHU

Moving south along the western coast of Kyushu from Hakata south, we find many *yabusa* sites. There are also similar sacred groves known by other names, typically including *-mori* (stand of trees, grove) or *-san/yama* (mountain). Many such groves or former groves now converted to shrines can be found in coastal areas of Kumamoto Prefecture.

In both the Satsuma and the Ōsumi Peninsulas of Kagoshima Prefecture, over one hundred *moidon* sacred groves have been identified. (*Moi* is *mori* [grove] and *don* is the honorific *dono*, meaning "venerable grove.") Most *moidon* sites are located alongside graveyards, and sometimes graves are located within the groves. Other than at the time of annual community worship, many local people avoid these sites out of fear of offending the deity within them. Cutting trees or branches or breaking them will invite divine wrath, so the sites are thick with vegetation.

TANEGASHIMA (AND TSUSHIMA AGAIN)

Moving into the Satsunan Islands, we find *garō* (also pronounced *garan* and *garo*) mountains. These sites are sacred groves, and their spirits protected the original land cultivator or were deities of local rivers and springs. Some *garō* groves feature a sacred tree in the center. The deities of *garō* sites are partly feared and partly reviled, and cutting wood there is prohibited. *Garō* mountain sites are related to Okinawan sacred groves, *obotsu* mountains in Amami-Ōshima, and the *moidon* of Kagoshima.

The island of Tsushima is also home to sacred groves called *garan*, an older name that became *garō* in Tanegashima. Tsushima *garan* groves are of ancient vintage and are similar in appearance and function to *shigechi* and *yabusa* groves. It is noteworthy that Tsushima is home to four types of sacred groves, *tendō*, *shigechi*, *yabusa*, and *garan*, all of which are similar in appearance and function to each other and to sacred groves in Jeju Island and mainland Korea. Tsushima appears to have been the major point outside Korea from which sacred groves spread to western Japan and the islands of the Ryukyu Arc. The presence so many different groves in Tsushima also indicates that it was a major regional conduit for shipping traffic and people.

KOREA

Busan, South Korea, is visible from northern Tsushima in clear weather. Just north of Busan, in Gyeongju, there are approximately twenty extant *dangsan* (*dang* mountain) sacred groves. There are other such groves throughout Korea, but these sites have been suppressed or otherwise put under pressure for centuries and have declined as a result.[4] Today, sacred groves called *dang* are most numerous and vigorous on the Korean island of Jeju, where 392 remain. These Jeju *dang* closely resemble Ryukyuan sacred groves.

The presence of a large number of sacred groves with similar characteristics throughout the zone extending from southern Korea to western Honshu, south through western Kyushu, and all the way through the Satsunan, Tokara, and Ryukyu Islands indicates that seafarers with a common culture traveled between these places and dwelled in them. Ideally, we would want to know when these groves first emerged. All evidence points to Korea as the place where sacred groves developed earliest.

APPROXIMATE DATES OF SACRED GROVE VARIETIES

Sacred groves are difficult to date because they typically lack formal buildings or associated written records. Although *yabusa* sites were originally groves without buildings, over the centuries many of them in Kyushu were transformed into Shinto shrines. In those cases, Yabusa or some variant of that name became the enshrined deity or one of several enshrined deities. A *yabusa* shrine in the Satsuma Peninsula has a building tag dated 1525.

Another outside Kagoshima City has a tag dated 1530. Because these sites were originally groves without buildings, they would have existed prior to and possibly long before the early sixteenth-century construction of shrine buildings.

The Korean *Account of East Sea Countries* (Sin 1471/1991) discusses *tendō* sites in Tsushima (called "sacred *dang*"). In the Korean context, sacred groves called *dang* or *dangsan* appear in ancient legends. Documents from the Goryeo and the early Joseon Eras described these sites and associated folk practices. Sacred mountains appear in Korean documents as far back as 1106, and the creation of mountain groves is mentioned as early as 1398.

The descriptions of the over seven hundred Ryukyuan groves listed in *Origins of Ryukyu* (1713) vary in terms of the amount of detail offered, but they sometimes include hints about when the groves were established. All these hints indicate a time prior to the establishment of a central state during the early sixteenth century. Similarly, the royal government did not create any groves. Given the available textual and archaeological evidence, all that can be determined as of this writing is that most or all Ryukyuan sacred groves were established during the fourteenth and fifteenth centuries.

In short, currently available evidence suggests that sacred groves originated in Korea and spread to western Japan and the Ryukyu Islands during approximately the late thirteenth to early fifteenth century, which was precisely the time of increased *wakō* activity within the region.

CHARACTERISTICS OF SACRED GROVES

Originally, many types of sacred groves functioned as open-air or more conventional grave sites for the founding ancestors of a community. It is likely that all or most of them originally functioned to enshrine the founders of a community and house their physical remains. Over time, groves and the deities enshrined there took on additional qualities or functions. Human bones have been found in nearly almost every Ryukyuan grove, and it is likely that one of their original functions was serving as grave sites. It is unclear to what extent, if any, Korean *dang* functioned as grave sites. It is noteworthy that there was a strong association in the Ryukyu Islands with the bones of important people being capable of bringing forth rain or otherwise influencing the course of nature. This interest in the power of bones probably originated in Korea. Another commonality was bone-washing funerals, which are emblematic of Ryukyuan culture but were also found in island Korea.

In the Ryukyu Islands, many sacred groves are located on hills or other elevated sites. Most consist of wooded areas, some surrounded by simple stone fences or walls. Some Ryukyuan groves prohibit men from entering them or from entering parts of them, and it is women who are in charge of sacred grove rites. Rites at groves are sometimes conducted in secret. (Public village rites and festivities are conducted in built structures called *kami ashiage*.) Cutting or breaking branches is prohibited in groves for fear of divine punishment. Ryukyuan groves often feature one or more sacred stones and, less commonly, a sacred tree. In some Yaeyama groves, deities or the humans created by deities to populate an island can emerge from the ground. Deities emerging from the ground is also characteristic of *dang* in Jeju Island.

Dang in Jeju Island and the Korean mainland consist mainly of a stand of trees. Vegetation and a variety of items accumulate in them because, once something is offered to the grove's deity, removing that item is inappropriate. *Dang* typically feature simple stone altars and contain no buildings. An unassuming stone fence or wall usually encloses the grove. Significantly, as at Ryukyuan groves and some of the Kyushu groves, women perform rites to the deities at *dang*. In these and other respects, Ryukyuan sacred groves and Korean *dang* closely resemble each other. All the varieties of sacred groves from Jeju and Tsushima through the southern Ryukyu Islands have or once had a large set of common characteristics.

The sacred grove zone maps out an interconnected maritime region. Although regarded as emblematic of classical Ryukyuan culture, sacred groves did not originate there. They came into the islands from the north, ultimately from Korea. Although most of the Gusuku Era migrants to the Ryukyu Islands came from Kyushu, western Kyushu had long been influenced by inflows of Korean people and culture. Furthermore, during the fourteenth and fifteenth centuries, Korean people came into the Ryukyu Islands, willingly or via human trafficking, owing to the activities of *wakō*. Importantly, the ranks of *wakō* included many Koreans or people of partial Korean ancestry.

Stone-Walled Fortresses (*Gusuku*)

During the fourteenth century, large-scale fortresses with impressively engineered sets of stone walls appeared at Nakijin in the north and at major harbors in central and southern Okinawa. Often called *castles*, these fortresses had walls that were strikingly high. Itokazu Fortress, for example, is 189 meters in elevation. The next highest are Tamagusuku Fortress (181 meters), Nakagusuku Fortress (167 meters), Ōzato Fortress (150 meters), Shuri Castle (130 meters), Zakimi Fortress (127 meters), and Katsuren Fortress (98 meters).

FIGURE 7.4. The walls of Gyeonghwon Fortress, a typical Korean mountain fortress (*left*), compared with the walls of Nakagusuku Fortress in Okinawa (*right*) (*left*, Wikimedia Commons, Korean Culture and Information Service, Wi Tack-whan, CC BY-SA 2.0; *right*, photograph by the author)

The rock with which the walls of these fortresses were made came from Okinawa. But what was the source of the know-how needed to build them? Let us consider the possibilities. Okinawan fortresses predate Japanese stone-walled castles by over a century, so Japan would not have been the source.[5] Perhaps people living in Okinawa figured out the engineering required for their construction on their own. This possibility seems unlikely given the speed and frequency with which well-made, large-scale fortresses appeared after 1300. Fortress-like walled cities had long existed in China. However, Chinese castles and city walls were of an entirely different character than Ryukyuan stone-walled fortresses. Chinese fortified cities were located in low-lying areas, and their walls consisted of baked bricks, not fitted stone.[6] It is also important to note that very few Chinese people ever settled in the Ryukyu Islands during the Gusuku Era and that we do not find strong Chinese cultural influence apart from the presence of large quantities of ceramics and other trade goods. What about Korea?

There are roughly twenty-four hundred extant examples of Korean mountain fortresses (K. *sanseong*), all built either before or during Ryukyu's Gusuku Era. Okinawan fortresses look almost exactly like Korean fortresses (fig. 7.4). Moreover, the range of functions of Korean fortresses was nearly identical to that of Okinawan fortresses. During the fourteenth and fifteenth centuries, many Korean people resided in Okinawa. Some were *wakō*, whose ranks included many Koreans, and some were the victims of *wakō* raids. The port of Naha was a major hub for human trafficking, and many Koreans came to Okinawa against their will. These Koreans, as well as people from the northern Ryukyu Islands, functioned in part as a labor force for the building of the fortresses. In short, stone-walled *gusuku*, five of which were registered on UNESCO's World Heritage List in 2000,[7] were modeled on Korean mountain fortresses.

Korea's Goryeo dynasty (918–1392) was a time when many older mountain fortresses were upgraded and newer ones built. Characteristics of Goryeo mountain fortresses include the following: they were constructed in high, mountainous areas; cliffs and steep drop-offs functioned as de facto fortress walls or as extensions of walls; most walls featured battlements; and the fortresses were built on scales larger than those of fortresses of previous eras (Korea Fortress Academy 2008a, 37). The same points apply to Okinawan fortresses, which appeared during the latter part of Korea's Goryeo Era.

Large walled fortresses in Okinawa consisted of either a series of laterally connected enclosures (e.g., Nakagusuku or Nakijin) or a series of concentric walled enclosures. Ryukyuan fortresses closely resemble Korean mountain fortresses with respect to the technical details of wall construction,[8] all the specific characteristics of Goryeo Era fortresses mentioned above, and their nonmilitary functions. Writing around 1460, the Korean castaway Ryang Seong described Shuri Castle as "fairly high, like capital castles in our country." Moreover, its gates "are also like those of our country," and its walls are like a meandering stream (*Joseon Veritable Royal Records* 2005, 144). Looking at photographs of walls, it is often impossible to determine whether the example in question is Korean or Ryukyuan. Large stone-walled *gusuku* appeared in Okinawa precisely at a time of extensive *wakō* activity in Korea. The *wakō* presence in the Ryukyu Islands functioned as a direct and indirect infusion of Korean people (technicians, slaves, *wakō*, others) and know-how, an example of *wakō* as agents of technology transfer.

Korean Impact

The Korean origins of sacred groves and stone-walled fortresses are not widely known, even among scholars. The distinctive Ryukyuan pottery of the Gusuku Era, *kamuiyaki*, was created using Korean technology and probably under the supervision of Korean technicians, at least during the initial phases of production. Okinawan-made copies of Korean tiles adorn the roofs of some of the buildings in Urasoe Castle, Shuri Castle, and Katsuren

Fortress. The first person (possibly fictive) to hold the title *king* in Okinawa, Satto, came from Korea, as did many members of the Satto group. Remnants of the Satto group perished in Korea around 1398. Korean pottery has been excavated at many archaeological sites from this era. In short, Korean cultural and technological influence on the Ryukyu Islands was profound. It is hardly surprising, therefore, that in inscription on the 1458 Sea Bridge to the Many Countries Bell the "excellence" of Korea is the first item listed with respect to contact with other countries.

This important Korean legacy in the Ryukyu Islands has been largely overlooked in the modern era for several reasons. First, the official histories were written well after frequent contact between the Ryukyu Islands and Korea had stopped. Moreover, at the time those histories were written, elite society in Okinawa was experiencing an influx of Chinese culture and technology. Largely for this reason, today it is common to imagine that the major cultural influences on the Ryukyu Islands came from Japan and China, overlooking Korea. Finally, the Korean presence was inextricably connected with the *wakō* presence in the Ryukyu Islands and human trafficking at the port of Naha. In 1957, Inamura Kenpu published an entire book on the *wakō* presence throughout the Ryukyu Islands with one of Japan's most prestigious academic presses (Yoshikawa kōbunkan). Nevertheless, it has had little influence. Most modern and contemporary scholars either ignore the topic of *wakō* in the Ryukyu Islands or assume that the *wakō* and the Ryukyuans were separate groups. Informed by the work of scholars like Inamura Kenpu (Inamura 1957) and Yoshinari Naoki and Fuku Hiromi (Yoshinari and Fuku 2006, 2007), I have argued in *Maritime Ryukyu* (2019) and elsewhere that the predominant drivers of Ryukyuan history during the fourteenth and fifteenth centuries were bands of *wakō*. For better or worse, these *wakō* linked the Korean Peninsula, western Japan, and the Ryukyu Islands.

The *Omoro sōshi* and Its World

The *Omoro sōshi* is, as we have seen, a collection of songs, some of ancient vintage. Geographically, these songs are mainly about the northern and central Ryukyu Islands, with occasional mention of other locations in the East China Sea region. The *Omoro* is often likened to Japan's *Manyōshū*.[9] In the context of analyzing the *Omoro*, scholars from the time of Iha Fuyū (1876–1947) have pointed out links between the content of particular songs and possible historical events. I have already put the *Omoro* to work as a historical source. The paragraphs below enhance our understanding of the collection itself and what it reveals about history, politics, culture, values, and lifestyles.

Today's *Omoro sōshi* consists of twenty-two volumes. The individual songs are numbered consecutively from 1 to 1,553. The first volume is dated 1531, and it was not until 1623 that the royal court finished compiling the remaining volumes. The *Omoro* we have today, however, is almost certainly different from the original in ways that we cannot know. The reason is that today's *Omoro* comes from a 1710 recompilation of the text from fragments in the wake of a palace fire. This reconstruction process likely resulted in some alteration of the original.

The *Omoro* is written in the classical language of the Shuri court, mainly using Japanese *kana* script to record the songs, although simple Chinese characters appear occasionally. (*Kana* is a syllabary, but we can think of it simply as an alphabet.) Buddhist priests from Japan were the main scribes who recorded the songs, at least for the first volume. Interpreting the *Omoro* is a specialized academic endeavor. The raw text would make little or no sense to modern readers, even those who might know Okinawan or other Ryukyuan languages.

The language of the *Omoro* is classical, courtly Okinawan. Classical Okinawan is closely related to classical and medieval Japanese. Nearly all the vocabulary in the *Omoro* songs consists of cognates of Japanese, and over 80 percent of it overlaps with Japanese of the Muromachi period (ca. 1336–1573). Other linguistic ingredients include terms from medieval Japanese dialects and some terms specific to the Ryukyu Islands. The meaning of some parts of some songs is in dispute among experts, and there are some words and phrases that currently remain undeciphered. The term *mishōgo*, "unknown word (or phrase)," comes up frustratingly often in the notes to *Omoro sōshi* translations or in *Omoro sōshi* dictionaries.

Omoro sōshi as Tribute to Shō Shin

There is a subtle but important underlying theme to the entire *Omoro sōshi*. The collection celebrates the accomplishments, power, and legacy of King Shō Shin. Shō Shin was the key figure in the transition from the era of trade kings to the emergence of Ryukyu as a centralized state and maritime empire. If we take the word *king* to mean the ruler of a centralized, bureaucratic state, then Shō Shin was Ryukyu's first king. Many of the songs in the *Omoro* celebrate the power and glory of local harbor-fortress pairs. The cumulative, larger effect of these songs is to glorify Shō Shin, who ended up ruling over all those celebrated harbors and fortresses. Similarly, many of the songs are from localities remote from Shuri, especially locations in the northern Ryukyu Islands. Nevertheless, the language of all the songs is courtly Shuri Okinawan. In other words, even the language of the songs serves to reinforce the power of Shō Shin and Shuri as Ryukyu's center. One of the lyrical names of Shō Shin is Ogyaka-omoi, "beloved son of Ogyaka." Ogyaka, Shō Shin's mother, orchestrated the palace coup that brought him to the throne at the age of twelve.

Omoro songs are not dated. The songs in volume 1 were, of course, composed prior to the 1530s. Other songs sometimes contain specific names or references to events that we can date. For example, consider the following song, which is somewhat unusual in that it mentions locations in the southern Ryukyu Islands:

> The deity of the sacred grove at Mt. Omoto
> Came from Kumejima
> Came to pacify
> The deity of the sacred grove at Mt. Omoto
> Came face-to-face with her father
> The venerable lord of Shuri grove [i.e., the king]
> Forever
> The venerable ruler [i.e., the king]
> All the way to the Yaeyama Islands
> All the way to Hateruma [i.e., all the Yaeyama Islands]
> Forever
> The venerable ruler
> All the way to Yonaguni
> All the way to Hateruma [i.e., all the Yaeyama Islands]
> Forever
> The venerable ruler
> Extends the rope
> Extends the line [i.e., brings them under his control]
> Forever
> The venerable ruler.

> (*Omoro sōshi*, 11-558)

Notice the first two lines indicating a connection between Kumejima and Mt. Omoto in Ishigaki. Recall the legend that three sister deities from Japan took up residence in the island of Kumejima, just west of Okinawa. After residing there for a while, one sister remained in Kumejima and became that island's *kimihae* deity. Another moved to Shuri and became the high priestess (*kikoe-ōgimi*). The other sister headed south and became the deity of Mt. Omoto, the tallest mountain on the island of Ishigaki in the Yaeyama group of the southern Ryukyu Islands. Moreover, according to legend, when an Okinawan army invaded Ishigaki in 1500, during Shō Shin's reign, the *kimihae* priestess (the human manifestation of the deity) was at the head of the invading forces. According to the story, when the defenders of Ishigaki saw the sister of their Mt. Omoto deity leading the opposing army, they lost their will to fight.

Prior to 1500, the southern Ryukyu Islands were politically independent of Shuri and Okinawa. In the song, the king in Shuri "extends the rope" to the Yaeyama Islands because it is about Shuri's conquest of the Yaeyama Islands, which began in 1500 and was probably completed in the 1520s. Therefore, the song was composed after 1500, probably a decade or two after because of the time required for Shuri to consolidate its hold over all the southern Ryukyu Islands. The king in the song is Shō Shin, the inspiration for the entire *Omoro sōshi* project. Notice also that this song was composed by the victors. It takes an event that was brutal and bloody and portrays it as noble—a common rhetorical device the world over.

There are other songs about the invasion of Yaeyama, including one from the first volume of the *Omoro* that conveys a stronger sense of the fighting. I translate the title *kikoe-ōgimi* in the song as *high priestess*. This priestess was established by Shō Shin, and she was one of the three sister deities/priestesses who came from Kumejima (and ultimately Japan). That may be one reason she is called "sibling ruler" in the song. The more obvious reason is that the high priestess was the king's sister (his principal wife in the eighteenth century and later). Notice also that most lines of the song are pairs saying the same thing using slightly different language. These pairs are common in *Omoro* songs. The song reads as follows:

> The high priestess
> Of the great country, of the venerable reign
> The venerable ruler [i.e., the king] resounds
> The resounding venerable one [i.e., the king]
> The venerable sibling ruler
> The venerable sibling person of renown
> [Has bestowed] great spiritual power on the soldiers
> [Has bestowed] great spiritual power on the soldiers
> The soldiers of Shuri grove
> The soldiers of Shuri and its precincts
> Venerable *Seyari-tomi* [ship name]
> Venerable *Teyori-tomi* [ship name]

Bewilder [i.e., make them lose the will to fight]
The Yaeyama soldiers
Bewilder
The Hateruma soldiers
Soldiers of Shuri grove
Cut [the enemy] like the dirt
Soldiers of Shuri grove
Cut [the enemy] like the dirt
The priestesses of the many harbors
Use your power to protect [the Shuri forces].

(*Omoro sōshi*, 1-33)

Although victory in battle is ultimately a matter of cutting the enemy like the dirt, notice the emphasis on the role of priestesses in bringing about this result. The high priestess, the sister of the king, along with the other priestesses, channels spiritual power into Shuri's soldiers. Conversely, they project disruptive power toward the enemy soldiers in Yaeyama. Notice the line "The priestesses of the many harbors." It alludes to the fundamental political geography prior to Shō Shin's time. Each harbor-fortress unit was home to one or more priestesses whose spiritual power helps that unit prosper. The emphasis on victory in war resulting from the intervention of priestesses is common throughout the *Omoro*.

Omoro sōshi versus the Official Histories

Taking a different slant on the question of the *Omoro*'s political significance, the pioneering *Omoro* scholar Iha Fuyū (1974–76, 6:217) concluded that, during the seventeenth century, the song collection came to be regarded as dangerous thought by the state. As a result, the early modern royal government kept the *Omoro* locked up (possibly one reason the entire collection was lost in the 1710 palace fire). Why might the *Omoro* have been dangerous? Because some of its songs are often sharply at odds with the content of the official histories. When the *Omoro* was compiled, there were no official histories. After 1650, however, the potential existed for tension between the two types of official texts, songs versus narrative history.

What about, for example, portraying the king as a pirate leader and praising a successful seizure of goods? The official histories portray Shō Toku as violent, and the 1725 edition of *Genealogy of Chūzan* specifically portrays him as a *wakō*. These works emphasize that he was utterly lacking in virtue and that therefore Shō Toku deserved to become the last king of his dynasty. Turning to the *Omoro*, however, consider the following song, which some scholars call the *"wakō omoro"*:

> Masarikyo [the captain] pilots the ship
> The king of Okinawa resplendently present
> Ukiagari [the captain] pilots the ship
> Do not think the oarsmen lack vigor in their rowing
> Do not think the oarsmen row dangerously
> The lord of the south is present
> The lord of the lords is present
> The impressive lady lord
> Spiritually powerful lady lord
> We offer splendid goods to our ancestors
> Offer splendid goods to our ancestors
> We did not obtain them by asking
> Did not acquire them by asking
> But by stealth
> By pilfering [*nosude*] we attained them
> And stashed them in wine jars
> Stashed them in sacred wine jars.

(*Omoro sōshi*, 10-546; partially repeated in 13-866)

There is some room for interpretation in this song, especially with respect to the lines about the oarsmen. Importantly, the part about seizing the goods and offering them to ancestors is clear. The verb I renter as *pilfering* would in modern Japanese be *nusunde* (robbing, stealing, improperly taking). Wine jars are a common symbol of wealth and prosperity in the *Omoro*.

In this song, the king himself and/or members of his inner circle celebrate the return from a successful raid. They are proud of what that have taken and ritually offer the goods to their ancestors. As noted above, Iha Fuyū once argued that the early modern royal government kept the *Omoro* text tightly controlled because *Omoro* songs often contradict the narrative in the official histories. Songs like this one lend support to Iha's claim.[10]

One consistent bias in the *Omoro* is that, except for enemy soldiers, it tends to praise any person, place, or topic appearing in the songs. Therefore, if a person, place, or thing of historical importance is not mentioned in the *Omoro*, that absence may be significant. We have already noted the absence of the three principalities and most of their associated trade kings. Returning to Shō Toku, the *Omoro* and the official histories seem to be in agreement about him because he is entirely absent from the *Omoro*. Conversely, the *Omoro* and the official histories appear to disagree in their assessment of Gosamaru and Amawari, who both died in 1458 during Shō Taikyū's wars to conquer Nakagusuku and Katsuren. The official histories regard Gosamaru a tragic hero, but he is absent from *Omoro* songs. Moreover, Amawari, Gosamaru's opponent, is a scheming villain in the official histories.[11] However, the *Omoro* praises Amawari, using language that places him on a par with the king.

Lords of the Water

The specific manner of *Omoro* praise for Amawari is especially intriguing. Amawari was on a par with the king because he handled the ultimate royal power object, a mother-of-pearl ladle. Indeed, the king is the only other person in *Omoro* songs who handles this ritual tool for controlling water.[12] Control of water—or the weather more generally—was the ultimate manifestation of power for a ruler in early Ryukyu. It is also a crucial element in the legendary biographies of several early kings. In the official histories, Shō Hashi destroyed the Sannan king Tarumi through shrewd wresting of control of the Kadeshi spring. In his official biography, Kanemaru had to flee Izena when his neighbors accused him of misappropriating water for his fields. Moreover, the king is known as *ukigumo* (floating clouds) in one *omoro*:

> Residing at Madama grove
> Living descendant of the sun, Ukigumo [the king].

> (*Omoro sōshi*, 3-90)

The *Omoro* also sings of a "lord of the windy clouds" (*aorikumo no aji*) who is a great conqueror:

> Lord of the windy clouds
> Known throughout the great country
> Conquers and returns
> Lord of the clouds who came down from the heavens
> Highest warrior at Shuri
> Highest warrior at the castle
> Attacks the wooden gate
> Attacks the metal gate

Attacks the wooden gate and breaks through
Attacks the metal gate and breaks through
[undecipherable line]
Pursues them to sacred places
And cuts down a hundred men
Cuts down seventy men [i.e., kills many people].

(*Omoro sōshi*, 10-519)

This lord is either the king or someone on a par with the king. The main point is that those who control the wind and the clouds are able to defeat their enemies in battle.

That Ryukyuan kings or other rulers portrayed themselves as sea lords with the power to control wind and rain is, on the one hand, to state the obvious. Nevertheless, it is important to keep this point in mind in connection with the *wakō* roots of early Ryukyuan power holders. It also helps explain the prominence of eagles in the *Omoro*. The eagle (*washi*) is a common metaphor for royal power in the *Omoro* and in Ryukyuan folk songs generally. Among other functions, eagles—often as a "power eagle" (*oni-washi*, lit. "demon eagle")—helped guide ships:

The power eagle soars above the sea
Herald above the mast
Protecting us
Crossing over the sea
The power eagle soars above the waves
Herald above the mast.

(*Omoro sōshi*, 13-967)

In other words, the power eagle had the ability to know what lies ahead—a scene invisible to crew members—and guide ships accordingly.

Eagles also served as power animals for kings on land, such as at the gate of Shō Hashi's base of power in Sashiki:

At the entrance to Sashiki
A power eagle
Is a splendid sight, flapping its wings
At the western entrance to Sashiki.

(*Omoro sōshi*, 19-1291)

Here, an eagle serves as a shamanic power animal for the lord of Sashiki in southern Okinawa. Priestesses enhanced and extended the power of kings and local lords. So, too, did eagles.

It is important to note that, in the ecological context of the Ryukyu Islands, eagles were imaginary creatures. Small eagles live in the Yaeyama Islands, but large birds of prey are not native to the Ryukyu Islands. They are found in Japan, but they are not associated with shamanic power animals or divine messengers, unlike, for example, the three-legged crow (*yatagarasu*) that famously guided the mythical Emperor Jinmu. Eagles are also found in Korea. There is at least one Korean example of eagles as power animals.[13] Eagles in the *Omoro* are yet another example of a northern cultural element and a northern orientation at the core of Ryukyuan culture, a point we have encountered previously.

Warfare and other forms of violent conflict are common themes in the *Omoro*, though they are often cast positively, for example, by praising one or another deity for making victory possible. Aoriyae is a powerful deity in Nakijin. Her likely origin was as a water-well deity in Kumejima. In Nakijin, Aoriyae became associated with wind, rain, and protection from storms. Control of water in various forms (wells, springs, storms) is a recurring theme in connection with powerful Ryukyuan men and women. By logical extension, Aoriyae was also a military deity. For example, in the *Omoro*, she was an "island-smashing priestess" (*shima-uchi-gimi*), with *island* meaning any defined community. Note also that there is no practical distinction between the deity and the priestess because the deity takes possession of the priestess during shamanic trances:

> Acclaimed Aoriyae
> Resounding Aoriyae
> Island-smashing Aoriyae forever.

> (*Omoro sōshi*, 12-685)

> Acclaimed Aoriyae
> Because you are an island-smashing priestess
> Aoriyae
> Provide for us a propitious day for our attack
> Acclaimed Aoriyae.

> (*Omoro sōshi*, 4-163)

Notice the constellation of related points. The ultimate indication of power is the ability to control water. Control of wells or springs is necessary for material well-being. Control of storms is a manifestation of great military power. Such control is sometimes attributed to especially powerful men. Typically, however, it comes through the ritual actions of priestesses, in whom powerful deities such as Aoriyae manifest themselves.

There are also examples of similar ideas outside the *Omoro*. For example, powerful local lords in the southern Ryukyu Islands typically discover springs or create wells. According to legendary material in the official histories, the military general and Shō Taikyū supporter Oni-Ōgusuku (d. ca. 1469) possessed such a potent voice that he was able to call down rain by singing sacred songs. The rains Oni-Ōgusuku summoned bogged down the armies of Amawari, thus giving Shō Taikyū's forces the upper hand in the warfare of 1458.

Shamanic Power

Shamanic trances, dances, and songs abound in the *Omoro*. Most of the shamans are women. For example:

> The shaman Seyaro-Kuniosoi
> Appears at Uezato grove
> The shaman Momotofumiagari
> Performs her dance
> The shaman Kearu-Kuniosoi
> The flourishing power of the sun
> The shining power of the sun
> Setting up a plentiful world
> Setting up a peaceful world.
>
> (*Omoro sōshi*, 12-719;
> repeated as 20-1350)

These shamanic women used their divine power in the service of a king or a warlord. The source of this power was the sun—or heaven—as a deity. Divine power resided above, according to the vertically oriented realm (*obotsukagura*) in *Omoro* songs. Shamanic women channeled this power and brought it down to earth.

The belief that a man's sister or some other female relative protects him spiritually (*onarigami shinkō*) became a prominent feature of Ryukyuan folk religion during the early modern era, and its roots extend further back in tome. Women in the *Omoro* dominate the spiritual realm, and priestesses use their power to protect the king, other rulers, or society in general. From Shō Shin's time on, the leading priestesses were nearly all royal relatives. However, men like Oni-Ōgusuku and Kanemaru possess their own spiritual power. Female shamans and priestesses added to that power. According to Korean observers of Shuri Castle during the fifteenth century, women armed with swords served as the king's bodyguard within the palace. Similarly, consider this song:

> The High Priestess Kikoe-ōgimi
> Resounding One of Great Spiritual Power
> Wearing red armor
> It is her sword striking, certainly
> That will resound throughout the country
> She has Tsukishiro in the lead
> She has the Knower of Things in the lead.

> (*Omoro sōshi*, 1-5)

Here, the high priestess is dressed as a male warrior participating in a procession. A sorcerer bearing the Tsukishiro stone precedes her. Tsukishiro was a form of the deity Hachiman (the deity of *wakō*). It was brought to Sashiki by the Samekawa group when it migrated to Okinawa from Kyushu, and there is a modern (ca. 1930s) Tsukishiro Shrine at the site of the ruins of Sashiki Fortress. The second Shō dynasty did not maintain any of the first Shō dynasty deities. Therefore, the song anachronistically transposed the high priestess back into the early fifteenth century, before she actually existed. There are some legends that do the same. During the time of Shō Hashi, the highest priestess in southern Okinawa was the Baten priestess. (Baten is an area adjacent to Sashiki.)

Spiritual Power, Sonic Power, the Sun, and Alcoholic Beverages

Excluding variations in spelling, there are seven different terms in the *Omoro* for "spiritual power." This section examines many of them. Readers unfamiliar with Japanese or Okinawan may find the sheer number of unusual words difficult to follow. The larger point, however, is to understand the way people in the early Ryukyu Islands tended to understand the spiritual power that flowed through their world.

The term *seji* indicates an enhancement of the abilities or power already inherent in people or things. *Se* (or *sei*) is similar but typically applies only to people, not objects. Someone referred to as having *se-ikusa* (enhanced abilities in warfare), for example, would be a soldier. *Sue* overlaps with the other terms but often suggests spiritual power by virtue of one's line of descent. The term *shii* functions the same way. For example, *teda-shii* indicates power by virtue of being a descendant of the sun (*teda*). The term *kyō* originally indicated a sacred space, and it commonly appears as *kyō-no-uchi* (within the sacred space). *Ke* (or *kei*) comes from what in modern Japanese would be *ki* (Ch. *qì*, "energy"), and *shike* indicates the trance-like state of a spiritual medium. Finally, *mono* (O. *mun*) usually appears as *ma-mono* (O. *ma-mun*) and indicates someone with deity-like power. Notice the importance of spiritual power in *Omoro* songs and the nuanced possibilities for expressing it.

These varieties of power or influence are often transmitted sonically, via singing, dancing, or drumming. The world of the *Omoro* songs abounds with sonic metaphors. Power resounds, echoes, booms, and reverberates. Vigorous dancing—which would produce a sonic effect (think of step dancing)—was one way to tap into divine power. The ultimate communion with the deities is the result of spirited singing or chanting, merging one's voice with the divine voice. Consider this typical example:

> The high priestess
> . . . .
> Merges her voice with that of [the solar deity] Terukawa
> Merges her voice with that of [the solar deity] Terushino
> Thereby pleasing Terukawa.
>
> (*Omoro sōshi*, 1-16)

In describing the role of religion at the royal court in the 1530s, the Chinese envoy Chén Kǎn (1534/1995) explained a ceremony involving a procession of three or five hundred (i.e., many) priestesses. They entered the royal palace and began to communicate with the deities. When one began to sing, the others joined her. Chén noted that the sound of their singing was indescribably powerful.

Male military leaders also sang in connection with their official duties. The Korean visitor Ryang Seong pointed out ca. 1456 that, when the king travels, a guard of three hundred mounted soldiers accompanies him. The leader of the soldiers sings songs that, to Ryang's ears, sounded like the melodies of agricultural songs. These songs were almost certainly *omoro*. During the sixteenth century, "*Omoro* Captain" (*omoro-sedo*) became a formal military post. Singing and power went hand in hand in classical Ryukyuan culture.

Another common manifestation of the merging of human and divine voices was a deity speaking through a priestess functioning as a shamanic medium. Both linguistically and conceptually, the terms for spiritual power *se* and *seji*, mentioned above, probably derive from the term *shike*, which refers to the trance state of a shamanic medium. This sonic manifestation of divine power may also be related to the ancient Japanese belief in the power of words to convey spiritual power (*kotodama shinkō*).

Alcoholic beverages were part of the process of divine communion, both conceptually and linguistically. Six different terms for alcoholic beverages appear in the *Omoro*: *miki, sake, kamenko, misago, shikechi,* and *seno* (variants are *se-no, sen,* and *seni*). Notice the last two of these terms. In the modern language of Kikaijima, the word *se* refers to the distilled liquor *shōchū*. There are twenty-eight examples of the priestess Se-no-kimi in the *Omoro*. In short, the term for "spiritual power," *se*, overlaps in meaning and pronunciation with *se* meaning "liquor." The same goes for *shike*, the trancelike state. *Shikechi* means "*shike* liquor."[14] Moreover, notice the *seni* variant of the word *se*. It also means "money" (*zeni*). The key point is that money (wealth), spiritual power, shamanic trances, and alcoholic intoxication are closely interrelated in the *Omoro* songs. Consider the following song about a wealthy local lord in Kumejima:

> The official in the south calls the tune [has things as he wants]
> . . . .
> In winter, he knows not of summer
> In summer, he knows not of winter
> He has plenty of liquor/wine [*sake*] in the wintertime
> He has plenty of liquor/wine [*shikechi*] in the summertime.
>
> (*Omoro sōshi*, 11-643)

Another *Omoro* song describes Eiso, a powerful ruler in the Urasoe area, as drinking wine year-round to indicate his prosperity. There would not have been much of a seasonal change of weather in Kumejima or Okinawa, and the frequent juxtaposition of winter and summer in *Omoro* songs is another indication of the northern roots of Ryukyuan culture. The main point is that this lord is so wealthy that he would not even notice the climate as he drinks all the alcoholic beverages he wants throughout the year.

A composite impression from the sample of songs we have seen thus far is that of seafarers who drank, danced, sang, partied, prayed, pillaged, and fought vigorously. They prized fine swords, nice jewels, and other luxury trade goods. The people of the *Omoro* preserved memories of older events in their songs, a common strategy among nonliterate people. There is no mention of an afterlife. Characters in the songs lived in the moment. The songs venerated the youthful vigor of the rising sun as well as conveying a sense that the sun always sets.

PART TWO

DEVELOPMENT AND TRANSFORMATION OF THE SHURI EMPIRE, 1490–1630

The official histories tend to locate state formation in the Ryukyu Islands at least a century early. The trade kings of the first Shō dynasty did not create a centralized state in Okinawa. The person who accomplished this feat was Shō Shin, toward the end of his long reign. Shō Shin came to the throne as a boy in the wake of a palace coup, and the first decades of his reign are characterized by official silence. Legendary evidence, which is all we have, suggests a struggle for power in which Shō Shin and his supporters prevailed by approximately the end of the 1490s. Shō Shin's struggle with legitimacy had reverberations that extended all the way to Ryukyu's disastrous war with Satsuma in 1609. The chapters in part 2 examine events from the time Shō Shin began to consolidate Shuri's empire to the decades immediately after the 1609 war. By roughly 1630, the foundation for the postwar, early modern era was in place.

For a much more detailed discussion of the topics in this section, including the long run-up to the 1609 war, see Smits (2019, chaps. 7–15). Akamine (2017, chaps. 3–4) also sheds light on this era. Among primary sources, the official histories become somewhat more useful for sixteenth-century and later material, but, of course, their content should not be taken at face value. Other key primary sources as they appear in the bibliography are Chén (1534/1995), Guō (1561/2000), Harada (2004), Hokama and Tamaki (1980), Ikemiya (2009), Ishigami (2014, 2018), *Joseon Veritable Royal Records* (2005), Kamei (1980), Kobata and Matsuda (1969), Kuroshima and Yara (2017), *Ming Veritable Records* (2001–6), *Omoro sōshi* (1972), Oshiro (1964), Taichū (1605/1988), Xià (1606/2001), and Yamashita (2007).

The following work has been especially important in informing my understanding of the sixteenth century and the early seventeenth: Akamine (1988), Burbank and Cooper (2010), China (2008), Dana (2008), Gi (2007), Harada (2003a), Hashimoto (2005, 2008), Ishigami (2000), Kamiya (1989), Kokuritsu rekishi minzoku hakubutsukan (2021), Komine (1998), Makishi (2023), Mamiya (2014), Murai (2019), Nagafuji (2000), Nakajima (2019,

2020), Ōhama (2005), Shimamura (2008), Takara (1982, 1987, 2011), Tomi-yama (1991, 2002), Tonaki (1992), Uehara (1992, 2009), Uezato (2000, 2002, 2009, 2010, 2012), Watanabe Miki (2012), Yano (2014), Yara (2017), and Yoshinari (2018). Especially important is work by Gi, Ishigami, Kamiya, Uehara, and Uezato on the structure of Shuri's military forces and the war of 1609, topics poorly understood in most Anglophone literature. This work forms the basis for my discussion of the war in *Maritime Ryukyu* (2019). I would also like to highlight Makishi's brilliant and meticulous work on connections between the *Omoro sōshi*, institutions, ritual, and ideology during the reigns of Shō Shin and Shō Sei. Finally, Nakajima's work brings a vast array of European sources to bear on the era, a perspective mostly absent in *Maritime Ryukyu*.

CHAPTER EIGHT

Shō Shin and the Shuri Empire

As the archaeologist Richard Pearson noted: "The Second Shō Dynasty could be seen to be the threshold of true state organization." By comparison, prior polities had been "well-developed chiefdoms" (2013, 237). The state that began to emerge toward the end of Shō Shin's reign marks the first time that the entire island of Okinawa came under the rule of a single center. Moreover, at almost the same time, Shō Shin's wars of conquest brought the rest of the Ryukyu Islands, from Kikaijima to Yonaguni, under Shuri's control. (Reconquest of some areas took place under some of Shō Shin's successors.) By around 1530, Shuri had become the center of a far-flung maritime empire.

Shō Shin

The most consequential king in Ryukyuan history was Shō Shin, and, as we have seen, he came to the throne at the age of twelve in a palace coup orchestrated by his mother, Ogyaka, and probably others who are now obscure. Some family background is needed for context. After Shō En died in 1476, his brother ascended the throne as Shō Sen'i. There were no formal rules for royal succession, and it is unclear whether Shō En ever stated a preference for who would succeed him. Recall that Shō En seized the throne in the wake of Shō Toku's death and that several previous kings had done much the same. In other words, whoever could seize the throne became king, regardless of his relationship to the previous king. We do not know exactly how Uncle Sen'i (from Shō Shin's perspective) came to the throne, but we have a better idea of how and why his short reign abruptly ended.

There is an especially revealing passage in *Reflections on Chūzan*. As background, Shō Sen'i was raised by his brother, who became Shō En. In the wake of Shō En's death in the second month of 1477, *Reflections* discusses the "solar deity Kimitezuri" even though Kimitezuri is actually the

name of a religious ceremony, not a deity.[1] According to *Reflections*, if Kimitezuri were to appear, it would indicate Sen'i as the choice of the deities.
Reflections then paints a scene whereby Sen'i is seated on the throne and
Prince Nakagusuku (Shō Shin) is standing beside him. The enthronement
ceremony soon took an ominous turn:

> In all previous cases, the High Priestess and lesser priestesses left Uchi-
> hara and stood facing east in front of the Kimihokori [building]. This
> time, however, contrary to the norm, they stood facing west. Then, start-
> ing with the ruler above and spreading downward, all present wondered
> what was happening. Spirits chilled, they clasped their hands, and their
> mouths turned dry. [Speaking through the priestesses, the deities] de-
> clared in an *omoro*: "Beloved child of the king in Shuri dances with the
> deities splendidly."[2] Hearing this song, Shō Sen'i regarded himself as lack-
> ing in virtue. He said that his bringing disrepute to the throne had pulled
> down Heaven's wrath on him. Having reigned for six months, he abdi-
> cated. (Shō Shōken 1650/2011, 56)

Uncle Sen'i might not have incurred heaven's wrath, but he definitely lost
out in the palace coup. Ogyaka had successfully put her son on the throne.

In an Okinawan context, the term *agari* refers to the rising sun, the
renewal of life, and the eastern direction. Therefore, priestesses would
normally face east when conducting state rites. By contrast, the western
direction was associated with decline, death, and the setting sun. When the
priestesses faced west, everyone in the audience knew that the sun had set
on Sen'i. *Reflections* explains that he "retired" to Goeku but lived less than
a month. The chapter on Sen'i ends by mentioning the story of the legendary Chinese sage king Yáo passing on the throne to the unrelated but virtuous Shùn, who passed it on to the unrelated but worthy Yŭ. It concludes:
"If the virtue of Shō Sen'i of our court indeed had exceeded that of Shō
Shin, then why on earth would the deities have acted contrary to people's
desires and cast Shō Sen'i out? Certainly, Shō Shin was one of the sages"
(Shō Shōken 1650/2011, 57).

Here, and in the passage about the enthronement rites gone awry, Shō
Shōken appears struggling to create a sensible narrative. He also appears
to have given up on doing so midway because the next chapter in *Reflections* is not about Shō Shin. Instead, it begins some fifty years later with
Shō Sei. By contrast, Sai On's 1725 *Genealogy of Chūzan* handles this material much more smoothly. What was the basic historiographic problem
here? Ryukyu's official histories seek to minimize violent disjunctions and
present Okinawan history as an orderly succession of kings who ruled by

virtue of their virtue. Therefore, framing and presenting Ogyaka's coup and Shō Shin's ascension to the throne were difficult. The coup was not only a challenge for later writers of history. It also presented a number of practical challenges to Shō Shin and his successors, and we will see examples throughout this chapter.

One challenge was partially religious. Shō Shin built several Buddhist temples, the most important of which was Enkakuji (円覚寺). Its name literally means "temple of [Shō] En's enlightenment." There are other Buddhist temples with this same name in Japan. However, given that Shō Shin's father was Shō En and that Shō Shin and his allies had killed Shō En's brother, the former king, the temple appears to have been built to appease Shō En's spirit. (It was destroyed in the 1945 Battle of Okinawa, and only the gate has been rebuilt.)

Furthermore, Enkakuji was part of a complex of religious structures. Adjacent to it was a shrine to the deity Benzai (Benzaiten). This deity appears to have arrived in Okinawa along with Kanemaru and his group around 1470. Benzai was a popular protective deity in Japanese ports, and she[3] became the main protector deity of Ryukyu in the religious hierarchy that Shō Shin established. Benzai's priestess was the *kikoe-ōgimi*, the high priestess. There is a shallow pond in front of the Benzai shrine, and Shō Shin put both the pond and the shrine to good use in solving another awkward problem.

A complete collection of Buddhist sutras (the Tipitaka) would have been highly prized in Shō Shin's time because the sutras would help ensure the stability and prosperity of a royal reign. Shō Shin inherited a full set, but it was problematic. The sutras had belonged to Shō Toku, the last king of the first Shō dynasty, whose family was killed by Shō En's forces. Moreover, the site in Shuri Castle where his wife and child were killed was afterward known as Kundagusuku and, at some point, became part of a popular royal bone cult. For Shō Shin, the sutras became the equivalent of toxic waste. He had them placed in a vault and the vault placed in the pond in front of the Benzai shrine. His intention was that Enkakuji and Benzai would, ideally, neutralize any adverse effect emanating from Shō Toku's sutras. Gradually, the sutras naturally rotted away as water leaked into their enclosure. Shō Shin obtained a new set of sutras from Korea (yet another Korean contribution to Ryukyuan culture) and placed them in a different temple.

Recall the legend of the three sister deities from Japan. One stayed in Kumejima and became *kimihae*. One went to the Benzai grove in Shuri to become the high priestess, the *kikoe-ōgimi*, and the other went to Mt. Omoto in Ishigaki. However, there had been powerful deities and priestesses in the Ryukyu Islands before the *kikoe-ōgimi* and her sisters arrived on the scene. How might Shō Shin integrate the new high priestess into existing networks of power? Adjacent to the Benzai grove, and across from Enkakuji, Shō Shin created a shrine, Sonohiyabu (園比屋武; also Sono-hyan). Today only the gateway remains. This shrine was directly linked to Kanahiyabu (金比屋武; also Kanahyan) Shrine in Nakijin. Recall that Na-kijin was the original Okinawan homeland of Kanemaru, and it was also the location of several powerful deities such as Aoriyae.

Shō Shin created a powerful trifecta of religious sites near Shuri Castle: Enkakuji, the Benzai shrine, and Sonohiyabu. This trifecta allowed Shō Shin to appease the spirit of his father, safely rid himself of Shō Toku's sutras, and link to the spiritual power of his Nakijin homeland. Where did he get the idea to do these things? Simply having survived the maelstrom of Okinawan royal politics suggests that he had good wits about him. Nev-ertheless, most rulers need good teachers and advisers. Shō Shin was prob-ably the first Ryukyuan king to receive a formal education in his youth. The Kyoto-born Rinzai Zen priest Kaiin Shōko (芥隠承琥, d. 1495) was his main tutor. Kaiin also wrote monument inscriptions and supervised much of the physical infrastructure of Shō Shin's Buddhist projects, especially Enkakuji. As a "black-robed minister" (kokue no saishō), he was an active participant in or at least had inside knowledge of the political upheavals of the era.

Starting approximately with Shō Taikyū's reign, Buddhist priests be-came increasingly close confidants and advisers to Ryukyuan rulers. By 1603, there were forty-six Buddhist temples in Okinawa. Seventeen existed by the start of Shō Shin's reign, twenty-four were established during the reigns of Shō Shin and Shō Sei, and one was established after Shō Sei.

Shuri, the Strong Center

Under Shō Shin, the Council of Three (Sanshikan [三司官], Hōshikan [法司官], or Yoasutabe [世司多部], and other names) functioned as the top-tier administrative and deliberative body. Other male officials were or-ganized according to a scheme whereby four hiki (引) formed one watch (ban [番]). There were three watches, each supervised by a member of the Council of Three. The term hiki refers to military units whose members also did other kinds of public work. Each hiki had its own hierarchy of officials and rank-and-file members (fig. 8.1).

Among female officials, the high priestess functioned analogously to the king and during the sixteenth century was his sister. Under her were three Ōamu (大阿母)—or Ōamu-shirare (大阿母志良礼)—analogous to the Council of Three. The three highest male and female officials were

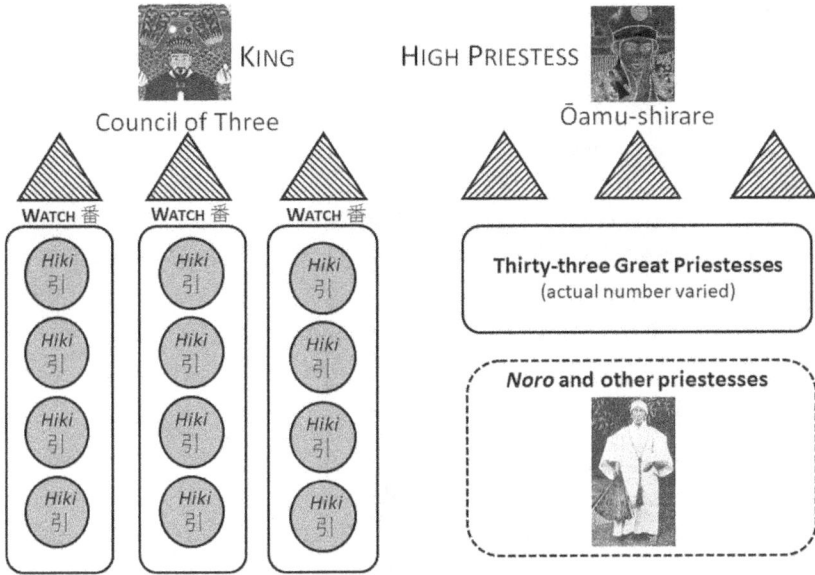

FIGURE 8.1. Simplified diagram of the structure of the central government in Shuri during the sixteenth century

each linked with the three core districts (*magiri* [間切]) surrounding Shuri: Mawashi, Haebaru, and Nishihara. The most prominent priestesses enjoyed a special status as part of the "thirty-three [great] priestesses" (*sanjūsan kun* [三十三君]).[4] A close look at the exact number of great priestesses listed in different sources reveals that there were between thirty-one and thirty-seven of them at various times. So thirty-three was not an exact number. The name probably derives from thirty-three being an auspicious number in Buddhism. Traditionally, these thirty or so top priestesses were associated with the protection of sea-lanes, and many *Omoro* songs portray them in this role.

Starting in the sixteenth century, the royal government formally appointed priestesses (*noro*) to each administrative district in Okinawa and other islands. A few of the appointment documents (*jireisho* [辞令書]) for priestesses and for male officials are extant. The example here is from 1541. It is an appointment document for a high-ranking official, written mostly in the *hiragana* syllabary. Consider the following line-by-line literal transliteration and translation (the English syntax is awkward in places):

[seal] shiyori no omikoto   Decree of Shuri
mawashi makiri no   of Mawashi District

kima no kanakusuku no	of Kanagusuku in Gima
satonushi tokoro ha [wa]	regarding the land set aside to
	provide for your official salary
hae no koori no	of the Hae administrative office
hitori ameku no ooyakumoi ni	to the Ōyakumoi [official title] of
	Ameku
tamawari mooshi sōrō	is granted
shiyori yori ameku no ōyakumoi	Ameku Ōyakumoi departing Shuri
ka kata e mairu	for [Kanagusuku]
[seal] Kasei [Jiājìng] 20 nen 11	
gatsu 6 nichi (1541)	

(Yara 2017, 72–73)

In other words, this document describes the salary details of the high-ranking official Ameku Ōyakumoi, who will take up office in Kanagusuku. He is part of the Hae administrative office, and his salary is based on a certain quantity of agricultural land set aside for this purpose. The document is written in Japanese (in a formal style called *sōrōbun*) and is dated according to the Chinese emperor's reign.

The royal court in Shuri produced similar writs of appointment for crew members of tribute trade ships, officials in the various *hiki*, local officials, and priestesses (*noro*). As of this writing, the earliest extant appointment document is from 1523. In other words, these documents came into use during the latter part of the reign of Shō Shin. We do not have any earlier examples of written documents used in domestic government administration in the Ryukyu Islands. In conjunction with appointment documents, the formal division of the Ryukyu Islands into administrative districts (*magiri*) became standardized. Shō Shin and his successors organized all the territory of the Ryukyu Islands and placed it under control of Shuri.

The process of making Shuri into a strong administrative center of the Ryukyu Islands included building new military facilities to bolster the defense of the Shuri-Naha area. Also crucial was the creation of a set of state religious ceremonies, which helped center Shuri ritually. Both the military infrastructure and the new state rites came into existence during the reigns of Shō Shin and Shō Sei. Although centered on Shuri, the network of spiritual power extended beyond the capital region. Court priestesses, for example, periodically visited the island of Kudakajima to perform rites. A network of new temples and shrines, including Sonohiyabu (Sonohyan) and Kanahiyabu (Kanahyan), linked Shuri with other spiritually powerful locations such as Nakijin.

A hierarchy of male officials developed during Shō Shin's reign, but the fine details are unclear. The general structure was the Council of Three just below the king. This council supervised officials known generically as *sedo* (勢頭), a term derived from *sentō* (船頭), "ship's captain." Each *hiki* was headed by a *sedo*, and the name of each *hiki* ended in *-tomi*, a suffix used for ship names (corresponding to *-maru* in Japan). The *hiki* institution directly reflected Ryukyu's maritime heritage. *Hiki* were multipurpose groups, its members serving the state as guards, soldiers, religious workers, civil engineers, and construction workers.

The system of titles and status ranks for male officials became more elaborate during Shō Sei's reign. Nevertheless, variation in terminology between the major sources, monument inscriptions, household records, and the investiture envoy Chén Kǎn's account (1534/1995) makes creating a detailed flowchart of Shō Sei's government difficult. However, moving to the end of the century allows us to glimpse the mature system before it changed during the seventeenth century. We know from the inscription on the monument Urasoe gusuku no mae no hi (1597) and other sources that there were six categories of elite social status. These categories were not themselves specific government offices, but they indicated eligibility for certain posts in the bureaucracy. They are listed below in descending order, with the approximate corresponding early modern term in parentheses.

Omoigwabe (Ōji [王子], prince)
Anjibe (Aji [按司])
Kanasome hachimaki (Ueekata [親方])
Sanban no ōyakumoi (Peichin/Peikumi [親雲上])
Satonushibe (Satonushi [里主])
Gerae akukabe (Chikudun [筑登之])

Notice that *satonushi*, a very high status early in the century, had become less prestigious by the end of the century. Clothing—and especially its color (e.g., caps and hairpins)—helped visually to distinguish these status ranks. Yellow indicates the highest rank (*Kanasome hachimaki* means "dyed golden cap"), followed by red, blue/green, and, finally, white. Like cap color, belt color also differentiated official status ranks.

Shō Shin and the Problem of Royal Legitimacy

The untimely death of Shō Sen'i brought no closure to conflict within the royal family. In the longer term, every royal transition from Shō Shin to Shō

Hō was contested in various ways, and the royal institution was especially weak during the war with Satsuma in 1609. Ogyaka's coup and Shō Shin's taking the throne set the stage for future instability. To understand this situation, some family details are necessary. The cast of characters other than Sen'i, Ogyaka, and Shō Shin includes Kyojin, the daughter of Sen'i and the principal wife (queen) of Shō Shin; Shō Ikō, the son from the union of Kyojin and Shō Shin; and Kagō, the consort of Shō Shin and mother of Shō Sei, Shō Shin's successor as king. First, notice that Shō Shin married the daughter of the man that he and his mother, in effect, assassinated. It would be fascinating to know more details and motives. It is, however, possible, although speculative, that Ogyaka pressured her son to marry Kyojin for the sake of appearances. As time went on, Kagō came to have an ever-greater influence on Shō Shin, and she worked to undermine Shō Ikō's reputation. Leaving out some intervening details, Shō Shin had by 1509 ordered the execution of his sixteen-year-old son. Shō Ikō survived by fleeing to Urasoe and living there in exile until his death in 1540. He thereby started the Urasoe branch of the royal family, and this branch would play a destabilizing role in the run-up to the 1609 war.

Shō Sei was Shō Shin's fifth son, and he became crown prince around 1508 or 1509.[5] His reign marked a major change in the process whereby the Chinese court formally and ritually recognized Ryukyuan kings (often called *investiture* in English). Shō Shin never received formal recognition by the Ming court, and prior to his reign there is no evidence that Chinese envoys traveled to Naha to perform investiture rites. From Shō Sei's reign on, the Chinese court sent envoys and an entourage to Okinawa to put on an elaborate display of royal investiture. Perhaps because of this significant upgrade in the Chinese court's investment of resources, and likely because of Shō Shin's legitimacy problems, the Board of Rites required leading Shuri officials to certify in writing that Shō Sei was indeed the legitimate heir to the throne. Thereafter, all Ryukyuan kings had to submit formal written verification of their legitimacy before investiture.

Forging Shuri's Empire

One of Shō Shin's projects was to legitimate himself and erase or minimize traces of problematic predecessors or family members. His creation of the Tamaudun royal mausoleum was one manifestation of these efforts. At the same time, Shō Shin was busy creating an empire. Forging an empire required much more than strengthening Shuri. It also required large-scale and expensive military campaigns to conquer the other Ryukyu Islands. Not surprisingly, none of the local powers in the other islands were eager to ship some of their wealth to Shuri each year for essentially nothing in return.

Focusing only on the invasions of Ishigaki and Kumejima, the conquered groups in both places were called *Kawara*.[6] Given that Shō Shin's forces conquered two Kawara groups in fairly quick succession, in *Maritime Ryukyu* I proposed: "The war that eliminated Akahachi's Kawara group in 1500 and the 1506 invasion of Kumejima were probably connected" (Smits 2019, 103). I would add that these wars were likely a battle for supremacy over the extended Kawara group. Specifically, Shō Shin's father had likely been a Kawara closely connected with Kumejima.

The group in Kumejima that Shuri defeated in 1506 (or thereabouts) was the Ishikinawa (O. Chinaha [伊敷索]). According to the account in the early modern chronicle *Gushikawa kyūki* (also *Kumejima Gushikawa-magiri kyūki*), the Ishikinawa group arrived in Kumejima as outsiders. Quite possibly, they were the original Kawara group in the Ryukyu Islands or the immediate descendants of that group. Despite what the official histories claim, it was not the case that Akahachi of Ishigaki or Ishikinawa of Kumejima were local rulers rebelling against an established state. More likely, these were two Kawara *wakō* groups that asserted their independence from the branch of the Kawara (Kanemaru and Shō Shin) that ended up in Shuri.

Of course, the larger situation involved more than an extended-family feud. For example, both Shō En and Shō Shin struggled to maintain good relations with the Ming court. It is likely that any moves they could make to gain control of the southern Ryukyu Islands and stem the tide of smuggling there would have helped them gain favor with Ming officials. During Shō En's reign, the Ming court reduced Ryukyu's permitted tribute missions to one every two years as a punishment for Ryukyuan abuses of the system and crimes that included arson and murder. It may have been a coincidence, but the tribute frequency was restored to once per year in 1507, just after Shuri's conquest of Kumejima. Moreover, by 1500, considerable wealth had accumulated in the southern Ryukyu Islands, and Shō Shin must have wanted a share of it. In that sense, he was like Shō Taikyū, who a half century earlier had sought to gain the wealth of Katsuren and parts of the northern Ryukyu Islands. One big difference was that Shō Shin's conquests, for the most part, held together.

By roughly 1530, the Ryukyu Islands had become a maritime empire with Shuri at its center. From Kikaijima and Amami-Ōshima in the northeast to Yonaguni in the southwest, Shō Sei's Ryukyu spanned approximately one thousand kilometers from east to west and approximately five hundred kilometers north to south. Transposed onto mainland Japan, the geographic span of Shuri's empire corresponds to the distance between Tokyo in the northeast and Fukuoka in the southwest. The territory was a potential source of strength for Shuri, which extracted taxes (tribute) from the rest of Okinawa and the other islands. Because this expanse of territory did not constitute an organic political unit, however, holding it together was difficult at times. Ryukyu as an empire consisted of territory united by military conquest and governed by officials loyal to Shuri.

During the 1450s and 1460s, Shō Taikyū and Shō Toku conducted military campaigns in the northern Ryukyu Islands. After repeated attacks, Kikaijima fell to Shuri in the 1460s. It is also likely that the Kasari Peninsula of Amami-Ōshima came under Shuri's direct or indirect control around this time. What follows is a list of military campaigns initiated by Shō Shin and some of his successors:

1500: Invasion and conquest of Ishigaki and nearby areas of Yaeyama

1490s and/or 1506: Conquest of Kumejima

1520s: Nakasone family, rulers of Miyako, toppled by Shuri

1520s: Conquest of Yoron by Okinawan forces (described in local legends)

1522 (with earlier campaigns likely): Conquest of Yonaguni

1535–37: Reconquest of Amami-Ōshima by Shuri after several rounds of fighting

1571: Possible invasion of Amami-Ōshima (major sources not in agreement)

1609: War with Satsuma (examined in a later chapter)

There are many details specific to each of these events, but notice the broad point that Shuri conquered the Ryukyu Islands militarily. At about the same time—the early sixteenth century—Shō Shin also conquered all Okinawa by force and diplomacy. The details are especially murky regarding Okinawa, and local legends are the main source. With this warfare in mind, let us briefly examine basic definitions of *empire*.

In his classic work, *Empires*, Michael W. Doyle emphasizes the nature of a relationship between two geopolitical entities. Specifically: "Empire . . . is a relationship, formal or informal, in which one state controls the effective political sovereignty of another political society. It can be achieved by force, by political collaboration, by economic, social, or cultural dependence" (Doyle 1986, 45). Applying this definition to sixteenth-century Ryukyu, the core region of Okinawa, with Shuri at its center, constituted a state. In terms of both culture and geopolitical units, outlying areas of Okinawa and the other Ryukyu Islands constituted different political societies. In a series of wars starting in 1500, these political societies were defeated militarily and came under Shuri's sovereignty. They include the domains of Oyake Akaha-chi (Ishigaki), Nakasone Toyomiya (Miyako), Onitora (Yonaguni), and the lord of Gushikawa in Kumejima. By 1520 or 1530, Shuri was the only state or major political community remaining in the Ryukyu Islands. It had become an empire through military force.

Shuri initiated systematic taxation and the extraction or wealth from the territories it conquered. Some of the appointment documents reveal parts of that system, but the best snapshot we have is from the Japanese Buddhist priest Taichū (袋中). Taichū stayed in Okinawa between 1603 and 1606 and wrote an account of local religion and customs called *Ryūkyū shintōki* (琉球神道記). In it, he recorded the arrival of tribute ships during one of the years he was in residence (which one is unclear) and the goods the ships brought to Shuri. In descending order of the total number of ships, they are as follows:

[Amami-]Ōshima (twenty ships): newly made tools, liquor, vegetables, and tax rice
Miyako (eighteen ships): superior cloth, lesser cloth, coarse hemp, rope for ships
Yaeyama (ten ships): white rice, barley
Kumejima (nine ships): cotton cloth, millet (*awa*), millet (*kibi*)
Kikaijima (five ships): polished rice, millet (*hie*), buckwheat

It is likely that the Amami-Ōshima ships included items from other north-ern Ryukyu Islands. There is no mention of the quantities of the goods or the size of the ships, but it is likely that these sixty-two ships made a signifi-cant contribution to royal wealth.

Shuri was able to collect wealth from the other islands in part because it created a network of agents in those places. Let us take Amami-Ōshima as an example. The situation there is described in an 1825 history of officials in Amami-Ōshima called *Renkanshi* that explicitly describes the Ryukyuan king as the "Shuri emperor" (*Shuri-tei*). Seven prominent households car-ried out local governance in Amami-Ōshima. A key part of this process was that these households sent children to Shuri to be raised by elite Oki-nawan families. At maturity, the children were appointed as local officials in Amami-Ōshima.

Local household records (*kafu* [家譜]) bear out the description in *Ren-kanshi*. First, consider the timing of the appearance of Shuri's agents in Amami-Ōshima. Someone named Tameharu became Shuri's agent in the Kasari Peninsula area in 1506, joined by a second Shuri-appointed agent in the nearby village of Ushuku later in Shō Shin's reign and a member of the

Kishitō-Ueekata lineage in the Kasari area around 1522. These early documented local officials all resided in the Kasari area, which was especially
wealthy. A song in the first volume of the *Omoro* describes the high priestess
praying to the heavenly deity Terukawa, who enables Shō Shin to conquer
Kasari (*Omoro sōshi*, 1-4). Most likely, by the 1520s Shuri consolidated its
hold on the Kasari Peninsula area as well as several other locations in the
northern Ryukyu Islands.

Zooming in to look at the Kasari lineage of Amami-Ōshima, the first to
arrive in Amami-Ōshima was Tameharu in 1506, when he was twenty-three.
Most likely he arrived from Okinawa as one of Shō Shin's agents. His successor, Tamemitsu (1508–ca. 1568), was an apprentice to Prince Nakagusuku
in Shuri before taking charge of Higashi (Higa) District in Amami-Ōshima
in 1533. Assuming this record is accurate, we see that Shuri's agents have
spread to areas beyond the Kasari Peninsula. Tameaki was third in the lineage, and he worked as "a servant to the emperor" in Shuri Castle before
taking up posts in Amami-Ōshima.[7] At this point, the pattern should be
clear. Young boys from prominent households in Amami-Ōshima (some of
which may ultimately have originated in Okinawa) apprenticed in Shuri to
maintain their orientation to the center. At maturity, they were assigned to
various districts or villages in Amami-Ōshima. Incidentally, the *-tame* element in these names refers to Minamoto Tametomo as a purported ancestor, the topic of chapter 16.

With these examples of Shuri as a strong political center in mind, consider the process of empire building described by Jane Burbank and Fred-
rick Cooper:

> The only way for a would-be king or tribal leader to become more pow-
> erful is to expand—taking animals, money, slaves, land, or other forms
> of wealth from outside his realm rather than from insiders whose sup-
> port he needs. Once this externalization of sources of wealth begins,
> outsiders may see advantages in submitting to a powerful and effective
> conqueror. Emboldened kings or tribal leaders can then use their new
> subordinates to collect resources in a regular—not raiding—way and to
> facilitate the incorporation of new peoples, territories, and trade routes
> without imposing uniformity in culture or administration. (Burbank and
> Cooper 2010, 9–10)

The sixty-two ships from the various Ryukyu Islands described above, all
bringing tax goods to Shuri, is one example of collecting resources in a
regular fashion. We will see detailed examples of resource extraction, the
"externalization of sources of wealth," in chapter 12. The transition from

harbor-fortress units serving as bases for traders and raiders to a central-ized bureaucratic state went hand in hand with collecting "resources in a regular—not raiding—way." One important point is that, although local of-ficials were often educated in Shuri, the Ryukyuan state made no effort to impose cultural uniformity on its empire. Its primary concern was resource extraction.

Shuri was not a benevolent master despite some claims that the various Ryukyu Islands willingly submitted to Shuri's control as part of the natural order of things. This romantic view has been asserted throughout modern history without any positive evidence. Here, for example, is Yanagita Kunio (1875–1962):

> According to conventional history, it is written that the Amami Islands became part of [the] Ryukyu [state] after 1471. However, this is truly a flawed interpretation. Whether the ruler of Chūzan [*Chūzan no yono-nushi*] received some trifling bit of tribute, or did not receive it, sim-ply fluctuated according to the times and the convenience of local *aji* households in the various harbors. Because the island people had long been wearing the same clothing and speaking the same language, ven-erating village deities in the same manner and according to the same seasonal cycle, the state (*kuni*) had been a singular entity since the be-ginning. . . . In other words, it is not that [the northern Ryukyu Islands] were conquered but, as grass and trees flutter in the wind, they willingly submitted. (1925, 70–71)

Here, Yanagita joins many other modern authors who have problematically portrayed the Ryukyu Islands as a tranquil land of submissive people, ignor-ing or minimizing the frequent warfare. With respect to Amami-Ōshima, not only did Shuri conquer it by force in the late fifteenth century, but armies from Okinawa also reconquered the island several more times dur-ing the sixteenth century. As we will see in chapter 12, Shuri's extraction of resources was brutal and severe throughout the early modern era, and a legacy of hostility toward Shuri in other Ryukyu Islands continues to this day. For example, a travel magazine featuring "beautiful" Amami-Ōshima opened its spread with a brief description of the islands' history, featuring conceptual drawings next to a paragraph of explanatory text. The fifteenth century through the seventeenth was the era of "control by the Ryukyu Kingdom," and the accompanying image shows Okinawan invaders beating the local population with staves ("Amami no rekishi" 2016, 20).

Approaching the matter from the perspective of anthropological field-work, Arne Røkkum makes a similar point, noting that the Ryukyu Islands

FIGURE 8.2. Statue of Oyake Akahachi resisting the Okinawan invasion
of Ishigaki in 1500 (photograph courtesy Shari Tamashiro)

becoming incorporated into a single state "may not have granted any com-
munality through collectively-held symbols" (Røkkum 2006, 47). It is important to bear in mind that, contrary to Yanagita's assertion, no common
cultural or political symbols (e.g., flags, religious figures, ideology, literary
works, etc.) ever bound the Ryukyu Islands together as a whole.

By the end of Shō Shin's reign in 1526, Ryukyu had become a state in the
sense that it was ruled by an organized, bureaucratic central government
backed by military power. It had also become an empire in the sense that
Shuri's military forces conquered the other islands and began to extract resources from them in a systematic manner. In *Maritime Ryukyu* (2019), I
discuss Shuri's post–Shō Shin empire at length over the course of two chap-

ters. Here, I note that the National Museum of Japanese History (Kokuritsu rekishi minzoku hakubutsukan) created a special exhibition, *Umi no teikoku Ryūkyū: Yaeyama, Miyako, Amami kara no chūsei* (Maritime empire Ryukyu: The Middle Ages from the standpoint of Yaeyama, Miyako, and Amami), that ran from March 16 to May 9, 2021. This exhibition represents an important step in examining Ryukyuan history critically and from perspectives other than that of kings and the royal court in Shuri.

There is a tendency to regard empires as large and powerful. Ryukyu was large in the sense of sheer expanse, and, during the first half of the sixteenth century, it possessed significant wealth and military capabilities. Nevertheless, size and power are largely beside the point. What matters is the nature of the relationship between Shuri and the other territories under its control. It is appropriate to regard the sixteenth-century Ryukyu Kingdom as an island empire, which is how Shuri or Okinawa is seen to this day by many residents of other Ryukyu Islands, both north and south. For example, Oyake Akahachi, who resisted the Okinawan invaders in 1500, has been and remains a hero in Ishigaki (fig. 8.2).

Culture and Royal Rituals

This chapter concludes with a few broad points about officially sponsored culture and rites during the era of Shō Shin and his successor, Shō Sei. Chinese and Southeast Asian material culture poured into the Ryukyu Islands during the fifteenth century as a result of private trade and the tribute trade. So too did certain forms of nonmaterial culture, although mostly from Japan. Starting at approximately the point of Shō Shin's emergence from the shadows at the end of the 1490s, Shuri Castle began to take on a Chinese-style appearance. There was genuine Chinese cultural influence on the sixteenth-century Ryukyuan court, but it was minor compared with Japanese cultural influences during the same time. As Ikuta Shigeru has pointed out, the establishment of temples staffed with Japanese priests and the use of *hiragana* to write Okinawan in public monuments are indications of a major wave of Japanese cultural influence (see Ikuta 1992, 292).

Perhaps most important with respect to official culture of this era were the newly created state rituals. Shō Shin and Shō Sei initiated agricultural rites, thus formalizing for the first time the idea of Ryukyu as an agricultural society (taxation, of course, also served this function). These rites, known generically as *shikyoma* or *mishikyoma*, included events like the Rice Ear Festival (Ine-no-ho matsuri) and the Barley Ear Festival (Mugi ho matsuri).

The most important official ritual, Kimitezuri, celebrated the arrival of an outside deity, Benzaiten, who linked the Aoriyae of Nakijin with the Aoriyae-sasukasa deity in Kumejima (notice again the central importance of Kumejima and Nakijin). These rituals were specific to the circumstances of Shō Shin's court, but they were not created from scratch. They much more closely resemble Japanese agricultural rites than agricultural rites of the Ming court. The prominence of female religious officials in official Ryukyuan rites would not have been found at any other royal court in the region, and it probably reflects the deep Korean folk roots of Ryukyuan religious culture.

These agricultural rites also became connected with solar worship during the time of Shō Shin and Shō Sei. It is at this time that the island of Kudakajima began to take on a sacred status, in part in connection with the legendary arrival there of grain. Royal worship of the rising sun began at Bengatake (Benzaiten) Shrine about a kilometer northeast of Shuri Castle. The sun rising in the east became associated with the renewal of royal power. Moreover, it appears that, starting in Shō Shin's time, the royal court began to promote a standardized version of *niraikanai* belief (the idea of power coming from across the sea), with *niraikanai* corresponding to the eastern direction and the rising sun. The merging of rising-sun worship with an official version of *niraikanai* appears to have been the reason for the rise to prominence of Seifaa utaki, just across from Kudakajima, as Ryukyu's holiest site. Seifaa utaki was the place best suited to this merger of solar worship and the official conception of *niraikanai*.

The Sixteenth Century

In 1556, Chinese military forces had repulsed a *wakō* force that attacked coastal Zhèjiāng Province. Driven off from its primary objective, the *wakō* sailed for Ryukyu.[1] The new king, Shō Gen, sent his navy to intercept them. According to *Ming Veritable Records*, the Ryukyuan force crushed the pirates, rescuing six Chinese who had been captured earlier, and repatriating them on the next tribute voyage. In official records, Ryukyuan military forces nearly always defeat pirates decisively and valiantly, and it is unclear precisely what happened during the 1556 battle.

Regardless of the details, the battle nicely illustrates Ryukyu's sixteenth-century transformation. The Ryukyu of the 1450s was a collection of local powers who, in many cases, were themselves pirates or potential pirates. A century later, it was a centralized kingdom that possessed an empire. Its broad interests coincided with those of other states in the region, and it occasionally took up arms against pirates.

The previous chapter examined the creation of Ryukyu as a strong centralized state and a maritime empire. This chapter examines major aspects of the politics, diplomacy, institutions, and cultural policies during the sixteenth century. I begin with what made the creation of Shuri's empire possible, military power.

Shuri's Military Power and Infrastructure

From approximately the 1490s, we have indications that Shuri was capable of projecting military power to distant locations. In the northern direction, an envoy to Korea reported that Ryukyuan forces frequently battled forces from Satsuma trying to encroach on Amami-Ōshima and that the Ryukyuans prevailed in eight or nine of ten of these battles or skirmishes. These points appear in a 1493 entry in *Joseon Veritable Royal Records*. Unfortunately, we lack further details about the situation. At the southern end of the Ryukyu Islands was Shuri's invasion of Ishigaki and possibly other islands in the Yaeyama group. According to the *Kyūyō* account, the Shuri force consisted of forty-six ships that attacked on two fronts. Unable to respond to the two-pronged attack, Oyake Akahachi and his forces went down to defeat. In other words, by 1500, Shuri was capable of projecting serious military force anywhere in the Ryukyu Islands.

The Chinese investiture envoy Chén Kǎn evaluated Shuri's military capabilities about thirty years later: "Both their blade weapons and archery weapons are strong and sharp. Bows are slightly longer than those used in China." Two hands are required to remove an arrow that has been shot into the ground. The range of arrows is two hundred steps. Armor is made from leather, and gongs and drums regulate military retreats and advances. Chén concluded: "Neighboring countries regard Ryukyu as a strong opponent" (1534/1995, 78).

The paragraphs below describe Shuri's military capacities and organization at two points in time, approximately 1550 and then six decades later during the war with Satsuma. The overall structure was the same at both points in time. Recall that *hiki* were organizational units that brought hundreds of people together for military service, civil engineering, or other types of labor. Shuri's forces most likely consisted of twelve *hiki*; however, we do not know the names of two of them. Four *hiki* combined to form one *ban* (watch), each under the command of a member of the Council of Three. Military forces drawn from the southern districts of Okinawa supplemented the three watches. Combined, these units protected the northern and southern shores of Naha Harbor, Naha itself, and Shuri Castle (fig. 9.1).

A military infrastructure supported the *hiki* and southern district forces. Shō Shin set up a central armory at Naha Harbor and enhanced the walls of Shuri Castle. In 1522, he built the Madama (or Madan) Road, which connected large areas around the harbor and facilitated the rapid movement of personnel and supplies. He also established an official to oversee artillery deployment. Shō Sei continued the enhancement of Shuri Castle, and, by 1546, its double walls were complete. He also constructed a new type of fortress. Yarazamori gusuku and Mie gusuku were artillery platforms located at each side of the relatively narrow entrance to Naha Harbor's deep channel. Hostile ships would come into range of both fortresses as they approached the channel. The fortresses also acted as anchors for a giant chain that could extend across the harbor mouth and hinder access of potentially hostile vessels.

Notice that both Shō Shin and Shō Sei devoted significant resources to ensuring that Shuri's forces could repel any conceivable attack on Naha Harbor and reinforcing Shuri Castle. This military buildup made perfect

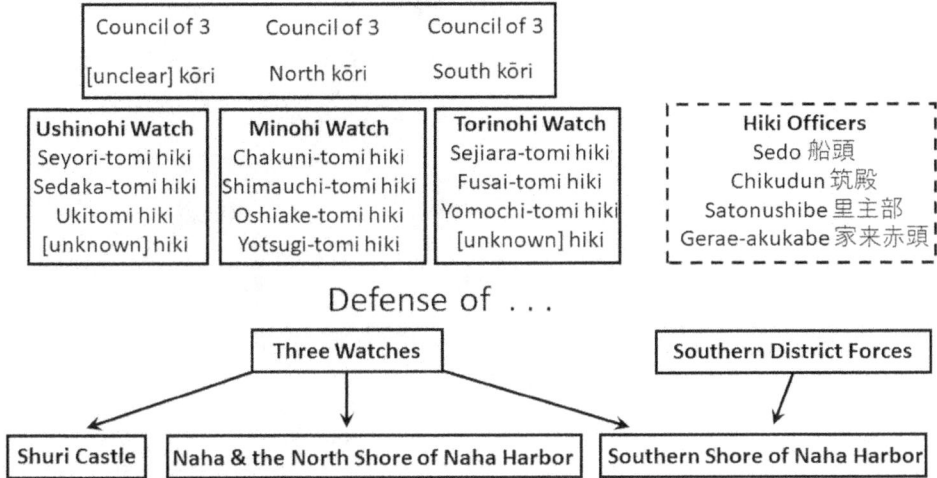

KING

Council of 3	Council of 3	Council of 3
[unclear] kōri	North kōri	South kōri

Ushinohi Watch	Minohi Watch	Torinohi Watch	Hiki Officers
Seyori-tomi hiki	Chakuni-tomi hiki	Sejiara-tomi hiki	Sedo 船頭
Sedaka-tomi hiki	Shimauchi-tomi hiki	Fusai-tomi hiki	Chikudun 筑殿
Ukitomi hiki	Oshiake-tomi hiki	Yomochi-tomi hiki	Satonushibe 里主部
[unknown] hiki	Yotsugi-tomi hiki	[unknown] hiki	Gerae-akukabe 家来赤頭

Defense of . . .

Three Watches

Southern District Forces

Shuri Castle

Naha & the North Shore of Naha Harbor

Southern Shore of Naha Harbor

FIGURE 9.1. Diagram of Shuri's military system during the sixteenth century

sense in the larger context of Shuri becoming the strong center of a maritime empire. One opportunity cost, however, was that an invading force approaching from anywhere other than Naha Harbor would face few obstacles until arriving at Shuri Castle—precisely what happened in 1609. Another problem with these arrangements was that, while Naha Harbor was well defended against an obvious naval assault, Shuri's officials were unable to prevent swarms of armed seafarers from Japan gathering at Naha to trade with the entourages of Chinese investiture envoys (which included many merchants). On the one hand, Shuri depended on these Japanese seafarers to purchase all the goods that Chinese merchants brought with them. On the other hand, the seafarers posed a safety and security threat.

The defenses of the Naha Harbor area consisted of a network of fortresses connected by the Madama Road (fig. 9.2). Yarazamori gusuku and Mie gusuku guarded the outer approach to the harbor channel. Iō gusuku (sulfur fortress) nearby was the central arsenal. It distributed weapons to the *hiki* and southern district soldiers as they assembled. Tomigusuku gusuku was located deep in the harbor and was a command-and-control center. Madama Road connected all these structures and Shuri Castle.

Ryukyu manufactured some of its own weapons, and acquired some firearms from China, but mostly imported weapons from Japan. Some weapons were hybrids. For example, many sword blades came from Japan, but the sword handles were of Ryukyuan design to facilitate wielding with one

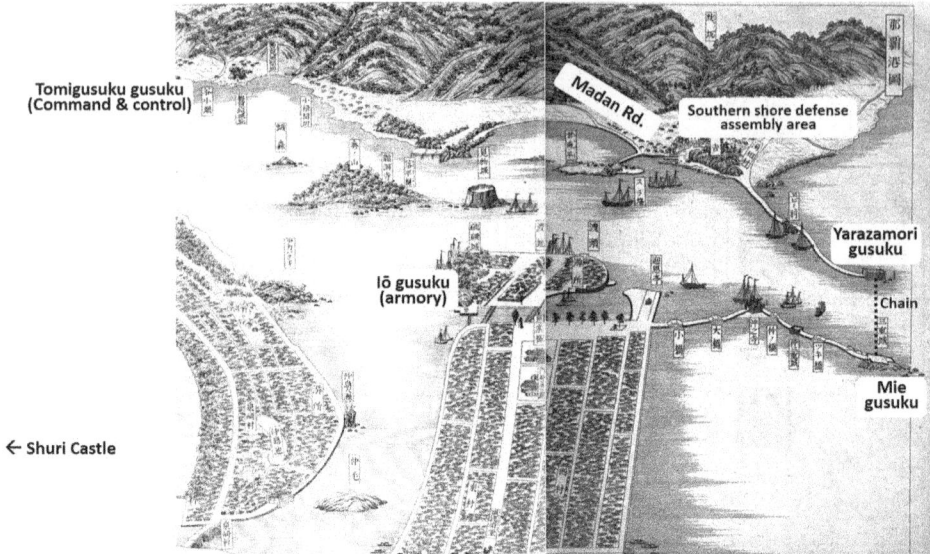

FIGURE 9.2. Main defense structures in and around
Naha Harbor (from Ijichi [1877, 86–87])

hand. Ryukyuans traded in weapons between these places, most commonly
bringing Japanese swords to China and Southeast Asia, where they were in
great demand.

Moving ahead to the run-up to the 1609 war with Satsuma, the military
infrastructure around Naha ensured that it was well defended against hostile ships. The *hiki* and southern district forces could muster as many as
three thousand soldiers on short notice. Okinawan swords were of high
quality. The arsenal at Iō gusuku also included bows and arrows, pikes,
halberds, and a type of hand cannon with three small barrels known as *hi-
yaa*. Armor, cavalry horses, and signal banners completed the equipment
profile. Writing in 1606, the Chinese investiture envoy Xià Zǐyáng was not
impressed with Ryukyuan military capacity in the face of what he regarded
as an impending invasion from Japan. Specifically, Ryukyuan swords and
armor were "hard and sharp," but the pikes were weak and good mainly
for decoration. The length of bows was approximately the width of house
eaves. Although arrows hitting the ground required both arms to pull out,
they did not travel very far (Xià 1606/2001, 193).

Superficially, the Ryukyuan military forces of 1609 were much like those
of the mid-sixteenth century when Shuri maintained control over all the
other Ryukyu Islands and occasionally defeated pirate incursions. However,
military technology advanced rapidly during the late sixteenth century,

especially in the realm of firearms. By the 1580s, Japanese armies routinely used muskets, but Ryukyuan forces possessed only unwieldy hand cannons. These weapons could sometimes be effective against fixed targets, and they played a role in suppressing a domestic revolt in 1592. On a fluid field of battle, however, they were nearly useless. When Ryukyuan forces faced off with invaders from Satsuma in 1609, it was the case of a Muromachi Era vintage military opposing soldiers with cutting-edge equipment and experience. As we will see, there were other factors beyond equipment that undermined Ryukyu's military effectiveness.

Although Ryukyuan military forces proved unable to fend off Satsuma's army in 1609, throughout the sixteenth century they were capable of maintaining Shuri's control over all the Ryukyu Islands. That control also included what today we would call *soft power.*

Shō Sei and the Creation of Royal Rites

The king's male and female officials managed Shuri's empire. Shō Sei and Shō Shin created a bureaucratic structure and a military infrastructure. Shō Sei added to Shuri's power by creating new state rites. They were agricultural ceremonies, loosely resembling Japanese imperial rites. As we have noted, the Ryukyu Islands were not capable of sustaining societies entirely or mainly on the basis of agriculture, especially cereal grains. Nevertheless, agriculture loomed large in official rituals and ideology. The prominence of agricultural state rites is another indication of the northern roots of Ryukyuan culture and population since the start of the Gusuku Era.

Specific agricultural rites depended on the natural cycle of each major grain. The general term for rites celebrating the first grains of the season was *shikyoma.* For example, the Rice Ear Festival (Ine-no-ho matsuri) took place during the fourth or fifth lunar month (different accounts give slightly different dates). In connection with this event, water from Cape Hedo in the northern tip of Okinawa was shipped to Shuri, thus tracing the movement of the deity Amamikyo (also Amamiku) according to official court mythology. The similar Barley Ear Festival (Mugi ho matsuri) took place on the fifteenth day of the second lunar month. As part of most agricultural rites, the three Ōamu priestesses (the female counterpart of the Council of Three) led processions of priestesses who conducted rites before the hearth deity at each of the three core districts around Shuri. The king led *hiki* officials to perform rites at the royal palace.

The following song from the *Omoro* was sung by priestesses at *shikyoma* grain rituals:

Amamikyo received the order
To descend to this big island [= Okinawa]
For all time
The beloved one of Ogyaka [= Shō Shin] has come
Shinerikyo received the order
To descend to this big island
Take the ears of grain and offer them up
May they have no blight on them!
Take the tips of the ears of grain and offer them up
May they have no blight on them!

(*Omoro sōshi*, 5-242; mostly repeated in 22-1508)

Interestingly, here the creator deity pair Amamikyo (female)/Shinerikyo (male) is linked with agriculture. Originally, the Amamikyo legend was about the founding of the physical world. Merging the origins of grain agriculture into the origin story was explicitly the work of the royal government during the sixteenth century, not a remnant of older folk memory. Notice also the presence in the song of Shō Shin, who is nearly on a par with the creator deities. As we have seen, he is the star of the *Omoro sōshi*, and this song is a good example.

Typical agricultural rites marked the three main phases of the cycle: the sowing of the first seeds, the initial ripening, and the harvest. Although some royal rites took place on Kudakajima, the legendary site where grains first arrived in Okinawa, most of the new sixteenth-century rituals focused attention on Shuri as the center of a prosperous kingdom. As formal functions of government, these rites originated during the reigns of Shō Shin and Shō Sei. Buddhist priests from Japan played a large role as advisers during these reigns (and later), and the Okinawan rites had general counterparts in Japan. It is highly likely, therefore, that Buddhist priests played a major role in fashioning the details of Ryukyuan state rites. Moreover, although we do not know precisely when solar deity worship originated in Ryukyu, its formal codification took place early in the sixteenth century (more on that below).

Although most of the new Ryukyuan rites celebrated agriculture, an important one was designed directly to enhance royal power and Shō Shin's newly created hierarchy of priestesses. It was called Kimitezuri (君手摩),[2] and it took the form of a royal procession. Kimitezuri celebrated the arrival of Benzaiten, an outside deity, who subsumed the other local deities. Benzaiten was the deity of the high priestess, the *kikoe-ōgimi*, herself a newcomer to Shuri. The deeper roots of the *kikoe-ōgimi* were the three sister deities of Kumejima. That island was also the origin of the *hiki* system, and it played a crucial role in institutions of the second Shō dynasty.

Diplomatic Difficulties

A 1475 edict from the Ming emperor to Shō En read: "King! Your envoys have already presented tribute at the capital and returned with the usual imperial largesse. Recently, officials in Fújiàn . . . have reported that the [Ryukyuan] delegation member Cài Zhāng [Sai Shō, 1445–1504, third-generation Kumemura resident] and others engaged in extreme unlawful acts such as murder and the theft of property on their return to Fúzhōu" (*Ming Veritable Records* 2001–6, 2:23 [no. 24]). It goes on to demand that Shō En hold these Ryukyuans accountable for their crimes. As punishment, the edict spelled out significant restrictions on future tribute trade, including a reduction in the frequency of tribute embassies from Ryukyu from one per year to one every two years.

The edict was prompted by a 1474 incident in which Chinese officials claimed that Ryukyuan envoys murdered the Fújiàn resident Chén Èrguān and burned his household compound down. This event caused Chinese officials to cut the frequency of Ryukyu's tribute trade in half. This move threatened the economic foundations of the court at Shuri at a time when trade with Japan had also become constrained because of the Ōnin War (1467–77).

The Chén Èrguān incident was part of a larger problem that had plagued Ryukyuan-Chinese relations since at least the early fifteenth century. Ryukyuans in China often behaved badly. According to Chinese records, their deeds included disorderly conduct, illegal trading activity, abuses of Chinese largesse, and serious crimes.[3] From the 1440s on, Chinese officials began gradually to put limits on the Ryukyuan tribute trade. The move in 1475, however, was a sudden, punitive change. Shuri pushed back vigorously against the edict, most likely with the assistance of Buddhist priests. A lengthy message in 1476, for example, explained why it would not have been possible for members of a Ryukyuan embassy to have committed these crimes. The Ming court was not impressed, which is probably why Shō Shin never received investiture. In 1478, an envoy from Shō Shin reported Shō En's death to the Chinese court. He also asked permission to resume annual tribute embassies. In denying the request, the Board of Rites responded in part with a rhetorical question. How could it possibly allow "outside barbarians" to profit from trade with China after Ryukyuan envoys had committed crimes as serious as murder and arson (*Ming Veritable Records* 2001–6, 2:24 [no. 33])?

In 1480, an imperial decree sent to Shō Shin made it clear that the restriction of tribute embassies was punishment for the crimes of Ryukyuans in China. The emperor complained of Ryukyuan envoys "sullying China" by improper behavior, citing a case in which Okinawans secretly purchased silk clothing featuring a dragon emblem that was intended only for Ming officials. According to the decree, clear proof of illegal activities such as these was the reason for the change in tribute frequency (*Rekidai hōan* 1994–2022, 1:28 [1-01-25]). The illegal clothing referred to a 1471 incident in which the Ryukyuan envoy Sai Ei (Ch. Cài Jǐng) was caught with the prohibited robes. He falsely claimed that Ryukyu's previous king (Shō Toku) had been allowed to use such clothing. These communications reveal serious tensions in Shuri's relations with the Ming court. These tensions had deep roots and persisted well into the seventeenth century.

Recall that the Ming court originally brought Ryukyu into the tribute system in the 1370s in an attempt to tame piracy and smuggling. Not surprisingly, bringing *wakō* to China resulted in illegal activity and abusees of Chinese trade terms, even though they were already highly favorable. Approximately a century later, in the 1470s, the Ming court had clearly become less tolerant of illegal behavior and abuses of the system. One of Shō Shin's challenges, therefore, was to restore good relations with China. There were several consequences of his creating a central state that expanded Shuri's control over all the Ryukyu Islands. The obvious one was the strengthening and enriching of what had hitherto been an unstable kingship. Additionally, especially after conquering the southern Ryukyu Islands, Shuri was in a better position to suppress illegal trade with China and exert tighter control over the tribute trade.

Shō Shin came to the throne just as Japan's decade-long Ōnin War was coming to a close. During the war, ships from Naha stayed away from Japan, so merchants from Sakai traveled to Naha to conduct trade. In other words, Ryukyuan trade with Japan had become economically important for certain Japanese merchants. In general, the Ōnin War diminished the power of the Ashikaga shoguns, but they retained importance for trade with China and Korea because, at least nominally, they held the title *king of Japan*. Recall that only someone holding the title *wáng* (king) could authorize trade with the Chinese and Korean courts. Although nominally trade kings, the Ashikaga shoguns did not actually control foreign trade during this era. Other powerful Japanese warlords—especially the Ōuchi based in Yamaguchi—did the trading. Ōuchi ships sent silver and copper ore to China and Korea on large ships, and, between 1518 and 1557, the Ōuchi controlled the "king of Japan" seal. Trade between the Ōuchi and Ryukyu also flourished during the sixteenth century.[4] The decline of the

Ashikaga shoguns changed the geopolitical dynamics in the seas around the Ryukyu Islands.

In Kyushu, Ashikaga weakness created a power vacuum that the Shimazu lords of Satsuma sought to exploit. Trade between the main Japanese islands and the Ryukyu Islands was active and economically significant. The Shimazu sought to increase their power, influence, and wealth by controlling the shipping between Japan and Ryukyu. Not only would such control likely benefit Shimazu coffers, but denying trade with Ryukyu to merchants in other Japanese territories—especially enemies of the Shimazu in Kyushu—was also part of Shimazu military strategy. Above all else, the Shimazu, in competition with entities such as the Ōuchi and the Ashikaga shoguns, sought to forge a direct trade connection with China. Ryukyu was in a position to facilitate this project.

Shimazu pressure on Ryukyu is often portrayed in survey histories as simple aggression. While Shimazu moves may have been aggressive at times, their goal was to work with Ryukyu to promote trade with China in the absence of *bakufu* power. Timing was also relevant. During Shō Shin's reign, Ryukyu was a significant regional military power, and the Shimazu were embroiled in warfare in southern Kyushu. When Shimazu Tadaharu (r. 1489–1515) attempted to convince Shō Shin to agree to confiscate the cargo of vessels entering Ryukyu without a Shimazu license, the king gave a noncommittal answer.

Changing circumstances, however, gradually impeded Ryukyu's ability to act independently. The Shimazu lords consolidated their power in Kyushu over the course of the sixteenth century. They probably would have conquered all Kyushu had it not been for the rise of Toyotomi Hideyoshi (1537–98) in the 1580s. Recall that Chinese-built ships sailing under the auspices of Ryukyu's kings conducted international trade in the context of the Ming Maritime Prohibitions. These prohibitions relaxed during the latter half of the sixteenth century. One result was that Chinese merchants could legally conduct trade under their own auspices. The pretense of conducting trade in the name of a Ryukyuan king became increasingly less relevant. Equally important, throughout the sixteenth century Europeans began to dominate the Southeast Asian trade, pushing out Ryukyuan merchants by about 1570.

The general trend as the sixteenth century went on was for Shimazu power to strengthen as Ryukyu's power weakened. Full ceremonial investiture of Ryukyuan kings (as opposed to investiture via documents) began with Shō Sei. This investiture process quickly became a financial burden for Shuri, which caused it to depend heavily on Japanese merchants. This process involved two Chinese envoys arriving in Naha with an entourage of assistants and merchants who brought with them trade goods.[5] The royal court and Ryukyuan elites were unable to purchase all the goods the investiture envoys and merchants brought to Naha for sale. The investiture embassy typically would not leave Naha until everything had been sold, and, the longer the envoys stayed in Naha, the greater the financial drain on royal coffers.

In this context, visiting Japanese merchants were essential to speed up and complete the process. Royal officials, however, struggled to maintain order when Japanese merchants were in port and often failed to do so. Furthermore, the Shimazu lords regarded trade in Ryukyu by Japanese from other Kyushu domains as a security threat and put pressure on Shuri to cooperate in stopping it. The rise of Hideyoshi exacerbated an already-difficult situation between Shuri and the Shimazu administration in Kagoshima.

Turbulent Royal Successions

Recall that one reason that Shō Shin's loyalists were able to oust Shō Sen'i is that there were no formal rules for royal succession. That situation persisted until soon after 1609. One result is that there appear to have been no smooth transitions among the first seven kings of the second Shō dynasty. Furthermore, Shō Shin's troubles with legitimacy cast a long shadow over his successors. Let us examine each king in succession.

Emerging from the shadow of his exiled half brother, Shō Sei received investiture from the Ming court after submitting written proof that he was the legitimate heir to the throne. Turning to the 1725 *Genealogy of Chūzan*, the succession from Shō Sei to Shō Gen was tumultuous. In the *Genealogy* account, Shō Sei lay dying in 1555 and summoned the Council of Three members Aragusuku Anki, Kunigami Keimei, and Gusukuma Shūshin. The king ordered them to support his designated heir, Shō Gen. Declaring Shō Gen weak, however, Kunigami and Gusukuma lobbied other officials to put Prince Ie on the throne instead. They were not successful, and the official account praises the loyal Aragusuku. Whatever actually transpired, it is clear that Shō Gen's ascension to the throne was fraught with conflict. This conflict persisted into the early years of Shō Gen's reign. His faction ultimately prevailed and exiled rival leaders to remote locations after consolidating power.

We do not know for sure when Shō Gen died because the sources are inconsistent. Some claim that he led an invasion of Amami-Ōshima in 1571, although we cannot be certain that this invasion actually took place. If it did, then it is possible that Shō Gen died from wounds or illness during the campaign. In any case, his death appears to have been protracted. According to *Genealogy*, he died on 1572.4.1, but Shō Ei did not become king until sometime in 1573. However, local household records suggest that Shō Gen was alive and active well after the fourth month of 1572. Specifically, he appointed officials in 1572.8.30 and again sometime in 1573. In short, his death took place sometime in 1572 or 1573, and it appears to have been protracted.

Shō Nei's coming to the throne was remarkable. He was a member of the Urasoe branch of the royal family, descended from Shō Shin's disowned son Shō Ikō. The official histories present differing accounts of Shō Nei's relationship to previous kings. His predecessor, Shō Ei, had two brothers, at least one of whom was alive when Shō Ei died at a young age. All indications point to a reaction against Shō Ei—possibly a coup—by officials who disagreed with his strongly pro-Shimazu (pro-Satsuma) policies. In any case, Shō Nei's struggle to solidify his power was long and divisive. Along the way, he faced an armed uprising in 1592 and a disastrous war with Satsuma in 1609.

Ogyaka's seizure of the throne on behalf of Shō Shin revealed factionalism within the royal family that never appears to have abated until sometime in the seventeenth century. Shō Shin's own reign includes decades of silence before he burst onto the scene at the end of the 1490s in a series of wars. Most likely he spent those decades consolidating power. By the time of Shō Gen's death, a major divide within the royal court in Shuri had developed, a pro-Satsuma faction facing off against an anti-Satsuma faction. Here, *Satsuma* refers to all the holdings of the Shimazu family, which usually included the provinces of Satsuma, Ōsumi, and Hyūga.

We can examine the pro- versus anti-Satsuma fault line through the lens of Satsuma's demand that Ryukyuan officials inspect Japanese ships entering Naha and confiscate the cargo of any vessel not authorized by Satsuma. Shō Shin, Shō Sei, and Shō Gen all ignored or politely set aside this demand. In other words, they were all anti-Satsuma.

Shō Ei was pro-Satsuma, or at least the officials who put him on the throne were. The king himself was only fourteen when he ascended the throne, and, as with most sixteenth-century royal reigns, several years were required for the new king and his supporters to consolidate power. Shō Ei devoted significant diplomatic and financial resources to mending the rift that had developed between Shuri and Satsuma during the 1570s. We also see Shō Ei's pro-Satsuma stance when looking closely at official correspondence. Whereas a letter from Shō Gen to Satsuma is dated "Great Ming [year, month, day]" and refers to Ryukyu as "Kyūyō" (beautiful Ryukyu), a similar letter from Shō Ei leaves out "Great Ming" and styles Ryukyu as "Shōkoku," meaning "small country" (Kuroshima 2016, 66). Satsuma responded well to the overtures of Shō Ei's administration and fully restored the commercial relations with Shuri that had been suspended since the early 1570s.

Shō Nei cooperated with both Satsuma and Toyotomi Hideyoshi early in his reign. He came under great pressure to do so, in part because Hideyoshi regarded the Ryukyu Islands as part of his territory. That cooperation included sending food supplies to support the contingent from Satsuma in Hideyoshi's 1592 invasion of the continent. Pushback from the Ming court in 1593, including the prospect of a truncated investiture ceremony, caused Shō Nei abruptly to change course. Not only did he become unwaveringly anti-Satsuma, but he refused even token cooperation with any Japanese entity, including the Tokugawa *bakufu* (after 1603). This stance led directly to a disastrous war in 1609, but, even after surrendering to Satsuma, Shō Nei resisted passively.

His successor, Shō Hō, realized that, if Ryukyu were to retain any autonomy, cooperation with Satsuma was essential. Not only did his administration collaborate with Satsuma; it also severely punished Ryukyuan officials who persisted in their anti-Satsuma stances. Notice, therefore, that, from Shō Gen through Shō Hō, each royal reign alternated between anti- and pro-Satsuma stances.

Solar Ideology

During the sixteenth century, a solar ideology developed around the king.[6] This ideology connected the king to the sun as a deity (*teda*, O. *tiida* and other terms). The details, however, have been subject to much debate among scholars. Typical formulations hold that the king was likened to the rising sun, that he was the son of the sun (*tedako*), or that he received spiritual and political power (*seji*) from the sun via the mediation of the high priestess.

Let us begin with the very idea of the royal line, which seems to have originated, like so much else, during the reign of Shō Shin. There is a basic contradiction in the sources regarding this matter. In monuments erected by both Shō Shin and Shō Sei, the kings of Okinawa are portrayed as descendants of Shunten (舜天), the founding king of the Tenson line. Shō Sei, for example, was the twenty-first generation since Shunten, according to a 1543 monument. Note that we have no evidence that Shunten or his two ostensible successors, Shunbajunki and Gihon, actually existed.

The *Omoro*, by contrast, emphasizes royal descent from Eiso, who was not biologically related to Shunten's line. Eiso probably did exist as a local ruler in the Urasoe area. However, his alleged accomplishments as stated in the official histories (e.g., organizing agriculture, initiating regular taxation) would clearly have been impossible in his day, as is the idea that he ruled over all Okinawa. Importantly, *Omoro* songs often refer to Eiso as a *solar king*, and, thus, Shō Shin or Shō Sei explicitly became descendants of the solar king Eiso in the context of those songs.

Urasoe Castle was located on high ground, and it had a direct line of sight to the sacred island Kudakajima. At the time of the winter solstice, the sun can be seen coming up directly in the middle of Kudakajima, at the site of the Kubō grove, which to this day is off-limits to ordinary people. A bright golden light radiates out from low-hanging clouds, creating a scene reminiscent of an oceanic paradise. The ceremony for reviving the sun at the winter solstice was called in Okinawan *ufu-tiida ishi,* and the name refers to the ceremony conducted while observing the sunrise over Kudakajima from Urasoe. Some scholars have proposed that this ceremony also functioned as a rite for the renewal of royal authority/potency. In other words, just as the sun renewed its strength at the time of the solstice, so too did the king, who was associated with the sun. This idea seems to be accurate, but what about the timing? When did solar rites of this type begin?

About one kilometer northeast of Shuri Castle is the shrine complex of Bengatake, consisting of a large shrine and a small one. Although it is now blocked by trees, at the time of the solstice the small shrine had a direct line of sight to the middle of Kudakajima. According to *Origins of Ryukyu* (1713), when it was impossible to perform rites on Kudakajima, they were performed at Bengatake. The deity name of the small shrine was Tenshi (天子), which could also be read as Tedako and also refers to the king (son of heaven, son of the sun). It turns out that this Bengatake shrine was where the king worshipped during years that he did not or could not go to Kudakajima. The rites in which the king participated were the *shikyoma* (grain) rites described earlier, and one of the major *shikyoma* rites took place at the time of the winter solstice.

The most likely sequence of development was that, originally, rites performed at Bengatake and Kudakajima were solstice rites. They celebrated the renewal of the sun's power and, by extension, the renewal of the king's power. Given that Benzaiten came to Okinawa with the second Shō dynasty, these solstice rites started with Shō Shin or possibly Shō En. And recall how Shō Shin was able to seize the throne—the priestesses performing enthronement rites all facing west instead of east. Later—probably during the reign of Shō Sei—the solstice rites became the basis for the *shikyoma* grain rites. According to legends, the same area of southeast Okinawa (Chinen/

Tamagusuku on Okinawa and Kudakajima just out to sea) was the precise area in which grain came into Okinawa from the north.

Niraikanai Ideology

One legend or religious belief found throughout the Ryukyu Islands and in other maritime areas is the idea of a phantom island (*maboroshi-no-shima*) located far out to sea. One example is the legend that Amamikyo came ashore in Okinawa from a "great eastern island." The home of that legend is Tamagusuku, in southeast Okinawa, and the place in which it plays out is the nearby shore of Hyakuna and the vicinity. The idea of a phantom island also exists in the northern Ryukyu Islands. In Okinoerabu and Tokunoshima, there is the idea that only people of strong faith will be able to view this phantom island (Agarihirashima) early in the morning on the first day after the solstice. It is located to the east where the sun rises, and it is a paradisiacal place of good fortune. Such phantom islands were also widely regarded as the abode of ancestral spirits.

In Yaeyama in the southern Ryukyu Islands, the phantom island is located, not to the east, but to the south. According to the South Hateruma (Paipateroma) legend, the people of Yaeyama were suffering under severe taxation imposed on them by Shuri (discussed in chapter 12). Seeking to save the people, an islander left home on a boat and floated atop the sea until he came on a prosperous island in which everyone seemed to be living comfortably and happily. It was South Hateruma. The man returned to his home island and prepared to escape to the island with forty or fifty villagers. However, a woman realized she forgotten her pot and went back to get it. When she got back, she was too late. The boat had left, and she clutched her pot in sadness. There was a field next to her, and it became known as Nabekaki (weeping pot) field. In Yonaguni, there is a similar legend regarding South Yonaguni (Paidunan). Because of the taxation details they mention, we know that these specific legends are from the early modern era, but the general idea of a phantom island to the south is older.

The term *niraikanai* (with local variations in pronunciation) is common in lore from all the Ryukyu Islands. It indicates a horizontal orientation, as opposed to *obotsukagura*, which indicates a vertical orientation. *Obotsukagura* refers to the heavens, *niraikanai* to the vast expanse of ocean beyond the reef line.[7]

There is a connection between likening royal authority to the rising sun in Okinawa, the idea of phantom islands, and the idea of *niraikanai*. The clue is in the official hierarchy of priestesses that Shō Shin established, with *noro* (Okinawa and Amami) and *tsukasa* (Miyako and Yaeyama) as the local tier. These women linked local areas to the royal court both directly and indirectly. The propagation of *niraikanai* ideas was part of this process whereby the royal court promoted a set of common cosmological ideas and appointed priestesses to promote those ideas throughout the empire. In this case, they promoted the idea of solar power coming into the Ryukyu Islands from across the sea to the east, the *niraikanai* direction, strengthening the king.

The *niraikanai* rites that these official priestesses performed were all similar, and the uniformity is an indication of Shuri's power. If these rites genuinely reflected local legends and practices, there would have been wide variations in them because the cultures of the various Ryukyu Islands varied significantly from one to the other. However, from Amami-Ōshima to Yonaguni, official rites performed by state-appointed priestesses shared a common core. For example, although in official rites *niraikanai* indicated the out-to-sea, horizontal dimension, in Yaeyama the equivalent terms in the local language (*niiresuku, niireisuku, niirō, niiruu*) indicated a very low place on the earth. There was, in other words, a mismatch between the official version of *niraikanai* and local beliefs about a divine territory with the same name but in a different location. Recall that, in the southern Ryukyu Islands, some creation myths featured deities who emerged from within the earth, that is, from *niraikanai* as understood locally.

We should not read too much into this example of *niraikanai*. It was not the case that officials in Shuri sought to make all culture uniform throughout their empire at the level of individual people or local communities. However, Shuri did seek—with substantial success—to implement a set of core ideas and rituals concerned with royal power at the level of government officials, even local ones.

There had always been beliefs about the sea throughout the Ryukyu Islands, but what we see in the *niraikanai* of the royal court was a new, standardized view of the otherworld. Specifically, *niraikanai* became standardized as the eastern direction out to sea, which fit perfectly with the emerging ideas connected with solar kings. In and around Okinawa, close to the imperial center, we find only this view. Far from the center in Miyako and Yaeyama, we find traces of phantom islands located to the south, not to the east, and a *niraikanai* at the bottom of the earth, not across the sea.

Similarly, Seifaa utaki, just across from Kudakajima, become the holiest grove early in the sixteenth century because of the royal government merging *niraikanai* concepts and solar worship. Seifaa utaki was the place best suited to this merger in terms of topography and geography. Shō Shin merged solar worship and ocean worship such that it was not the sun in the heavens but the sun rising from the eastern sea to which the king was likened. The creation of official ideologies and rituals was a crucial component of a centralized state. In the face of changes brought by the war with Satsuma in 1609, the royal government expanded the process of ideological production during the early modern era, as we will see.

CHAPTER TEN

War with Satsuma and the Immediate Aftermath, 1570–1650

A major turning point in Ryukyuan history was the war between Ryukyu and Satsuma early in 1609. Modern and contemporary writers who inaccurately claim that Japan annexed an independent kingdom in 1879 either are unaware of this event, are unaware of its importance, or choose to ignore it. The war resulted in vast substantive changes behind the scenes but fewer changes on the surface.

The 1609 war was not a capricious or inevitable invasion of the Ryukyu Islands. It had a long and complex run-up, and, almost until the last minute, it could have been averted. Once it was under way, despite some fierce resistance in Tokunoshima and in the Shuri-Naha area Satsuma's victory was swift and decisive. The result was that all the Ryukyu Islands became the territory of Satsuma, formally recognized as such by the Tokugawa *bakufu*. The northern Ryukyu Islands came under direct administration of Satsuma. With *bakufu* approval, Okinawa and the southern Ryukyu Islands posed as an independent country to preserve the tribute trade. The war also accelerated domestic changes that were already under way. This chapter examines the causes of the war, the war itself, and the major changes that the war either produced or accelerated. In other words, it examines the transition from what Japanese historians typically call *old Ryukyu* (*ko-Ryūkyū*, 古琉球) to early modern Ryukyu (*kinsei Ryūkyū*, 近世琉球).

The Great Days of Chūzan

The period from the 1520s to the 1530s was when Shuri's empire became fully formed, and these decades marked the peak of its economic prosperity. George H. Kerr (1958/2000) called the sixteenth century the "great days of Ch[ū]zan." There are problems with this characterization. First, it is clear that, by 1570, Shuri had become impoverished. In other words, its great days lasted only a few decades, not an entire century or more. Moreover, *Chūzan* is a vague term. To be more precise, Shuri gained power and wealth as a result of bringing the other Ryukyu Islands under its control and extracting wealth from them. For the people living on those other islands, however, the early sixteenth century was a time when Shuri began to appropriate their resources. From the standpoint of many northern and southern islanders, the mid- to the late fifteenth century would not have been great days. After 1609, Satsuma imposed direct taxation on the northern Ryukyu Islands, a taxation that eventually became severe. In response, Shuri pressed the southern islands even harder than it had during the sixteenth century. In short, the great days of Chūzan were much greater for a few Okinawans in the capital area than they were for most denizens of the Ryukyu Islands as a whole, and they were short-lived in any case.

The world underwent major changes during the sixteenth century in ways that affected the Ryukyu Islands. The first trend was a decline in Ryukyu's tribute trade with China, especially the offshoot of the tribute trade that extended into Southeast Asia. It is common to read that Ryukyuan sailors traded throughout Southeast Asia during the fifteenth and sixteenth centuries. That point is accurate, but only in a limited sense. Recall that a major function of Okinawan trade kings was to provide cover for Chinese ships conducting international trade despite the Maritime Prohibitions. The Ming court and some privileged Chinese merchants gave ships to Ryukyuan kings. However, these ships came with a Chinese captain and crew. Technically, the ships sailed on behalf of Ryukyuan kings, and, indeed, there were Ryukyuans on board these ships: crew members, merchants, and envoys. But the Chinese officers had ultimate control of the vessels. Although this is not a perfect comparison, the situation resembled the modern and contemporary use of flags of convenience in maritime commerce. Voyages were profitable for Ryukyuan kings and their associates as well as for select Chinese merchants. However, these voyages to Southeast Asia in connection with the tribute trade were not the independent actions of Okinawan entities.

The sailors of Miyako Island, by contrast, were independent, private entrepreneurs and mariners. Using lumber from the Yaeyama Islands, shipwrights in Miyako constructed Japanese-style vessels called *Uruka ships* (*Uruka miuni*, 砂川ミウ二) that made their way to China and to parts of Southeast Asia. So there were indeed Ryukyuans who sailed independently to Southeast Asia for trade, but they were from Miyako, not Naha. Shō Shin's conquest of that region, starting in 1500, greatly curtailed the voyages of the Uruka ships. At almost the same time, another force began to curtail trade with Southeast Asia. In 1510, Goa fell to Portuguese conquerors. It was the beginning of Spanish and Portuguese colonization of Southeast Asian trading ports. By the early 1570s, this conquest was largely complete. At the same time, Ryukyuan presence in Southeast Asia came to a stop, except for one voyage in 1577 and another in 1606.

Recall that the Ryukyu Islands had long been home to trading-and-raiding societies. It was wealth from trade, not from agriculture, that permitted the formation of an empire centered at Shuri. The loss of Southeast Asian trade was a significant economic blow to Shuri. So, too, was the Ming court's relaxation of the Maritime Prohibitions in 1567. After that time, it became much easier for Chinese merchants to conduct trade without having to pretend to do so under the auspices of a Ryukyuan king. Chinese merchants quickly took over trade with Southeast Asia.

Another change in world circumstances was the result of Spanish silver mines in the Americas. Spanish silver from the Americas flooded into world markets and became a de facto world currency. Spain, however, was bound by a 1494 treat not to trade directly with China from its base in the Philippines. Moreover, Chinese silk and Japanese swords were in high demand throughout the region, and there were different exchange rates for gold and silver in different places (1:13 in Spain, 1:6 in China, 1:9 in Japan). Merchants based in the Ryukyu Islands were able to conduct private trade that took advantage of these exchange rate differences, and they occasionally filled in gaps for high-demand commodities. There are no Ryukyuan, Japanese, or Chinese records that discuss such trade in much detail, but Spanish records frequently mention it.[1] In short, although worldwide changes disrupted Ryukyuan trade, generally for the worse, they also created some new avenues for potential profit.

In this way, an increase in private trade appears to have partially offset the decline in the tribute trade. There was, however, an important difference. Even though the tribute trade included (or masked) a large private component, it was formally a government-to-government undertaking, and it generally enriched Shuri's coffers. A strong centralized state and empire had barely come into stable existence when, in the mid-sixteenth century, Shuri came under increasing economic pressure. As stated above, the so-called great days of Chūzan lasted only several decades. The last half of the sixteenth century was a time of steady economic decline for Shuri.

Diplomatic Tensions

Prior to the establishment of a centralized state, trade kings in Okinawa conducted formal diplomacy with the Chinese court on a modest scale. They dispatched tribute embassies, asked for and received investiture (a process conducted via documents before Shō Sei), and sometimes made other requests. For example, after the war between Shiro and Furi in the 1450s, Shō Taikyū asked for a replacement royal seal because the previous one had melted when part of Shuri Castle caught fire. It is unlikely that these trade kings were capable of drafting diplomatic correspondence and documents themselves, if, indeed, they were literate at all. This sort of work was done by Chinese merchant-officials residing in Kumemura (久米村) or, as time went on, by their descendants. As time and generations passed, these descendants became less Chinese and more Okinawan in terms of culture. Therefore, during the sixteenth century, Buddhist priests from Japan played an increasingly important role in mediating Chinese-Ryukyuan diplomatic interactions. Moreover, priests had long played a key role in diplomacy between the Ryukyu Islands and Japan and Korea.

From the time of Shō Hashi, Okinawan kings enjoyed cordial relations with Japan's Muromachi shoguns. The shogunate established an office to deal with Ryukyuan vessels, and merchants based in Sakai (near Kyoto) played a major role in trade with the Ryukyu Islands. During the years of the Ōnin War (1467–77), few Ryukyuan ships were willing to sail to Japan because of disordered conditions, especially in the area near Kyoto. Merchants from Sakai sailed to Naha instead, indicating the high importance of Ryukyuan-mediated trade for merchants in Japan.

In 1481, during the reign of Shō Shin, but prior to his emergence as a strong ruler, the Ryukyuan court began dispatching *ayabune* (decorated ships, 綾船) to the court of the Muromachi shogun for special occasions. After the Ōnin War, the power of the shoguns was greatly diminished, eclipsed by the Ōuchi lords of western Japan based at Yamaguchi. Nevertheless, until the formal end of the Muromachi *bakufu* in the 1570s, Ryukyuan kings maintained cordial relations with the Ashikaga shoguns.[2] It is important to note that this relationship was casual, almost like that of an older brother (the shogun) and a younger brother (the trade king, or *Ryūkyū yononushi* [琉球世の主], as the shogun referred to him). The relationship made no serious demands on Ryukyuan kings or on the crews of Ryukyuan ships. This point is important. Whether at the level of heads of state or at any other level, despite having interreacted with the Muromachi *bakufu*, Ryukyuans were not familiar with the demanding protocols that governed diplomacy between samurai warlords.

During the 1550s, Shimazu Takahisa (1514–71), aware that Shuri occasionally dispatched decorated ships to Kyoto, began to demand that it do the same vis-à-vis the Shimazu lords in Satsuma. Shuri replied that it lacked the resources to maintain diplomatic relations with nearby countries, and this claim was almost certainly accurate. Despite initially refusing to do so, in 1559 Shuri dispatched a decorated ship to Kagoshima. This dispatch opened the door to future problems. Because it sent a ship in 1559, the Shimazu lords expected that Shuri would do so thereafter on occasions such as a new Shimazu ruler assuming office or having accomplished something important. Diplomatic protocol required that these ships bring with them valuable gifts. The Shimazu lords would reciprocate, but diplomacy between Shuri and Kagoshima was a net drain of resources for Shuri. Moreover, recall that Shuri was inexperienced in serious diplomacy in a Japanese context.

In 1568, a disabled ship from Miyako drifted into Kaseda in Satsuma. Shimazu Takahisa instructed his officials to return the crew to their homeland. Doing so was standard procedure. Shimazu also returned the ship's cargo, something that was *not* standard procedure. Under prevailing customs in Japan, the lord of the place into which disabled ships drifted was entitled to keep the cargo. In many cases, the value of the cargo would offset the expense of caring for and returning the crew. In response to this gesture, Shuri dispatched a Buddhist priest to Satsuma as an envoy of thanks. So far, so good. Soon thereafter, however, matters became unpleasant.

Recall that there was a fairly long and unclear period of transition between the reigns of Shō Gen and Shō Ei around 1572–73. The transition came at a particularly bad time because, in 1570, a messenger from Satsuma arrived with news that Shimazu Yoshihisa (1533–1611) had succeeded to the headship of the Shimazu household. The proper response would have been to send a congratulatory decorated ship within a year. Two years out, there was no ship. Additionally, in 1572, an envoy from Kagoshima came to Ryukyu with letters complaining about unauthorized trade. This complaint was one manifestation of insistence by Shimazu that any Japanese ships permitted in Naha for trade must present written authorization from Satsuma. Recall that this demand was long-standing and that Shō Shin had politely ignored it. He was able to do so because Shuri was militarily powerful and economically wealthy in the 1520s and 1530s. That was no longer the case by the 1570s. Shimazu forces were also almost constantly at war with some other power in Kyushu in the 1570s. Attempts to regulate ship traffic between Kyushu and Naha were part of a larger Shimazu effort to consolidate power in Kyushu.

The belated Ryukyuan diplomatic embassy did not set sail until 1575. Despite the embassy being welcomed by fireworks on arrival, things did not go well. Officials in Kagoshima presented the Ryukyuan ambassadors with a lengthy list of complaints. Some were about lapses in etiquette. Other were more substantive, for example, not working with Satsuma to regulate ship traffic. One article complained that Ryukyuan officials had beheaded the first mate of the ship *Kuniyoshi-maru* when it was in Naha. It would be fascinating to know the details of this matter, but all we have are the exchanges from 1575.[3] In addition to the formal complaints, other issues emerged. For example, officials in Satsuma grumbled that the gifts brought by the Ryukyuans were significantly less valuable than those brought on previous voyages. The Ryukyuan envoys proffered as an excuse the difficult and extended period of royal transition from Shō Gen to Shō Ei. Amid this diplomatic wrangling, Shimazu officials made the claim that Shōgun Ashikaga Yoshinori (1394–1441) had granted Shimazu Tadakuni "the portal to the Ryukyu Islands." The original meaning of this vague phrase is unclear, but, over subsequent decades, it transformed into a claim by Satsuma that the Ryukyu Islands had been territory of Satsuma since 1441.

When the Ryukyuan envoys initially presented written replies to the complaints, officials in Kagoshima rejected them and demanded better answers. The wrangling was intense, and one of the envoys collapsed from the pressure and had to be caried to a nearby temple. Ultimately, the two sides arrived at agreements or tentative agreements, and the theatrical aspects of the embassy could proceed (a formal audience with Yoshihisa, a banquet, gift exchanges, etc.). Matters were not well, however, and Yoshihisa imposed a ban on ships from Satsuma sailing to Naha.

Shō Ei and his allies needed a few years to consolidate his hold on the throne. In addition to whatever other matters may have been at play, Shō Ei was a young teenager when he became king. He and his officials actively worked to reduce tensions with Satsuma, starting in 1577. The next year, he sent a well-stocked decorated ship to Kagoshima. Significantly, the Ryukyuan ship contained additional gifts that amounted to the exact shortfall officials in Kagoshima had complained about in 1575. In a dramatic gesture of goodwill, Shimazu dispatched the *Kuniyoshi-maru* to Naha in 1579, the same ship whose first mate had been beheaded in Naha. The vessel's arrival indicated that good relations between Shuri and Kagoshima had been restored. The situation continued until Shō Ei's untimely death in 1588.

Unless relevant new documents are discovered, we will never know the details about why Shō Nei came to the throne despite at least one of Shō Ei's brothers having been alive in 1588. On creating the Tamaudun (玉陵) mausoleum for his family, Shō Shin explicitly prohibited Shō Ikō's remains from being interred there. That is why both Shō Ikō and Shō Nei are buried in Urasoe. Bones and burials were a very important matter in Okinawa, so it is clear that Shō Shin went to great lengths to relegate Shō Ikō and his descendants to the sidelines. But, with Shō Nei, the exiled branch of the family returned to center stage.

A backlash against Shō Ei's strong pro-Satsuma policies probably brought Shō Nei to the throne. Moreover, Toyotomi Hideyoshi had defeated Shimazu armies in 1586. That event may have emboldened the anti-Satsuma faction at the royal court. Why exactly Shō Nei garnered sufficient support to take the throne, however, is less certain. Importantly, throughout his long reign, Shō Nei was never able to unite the entire royal court behind his rule.

Shō Nei's Turbulent Early Years

There was much diplomatic activity between 1588 and 1592, driven by demands made by Toyotomi Hideyoshi. Hideyoshi had unified all Japan under his rule, the first time the country had been geopolitically unified in over a century. He had big plans. He sought to invade and conquer China via the Korean Peninsula, and his ambitions extended as far as India. To give a brief summary, Hideyoshi's first invasion of the continent took place in 1592. He regarded the Ryukyu Islands as part of his territory and insisted that they assist with the project. Shō Nei agreed to provide a substantial portion of the food for the Shimazu forces. At the same time that Shuri committed to material support for Hideyoshi's invasion, Ryukyuan envoys also warned officials in China that an invasion was imminent. It is possible that the warning was of some help to the Ming court, but we do not know how seriously it was taken.

Also in 1592, an armed revolt against Shō Nei broke out in or near the capital. Those events were probably connected. Most likely, the Jana revolt of 1592 reflected anger on the part of Okinawan elites at the heavy resource burden they had to shoulder so that Shuri could procure and send food to the force from Satsuma in Korea. In this context, recall that agriculture in the Ryukyu Islands was poorly developed. Even after leaning heavily on prominent families, Shuri was unable to obtain all the food supplies it promised just prior to the invasion. One result was serious hunger on the part of the Shimazu forces, which many of them remembered for a long time. Shuri did eventually ship all the food supplies that it promised, but the price had been very high in several respects.

For one thing, there was a significant turnover of top Ryukyuan officials in Shō Nei's government, starting in 1592. The Council of Three remained unstable throughout the 1590s and the first decade of the seventeenth century. Recall that the priest Taichū resided in Okinawa between 1603 and 1606. Sometime during that period, he reported the appearance of an anonymous tract slandering the king and his officials. Shō Nei's government

apparently spent considerable energy trying to track down those responsible and eventually exiled a group it deemed at fault to a remote island. In
short, the Ryukyuan court and elite families were in a state of turmoil during the years leading to 1609.

There was even more fallout from Shō Nei's providing food for the contingent from Satsuma in Hideyoshi's invasion forces. Chinese officials and/
or merchants quickly became aware of it, and word spread widely (we have
documentary evidence). The Ming court decreed that Shō Nei's investiture
ceremony would not take place in Okinawa and instead would be held re-
motely, in China. The ostensible reason was safety during wartime. However, Shō Nei interpreted the Ming court's actions as punishment, and he
was probably correct. He sent repeated envoys to China who darkly hinted
that, if he were not given a proper investiture in Okinawa, he might lose
power and Ryukyu could drift into Japan's orbit. In the end, the Ming court
decided to support Shō Nei, but the Chinese envoy who crossed over to
Okinawa in 1606, Xià Zǐyáng, was scathing in his criticism. He stated that
Ryukyuan officials were arrogant and that the royal court merely goes
through the motions of maintaining ties to the Chinese court. He also noted
that Shuri was insufficiently prepared for war with "Japan" (by which he
meant Satsuma) and predicted that Ryukyu would soon be humbled as a
result (see Xià 1606/2001). On this last point, at least, he was correct.

Notice also that Xià's criticism constitutes one more example of the
friction, sometimes even enmity, that characterized relations between the
Ming court and Shuri throughout the fifteenth and sixteenth centuries.
Characterizations of Shuri's relationship with China as smooth and ami-
cable, common in both Anglophone and Japanese literature, are inaccurate.

Anglophone writers occasionally use the term *suzerain* in reference to
the Ming court and Shuri's relationship to it. Although this term can be
vague, in its basic dictionary definition of one sovereign, or state, having
a degree of control over another state that is otherwise internally autonomous, it is problematic. Recall that participation in the tribute trade originated as a Ming antipiracy policy and quickly became a way to circumvent
the Maritime Prohibitions in a controlled manner. As the Sea Bridge to the
Many Countries Bell inscription stated, the relationship was mechanical
and functional. Moreover, Ryukyuans abused the system frequently, and
Shō Nei essentially blackmailed the Ming court to grant him investiture.
All indications are that Xià's assessment was generally accurate. Relations
between Shuri and the Ming court had long been strained. As we will see,
one reason that tributary relations between Shuri and Beijing (under the
Qing) became relatively smooth was because Satsuma provided the necessary financing. Although Chinese merchant-officials were involved in Shō

Hashi's rise to prominence in the 1420s, at no time did China ever exert political control over the Ryukyu Islands.

Another source of strain with China during approximately the 1590s was the frequent appearance along the Chinese coast of suspicious vessels. They were suspicious in the sense that their crews appear to have been Japanese, the vessels contained illicit trade goods, and sometimes armed crews fought back against Chinese coastal patrols. The circumstances of each case are complex, and Watanabe Miki has examined them in detail (Watanabe Miki 2012, 24–64). In many cases, closer examination by Chinese officials revealed the presence of crew members from various parts of the Ryukyu and Tokara Islands (or people posing as such), sometimes with Chinese and Japanese from Kyushu in the mix. On repeated questioning, the crews usually came around to claiming that they were Ryukyuans traveling to China on official business. Such claims seemed very strange on the surface. The crews of intercepted ships were typically poorly dressed and had no documents. Sometimes they professed to have come to warn Chinese officials of Japanese invasion or raiding plans.

These suspicious ships and their crews looked and acted like pirates from Japan, but they asserted—or at least eventually asserted—that they were Ryukyuan envoys. Often their stories and claimed identities changed each time a new official questioned them. Neither Chinese officials nor the Japanese interpreters who assisted them were able to figure out definitively whether the crews were Ryukyuan or Japanese. The interpreters claimed that the language, clothing, and general customs of Ryukyu and Japan were so similar that they could not distinguish between them. Almost certainly these sailors were indeed smugglers, and they were a blend of local coastal people. They would have been familiar with the local cultures and languages of western Kyushu, the Ryukyu Islands, and to some extent southern China. The cases are fascinating in their own right, but they also serve as another indication of the confusion that prevailed during Shō Nei's reign, when so many pirates or shady characters were able—ultimately with considerable success—to pose as Ryukyuan envoys to China during the 1590s.

Shō Nei was under pressure from all sides. Hideyoshi possessed overwhelming military might, and he regarded the Ryukyu Islands as his possession, occasionally threatening to give the islands to one or another of his retainers if the Shimazu lords and Shō Nei failed to do his bidding. Indeed, at one point he even started to do so in writing but changed his mind at the last minute. The Ming court was unhappy with Shō Nei's support for Hideyoshi and Shimazu, especially the food aid. Closer to home, Shō Nei faced severe opposition by many prominent Okinawans. The times were perilous, and the king had no good options.

Pause for Perspective

At this point, it is useful to review several centuries of Ryukyuan history in broad strokes. During the Gusuku Era, waves of migrants from Japan and to a lesser extent Korea swept into the Ryukyu Islands, fundamentally altering their culture and population. During the fourteenth century, *wakō* powers based in harbors in the Ryukyu Islands became powerful and traded directly with harbors in Korea, Japan, and China via interconnected maritime networks. During the 1370s, Okinawa sprouted several trade kings and royal relatives who participated in the tribute trade under extremely favorable conditions. This situation was the start of a successful long-term campaign by the Ming court to tame *wakō* by buying them off, making them dependent on Ming largesse, and then reducing that largesse.

The tribute trade was itself quite profitable, and private trade in connection with it was potentially even more profitable. To fuel this private trade, Okinawan powers mobilized their networks throughout the East China Sea region to procure goods from places like Japan, Korea, and Southeast Asia (via Miyako) to sell in China. This profitable situation led, however, to violent warfare in Okinawa from the 1380s through the 1420s—the Three Principalities Era—and beyond. During the fourteenth and fifteenth centuries, powerful trading-and-raiding groups operated in the Ryukyu Islands. Some of these groups held or used the Chinese title *wáng* (king), which permitted them formally to participate in the tribute trade. None of these people, however, ruled over the entire island of Okinawa, nor did Okinawa have a central government. Moreover, except for Kikaijima and the Kasari Peninsula of Amami-Ōshima during the late fifteenth century, the other Ryukyu Islands were politically independent of Okinawa or any specific Okinawan power.

This situation changed decisively between the late 1490s and the 1530s. By the late 1490s, Shō Shin had consolidated his position within his family and at Shuri. He then set out to subdue the rest of Okinawa and nearly all the other Ryukyu Islands. Profit from the tribute trade formed the economic basis for these conquests, and there were other factors at play. Shō Shin lived a long life. All indications are that he was a shrewd politician and an effective military commander. He created a strong centralized state based in Shuri, and he created a maritime empire encompassing the other Ryukyu Islands. He also created important social and cultural institutions. His fifth son, Shō Sei, followed up on the project. Within a few decades, the Ryukyu Islands had transformed from a disorganized frontier region to an empire with considerable military and economic strength. To use a boxing metaphor, the Ryukyu Islands were punching above their weight at this time.

The underlying foundation for this wealth and power was not agriculture or any valuable natural resource except sulfur. It was a constellation of unlikely circumstances. The Ming dynasty had formally outlawed foreign trade, even though, in practice, such a ban was unsustainable. Foreign trade did, in fact, have to occur. The main solution was to use the port of Naha as a de facto shipping corporation. The Ming court, in cooperation with certain merchants, operated a fleet of trading ships under the ostensible auspices of Ryukyuan trade kings. These hybrid Ryukyuan/Chinese ships sailed as far afield as Southeast Asia. When European powers took over the ports of Southeast Asia and the Ming dynasty relaxed its Maritime Prohibitions in the late sixteenth century, the basis for Shuri's wealth mostly collapsed. There were still some trading opportunities, and there was some carryover of wealth accumulated from the great days of Chūzan, but, by the time Shō Nei became king, Shuri's empire was barely hanging together.

During the peak of Ryukyuan prosperity, 1490s–1540s, warfare in Japan was frequent, and de facto power shifted to the Ōuchi territories in southwestern Honshu and northwestern Kyushu, whose wealth was also based on maritime trade. This situation permitted Ryukyu partially to offset decline in the tribute trade. However, by the 1580s, the Ōuchi were gone, and Japan was geopolitically reunited and powerful. The economically weakened Shuri Empire was in no position to assert itself. Nevertheless, that is what Shō Nei did.

The Road to War

Tokugawa Ieyasu became the most powerful person in Japan in 1600, and the *bakufu* he established lasted until 1867. One of his main goals was to reestablish foreign relations with the major states in the region. With difficulty, he succeeded in establishing relations with Korea even though Hideyoshi had invaded the peninsula. Negotiations with Ming China dragged on for years and ultimately failed. Chinese merchants did business in Nagasaki in large numbers during the Tokugawa Era, but there were no formal state-to-state diplomatic relations between the Tokugawa *bakufu* and Chinese courts (initially the Ming, then the Qing).

Satsuma was on the losing side in the Battle of Sekigahara in 1600, but it managed to survive. Battlefield losses to both Hideyoshi and Ieyasu, however, had impoverished Shimazu territory. Planners in Satsuma began to consider the possibility of seizing the northern Ryukyu Islands to enhance revenue.[4] Any such move would require *bakufu* approval. Meanwhile, Tokugawa Ieyasu was working hard to forge diplomatic relations with the Ming court. He thought that the Ryukyuan king should be willing to function as a go-between in the process. This idea made sense on the surface, but recall the severely strained relations between the Ming court and Shō Nei.

In Okinawa, Shō Nei dug in his heels. He had indeed cooperated— begrudgingly but substantively—with Hideyoshi's invasion project. That support resulted in an armed revolt at home and suspicion on the part of the Chinese court. From 1593 on, Shō Nei became determined never again to cooperate or appear to cooperate with any Japanese political entity. This is not to say that he harbored any dislike for Japan or the Japanese people. Quite the contrary, many of his closest confidants were mainland Japanese. Taichū was one of them, as were the priest Kian Nyūdō (喜安入道, 1566– 1653), from Sakai, the physician Yamazaki Nikyūshusan (山崎二休守三, 1554–1631), from Echizen in northern Honshu, and Tōma Jūchin (当間重陳, 1591–1676), from Kokubu in Ōsumi. And there were others. Indeed, Shō Nei may have preferred distant outsiders over the faction-ridden world of the royal court at Shuri. His personal fondness for specific Japanese people not- withstanding, Shō Nei refused to cooperate with political powers in Japan, and he ignored or rejected repeated requests by Shimazu to mediate be- tween the Ming court and the Tokugawa *bakufu*.

For the leaders in Kagoshima, this situation was potentially win-win, although not equally so. If Shō Nei were to agree to use his good offices, Shimazu would get credit for the breakthrough in Ieyasu's eyes. If he re- fused, the *bakufu* was likely to approve Satsuma's plan to seize the northern Ryukyu Islands. All indications are that Shimazu's preference was for Shō Nei's cooperation with the *bakufu*. Shimazu Iehisa tried very hard to gain it, sending letter after letter, each one more strongly worded, as well as a special envoy. Shō Nei probably did not have the clout with China to be of much use, but, even if he had attempted to mediate, he probably could have averted a disastrous war.

When the war got under way, Satsuma won quickly and decisively. Why, therefore, did Shō Nei think that he could stand up to Satsuma so firmly? Of course, we cannot know what was in his mind with certainty, but there are several relevant factors to consider. First, simply in terms of numbers of troops and infrastructure around Naha, Ryukyu's military appeared fairly strong, especially for defense purposes. Indeed, the Shimazu forces ex- pected and prepared for a much longer and more costly war than the one that actually took place. Next, Shimazu issued so many threats during the early seventeenth century that the Ryukyuan court probably assumed that they would never amount to concrete action. In 1606, when the investiture envoy Xià Zǐyáng asked Ryukyuan officials about the possibility of an invasion, they replied that the great distance from Kyushu would make an invasion untenable (see Xià 1606/2001). Furthermore, Ryukyu was protected, they claimed, by a powerful deity (Benzaiten). The Okinawan officials' thinking made sense, at least within their small circle. Consider that, after Benzaiten came to Ryukyu with the second Shō dynasty, Shuri's forces had been victorious in one battle after another since the 1490s. Benzaiten's arrival coincided with past military victories, and people routinely confuse correlation with causation. Okinawan officials might genuinely have believed that Benzaiten's power was militarily effective.

One other psychological factor may have been at work. Ming Chinese forces vigorously opposed Hideyoshi's invasions of Korea. Of course, they did so for their own defense. In other words, for the Ming court, fighting in Korea was preferable to fighting in China, Hideyoshi's ultimate target. China did not normally lend military support to tributary states. Nevertheless, it is possible that some Ryukyuan officials thought that Chinese aid or even the possibility of it would keep any northern invaders at bay. If this was their idea, they were wrong. As we have seen, Chinese officials did not think very highly of Ryukyu at this time, and, in any case, Chinese defense of Korea was a peculiar circumstance in which a tributary country was of direct military significance for the Ming court.

The Fighting

The military phase of the war took place over roughly one month, from the fourth day of the third lunar month (3.4; dates appear this way hereafter) until approximately 4.5. The force from Satsuma consisted of approximately three thousand well-armed soldiers in ships, some of whom were veterans of the many military campaigns of the era. They were under the command of Kabayama Hisataka. The fleet set sail from Yamakawa at the southern edge of the Satsuma Peninsula in support of the goals of conquering the northern Ryukyu Islands, conquering Okinawa, and forcing the king to sign surrender documents. The overall plan was to seize the northern Ryukyu Islands, administer them directly, and make the king subordinate to Satsuma and, therefore, the Tokugawa *bakufu*. The *bakufu* formally approved this plan.

Because Ryukyuan military forces seemed potentially formidable, commanders from Satsuma made detailed preparations. They were under pressure to achieve a decisive and swift victory to keep costs down and avoid political complications. They proved successful in doing so, and figure 10.1 illustrates the major landings and battles.

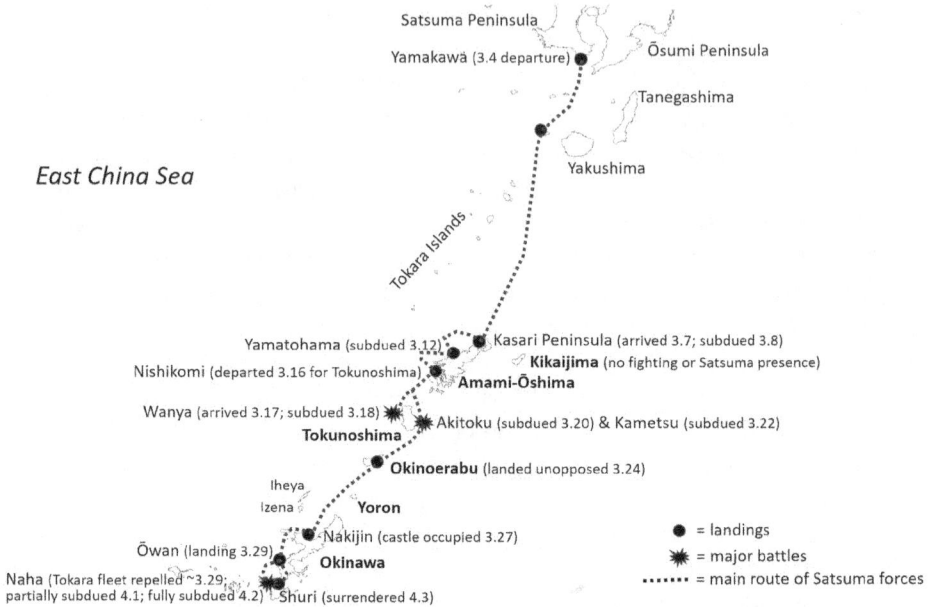

FIGURE 10.1. Major landings and battles during the 1609 war with Satsuma

Arriving at the Kasari Peninsula of Amami-Ōshima on 3.7, the forces from Satsuma encountered no organized defenses and quickly took control of the region. Most of the local residents had fled into the nearby mountains. Shuri's local official surrendered immediately, and he encouraged his peers elsewhere on the island to do the same. According to official records, that official's salary doubled after Satsuma took control, and all the other officials who cooperated benefited from increased pay. It is possible that agents from Satsuma contacted some or all of Amami-Ōshima's local officials in advance of the soldiers landing.

In the meantime, Hachimine Peichin had been sent by Shuri to report on the situation. Witnessing the collapse of Kasari, he took a fast boat to Okinawa, arriving on 3.10. Hachimine's report prompted rumors and panic. Shō Nei dispatched a priest as an envoy to Amami-Ōshima in the futile hope of negotiating a settlement before Satsuma's forces reached Okinawa.

The next landing of soldiers—which took place on 3.12 at Yamatohama, in the middle of the western coast of Amami-Ōshima—encountered a similar situation, that is, local officials surrendering without a fight and being rewarded. One source claims that a local official organized peasants to erect barricades, which gunfire quickly breached. In Kikaijima, Shuri's local official witnessed the invasion. He sailed to Amami-Ōshima and surrendered his island in advance of any possible landing. Events at this point indicate no significant defense preparations on Amami-Ōshima or a will on the part of the local population to fight.

The conquest of Amami-Ōshima took place on 3.16, when the fleet arrived at Nishikomi on the southwestern coast. That same day, part of the fleet departed for Tokunoshima, the rest being kept in Amami-Ōshima by poor weather. The invaders met a much more hostile reception on Tokunoshima. As background, rumors of an impending invasion by Satsuma had been circulating for several years prior to 1609. While the overall response in Shuri was to ignore the threat, it is possible that, in the highly polarized political environment, some Ryukyuan officials did press ahead with limited defense preparations. A prominent official arrived in Tokunoshima from Shuri as early as 1608, and, when the invaders came ashore, Ryukyuan soldiers and local people put up a vigorous but ultimately ineffective defense in several locations. Forces arriving at Wan'ya, on the northwest coast, faced as many as one thousand defenders, although many of them were armed only with homemade weapons. When a force of about two to three hundred troops waded ashore, they routed the defenders and took roughly fifty heads. Intense fighting took place two days later at Akitoku Harbor in the southeast part of the island (fig. 10.2). Ryukyuan soldiers, remnants of the Wan'ya battle, and local militia armed with homemade weapons attacked the invaders at the beach. Initially, these defenders pinned down Satsuma's

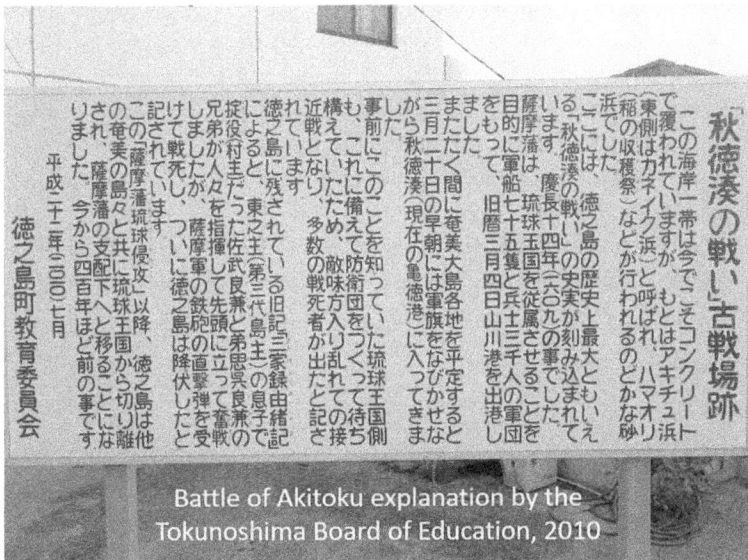

FIGURE 10.2. A brief history of the Battle of Akitoku (photograph by the author)

forces and inflicted some casualties on them. When they were able to bring their muskets to bear effectively, however, the invaders crushed the island's defenses.

The text in figure 10.2 reads:

"THE BATTLE OF AKITOKU BAY" OLD BATTLE SITE

This stretch of the shore is now covered in cement. However, it was originally called Akichu-hama (the east side was called Kaneiku-hama), and it was a calm, sandy beach where the Hamaori (rice harvest festival) was carried out.

Here are written the historical facts of what could be called the greatest [battle] in the history of Tokunoshima, the Battle of Akitoku Bay. It took place in Keichō 14 (1609). With the goal of subduing the Ryukyu Kingdom, Satsuma sent seventy-five military ships and a force of three thousand soldiers. They set sail from Yamakawa Harbor on the fourth day of the third month in the old [lunar] calendar.

On subduing every part of Amami-Ōshima in short order, on the morning of 3.20, military flags aloft, they entered Akitoku Bay (present-day Kametsu Bay).

Knowing what was to come, a defense squadron of the Ryukyu Kingdom was assembled and waiting. Thus, when the enemy entered [the beach], a melee of close-range fighting broke out. [Sources] record large numbers of people killed in the battle.

According to *Sankeroku yuishoki*, an old historical source from Tokunoshima, the village leader Saburagane, son of Higashi-no-shu (third-generation island head), and his younger brother Meguragane took charge and fought fiercely in front of their men. However, they took direct hits from muskets and died in the fighting. Eventually Tokunoshima surrendered.

After Satsuma's invasion of Ryukyu, Tokunoshima, along with Amami-Ōshima, was severed from the Ryukyu Kingdom and came under the direct control of Satsuma. It happened four hundred years ago.

Tokunoshima Town Board of Education

There was one more battle—at nearby Kametsu—probably on 3.21, and Ryukyuan officials fled into the mountains afterward. The next day, members of the invasion force hunted for them. Shuri's top official fell into their hands and agreed to cooperate.

Ascertaining casualty counts is extremely difficult. Roughly two to three hundred Ryukyuan soldiers died in the Tokunoshima battles, but the real death toll was probably much higher. Official records would have counted only formal soldiers wearing armor and helmets, not members of local militias. One interesting measure of the impact of the fighting comes from a local official on the island writing in 1682 or 1683 who noted that some elderly survivors of the Akitoku battle still got together to talk about it.

Local officials on Okinoerabu were confident that the invaders' large ships would not be able to land there because of the reefs that surrounded the island. However, an unusually high tide permitted some of the force to land at China (知名) Harbor at the southern end of the island. Shuri's surprised official surrendered without a fight on 3.24.

The fleet bypassed the island of Yoron and arrived Kouri, a small island near Unten Harbor on 3.25. Unten was the gateway to Nakijin, and, on 3.27, the invasion force occupied Nakijin's imposing fortress, which had been abandoned. As Satsuma's forces were entering northern Okinawa, Shō Nei dispatched peace envoys, the priest Kikuin and the Council of Three member Nago Ueekata Ryōhō. Nago became a hostage, but General Kabayama refused to negotiate with the pair at Nakijin. Kikuin rushed back to Shuri, and blood from his feet stained his robes, according to Kian Nyūdō's diary, *Kian nikki* (see Ikemiya 2009). Kikuin arrived in Shuri only slightly ahead of the invasion force.

The events described above differ significantly from the version relayed in a letter that Shō Nei sent to the Ming court approximately a month after he surrendered. The main purpose of the letter was to inform the court that Ryukyu would not be able to send a tribute embassy on account of the invasion and portray Ryukyu in the best possible light. Shō Nei presented himself and his generals as putting up a vigorous defense. In the case of Nago Ueekata, for example, the letter portrayed him as leading an army of one thousand that fell victim to a diabolical ruse on the part of the invaders. Defiant as a prisoner, Nago denounced the invaders and declared that he had no fear of death. Impressed by his patriotism and zeal, Satsuma's commanders spared Nago's life.

Shō Nei's account of Nago's bravery was fanciful, but there may have been some fighting in the vicinity of Nakijin as Satsuma's forces arrived. The main evidence is that the top Okinawan commander in the region, Shō Kokushi, died the day after Nakijin Castle was occupied. He was only twenty-eight at the time. Whatever resistance Shō Kokushi and the forces he commanded were able to mount, however, did nothing significantly to slow the pace of the invasion.

According to Kian's diary, the king was visibly shaken when the blood-soaked Kikuin appeared and reported that Satsuma's soldiers would soon be in the capital. Some young officials in the palace resigned themselves to fighting and rushed to Naha. Presumably, they assumed that the invaders would push their way into the harbor. Knowing that the harbor was well defended, however, the bulk of the force landed at Ōwan in Yomitan and marched overland to Shuri. Because the capital defenses were all focused on the possibility of a seaborne invasion through Naha Harbor, there was no significant infrastructure other than Shuri Castle itself to defend against an overland invasion.

However, there was a naval battle. Kabayama sent some of his fleet to test the harbor defenses. As the ships approached, the *hiki* forces manned their battle stations. The Council of Three member and main architect of Ryukyu's disastrous prewar stance Jana Ueekata Teidō led roughly one thousand soldiers to defend the harbor shoreline. Tomigusuku Ueekata, standing in for the indisposed Nago Ueekata, led another force of about one thousand to the harbor area, while Urasoe Ueekata, a close ally of Jana, supervised the defense of Shuri Castle. When the ships arrived, they were met with the roar of artillery from Yarazamori and Mie Fortresses, and a great chain across the harbor impeded their progress. Local people in the area fled in panic. According to Shō Nei's letter to the Ming court, the enemy "dead were too numerous to count" (Smits 2019, 231), but all other sources indicate a low casualty count and only moderate damage to the attacking ships. Though brief and not ultimately decisive, the initial battle for Naha Harbor was the sole Ryukyuan victory of the war.

The harbor battle had the effect of drawing Ryukyuan forces away from Shuri Castle. As that battle raged, Shimazu forces approached the outskirts of Shuri. At Taihei bridge, Goeku Ueekata led a cavalry force of about one hundred to defend it, but gunfire scattered them. According to the king's letter to China, the invaders approached from the north, burning everything in their path. Shō Nei blamed the limited resources of a small country for the defeat: "When we sent our forces to the north, we lost in the south, and when we attacked in the south, we lost in the north" (Smits 2019, 231). Again, this version of events portrays Ryukyu's military forces as effective and brave but badly outnumbered. If anything, however, the Ryukyuan forces had a numerical advantage. What they lacked were effective weapons and experience in overland fighting. They also lacked firm political unity within the royal government.

Most Ryukyuan defenders retreated to Shuri Castle, which was soon surrounded. Some Shimazu soldiers attempted to force their way into the castle at Iri no Azana (a tower), but a Ryukyuan force beat them back.

This force was led by Yamazaki Nikyūshusan, a recent immigrant from Echizen and one of Shō Nei's Japanese confidants. This point may be obvious to those familiar with premodern Japanese history, but notice that in this era military loyalties were not tied to abstractions such as "Japan" or "Ryukyu." Instead, they were personal. Yamazaki put his life on the line for Shō Nei, and, after surrendering, Shō Nei paid a large ransom to spare Yamazaki's life.

The end came swiftly during the first few days of the fourth month. On 4.1, Urasoe Castle fell, and Satsuma's fleet entered Naha Harbor. Large parts of the capital region had gone up in flames. Available sources indicate that at that point Jana and Urasoe continued to fight but that many top members of the Ryukyuan government were hiding in nearby mountains, having fled when Kikuin arrived with the news that the invaders were nearly at Shuri's doorstep. The flight of many top officials further indicates Shō Nei's tenuous hold on the royal government.

As for Jana's force defending Naha, it appears to have withdrawn to the Kememura area of Naha Harbor and continued to fight throughout 4.1 and 4.2. It is unlikely that Jana led the people of Kumemura to resist, as some legends have claimed. More likely, the remnants of his army, the one drawn from the southern districts, continued to resist for approximately one full day after Naha Harbor fell.

After ascertaining that he could retain his throne, on 4.3 Shō Nei agreed to surrender. Scattered resistance continued for a day or two afterward. In light of the decision to surrender, we can identify several groups among the top Okinawan officials. We might refer to Ōzato Aji, Kunigami Aji, Gusukuma Ueekata, Mabuni Ueekata, and the others who fled and hid in the mountains as *the cowardly faction*. Not surprisingly, their reputation and careers suffered after the war. A large number of officials stood by Shō Nei but supported the decision to surrender. They included Prince Gushikami, Nago Ueekata, Kikuin, and Ikegusuku Anrai, who was instrumental in crushing the 1592 revolt against Shō Nei. Jana Ueekata and Urasoe Ueekata, both Council of Three members and highly influential in the run-up to the war, advocated continued resistance. Their group included about seventeen others. Kian Nyūdō and Yamazaki Nikyūshusan stood by Shō Nei throughout the war and its aftermath, although we do not know whether they advocated surrender on or around 4.3.

Was further resistance a viable option? The short answer is no. On 4.1, Shuri Castle was full of armed soldiers, many of whom appeared eager to fight. The castle itself was an impressive fortress. Although it would eventually have fallen, Okinawan defenders could have delayed the process. It is unlikely, however, that such a delay would have benefited Shō Nei or his

government. Although some modern folklore portrays Shō Nei has having surrendered for the benefit of the ordinary people, all indications are
that he did so to save what was left of his throne and capital after intermediaries assured him that Satsuma's main goal was to seize the northern
Ryukyu Islands.

Immediate Postwar Decades and Their Significance

Overall, the war was a disaster for Shuri. However, as is often the case in
such situations, the suffering was disproportional among social groups. Although he had to spend some time in Japan, where he was treated very well,
Shō Nei kept his throne. Most of the officials who remained loyal to Shō
Nei during the fighting enjoyed continued high status. Satsuma's generals
wanted to behead Yamazaki Nikyūshusan, who was probably the most effective general on the Ryukyuan side, but Shō Nei protested vigorously and,
as we have seen, paid a large ransom for his life. Jana Ueekata was the main
architect of Shuri's disastrous course of action and arguably lacked good
judgment. Nevertheless, he stood for his principles to the end. When it
came time for the Council of Three members to sign surrender documents,
Jana refused and lost his head as a result.

In a theme that will recur in subsequent chapters, it was ordinary people who suffered the most. Elite Okinawans in Shuri and Naha gradually
adapted to Satsuma's control and became skilled at leveraging Shuri's connections to China to create a measure of autonomy and other benefits for
themselves. However, life for most ordinary people throughout the Ryukyu
Islands became more difficult after 1609.

It is important to note that the entire Ryukyu Islands became Satsuma's
territory after the war. The northern islands came under Satsuma's direct
administration, while Okinawa and islands to the south remained within
Shuri's empire. But Shuri was no longer independent and never would be
again. Among other obligations, it paid a substantial yearly tax to Satsuma.
This and other factors explained in subsequent chapters resulted in the severe taxation of the Okinawan countryside and even more severe extractions from the southern Ryukyu Islands. Satsuma's officials levied taxes on
the northern Ryukyu Islands, and this tax burden became heavier over time.
In the nineteenth century, after sugar became the main cash crop there,
many denizens of the northern Ryukyu Islands were reduced to slavery-
like conditions.

From the standpoint of Shō Nei and his government, the immediate
postwar years were a time of confusion and anxiety. Shuri struggled with

damage control. Shō Nei and an entourage set off for Japan, where they would remain for almost three years. Nago Ueekata emerged as the leading official in Shuri, and he took charge of the government while the king was absent. Even after Shō Nei's return in 1611, the status of his throne and the Ryukyuan state in general remained unclear. Officials from Satsuma moved quickly to take control of the northern Ryukyu Islands, and, by 1611, that process was well under way. Back in Shuri, Shō Nei continued passively to resist Satsuma's demands that Ryukyu serve as an intermediary with China. He was able to do so in part because the Ming court had essentially suspended its relations with Ryukyu and in part because, if those relations were ever to be restored fully, Ryukyu would have to appear to be an independent state. I examine this complex dynamic in later chapters. During the 1630s, King Shō Hō initiated a policy of cooperating with Satsuma to pursue potentially profitable tribute trade with China. The transition from the Ming to the Qing dynasties in the 1640s created further confusion, making it hard for Satsuma to profit from Ryukyu's tribute trade.

As acting head of state, Nago Ueekata sent a message to the Chinese Board of Rites, the entity that dealt with foreign affairs. That message repeated many of the claims that Shō Nei had made in his letter. However, Nago's message stressed that Satsuma has been merciful and that Ryukyu was working hard to restore good relations with Japan. Nago's message also made the claim that the invaders had intended to continue south and capture Taiwan, but vigorous remonstrance by Ryukyuans had caused a suspension of those plans. Moreover, the threat to Taiwan would abate for the long term if Ryukyu were able to forge peaceful relations with Japan. Satsuma, of course, had no interest in invading Taiwan. In his letter, Nago was trying to convince the Chinese court that Ryukyu prevented an invasion of Taiwan and good relations between Ryukyu and Japan would ensure that no such invasion would happen in the future. It was a clever ploy, although it probably had little or no effect.[5]

The attempts by Shō Nei and, later, Nago Ueekata to reassure the Ming court do not appear to have gone well. For example, in 1612.7.7, the Fújiàn grand coordinator stated that, even though Shō Nei had returned to his country, Ryukyu was still under Japanese control. The supervising secretary of the Office of Scrutiny for War responded to the grand coordinator: "As for this Chūzan king, why in the world would he, after being spared death and released from captivity, suddenly forget the power of Japan and revere the righteousness of far-away China? . . . It is clear that Japan tells him what to do" (*Ming Veritable Records* 2001–6, 3:18 [no. 63]). These views were essentially correct, and the Ming court was wary of the situation. In 1612, it set the tribute frequency to once in ten years. After repeated entreaties by

Ryukyuan diplomats, in 1622 the frequency was changed to once every five years. Ten years later, the prewar frequency of once every two years was restored, soon to be disrupted by the decline and fall of the Ming dynasty. As we will see, during the seventeenth century, Ryukyu's government cultivated an elite group of China specialists at Kumemura. They gradually developed expertise in curating Ryukyu's image vis-à-vis China, and suspicion of Japanese control over the islands seems to have faded by the eighteenth century.

While Shō Nei was away in Japan, agents of Satsuma conducted the first systematic survey of Ryukyuan agricultural productivity. There would be others. These surveys indicate a crucial change in Ryukyuan society. Foreign trade had over the course of the sixteenth century become gradually less profitable. The war and its aftermath curtailed trade possibilities even further and isolated the Ryukyu Islands. From this point on, the Ryukyu Islands had to rely on their own resources—mainly agriculture—to survive. Specialty crops such as turmeric (*ukon*) and sugar proved to be economically valuable, and the introduction of sweet potatoes in the early seventeenth century helped stave off starvation during times of famine. Nevertheless, cereal-grain agriculture was poorly developed and would remain so, a point I revisit in subsequent chapters.

In conjunction with its initial agricultural survey, in 1611 Satsuma issued a set of directives regarding territory, authority, finances, and certain cultural matters in Ryukyu (now meaning Okinawa, nearby islands, and the southern Ryukyu Islands). In the economic realm, taxation, productivity, and related matters came to be measured in units of rice (*koku* and other measures), as was the norm throughout Japan. (One *koku* was roughly 150–60 kilograms.) Very little rice was grown in the Ryukyu Islands, but other grains such as wheat and millet and other agricultural products were converted to units of rice according to a formula. Later chapters examine taxation in more detail. Ryukyu's assessed annual productivity was 110,304 *koku*, which was roughly the size of a medium domain of a *daimyō* (warlord). Eventually, the *bakufu* recognized this productivity as part of Satsuma's total, thereby inflating Satsuma's *kokudaka* (assessed productivity).

In principle, 21,218 *koku* of Ryukyu's total—just under 20 percent—went to Satsuma as an annual tax. The actual tax burden, however, was closer to 25 percent of total productivity because the royal government also paid taxes in cloth, cowhide, and other local goods. It was common in *daimyō* domains for lands accounting for roughly 40 percent of productivity to support the lord and his family and the remainder to support his retainers. Satsuma divided Ryukyu's *kokudaka* similarly but with more going to support the royal family. Of the 89,086 *koku* remaining after what went to

Satsuma, 50,000 *koku* (56 percent) was earmarked for the royal family and the rest apportioned among titleholding elites. Should productivity exceed that amount, the excess would go to the royal family.

Notice that the fundamental framework of the postwar royal government ensured that it would always be short of resources and that it would function as a de facto oppressive force, extracting as much as possible from the farmers in Okinawa and other islands. This heavy extraction, which I examine in subsequent chapters, was one reason that no popular opposition ever developed to Japan's formal annexation of Ryukyu in 1879. In other words, most ordinary people in Ryukyu did not identify with the royal court and suffered under its governance.

During the early modern era, Satsuma gained favored access to Chinese products and intelligence via Ryukyu. This access to China became especially valuable after 1630, when Tokugawa Iemitsu (r. 1623–51) moved to regulate and restrict Japan's foreign relations. These policies are often, though problematically, called *sakoku* (closed country) by modern historians. It is important to bear in mind, however, that, in 1609 and soon thereafter, these developments of the 1630s could not have been anticipated. The immediate goal of Satsuma during the second decade of the seventeenth century was to seize the northern Ryukyu Islands and incorporate them into its administration. Satsuma's use of Shuri as a trade and information portal to China was an afterthought. Moreover, the process required several decades to mature and become viable.

Summarizing the major administrative changes in the northern Ryukyu Islands, in 1610 Satsuma's Ōshima daikan replaced Shuri's top official in Amami-Ōshima. In 1613, the title of this official, who was in charge of all the northern Ryukyu Islands, changed to Ōshima bugyō. Three years later, Satsuma established the Tokunoshima bugyō to administer Tokunoshima, Okinoerabu, and Yoron. In other words, from 1616 one *bugyō* supervised Amami-Ōshima and nearby small islands while another supervised Tokunoshima, Okinoerabu, and Yoron. In 1623, village-level officials under these *bugyō* (commissioners) were appointed from locally prominent families. According to a 1621 survey, the total productivity of the northern Ryukyu Islands was 43,257, about 40 percent of Shuri's remaining empire (Okinawa and the southern islands).

The post-1609 geopolitical situation became more complex in ways that I explore in subsequent chapters. Sixteenth-century Ryukyu is best characterized as a maritime empire, and Satsuma (the various territories of the Shimazu family) also functioned as an empire from the seventeenth century on. Kagoshima was the center of Satsuma's empire. Although the northern Ryukyu Islands were directly administered by agents from Kagoshima, they did not have quite the same status as the core Shimazu territories of Satsuma, Ōsumi, and Hyūga. Shuri was subordinate to Satsuma, and an official from Kagoshima was always present on Okinawa. However, in most routine matters, the royal government in Shuri continued to administer Okinawa and the southern Ryukyu Islands. And this whole complex of Shimazu family territories was, ultimately, subordinate to the Tokugawa *bakufu*. After 1609, Shuri's (reduced) empire was an empire within an empire, all within the larger Japanese state, itself a patchwork of shogunal land, *daimyō* domains (*han*), and other types of land (collectively, the *bakuhan* state). The most peripheral region in this complex arrangement was the southern Ryukyu Islands, and they suffered under especially severe extraction pressure. Overall, the living conditions of ordinary people outside the Naha-Shuri capital region did not improve after 1609 and often worsened.

PART THREE

THE MATURE THEATRICAL KINGDOM AND ITS COLLAPSE, 1630–1880

Early modern Ryukyu is a fascinatingly complex entity, prone to misunderstanding. One key point to bear in mind is that the modern Western-derived logic of state sovereignty (often called the Westphalian system) does not apply to the theatrical kingdom that was Ryukyu from the 1620s through the 1870s. Very briefly, all the Ryukyu Islands became the territory of Satsuma after the 1609 war, and Satsuma was a domain in Japan's so-called *baku-han* state headed by a shogun. Within this multilayered arrangement, the northern Ryukyu Islands were administered directly by Satsuma. Shuri's empire survived in the form of Okinawa, nearby islands, and the southern Ryukyu Islands, which pretended to be an independent kingdom vis-à-vis China and eventually some other countries. The officials in Kumemura who dealt with China became by the nineteenth century extraordinarily good at controlling the theatrical aspects of the Ryukyuan-Chinese relationship.

Internally, the ideological foundations of the kingdom transformed, with the king increasingly portrayed as a Confucian sage and ritually acting much like a small-scale version of a Chinese emperor. In this context, agriculture became the basis of the kingdom's economy, both rhetorically and in fact, even though the Ryukyu Islands remained a location poorly suited to agriculture. This situation, plus Satsuma's control, created a crushing burden of taxation on peasants, especially in the southern Ryukyu Islands. In the northern islands, the advent of sugar cultivation led to conditions akin to slavery by the 1830s.

The early modern era was a time of contradictions—or at least tensions—at many levels. While Ryukyu's peasantry sank deeper into poverty, among Okinawa's urban aristocrats literature, drama, music, scholarship, and other forms of high culture began to thrive. The chapters in part 3 examine post-1609 reforms by Shō Shōken and Sai On, the development of new institutions of governance and education, ideological and ritual transformations, the misery of ordinary people and the main causes of that misery, the collapse of the kingdom's economy, several aspects of high culture, approaches to portraying Ryukyu and its past, and the fascinating story of the Tametomo legend as it pertains to the Ryukyu Islands.

Written documents for the early modern era are plentiful. Therefore, researchers will want to consult major primary source collections and series such as Hateruma Eikichi's thirty-five-volume *Ryūkyū bungaku taikei* (2022) and many of the twenty-nine volumes in the Naha-shi shiminbunka-bu rekishi shiryōshitsu's *Naha-shi shi*, which includes extensive household records and other primary sources (see Naha-shi shiminbunka-bu rekishi shiryōshitsu 1966–2004). Also important are Okinawa-ken Okinawa shiryō henshūjo and Okinawa-ken Kyōiku iinkai (1981–89), Sakihama (1986), the twenty volumes in the *Ryūkyū ōkoku hyōjōsho monjo* series (Ryūkyū ōkoku hyōjōsho monjo henshū iinkai 1988–2003), the official histories, the writings of Sai On (1984), Satō (2016), and Shō Shōken (Shō Shōken 1673/1981), records of Chinese investiture envoys, and potentially many other works. The early eighteenth century was a time of vigorous academic and literary activity in Okinawa. For an analysis of this activity and authoritative modern Japanese translations of key works, see Shimaura, Okogi, and Yara (2022). For a complete record of petitions to Tokyo on behalf of the royal court during the 1870s, see Nishizato (1992b). Because primary sources are so numerous, as a practical matter I often recommend that researchers first read some of the major secondary literature on a topic, thereby learning which primary sources are relevant.

Despite a wealth of primary sources, there are still many gaps. One example is the day-to-day details regarding taxation and legal matters. Many of the sources on which scholars have relied were written during the Meiji Era by mainland officials charged with reporting on the old system in preparation for integrating Okinawa Prefecture into the rest of Japan administratively and legally. Kinjō (1903/1953) is one example, and Kurima (2022) discusses many others.

In English, my first book, *Visions of Ryukyu: Identity and Ideology in Early-Modern Thought and Politics* (1999) has held up well, although I would like to rewrite the first and last chapters to accord with my current understanding of the big picture of Ryukyuan history. That book is a close study of the ideological and practical impacts of certain forms of Confucian thought in early modern Ryukyu, especially among Shō Shōken, Tei Junsoku, and Sai On. Its bibliography includes many of the major studies of early modern Ryukyu through the mid-1990s and complements the Japanese secondary sources listed below. Several of my articles or book chapters also deal with early modern topics. Regarding the end of the kingdom, see Smits (2001, 2015a).

Regarding other work in English, Akamine (2017) provides excellent coverage of the early modern era, especially relations between China and Shuri, albeit to the exclusion of many other topics and many other parts of the Ryukyu Islands. One strength of Akamine's work is his discussion of the military situation aboard Ryukyuan ships sailing to China. Another important work in English is Edwards (2015), which is a deeply contextualized study of Okinawan musical drama. An excellent study of this topic in Japanese is Itaya (2015). Marco Tinello (see Tinello 2018, 2022) provides a detailed look at Ryukyuan foreign relations during the final decades of the kingdom.

There remains a relative dearth of quality Anglophone material on the early modern era, although it is slightly more plentiful than the material on earlier time periods. Existing literature is weighted heavily toward Ryukyuan-Chinese relations. While that is an important topic, there are many other topics of equal or greater importance still accessible only in Japanese and, therefore, less likely to be known in Anglophone academic circles. A select list of important secondary sources includes Araki (1980), Dana (1984, 1992), Fuma (1999), Harada (2003b), Harada (2017), Higa and Sakihama (1965), Kurima (2015), Matsushita (1983), Naze-shi (1996), Nishizato (1992b), Ōhama (1971), Ōishi, Takara, and Takahashi (2009), Ōyama (1996), Ryūkyū shinpōsha (1989, 1990), Takara (1989), Tinello (2018, 2022), Tomiyama (2004), and Watanabe Miki (2011, 2012). Of these works, Tomiyama (2004) is a masterpiece of detailed and thoughtful scholarship, although now slightly out of date. Complementing Tomiyama (2004) is Uehara Kenzen's detailed study of trade and economic exchanges at every level during this period (see Uehara 2016). Another leading scholar of early modern Ryukyu is Watanabe Miki, whose prolific work has won several awards. To keep up with her work and that of other scholars, see Watanabe Miki (n.d.).

[CHAPTER ELEVEN]

The Era of Shō Shōken and Sai On

Haneji Chōshū (1617–75) is commonly known as Shō Shōken (向象賢).[1] He was part of the first generation of Ryukyuan elites who received classical educations and, thus, exposure to the major works of Chinese and Japanese literature. He also came of age at a pivotal time, when elite society was still adrift following the 1609 defeat. The author of Ryukyu's first official history, he became the leading government official in the kingdom. In that capacity, he attempted a variety of reforms.

Sai On (蔡温, 1682–1762) was the son of Sai Taku (蔡鐸, 1645–1725), a prominent resident of Kumemura (O. Kuninda). Recall that Kumemura was the neighborhood in Naha where Chinese merchant-officials and some Koreans resided during the fourteenth and fifteenth centuries. As time and generations passed, Kumemura residents gradually lost their Chinese or Korean character. Moreover, because of the substantial reduction in the tribute trade during the late sixteenth century, the population of Kumemura became very sparse. Sai Taku was part of the first generation of Okinawans from outside Kumemura who, with government financial encouragement, moved to Kumemura, took Chinese names, and devoted themselves to mastering classical Chinese, Chinese poetry, and the other skills required to conduct diplomacy with China. Sai Taku and the other Okinawans who relocated to Kumemura in the seventeenth century became proficient, to varying degrees, at performing Chinese high culture. Sai On was part of the second generation of recent Kumemura transplants, and he lived at a time when the influence of Kumemura on Shuri politics was especially strong.

Sai On was Ryukyu's most radical reformer. He was a Confucian scholar with a pragmatic bent, and he approached governing and every-thing else with a thoroughgoing rationalism. He sponsored environmental and social engineering programs, agricultural reform, educational reform, and more. He was not always successful, and he made power-ful enemies. Nevertheless, the Ryukyu Kingdom attained the peak of its

224 < THE MATURE THEATRICAL KINGDOM, 1630–1880

post-1609 prosperity during the period ca. 1750–70, in part because of his activities.

Ethnogenesis

The creation of a centralized state in the sixteenth century created the possibility of ethnogenesis, the formation of an ethnic group. Ethnogenesis can come about as the result of group self-identification or because people outside a group begin to recognize it as a distinct ethnicity. The 2002 *Dictionary of the Social Sciences* defines ethnogenesis as follows: "The process by which a distinct ethnic or group identity emerges out of other, potentially diverse, identities. The concept places an emphasis on the processes of syncretism, or cultural blending, and consequently critiques the notion of authentic, unchanging cultures" (Calhoun 2002, s.v. "ethnogenesis"). With this definition in mind, consider the question, Did an ethnic group known as *Ryukyuans* exist around the year 1500? At that time, in written documents the word *Ryūkyū* meant the island of Okinawa, but let us use *Ryukyuans* in the modern sense of any resident of the Ryukyu Islands. Would ordinary people around 1500 living in, for example, Kikaijima, Okinoerabu, Kumejima, Miyako, or Ishigaki have thought of themselves as all belonging to a common ethnic or cultural group? We have encountered no indication thus far. Equally relevant, did outside people regard the residents of the various Ryukyu Islands as constituting a single ethnic or cultural group? Again, there is no evidence of such a thing in 1500 or even in 1600.

The presence of a centralized state was not sufficient to cause ethnogenesis. However, conditions that prevailed during the early modern era did result in the creation of new ethnic groups—not necessarily in terms of objective reality but in terms of people's imaginations. Importantly, ethnogenesis did not happen at the same time for all social groups and in all locations. It occurred first among the social elites of the Naha-Shuri area during the seventeenth century. Among ordinary people in Okinawa, it took place during the latter half of the nineteenth century. In the northern Ryukyu Islands, it followed its own logic, as we will see. Moreover, by the nineteenth century and possibly earlier, people in the mainland of Japan began to develop a consciousness of Ryukyuans (typically meaning Okinawans) as a distinct group. This chapter examines some of the conditions that promoted ethnogenesis among elites. Later, I survey the formation among ordinary people of geoethnic identities that extended beyond their local villages and towns.

Ryukyu (Mostly) Closed Off

One common notion about the 1609 war is that it caused the Ryukyu Islands to become part of Japan. In this thinking, prior to 1609 the Ryukyu Islands were independent of Japan, and after 1609 they were a de facto part of that state. This idea is partially accurate, but the situation was more nuanced. During the early modern era (i.e., the Tokugawa period, ca. 1600–1868), "Japan" was a collection of several hundred warlord (*daimyō*) domains with shogunal land mixed in here and there (about 20 percent of the total). The *bakufu* or shogunate was more powerful than any warlord domain, and it conducted foreign affairs in cooperation with certain domains like Satsuma and Tsushima. However, early modern Japan lacked a strong centralized state. So, yes, in 1609 the Ryukyu Islands became part of this *bakufu*-dominated geopolitical patchwork, usually called "the *bakuhan* state." However, to understand the status of the early modern Ryukyu Islands we need to examine some details (fig. 11.1).

Setting aside political boundaries, and looking simply at flows of people and culture, the Ryukyu Islands had been part of Japan since they became Japonic in the eleventh century. They were a frontier region of the main Japanese islands and, to a lesser extent, of Korea and other parts of the East China Sea region. Activity along maritime routes and major political upheavals in the East China Sea region caused migrations into different parts of the Ryukyu Islands at different times. The Ryukyu Islands were linked into the wider East China Sea region. The big difference after 1609 (or, more accurately, after about 1620) was that the islands became relatively isolated because Satsuma and the *bakufu* placed significant limits on the movement of ships and people into and out of them.

Before 1609, the Ryukyu Islands were open to Japanese ships and people, and ships from the Ryukyu Islands freely traveled to Japan. After ca. 1620, however, the Ryukyu Islands became mostly closed off from Japan. The new Shimazu overlords prohibited any Japanese from traveling there without permission. With approval, some Ryukyuans traveled to parts of Japan (usually Satsuma) to study technical subjects, and some traveled to Edo with personnel from Satsuma for diplomatic purposes. However, residents of the Ryukyu Islands were no longer free to travel to Japan or elsewhere in the region. Therefore, the free flow of people between the Japanese mainland and the Ryukyu Islands stopped early in the seventeenth century.

Defeat in war and the resulting changes rendered the older trade-based modes of economic activity mostly obsolete. Ryukyu's location was once an

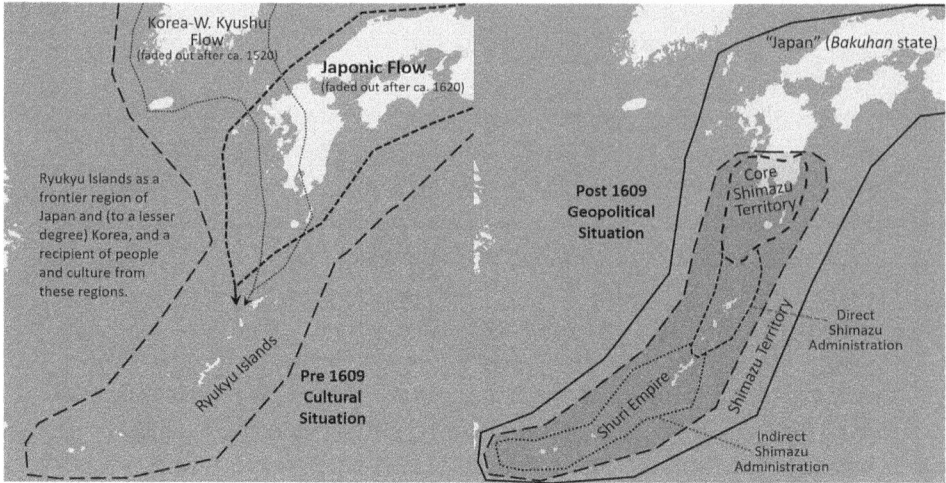

FIGURE 11.1. General flows of culture into the Ryukyu Islands
before 1609 and the geopolitical situation after 1609

economic asset, but it became a liability. More than ever before, the people
living in the Ryukyu Islands had to rely on their own knowledge, skills, and
resources. It became necessary for them to enhance their knowledge and
skills, create new resources, and make better use of available resources.
During the early modern era, leaders like Shō Shōken and Sai On determined to create new societies in the Ryukyu Islands, societies whose economic basis was agriculture.

Vis-à-vis China, the royal court at Shuri pretended that nothing significant had changed after 1609. In other words, Ryukyu posed as an independent country. Sometimes this posture required a high degree of theatrics.
For example, when Chinese investiture envoys were in Okinawa, delegations from each of the northern Ryukyu Islands would travel to Naha to
greet the Chinese party and pretend that they were subjects of the Ryukyuan
king. Before the arrival of Chinese envoys, Satsuma's official charged with
overseeing Ryukyu and his staff left the Shuri-Naha area and went into hiding so that Ryukyu would not appear connected with Japan in Chinese eyes.

Some Ryukyuans from Kumemura studied technical subjects in Fújiàn
Province or nearby areas, a smaller number studied in Beijing, and some
traveled to China as diplomats connected with the tribute trade. Significantly, during the seventeenth century, the tribute trade with China became
a net financial drain on Shuri's royal government. Select individuals in both
Okinawa and Satsuma were able to profit from the trade, but sustaining the
whole endeavor required a significant influx of money and prized goods

from Satsuma. Simply stated, Satsuma increasingly took over the financing of Ryukyu's tribute trade with China.

After 1609, the Ryukyu Islands lost their independence, but they did not become the *direct* territory of the Tokugawa shoguns or of Japan. They became the territory of the Shimazu family. Large *daimyō* such as the Shimazu sometimes parceled out parts of their territory to be administered by local retainers. Applying the classic language of European feudalism to Japan, some historians call this practice *subinfeudation*. The king in Okinawa became one of these Shimazu retainers. So far, this description may seem straightforward and easy to map out in a flowchart. In practice, however, things were not so simple as figure 11.2 suggests.

The Tokugawa *bakufu* exercised supreme authority with respect to foreign relations. In that capacity, especially after the fall of the Ming dynasty around 1644, the *bakufu* issued orders concerning Ryukyu. In other words, the *bakufu* regarded the Ryukyu Islands as part of its jurisdiction with respect to foreign policy, even though officials from Satsuma implemented the relevant *bakufu* orders. Therefore, the Ryukyu Islands were both *bakufu* territory and Shimazu territory, depending on the context. Okinawa and the southern Ryukyu Islands posed as an independent country vis-à-vis

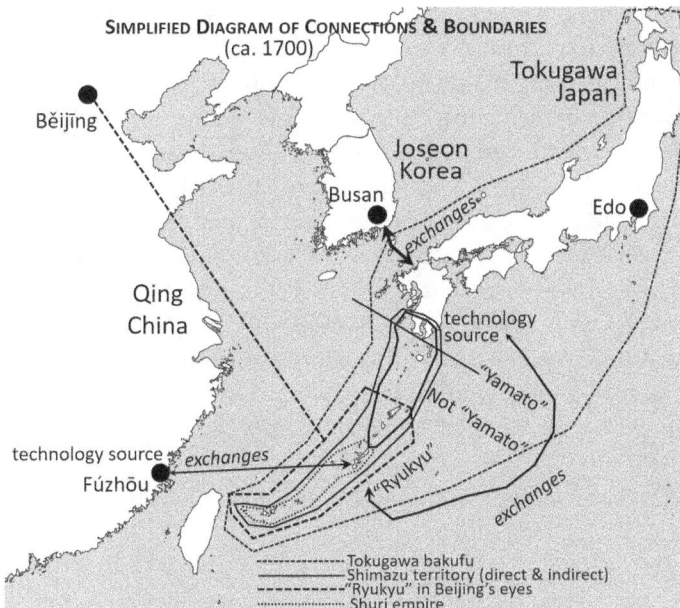

FIGURE 11.2. Diagram of the major connections and
boundaries in the East China Sea region ca. 1700

China, and, in that context, Shuri pretended that the northern Ryukyu Islands were still part of its territory. The royal government in Shuri exercised day-to-day governance over Okinawa and the southern Ryukyu Islands. The precise balance of administrative authority between Shuri and Kagoshima vis-à-vis these islands fluctuated over the years as circumstances changed (for a nuanced analysis, see Tomiyama 2004).

The Ryukyu Islands were the site of several overlapping Japanese political jurisdictions. Although exchanges were closely regulated, the Japanese mainland and China—especially southern China—functioned as sources of technological know-how (medicine, agriculture, papermaking, other manufacturing, calendar making, etc.) for Ryukyuans. Moreover, also under controlled conditions, trade took place between different Ryukyu Islands and with Kagoshima and southern China. Ultimately, some of the products Ryukyuans obtained in China ended up for sale in large Japanese markets such as Osaka. Therefore, the Ryukyu Islands continued to function as conduits of regional exchange, but the volume of exchange shrank significantly during the early modern era.

The term *Yamato* is common in *Omoro sōshi* songs and in early modern documents. Depending on the context, it could indicate Japan as a whole or the southern edge of Japan.[2] By convention, this edge was a line passing through the southern tip of the Satsuma Peninsula. When Mt. Kaimon, a volcanic peak 924 meters above sea level, came into sight aboard a northbound ship, the crew knew it had reached Yamato. In this context, *Yamato* indicated the mainland of Japan as opposed to the southern islands (Tanegashima, Yakushima, and points south). Depending on context, *Ryukyu* could mean the Ryukyu Islands, starting at Amami-Ōshima and Kikaijima, or, more commonly, the island of Okinawa. Interestingly, the Tokara and Satsunan Islands existed in an intermediate zone that was neither fully Yamato nor fully Ryukyu. It is important to keep in mind that this terminology reflects premodern and early modern concepts of geography among southern islanders and residents of southern and western Kyushu. It had no legal significance in the modern (Westphalian) sense of sovereign political boundaries. Attempts to map modern concepts onto early modern Ryukyu or Japan, or the reverse, are highly problematic.

What follows is a summary of the major interactions between the court at Shuri and other locations in the region:

1. Shuri sent regular trade/diplomatic embassies and students to China.
2. China sent periodic investiture embassies to Okinawa.

3. Shuri sent periodic diplomatic embassies to the *bakufu* in Edo (eighteen between 1634 and 1850), always accompanied by officials from Satsuma. A typical reason would be to congratulate a new shogun.
4. Via Satsuma, Shuri received periodic orders from the *bakufu* designed to calibrate its relationship with China.
5. A few Okinawans spent time in southern China or in southern Japan studying technical subjects.
6. Satsuma provided funds to Okinawans in the China-bound tribute embassies for them to purchase certain goods in China. Typically, Satsuma's officials sought to sell those goods at a profit in Osaka and other urban markets in Japan.
7. Okinawans who had been to China as part of official embassies provided information on conditions there to officials in Satsuma, who sometimes passed this information on to the *bakufu*.

Notice that, by modern standards, some of these items would seem contradictory. The early modern logic of state sovereignty and relations between states was different. For example, states did not regard each other, in principle, as equals. It was natural and normal for small states to subordinate themselves to one or more larger states.

Most survey histories refer to Ryukyu's early modern situation as one of "dual subordination" to Japan and China (*Nisshin ryōzoku* and other terms). This formulation is not entirely wrong, but it is overly simplistic because the two relationships were not symmetrical. The nature and details of each differed significantly. The key points are as follows:

1. Ryukyu's relationship with the Qing court was *instrumental* in character. Qing China was a source of potential material wealth and potentially useful technologies (e.g., know-how regarding medicine, sugar refining, shipbuilding, etc.). Crucially, the China connection allowed Ryukyu to maintain some degree of autonomy vis-à-vis Satsuma and the *bakufu* (explained in the next section).
2. Ryukyu's relationship with Japan was dual layered. The Shimazu lord was Ryukyu's immediate overlord, but the *bakufu* was the ultimate source of authority. Moreover, the interests of Satsuma and the *bakufu* did not always coincide. Therefore, Ryukyuan diplomats sometimes had to tread carefully, cooperating with Satsuma (or appearing to do so) while also appeasing (or appearing to appease) the *bakufu*. Also, if China were ever to sever its relationship with Ryukyu, there would have

been no reason for Satsuma and the *bakufu* to continue preserving the kingdom.

3. Ryukyu's relationship with the *bakufu* in particular included theatrical elements, which also enhanced the prestige of Satsuma. Ryukyuan entourages paraded through the streets of Edo in Chinese attire, with a band of musicians playing Chinese music. In other words, the Ryukyuans presented themselves as exotic foreigners during public displays in Edo and along their route to Edo.[3]

4. The higher levels of Qing officialdom do not appear ever to have taken a careful look at Ryukyu. Otherwise, the Qing court would have been aware of Ryukyu's close connections with Japan. Indeed, all Chinese investiture envoys knew of those ties with Japan, but they prudently chose not to say much about it. When the Qing court finally found out the truth in the 1870s, leading officials appear genuinely to have been shocked.

It is mainly for these reasons that I refer to the early modern Ryukyu Kingdom as a *theatrical state*. The concept of a theatrical state does a much better job of encapsulating the prevailing situation than does the standard dual subordination formulation that dominates the academic literature. To understand the theatrical state, it is necessary to appreciate that China suddenly became crucial for Ryukyu's continued survival as something other than just another Japanese domain.

China as Shuri's Lifeline

Recall Sai Taku, mentioned at the start of this chapter. In 1645, he was born into the family of Kanagusuku (金城) Peichin of Shuri. However, at age eight, he was adopted into the household of Sai Kin (蔡錦) of Kumemura. This move was part of a government policy to encourage the best and the brightest of elite urban Okinawan society to settle in Kumemura, take Chinese names, master certain aspects of Chinese high culture, and serve as diplomats to strengthen Ryukyu's ties with China. Sai Taku's many accomplishments included writing the 1701 version of *Genealogy of Chūzan* in classical Chinese.

The early modern royal government was never wealthy, but it put significant resources into reviving Kumemura as a center of Chinese expertise. The basic reason was simple. Ryukyu's ties with China became the main reason that Ryukyu remained in business as a kingdom, as opposed to becoming just another piece of Shimazu territory in the manner of the northern Ryukyu Islands. What saved the kingdom was the failure of talks between

Tokugawa Ieyasu and the Ming court in 1615. In the end, Ieyasu refused Ming demands that the shogun's court become a tributary state. With no formal diplomatic ties between the *bakufu* and the Chinese court, Ryukyu's ties to China suddenly became highly valuable.

For the *bakufu*, the Ryukyu Islands could serve as a source of direct information about China. The *bakufu* did not need the Ryukyu Islands as a source of goods from China because Chinese merchants did business in Nagasaki, a *bakufu*-controlled city. For the Shimazu, by contrast, Ryukyu's link to China was an opportunity to gain access not only to information but also to coveted Chinese goods. Because Satsuma could not appear to be competing directly with the *bakufu* economically, disposing of those goods required some care. Nevertheless, Ryukyu had the potential to bring substantial profit to Satsuma through trade with China.

However, in 1609 and for some time thereafter, relations between Ryukyu and China were at a low point. Kumemura had nearly died out, and Ryukyuans with sufficient expertise to deal with China were scarce. Long gone were the days when Chinese merchant-officials took care of all the tribute trade paperwork and details. Ryukyu badly needed people with expertise in China to ensure that the tribute trade survived and, ideally, flourished. That is why the royal court offered comparatively high stipends to promising sons of non-Kumemura elite families who would relocate to Kumemura and undertake the rigorous training needed to become proficient in Chinese high culture.

One of the most persistent misunderstandings about the Ryukyu Islands—one especially common in today's China—is that they were fundamentally Sinitic with respect to culture.[4] As we have seen repeatedly, the Ryukyu Islands are fundamentally Japonic with respect to culture, with a deep layer of Korean influence and even some Austronesian bits and pieces in the mix as well. Chinese cultural influences came to the Ryukyu Islands quite late, mostly from the late seventeenth century on. Moreover, although a few aspects of Chinese culture did spread among ordinary people, the greatest Chinese cultural impact was on the elite members of post-1609 Kumemura society, a tiny subset of the population.

Maintaining problem-free ties to China was not solely a matter of cultural expertise. Subterfuge was also necessary. It was crucial, for example, that Ryukyu's connections to Satsuma be hidden from Chinese eyes. Ryukyu had to *appear* to be an independent state even though it was not one. Moreover, it had to appear culturally distinct from Japan whenever Chinese were at hand, even though it was culturally akin to Japan. These related contradictory requirements became the basis for the mature, early modern iteration of the theatrical state.

The Theatrical State (Performing Ryukyu)

Soon after 1609, Satsuma enacted cultural policies. For example, decrees forbade Ryukyuans—even in the northern Ryukyu Islands—from taking Japanese names and wearing Japanese clothing. Later, the rules became more elaborate. For example, any Japanese written materials or material with Japanese imperial reign dates on them were to be hidden whenever Chinese investiture embassies were in Okinawa or on their way. Satsuma's official in Okinawa and his staff went into deep hiding at such times. Ryukyuan officials had to memorize stock answers to give in response to any questions by Chinese about Ryukyu's relationship with Satsuma or Japan. When Chinese investiture embassies were in Okinawa, the northern Ryukyu Islands were required to pretend that they were still part of the Ryukyu Kingdom. Each island would send a well-coached delegation to Shuri for this purpose. Incidentally, it was Shuri that initiated this practice, sending a message to Satsuma in 1626 explaining the need for it and asking for financial assistance in lodging the northern islands envoys.

Consider names. In many cases, there was no clear line between Japanese names and Ryukyuan names, especially when so many elite households in Okinawa and elsewhere traced their ancestry to different parts of Japan. Still, some examples are obvious. Before 1609, the most common male childhood name[5] in many parts of the Ryukyu Islands was Yamato or a name containing Yamato (山戸 or other characters). For example, during the war with Satsuma, one of the sons of Urasoe Ueekata slipped out of Shuri Castle after Shō Nei's surrender, continued fighting, and lost his life. His name was Mayamato (lit. "genuine Yamato"). Naturally, this custom of naming boys Yamato came to a quick end in the early seventeenth century. For the same reason, distinctively Japanese-sounding male names like Goemon, Rokubei, or Magohachi (recall Guraru Magohachi of Okinoerabu, ca. 1350–1400) faded away or never came into use.

When Ryukyuan embassies traveled to Edo to congratulate a new shogun or for some other reason, they dressed in Chinese clothing, played Chinese music, and were required to pretend in public that they could not understand Japanese. However, in private or in certain formal ceremonial occasions vis-à-vis the shogun, the envoys spoke Japanese. Notice, therefore, that a high degree of Chinese cultural expertise became necessary not only when dealing with Chinese officials either in Okinawa or in China but also when traveling to Edo. When Ryukyuan embassies set out for either China or Japan, they literally performed a certain version of Ryukyu. It was theater, and the performances were of existential importance.

This theatrical dimension was not entirely new. Since the 1370s, certain Ryukyuans performed the role of king (or royal uncle in the case of Sannan). Doing so, however, was relatively simple. The Chinese merchant-officials took care of the paperwork, and officials in China do not appear to have asked many questions. Starting with Shō Sei, the Ming (and later Qing) court began sending investiture envoys and an entourage to Okinawa. In this context of expending greater resources on the investiture process, the Ming court began to demand formal verification by Ryukyuan officials that the person claiming to be king really was widely recognized as such by other elite Okinawans. The level of performative tension increased significantly during the seventeenth century. Ryukyuan officials had to carry out directives from Satsuma while they were in China[6] but at the same time give no indication that Ryukyu was connected with Japan. It was sometimes a difficult balancing act, and there were serious lapses. In general, however, Ryukyuan elites became increasingly skilled actors in every sense.

Did all the effort to hide Ryukyu's Japanese connections from Chinese eyes succeed? No. Japanese culture was so pervasive that Chinese investiture officials realized Ryukyu was closely connected with Japan. However, they do not appear to have known—or tried to know—the details. For example, they usually noted the cultural influence of Japan, but they were not aware of a specific connection between Ryukyu and Satsuma. These officials held a relatively low rank at the Chinese court, and they probably realized the importance of being prudent for the sake of career advancement. They were aware of a Japanese cultural presence and possibly more, but they chose to look away and make no serious inquiries.

As Ryukyuan officials adapted to the early modern situation, they became increasingly skilled at using Ryukyu's China connection to extract concessions from Satsuma, particularly in the financial realm. By the nineteenth century, Ryukyu's tribute trade was funded almost entirely by Satsuma. At the state-to-state level, it was a money-losing enterprise, but elite Ryukyuans and well-placed merchants and officials in Satsuma profited from the extensive private trade that took place in connection with tribute embassies.

What about the broader question of the status of the Ryukyuan state during the early modern era? First, it was not an independent state. This point should be obvious to readers of these pages, but journalists or others with a superficial understanding of history sometimes characterize early modern Ryukyu as an independent country. In China, it has gradually become the norm to claim, on the basis of their participation in the tribute system, that the Ryukyu Islands were Chinese territory. This is an inaccurate portrayal of the nature of the tribute trade, but it was prompted by geopolitical concerns and rising Chinese power (see the final chapter).

The early modern Ryukyu Kingdom was not independent, but it was substantially autonomous with respect to domestic matters. It issued laws and regulations, maintained police and judicial organs, taxed its territories heavily, maintained written records, performed ceremonies of state, regulated forest resources, and generally did all the things a typical state at the time would do. In this sense, the Ryukyuan state was much like a domain government in Japan, except that it was part of and paid taxes to a larger domain government. All the functions of government that Shuri carried out could have been carried out by Satsuma's own organs of state. For reasons we have seen, however, it was essential that Ryukyu appear to function as an independent state to maintain its valuable ties with China.

A Time of Firsts

From the late seventeenth century on, Shuri's royal government made several attempts to create new communities within its territories for better economic efficiency. This process included the creation of new villages or the consolidation or rearranging of others. It also involved adapting new technologies; changing or attempting to change customary practices, laws, and procedures; and sometimes creating new institutions. Reading through *Kyūyō* provides a good sense of the nature and pace of social change. It is striking how many entries from around 1650 on begin with or include the phrase *for the first time*. Starting with the reign of Shō Shitsu, and going through the reign of Shō Kei (thus including Shō Shōken and Sai On), here is a long but partial list of these firsts in chronological order that provides a sense of this phenomenon (especially important or interesting items are flagged by an asterisk):

SHŌ SHITSU (1648–68)

An official in charge of banana fiber cloth is established.*
The practice of the tea ceremony (*sadō*) is (re)established.
Festivities by the mourners at funerals are discouraged.
Members of rural households are prohibited from relocating to Naha,
    Shuri, Kumemura, or Tomari.*
An official known as the *head envoy* is created.
People of *aji* status are permitted to wear gold hairpins.

Royal government officials at Ōgusuku and Taketomi in the Yaeyama
Islands are established.

A mortuary area at the temple Kōtokuji is established.

An official is put in charge of sugar.*

It is decided that the crown prince and his younger brothers will visit the
court on the first and fifteenth days of the month.

Brothers of the king are permitted to take the king's place in offering
incense at mausoleums or shrines.

The study of medicine is established in Miyako Island.*

A forestry official is established in the Nakagami region.*

Officials promoted to positions in Miyako or Yaeyama must give formal
thanks on accepting.

Mourning attire is standardized.

A blacksmith is established in each county at government expense.*

Trees are cultivated in Wakasa.

The various officials are divided into status ranks.

SHŌ TEI (1669–1709)

Officials in charge of forestry, stone working, and iron work are permitted
to wear knotted sleeves.

The manner of worship at the mausoleum at Sōgenji is established.

An official in charge of tools is established.*

Buddhist priests are required to pay new year respects to the royal court.

Shuku Aiden went to Fújiàn to study artillery methods.*

The post of secretary for the Monobugyō (a major government division) is
established.

Three-axle sugar-refining machinery is established in several locations.*

A Confucian temple is established in Kumemura.*

It is decided which officials will be dispatched to Chinen, Tamagusuku,
and Kudakajima (for the performance of rituals).

The practice of the king and the high priestess worshipping at sacred
groves (in Kudakajima) is revised such that a royal representative takes
the king's place.*

The queen becomes high priestess (not the king's sister).*

The royal kitchen is established.

It is determined that the king and crown prince will visit the Confucian
temple during the first two days of the new year.*

A forestry official is established in Kunigami.*

Tei Meiryō goes to Fújiàn to study the method of facial physiognomy.

A secretary is added to the office of roof tile commissioner.

(There are several entries about government posts being eliminated.)

Surnames are bestowed on local officials.

The position of head of Kumemura is established.

Those who have recently established their credentials for noble lineages are allotted copper or silver hairpins.*

Winter and summer attire for officials and the common people is established.

Six people are established as secretaries to the Hyōjōsho (the supreme council).

Two forestry commissioners are established.*

Black ink squares are manufactured in Ōmine in Naha.*

An emergency storehouse is created and stocked with rice and (copper) cash.

REIGN OF SHŌ KEI (1713–52)

Council of Three Members rotate their duties and use individual seals for official business.

Inkstones are manufactured in Wakasa.*

A master physician and his assistants make rounds of the royal palace.

Lanterns and umbrellas are manufactured at Asato (in Shuri).*

Gunpowder is stored in the stone vault at Omonogusuku.*

Posthumous portraits of all previous kings are hung.*

The names of people from the various districts (= rural areas) are prohibited from being entered into the household registers of the residents of Shuri, Naha, Tomari, and Kumemura.*

Shō Juyū (= Tamagusuku Chōkun) is ordered to take matters that happened in the country and make them into stage drama.*[7]

All noble households are required to revise their household records (kafu) once every five years.

Six junior inspectors are appointed and charged with improving (people's) customs (= behavior).*

Silver objects are manufactured in Tomari.*

Members of noble households are permitted to pursue occupations as painters, chefs, and skilled craftsmen.*

The king orders Bu Jiyū to build irrigation ditches in southern Okinawa to bring water from springs and rivers to farmers' fields.*

The Blacksmith Bureau begins making (horse) bits and related hardware.*

Two field officers of the rice commissioner are added.*

Vermilion (dye or ink) begins to be manufactured in Naha.*

The royal mausoleum is changed to the great hall at Enkakuji.

People in rural areas are prohibited from becoming government officials.

Offering liquor before the Buddhas is prohibited.

Constructing tombs below the facilities for praying for rain in Kinjō is
    prohibited.*[8]

(There are several entries about eliminating various official government
    positions.)

Sai Kōbo manufactures charcoal.*

Maaran ships are built in Kumejima.*

The use of torture when questioning (suspects) of noble rank is halted.*

The formation of mutual aid societies (moai) has benefited the
    (impoverished) nobility.*

Forestry commissioners are established in every locality.*

The construction of kaisen (large ships) is planned.*

An agency to maintain and observe the water clock is established with six
    staff members.*

The position of classical Chinese compiler is established in Kumemura.

Six physicians are placed in the palace.*

Ash powder is applied to the castle walls to defend against burglars.*

Physicians are sent to Miyako and Yaeyama to treat disease.*

Many of the first-time entries are about the creation, consolidation,
or elimination of administrative territories, usually villages or counties
(gun). I have not included those kinds of entries in the list offered above.
Another common category is matters of ceremony and propriety. These
include who worships at which shrine at what times and in which manner, who is permitted to wear certain types of clothing, who participates
in certain ceremonies, which kinds of officials belong to which court ranks,
and so forth. I have included only a few of these types of entries as examples. Let us now arrange the items asterisked in the list offered above into
categories:

REGULATION AND ENCOURAGEMENT OF AGRICULTURE

The study of medicine is established in Miyako Island.

An official in charge of banana fiber cloth is established.

Members of rural households are prohibited from relocating to Naha,
    Shuri, Kumemura, or Tomari.

An official is put in charge of sugar.

A blacksmith is established in each county at government expense.

An official in charge of tools is established.

Three-axle sugar-refining machinery established in several locations.

The king orders Bu Jiyū to build irrigation ditches in southern Okinawa to
  bring water from springs and rivers to farmers' fields.
The names of people from the various districts (= rural areas) are
  prohibited from being entered into the household registers of the
  residents of Shuri, Naha, Tomari, and Kumemura.
Two field officers of the rice commissioner are added.
Physicians are sent to Miyako and Yaeyama to treat disease.

Although it might not be obvious at first glance, all the items listed above
are related to agriculture. One of the great challenges for the royal government during the early modern era was to create an agricultural society amid
the wreckage of the previous trading society. Whether that project ever succeeded is debatable because most parts of the Ryukyu Islands are poorly
suited to the production of cereal grains such as rice, barley, and millet.[9]
The items concerning the study of medicine in Miyako and the dispatching of physicians to Yaeyama also pertain to agricultural productivity. A severe and often deadly form of malaria was endemic to the southern Ryukyu
Islands, and those islands became a major source of food production for
Shuri (rice and other grains from the southern Ryukyu Islands went to Okinawa). Shuri levied heavy taxes on the southern islands (discussed in the
next chapter), and, therefore, it was in Shuri's financial interest to maintain
as large and as healthy a population there as possible.

Infrastructure improvements, such as irrigation ditches, played an important role, as did the appointment of officials to oversee different aspects
of agriculture. The items about blacksmith facilities and tools are also part of
the agricultural infrastructure. Life in the countryside was severe, and people in rural villages sought to leave their farms for urban areas. To maintain a
population of laborers in the countryside, the royal government prohibited
rural dwellers from migrating to Okinawa's main urban area (the capital
region of Shuri, Naha, Tomari, and Kumemura). Finally, in the seventeenth
century, sugar became established as a cash crop. The royal government
monopolized sugar production, and sugar became a major source of revenue as time went on. It was also a tax crop, and, by the eighteenth century,
approximately 60 percent of Shuri's tax revenue from Okinawa came in the
form of brown sugar and turmeric (as measured in silver).

REGULATION AND ENCOURAGEMENT OF FOREST
RESOURCES AND SHIPBUILDING

A forestry official is established in the Nakagami region.
A forestry official is established in Kunigami.

Two forestry commissioners are established.
Forestry commissioners are established in every locality.
Maaran ships are built in Kumejima.
The construction of *kaisen* (large ships) is planned.

The thick forests of northern Okinawa were a vital resource of the lumber needed for the construction of government buildings (e.g., most of Shuri Castle burned down in 1709) and for shipbuilding. However, until the early modern era, there had been no government regulation of forest lands, and, by the early eighteenth century, forest resources had become badly depleted. Although forest regulation predates him, Sai On made especially vigorous and successful efforts to conserve and nurture forests.

One effect of the Ming policy of providing ships for the tribute trade was that, except perhaps in Miyako, shipbuilding in the Ryukyu Islands died out.[10] During Sai On's era, shipbuilding returned. Ryukyuans studied shipbuilding in Fújiàn, and forestry conservation policies ensured a supply of lumber. Maaran ships were of medium size and typically served to transport people and goods (especially tax goods) between different islands. *Kaisen* (楷船) were large, although not as large as typical Chinese ships. They were suitable for tribute embassies and for sailing to Kagoshima.

ADDRESSING POVERTY AMONG THE NOBILITY

Black ink squares are manufactured in Ōmine in Naha.
Inkstones are manufactured in Wakasa.
Silver objects are manufactured in Tomari.
Members of noble households are permitted to pursue occupations as
    painters, chefs, and craftsmen.
The Blacksmith Bureau begins making (horse) bits and related hardware.
Vermilion (dye or ink) begins to be manufactured in Naha.
Lanterns and umbrellas are manufactured at Asato (in Shuri).
Sai Kōbo manufactures charcoal.
The formation of mutual aid societies (*moai*) has benefited the
    (impoverished) nobility.

During the late seventeenth century and into the early eighteenth, the government in Shuri created a formal nobility from the ranks of urban dwellers. Families whose past members included government officials (anyone who had received a formal appointment document) during the sixteenth century or earlier submitted genealogies and relevant documents to a central office for vetting and approval. The formalization of the ranks of the nobility was part of a broad trend to standardize society in as many ways as possible.

Having created a formal nobility, the royal government and the nobles faced a new problem: poverty. There were too few government jobs to employ all the nobles, and, indeed, many *Kyūyō* entries from this era are about cutbacks in government positions. Sai On attacked this problem head-on. First, he encouraged the creation of new types of skilled manufacturing. Next, he permitted and encouraged nobles to work in such industries or as skilled craftsmen. Customarily, nobles worked only as government officials, and that was the ideal situation in classical Confucian-inspired thinking. However, Ryukyu simply could not afford to employ all or even most nobles as government officials. Instead, Sai On stressed the value of productive work itself as a virtue. Eventually, he created a program to relocate impoverished nobles to the countryside. There, they created nobles-only farming villages (called *yaadui*). Mutual aid societies were another innovation of this era. They spread to ordinary people and still exist today.

CHANGING THE IDEOLOGICAL BASIS OF ROYAL AUTHORITY AND OF SOCIETY

A Confucian temple is established in Kumemura.

The practice of the king and the high priestess worshipping at sacred groves (in Kudakajima) is revised such that a royal representative takes the king's place.

The queen becomes high priestess (not the king's sister).

It is determined that the king and crown prince will visit the Confucian temple during the first two days of the new year.

Posthumous portraits of all previous kings are hung.

Constructing tombs below the facilities for praying for rain in Kinjō is prohibited.

An agency to maintain and observe the water clock is established with six staff members.

Six physicians are placed in the palace.

Shō Juyū (= Tamagusuku Chōkun) is ordered to take matters that happened in the country and make them into stage drama.

Six junior inspectors are appointed and charged with improving (people's) customs (= behavior).

Both Shō Shōken and Sai On had formal training in the body of learning we commonly call *Confucianism*.[11] Typically, they did not publicly criticize the older solar ideology and religious practices based on the transmission of power (*seji*) to male rulers by priestesses. However, they worked structurally to undermine such ideas and practices and to refashion kings as Confucian sages. Sai On especially also endeavored to reform society and customary behavior, something we might call *Confucian social engineering*. His success in this realm was limited.

Shō Shōken was embarrassed at the custom of the king personally traveling to Kudakajima to worship there in a manner subordinate to the high priestess. He managed to alter the practice in the name of the king's safety. Instead, a representative went to Kudakajima in place of the king. Moreover, the high priestess changed from having been one of the king's sisters to being his primary wife, that is, the queen. The move severed the *onarigami* (sister-as-protector) connection. The notion that sisters possessed protective spiritual power vis-à-vis their brothers was something many Confucian reformers would have regarded as a baseless belief unmoored from the rational laws of nature.

The establishment of a Confucian temple in Kumemura was a major change, and a formal visit there by the king during the new year was of symbolic importance. The king, in effect, acknowledged Confucian principles as the basis of royal authority and elite society. Ryukyuans of all social strata relied heavily on magic or sorcery for the treatment of disease and much else. Sai On encouraged people to rely on properly trained physicians instead, although it is unlikely that many Ryukyuans abandoned traditional practices. One example of superstitions practices that Sai On sought to combat was the belief that noble bones attract rain. That is the reason for the prohibition of elite grave sites near the place where the king formally prayed for rain, although Sai On justified the move in terms of hygiene.[12] More broadly, Sai On sought to regulate the workings of society, which is one reason he placed great importance on measuring time accurately.

Another manifestation of Confucian ideology was the creation of a dramatic art form known as *kumiodori* (組踊). Recall that, to a large extent, the narratives in the official histories took the form of a Chinese-style morality play. With state encouragement, Dance Commissioner (*odori bugyō*) Tamagusuku Chōkun (玉城朝薫, 1684–1734) selected episodes from Ryukyu's past as described in the official histories that were morally uplifting. A student of *nō* and other forms of Japanese drama, Tamagusuku turned the episodes into stage drama. Who was the primary audience? Visiting Chinese investiture envoys, who were routinely entertained by *kumiodori* performances as well as other forms of stage drama. *Kumiodori* is a literal example of performing a certain version of Ryukyu for outside consumption.

STATE-SANCTIONED VIOLENCE

Shuku Aiden goes to Fújiàn to study artillery methods.
Gunpowder is stored in the stone vault at Omonogusuku.
Ash powder is applied to the castle walls to defend against burglars.
The use of torture when questioning (suspects) of noble rank is halted.

After 1609, the *hiki* system faded away, but Shuri still maintained some military capabilities. The main reason for this was pirates, who infested the China coast throughout the early modern era. Ryukyuan ships sailing to China were armed, and the crews underwent military training prior to departure. A high level of readiness against potential pirate attack was also required when Chinese investiture envoys sailed for Naha. *Kyūyō* passages provide detailed accounts of naval battles with pirates, and they inevitably describe Ryukyuan crews as fighting valiantly. Even taking such descriptions with a grain of salt, it is certain that pirate attacks remained an ongoing problem and that Ryukyuan crews sometimes found themselves in serious battles.

The government also maintained police officials, and crime of various degrees of severity was always present. Theft was most common, at least according to existing records. The era of Shō Shōken and Sai On saw a number of significant judicial reforms. For example, the government officially took a position of skepticism regarding accusations of sorcery, although, technically, sorcery remained a crime. High-ranking officials were generally free to speak their minds in deliberative situations. Once a decision had been made, however, opposing it could lead to serious repercussions. If, indeed, the use of torture on elites did stop during the eighteenth century, it seems to have made a return later. Several prominent members of Kumemura, for example, faced torture in connection with the 1797 *Kanshō sōdō* (官生騒動) (examined in a later chapter). Early modern Ryukyu may have been a theatrical state, but its government carried out all the usual state functions, including violence.

Importance of the Ming-Qing Transition

The Ming dynasty fell in 1644, giving way to the militarily powerful Manchu Qing dynasty. Concerned that severing the Ryukyu-China trade connection might invite trouble, the *bakufu* decreed that Ryukyu should continue trade and other activities with China as before. In 1663, the Qing Kāngxī emperor sent envoys to invest Shō Shitsu, who had been on the throne since 1648. On the surface, Ryukyuan-Chinese relations looked the same, but the Ming-to-Qing transition changed the international context in ways that had an impact on Ryukyu. For example, it caused Ryukyu's connection with Japan's *bakuhan* state to move in the direction of greater concealment. A second change was that the *bakufu* developed a more conspicuous sense of Ryukyu as its protectorate. For example, in 1670, pirates based in Taiwan and loyal to Zhèng Jīng[13] attacked and severely damaged a Ryukyuan tribute ship off the coast of China. On discovering this matter, *bakufu* officials in Nagasaki extracted three hundred *kanme* of silver as a fine from vessels under Zhèng's command and sent the money to Ryukyu. (One *kanme* is equivalent to approximately 3.75 kilograms.) In 1671, the *bakufu* explained to Holland that Ryukyu belongs to Japan and prohibited any piratical activity against Ryukyuan vessels.

Note again the sense of paradox, at least by modern reckoning. Vis-à-vis the Qing dynasty, the *bakufu* (with cooperation from Satsuma and Ryukyu) kept Ryukyu's relationship with Japan concealed. Vis-à-vis Holland, however, and more generally, the *bakufu* asserted dominion over the Ryukyu Islands. It is important to keep two points in mind regarding this situation. First, Ryukyu was badly defeated in its war with Satsuma in 1609. One result of the war was Ryukyu's subordination to Satsuma and, therefore, to the *bakufu* as well. Second, modern notions of state sovereignty do not apply very well either to China's tributary system (e.g., it would be absurd to claim that Korea was Chinese territory on the grounds that Korea had long been a tributary state) or to the *bakufu*'s similarly designed system of foreign relations. Sorting out state boundaries took place during the 1870s and 1880s, after modern Western notions of sovereignty began to influence regional statecraft.

Shō Shōken (Haneji Chōshū)

In 1663, Shō Shitsu was the first king to receive Qing investiture. The next year, he dispatched to China the Council of Three member Chatan Chōhō as Envoy of Gratitude and Eso Jūkō as Envoy of Congratulations. Their cargo included a precious gold wine jar provided by Satsuma as a gift to the emperor. The events that became the Chatan-Eso incident of 1664 are complex in their details. The gist of the matter is that Ryukyuans dressed as Chinese pirates attacked Chatan and Eso's vessel, almost certainly with prior knowledge by some members of the crew. The incident involved theft, poisoning, blackmail, and the murder of some of the crew by other Okinawans. The jar and much of the cargo were lost. Among other things,

Satsuma ordered Chatan and Eso executed and their families banished to remote locations. The incident caused the downfall of the Council of Three member Kanegusuku Ryōsei as well as Prime Minister (*sessei*, O. *shisshii*, 摂政)[14] Gushikawa Chōei. In the aftermath of this debacle, Shō Shōken became prime minister in 1666.

After *bakufu*-Ming negotiations broke down, Satsuma took over direct management of Ryukyu's tribute trade. Satsuma's officials bet on the profitability of trade with China via Ryukyu, but, even as late as the mid-1660s, things had not gone very well. Stubborn refusal to cooperate on the part of many Okinawans (e.g., the Chatan-Eso incident) combined with poor trade conditions during the protracted Ming-to-Qing transition brought Satsuma to the verge of bankruptcy. One effect was that Satsuma restored the authority to direct the tribute trade to Shuri's royal government. At that time, however, the sugar monopoly was in its early stages, and the royal government had no major source of revenue other than trade with China. Therefore, it could not afford to conduct this trade without continued backing from Satsuma.

Shō Shōken saw that large areas of Ryukyuan society had been in decline since 1609. Clearly, major reforms in society and government were needed, reforms similar to those Satsuma had recently carried out in Kyushu. It was as if the Ming-to-Qing transition functioned as a wake-up call. The world was changing, and it was necessary to adapt. Shō Shōken had the full backing of Satsuma, and the Chatan-Eso incident cleared away many of his potential rivals within the government.

We can divide Shō Shōken's reforms into two broad categories. First was reorganizing the structures of authority and, concomitantly, reorganizing the formal aspects of official office holding such as perks, costume, ranks, rituals, etc. These reforms disrupted or ended customs that had long prevailed at the royal court. Shō Shōken insisted on a clear distinction between private matters within the royal palace and public matters of state. Among other things, he reformed (by greatly reducing) long-standing gift-giving customs. One other move regarding reorganizing the structures of authority was that, along with the Council of Three, he decreed that henceforth all government officials must meet minimum qualifications with respect to practical and cultural knowledge. Specifically, they must possess writing and equestrian skills and be conversant with the literary arts, arithmetic, Chinese music, calligraphy, Okinawan music, medicine, the culinary arts, protocol, the tea ceremony, and flower arrangement. Whether this decree was rigorously enforced we do not know. In any case, this list is a good snapshot of the ideal skills and knowledge that members of the Ryukyuan nobility should possess as of the late seventeenth century.

Second, Shō Shōken reformed and stabilized the royal finances in four respects. First, he revived the tribute trade by arranging to have two ships sent with each embassy (the tribute ship and its escort) and by investing money borrowed from Satsuma. Next, he made the production of sugar, turmeric,[15] and other specialty products a royal monopoly. Third, he adjusted the agricultural base to broaden the tax base. He encouraged bringing more land under cultivation by reducing corvée labor service requirements, thus affording farmers more time and energy to cultivate. Specifically, he tried to make conditions favorable for small farmers by reining in abuses by local officials. He required that that peasant laborers be compensated, and he prohibited local officials from requisitioning goods on the spot or loaning money at high interest rates. Closely related, the fourth aspect of his financial reforms was strengthening central government control over localities and, thus, curbing local abuses. In Okinawa, villages were combined or split as needed to reorganize districts. Vis-à-vis the southern Ryukyu Islands, there was an effort for Shuri to assert more direct control instead of going through intermediaries, who inevitably took a cut for their work.

Such aggressive encouragement of opening new farmland may seem like an obviously good idea. However, major changes in land use almost always lead to unintended consequences. The push to bring more land into cultivation reduced the land available for gathering grass or cutting trees for fuel, and it worsened soil erosion problems. For these reasons, in 1689, the government prohibited further land reclamation. This inherent limiting dynamic with respect to harvest sizes (more land reclamation leads to greater problems with fuel and erosion) was something from which small-scale island societies like Okinawa or the other Ryukyu Islands could not escape.

Another problem was that the labor force in the countryside was often too small even to work existing land effectively. As the agricultural population moved about, households became less productive or even collapsed as peasants absconded from villages. Regulations in 1697 acknowledged that sometimes it was necessary for farmers to sell their labor in villages other than their own but decreed that, henceforth, such activities must occur only within one's district (*magiri*). The regulations also prohibited rural people from relocating to Shuri, Naha, or Tomari. Reclaimed land became the object of buying and selling, and the increased frequency with which peasants sold their labor elsewhere suggests that a cash economy was beginning to operate in the countryside. (Scholars have debated the extent to which the early modern domestic economy became monetized, with some arguing that cash circulated only in the Shuri-Naha urban area.) A great famine in 1709, which killed roughly three thousand people in Okinawa, highlighted Ryukyu's problems with agriculture.

Sai On

Sai On's major activities coincided with King Shō Kei's reign. The relationship between these two men was outstanding, each working in complementary ways toward the same goals. Sai On promoted infrastructure improvement and policies aimed, at least in his mind, at the rational reorganization of society at many levels, from the landscape to people's behavior. In addition to being an aggressive politician, Sai On was a scholar. In his later years, he became a prolific writer, penning some works of practical guidance for government officials and some of a more scholarly or philosophical nature. In the interest of brevity, here I examine only a few of his activities as a reformer (for more details, see Smits 1999).

Sai On had a deep appreciation for the circulation of commodities and the capacity of demand to stimulate production. One aspect of his economic policies was to eliminate or reduce barriers to commerce and occupational restrictions. The best example is the policy of encouraging crafts and manufacturing enterprises in the Naha area as employment opportunities for nobles who were not employed as government officials. In general, during the eighteenth century there was a tendency among Confucian thinkers throughout East Asia to appreciate the positive power of economic markets.[16] Sai On was part of this trend, and he was aware of some of the social and economic reforms taking place in Japan and China.

That said, however, Sai On was not a libertarian. He was greatly concerned with attempting to regulate personal behavior, and he never lost an opportunity to rail against consuming alcoholic beverages. He promoted policies to extract more work from peasants, and, although he was generally not successful, he pressed the government to outlaw what he regarded as superstitious practices. During his time in office, and for some time thereafter, it was common for the central government to force people in the countryside to relocate to enhance the efficiency of agricultural production. Sometimes these relocations involved great distances. While these relocations were rational in some sense, they came at a great cost in human suffering. The most notorious example was the forced relocation of people from Okinawa to Yaeyama. Although it is unclear whether Sai On personally ordered such relocations, they took place while he was in power, so he must have known about and approved them.

Another of Sai On's policies—one that was generally effective—was to create a system of forest management extending throughout the Ryukyu Islands. The system used local incentives as leverage to gain the cooperation of ordinary people. Ryukyu's forests began to flourish, and the tall,

FIGURE 11.3. Sai On pines in northern Okinawa in 1989 (photographs by the author)

impressive stands of pines that resulted from his polices are called *Sai On narabi matsu* (Sai On pines; see fig. 11.3). Sai On also sponsored major environmental engineering projects for flood control and irrigation.

On balance, Sai On's policies delayed the economic collapse of society but made him many enemies. During his lifetime, Sai On was able to keep these enemies at bay, but, after his death, clashes between proponents and opponents of his ideas disrupted elite society. By the mid-nineteenth century, Ryukyuan society had become desperately poor and was on the verge of collapse. This situation is one reason that, when the kingdom fell in 1879, only its officials mourned.

POPULATION, PRODUCTIVITY, TRADE, AND FINANCES

According to the Kanbun survey of 1637, there were 54,400 men in Ryukyu (Okinawa and the southern Ryukyu Islands) and 57,196 women, for a total population of 111,596. Sai On estimated the population of Ryukyu to have been 200,000 ca. 1716, although that was probably on the high side. In 1879, the population was 310,540. Today, the population of all the Ryukyu Islands combined is about 1.5 million.

A survey in 1612 of all Satsuma's territory revealed a total agricultural productivity of 7,132,157 *koku* for Satsuma, Hyūga, Ōsumi, and Ryukyu. (Again, one *koku* was roughly 150–60 kilograms.) Ryukyu's productivity was 113,101 *koku*, a tiny fraction. According to a 1634 survey, this figure was down to just under 95,000 *koku*, rising to nearly 124,000 *koku* in 1726. Sai On's policies undoubtedly increased productivity to some degree, but, unfortunately, we do not have survey data for the late eighteenth century. The 1634 figures for the specific islands in *koku*, indicating the relative productivity of each, are as follows (notice that, after Okinawa, the Miyako and Yaeyama island groups were the second- and third-highest producers in relative terms; much of the grain they produced ended up in Okinawa as tax): Izena, 771; Ie, 3,777; Okinawa, 65,539; Kerama, 210; Tonaki, 47; Aguni, 754; Kumejima, 3,813; Miyako, 12,917; and Yaeyama, 6,801. From a 1728 document called *gozaisei* (御財政), we know that the main sources of royal government silver revenue were sugar (437+ *kanme*) and turmeric (256+ *kanme*), totaling about 60 percent. Other sources of silver included high-quality cloth (*Ryūkyū jōfu*, 琉球上布), *awamori* (white liquor), *kaininsō* (seaweed, 海人草), indigo, and *hazeyu* (similar to soy sauce, 櫨油). Sugar was the most important commodity.

Peasants were required to send all sugar they produced to Shuri as tax. Ryukyuan sugar was sold to select merchants in Satsuma for cash. Ryukyuan officials in Kagoshima typically used much or most of this cash to purchase commodities, usually through the same merchants to whom they sold the sugar. Most of whatever cash remained went into a government store-house in Shuri. The sugar sold in Satsuma was shipped to Japan's Inland Sea ports or to the Kyoto market or Osaka. Kyoto was also the main market for turmeric.

Trade with China and Japan remained essential for Ryukyu. During the early modern era, however, the items bound for the Japanese market were mainly certain specialized agricultural products from Ryukyu, an indication of an increase in domestic production capabilities. Many of the products—and the cash obtained by trading in Japanese markets—found their way indirectly to China via the tribute trade. Economically, the *bakufu*, Satsuma, and Ryukyu became ever more tightly connected as the early modern era went on.

In 1683, the lifting of Qing restrictions on trade with Japan resulted in a vast increase in Chinese ships coming to Nagasaki and a vast outflow of silver from Japan to China. In response, in 1685, the *bakufu* ended its earlier policy of free trade at Nagasaki and implemented a more restrictive set of rules. Significantly, these restrictions applied to both Nagasaki and Ryukyu. Notice again that the *bakufu* regarded Ryukyu as territory that it was willing to regulate. Although the *bakufu* tried to cover Nagasaki and Ryukyu with the same net of control, in practice conditions in Ryukyu were different. For example, in the wake of currency debasements during the late seventeenth century and the early eighteenth, the *bakufu* granted Satsuma permission to mint silver coins of original purity for trade purposes. Moreover, certain marine food products increasingly made their way from Japanese markets to Ryukyu for export to China.[17] As time went on, Satsuma gained the upper hand vis-à-vis the *bakufu* regarding control of Ryukyu-connected trade.

The Nobility

We have seen that, during the early modern era, the royal government created a formal class of nobles. This group was called *yukatchu* (lit. "good people," 良人) and by other names, including *samuree* (from *samurai*). Nobles possessed household records (*kafu*, 家譜), copies of which were held by a central government office. Members of the nobility received formal court rank, modeled after the classic Japanese system of ten ranks, each divided into senior and junior. These ranks corresponded to formal titles such as *aji* (按司), *ueekata* (親方), *peichin* (親雲上), *satonushi* (里之子), and *chikudun* (筑登之). It was possible for wealthy urban commoners to purchase noble status. Such people were called *shinzanshi* (新参士) in documents, and they typically lacked formal court rank. Although it does not cover every possibility, table 11.1 summarizes the relationship between status, title, court rank, official positions, and several other variables.

There was a strong linkage between urban residence and noble status. Because local government officials did not live in the capital region, they were not members of the nobility. The titles of local officials were (in descending order): *jitōdai* (地頭代), *bujitō* (夫地頭), *sabakuri* (捌理), and *tikugu* (文子). (*Sabakuri* was subdivided into four titles and *tikugu* into numerous titles.) Even *jitōdai* were commoners. However, because they supervised entire districts (*magiri*), while in office they were given the relatively lofty title *peichin*.

Final Remarks

This chapter surveys some of the major changes that took place in the Ryukyu Islands during the seventeenth and eighteenth centuries. These changes occurred within the broader context of major changes in the East China Sea region, especially the fall of the Ming dynasty in China and the establishment of the *bakuhan* system in Japan. Notice that, even though early modern Ryukyu was a vastly different place compared with previous iterations of Ryukyu, the general point about regional political upheavals affecting the islands still holds. One important difference is that the Ryukyu Islands had become comparatively isolated insofar as unrestricted movement of people between the islands and Japan (and other countries) was

TABLE 11.1. Status ranks, titles, official offices, accoutrements, and territory of the Shuri and Kumemura nobility during the early modern era

Status	Title	Rank	Office	Kumemura	Hairpin	Cap	Territory
Royal family	Prince (王子)	N.a.	Prince (王子)	N.a.	Gold (金簪)	Red base floating 5-color weave	Aji jitō (按司地頭) (one district)
	Aji (按司)	N.a.	Aji (按司)	N.a.	Gold (金簪)	Red base floating 5-color weave / Yellow base floating 5-color weave	Aji jitō (按司地頭) (one district)
	Ueekata (親方)	Senior First	Purple floating weave Council of Three (紫地浮織三司官)	N.a.	Gold	Purple base floating 5-color weave	Full jitō (総地頭) (one district)
		Junior First	Council of Three (三司官)	N.a.	Gold	Blue base floating 5-color weave	Full jitō (総地頭) (one district)
		Senior Second	Council of Three in Waiting (三司官座敷)	Council of Three in Waiting	Gold	Purple base floating weave	Assistant jitō (脇地頭) (one village)
		Junior Second	Purple Official (紫官)	Murasaki-kintaifu (紫金大夫)	Gold	Purple	Assistant jitō (脇地頭) (one village)
Elite nobles	Peikumi (親雲上) · Peichin (親雲上) Satonushi Peichin (里之子親雲上) Chikudun Peichin (筑登之親雲上)	Senior Third	Mōshikuchi (申口)	Murasaki-kintaifu (紫金大夫)	Gold head, silver stem (金簪茎銀簪)	Purple	Assistant jitō (one village)
		Junior Third	Mōshikuchi-za (申口座)	Mōshikuchi-za	Silver (銀簪)	Yellow	
		Senior Fourth	Investigative Official (吟味役) Head of Naha (那覇里主)	Mōshikuchi-za	Silver (銀簪)	Yellow	Assistant jitō (one village)
		Junior Fourth	Official in waiting (座敷)	Official in waiting		Yellow	N.a.

Ordinary nobles	Peichin / Satonushi-Peichin / Chikudun-Peichin	Lower kōri administrator (下庫理当)	Senior Fifth	Lower kōri administrator	Silver	Yellow	N.a.
		Administrator in waiting (当座敷)	Junior Fifth	Administrator in waiting			
	Peichin / Satonushi-Peichin / Chikudun-Peichin	Lower kōri sedo (下庫理勢頭)	Senior Sixth		Silver		
		Sedo in waiting (勢頭座敷)	Junior Sixth	Sedo in waiting			
	Peichin / Satonushi-Peichin / Chikudun-Peichin	Satonushi-Peichin (里之子親雲上)	Senior Seventh	Satonushi-Peichin	Silver		
		Chikudun-Peichin (筑登之親雲上)	Junior Seventh	Interpreter-Peichin (通事親雲上)			
	Satonushi	Lower kōri Satonushi (下庫理里之子)	Senior Eighth		Silver	Red	
		Junior Satonushi (若里之子)	Junior Eighth	Interpreter (通事)			
	Chikudun	Lower kōri Chikudun (下庫理筑登之)	Senior Ninth		Silver	Red	
	Chikudun	Chikudun in waiting (筑登之座敷)	Junior Ninth	Interpreter			
	Shi (子)	Shi	No rank	Talent (秀才)	Copper (銅簪)	Blue/green	
	Niya (仁屋)	Niya	No rank	Junior Talent (若秀才)			

Note: "N.a." = "not applicable."

no longer possible. Nevertheless, they still functioned to some degree as maritime conduits connecting Japan and China.

One effect of this relative isolation was to encourage distinctively Ryukyuan forms of culture to develop. Ryukyuan languages diverged from mainland Japanese languages at a faster pace during the early modern era. Satsuma's cultural policies also encouraged Ryukyuan cultural distinctiveness in connection with state theatrics. Certain new forms of culture such as *kumiodori* were actively created during this era, sometimes to serve social or political ends. Perhaps the most important long-term change, however, was poverty. Although there were local variations in circumstances and reforms of some effectiveness, the general trend from 1600 to 1879 was a lower material standard of living for ordinary people and even elites. This situation also played a major role in the region's modern history, as we will see.

CHAPTER TWELVE

Extracting Resources from the Northern and Southern Ryukyu Islands

Between roughly the 1520s and 1609, Shuri systematically extracted resources from the other Ryukyu Islands. To facilitate that process, agents from Okinawa oversaw the local officials who collected taxes and performed other basic governance functions. Shuri also installed officially appointed priestesses throughout its territory. After 1609, the same basic dynamic prevailed but with some important changes. First, the size of Shuri's empire shrank because all the northern Ryukyu Islands came under Satsuma's direct administration, outside Shuri's jurisdiction.[1] Second, the northern Ryukyu Islands and the rest of the Ryukyu Islands developed along different paths from the seventeenth century on. Third, the combination of the loss of revenue from the northern islands and the requirement that Shuri pay a substantial annual tax to Satsuma put severe financial pressure on the royal government. Fourth, recall that in the sixteenth century Shuri's wealth derived mainly from trade, not domestic production. The curtailment of trade as the sixteenth century progressed had already shrunk Shuri's economic power by 1609, one reason it fared so poorly in the war. The war and its aftermath curtailed trade even further, thus imposing additional financial pressure. One result of this situation was that the royal government tried to increase and diversify agricultural productivity, as we have seen.

This chapter focuses on the northern and southern Ryukyu Islands in light of the circumstances described above. In the southern islands, the general trend was an increase in Shuri's oversight, for example, occasional census taking and an increase in the severity of taxation. The northern islands were generally better off under Satsuma's direct control until sugar became established as the main crop there. The profitability of sugar resulted in severe resource extraction and concomitant human misery during the nineteenth century.

In 1986, the Amami-Ōshima-born historian Ōyama Ringorō (大山麟五郎) made the following comment about folk songs in the context of an academic panel discussion with two other scholars: "The traditional folk songs of Amami-Ōshima involve a full-throated type of singing in which the tendons of the singer's neck stand out. They are not for singing in the daytime. At nightfall, or even at dawn, with the door closed and lit by a faint lamp, the singer sings them while shedding tears. . . . It is unfortunate that, recently, folk singing has become a pleasant parlor artform" (Tanigawa 1986, 71). Moving to the other end of the Ryukyu Islands, here is a children's song from Yonaguni called *Ami ya fuihinna* (Rain, please don't fall, 雨や降いひんな) and featuring an older girl taking care of her younger sister while their parents are toiling:

Under the northern banyan tree
A cow's saddle on a goat; a horse's saddle on a cow
The warp is insufficient; the weft is insufficient[2]
[For the sake of our toiling parents] I beg you rain—please do not fall!

Roosters report the time of day
Our parents trample the morning dew and return soaked in the evening dew
They cannot survive the voice of heaven, the command of our overlords
Nor are they able to die
I beg you rain—please do not fall!

(*Churashima Okinawa* 2008)

The context of this bitter song is oppressive taxation within a system not abolished until 1903.

In 1990, the newspaper *Yaeyama mainichi shinbun* published an interview with a woman who was 105 at the time and had formally gone through the taxation procedure on Taketomi Island three times between ages of fifteen and eighteen. Part of the interview was about the reluctance of parents to give birth under conditions akin to slavery. The more children a family had, the harder it was for parents and children to fulfill their duties. Not wanting to burden their children with the same hardships, and because having children would be a burden vis-à-vis required work, many mothers feared they could not handle the responsibilities. The first measure many took was to make a decoction of the Chinese lantern plant, a medicine that would prevent conception. However, if they did become pregnant, in many cases the newborn baby would be covered with a giant clam shell and buried alive. Behind the living room where the interview was taking place was the grave for babies who had been disposed of this way. An informant from Nakasuji Village recounted several stories of babies being picked up from under shells and raised (Okinawa kokusai daigaku, Nantō bunka kenkyūjo 2003, 241–48).

The following description comes from Kumejima at the end of the eighteenth century, and it makes a similar point: "Women as old as forty are up till one or two at night in the weaving building making cloth, and elderly women are terribly busy preparing their food. When they return home, they all put their heads together and wonder how this situation will ever end. They heave a sigh and wonder how to make things better" (Iha 1974, 1:138).[3] On the island of Kumejima, pongee (*tsumugi*), fabric made from threads of raw silk, was the main tax.

Most survey histories state that Shuri imposed an especially cruel form of taxation on the southern Ryukyu Islands, a poll tax (head tax, per capita tax, J. *nintōzei* or *jintōzei*, 人頭税). In such a system, the same tax is levied on all individuals in certain age ranges, regardless of their ability to pay. In today's southern Ryukyu Islands, Shuri's poll tax remains a vivid symbol of oppression and discrimination. We will see, however, that the situation was somewhat more complex and that the term *poll tax* is technically a misnomer. Let us begin, however, with modern and contemporary perceptions of the early modern past, focusing on the island of Yonaguni, also known as Dunan.

Perceptions from the Southern Ryukyu Islands

On the morning of October 31, 2019, the major structures of Shuri Castle, a UNESCO World Heritage site, caught fire and burned. Many valuable items of historical significance inside perished in the flames. Faulty wiring and the lack of a sprinkler system were to blame.

Almost a year later, Shiroma Ari, a reporter for the Naha-based newspaper *Okinawa taimusu*, went to the island of Yonaguni to get a sense of attitudes there about Shuri Castle. He reports having been stunned by the animosity he encountered toward the castle and the kingdom it represented. For example, Shiroma interviewed Sakihara Yōnō, a former education superintendent in Yonaguni. In the resulting article, Sakihara is quoted as saying, "The annexation of Ryukyu [*Ryūkyū shobun*, 1879] is written about only as an event in which Shuri people lost their special privileges. [But] it was a case of the people of Miyako and Yaeyama, who suffered under the poll tax, gaining freedom of occupation and freedom of movement." Noting that, even today, excessive interference from Tokyo and Naha hinders the ability of the local community to create economic opportunities, Sakihara lamented that the postwar marginalization of places like Yonaguni has added another layer of sorrow on top of the legacy of severe taxation. The residents of Shuri ate the grain grown in Yonaguni and wore clothes made from the

FIGURE 12.1. A public marker at the Kubura-bari site in
Yonaguni describing the "cruel practice" of forcing pregnant
women to jump across the gap between the two rocks
(Silvia Groniewicz / Alamy Stock Photo)

tax cloth produced there. Moreover, Shuri Castle was built by laborers from
places like Yonaguni. "I think of Shuri Castle with malice," Sakihara said.
In light of such comments, Shiroma wrote that the mass media in Okinawa
has a problematic "Yamato [mainland Japan] versus Okinawa" mentality. He
opined that it is not acceptable to push a Naha-centered set of values onto
other communities within the Ryukyu Islands. Noting that the dragon pillar
at Shuri Castle, which survived the fire, was made from stone quarried in
Yonaguni, Sakihara declared that the pillar represents "the strength of the
oppressed" (Shiroma 2020).

The terms *tunguda* (トゥング田), *isshōda* (一升田), and *hitomasuda* (lit.
"human measuring field," 人桝田) refer in Yonaguni to a purported method
of tax relief brought about by culling weak and disabled people from the
population. According to local lore, all men aged fifteen to fifty would be
called, suddenly and without warning, to an emergency gathering in a field
some distance from the village. Those unable to get there or who arrived
late and could not fit into the field were killed (there are different versions
of the details). In other words, the call to assemble in the field was a way of
culling weak or infirm men from the population.

For women in Yonaguni, there was a similarly grim measure of physical strength. It was a rock formation called Kubura-bari (久部良バリ; see
fig. 12.1). According to legend, pregnant women were required to leap
across a gap between two large rock outcroppings to demonstrate their fit-
ness. Those unable to leap across the gap (the -*bari*) fell to their deaths.

Nearby the site is a statue of the bodhisattva Jizō to appease the spirits of those who did not make it across.

Did such things actually happen? There is no definitive evidence either way. The key point is that, even if they are exaggerations, these legends reflect suffering under a heavy tax burden. As James Rhys Edwards notes: "On several occasions during the eighteenth century, peasants in Yonaguni and Hateruma-jima are reported to have committed mass suicide in protest of tax burdens that had driven them to the brink of starvation. In nineteenth-century Miyako, peasants repeatedly petitioned against the onerous per capita tax, sometimes clashing violently with local officials. Throughout the entire Ryūkyū Kingdom period and after annexation, indebted families regularly indentured their sons and daughters as manual laborers or prostitutes; infanticide was not unheard of" (Edwards 2015, 64–65). In short, many modern and contemporary residents of Yonaguni or elsewhere in the southern Ryukyu Islands regard the early modern past as a time of great cruelty and hardship.

The term *Ryukyu Kingdom* became popular in Okinawa in connection with tourism and local pride, especially after the reconstruction of Shuri Castle in 1992. It also commonly appears in Anglophone writing about the Ryukyu Islands, including my own earlier work. In the typical Okinawan context, or in English, *Ryukyu Kingdom* has positive connotations. However, this term is not widely used in either the northern or the southern Ryukyu Islands. When it is used in these places, it typically does not carry positive overtones. In the southern Ryukyu Islands, bitter memories of heavy taxation permeate literature, songs, and the historical consciousness.

In the context of discussing local concepts of nature in contemporary Yonaguni, the anthropologist Arne Røkkum makes a similar point: "Under a heavy poll tax regime, and as far into the present as at the beginning of the 20th century, the southern islanders toiled in the fields to produce rice they could not afford to eat themselves. Over and over again the head of the *tumujâ* [festival house] would return to this topic, as when saying that the moon had to be an object of prayer due to people's dependence on its light to work far into the night" (Røkkum 2006, 66). Much of the rice (the most prized grain) and other grains consumed by urban Okinawans during the early modern era was produced by people in the southern Ryukyu Islands in conditions akin to involuntary servitude. Recall from the previous chapter Shuri's concern with placing physicians in those islands. It was not an act of benevolence. Less illness meant higher tax revenue.

On the island of Miyako, there is a stone called *Nintōzei-seki* (poll tax stone). According to local lore, probably apocryphal, prior to the tax being imposed on the basis of age, it was imposed on people who had reached the height of the stone. According to the explanation posted nearby the stone:

> In *Kainan shōki*, the ethnologist Yanagita Kunio, who visited Miyako in 1918, called this stone pillar "measuring stone." He introduced the legend whereby "tax was assessed when a person reached the height of this stone." In 1637, the Ryukyu Kingdom initiated a poll tax system in the southern Ryukyu Islands. It levied a tax (in millet or textiles) based on the population, assessed at the discretion of local officials. However, in 1659, instead of the tax varying with increases or decreases in population, it was changed to a "fixed value per person tax," and, in 1710, the age range was fixed at fifteen to fifty (men paid in grain, women in textiles). This tax was eliminated on January 1, 1903, in conjunction with the implementation of a new tax system.

Is this description accurate? Partially. Taxation was, indeed, severe, and population was a variable in calculations of the tax burdens for communities. However, there was no poll tax in the sense that every individual was required to pay an identical tax either in grain or cloth. Indeed, the origin of the term *jintōzei* (lit. "poll tax") appears to have originated not in the early modern era but in the 1890s. Official reports from the Meiji Era (mis)characterized taxation in the southern Ryukyu Islands as *jintō haibu zei* (人頭配賦税), which literally means "tax assessed per capita," or *jintōzei* for short (see, e.g., Kinjō 1903/1953, 39). In other words, modern people read this term back in time anachronistically. The actual tax system was, however, more nuanced, albeit still severe. Let us take a closer look at taxation, focusing on the Yaeyama Islands.

Taxation in the Yaeyama Islands

Examining taxation in the Yaeyama Islands, let us start with data from the head of the Bureau of Revenue from the period 1789–1801. The figures are similar to the information found in the only other extant document dealing with royal revenue, *gozaisei* (1728).

To calculate the basic grain tax burden, take the main annual (rice-equivalent) grain tax for the Yaeyama Islands, and divide by the percentage of Yaeyama's population ca. 1800. The total population of the Ryukyu Kingdom was about 155,637 in 1800. Yaeyama's population in 1803 was 15,858, which is very close to its population in both 1798 (15,957) and 1810 (15,533) (Dana 1984, 52–53; Takara 1982, 23 [table 2]). Therefore, as of approximately

1800, the Yaeyama Islands constituted 10 percent of the kingdom's population and paid 13 percent of the basic grain tax. The real burden on Yaeyama residents, however, was substantially heavier than the 3 percent differential because of the way taxation was assessed, the prevalence of malaria, and the relative lack of resources and because extra and ad hoc taxes were particularly heavy. Moreover, for the Yaeyama Islands, the grain tax was only 40 percent of the total regular tax assessment. The other 60 percent consisted of processed goods, mainly cloth. Depending on location, processed goods could include sugar, indigo, turmeric, cotton floss, and woven cloth. The percentage of processed goods in the total regular tax assessment for each region of the kingdom was roughly 50–60 percent for Okinawa and nearby islands, 60 percent for the southern Ryukyu Islands, and 80 percent for Kumejima (whose economy was dominated by pongee production).

It is also important to note an overall trend. Throughout the nineteenth century, the population of Yaeyama decreased in absolute terms and relative to the total population of the kingdom. By 1871, the Yaeyama Islands shouldered a similar 13 percent grain tax burden but with only 7 percent of the kingdom's population. Although Yaeyama was especially hard-pressed, the general trend throughout all parts of the kingdom during the nineteenth century was for the already high tax burden to climb even higher. As we will see, by the time the kingdom came to an end in 1879, it was no longer economically viable.

Was It a Poll Tax?

Was there a special and especially cruel form of taxation—a poll tax—imposed on the southern Ryukyu Islands, one that was different from the taxation imposed on Okinawa? In *There Was No Poll Tax* (*Jintōzei wa nakatta*), the agricultural historian Kurima Yasuo argues that the answer is no, albeit with some qualifications (see Kurima 2015). I agree with Kurima on this important point. In more recent work, he has argued that the tax burden on individuals during the early modern era was not especially severe (Kurima 2022). I do not agree with this conclusion.[4]

In 1633, starting in the island of Miyako, Shuri's officials conducted a census. The next year, the tax rate for grain and cloth was established on the basis of population. As a result of subsequent censuses, it was adjusted to account for population fluctuations. This taxation method was called *zugake* (頭懸), which means roughly "based [on the number of] heads." In 1659, however, population-based adjustments stopped, and the total tax remained unchanged. At this point, the tax might appear to have been a poll tax, especially given its (modern) name. However, there was never a fixed per capita assessment that was the same for all adults or even all men or all women. Government officials levied taxes at the village level, and it was the responsibility of each village to pay the assessed tax. In other words, the unit of taxation was the village, not the individual. This point applied throughout the kingdom.

Initially, men and women were graded into four categories on the basis of local officials' subjective judgment of their capacity to work. In 1711, tax allotments became more systematic, being now based on a person's age and the productive capacity of that person's village. In Yaeyama, the four age grades were (for both men and women): top (ages twenty-one to forty), middle (ages forty-one to forty-five), lower (ages forty-six to fifty), and lowest (ages fifteen to twenty). The burden was further adjusted on the basis of one of four grades of basic agricultural productivity applied to each village. The total range of the tax one might be assessed in Yaeyama, with all the factors taken into consideration, was sixteen units (the top age group in a top productivity village) to four units (the lowest age group in a lowest productivity village). In Miyako, the range was similar. Local officials were exempt from taxation, and certain specialty occupations such as tile smith, tofu maker, or physician typically paid a tax in cash.

Compared with taxation in Okinawa, taxation in the southern Ryukyu Islands was somewhat more rigid. It would not be possible concisely to describe the system of taxation in Okinawa at the village level because there was so much variation in tax-related customs and land allocation practices from village to village. In Okinawa, officials levied taxes on villages, and it was up to each village to work out the details.[5] In the southern Ryukyu Islands, taxation practices were more uniform and systematized. Of course, the distinction between a poll tax and a tax rate based on (outdated) population statistics could be regarded as a matter of semantics. The more important point is that, whatever the system, the de facto individual tax burden throughout the kingdom was severe and that, in the southern Ryukyu Islands, there was less flexibility at the level of households and individuals with respect to how villages met their tax quotas.

There is one other important point to be made with respect to taxation, whether in Okinawa or in the southern Ryukyu Islands. In both places, corvée labor formed the major part of any individual's tax burden. For example, in a typical village in Okinawa, agricultural land was allotted among village households from a fixed pool. Typically, each household's allotment was enough to provide its basic food and other resources. Importantly, the products from this type of land were not meant to be used for tax purposes. Agricultural taxation took the form of corvée labor, with groups of mobilized peasants doing such tasks as maintaining infrastructure, working in fields set aside for the income of local and central government officials, and producing tax-specific products such as sugar and turmeric. Importantly, in typical corvée arrangements, each person of a certain age was assigned the same number of days of labor even though individual productivity per day necessarily varied. As Kurima (2015) points out, this arrangement—equal days of labor per person—did resemble a poll tax.

Recall also that, in the southern Ryukyu Islands, cloth production constituted the larger part of the tax burden. Most cloth production took place as corvée labor at village production facilities under the supervision of village officials. Because cloth production by village women required teamwork and a division of labor, a specific bolt of cloth was the product not of a single woman but of several. In actual practice, therefore, cloth production was not a poll tax in the sense that each individual was required, by herself, to produce a certain quantity of cloth. On the other hand, it resembled a poll tax in that all the women in an age bracket were required to perform the same number of days of labor.

There are many other taxation details, but what I have described here is the basic system. One further note is that the government in Shuri did grant concessions in cases of major natural disasters or other emergencies. For example, the total tax burden for Yaeyama was lowered after the Meiwa tsunami and the resulting sharp drop in population (discussed later in this chapter). Nevertheless, natural disasters tended to increase per capita tax burdens because tax reductions were rarely commensurate with population loss or other factors that negatively affected production.

Overall, the extraction of resources and social restrictions connected with that extraction put many islanders into a condition of de facto involuntary servitude. Not only did most of the population labor on behalf of Shuri, but young women also sometimes found themselves in sexual relations with Okinawan officials, either on an ad hoc basis or more formally as *uyanma* (J. *genchi tsuma*), local "wives" of Okinawans. Depending on personalities and circumstances, a range of outcomes was possible, but, overall, conditions in the southern Ryukyu Islands created an atmosphere conducive to sexual abuse. Pulling together folk songs from the islands dealing with taxation, there are eight categories based on content (number of songs in parentheses): protest songs about adversity (fifteen), songs describing the payment of taxes (ten), songs about the lives of *uyanma* (ten), songs harshly critical of *uyanma* (two), songs about the tragedy of forced relocation (five), songs about the sadness of separation from *uyanma* (two), songs about the desire to drink alcoholic beverages to one's content with what is left over from taxes (three), and children's songs (four) (Okinawa kokusai daigaku, Nantō bunka kenkyūjo 2003, 266–79). Notice that three categories and fourteen songs are about *uyanma*.

The Northern Ryukyu Islands under Satsuma's Direct Control

In the northern Ryukyu Islands, the common term referring to the time when the islands were part of Shuri's empire is *Naha(n)-yu* (the reign of Naha, 那覇世).[6] While we should not read too much into names, notice that the emphasis is on the port of Naha, not the royal palace in Shuri. After 1609, the northern Ryukyu Islands entered the "reign of Yamato." The reign of Yamato in Amami-Ōshima can, on the basis of events, be divided into four logical time periods: 1609–90, 1690–1747, 1747–1830, and 1830–67. Summarizing the narrative in general terms, the standard of living in the northern Ryukyu Islands either improved slightly or remained largely unchanged into the eighteenth century. However, as sugar came to dominate the islands' economies, the conditions of life for ordinary people declined, eventually severely. Satsuma's officials began experimenting with sugar production around 1690, and, in 1747, sugar-based taxes replaced rice-based taxes. In 1830, Satsuma instituted a policy whereby the domain government was the exclusive buyer of island sugar, thereby initiating a period of intense misery. Let us look at each period in turn.

1609–90: REORGANIZATION AND ECONOMIC GROWTH

The geopolitical districts (*magiri*) from the reign of Naha carried over into the reign of Yamato. Within each district were a number of villages, which in documents were often called *hō* (方). A commissioner from Satsuma—*bugyō* (奉行) before 1633[7] and *daikan* (代官) after 1633—oversaw local officials drawn from prominent island families. Such officials typically carried the title *yohito* (与人) or *yokome* (横目). One post-1609 change is that these local officials were rotated much more frequently (once every three years was typical) and more widely to prevent their becoming entrenched in a single locality. Official political ties with Shuri were cut, but private trade with the rest of the Ryukyu Islands continued. Figure 12.2 maps major exchanges in the zone from Okinawa to Satsuma.

By 1633, sweet potato cultivation reached Amami-Ōshima from Okinawa (ultimately from China via South America). Sweet potatoes had many advantages as a staple food, and they hold up much better to drought or severe winds than do cereal grains. Moreover, the use of sweet potatoes as a major local food source meant that all irrigated fields could be devoted to rice

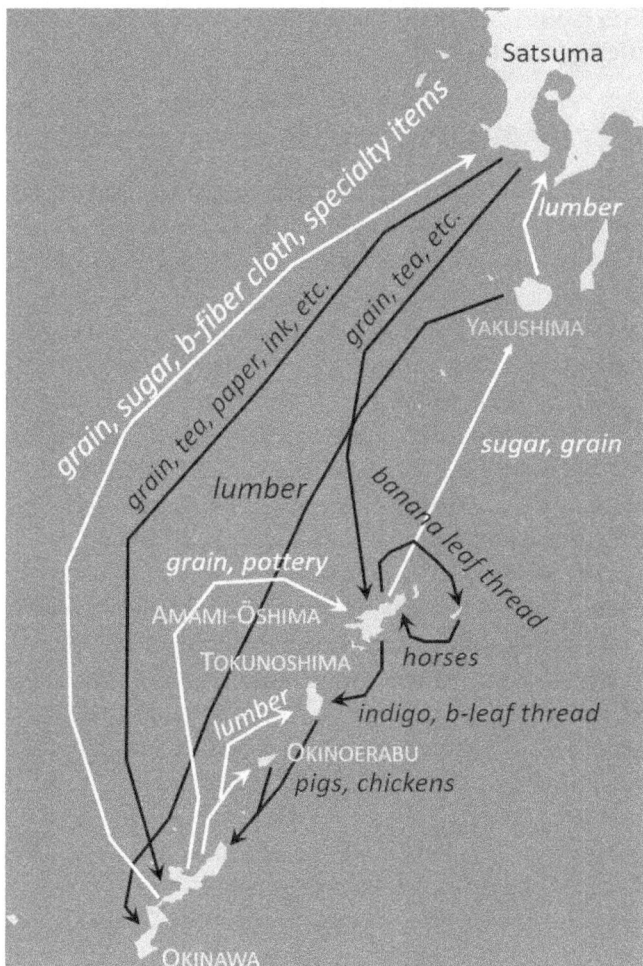

FIGURE 12.2. Major commercial exchanges among and between Okinawa, the northern Ryukyu Islands, and Satsuma in the nineteenth century

production, a potentially valuable trade product. Local products purchased by the domain included palm bark (used in shipbuilding), bishopwood (*akagi*), sweet potatoes, matts, bananas, and white liquor (*shōchū*). In general, taxes in Amami-Ōshima were higher than they were before 1609, but productivity was greater, as was, thus, the ability of people to pay.

According to a 1659 survey, the population of the northern Ryukyu Islands was 62,304, with 23,605 living in Amami-Ōshima. Notice that, in the northern Ryukyu Islands, the population was much more evenly spread out than it was in the formal Ryukyu Kingdom, where the population was highly concentrated in southern Okinawa.

1690–1747: BENEFICIAL SUGAR

In 1690, two local officials in Yakiuchi District (today's villages of Uken and Yamatohama) went to Okinawa and came back with sugarcane and sugar-making know-how. In 1706, brown sugar from the northern Ryukyu Islands was first sold on the Osaka market. From 1713, Satsuma's officials pursued a policy of forcing peasants in Amami-Ōshima to cultivate sugarcane and requiring them to sell a fixed quantity to the domain at a set price. However, at this stage, sugar growers had plenty left over to sell privately, and sugar prices tended to rise. Under these circumstances, sugar cultivation became profitable for peasants. On the other hand, rice cultivation did not do well. One reason was that, in Amami-Ōshima, soil suitable for rice cultivation is scarce, being found mainly in the Kasari Peninsula. Second, rice from the Ryukyu Islands was considered the lowest grade in Japan's markets and, thus, fetched a low price. Finally, local priestesses had designated many of the island's springs, streams, mountain fields, and shorelines as sacred places into which ordinary people were prohibited from entering.

Starting in 1691, Satsuma's policy was for local island officials to travel to Kagoshima once every three years. On arrival, they would lodge at a residence set aside for them and be eligible for a meeting with the domain lord if he was in residence (i.e., if he was not in Edo). There was an (Amami-) Ōshima residence, a Kikaijima residence, etc. Similarly, the Ryūkyū-yakata in Kagoshima was an official residence for officials from Okinawa. During the voyage to Kagoshima, when the ship carrying local officials came within sight of Mt. Kaimon (the southernmost peak of the Satsuma Peninsula)— that is, when Yamato came into sight—a peculiar ritual called *shankurume* would begin. The passengers—the local officials—were bound with ropes, hoisted up to the top of the mast, and then lowered to the bottom of the ship's hold. They would then give *shōchū* (white liquor) and pork to the ship's crew, who would in return release them. The origins of this custom are unclear, but it could be regarded as a small-scale performance of northern-Ryukyuan-ness and, of course, subordination to Satsuma.

In response to a decree by Satsuma prohibiting Japanese surnames throughout the Ryukyu Islands, many prominent households did not actually change their names. They simply changed the way those names were written. For example, Maeda went from 前田 to 真栄田 and Yokota from 横田 to 与古田. If Chinese visitors ever saw these three-character surnames, they would not appear to be Japanese. Furthermore, some residents of the northern Ryukyu Islands traveled to Okinawa when Chinese investiture envoys were in Naha, and others engaged in clandestine trade (*mitsu bōeki*). Such traders found it more convenient to use single-character surnames, which appeared to be Chinese and could easily be read as such if seen by a literate Chinese person. Thus, even today, they are common in the northern Ryukyu Islands. Some typical examples are Kotobuki (壽), Yoshimi (嘉), Sakae (栄), Megumi (恵), Iwai (祝), Inori (祷), Inori (祈), Inori (禱), Katsu (勝), Nobori (昇), and Fuku (福). While there is probably no reliable way to verify this point, the prominence of single-character surnames suggests that a considerable frequency and volume of illicit trade, quite possibly in covert cooperation with Satsuma's officials, took place via the northern Ryukyu Islands.

1747–1830: SUGAR—FROM BENEFITING THE ISLANDERS TO BENEFITING THE DOMAIN

During the eighteenth century, the market price of rice was relatively low and the price of sugar high. Therefore, in 1747, all rice or grain taxes were converted to sugar taxes. Small quantities of rice were still grown, but the lack of local cereal grains made deadly famines more common, especially in Tokunoshima. Whether in response to famine or simply as a supplement to the food supply, the northern Ryukyu Islands began to import grain from Okinawa. Our records are not granular enough to know with certainty, but it is quite possible that some rice or (more likely) millet grown in the southern Ryukyu Islands as tax ended up being consumed in the northern Ryukyu Islands.

In 1777, sugar became a domain monopoly, and private sales were prohibited. That policy was rescinded ten years later because of pushback from powerful merchants. In 1818, another attempt at creating a monopoly was short-lived because of other unanticipated problems. In the meantime, sugar-making equipment and know-how advanced rapidly in the northern Ryukyu Islands. By the early nineteenth century, they began to produce more sugar than Okinawa did.

1830–67: THE BITTER TASTE OF SUGAR

In 1830, Satsuma's government imposed a strict sugar monopoly on all the northern Ryukyu Islands and enforced it vigorously. Local officials purchased sugar locally, within the islands. They became increasingly tyrannical under pressure from higher up the chain of authority to deliver more sugar. Punishments for peasants who resisted or ignored orders included forced labor on road maintenance projects. Sugar is notoriously demanding because, once the cane is cut, the sugar content of the juice steadily diminishes. Crushing the cane is dangerous, but there is intense pressure to do the job quickly. Anyone who was negligent in any aspect of the process was subject to punishment. Cutting the cane stalks too high above the ground, for example, might result in the offender(s) being put into stocks (fig. 12.3). Illegal private sugar sales were, at least in principle, punishable by death.

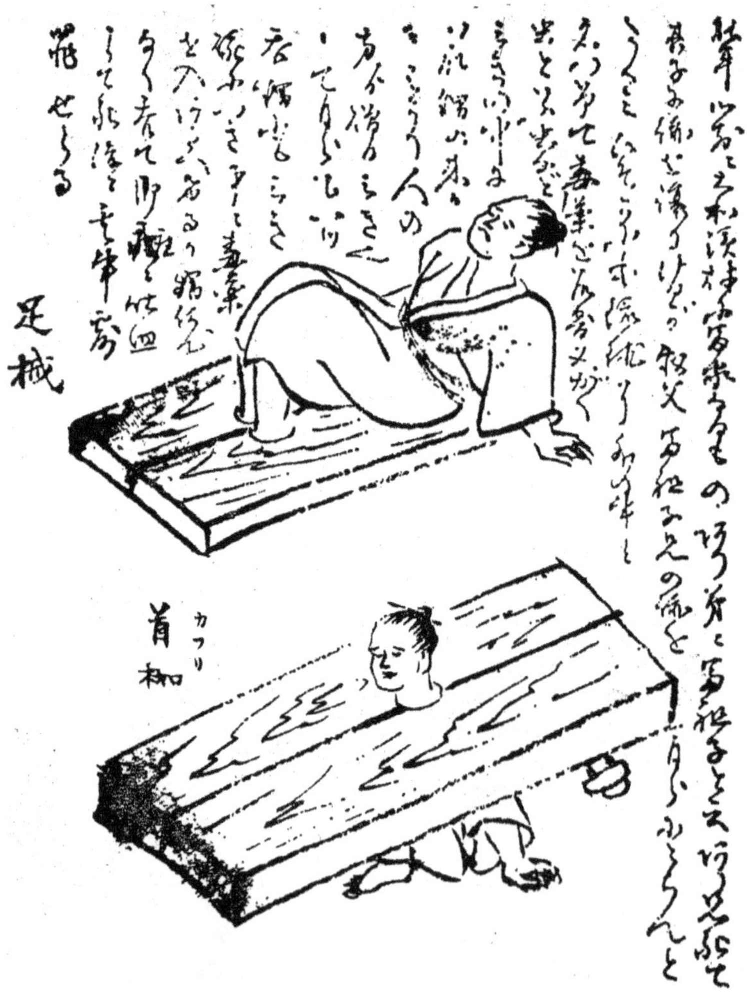

FIGURE 12.3. A depiction of ankle and neck stocks used to punish denizens of the northern Ryukyu Islands who were deficient in sugar production (among other possible offenses) (from Nagoya Sagenta 1855/1984, 2:60)

TABLE 12.1. Typical commodities and their price in sugar ca. 1830–35 in the northern Ryukyu Islands

| Item | Price in *kin* (斤) of sugar (1 *kin* ≈ 600 grams) | |
	1830	1835
Bundle of paper	25	28
One smoking pipe	18 (higher quality) 15 (lower quality)	
Pair of small (thin) writing brushes	5 (higher quality) 3 (lower quality)	
One *furoshiki* cloth	28	
2 *to*, 8 *shō* (roughly 50 liters) of soybeans	150	
One *tan* (roughly 992 square meters) of cotton cloth	45 (higher quality) 40 (lower quality)	
100 2-*sun* (roughly 6-centimeter) nails	6	4
One umbrella	18	
One round pot	200	
One *kin* (roughly 600 grams) of candle (or candlewax)	20	20
Three *gō* (0.54 liter) of rice	1.52	1.0
One *kin* (roughly 600 grams) of tea	25 (higher quality) 22 (medium quality)	
One *kin* (roughly 600 grams) of tobacco	25 (higher quality) 18 (medium quality)	

Moreover, to prevent the possibility of profit from private sugar sales, Satsuma prohibited all circulation or use of money within the northern Ryukyu Islands. Sugar became the only local currency, and every daily-use item or commodity became priced in terms of sugar. Those prices were set by the domain to profit the domain, and the price of sugar within the islands was set to only about one-fourth its true value in the Osaka market. The difference was profit for the domain, garnered at the cost of vast human misery in the islands. To take a specific commodity example, one *kin* (斤)—approximately six hundred grams—of high-quality tea cost twenty-five *kin* of sugar, or very roughly US$50.00–US$60.00 (as of this writing). For other examples, see table 12.1.

Because of the exclusive focus on sugar, nearly all food and daily-use items had to be shipped into the islands from Kagoshima. In 1855, twenty-two ships sailed to the islands filled with grain, and thirty-three sailed filled with daily-use goods. The domain in general, along with specific merchants, profited from these commodities, while the people of the islands barely sustained themselves. Some sunk into involuntary servitude.

An important cost of the sugar policy was an increase in the number of un-free people. *Yanchu* (家人) were people who could not pay their sugar taxes and, therefore, had to sell themselves into servitude to a wealthy household for a term of five or ten years. Some had once obtained loans against their taxes but then had to sell themselves when they could not repay the loans. Some terms of servitude were unlimited. We could call some *yanchu inden-tured servants*, but some of them were functionally little different from slaves.

As a rough idea of the money involved, a period of indentured servi-tude corresponded to between fifteen hundred and two thousand *kin* of sugar. Two thousand *kin* of sugar was equal to about ten *koku* of rice. Con-verted into 2011 currency, this ten *koku* of rice would be roughly ¥600,000 or US$5,300. In other words, it would have cost about $5,000 in 2011 dollars— and more today—for a person to buy out or redeem a standard period of servitude. Moreover, in a society in which most people barely survived from year to year, $5,000 would represent a quantity of wealth that only a few elites would have been able to amass.[8]

Other than for local officials, travel to the mainland was prohibited for residents of the northern Ryukyu Islands (with exceptions for medical treat-ment) after the establishment of the sugar monopoly. Note that there are several small islands near Amami-Ōshima in addition to the larger islands of Kikaijima, Tokunoshima, Okinoerabu, and Yoron. Travel between all these places was typically by locally made boats known generically as *sabani*, *sabune*, and other similar names. These vessels were also used for fishing, which was a valuable supplement to the food supply. The simplest boats were dug out of a single log, whereas larger ones were made from planks. Such boats could be lashed together for stability. They could be rowed or powered by simple sails. These vessels were in common use well into the twentieth century.

In the realm of land use, the basic pattern was to create as many fields as possible and devote them to sugar production. Any remaining land on which something could be planted was devoted to sweet potatoes, which were sturdy and needed relatively little active cultivation. These potatoes were literally a lifeline. Throughout Japan at this time, the typical agricultu-ral tax rate was 50–60 percent of the crop. In Satsuma, including the north-ern Ryukyu Islands, it was 80 percent (with 20 percent left to the farmers). Extractions reached a peak of severity during the 1850s and 1860s because of the massive expenses Satsuma incurred in its purchase of European weap-ons and ships and because other parts of Japan began to produce sugar, thereby reducing Satsuma's profit margin.

Life in Amami-Ōshima's "sugar hell" (*satō jigoku*) was miserable for most ordinary people, and the island was also a common destination for people from Satsuma sentenced to banishment. In 1852, for example, there were 346 such banished people. Saigō Takamori is probably the most famous resident of Satsuma banished to Amami-Ōshima. Nagoya Sagenta (名越左源太, 1820–81), a samurai, was banished there in 1850 owing to his part in a plot connected with domain politics. He spent five years interacting with local people and describing local customs, work, and wildlife. The result was a valuable source, *Nantō zatsuwa* (Southern islands miscellany, 南島雑話) (see Nagoya 1855/1984). According to Nagoya's count, in 1852, there were 1,089 local officials (*shima yakunin*, 島役人)—including village-level officials—in Amami-Ōshima, 2.8 percent of the population. The number of officials from mainland Satsuma in the island would typically have been fewer than 10.

A three-tier customary social status system prevailed. At the top were the *yukarichu* (connected people 由縁人), prominent households that date back to the reign of Naha or that rose to prominence after the island became part of Satsuma. These households produced local officials. They also ran what were, in effect, large sugar plantations. At the bottom were the *yanchu*, servants and laborers for these elite households and the laborers who worked their plantations. In between were the *jibunchu* (people unto themselves, 自分人), the commoners who mainly performed agricultural work.

Despite the misery that prevailed in the northern Ryukyu Islands, from 1830 on the population increased, as did the number of boats. People are adaptable, and it appears that many denizens of the northern Ryukyu Islands managed to adjust to the severe conditions.

Sugar extracted from the northern Ryukyu Islands and the islands' people helped Satsuma become financially solvent and purchase advanced weapons. Therefore, it could be argued that the northern Ryukyu Islands provided some of the raw economic power allowing Satsuma to spearhead the 1868 Meiji Restoration and the events leading up to it.

Administrative Structure in the Miyako Islands

As we have seen in the northern Ryukyu Islands, historical periodization from a local perspective produces a distinctive chronology. In Miyako, the earliest era was an "age of warfare" (*senran jidai*). Because there are no written records from this time and most events were passed down as legends, it is hard to know when it began. A rough estimate is 1250–1300. This era is also known as *the time of heroes* because of dramatic battle stories involving the Yunahabara group and Meguromori Toyomiya. In the late fourteenth century, Miyako entered the Toyomiya Era. *Toyomiya* (豊見親) is a title similar to *aji* in Okinawa, and it would have been pronounced *tuyumiya* locally. According to the Shuri-centered narrative, a young man from Miyako named Masaku sailed to Naha, learned the superior ways of Okinawa's capital region, and initiated formal relations between Chūzan (based at Urasoe Castle) and Miyako. He later became Yonaha Sedo Toyomiya. In the official narrative, Yonaha became the first overlord of Miyako, although he was only one of several powers in the Miyako Islands at this time.

The most famous *toyomiya* was Nakasone (仲宗根). In 1500, Nakasone was an ally of Shō Shin during Shuri's invasion of Yaeyama. However, he and his family disappeared soon thereafter. According to the official histories, they were accused of committing various crimes soon after 1500. In other words, after making use of Nakasone to conquer Yaeyama, Shō Shin moved against him. In the decades after 1500, Shuri installed a variety of officials and priestesses in the southern Ryukyu Islands and began systematically taxing the territory. After the downfall of Nakasone and his family in the early sixteenth century, the title *toyomiya* was abolished.

In post-1500 Miyako, the three officials sent from Shuri represented the highest administrative tier. One was based at Hirara, another at Shimoji, and a third at Uruka (Sunagawa). One term for them was *kashira* (chief, head). Their more formal title was *Shuri ōyako* (首里大屋子), and it was usually abbreviated as *Ōya* (大親). The early sixteenth century was start of the Ōya Era. There were two broad social classes among the islanders. The *yukarichu* were the elites, from whom village-level local officials were drawn. The rest were considered commoners.

During the eighteenth century, posts for additional officials from Shuri were established, and they were distributed more widely to include the islands of Irabu and Tarama. The main government office was the Kuramoto (蔵元), and its offices included the Shinoboseza (the grain-tax collection bureau), the Funateza (the construction [shipbuilding etc.] bureau), the Tokorozukaiza (the village expenses bureau), the Kanjōza (the recordkeeping bureau), the Keizuza (the household records registry), the Kōfuza (the cloth-tax collection bureau), the Nōmuhō (the agriculture bureau), and the Somayamahō (the forestry bureau). The organization of the Yaeyama Islands was similar.

In short, Shuri controlled the southern Ryukyu Islands tightly through central government officials stationed in the islands, local government offices that were extensions of the royal government, and the local elites who served Shuri as local officials. Proclamations from Shuri sometimes warned officials in the southern islands not to abuse the peasants by extracting extra labor or taxes from them. In such cases, Shuri's main concern was that local officials would enrich themselves at the expense of the peasants, thereby cutting into its own revenue. From Shuri's perspective, the ideal situation was hardworking, healthy peasants who pay their taxes in full and on time and are administered by efficient, loyal bureaucrats who refrain from taking advantage of opportunities to line their own pockets. Reality typically differed.

Relocations and Disasters in Yaeyama

The government in Shuri was in a difficult position. Satsuma drained off a substantial portion of its resources via annual taxes. It also put resources back into Shuri by funding the tribute trade with China, so the situation was not simply a one-way extraction. Nevertheless, even under relatively good conditions, royal government finances were precarious, and Shuri sought to extract maximum possible grain, cloth, and other taxes from its territories. As we have seen regarding Shō Shōken's agricultural policies, increasing yields was not simply a matter of opening up new land for cultivation. Opening new land incurred opportunity costs such as less land being available for fuel or lumber. Moreover, labor was more often a limiting factor than was land. Some villages had populations too large for maximum agricultural efficiency, and others had more land than there were people to farm it. During the eighteenth century, therefore, Shuri forcibly relocated peasants to increase productivity. On the one hand, forced relocations were a rational reallocation of resources, but, on the other hand, at the level of households and individuals they increased human misery.

Looking at the Yaeyama Islands, the major examples of relocation prior to the crucial year of 1771 (see Tamura 1927/1977, 146–49) are as follows (-*son* [村] means "village"):

1722: 400 from Kuroshima-son to Nosoko (野底) in Miyara-son to create Nosoko-son

1722: 700+ from five villages in Ishigaki to create Tōzato-son (桃里村)

1722: 600+ from Kohama and other small islands to create Takana-son (高那村) in Iriomote

1734: 74 from Taketomi-son in Iriomote sent to Yarabu-mori to create Haemi-son (南風見村) (in the vicinity of the Nakama River in Iriomote)

1737: 533 from a village in Tōnoshiro (Ishigaki, today's Banna Park area) combined with 87 of the original inhabitants of Nagura-son (名蔵村) to create a village of 600+

1750: 960 from Ishigaki-son to create Arakawa-son, then 1,500 from
Tōnoshiro to create Ōkawa-son, 185 from Hirae-son to create Maezato-
son, 400 more from Hirae-son plus 400 from Ōhama-son to create
Nakahara-son, and 686 from Shiraho-son to create Maja-son (真謝村)
1753: 48 from Ibaruma-son, 100 from Shiraho-son, and 200 from
Taketomi-son to create Ara-son (安良村)
1755: 200 from Hateruma to create Sakiyama-son (崎山村) in Iriomote

Notice that, particularly during the years of Sai On's tenure in office, the
relocation of people was extensive.

Disaster struck the Yaeyama Islands in 1771 in the form of the Meiwa tsunami (or Great Yaeyama tsunami). It killed over nine thousand people and
disrupted villages, property, and infrastructure. A massive burst of relocation followed in the wake of the tsunami, but, during the early modern era,
the population never recovered. It declined steadily and reached pre-1771
levels only in the 1920s. The numbers for Yaeyama's population over the
years are 27,241 in 1771 (before the tsunami), 18,119 in 1775, 15,957 in 1803,
11,216 in 1854, 16,900 in 1912, and 31,493 in 1923.

Another way to look at the relocation picture is to compare the number
of villages in 1629 to the number in 1902, just before the old tax system was
abolished, by district (*magiri*): Miyara went from eight to eleven, Ōhama
went from ten to nine, Ishigaki went from seven to eleven, and Yonaguni
remained unchanged at one. Notice that, even though the population of
the region suffered a major reduction in 1771 and had not recovered even
by 1902, the total number of villages grown from twenty-six to thirty-two.
This was the result of social engineering by Kuramoto officials to increase
agricultural efficiently.

The forced relocation of people was not unique to the Yaeyama Islands.
It took place throughout Shuri's jurisdiction, including on the island of Okinawa. In Yaeyama, however, relocations were extensive, and they have often been cited in modern times, along with the so-called poll tax, as a source
of past misery.

Table 12.2 outlines major outbreaks of deadly disease, famine, or other
natural disasters in the Ryukyu Islands, leaving out the Meiwa tsunami of
1771. Notice that, during the nineteenth century, deaths from famine and
disease increased in frequency all over the Ryukyu Islands. To some extent,
it may have been random bad luck, but from other evidence we know that
agriculture everywhere in the islands was underproducing and under constant stress. In other words, food insecurity contributed to the population
becoming ever more susceptible to the ravishes of famine and disease.

TABLE 12.2. Major outbreaks of deadly disease, famine, and other natural disasters in the Ryukyu Islands

Year	Type of disaster	Specific location (if known or applicable)	Deaths (if known)
1709	Famine from typhoon	Okinawa	3,199
1772	Smallpox	Okinawa	4,560
1776	Famine	Yaeyama Islands	3,733
1802	Epidemic disease		425
1816	Famine		1,563
1825	Famine		3,358
1827	Famine		
1832	Famine from typhoon and disease		3,928
1838	Typhus and other diseases		10,856[a]
1852	Famine from storms and drought	Miyako	3,000
1854	Fever-causing disease	Miyako and Kumejima	
1879	Cholera		6,400

Note: The numbers of total deaths are taken from Nakagawa (2005, 72).

[a] 636 in Yaeyama.

Causes of Misery

As in the northern Ryukyu Islands, during the nineteenth century life in the southern Ryukyu Islands became increasingly difficult for ordinary people. Moreover, the old taxation system continued until 1903, well past the end of the kingdom. The delay in abolishing the old tax system is one reason early modern taxation is remembered to this day as having been especially cruel. Which entity was responsible for inflicting so much misery on the people of the southern Ryukyu Islands? There is no simple answer because several factors combined to worsen the situation for ordinary people.

First was Satsuma. There were no officials from Satsuma stationed in the southern Ryukyu Islands, but, soon after 1609, these islands became Satsuma's territory in the eyes of the *bakufu*. All the domains in Japan at this time tended to prioritize tax collection and revenue enhancement. Satsuma, however, was especially willing to press its farming population—especially islanders—for revenue. The southern Ryukyu Islands had been relatively wealthy conquered territory in the sixteenth century, thanks to the century or so of direct trade with China (ca. 1400–1500). In 1500, Shuri envisioned the islands as a source of wealth, and this situation did not fundamentally change after 1609. Therefore, Satsuma's tax on Shuri fell disproportionately heavily on the people of the southern Ryukyu Islands as it got passed down.

Especially if we apply contemporary ideas about what governments should and should not do, it is easy to assign blame to both Satsuma and Shuri for rapacious taxation. However, we should not forget the role of local officials. In both the northern and the southern Ryukyu Islands, these people tended to abuse their power and privileges to enrich themselves at the expense of the other villagers. In 1768, the high-ranking official Yoseyama Ueekata was dispatched from Shuri to investigate conditions in Yaeyama. He reported that local officials abused the peasants and sought to enrich themselves. As a result, peasants were unable to work efficiently and pay their taxes fully. Owing to Yoseyama's report, Shuri issued strongly worded warnings to local officials and permitted peasants to report abusive overlords to police officials. It also created three districts in Yaeyama (previously all the islands had been one district). It is unlikely, however, that any of these measures did much to lessen the peasants' misery. The power of local officials was deeply entrenched, and Shuri lacked the resources fully to control them. Even the modern Japanese state lacked such resources until ca. 1903.

Like *yanchu* in the north, many peasants in the south became de facto servants of their local officials. It is unlikely that all local officials were abusive, but there was little or no counterbalance to those who were. The cloth tax was especially vulnerable to abuse by local officials. Because cloth weaving requires special equipment, the typical arrangement was that women worked at a communal weaving hut throughout the day under the constant supervision of local officials. This was forced labor, little different from factory slavery, and sexual abuse was always a potential and sometimes an actual problem. Another source of misery was the forced relocations, described above, which disrupted many lives.

While government at each level (local officials, Shuri, Satsuma) played a major role in increasing the suffering of Ryukyuan peasants, especially during the nineteenth century, so too did natural disasters. Natural hazards include phenomena in the environment such as seismicity, fierce winds accompanying storms, disease-causing microorganisms, and so forth. When these hazards intersect with human societies, they might cause significant death and destruction. In that case, the result is a natural disaster.

The initial cause of most of the famines outlined in table 12.2 was adverse weather. In the Ryukyu Islands, adverse weather could mean floods, droughts, high winds, or some combination of the three. In addition to deadly epidemic diseases, malaria has afflicted the Ryukyu Islands from ancient times through the early 1960s. The disease was known by a variety of names in premodern texts, and there are three types. First is tropical malaria, the most severe type, which mainly infected people in the southern Ryukyu Islands. This type typically flares up on a daily basis and was often fatal. There are two other varieties of malaria found in Okinawa and farther north. In one, occasional flare-ups last for up to three days, and, in the other, they last for up to four days. Although these forms of malaria are rarely fatal, those infected usually suffered periodic repeat outbreaks.

Agriculture: A Fundamental Problem

The factors outlined above have been discussed by many scholars of Ryukyuan history. Together, they constitute a perfect storm of misery that increased in intensity throughout most of the nineteenth century. There was, however, another fundamental problem that most scholars overlook (exceptions include Asato 2010, Kurima 2013, and Yoshinari 2020). The Ryukyu Islands lack the capacity to support large agricultural societies. An agricultural society (J. *nōkō shakai*) is one in which agriculture forms the basis of the economy, generates the majority of wealth, and contributes to social complexity and state formation or maintenance.

Scholars have long assumed that, because agriculture *existed* in the Ryukyu Islands as early as the eleventh century, these islands necessarily became agricultural societies. Agriculture, including animal husbandry, was an important component of the food supply, but there is no strong evidence that agricultural surpluses provided the wealth that powered the formation of a kingdom. As we have seen, it was trade—or trading and raiding—that generated this surplus wealth.[9]

During the early modern era, the trade component of the economy was vastly reduced and concentrated in the hands of Shuri-Naha area elites. The vast networks of local powers who had once engaged in regional trade were long gone. All that was left for generating a taxable profit was agriculture and local skilled crafts. Reformers like Shō Shōken and Sai On tried hard to make agriculture work, that is, to make Shuri's territories into a collection of viable agricultural societies. However, eighteenth- and nineteenth-century records indicate that these reforms never succeeded on a large scale. Yields were often insufficient in part because fertilizer and metal tools were in short supply. Many farmers worked with wooden tools. At best, metal tools consisted only of small sickles and spades. Metal hoes and plows were either nonexistent or very rare. Metal-edged hoes came into common use only during the twentieth century. Furthermore, most Ryukyuan soil is poorly suited to agriculture, especially when it comes to cereal grains (rice, wheat, millet, etc.). Even where the soil was good or at least adequate, a substantial input of fertilizer and labor was needed to produce crops on a large enough scale to pay taxes and have something left over. As we have seen, sugar and turmeric made up more than half of tax revenues in Okinawa by the eighteenth century, another reflection of the poor state of cereal-grain agriculture.

During the early modern era, Chinese envoys periodically traveled to Naha to invest new kings. While there, they typically took notes about conditions in Okinawa and then published book-length reports on returning to China. Their accounts all indicate that Okinawa was poorly suited to agriculture. For example, Guō Rǔlín was the envoy for Shō Gen's investiture. In *Jūhen shi Ryūkyū roku* (Revised record of an envoy to Ryukyu), he observed that the landscape in the countryside was rocky and that the soil was sandy and impoverished (see Guō 1561/2000). People raised cows, sheep, chickens, and pigs, but the animals were so thin that they were of little use as food. The people were inept at agriculture, and they rarely used fertilizer. People's meager grain consumption put them on the verge of starvation, and they rarely ate fish or meat. Shō Ei's investiture envoys, Xiāo Chóngyè and Xiè Jié, made nearly the same observation in 1579. In 1721, the envoy Xú Bǎoguāng noted in *Chūzan denshinroku* (Record of Chūzan communications) that there were significant environmental constraints on Okinawan agriculture (see Xú 1721/1982). Farmers sowed seeds in the ninth and tenth lunar months and harvested during the fifth. This unusual cycle was the result of the severe wind- and rainstorms that regularly occur during the sixth month and damage crops. Discussing agricultural tools, Xú pointed out that spades were small and that mountain fields were irrigated only by rainwater. Wet fields must therefore be located under a spring because rivers and ponds are subject to saltwater intrusion and thus cannot be used for irrigation.

Today, sugarcane, pineapple, and other warm-climate crops constitute part of the economy of Okinawa and Kagoshima Prefectures. Cereal-grain agriculture, however, has faded away to almost nothing in Okinawa and the southern Ryukyu Islands. Such grains are produced elsewhere—whether in Japan or elsewhere in the world—and shipped into the islands. In short, the project of creating an agricultural society during the early modern era was probably doomed to fail from the start.

Conclusion

Throughout the early modern era, Shuri extracted resources from the outlying areas of what remained of its empire. Those extractions were heavy, and, in relative, per capita terms, they tended to increase over time. The nineteenth century was a time of increasing poverty and human misery in both the northern and the southern Ryukyu Islands. In the northern islands, the profitability of sugar consigned most of the population to lives of poverty and backbreaking labor. Moreover, the policy of prohibiting the use of money and travel to Kagoshima reinforced a consciousness of division between Ryukyuans, on the one hand, and denizens of Satsuma, on the other.

Although Shuri made several attempts to create viable agricultural societies in its territory, the odds were stacked against that endeavor owing to the physical environment. Environmental constraints and natural disasters kept agricultural production low. During the nineteenth century, the situation became steadily worse, especially in the southern Ryukyu Islands. By the end of the century, as we will see in more detail, the Ryukyu Kingdom had become a de facto failed state.

When Japan's Meiji state moved definitively to create Okinawa Prefecture out of the kingdom in 1879, some Okinawan elites protested and passively resisted. Importantly, however, the move did not cause any popular opposition. By the late nineteenth century, there was little or no loyalty to or nostalgia for the regime in Shuri among ordinary people in Okinawa, and Shuri's control was positively despised by peasants in the southern Ryukyu Islands—as well as by their modern descendants.

CHAPTER THIRTEEN

The Mature Kingdom

By the late eighteenth century, Sai On's reforms had modestly improved the economic basis of the government in Shuri. However, the 1771 Meiwa tsunami was a major setback, and the whole project of a viable society based on agriculture was precarious. Nevertheless, as the year 1800 approached, the situation in Okinawa and the southern Ryukyu Islands was relatively stable. During this relatively stable era—between 1789 and 1835—the royal government established formal educational institutions from the elementary to the advanced levels in the Naha-Shuri area. This chapter examines Shuri's royal government in its mature form, during the early and mid-nineteenth century.

Mature Central Government Structure

The topic of the government in Shuri has come up many times thus far. We have examined the top part of the government—the king, the prime minister (*sessei*), and the Council of Three—but what about the rest of it? Figure 13.1 offers a broad outline of the government in its mature form, that is, in the early nineteenth century.

Notice the main features. Under the king was a deliberative body, the Council of State, which formulated policy. To carry out those policies, and for the routine management of the government, there were two broad divisions, one concerned with finance and the other with everything else. Under the Division of Finance were three departments, and under the Division of General Governance were four departments. Let us take a closer look at these seven departments and the offices within them. The list of offices, translated freely to highlight their main functions, indicates the specific functions and the priorities of the mature early modern royal government.

Under the Department of Revenue were thirteen offices handling the following areas:

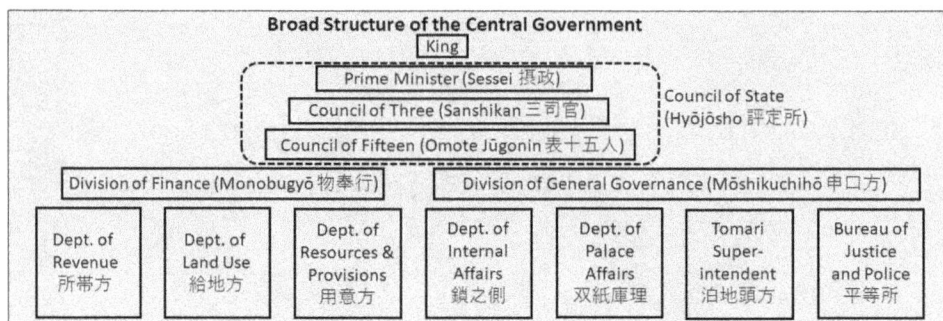

FIGURE 13.1. Diagram of the major administrative divisions
of the mature government of the Ryukyu Kingdom

Agriculture (田地方)
Revenue from land subject to periodic redistribution (取納座)
Revenue from reclaimed land (*shiakechi*) not subject to redistribution
(請地方)
Granary (米蔵)
Tax grain bound for Satsuma (仕上世座)
Tax grain from the southern Ryukyu Islands and Kumejima (宮古蔵)
Strong room for taxes paid in cash (銭蔵)
Budget (賦方)
Tax goods inspection (座検者方)
Sago palm office (蘇鉄方)
Paper (supply and manufacture) (紙座)
Manufactured goods and produce (諸製方)
Lacquer/wax trees (Japan wax tree, 櫨垂方)

Most of these offices are straightforward. Taxes paid in produce and finished goods necessitated officials charged with inspecting the quality of the
items in questions. Several offices were concerned with specific resources
such as the trees with valuable sap. During the early modern era, Ryukyu
provided many such trees to the Japanese mainland. Papermaking was one
of the industries that developed as part of Sai On's initiatives. Sago palms
(*sotetsu*, 蘇鉄) grow plentifully throughout the Ryukyu Islands. They were
used for erosion and wind control, and their barely edible fruit functioned
as a food of last resort in times of famine. This plant figures in Ryukyuan history again during the 1920s.

Within the Department of Land Use were seven offices handling the following areas:

Land assessment (高所)
Salary lands (lands that provided stipends for officials) (給地座)
Tax cloth from the southern Ryukyu Islands and Kumejima (用物座)
Shipbuilding (船手蔵)
Auditing (勘定座)
Tools and utensils (道具当)
Emergency relief (救助蔵)

Most of the offices are concerned with land use in some manner. The raw material for shipbuilding came from forest lands, which were supervised by the Department of Resources and Provisions.

The Department of Resources and Provisions (lit. the Readiness Department) included six offices handling the following areas:

Reserve granary (用意蔵)
Sugar production (a royal monopoly) (砂糖蔵)
Forest management (山奉行所)
Palace pantry (料理座)
Palace kitchen (大台所)
Tax debt collection (催促方)

In addition to supplying the royal palace with food, this department supervised an essential natural resource (forests) and the dominant source of revenue (sugar). The office handling tax debt collection seems out of place in this department, and there is very little information about it. Its name literally means "urging bureau," and its main function seems to have been to press for the payment of back taxes—somewhat like a modern collection agency.

Looking over the list of offices on the financial side of the government provides an overview of the main sources of revenue and some of the large or potentially large expenditures (the royal palace, taxes to Satsuma, shipbuilding, and local emergency relief). Notice that several offices were devoted to extracting resources from the other islands.

Moving to the Division of General Governance, the Department of Internal Affairs included ten offices handling the following areas:

Genealogical records (系図座)
The magistrate of Naha (那覇里主所)
The magistrate of Kumemura (久米村方)
The State Academy (国学)
The Confucian academy (Meirindō) in Kumemura (久米村明倫堂)

Schools in the three districts of Shuri (首里三平等学校所)
Schools in the four neighborhoods of Naha (那覇四町学校所)
School in Tomari (泊村学校所)
Schools in each neighborhood of Shuri (首里各村学校所)
The supervisors of harbors (諸浦在番)

Notice the many educational institutions. Most were very recent additions of nineteenth-century vintage, a follow-up to Sai On's call for the government to establish schools. The top institution was the state academy (roughly like a university), followed by the schools in the three districts of Shuri (middle or high schools) and then the schools in neighborhoods (elementary schools). The spread of formal education outside Kumemura resulted in an unpleasant incident described later in this chapter.

The Department of Palace Affairs included six offices handling the following areas:

Inner palace affairs (下庫理)
The royal library and documents (書院)
The storehouse (納殿)
Fine crafts and royal utensils (小細工奉行所)
Shells and shell products (貝摺奉行)
The stables (厩方)

The royal library and document office took care of the king's official correspondence. It also supervised certain other specialized palace functions. For example, royal physicians worked from this office. The storehouse procured specialty items for the royal household.

The Tomari Superintendent included eight offices dealing with the busy port of Tomari, just above Naha. (Tomari was the port for smaller ships and traffic to and from other Ryukyu Islands.) Several major industries and religious buildings were also located there. The eight offices handled the following areas:

Temples and shrines (寺社座)
Household registry (大与座)
Police inspector (総横目)
Magistrate of Tomari (泊村方)
Maintenance and repair (普請奉行所)
Blacksmith foundry (鍛冶奉行所)
Rooftile works (瓦奉行所)
Fire department (総与力)

Finally, the Bureau of Justice and Police was the main enforcement agency of the kingdom's first official penal law code, *Ryūkyū karitsu* (1786).[1] It operated under a set of formal rules for trials, *Kyūmei hōjō* (1786), and it also guarded the royal mausoleum, Tamaudun. In practice, it handled only major cases because minor crimes and civil disputes were usually dealt with locally. Typically, the Council of State approved serious judicial penalties before they could be caried out.

Female Religious Officials

All the officials who headed or staffed the government offices listed above were men. Roughly paralleling this hierarchy of male officials was a hierarchy of female religious and spiritual officials who carried out regular duties connected with the rituals of state (fig. 13.2). They also performed extraordinary duties as needed in times of emergency.

The *kikoe-ōgimi*, the high priestess, was roughly the counterpart of the king. The high priestess was a relative newcomer historically, arriving in Okinawa with the second Shō dynasty. One of Shō Shin's major accomplishments was to elevate the high priestess above the other, older regional priestesses. During the sixteenth century and the early seventeenth, the high priestess was one of the king's sisters. In that capacity, she channeled vitality and power (*seji*) from the sun and transferred it to the king (fig. 13.3). In this arrangement, the king's sister was essential for the king's spiritual potency. The *kikoe-ōgimi* was not herself the solar deity. Instead, she was the human avatar of Benzaiten, a powerful protective deity commonly associated with large bodies of water. In that capacity, she had the ability to take the sun's power and pass it on to the king via special rituals.

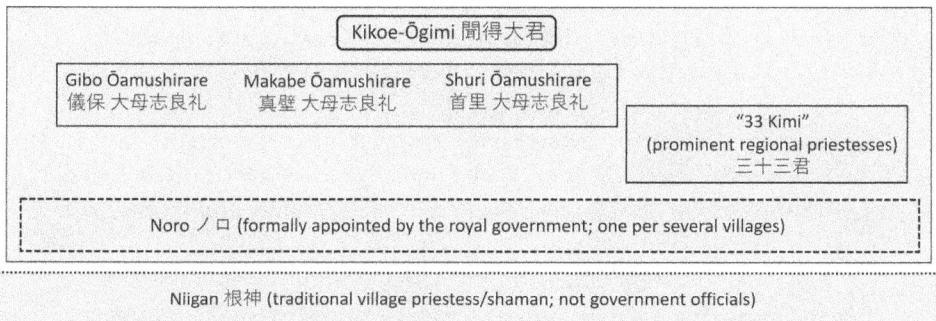

FIGURE 13.2. The basic organization of the religious hierarchy of the mature Ryukyu Kingdom

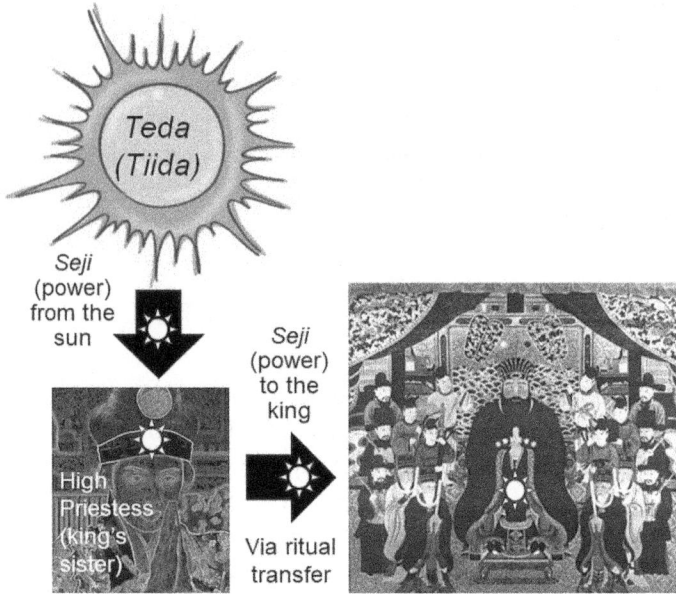

FIGURE 13.3. The dominant conception of supernatural
power flow until ca. the late seventeenth century

This arrangement began to change with Shō Shōken and especially Sai On. That the king derived his power via a female intermediary was not compatible with a Confucian outlook. Therefore, reformers like Sai On worked to transform the king into a Confucian sage. The *kikoe-ōgimi* remained in place, and, because Confucians tend to put much stock in rituals, she continued to perform the usual religious rites. Someone like Sai On would have regarded these rites as having no power in and of themselves. Their benefit was to put the minds of the superstitious common people at ease. In this new Confucian-inspired context, the queen took over the role of high priestess. In this context, the *kikoe-ōgimi* transformed from an essential enabler of royal power to being clearly subordinate to the king.

Under the *kikoe-ōgimi* were the three top priestesses of Shuri, the *ōamushirare*. Also under the high priestess but slightly lower in status were the "thirty-three *kimi*," the prominent regional priestesses such as the Nakijin Aoriyae and Kumejima's *kimihae*. Recall that the number *thirty-three* was not exact. In this context, it means "various" or "numerous."

Noro were royal appointees at the district level throughout the Ryukyu Islands. Even after 1609, *noro* in the northern Ryukyu Islands continued to be appointed by the king in Shuri. Satsuma tried to abolish the practice, but local opposition proved too strong. The southern Ryukyu Islands did not have a tradition of *noro*. Known there as *tsukasa* (司), these official priestesses arrived in the southern Ryukyu Islands soon after Shuri conquered them in 1500.

At the level of individual villages, the prominent religious figure was a woman known as *niigan* (J. *negami*, lit. "root deity"). Typically, she was regarded as a descendant of the founding family of the village. The founder of the village was typically enshrined at a local sacred grove, and the *niigan* performed rites there. Recall that sacred groves originated in the Korean Peninsula. *Niigan* were part of this older stratum of culture. Although relations between *niigan* and *noro* could be tense in some circumstances, by the time of the mature kingdom these two types of priestesses coexisted without much difficulty.

Female shamans and sorcerers known as *yuta*, however, came under severe pressure from the royal government during Sai On's tenure. Whereas *niigan* fit nicely into a framework of ancestral veneration, serious Confucians tended to regard shamans and sorcerers, male or female, as charlatans. In the official view, resources spent on *yuta* were wasted. However, most Ryukyuans—even many high-ranking officials—were not serious Confucians. Well into the twentieth century, *yuta* were popular among Okinawans from all walks of life. Their services could potentially cure disease or promote a household's prosperity. Deeply rooted in local culture, such women (and some men) who perform the mantic arts could not be eliminated by Shuri's decree.

The Mature Image of the King

Starting with the second Shō dynasty, Okinawan kings appeared in posthumous portraits called *ogoe* (御後絵). Compare the two portraits reproduced in figure 13.4. There are several important differences in the portrayals these two kings. First, notice the size of the king relative to his ministers and attendants. In relative terms, Shō Tei is larger than Shō Nei. Notice the background of Shō Nei. It is the waves of the sea with the sun and moon overhead. In Shō Nei's time, kings were still lords of the sea, a carryover from the era of *wakō* and trade kings. By contrast, Shō Tei was not portrayed as a seafaring monarch. Instead, he was cast as a Chinese-style emperor. In front of him and his tiny ministers is a ritual vessel known as a *dǐng* (鼎, J. *tei*). It is the classical Chinese symbol of a monarch's authority. By 1709, classical Chinese symbolism had become prominent at the royal court.

FIGURE 13.4. A comparison of posthumous portraits of Shō Nei
(r. 1589–1620; *left*) and Shō Tei (r. 1669–1709; *right*) indicating
changes in royal symbolism (Wikimedia Commons)

FIGURE 13.5. A comparison of posthumous portraits of
Shō Tei (r. 1669–1709; *left*) and Shō Iku (r. 1835–47; *right*)
indicating changes in royal symbolism (Wikimedia Commons)

Next, compare the two portraits reproduced in figure 13.5. Notice that
Shō Iku's crown has nearly twice as many rows of jewels as Shō Tei's.
Moreover, there are dragons on Shō Iku's robes, another classical Chinese
symbol of royal authority. During the sixteenth century, kings retained
links—even if only of a symbolic nature—with their seafaring *wakō* legacy.
They also depended on a sister to transmit cosmic power to them. By the

late seventeenth century, during the era of Shō Shōken, kings were beginning to transform into Chinese-style monarchs. By the nineteenth century, mainly as a result of Sai On's reforms and influence, the symbolic imperial transformation of kings was complete. In terms of optics, they were very nearly on a par with Chinese emperors.

Activist Kings

Although technically retired, Sai On served as an adviser to Shō Boku during the early years of his reign. Shō Boku vigorously extended or preserved many of Sai On's policies. For example, he promoted the royal cult, establishing a hall for the veneration of royal ancestral tablets, and initiating a yearly feast before the royal graves at Tamaudun. Like Sai On and Shō Kei did, he toured the northern forests of Okinawa and later insisted that the Council of Three do the same. During his reign, Ryukyu's first comprehensive law code, *Ryūkyū karitsu*, was written and promulgated. It closely resembled China's Qing legal code. *Ryūkyū karitsu* includes one volume of cases of exemplary conduct, and it specifies rewards for such conduct. The code includes eighteen volumes of laws, prohibitions, and penalties, occasionally including past cases as illustrations.

During Shō Boku's reign, serious problems began to emerge. The Meiwa tsunami in Yaeyama was one. Also, by 1791, the royal government had become seven thousand *kanme* of silver in debt to Satsuma. The king forced wealthy households to extend loans to the government that would never be repaired. He also allowed a hitherto unprecedented number of wealthy commoners to purchase noble status (they became *shinzanshi*) to raise revenue. Nevertheless, royal finances remained precarious, and Ryukyu's government was in debt to Satsuma from this point until the end of the kingdom.

Like Sai On, Shō Boku worked to shore up Ryukyu's ever-fragile agricultural base. His government undertook surveys and dispatched special troubleshooting agricultural officials called *gechiyaku* (下知役). Such efforts were only minimally effective.

Shō Boku's young and enthusiastic successor was Shō On, named after Sai On. Shō On ascended the throne at age twelve and died at age nineteen. According to legend, he was poisoned by his enemies. Who might those enemies have been?

The Qing court permitted Ryukyu to send four students at a time to China's National Academy (Guózĭjiān). They received a high-quality education at the expense of the Qing treasury. Such students were known as *kanshō*

288 < THE MATURE THEATRICAL KINGDOM, 1630–1880

(官生, Ch. *guānshēng*). In 1798, Shō On changed the *kanshō* selection process. Instead of all four students being selected from Kumemura, two would be selected from among qualified young men in Shuri. The idea for this change may have come from Sai Seishō (1737?–98), a Confucian scholar and relative of Sai On. He became Shō On's tutor about a year before the king announced the new policy. In any case, this change did not represent a spur-of-the-moment decision. The previous year, the Council of Fifteen (see fig. 13.1 above) approved the idea, and Kumemura officials were given a chance to respond. They took four months in doing so, and, by the time they did, the decision had already been made. Kumemura was in some sense a victim of its own success. It had long held a monopoly on Chinese learning, while the Shuri elites focused on Japanese arts and literature. However, Chinese learning prospered in Shuri during Shō Boku's reign to the point that Shuri could also provide *kanshō*. The residents of Kumemura feared for their livelihoods, and their reaction was violent.

Nearly all Kumemura's residents signed a petition opposing the new policy. However, Sai Seishō and the prominent scholar Tei Kōtoku refused to do so. The Council of Three rejected the petition and ordered the head of Kumemura to cease opposing the new policy. At that point, Kumemura residents rioted. They attacked the residences of Sai Seishō and Tei Kōtoku and hurled excrement at them. The Kumemura leadership even sent a letter of protest to Satsuma's top official in Okinawa—oddly reminiscent of Heshikiya Chōbin (see chap. 15). The matter is known as the Kumemura Disturbance (*Kumemura sōdō*) or the Kanshō Disturbance (*Kanshō sōdō*).

The reaction from Shuri was swift and severe. Police agents rounded up the ringleaders over the course of several days. One of the ringleaders, Matsunaga Peichin, was banished to Kumejima. All the others were banished to remote locations. The other participants in the rioting were forced to retire from public life and become Buddhist monks. Kumemura's influence suffered a major setback, one from which it never recovered.

Soon thereafter, a second shock arrived when Shō On's government established the State Academy (Kokugaku, 国学) in Shuri as well as plans for a mid-level school in each of the three districts of Shuri. These schools offered a classical Chinese-style curriculum to Shuri's elites, further eroding Kumemura's monopoly on high-level Chinese learning. Kumemura was not out of business, however. The purpose of the State Academy was to train potential government officials. The purpose of Meirindō, the Confucian academy in Kumemura, was to train diplomats for service in China.

At the time of the founding of the State Academy, Shō On issued a statement of principle. Henceforth, merit, not heredity, would be the most important criterion for selecting officials: "Without consideration of whether his lineage be exulted or base, if someone accumulates meritorious deeds, works hard at scholarship, and proposes plans that are beneficial to the country, then even if he be the son of a commoner, I will raise him up and make use of him. On the other hand, if someone fails his exams, indulges excessively in leisure, and fails to abide by wise teachings, then even if he be the son of a high-ranking *yukatchu*, I will have him dismissed and removed from office" (quoted in Smits 1999, 139). These were strong words from the young king, portending radical social change if they had been put into practice.

In the context of early modern Japan, the intellectual historian Watanabe Hiroshi has aptly characterized Confucianism as having been "dangerous thought" (Watanabe Hiroshi 2012). Confucian thought prioritized earned merit over hereditary social status. Institutionalized Confucianism tended to undermine hereditary privilege. Here we see the same potentially disruptive impact in the context of elite Okinawan society. There would have been a long list of capital-area elites happy to see Shō On depart this world at the tender age of nineteen.

Relations with China and Making Good Impressions

For the royal government, the main point of the tribute trade was that it enabled Ryukyu to remain in business as a kingdom. The connection with China was the very basis of Ryukyu's continued existence. China also became a valuable source of knowledge and new technologies. In addition to the *kanshō*, who studied in Beijing, young men from Kumemura often studied specific subjects in southern China, a phenomenon called *kingaku* (勤学). Topics of study included language, music, painting, navigation, the calendar, astronomy, medicine, agriculture, silk production, and more. A few specific examples of Ryukyuans in China and the subjects they pursued follows:

1678: Sai Chōkō (蔡肇功), calendar science
1623: Ma Heikō (麻平衡), sugar production methods
1663: Riku Tokusen (陸得先), producing white sugar and rock candy
1668: Gi Shitetsu (魏士哲), lip repair surgery
1714: Tei Junsoku (程順則), brought *Rikuyu engi* (六輸衍義) (a morality primer) and other Chinese texts to Okinawa and Japan; wrote a guide to maritime navigation
1743: An Mōtoku (晏孟得), tongue surgery

Pragmatic knowledge, technologies, and products came into early modern Ryukyu from both Japan and China. One of the most important Chinese contributions (in the seventeenth century) was sweet potatoes, which then spread from Ryukyu to the Japanese mainland, enhancing food security in all places.

Chinese ships sailed to Naha to invest new kings. Such investiture missions were a severe strain on royal finances. After taking the throne, therefore, kings often had to wait years or decades before they received investiture. The reason for the financial strain was that the Chinese entourage arrived not only with diplomats but also with merchants, sailors, and merchandise. Only the envoys received a salary from the Chinese government. Everyone else came to Okinawa without pay, expecting instead to profit from sale of the merchandise. The merchants and sailors were lodged at Shuri's expense and would not leave until the royal government had purchased all the merchandise. Haggling over prices sometimes became violent. One of Sai On's accomplishments, for example, was deescalating a dispute in 1719 over the valuation of Chinese goods during Shō Kei's investiture that came to be known as the valuation incident (*hanga* [J. *hyōka*] *jiken*, 評価事件).

Skill in diplomacy and the general management of Ryukyu's relations with China was difficult to acquire, in part because of the language demands. At a minimum, Kumemura residents had to master spoken Chinese with respect to formal, ritual situations. Ideally, they learned to speak Chinese freely, although many clearly did not. For example, the first thing that Sai On did in de-escalating the valuation incident was to insist that all communication be conducted in writing to avoid misunderstandings. Furthermore, a good diplomat would be able to write classical Chinese poetry, which lubricated the gears of diplomatic and cultural exchange. Poetry exchange accompanied many diplomatic situations, and the presentation of poems as gifts was a common practice. In 1761, a group of Ryukyuan students in Beijing made a good impression on their hosts by presenting a book of poems they wrote in honor of the empress dowager's seventieth birthday.

By 1800 or so, Kumemura residents were well attuned to a variety of best practices in handling relations with China. One interesting example is the arrangement of the ancestral tablets of the Chūzan kings. The customary Chinese *zhāo-mù* (昭穆秩序) order (fig. 13.6) put the dynastic founder in the middle, the even-numbered reigns to his left (*zhāo*), and the odd numbered reigns to his right (*mù*). The Okinawan arrangement logic, by contrast, had the most important founding figure (Shunten) flanked by the founders of two ancient lines, Eiso and Satto, followed by the kings of the current second Shō dynasty (fig. 13.6). Moreover, there was a Buddhist manner of arranging the tablets that also differed from the Chinese order. Okinawans became aware that Chinese envoys regarded their arrangement

The "proper" Chinese zhāo-mù order that spreads outward chronologically from the first king

2nd Shō 1st Shō & Earlier Gihon Shunten Eiso Shunbajunki 1st Shō & Earlier 2nd Shō

先王廟神主昭穆図

The Ryukyuan order of royal tablets associating the 2nd Shō dynasty with Eiso, Shunten & Satto

1st Shō & Earlier 2nd Shō Satto Shunten Eiso 2nd Shō 1st Shō & Earlier

歴代有功王叔

FIGURE 13.6. The Chinese *zhāo-mù* order for arranging royal tablets (*top*) compared with the Ryukyuan order (*bottom*)

of Chūzan kings as haphazard. Bear in mind that, vis-à-vis China, there were no first Shō dynasty, no second Shō dynasty, and no other different lines of kings. Instead, all the kings from the mythical Shunten on formed a single, continuous lineage.

As a result, from about 1719 on, the procedure was that all sets of royal tablets—even those in the royal temple Sōgenji—were arranged in the standard Chinese order but only during visits from Chinese envoys. After the envoys left, the tablets went back to their Okinawan arrangement, which emphasized the legitimacy of the second Shō dynasty. This is a perfect example of the theatrical state in action.

Perhaps the best example of theater designed to enhance Ryukyu's image in the eyes of Chinese investiture officials was literally theater. *Kumiodori* was a combination of drama and music, with content derived from local Okinawan legends. Its creator, Tamagusuku Chōkun, had traveled to Japan five times, studying dramatic arts such as *nō, kyōgen*, puppet theater, and *kabuki*. The first known performance was in 1719, at a banquet to entertain the investiture envoys.[2] One of the plays the envoys watched was *Nidō tekiuchi* (Two boys avenge their enemy, 二童敵討), which was based on the conflict between Gosamaru and Amawari. In it, the sons of the unjustly destroyed Gosamaru kill the scheming Amawari, who had wrongly convinced the king that Gosamaru was plotting rebellion. The play transformed the violent events connected with Shō Taikyū's expansion of his territory in the 1450s into a cultural drama highlighting loyalty and filial piety.

Another *kumiodori* performance was *Kōkō no maki* (Tale of filial piety, 孝行之巻), which was particularly suited to the task of creating and conveying a sense of deeply ingrained Ryukyuan virtue. Set in the time of the legendary King Gihon (r. 1249–59), a filial son and daughter from a poor household offered themselves as sacrifices to appease a fierce dragon and, thus, provide money for their family. It was the daughter who had to make the ultimate sacrifice, thus resonating with Chinese tales of dutiful women who sacrifice their lives. However, owing to her steadfast filial piety, the cosmic forces intervened to provide a happy outcome for everyone involved. In 1800, the envoy Lǐ Dǐngyuán (李鼎元) saw this episode and was moved by it. He devoted considerable space in his writing to summarizing and quoting from the play. At the end, he commented that for heaven to reward filial behavior is deeply satisfying.

There was at least one more event that Lǐ found deeply satisfying. The eleventh day of the tenth month was his mother's birthday. He had intended to keep this matter to himself and did not tell anyone. Ryukyuan officials had done their research, however, and royal envoys surprised him with gifts of five elegant fans, an incense burner, and a commemorative longevity manuscript. The event led to a celebratory feast with the Ryukyuan envoys, and of course it enhanced Ryukyu's image as a small but highly refined kingdom worthy of Chinese esteem. Ryukyu's China handlers had by the nineteenth century become experts at their work. Indeed, that expertise has contributed to misconceptions about the nature of the relationship between Ryukyu and China, some of which persist to this day.

Ethnogenesis

In internally generated ethnogenesis, groups of people come to define themselves as ethnically or culturally distinctive vis-à-vis other groups of people within their frame of knowledge. In externally generated ethnogenesis, people outside a group begin to regard that group as a distinct ethnic or cultural entity. The existence of a state or a country is not required for ethnogenesis, but the presence of one can increase its likelihood.

Consider the matter of personal identity. With what geographic or cultural entity or structure might someone living in the Ryukyu Islands have identified? One possibility is one's village. Indeed, villages in Okinawa were such tight-knit communities that sexual relations or marriage outside the village were often prohibited by village rules. Similarly, one might identify with a district (*magiri*, roughly a county), and a variety of rules prohibited certain interactions between people of different districts.

I examine the poet Onna Nabe in chapter 15. Poems attributed to her indicate a strong identity with the Yanbaru region, and her name itself refers to her district, Onna. She was sensitive to the sociocultural divide between her and people from Shuri. Did any of Onna Nabe's poems or those of other poets like Yoshiya Umitsuru hint at possessing a Ryukyuan or an Okinawan identity or something similar? The short answer is no, but that does not necessarily mean that neither woman was conscious of being Ryukyuan. However, even if they were, their identification with Onna District and the region around it seems to have been paramount.

It may be useful to consider the extent to which people living in the Japanese islands identified as Japanese. If we were to zoom in around the year 1900, modern school systems, flags, anthems, newspapers, and a variety of other social phenomena and institutions constantly reinforced a Japanese identity. The vast majority of ordinary people from Hokkaidō through the bottom of Kyushu and further south would have regarded themselves first and foremost as Japanese. They might also have embraced a local identity, but it would have been subordinate to the national identity. Were a reporter to ask such people to define *Japanese identity* precisely, most likely there would be no single response, although certain themes would have been common, for example, something about the emperor or about uniquely possessing the virtues of loyalty and filial piety. Regardless of how they might define or imagine the details, in 1900 nearly everyone in Japan embraced the label *Japanese*.

What about the year 1800? Nearly all the elements that combined to create a Japanese identity in 1900 would have been absent or very faint in 1800. It is possible that some farmers vaguely understood that they lived in a place called *Japan*, but their primary identities would have been to village, domain, or province. Indeed, the very word *country* (*kuni*, 国) almost always referred to a province or *daimyō* domain. In 1800, there were "countries" all over the Japanese islands. By 1900, however, there was only one country in the Japanese islands, Japan. For most people around the world, primary modern or contemporary identities with nation-states are relatively recent historical constructs.

In the Ryukyu Islands, ethnogenesis took place at different times in different places among different social groups. Moreover, the characteristics that different groups imagined as fundamental to their ethnos varied as well. What follows is a brief summary.

The first group to regard themselves explicitly as Ryukyuans were the elites of the Shuri-Naha area. Let us regard as elite those members of society who were literate and relatively wealthy or influential. In this sense, the term *elite* would include most of those with formal noble status and most commoners who worked as local government officials. Such elites constituted roughly 8–10 percent of the population. Among these people, consciousness of being Ryukyuan may have existed faintly during the sixteenth century, but it became strong over the course of the seventeenth century.

This Ryukyuan identity was concentrated geographically in the capital region and does not seem to have extended farther than the island of Okinawa, except among some of Shuri's officials in other islands. To be clear, ordinary people in the southern Ryukyu Islands were painfully aware of the existence of Shuri and the king, but there is no evidence that they identified themselves positively with that polity.

The next group were the denizens of the northern Ryukyu Islands. They became aware that they were Ryukyuan early in the nineteenth century, possibly earlier. The main reason is a lack of integration with the rest of Satsuma and, indeed, forced isolation during the sugar hell years of the nineteenth century (see chap. 12). Documents produced in the islands and in Satsuma during the nineteenth century routinely made distinctions between Ryukyuans and Japanese, and those distinctions mattered in certain circumstances.

The last group in which a Ryukyuan ethnogenesis took place was ordinary people in Okinawa and the southern Ryukyu Islands. Interestingly, their Ryukyuan identity formed at the same time and for the same reasons as did their Japanese identity. They became both Ryukyuan and Japanese simultaneously, starting in the 1880s. Let us look more closely at Okinawa.

Watanabe Miki has examined the formation of Ryukyuan elite identity during the early modern era from several angles (Watanabe Miki 2012, esp. 264). Ryukyu's international status within East Asia helped constitute its elite domestic society. For example, during the eighteenth century, a consensus of the nature of formal elite status and duties developed within the government. Ryukyuan elites bore the responsibility of fulfilling the kingdom's obligations to China and Japan, a duty made possible by superior knowledge and behavior. Those who excelled in this function were eligible for promotion or other formal rewards from the state. Similarly, elites bore the responsibility of maintaining and enhancing Ryukyu's reputation (*o-gaibun*, 御外聞) vis-à-vis its larger neighbors. They did so by carrying out trade and diplomacy in a ritualistically correct way and through their cultivation of the literary arts and other relevant knowledge domains. Skillful handling of diplomacy with China and *kumiodori* were examples of elite Ryukyuans curating the kingdom's image. This process constantly reminded them that they were Ryukyuan. Ryukyuans may not have been radically different from Japanese (with whom they shared a fundamentally Japonic culture) or Chinese (with whom they shared universalizing Confucian ideas and a literary high culture). Nevertheless, it was a meaningful category of identity.

What did it mean to be Ryukyuan for an elite Okinawan? There are multiple possible answers, but we can gain some insight into the matter by looking at the rhetoric of the 1870s produced as these elites resisted full incorporation into the new Japanese state. The *shobun* era (ca. 1870s) rhetoric of Ryukyuan elites is notable for defining Ryukyu not as a sovereign state in a modern sense but as a state defined in terms of its relations with China and Japan. Ryukyuans arguing against annexation typically characterized China and Japan as Ryukyu's mother and father. Ryukyu should continue to exist as a distinct kingdom, they argued, so that it could carry out its obligations to each of its metaphoric parents.

Ordinary islanders were well aware of Shuri's existence. After all, they toiled to pay its taxes. For the most part, however, they did not identify with Shuri on a personal level. They identified primarily with their villages. Only after being told, in the nineteenth century and later, by teachers and local officials to stop behaving like Ryukyuans and start behaving like Japanese did most rural Okinawans realize that they were both these things.

Consider a few other relevant points regarding ethnogenesis or national identity. No common language bound Ryukyuans or Okinawans together. Ordinary people in Nakijin could not communicate with people from the Shuri-Naha area. Similarly, the linguistic gaps between the Miyako Islands and the Yaeyama Islands were even greater. Today, standard Japanese is the language that all the Ryukyu Islands have in common, and, were Okinawa Prefecture to give official status to one of the Ryukyuan languages, large numbers of prefectural residents would not understand it. Symbols of royal authority were largely limited to the vicinity of the court itself or its obvious extensions such as ships. There were no common symbols of Ryukyu, such as flags or anthems, that circulated throughout the kingdom. Rugged terrain and a lack of roads and transportation infrastructure served to isolate communities within the larger islands. Before ca. 1880, few ordinary islanders would have had more than a rudimentary knowledge of China and Japan or a sense of Ryukyu as a part of a larger East Asia.

The story of what happened when prevailing local identities in Okinawa were submerged into dual Ryukyuan and Japanese identities is both fascinating and mostly unhappy. I return to it later chapters.

Europeans and the Myth of Ryukyuan Pacifism

As we have seen, by the nineteenth century Ryukyuan officials had become highly adept at manipulating the kingdom's image vis-à-vis outsiders. The most important group of outsiders was Chinese investiture envoys. During the nineteenth century, Europeans also entered the picture. Starting in the early nineteenth century, European ships made their way to Naha with increasing frequency. These visits produced a variety of reports about the inhabitants of Okinawa, some of which were published and reached an audience of armchair travelers. The relative obscurity of Ryukyu added to its exotic appeal. With the upheavals of the Napoleonic Wars seared into their memories, many European officers were much interested in the possibility that, somewhere in the world, a genuinely pacifist society might exist. When they got to Naha, at least some European sailors thought they had found it.

According to an uncritical summary of these accounts by George H. Kerr: "The visitor [to the Ryukyu Islands] was invariably struck by the absence of arms or incidents of violence, by the unfailing courtesy and friendliness of all classes, by the intelligence of the gentry, and by the absence of thievery among the common people" (1958/2000, 250–51). Kerr quotes European writings at great length, taking their contents at face value. Because he did not read Japanese, he depended on assistants to translate or summarize Japanese material. His general history of Okinawa was and remains highly influential in Anglophone circles, but it did not reflect the state of Japanese-language scholarship on Ryukyu even in the 1950s. The *hiki* system, for example, receives no mention even though Iha Fuyū had already published on this topic some two decades earlier. In short, Kerr seems to have had no knowledge of Ryukyuan military affairs and found the nineteenth-century European reports of a pacifist society convincing. I make these points not to criticize Kerr, who did the best he could within the limitations of his circumstances. It is important to note, however, that his book has been and continues to be a prominent vehicle for perpetuating a myth of Ryukyuan pacifism.

A major development of the myth came from the visit to Naha in 1816 of two British ships, the *Lyra* and the *Alceste*. The ships were on a mission to survey parts of the Korean coast and the Ryukyu Islands, and they stayed at Naha from September 15 through October 27. Several members of the crew noted their observations of Okinawa, but Basil Hall, the captain of the *Lyra*, and John M'Leod, the physician on board the *Alceste*, wrote lengthy accounts that were later published and widely read. These accounts gushed with praise over the kindness, gentleness, and intelligence of the Okinawans, whose behavior contrasted with the alleged boorishness and arrogance of "the Chinese." According to Hall and M'Leod, Okinawa was a land of peace and serenity. Its residents bore no weapons, and its people committed no crimes. According to Hall: "We never saw any punishment inflicted at Loochoo [Ryukyu]; a tap with a fan, or an angry look, was the severest chastisement ever resorted to, as far as we could discover" (quoted in Kerr 1958/2000, 255).[3] Note the important qualifying phrase "as far as we could discover." Hall and his crew were watched at all times, and they saw only what their Okinawan handlers wanted them to see. Hall's account of social order enforced by fan taps was destined to be repeated many times, and it remains a potent image to this day.

It is likely that Hall's account is accurate as far as it goes. Why would Hall and the other crew members, whose movements were restricted to a small area, ever have had occasion to observe police and judicial activities during their short stay? Obviously, Hall was unaware of Shuri's judicial department, the Hirajo, its police forces, or Ryukyu's detailed law codes. Likewise, he was unaware that offenders against these laws or government policy had been arrested, tortured, fined, exiled, had their property confiscated, and/ or faced the death penalty.[4] It is hardly surprising that the accounts of Hall and M'Leod would have appealed to Europeans in the wake of the Napoleonic Wars—or to anyone for that matter. Interestingly, when Hall described Okinawa to Napoléon himself (in exile at St. Helena) and claimed that the place had never experienced warfare, Napoléon found Hall's tale absurd. Perhaps he had a vested interest in warfare, but, as we have seen at great length, the Ryukyu Islands had been the scene of warfare for centuries. Napoléon was correct.

At the end of the nineteenth century, Basil Hall Chamberlain, a relative of Captain Hall and a noted authority on Japan, visited Okinawa Prefecture briefly and published a lengthy analysis in the *Geographical Journal*. His account of Ryukyuan history vigorously endorsed the myth of Ryukyuan pacifism. Part of his account reads: "In some important respects the country really deserved the title bestowed upon it by a Chinese emperor in 1579, and is still proudly inscribed on the gate of its capital city, the title of 'The Land of Propriety.' There were no lethal weapons in Luchu, no feudal factions, few if any crimes of violence. . . . Confucius' ideal was carried out—a government purely civil, at once absolute and patriarchal, resting not on any armed force, but on the theory that subjects owe unqualified obedience to their rulers" (Chamberlain 1895, 310–11). Here, of course, Chamberlain takes the descriptions of Hall and M'Leod and explains them in terms of classical Confucian values. In his version, Ryukyu was not only a rare or unique example of a society without war, weapons, or aggression but also a rare or unique instance of a Confucian paradise.

Later in his account, Chamberlain restated the matter in terms of the prevailing tenets of the racial "science" of the day. After discussing the physical qualities of Ryukyuans in some detail and comparing them with those of Japanese, he concludes: "The most prominent race-characteristic of the Luchuans is not a physical, but a moral one. It is their gentleness of spirit, their yielding and submissive disposition, their hospitality and kindness, their

298 ‹ THE MATURE THEATRICAL KINGDOM, 1630–1880

aversion to violence and crime. Every visitor has come away with the same favourable impression—Captain Broughton, whom they treated so hospitably on the occasion of his shipwreck in 1797; Captain Basil Hall, Dr McLeod, Dr Guillemard—even the missionaries, poor as was their success, and all the Japanese. For myself, I met with nothing but kindness from high and low alike" (Chamberlain 1895, 318–19). Like Chamberlain, today's advocates of the myth tend to speak of *the* Okinawans or *the* Ryukyuans as if they were and are a singular entity. Instead of relying explicitly on nineteenth-century notions of racial or national characteristics, the contemporary preference is to rely on a romantic version of history.

When encountering statements like those by Chamberlain, Kerr, and a host of modern popularizers of the myth, it is a good idea to recall not only the warfare of the past but also the suffering of so many people in the Ryukyu Islands who toiled to pay taxes to Shuri or Satsuma. No doubt a semitropical chain of islands in which everyone lived happily and peacefully amid warm breezes is an appealing image. However, ignoring social realities, whether in the present or in the past, is a poor foundation either for dealing with the world effectively or for improving it.

Centers versus Edges

The region of East Asia underwent a massive upheaval during the latter half of the nineteenth century. The major contributing factors were the weakening of each major early modern state in the region, the Joseon dynasty in Korea, the Qing dynasty in China, and the Tokugawa *bakufu* in Japan. At the same time, imperialism was in high gear throughout much of the world, and European powers became increasingly assertive in East Asia. Of the major states, Japan was the nimblest in adapting to the new situation. After relatively modest bloodshed, the Tokugawa *bakufu* gave way to a new, centralized state between 1867 and 1869. After the defeat of the Satsuma Rebellion in 1878, Japan's Meiji state was firmly entrenched. Less than a year later, it created Okinawa Prefecture.

To understand this era of rapid change, we should contrast the early modern logic of foreign relations and geopolitics with the significantly different modern logic. The early modern logic focused on relations between important centers or points. It was almost as if, the larger and more powerful a center was, the stronger its gravitational force. There was some concern for clarifying boundaries, but most early modern states tolerated considerable fuzziness at their edges. For example, it was never entirely clear how much of Hokkaidō was Japanese territory and how much Ainu. The greater

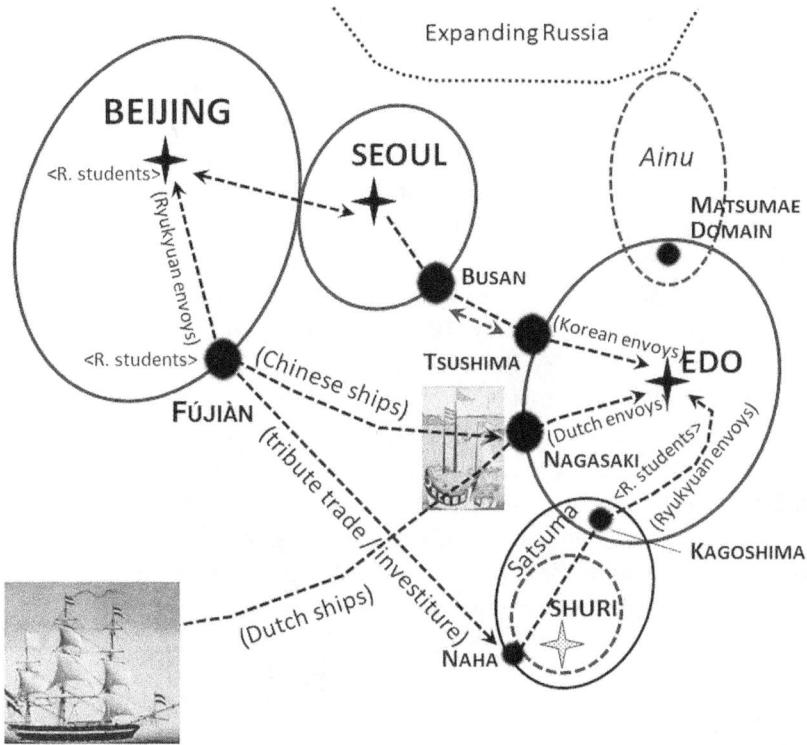

FIGURE 13.7. Diagram of regional centers (capitals) and portals (ports) through which diplomatic and commercial exchanges took place during the early modern era

concern was specific trade conditions between Ainu and Japanese who lived in the northern frontier. Similarly, the boundary in the south of Japan was unclear. Where, exactly, did Satsuma or Yamato end and Ryukyu begin? The Tokara Islands? Amami-Ōshima? Yoron? Yonaguni? Throughout the early modern era, there was extensive travel and commerce throughout the Ryukyu Arc. That some of the islands were administered by Satsuma and others by the court in Shuri mattered little for most purposes. Similar situations prevailed all over the region.

Figure 13.7 offers a schematic diagram of the major web of regional international relations during the early modern era. Diplomatic and commercial ties were formed between centers, some larger than others, and via seaports or land ports. The major centers were Edo, Seoul, Beijing, and, to a lesser extent, Shuri. The major portals were Nagasaki, Tsushima, Kagoshima, Busan, northeast China, Fúzhōu, Naha, and Hokkaidō. The centers and portals were prominent, but the edges of states were frequently vague. Where in the ocean, for example, did Japanese waters stop and Korean waters begin? Land boundaries were potentially more obvious, but even they were often unclear.

With the arrival of aggressive Europeans, clearly defined edges quickly became important. States had to define their territory clearly or risk encroachment by ambitious outsiders. Japanese leaders realized this situation rapidly. They moved to ensure that Hokkaidō was within Japan and clarify the boundary between Russia and Japan's northern islands. This process also led to the formal annexation of Ryukyu. A theatrical state like Ryukyu made sense in the early modern era. In the modern world, however, it was not viable. Given that the Ryukyu Islands had been part of Satsuma since the early seventeenth century, the new Meiji state moved formally to incorporate them into Japan on that basis, thus clarifying its southern edge.

With respect to the Ryukyu Islands, however, two different tendencies worked against each other. On the one hand, vis-à-vis the world, Tokyo unambiguously declared that the Ryukyu Islands were and had long been Japanese territory. In making this claim, it emphasized the 1609 war and the surrender documents that Ryukyuan officials signed. On the other hand, it was not able easily to weave this territory and its people into the broader social or economic fabric of modern Japan. The result was a long, awkward, and painful transition period. Several subsequent chapters examine these matters in more detail.

CHAPTER FOURTEEN

The *Ryūkyū shobun* and the Creation of Okinawa Prefecture

Throughout the latter half of the nineteenth century, the agricultural economy of Okinawa and the southern Ryukyu Islands continued to decline. European and US ships began to appear more frequently in the region, and some weighed anchor at Naha. This situation added stress to the theatrical state, which now had to conceal its connections with Japan from both Chinese and Western eyes. One result was that, when pressed by Matthew Perry, Ryukyu signed a simple treaty with the United States, followed by nearly identical treaties with France and Holland.

The collapse of the Tokugawa *bakufu* and its replacement by Japan's Meiji state led in the 1870s to a process called the *Ryūkyū shobun* (the disposition of Ryukyu, 琉球処分; hereafter *shobun*). The *shobun* was mainly the result of Japan's new leaders placing a high priority on clarifying boundaries, motivated by a fear of imperialist encroachment. Tokyo's leaders decided that the Ryukyu Islands must become formally and publicly incorporated into Japan, but there were three main obstacles: the treaties with the United States, France, and Holland, the tribute trade with China, and passive resistance by the king and his officials. These obstacles, combined with major events within Japan—such as the abolition of the domains, the abolition of samurai, and several uprisings—delayed the formal designation of the kingdom as Okinawa Prefecture until 1879.

The period following the 1879 annexation and lasting through the rest of the century was characterized by the policy called *kyūkan-onzon* (旧慣温存). This term refers to the preservation of certain institutions and governing practices from the days of the kingdom. The main reason for this policy was to persuade elite Okinawans to cooperate with the new order. It also reflected the initial weakness of Okinawa Prefecture's fledgling government. Continuation of the tax system in the southern Ryukyu Islands until 1903 is perhaps the most notorious example of *kyūkan-onzon* policies.

Even after Tokyo created Okinawa Prefecture and persuaded many former Ryukyuan officials to work for it, some elite Okinawans continued to dream of some kind of restoration of the kingdom. Moreover, international pressure led in the 1880s to negotiations between Tokyo and Beijing over the Ryukyu Islands that were inconclusive. Japan's decisive defeat of China in 1895 effectively put an end to the possibility of major change in the status of Okinawa Prefecture. This chapter examines the turbulent era from the 1870s to the end of the nineteenth century in the context of the establishment of Okinawa Prefecture.

The *Shobun* Process

The *shobun* was a complex, multifaceted process that did not conclude fully until shortly after Japan's 1895 victory in the First Sino-Japanese War. It was an attempt by the Meiji state to clarify the geopolitical status of the Ryukyu Islands with respect to Western notions of sovereignty. The process began in 1872 and soon led to a high-level Meiji government decision formally to annex the kingdom. Needless to say, the *shobun* was a major turning point in the trajectory of Ryukyuan/Okinawan history. It can also serve as a useful lens through which to view larger changes within Japan and East Asia. By the early 1870s, Japan's leaders had become well aware of the need to clarify and enhance their country's autonomy. By contrast, Ryukyuan and Chinese notions of interstate relations continued to reflect a worldview in which states interacted with each other on the basis of family-like webs of relationships (Ch. *lǐ*; J. *rei*, 礼; ceremonial forms, propriety, rites, etc.), not as independent, sovereign entities. In practice, of course, both international relations as *lǐ* and international relations governed by law were but two different styles of articulating differences in power. Nevertheless, that Japan very quickly adopted the vocabulary and outlook of the Western powers is significant, and the *shobun* was Tokyo's first practical application of Western-style international law within the international arena.

At the level of individuals, the official logic of the *shobun* required that Ryukyuans be or quickly become Japanese because they had really always been Japanese. Most mainland Japanese accepted this idea at a basic level, and most islanders were at least not opposed to becoming Japanese. However, a dominant mainland view of the islanders as culturally backward quickly developed. The creation and early history of Okinawa Prefecture bring into focus contradictions inherent in the very idea of Japanese as a stable, coherent, naturally occurring entity to which someone might belong—as well as, of course, Ryukyuan, Okinawan, and other identity categories.

The Road to Annexation, 1872–79

In the wake of the 1609 war, Ryukyuan officials signed surrender documents. Among other matters, these documents made clear that the king was now a vassal of the lord of Satsuma. Soon thereafter, the *bakufu* recognized the Ryukyu Islands as part of Satsuma's holdings, and all the assessed agricultural productivity of the islands counted toward Satsuma's total assessed productivity. In short, Ryukyu became part of the *bakuhan* state soon after 1609.

Immediately after coming into existence ca. 1868, the new Meiji state was too busy with the urgent business of consolidating its power to concern itself with Ryukyu. When the central government formally abolished the Tokugawa Era domains in 1871, it decided tentatively to treat Ryukyu as part of Kagoshima Prefecture for administrative purposes. Early in 1872, however, Japan's leaders came to the realization that Ryukyu's vague status as a kingdom with obligations to Japan and China would have to be resolved. The theatrical state was no longer viable. Also of concern to officials in Tokyo was that the Ryukyuan court had signed treaties with three Western countries.[1]

The specific matter that prompted concern about clarifying Ryukyu's status was a report to the Foreign Ministry concerning a vessel from the island of Miyako that had run ashore in a remote part of Taiwan. Evidently, Taiwanese natives had killed most of the crew. The question of how to respond to this incident touched off a general discussion of Ryukyu's status and possible approaches to clarifying (i.e., *shobun*-ing) it. One result was a message to the Ryukyuan court, sent via Kagoshima Prefecture, that Ryukyuan envoys should visit Tokyo for discussions with Foreign Minister Soejima Taneomi.

The political rhetoric of the early Meiji state contained an interesting mixture of appeals to both modernity and antiquity. When Prince Ie and Ginowan Ueekata went to Tokyo in 1872 to meet with Soejima, they were aware of the Japanese political slogan *ōsei fukko*, which translated roughly as "restoring the ancient rule of the sovereign," and the general rhetorical stance of the Meiji state as the restorer of the proper lines of authority that centuries of Tokugawa rule had obscured. They were hopeful, therefore, that Japan's new rulers would restore Amami-Ōshima and other northern Ryukyu Islands to the king's domain. Such thinking proved to be entirely misguided. Insofar as the Meiji state invoked the rhetoric of restoring the old, in the course of the *shobun* it was to state that Ryukyu had long been a dependency of and thus a territory of Japan.[2] The Ryukyuan envoys came away from their meeting with Soejima believing that he was sympathetic to their point of view. He was not.

Instead, Soejima recommended to the government that it settle the ambiguities in Ryukyu's status by replacing Satsuma's former resident supervisor office with a branch office of the Foreign Ministry. Furthermore, Meiji officials produced an imperial decree declaring the Ryukyuan monarch, Shō Tai, "king of Ryukyu domain" (*Ryūkyū han-ō*). The Ryukyuan envoys interpreted the new title as an instance of the Japanese emperor replacing Satsuma as Ryukyu's overlord to the north. Ryukyuan acknowledgment of the designation *han* (domain), however, played into the hands of Meiji officials seeking to abolish the kingdom. In this logic, if Ryukyu were a *han* and all the other *han* had recently been eliminated and incorporated into prefectures, the same could and should happen to Ryukyu.

Was it the case, therefore, that by mid-1872 the entire leadership in Tokyo had decided to annex Ryukyu and make it a prefecture? It was certainly the Meiji state's intention to bring Ryukyu firmly under its control. It was probably not until 1874, however, that the relevant officials agreed on formal annexation as the plan. Furthermore, it was not until early 1875 that the majority of Ryukyuan officials realized that Japan's government sought to annex the kingdom, now technically the domain, and make it a prefecture.

In the seventh month of 1874, a branch office of the Home Ministry replaced the Foreign Ministry branch office in Okinawa. In retrospect, this change seems an obvious move in the context of the Meiji state asserting that Ryukyu was Japanese home territory. However, many Ryukyuan officials misinterpreted it as Japan facilitating Ryukyuan-Qing relations by changing to a less ominous form of official presence in Okinawa. Unbeknownst to Ryukyuan officials, between the time of the declaration of Ryukyu domain and the replacement of the Foreign Ministry office with the Home Ministry office, Japanese officials had been discussing Ryukyu and related matters with representatives of the three countries that had signed treaties with the kingdom and with China.[3]

Particularly important at this point was the diplomatic activity between China and Japan in connection with the ill-fated Miyako vessel mentioned above. Sometimes called the *Taiwan incident*, the attack on the Miyako crew and its aftermath facilitated the Meiji government's *shobun* efforts. Almost as soon as the incident became known in Japan, Kagoshima Prefectural Counselor Ōyama Tsunayoshi formally recommended to the central government that the responsible aboriginal group be chastised immediately in an overseas demonstration of imperial authority. Early in 1873, Foreign Minister Soejima went to Beijing and asked about the incident. He received a reply from the Chinese court stating in part that the Taiwanese aborigines lay outside the bounds of Qing governance. In other words, the Qing government disavowed any responsibility for the actions of the Taiwanese natives.

Although this answer did not amount to Qing agreement with Japanese plans, on Soejima's return the Meiji leaders begin final preparations for an attack on Taiwan to demonstrate their resolve to protect Japanese subjects.

When news of the impending attack reached foreign embassies, several European countries and the United States expressed reservations. In response to this diplomatic pressure, the central government ordered the expedition delayed. However, the expedition commander, Saigō Tsugumichi, ignored these orders, possibly with tacit central government agreement, and set sail on 1874.5.3. Thus began the Meiji state's first foreign military campaign, the Taiwan Expedition. Vigorous Qing protests eventually resulted in the withdrawal of Japan's soldiers, though not before gaining formal Chinese recognition that the murdered Ryukyuans were Japanese subjects. Furthermore, the Qing court agreed to pay some of the costs of Japan's expedition and provide money for the families of the victims.

In response to strong Qing reaction to Japan's invasion of Taiwan, Ōkubo Toshimichi went to China in the fourth month of 1874 to negotiate a settlement. While there, he was embarrassed by the appearance of a Ryukyuan tribute embassy in Beijing. The embassy was part of the regular schedule of tribute-related diplomatic activities. Naturally, the appearance of the embassy had the effect of weakening the persuasiveness of Ōkubo's argument vis-à-vis the Qing court that Ryukyuans were Japanese subjects. Remember, too, that, while individual Chinese investiture envoys had encountered evidence over the years that Ryukyu was closely linked with Japan, the Qing court was unaware of it. Leading Qing officials appear genuinely to have thought that Ryukyu had been an independent state, participating in tribute relations with China of its own accord. The appearance of the Ryukyuan embassy impressed on Ōkubo the urgency of bringing Ryukyu's relationship with China to an immediate end.

The following month, the Meiji government summoned two high-ranking officials, Yonabaru Ueekata and Ikegusuku Ueekata, to Tokyo. They were part of the so-called progressive faction (*kaimeiha*) of the royal government, which tended to support cooperation with the Meiji state. In contrast with the 1872 visit of Ginowan Ueekata and Prince Ie, who had been treated like foreign dignitaries, the simple, businesslike reception of Yonabaru and Ikegusuku indicated the changed status of Ryukyu in the eyes of Meiji officials. The visit agenda included tours of factories, schools, military training facilities, and other concrete examples of Japan's modernity. It was the Meiji state's hope to impress on Ryukyu's leading officials the advantages of incorporation into Japan and the futility of resistance.

It is important to pause and note that some Japanese central government officials opposed annexing the Ryukyu Islands, at least initially. Their

opposition was practical, not ideological. Annexing Ryukyu, an impoverished chain of islands relatively far from the mainland, would be too expensive for the resource-poor Meiji government. Ultimately, however,
geopolitical and military considerations contributed to a consensus in favor
of annexation.

At about the same time that the Ryukyuan officials were in Tokyo,
Ōkubo put his government's French legal adviser, Gustave Boissonade,
to work on the technical details. His response was threefold. First, in the
course of negotiations over the Taiwan incident, China had recognized
Japan's sovereignty over Ryukyu. Second, the Meiji state should not force
the issue but instead take gradual steps to persuade the Ryukyuans of the
advantages of Japanese sovereignty. In this connection, the king should
be made to visit Tokyo. Third, Ryukyu's tributary relationship with China
must stop immediately (Arakawa 1981, 8–9). In the end, however, this
course of action did not succeed in securing the willing compliance of
Ryukyu's government.

Therefore, early in 1875, Matsuda Michiyuki was appointed to carry out
the *shobun* along the lines outlined in Boissonade's recommendations. Matsuda met with Ryukyuan officials and ordered that the king travel to Tokyo
to express thanks for Japan's efforts in Taiwan on Ryukyu's behalf. He also
ordered that contact with China must stop and that, because it is vulnerable
to foreign imperialist ambitions, Ryukyu must allow Japanese troops from
the Kumamoto military command to be stationed there. Although affiliated
with the progressive faction, the Ryukyuan envoys in Tokyo were shocked
by Matsuda's orders. The Meiji state's true intentions finally dawned on
them, and they quickly sent word back to Okinawa. They refused formally
to agree to Matsuda's orders on the grounds that they lacked the authority
to do so without discussing the matter with the king and other officials.
Matsuda's response was to travel to Okinawa with Ikegusuku and Yonabaru.
Thus began the first of three visits by Matsuda.

In the seventh month of 1875, Matsuda met with Prince Nakijin, the
king's representative, and ten high officials. He did not meet directly with
Shō Tai owing to alleged illness on the king's part. As part of his attempts
to forestall the annexation, Shō Tai frequently refused meetings on the
grounds of illness. Matsuda issued a set of orders that included severing
all connections with China, using Meiji reign dates in all official documents and correspondence, and allowing surveys by officials from Japan.
Surprised by these orders, Ryukyu's top officials decided to accept some of
them but reject the orders of fundamental importance, especially the severing of relations with China. However, Matsuda refused to accept any answer
other than complete acceptance of the list of directives, and for the next

two months there were repeated rounds of Okinawan court rejections and Matsuda's refusal to accept them.

At this point in the *shobun* process, some Ryukyuan officials began to indulge in wishful thinking that somehow China would intervene to save the kingdom. In the middle of the ninth month of 1875, a steamship anchoring in Naha brought news of a Chinese newspaper report that the Qing court had ordered a warship to sail for Okinawa. On learning of the rumor, Matsuda's patience ran out, and he demanded a final, positive answer. However, buoyed by the rumor of Qing intervention, the Ryukyuan court refused to agree to all Matsuda's demands on the grounds that they would be unacceptable to China. Matsuda responded with an angry letter to the king declaring him and his court to be in rebellion and threatening to report the same to the Meiji government on his return.

The king initially decided to issue a decree calling for Ryukyuans to respect the orders of the court (Tokyo), but vigorous protests from top officials persuaded him to hold back. Hearing that the king had sent two envoys to meet with Matsuda, crowds of protesting nobles in and around Shuri Castle became angry. They pursued the envoys, intercepted them, and brought them back to Shuri. Matsuda, guessing that he might be in danger, laid low until the crowds of Ryukyuan officials dispersed.

Notice the source of opposition to Matsuda and to annexation: officials of Shuri's government. These officials were afraid of losing their privileged positions. Nearly all Okinawan opposition to the *shobun* came from officials. A few were motivated by deep loyalty to the king or kingdom, but, as we will see, most were willing to work for Japan if the price was right.

As a result of such spirited opposition, Matsuda softened his position slightly. He agreed to withhold his final report and allow one or more Ryukyuan envoys to travel to Tokyo to make one final appeal to the Meiji government that Ryukyu be permitted to continue its relations with China. He insisted, however, that, in his letter requesting the appeal, the king agree that Ryukyu would abide by whatever decision the Meiji government made. In the ninth month of 1875, Ikegusuku and Yonabaru made a second trip to Tokyo to represent the king.

During the course of the *shobun*, Ryukyuan officials petitioned the Meiji government repeatedly, particularly with respect to what they correctly regarded as the key to the kingdom's continued existence, the maintenance of tributary relations with China. The rhetorical strategy of these petitions was almost always identical, namely, deploying metaphors of familial obligation. The Ryukyuans spoke of their country's "dual obligations" to China and Japan, which they likened to Ryukyu's mother and father (fig. 14.1). This dual obligations rhetoric appears to have influenced

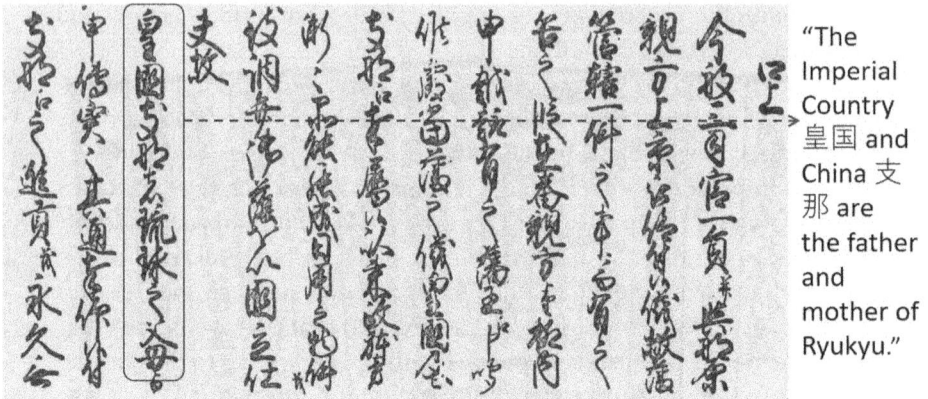

"The Imperial Country 皇国 and China 支那 are the father and mother of Ryukyu."

FIGURE 14.1. Part of a petition to the government in Tokyo, 1875
(from Shinzato, Taminato, and Kinjō 1972/1983, 156)

modern and contemporary understandings of early modern Ryukyu. As discussed previously, in my view the theatrical state model has better explanatory power.

That Ryukyu had been carrying out these relations with both China and Japan for centuries was, for Ryukyuan officials, a strong argument against their sudden curtailment. However, traditional ways of imagining the kingdom—based loosely on a China-dominated East Asian order—had become untenable by the 1870s. Instead, international law, supported, of course, by the guns of the imperial powers, had become the dominant language of interstate relations, and the Meiji state spoke this language.

The new language of sovereignty and international law did have some room for moral arguments even if they were often self-serving justifications. For example, progress, modernity, good government, civilization, and so forth often justified one state taking control of another. Matsuda's arguments in favor of a swift, decisive *shobun* of Ryukyu often took such an approach. On his return to Tokyo in late 1875, for example, Matsuda emphasized in his written recommendations that Ryukyu's royal government was antiquated and unjust. The oppressed people of Ryukyu, in other words, deserved the enlightened, modern government of the Meiji emperor.

Matsuda was certainly correct that the royal government was oppressive when it came to ordinary Okinawans and others living in the Ryukyu Islands. As Eiji Oguma notes: "Though ordinary Okinawan residents had no feelings of allegiance towards the Japanese government, . . . they had scant affection for the Ryukyu Dynasty's samurai class that had dominated them"

(Oguma 2014, 6). Unfortunately for such people, rule by the Meiji state did not result in a significant improvement in their quality of life, as we will see.

If talk of modernity, good government, etc. was one major rhetorical strategy of the Meiji state, the other was the rhetoric of sovereign authority. After the Meiji government rejected the petition of Yonabaru and Ikegusuku, the two Ryukyuans refused to agree to Matsuda's demands because they claimed that they had arrived in Tokyo only with the authority to petition. And petition they did, repeating ad nauseam the argument about Ryukyu's filial obligation to both parents. Fed up with such delaying tactics, in the fifth month of 1876 the Meiji government transferred all remaining legal authority from the king to the Home Ministry, ordered all Ryukyuan officials in Tokyo to return to Okinawa, and transmitted to Ryukyu the following decree from Grand Minister of State Sanjō Sanetomi: "The ritual subordination of Ryukyu domain to the Qing court is a great problem for our national polity (*kokutai*) and sovereignty. Its abolition is based on careful consideration. Because the resistance of a single domain is not appropriate, from now on, no matter how much it may appeal, [these appeals] will not be accepted" (quoted in Arakawa 1981, 19). The course of Okinawa's history during the late nineteenth century and the early twentieth suggests that Sanjō's argument on the grounds of sovereignty and state authority, not Matsuda's emphasis on progressive government, was closer to the true intentions of the Meiji state.

At this point, Japan's annexation of Ryukyu was nearly assured. Only two things might have prevented it. One was vigorous opposition by a major foreign power. The other was the collapse of the Meiji state. The latter nearly happened, and the quelling of rebellions occupied Japan's central government during much of 1876 and 1877. Even after Saigō Takamori's uprising collapsed in 1877, the central government had to deal with its financial consequences. The assassination of Ōkubo Toshimichi in the fifth month of 1878 also served to divert central government attention from the "Ryukyu problem." Having been given a brief respite from Japanese pressure, Ryukyuan officials began sailing to China to petition the Qing court for assistance. Although the ailing Qing dynasty had much greater concerns than the fate of a small tributary state, the envoys' rhetoric of loyalty and filial obligations found sympathetic ears among some Chinese officials.

Late in 1878, when the Meiji state accepted a plan devised by Matsuda for the fast and decisive annexation of Ryukyu, the Qing representative in Tokyo, Hé Rúzhāng, vigorously criticized the move. He also proposed to his own government that China send naval vessels to Ryukyu to reinstate tributary missions and prevent a Japanese takeover. As a result of protests by Hé and the Qing court, Tokyo agreed to start negotiations with China over Ryukyu. In the meantime, however, it was determined to carry out the annexation.

Early in 1879, Matsuda went to Okinawa to give the royal government one last chance to agree to the annexation voluntarily. The response from the king and his officials was a firm rejection. About two months later, a ship bearing Matsuda, other Home Ministry administrative personnel, and several hundred police and soldiers from Kumamoto appeared in Naha Harbor. Two days later, Matsuda read two short orders to Ryukyuan officials assembled in Shuri Castle: the domain has hereby come to an end, and the former domain king shall move to Tokyo. Four days later, on March 31, 1879, Shō Tai left Shuri Castle and boarded a ship for Tokyo. The government's formal declaration of annexation came four days later on April 4.

Incidentally, the repeated petitioning by the royal court, always invoking the same basic argument, may seem to have been a pointless strategy, and in some sense it was. However, it makes better sense in historical context. Throughout the eighteenth and nineteenth centuries, Ryukyuan officials often repeatedly petitioned Satsuma about various matters. When a petition was rejected, they often persisted in the petitioning process until fully or partially successful. For example, leaving out many details, in the 1790s Ryukyuan officials repeatedly petitioned that Ryukyuan embassies to Satsuma or Edo travel in Okinawan-made maaran ships, not Satsuma's ships. By 1812, Satsuma removed all restrictions on the use of maaran ships for this purpose (Tomiyama 2004, 219–22). The repeated petitioning during the 1870s, therefore, was a strategy that had been successful in the recent past.

Resistance of Officials and the *Kyūkan-onzon* Policy

Although Tokyo had ousted the king and taken control of Shuri Castle, the Meiji state was unprepared immediately to administer the Ryukyu Islands. Instead, it expected that most of the former kingdom's officials would remain at their posts. Two days after the official creation of Okinawa Prefecture, its governor, Nabeshima Naoyoshi, declared that, although the offices of the former kingdom had been eliminated, local officials shall remain on the job, carrying out their duties as before. Most, however, refused to cooperate with the new regime.

This initial show of resistance encouraged others. The former officials agreed to the following pact: "Those who obey Japanese orders and serve the Japanese government will be beheaded. Anyone executed by the Japanese government for refusing to cooperate shall be assured that his family will receive money from a pool of funds and will be cared for." Soon

FIGURE 14.2. Absconders—Ryukyuans living in Fúzhōu, China—during the *shobun*
era, three of whom appear with Qing hairstyles (from Takara and Dana 1993, 119)

thereafter, Matsuda called together local Okinawan officials to berate them
for abandoning their duty. One by one, each came forward and, claiming
poor health, turned in their resignations. Many lower-ranking officials did
the same. There was, in short, initial widespread passive defiance of Japanese control by (former) government officials (Arakawa 1981, 34–36).

Confounding matters further, some of these officials and other elite
Ryukyuans sailed to China. There, these "absconders" (*dasshinjin,* 脱清人)
lobbied Chinese officials to intervene on Ryukyu's behalf, thereby compli-
cating and drawing out the *shobun* process (fig. 14.2). The practice of fleeing
to China in response to policy changes continued throughout the nineteenth century. The implementation of military conscription in Okinawa in
1898, for example, caused a wave of absconders. It was to stem the flow of
Ryukyuans fleeing to China and restore basic governance that in 1879 and
1880 Japanese officials agreed to continue temporarily certain kingdom-era
practices in return for cooperation from former officials. Retroactively, this
policy came to be called *kyūkan-onzon.*

The *kyūkan-onzon* policy worked as intended. Ōwan Satonushi Chōkō
provided a firsthand account of the rapid change in attitude. He noted
the speed with which most Okinawan officials embraced—or at least
tolerated—Japanese control. In his view, the Okinawan nobility had grown
lazy and useless from the effects of hereditary privilege. Furthermore, officials regarded the peasants under them as little more than farm animals.

They loaned money to peasants at usurious rates and often by force. Ōwan explicitly likened the Japanese conquerors to liberators and portrayed his own cooperation with the new order as an act of benevolence (Arakawa 1981, 53–55).

Many former officials began quietly to cooperate with the new regime, while others continued passive resistance. According to Kishaba Chōken (1840–1916), former officials secretly began to present themselves to the prefectural government office for employment. By day, they pretended to resist the Japanese administration, but they made employment inquiries by night (see Kishaba 1980).

Loyalties in immediate post annexation Okinawa were complex, and Japanese power intersected long-festering divisions within elite Okinawan society. The *kyūkan-onzon* policy garnered enough elite Okinawan support for the new order to ensure a moderately smooth incorporation of the former kingdom into Japan's larger governing structures. Despite some of the violent rhetoric by former royal officials, the transition went forward with little actual violence. The main reason was that the kingdom had virtually no support outside its own officials and others who profited from it. Most Ryukyuans suffered under high tax rates and abuses by local officials, including the forced loans that Ōwan mentioned. The vast majority of them were willing to cast their lot with Japan because doing so could not be worse than their current situation.

The literal meaning of *kyūkan-onzon* is "the preservation of old customs," but that is misleading. The policy did not preserve customs or culture (*kan* or *shūkan*) in the usual sense. In the cultural realm, government policy was Japanification from the start (fig. 14.3). Instead, *kyūkan-onzon* sustained institutions connected with taxation and governance. In return for the continuation of customary social privileges and stipends, former royal government officials administered the old land distribution system and taxation system and maintained order in the countryside.

Historians of modern Okinawa have tended to interpret *kyūkan-onzon* as either a calculated move by the Meiji state to exploit Okinawa (e.g., by pressuring farmers to grow more sugar and sell to Japanese corporations) or a temporary expedient of little long-term significance. These different views are subsets of radically different conceptions of Okinawa's economic situation during the early decades of Japanese control.

One view is a narrative of Ryukyuan victimization. The locus classicus of the view of the Meiji state as willfully exploiting Okinawa was Shinjō Chōkō's 1925 *Dying Ryukyu* (*Hinshi no Ryūkyū*). This work also popularized the term *sago palm hell* (*sotetsu jigoku*) to describe the widespread famine conditions prevailing at the time. The Russian Revolution also loomed in

J. Kyō wa, makoto ni, nodokana tenki, de gozarimasu.
O. Chū ya, makoto [makutu] ni, ee teshichi, deebiru.
(Today, the weather is indeed calm.)

Okinawa taiwa, a
Language primer,
1880

沖縄對話
第一章　四季ノ部
第一回　春

今日ハ誠ニ長閑ナ天氣デ、ゴザリマス

明治十三年
四月八日出版届
十二月出版

沖縄對話

沖繩縣學務課編纂

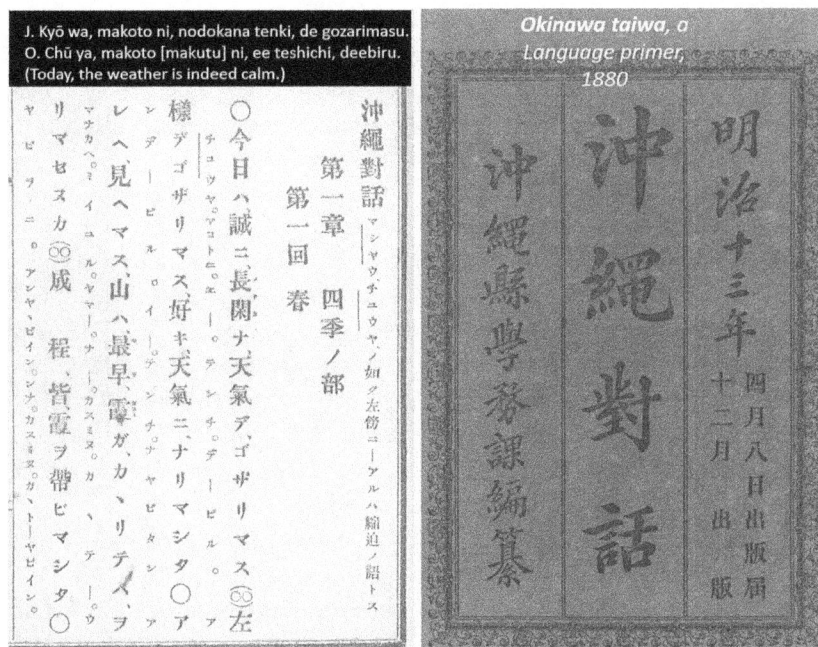

FIGURE 14.3. Translation and transliteration of the first line
of an 1880 language primer used in Okinawa Prefecture

the background. In the 1920s, many Okinawan scholars came to regard socialism as the wave of the future and set about discovering protosocialistic institutions in Ryukyu's past. During the 1920s and 1930s, major scholars like Iha Fuyū, Shinjō Chōkō, and Oyadomari Kōei reinterpreted the annexation of Ryukyu. Instead of it being a liberating event, a view they once held, they recast it in terms of a powerful outside entity exploiting or robbing Okinawa and destroying worthy, protosocialistic institutions like land (re)distribution systems. Subsequent history—especially the Battle of Okinawa, the long US occupation, and the continuing disputes over military bases—has provided abundant material for the continuation of this narrative of victimization.

In its postwar form, the argument that, from the 1880s on, the residents of Okinawa Prefecture paid more per capita in taxes than did residents of any other prefecture while receiving less from the central government than did residents of any other prefecture is known as the Kinjō-Nishizato hypothesis. It was an updated version of the victimization narrative established during the 1920s and 1930s. During the 1960s and 1970s, Kinjō Seitoku, Nishizato Kikō, and Shinzato Keiji used statistics to advance the

view that Tokyo's relationship with Okinawa was fundamentally exploitative. Among other things, they argued that this exploitation was a means
by which Japan's central government amassed the capital necessary to fuel
mainland industries. For the major essays establishing this interpretation,
see Kinjō (1969/1989) and Nishizato (1969/1989).

Directly criticizing the Kinjō-Nishizato hypothesis, Araki Moriaki argued that, in its early years, Okinawa Prefecture received much more from
the central government than its people paid in taxes. The central government used general revenue to make up the frequent deficits of the prefectural government. Furthermore, the Meiji government paid an artificially
high price for Okinawan sugar during the entire *kyūkan-onzon* era, a de
facto subsidy. In short, Araki deployed statistics to argue precisely the opposite of the Kinjō-Nishizato hypothesis. According to Araki, Okinawa was
actually a drain on central government finances, not a positive source of
central government revenue (see Araki 1980, esp. 218–25).

These polar opposite positions (the Nishizato-Araki debate for short)
have dominated the basic framework of interpretations of modern Okinawan history for decades. There have been some attempts to move beyond
them or find ways to reconcile them, but so far with relatively little success
(see esp. Ōsato 2003).

From the standpoint of the typical peasant, becoming Japanese during
the *kyūkan-onzon* era was not a change for the better. Peasants continued to
suffer under a heavy burden of taxes in cash, produce, and/or labor service,
and they enjoyed few or none of the opportunities for social or economic
advancement available to mainland Japanese. In the prewar decades, all
the governors of Okinawa Prefecture were appointed by Tokyo. Okinawa's
second governor, Uesugi Mochinori (who served from May 1881 to April
1883), tried to bring relief to the masses of impoverished Okinawans. He
vigorously and repeatedly petitioned the central government to permit him
to reorganize and streamline local administration. His aim was to curtail
administrative expenses throughout the islands by reducing unnecessary
layers of local government, phasing out support for the former nobility, and
using the savings to fund education and promote industry. None of his proposals required any additional expenditure from Tokyo, but Tokyo rejected
them as being premature. Uesugi may have made at least some Okinawan
elites nervous, for it was during the two years of his administration that the
largest number of former officials of the kingdom fled to China. His successor, Iwamura Michitoshi, reversed all his policies.

In light of Tokyo's refusal to approve Uesugi's approach and his rapid
replacement with Iwamura, it is clear that for the Meiji state the main goal
of the *shobun* was to clarify and extend Japan's southern boundaries, not

to alleviate the suffering of ordinary people. While the welfare of Okinawans often came up as an argument for bringing the kingdom to an end, once that happened Tokyo seems to have lost interest in the plight of its newest citizens.

The *kyūkan-onzon* policy was generally successful in gaining sufficient cooperation from Ryukyuan elites and local officials that tax collection and social control continued largely as before. Of course, not all Ryukyuan elites were willing to collaborate with the new rulers, and some of them settled in China at the former Ryukyuan embassy/trading center in Fúzhōu. There, they lobbied for Qing intervention on Ryukyu's behalf, and a few remained in China until their deaths.

Qing-Tokyo Dispute over the Ryukyu Islands

As early as 1877, Chinese officials were aware of Japanese intentions to annex or closely control the Ryukyu Islands. In that year, for example, a Ryukyuan envoy conveyed a message from King Shō Tai explaining that Japanese pressure made sending tribute impossible and asking that China bring up Ryukyu as a formal diplomatic issue with Japan. The Okinawan royal court had the strong support of Ambassador Hé Rúzhāng. Furthermore, Lǐ Hóngzhāng, possibly China's most influential official at the time, sympathized with Shuri's plight. Lǐ, however, was also firmly committed to a policy of Sino-Japanese cooperation. Although he hoped to preserve a viable domain for Ryukyu's king, he was unwilling to sacrifice good relations with Japan for this goal.

The annexation of Ryukyu took place shortly before word reached China that former US president Ulysses Grant planned to visit China and then Japan. In Lǐ's eyes, Grant was ideal as a possible mediator regarding Ryukyu. When Lǐ and Grant met in Tiānjīn, their main concern was the future of Sino-Japanese relations. Lǐ also pointed out to Grant that disputes over Ryukyu might adversely affect Sino-American shipping and trade and that China's concern in this matter was with land and boundaries, not continuing to receive tribute from Ryukyu. However, about twenty days after the meeting with Grant, Lǐ had a series of talks with Ryukyuan envoy Kō Tokkō that convinced him that restoring the royal government was indeed a desirable goal (contrary to what he had told Grant).

In Japan, Grant emphasized Lǐ's point that, because the sea-lanes in and around the Ryukyu Islands were vital for international commerce, clarification of state boundaries was desirable. By this point in the informal talks between Grant, Japanese officials, and other interested parties such as the

US ambassador to Japan, proposals to divide the islands into two or three parts had come up. Because of strong Japanese resistance to such an idea at the time of his departure, however, Grant declined to propose a concrete solution to the Ryukyu dispute, calling instead simply for talks between Japan and China. Face-to-face talks began in 1880.

Japan's initial envoy was the scholar of Chinese literature Takezoe Shin'ichirō. Aware of Li's desire for Sino-Japanese cooperation, Takezoe emphasized that Ryukyu was strategically important and that Japan received nothing but an added burden in taking over the territory. That Japan did so, he added, was a good thing for China since Japanese control prevented other less trustworthy countries from seizing the islands. Aside from promoting Japan's interests, Takezoe's initial arguments stressed what might be called *objective geopolitical concerns*. Although Li shared these concerns, he was also swayed by the subjective or emotional arguments of the Ryukyuan elites in exile. In response to Li's desire to preserve some measure of royal sovereignty, Takezoe tried to cast the issue as an either-or choice between assisting Ryukyu and cooperation with Japan.

Several rounds of communications ensued between Takezoe, Li, and others, and proposals for dividing the Ryukyu Islands emerged in these discussions. By the time formal negotiations began in August 1880, China advocated a three-way division of Ryukyu, with Japan possessing the northern Ryukyu Islands, the Ryukyuan king possessing Okinawa and the surrounding small islands, and China possessing Yaeyama, Miyako, and the nearby islands. Li and other major Chinese officials thought that, in such a case, China would return Yaeyama and Miyako to the king after the situation had stabilized. If implemented, this proposal would have left things little changed from the arrangement that prevailed during the Tokugawa period except that the Ryukyuan monarch would be more secure in his position. Japan, of course, rejected the Chinese proposal but expressed a willingness to allow Yaeyama and Miyako to go to China in return for China's government granting Japan more favorable terms in the treaty of amity and commerce between the two countries. Early on in the negotiations, the Chinese side showed a willingness to agree to a two-way division of Ryukyu along these lines.

It was Tokyo's push to revise its treaty of amity and commerce with China to allow unrestricted Japanese residence and most-favored nation status that most occupied the time and energy of the negotiators. On October 21, 1880, the two sides reached an agreement. The resulting draft treaty generally reflected Japan's position during the negotiations. With respect to Ryukyu, the Miyako and Yaeyama island groups were to go to China in return for Chinese trade concessions to Japan. Stated bluntly, Tokyo bartered away part of the Ryukyu Islands to China in return for favorable terms for trade and commerce. The best interests and the will of the people living in the southern Ryukyu Islands were irrelevant.

Lǐ and Shishido Tamaki, Japan's lead negotiator, agreed to ratification within ten days and a formal exchange of treaties within three months, but ratification never took place. Leaving aside the many details of who argued what and when, the draft treaty sparked significant debate among Chinese officials, Okinawan exiles in China, and Okinawans in Tokyo, including Shō Tai. The controversy was of sufficient magnitude that the Chinese emperor and many Qing high officials decided that a rush to ratification was unwise and that the treaty should be negotiated further.

Throughout this process, there was vigorous and influential participation by elite Okinawans. Nishizato Kikō has argued that a clear understanding of the events of the early 1880s requires that this Okinawan participation be factored into the larger picture. Lǐ, for example, changed his mind about rapid ratification after hearing a tearful plea from Kō Tokkō that the two-part division of Ryukyu would be equivalent to the kingdom's destruction. Kō and many other Okinawans apparently had no desire to preside over Yaeyama and Miyako. They argued that the southern Ryukyu Islands were simply too small and resource barren to serve as the physical foundation of a viable kingdom. Although we cannot know the full contents of his mind, it is also possible that Kō and other, like-minded Okinawans knew how unpopular any iteration of the kingdom would be among the residents of the southern Ryukyu Islands. In Tokyo, Shō Tai expressed similar doubts. Although some prominent Okinawans did support the two-way division as specified in the draft treaty, many vigorously opposed it. According to Nishizato, it was this Okinawan opposition, filtered through officials like Lǐ, that ultimately caused China to advocate renegotiation (Nishizato 1992a, 45–55).

Thereafter, the matter of a possible division of Ryukyu between Japan and China in the context of Chinese trade concessions to Japan remained unresolved. In 1884, China and France came to blows over Vietnam, and China was also heavily involved in a three-way struggle with Russia and Japan for domination of Korea. With such pressing problems close at hand, the Ryukyuan question languished. All the while Tokyo consolidated its control.

The First Sino-Japanese War and the Ryukyu Islands

On the eve of war between China and Japan, an 1894 central government report analyzing Okinawan society identified two different anti-Japanese factions. A "black faction" (*kuro-tō*) favored total affiliation of the Ryukyu Islands with China. A "stubborn faction" (*ganko-tō*) sought to restore the previous dual relations with China and Japan. To confuse the political lines, not all supporters of the *kaika-tō* (roughly, "modernizers") had given up on the idea of some kind of restoration of the old royal domain.

The report concluded that the image of China in Ryukyuan eyes had always been positive while the image of Kagoshima had long been negative. Therefore, among Ryukyuans there was a tendency to view China and the mainland of Japan differently. The black and stubborn factions, however, were not rooted in this perception. Instead, they were vehicles for former elites to try to regain personal profit and authority. The report further stated that the black faction members generally understood the trend of the times but could not bring themselves to cooperate with the new order. The conclusion was that, should a Qing army invade the Ryukyu Islands, it would be difficult to predict its reception by local residents.

Indeed, when war broke out, the stubborn faction became quite animated by the possibility that "Great Qing" would liberate Okinawa. Despite the divisions outlined in the government report, a distinction between the stubborn faction and the black faction does not appear to have been clear-cut. Newspaper reporters, for example, often lumped the two together as the "black-stubborn faction" (*kokugan-tō*). When the war started, stubborn faction partisans held twice-monthly meetings in shrines and temples to offer prayers for a Chinese victory. In contrast, *kaika-tō* modernizers praised the pro-Japanese articles appearing in the newspaper *Ryūkyū shinpō*, which had been established the previous year.

In the guise of praying for the health of the deposed king, Shō Tai, stubborn and black faction sympathizers made the rounds of the major religious sites to pray for a Qing victory. While doing so, they wore the ritual attire of former Shuri court officials. A well-known *ryūka* (Ryukyuan verse, 琉歌) of the stubborn faction went:

開化断髪やなまや威張らちょけ, 黄色軍艦の入らばだいもの

The *kaika-tō* bastards with their cropped hair are strutting around now,
Just wait until the yellow ships of the Qing navy enter into our ports!

(quoted in Smits 2015a, 167)

When a headline in the *Ryūkyū shinpō* read "Victory for Japan, Qing Is Defeated," the stubborn faction regarded it as fake news and refused to believe that Japan had prevailed.

The wartime dispute between pro-Chinese and pro-Japanese factions was mainly an elite phenomenon. Ordinary Okinawans, not to mention people in other islands, were mostly passive observers. After the war, these political divisions continued to exist, not because anyone continued seriously to believe that China would or could liberate Okinawa from Japan, but because the political divisions were rooted in Okinawan society itself.

One significance of Japan's victory was that in the international arena all the Ryukyu Islands became indisputably Japanese territory. Within Okinawa, the *kyūkan-onzon* era began to wind down, ending entirely when stipends to former elites ceased in 1910. By ca. 1896, nearly all Okinawans would have realized that they had no choice but to embrace a Japanese identity, even if begrudgingly. Moreover, as in the rest of Japan, a middle class began to emerge in Okinawa. It was oriented firmly toward Japan and Japanese culture, and its members' most persistent demand was for greater educational opportunities.

Nevertheless, while some elite Okinawans recognized that the kingdom would never be restored to its past form, they still harbored some hope that a modified version of it might return. One prominent example was the Kōdōkai, a group founded in 1896 by Shō Tai's second son. The Kōdōkai argued that the cultural differences between Okinawa and the rest of Japan warranted a long transition period if Okinawa was ever to become moderately prosperous. The group made the dubious and self-serving argument that, should Tokyo restore members of the Shō family as governors, the majority of the people would rally behind them. (Recall that the royal family had very little support among ordinary people.) In this capacity, the former royal family would lead Okinawa toward gradual cultural and institutional union with the rest of Japan. A petition to this effect was drawn up, and it garnered the signatures of many of the elite. A delegation presented it in Tokyo, but the central government rejected it immediately. Thereafter, the movement to restore the Shō family to leadership quickly dissipated.

Ethnogenesis Revisited

Resistance to Tokyo and negotiations between the Qing and the Japanese governments was the result of the activities of elite Okinawans determined to preserve their privileges and economic security. The *kyūkan-onzon* policy brought enough of these elite Okinawans on board that the transition from kingdom to prefecture was moderately smooth, albeit protracted. In the short term, however, there was little by way of transition for ordinary people. Most of them continued toil in fields poorly suited to agriculture or to weave cloth to meet severe tax obligations. Ordinary Ryukyuans had no love for the kingdom, but their becoming Japanese citizens, initially at least, made little difference in their lives.

Pulling several themes together, let us briefly revisit the question of ethnogenesis. Outside the Shuri-Naha urban area, ordinary people living in the Ryukyu Islands had been well aware of the kingdom in Shuri. They paid taxes to it, but they did not derive a sense of personal identity from it. Looking at the Ryukyu Islands from the Japanese mainland, many people conceived of Ryukyuans as constituting a distinct ethnic group. There were a variety of ideas about Ryukyuans, but one conception common in mainland Japan was that Ryukyuans were closely related to Japanese ethnically (*racially* in the terminology of the time) but less modern. A closely related idea was that the Ryukyu Islands were a kind of storehouse of ancient Japonic culture, an idea that ethnologists (folklore scholars) such as Yanagita Kunio and Orikuchi Shinobu popularized in the 1920s and 1930s. In this view, the inhabitants of the Ryukyu Islands were of interest both academically and as an exotic branch of the larger Japanese family, but they were not yet ready to shoulder the burdens of modern society.

The long period of isolation from Japan that began soon after 1609 had indeed accelerated cultural distinctiveness and differences within the Ryukyu Islands and between the islands and the mainland. During that same period, in Japan's urban areas newspapers and other mass media helped bring the diverse parts of Japan into conversation with each other. Thanks mainly to print culture, by the early nineteenth century a sense of Japanese identity had emerged in urban areas. This early modern identity differed in important ways from Japanese identities that developed during the modern era, but its existence smoothed the process of people throughout Japan identifying with new concepts of national identity and citizenship.

By contrast, no broadside newspapers or any form of popular print culture emerged in the Ryukyu Islands during the early modern era. Not only did Ryukyuan culture and Japanese culture drift further apart after 1609, the various cultures and societies within the Ryukyu Islands remained substantially isolated from each other. As we have seen, boats and small ships plied the waters between the Ryukyu Islands for trade. However, most rural villagers lived in relative isolation. By the time that schools and other formal social institutions made appearances in rural villages, Okinawa Prefecture had come into existence. The sense of identity that developed after the 1880s was an overdetermined Ryukyuan-Japanese dichotomy. In other words, the majority of residents of the newly minted Okinawa Prefecture became aware of being Ryukyuan and Japanese simultaneously.

CHAPTER FIFTEEN

Literature, Drama, and Official Portrayals of Ryukyu

By the eighteenth century, dramatists, poets, artists, and academic writers had emerged in Okinawa. Most were grounded in Japanese literature because it was much easier to master than Chinese. In Kumemura, however, the skill of Tei Junsoku (1661–1734) in classical Chinese poetry was such that some of his poems were known in China. The following sections briefly examine three literary figures: Onna Nabe (O. Nabi or Nabii, 恩納なべ); Yoshiya Umitsuru (吉屋思鶴), also known as Yoshiya Chirū (吉屋チルー), a courtesan;[1] and Heshikiya Chōbin (平敷屋朝敏, 1701–34), a playwright, a scholar of Japanese literature, and a tragic opponent of Sai On. The chapter concludes with sections examining several manifestations of official portrayals of Ryukyu.

Onna Nabe

Terminal dates unknown, Onna Nabe (Nabe of Onna) was an approximate contemporary of Sai On, active in the latter half of the eighteenth century—if in fact she existed. It turns out that there is no proof that she did, nor can we say with certainty which poems she wrote. Scholars have tended to take any short poem from the late eighteenth century and attribute it to her unless it was clearly someone else's. In any case, a certain body of poems has come to be associated with her, so we will assume that she either composed or frequently recited them and, of course, that she existed. Her home was Onna District on the west coast of central Okinawa.

One of her poems praises the king in connection with the construction of a new ship:

恵みある御代にはぎけたる御船ももと幾旅もさびやかないさめ

The ship that has been built during the bountiful and well-governed reign of the king could make hundreds of voyages and never suffer any damage.

(Fuku 2010, 19)

We do not know the poem's context, but, during Shō Kei's reign, there had been a revival of shipbuilding in Okinawa after a long hiatus. Moreover, in the Ryukyu of the *Omoro sōshi*, women with shamanic powers were seen as protectors of ships. This poem is one reason for speculation that Nabe may have been a priestess.

Nabe is known mainly for love poems and poems that are critical of the many rules and restrictions governing early modern Okinawan society:

恩納岳あがた里が生まれ島もりもおしのけてこがたなさな

On yonder side of Mt. Onna is the village in which my love was born. I want to sweep away that annoying mountain and pull his village this way.

(Fuku 2010, 22)

The theme of lamenting natural features for blocking access to one's beloved can be found in *Manyōshū* (e.g., vol. 2, no. 131), an ancient collection of Japanese verse. Resemblances between Ryukyuan literature and classical Japanese literature are common, sometimes because there is a direct connection and sometimes because most producers of Ryukyuan works were steeped in Japanese classical literature and drew on it consciously or unconsciously.

The term *shinugu* refers to sacred dancing performed in rural villages to venerate or influence the deities of the sea and mountains in the hope of a bountiful harvest. Indirect evidence indicates that women danced before the deities naked and in a trance-like state known as *shike* as they communed with them. Men were forbidden from being present at the sites of such dances.[2] After the dancing, most villages got together for celebrations that could last late into the night. It appears that *shinugu* dancing was prohibited, at least in Okinawa, during Shō Kei's reign. The prohibition came the year before his investiture, on the grounds that such dancing was an embarrassing and vulgar custom and that there was a chance visiting Chinese envoys might find out about it. If, indeed, hiding *shinugu* dancing from Chinese eyes was the motivation, the prohibition is a good example of the theatrical state in action. Even if this particular reason was not at play, the general tendency of Sai On and Shō Kei was to suppress local agricultural festivals on the grounds that they wasted time, energy, and resources better devoted to sober hard work.

In that context, another of the poems attributed to Nabe is the following:

あねべたやよかてしのぐしち遊でわすた世になればおとめされて

My older sister could dance with the deities and enjoy herself. But, in our time, such enjoyment has been prohibited.

(Fuku 2010, 30)

Similarly:

あまん世のしのぐおゆるしめしやうれ

[Said to the top local official:] Please transmit this petition from the young people: Please allow us to dance with the deities as in the days of old.

(Fuku 2010, 33)

The following verse is probably her most famous:

恩納松下に禁止の牌の立ちゆす恋忍ぶまでの禁止やないさめ

Under the pine tree in front of the Onna local government office stands a board of prohibitions. It is doubtful, however, that among them is a prohibition of love. [So we need not fear pursuing it.]

(Fuku 2010, 36)

This poem hints at the tenor of the late eighteenth century. Confucian moralists in the government issued frequent prohibitions as part of social engineering campaigns to change the attitudes and behaviors of ordinary people in the countryside. They were largely unsuccessful.

At least in the poems attributed to her, Nabe often proclaimed the beauty of her native area. She was also conscious of the cultural differences between a relatively remote, rural area like Yanbaru and Shuri and its surrounding urban area. Urban dwellers often exhibited a strong sense of superiority. Consider the following:

首里親国人や見る間のかなしやあがたとんなれば我事いゆらだぅ

It is only when I am face-to-face with a person from the venerable capital, Shuri, that he cherishes me. When we are apart, he speaks ill of me.

(Fuku 2010, 52)

The precise context of the following, final example is unclear:

わ山国習ひの田畑しゆる外にのの思のあゆが首里の主の前

Do you think it is the custom of us mountain dwellers to think about anything other than cultivating fields?—oh venerable man from Shuri!

(Fuku 2010, 54)

One possibility is that Nabe wrote the poem to or about a man from Shuri who had passed through the area, most likely someone acting in an official capacity.

There are several more poems with the same or nearly the same beginning (a reference to "humble mountain dwellers") and ending ("venerable man from Shuri"). In one, the venerable man is told to make do with a simple straw mat because there is nothing better at hand. Another makes a similar point about using a pine stump in place of "the pillows available in Shuri and Naha." Another asks the man to play the *sanshin* for the benefit of those who dwell in the mountains. Among other things, the poems attributed to Nabe provide a glimpse of some of the social complexities and perceived lifestyle differences in eighteenth-century Okinawa.

Yoshiya Umitsuru (Yoshiya Chirū)

The name *Yoshiya* appears to have come from the 1518 Japanese verse collection *Kanginshū* (閑吟集). Yoshiya was sold to a brothel in Naha as a child from her home in Yomitan, in the same area as was Onna Nabe's residence. Her life was unhappy, and, according to local lore, she died of grief at age eighteen. It is not clear precisely when she lived, but a range of about 1650–1700 seems reasonable. As with Nabe, it is uncertain whether all the poems attributed to her were actually her compositions.

The context of the following poem is that, as a child, Yoshiya is leaving her home and crossing the bridge over the Hija River:

恨む比謝橋やわぬ渡さともて情けないぬ人のかけておきやら

That awful Hija bridge! Some heartless person must have thought
of me crossing it and then built it [for that purpose].

(Fuku 2010, 61)

Here, the bridge is a concrete symbol of the two different worlds Yoshiya
inhabited. One was the world of her home village, which she tended to idealize in her poems, and the other was the world of the Nakashima brothel
(*Nakashima yūkaku*, 仲島遊郭) near the edge of Naha Harbor.

At Nakashima Yoshiya writes:

寄辺ないぬものや海士の捨小舟つく方ど頼むつなぎたばうれ

An unmoored thing, [I am] a diver's abandoned boat. Please hold
on to me as you would secure a boat.

(Fuku 2010, 64)

There is a legend that, on hearing this poem, the proprietress of the brothel
reached out and hugged Yoshiya. In any case, notice that the basic metaphor here is that Yoshiya is comparing herself—or, more specifically, her
body—to a boat that drifts here and there for customers to board.

Similarly, in another poem Yoshiya describes the experience with her
first customer:

あらはぎの舟にかれよしの乗り衆よべの夜走らしや波も静か

A fine customer boards a newly built boat. On last night's voyage,
the waves were quiet, and the heading was calm.

(Fuku 2010, 67)

Here, she compares herself to a newly built boat and reports that her first
night with a customer went smoothly. The metaphor of a woman as a boat
and a man boarding it was not unique to Yoshiya's poems. It comes up in
three poems attributed to Nabe, and there was a long tradition throughout
the Ryukyu Islands of likening ships to women, and vice versa.

Yoshiya's first encounter with a customer may have gone smoothly, but
she hated her life in Naha. For example:

あんま主やよかて生まれ島いまぬ我身や仲島のあらの一粒

Mother and father are happy in their hometown, while I live a
wretched existence at Nakashima, like a cast-off piece of rubbish.

(Fuku 2010, 68)

And:

育てらね親ののよで我身産ちゆて花におし出ぢやちよそにもます

My parents, who could not raise me. Why did you give birth to me, sell
me to a brothel, and subject me to the suffering of being the plaything
of others?

(Fuku 2010, 69)

Recall the case of *yanchu* in the northern Ryukyu Islands. In Okinawa, the
rules of most villages stated that, when a household could not pay its share
of taxes, its property would be sold first, then its people. A common order
of sale in such cases was the wife of the household head, the children of the
household head, and then the household head himself, depending on the
extent of the debt. However, we do not know the specific circumstances
whereby Yoshiya ended up as she did.

In the following poem and others, Yoshiya idealizes life in her agricultural village, but she mentions no specific people other than her parents:

島もとなどなとこばもそよそよと繋ぎある牛の鳴きゆらとめば

The village [*shima*] is quiet, without any kind of sound. Palm fronds
[*kuba*] are faintly swaying in the soft breeze. Turning around with
no particular thought, I imagine that a tethered cow cannot bear the
loneliness and cries out.

(Fuku 2010, 70)

Of course, her thoughts about her parents were complicated. Also, notice
her commenting on the scene from the emotional perspective of a cow.

In another poem, Yoshiya talks to a cicada:

おどろくなあささ食はゆんであらぬ肝かなしやあてど抱きや見ちやる

Cicada! Don't be afraid. It is not that I will eat you. It's just that
you are cute, so I thought I would pick you up and hold you.

(Fuku 2010, 77)

As with most of her poems, there is a legendary context. Supposedly, while
on her way to the brothel, she saw a mantis about to attack a cicada. She
sang or spoke this poem, which scared the mantis away.

According to legend, Yoshiya charmed many of her customers with her
exquisite sensibilities, artistic talent, and sensual beauty. She fell in love
with the *aji* of Nakazato, but, on hearing that a wealthy man with the peculiar name Kurokumo-dun (Lord Blackcloud, 黒雲殿) had bought out her
contract, she stopped eating, wasted away, and died. Consider this poem:

おぞで取て投げるとがもないぬ枕里が面影や夢にしちゆて

I saw my lover's image in a dream. Waking to realize it was only
a dream, I hurled the blameless pillow.

(Fuku 2010, 90)

Heshikiya Chōbin popularized Yoshiya's story, or at least certain versions
of it. By the early eighteenth century, Yoshiya-related legends were in wide
circulation in elite society in Shuri.

Heshikiya Chōbin

Heshikiya's title was Neha Peichin (弥覇親雲上). His father died when
Heshikiya was young, and he was tutored in Japanese literature by his ma-
ternal grandfather. He wrote four short novels (*monogatari*) in a style of
classical Japanese today called *gikobun*. They are *Record of an Impoverished
Household* (*Binkaki*, 貧家記), *Many Talents* (*Manzai*, 万才), *Tale of Young
Grass* (*Wakagusa monogatari*, 若草物語), and *Beneath the Moss* (*Koke no
shita*, 苔の下). The atypical *kumiodori* drama *The Fate of Washwater* (*Te-
mizu no en*, 手水の縁; also translated as *The Bond of Water in Hands*) is also
attributed to Heshikiya, although he might not have been the author.

Tale of Young Grass is set in Japan. The protagonist is a samurai and a
poet, Ozasa Tsuyunosuke, whose name includes the world *dew*, a favor-
ite metaphor of Heshikiya. Ozasa fell in love with a courtesan, Wakagusa
(Young Grass). However, after her contract was sold, the two decided to

kill themselves together. *Beneath the Moss*, set in Okinawa, is essentially one version of the legend of Yoshiya and the Nakazato Aji. When their love was thwarted, she stopped eating and killed herself, and the *aji* resolved to do the same. *Record of an Impoverished Household* is semiautobiographical. A noble falling into poverty left Shuri to spend a year in the countryside. Heshikiya's observations of rural life take the form of poems. Shirōtarugane is the protagonist of *Many Talents*. He is handsome, learned, and possessed of great musical talent. He falls in love with a beautiful woman, but her father has already promised to marry her to another household. He kills himself, and she almost does the same when a deity appears and saves the day, restoring Shirōtarugane to life, and the two live happily ever after. Notice that a happy ending in this situation requires divine intervention.

Space does not permit an analysis of Sai On's Confucian philosophy (on this topic, see Smits 1999). Simply stated, however, Sai On stressed that through hard work people have the power to make their own destiny at the level of both the individual and the society. One of his mottoes could have been, Never give up! For example, Gihon was a legendary king who abdicated the throne after a series of natural disasters. Shō Shōken praised Gihon's selfless virtue for abdicating, but Sai On regarded him as a quitter and a terrible example. With this point in mind, notice Heshikiya's worldview. He was acutely aware of the structural barriers to happiness, and he tended to be fatalistic. Moreover, he delighted in people of vastly different social statuses falling in love, as with Yoshia and her *aji*. Similarly, *The Fate of Washwater* is a drama about illicit love. In terms of their sensibilities, it is difficult to imagine greater opposites than Sai On and Heshikiya Chōbin. Moreover, there is evidence that Heshikiya and Sai On were competitors in other realms. Heshikiya was exiled to the countryside because of rumors that he was having an affair with one of the king's daughters, a daughter Sai On's son would later marry.

The details are unclear, but the best evidence is that Heshikiya and Tomoyose Anjō (友寄安乗) became the leader of a group of Shuri literati who opposed Sai On's administration and his reforms. This animosity culminated in Heshikiya and Tomoyose delivering a letter criticizing Sai On to Kawanishi Hiraemon, an inspector from Satsuma in Okinawa.[3] Their gambit was a disaster. Sai On had the full support of Satsuma, and, in the sixth month of 1734, Heshikiya, Tomoyose, and thirteen others were executed at Ajiminato. The wives and children of all involved were made commoners, and all the sons were banished to Yonaguni. Even grandsons were banished, extending the punishment out to three generations.

The Heshikiya-Tomoyose incident was a remarkable purge, and it indicates that something of the utmost gravity had happened. The royal government sought to bury the matter. Household records were purged of the names of those executed (although two records have survived that provide some information). It appears that the swift punishment and documentary coverup prevented Heshikiya, Tomoyose, and their group from becoming martyrs for a cause.[4] Over the decades, scholars have speculated about the details of the incident. More recently, amateur historical detectives have created detailed websites purporting to reconstruct the relevant events. The takeaway point, however, is that there was a major clash of factions in the capital area. Heshikiya and his partisans, all prominent Shuri elites, tried to oust Sai On and his supporters or perhaps even to reduce the extent of Satsuma's control. They failed miserably. In general, Sai On's vision for Ryukyu prevailed, but there were other dissenters, both during Sai On's lifetime and in the next generation.

Official Presentations of Ryukyu

Many of the performing arts—music, dance, and drama—associated with Okinawa or other parts of the Ryukyu Islands have their roots in the early modern era. The same goes for karate and related martial arts. That said, in many cases the present forms of specific performance schools and martial arts styles underwent significant change during the modern era. Tracing the precise lineage of many art forms is difficult, and legend often fills in for a lack of verifiable information. A comprehensive survey of the performing arts is beyond the scope of this book.[5] This section is limited to a brief consideration of some of the ways in which elite Okinawans, in effect, presented the Ryukyu Kingdom to their own society and to the world, that is, to China and Japan. The material here is an extension of topics already mentioned in previous chapters.

THE OFFICIAL HISTORIES

We have encountered Ryukyu's official histories many times. Although these works can be useful as guides to the past if read critically, they should not be taken at face value. The process of creating the portions of the official histories dealing with material prior to the sixteenth century was similar to the creation of *fudoki* (gazetteers) in ancient Japan. Officials went out to the provinces, collected tales, cast them in formal language, and dressed them in the ideology of the ruling group. This was an ideological act, not a case of simple transcription.

Recall that there are significant differences between the specific official histories. These differences in part reflect different sources. In 1725, Sai On had access to official Ming records, whereas previous authors did not. Moreover, he was a better writer than Shō Shōken, and he benefited from the being able to start with Shō Shōken's work and Sai Taku's revision of it. *Reflections on Chūzan* is full of awkward passages. By comparison, Sai On's *Genealogy of Chūzan* smooths over difficult material and awkward events. Sai On claimed that his *Genealogy of Chūzan* made no use of legends, but that was not accurate. First, even the most basic narrative—the one Shō Shōken created—was based on legends. Additionally, in some cases, Sai On included legends in his text as appended notes. Nevertheless, it appears that he genuinely sought to avoid using legends as sources, at least in the main text of *Genealogy*.[6]

Kyūyō, by contrast, is different from any of the other official histories. Tei Heitetsu (鄭秉哲, 1695–1760) was the editor of both *Ryūkyū kyūki* (琉球旧記, 1731) and *Kyūyō*. *Kyūki* was ostensibly a classical Chinese translation of *Origins of Ryukyu* (1713). Its contents are very similar to those of *Origins*, but there are differences between the two texts. At its core, *Kyūki* is based on legends. Similarly, *Kyūyō* took all the legendary material that formed the core of previous official histories, added legendary material from *Kyūki*, and fashioned it into historical narratives. Any legends that were left over became appended to *Kyūyō* in a supplementary volume called *Irōsetsuden* (Ancient legends, 遺老説伝).[7]

APPROPRIATION OF LEGENDS

Consider the process of legend consolidation in *Kyūyō* and *Irōsetsuden*.[8] Local legends from all over the territory of the Ryukyu Kingdom were pulled together under a national banner. One indication is language. Although the legends would have been known only in their local languages (the language of each island in the Ryukyu Arc is distinct and Japonic), in *Irōsetsuden* they all appear in classical Chinese. Only a few elite Ryukyuans would have been able to comprehend them, and no reader would have been able to hear them via the written text.

For example, the story of Toyomi Ujioya of Irabu Island (in the Miyako group) bravely entering a giant shark's body and cutting it open from the inside to save his village was the act of a Miyako hero who became a Ryukyuan hero. *Irōsetsuden* (no. 37) characterizes Toyomi's deed in terms of universal, heavenly principles. This process of Ryukyuanizing local legends is one indication of ethnogenesis among elite Okinawans.

A less dramatic origin tale of the Tomori grove from *Irōsetsuden* (no. 136) tells of an immigrant from Yamato. He was virtuous and kind, and he promoted agriculture. When he died of illness, he was buried in Tomori grove, and he manifest himself as a deity to protect the village. The villagers worshipped him as Yamato-hokora sendō-den ganashi. In this way, people from mainland Japan also become part of the tale of "beautiful Ryukyu" (the meaning of *Kyūyō*).

Let us take one more example from *Irōsetsuden* (no. 62). In Kawamitsu Village in Miyako, a heavenly goddess appeared at Sumiya grove. Her name was Teniya-ōtsukasa, and she became the wife of Merima Aji. The couple had three daughters and a son. The father soon died, and the mother raised all four children. The third daughter, Makanasu, was a filial child who stayed by her mother's side and did not wander outside the house. Nevertheless, inexplicably, she became pregnant, and her pregnancy lasted thirteen months. The family was surprised and concerned. A boy was born, but soon two horns grew out of his head, his eyeballs sank down, and his hands and feet resembled the feet of a wild goose. He was named Merima-tsuno-kawara (Horn-headed Merima). At age fourteen, he, along with his mother and grandmother, flew up into the sky on a white cloud. Later, they appeared at Mt. Merima, and the villagers in the vicinity worshipped them, resulting in Merima sacred grove.

The original written version of this tale is in *Miyakojima kyūki* (Ancient record of Miyako Island). In that version, the whole family was embarrassed about the pregnancy and deformity, and they fled from the village in shame. Notice that, in *Irōsetsuden*, the story is meant to explain the origins of a sacred grove. The bizarre details probably made it unsuitable for inclusion in the main text of *Kyūyō*, which also includes origin stories of sacred groves.

The main point of these examples is that, once legends leave local oral traditions and become written down in official or semiofficial collections, they change character and acquire ideological qualities. The tales in *Irōsetsuden*, as bizarre as many of them may seem, nevertheless convey certain messages that resonated with the interests of Shuri and its empire. Notice especially the ability of works written in the center—the Shuri-Naha area—to appropriate events, sacred spaces, and heroic figures from elsewhere in the Ryukyu Islands.

KUMIODORI

The royal court put *kumiodori* performances to good use in entertaining and impressing Chinese investiture envoys. The audience for *kumiodori* also included elite Okinawans in the capital area. The basic plot material for many but not all *kumiodori* came from Ryukyuan history and legend, as codified in the official histories and *Irōsetsuden*. Also influential in terms of plot material, style, and overall dramatic structure and style was *nō* (Noh) drama. Like *nō*, *kumiodori* feature a chanting chorus, and all characters are portrayed by men. By far the most common theme in the approximately forty *kumiodori* produced during the early modern era is loyalty and filial piety, reflecting a Confucian influence.

James Rhys Edwards describes *kumiodori* structure was follows:

> Nearly all kumiodori begin with a monologue in which the main char-
> acter or characters introduce themselves. A dialogue between the main
> characters follows, then a traveling scene or scenes (*michiyuki*), dur-
> ing which secondary characters enter and exit and plot complications
> emerge. The third scene is a climactic reunion or confrontation, followed
> by a celebratory final dance. It is possible to analyze this structural pat-
> tern as a variation on the "introduction–break–rapid crisis" (*jo-ha-kyū*)
> template employed in mainland Japanese performing arts, and/or as a
> variation on the "introduction–development–turning point–resolution"
> (*kishō-tenketsu*) template employed in Chinese and Japanese poetry and
> rhetoric. These concepts were salient in aesthetic thought and practice
> throughout the Sinocentric world, and [Tamagusuku] Chōkun would
> have been aware of them.

The metrical structure of *kumiodori* consists of an "8.8.8.6 mora, with occasional switches into other meters to obtain an effect of urgency—[and]
is derived from that of *ryūka*, the court's primary indigenous literary medium": "Like Japanese *waka*, *ryūka* are richly intertextual, frequently making use of allusive devices such as fixed word-associations (*engo*), allusive
plays on words (*kakekotoba*), and seasonal words (*kigo*)" (Edwards 2015,
107, 108 [Japanese characters removed]). In short, *kumiodori* drew on a
wide range of Japanese and Ryukyuan literary and dramatic traditions, re-
combining elements in interesting and imaginative ways. As an impressive
art form, *kumiodori* was a superb means of presenting Ryukyu to both domestic and foreign audiences.

OFFICIAL RITUAL

During the sixteenth century, the royal rituals created by Shō Shin and Shō
Sei derived in a general way from ritual practices common in Japan.[9] During
the early modern era, commensurate with the new basis of royal authority,
China became the dominant model for royal ceremonial. One result was
significant changes or additions to state rituals. One example is rites at the
Confucian temple in Kumemura. The temple was completed in 1676, and,

from that time, the head of Kumemura presided over the new year rites, the spring and autumn rites, and other important ritual events. These rites were initially held by and for the residents of Kumemura and held no broader significance. In 1719, however, the royal government in effect nationalized them, sending members of the Council of Three to the Confucian temple to preside over the new year rites. This development was an indication both of the growing influence of Confucianism in general and of the increasing importance of Kumemura within Okinawa.

The other major change was to the new year rites at the royal court. The original rites, created in the sixteenth century, were based on the Japanese calendar and elements derived from such Japanese practices as *onmyōdō* (yin-yang) divination, *shugendō*, and Shingon and Zen Buddhism. For example, the king faced a different direction each year, the choice of direction being based on divination to determine which was the most propitious. In 1719, the rites were revamped such that the king always faced north so he could pay respects to the emperor in Beijing. Moreover, the text of the prayers that he recited closely resembled prayers the Chinese emperor recited. However, the Ryukyuan rites were not an exact copy. There was no grand altar of heaven and earth, for example, just a smaller platform more similar to the simple altars at sacred groves and local temples.

The revised new year rites were controversial. The basic issue was the extent to which the Okinawan king could or should perform the same actions as the Chinese emperor. One issue was the king's worship of heaven and earth. Confucian purists in Kumemura objected to the royal worship of heaven, earth, and key celestial bodies such as the North Star on the grounds that such worship was or should be the sole prerogative of the emperor. The same issue came up in Korea, with the result being that royal veneration of heaven and earth took place there only when there was an extraordinary emergency. In the case of Ryukyu, however, the kings venerated heaven and earth each year. The main reason appears to have been the influence of earlier traditions. Recall solar worship. *Heaven* (O. *teni*) was another term for the sun, the former source of royal power. For the king not to venerate heaven would have been too severe of a break with the past.

Recall the practice of rearranging royal mortuary tablets just prior to the arrival of Chinese investiture envoys (see chap. 13). This matter was part of a larger overhaul of royal mausoleum rites that took place between about 1690 and 1730. The details of the new arrangements and arguments about them are too complex for my purposes here, but consider some of the relevant issues. One was how to deal with certain royal relatives, especially the fathers of kings who had not been kings themselves (e.g., Shō I, who was Shō Nei's father) and crown princes who died before they could become king. Ultimately, such figures were treated ritually as if they had been kings, but their tablets were not always placed in the main royal temple (there was extensive argument over this matter). There were also special rites for kings deemed particularly important and potent, but the decision as to which kings should be in this category was not always obvious. In 1691, for example, Shō Hashi and Shō En were added to this select group of kings, but, previously, they had not been considered to have sufficient gravitas. Kumemura officials were deeply involved in the new mausoleum rites, but their opinions often clashed with those of officials from the royal government in Shuri. Okinawan elite society was complex.

When mausoleum-related matters eventually settled down into a rough consensus, there was the division of labor among the temples. Enkakuji became the mausoleum of the kings of the second Shō dynasty, and the rites performed there were Buddhist. Sōgenji was the mausoleum for the entire line of kings from (the legendary) Tenson on, and, although it was a Buddhist temple, the rites held there were Confucian. Ten'ōji became the mausoleum for the queens of the second Shō dynasty, Tenkaiji was used for other varieties of state ceremony, and Ryūfukuji became the mausoleum for the (real or imagined) queens of Tenson through the first Shō dynasty.

Ryukyuan crown princes and likely crown princes went to Satsuma for extended visits. There, they were involved in a variety of ritual-like activities, including visits to the Confucian temple in Kagoshima, visits to Tsurumaru Castle, a variety of formal banquets, watching of *nō* plays, art viewings, and more. Throughout these visits, there was no ritual subordination. The crown princes were treated like guests of honor. It was a type of bonding, and one goal seems to have been to impress the future king with the power, grandeur, and largesse of Satsuma such that he would want to cooperate with the theatrical state system.

[CHAPTER SIXTEEN]

The Tametomo Legend

When diverse sources and prominent people repeat something often enough, it can become widely accepted as truth, even without a shred of good supporting evidence. Such was the case with the Tametomo legend in the Ryukyu Islands.[1] Its origins hark back to the twelfth century, and the legend underwent transformations between then and the modern era. During the early twentieth century, it became enshrined as historical fact in school textbooks and popular culture. Japan's wartime defeat in 1945 brought an abrupt end to official support for the legend as historical fact. Soon thereafter, popular belief in it faded as well.

The basic modern version of the legend is as follows. Minamoto Tametomo was a Japanese warrior of almost superhuman strength. His branch of the Minamoto family descended from Emperor Seiwa (r. 858–76). When Taira forces defeated the Minamoto armies in 1156, Tametomo was exiled to the Izu Islands. He escaped, made his way to the Ryukyu Islands via Kyushu, and entered Okinawa at Unten Harbor near Nakijin. He then moved to southern Okinawa and married the sister of a local warlord, and she gave birth to a son. By that time, however, Tametomo had left Okinawa to return to mainland Japan. This son became Okinawa's first king, Shunten (r. 1187–1237). Shunten's line of kings lasted only three generations, ending with a king named Gihon. However, omitting the complex details, the 1725 version of *Genealogy of Chūzan* linked Shunten's line of kings with the second Shō dynasty. The bottom line was that Ryukyu's first and last king as well as all the kings of the second Shō dynasty were very distant relatives of Emperor Seiwa thanks to Tametomo's brief sojourn in Okinawa.

Some modern and contemporary writers have claimed that the Japanese government foisted this fanciful tale onto Okinawa for political purposes. It did not. On the contrary, people in the Ryukyu Islands have nurtured and embraced some version of the Tametomo legend since as early as the Gusuku Era. The legend was prominent in the islands for centuries. This chapter traces its development from inception to the twentieth century.

Cast of Characters

In the basic narrative of Japanese history, the half brothers Minamoto Yoshitsune (ca. 1159–89) and Minamoto Yoritomo (1147–99) figure prominently. As young men, they led the Minamoto forces in the Genpei War (1180–85) and emerged victorious. Yoritomo went on to found the Kamakura *bakufu* (shogunate). In the process, however, he eliminated Yoshitsune, falsely accusing him of treason. One result is that Yoshitsune has enjoyed popular acclaim as a tragic hero. Moreover, all manner of fantastic legends about him can be found. In one, for example, he did not die but instead fled to the Asian continent. There, he became Genghis Khan. In the early twentieth century, many Japanese believed this wild claim.

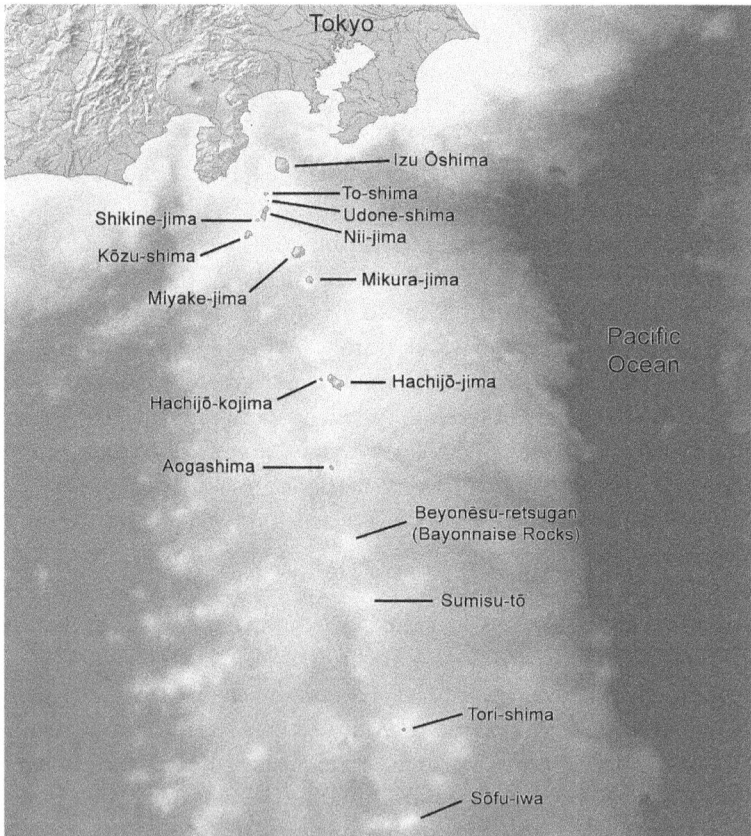

FIGURE 16.1. The Izu Islands

Minamoto Tametomo (1139–70) was of the previous generation. He fought in the Hōgen Rebellion of 1156, which was an earlier round of warfare between the Minamoto and the Taira. While they prevailed in the Genpei War, in the Hōgen Rebellion the Minamoto went down to defeat. Reliable details about Tametomo are few, but, after the Minamoto defeat, he was exiled to Ōshima in the Izu Islands. There, he either killed himself or died battling the forces of an opponent, Kudō Shigemitsu. In either event, he died somewhere in the Izu Islands (fig. 16.1). Ōshima and Hachijōjima are the main possibilities. Tametomo was also known as Chinzei Hachirō Tametomo, and this version of his name is common in Tametomo legends in the Ryukyu Islands.

Legends developed about Tametomo to the effect that he did not die in the Izu Islands. Instead, he crossed over to an island called *Onigashima* (Island of demons) and carried on the fight. Later legends placed him in Higo Province (Kumamoto Prefecture), a location with extensive ties to the Ryukyu Islands. Even later, sixteenth-century legends placed him in the northern Ryukyu Islands and Okinawa. According to legends of this vintage, while in Okinawa, Tametomo briefly ruled the island before returning to the mainland of Japan. In 1650, *Reflections on Chūzan* stated that Shunten, Okinawa's first king, was the son of Tametomo and a sister of the ruler of Ōzato in southern Okinawa.

Geographic Distribution of Tametomo Legends and Their Influence

There are two main clusters of legends about tragic Minamoto warriors. According to Harada Nobuo (2017), the legend of Minamoto Yoshitsune (a generation *after* Tametomo) is found in forty-two prefectures and urban districts throughout Japan, and there are a total of 508 specific manifestations of it. The geographic distribution of legends about Minamoto Tametomo includes thirty-six prefectures and urban districts and 196 specific instances. Most of the Yoshitsune legends are found in northern Japan (Hokuriku, Tōhoku, Hokkaidō), while most of the Tametomo legends are found in Kyushu, the Izu Islands, and the islands of the Ryukyu Arc.

Notice that, in an early iteration of the legend, Tametomo left Ōshima and traveled to Onigashima. There is no island in the Izu group with that name. Onigashima resonated with both Kikaijima and Okinawa, which many Heian-period Japanese regarded as a land of savage cannibals.[2] There is another important link between Tametomo and southern Kyushu. Ata Tadakage, a powerful local ruler of the Manose River area of the Satsuma

Peninsula was Tametomo's father-in-law. There are legendary accounts to the effect that, after a failed rebellion, Tadakage fled to "Kikai," a name that could mean Kikaijima or any of the Satsunan Islands. Tametomo married his daughter. Notice the plot outline. A powerful outsider arrives and marries the daughter or sister of a powerful local ruler. Legends featuring this basic plot gradually spread throughout the southern islands all the way down to Okinawa.

In Onozu, in northwest Kikaijima, is found the Karimata Spring. According to legend, this is the first place Tametomo set foot on land after setting out by ship from Ōshima in the Izu Islands. A shrine to the deity Hachiman was established at Onozu in connection with this legend.[3]

Surveying some examples of Tametomo legends in the northern Ryukyu Islands, the Saneku Sanjirō shrine in Saneku, Kakeroma Island (just south of Amami-Ōshima), enshrines a powerful giant of a man, Saneku Sanjirō. He was the offspring of Tametomo and a local woman, conceived when Tametomo came through the island. According to *Nantō zatsuwa* (see Nagoya 1855/1984), Tametomo resided in Naze (Amami City) for about three years and then lived in Kakeroma. A local song there tells of a "scion of Yamatogusuku," which refers either to Tametomo or his offspring. *Yamato* is a general term for Japan, and *-gusuku* in this context is an honorific suffix. So the name means something like "Venerable scion of Japan."

In Tokunoshima, on the top of Inutabu peak, there are two rocks on which Tametomo purportedly sat while gazing out at Okinawa. There is a Yamatogusuku in Amagi District, and there is a shrine to Tametomo atop Amagi peak.

In Okinoerabu, there is a legend that Tametomo built a mansion at Gusukume in Ajifu. Moreover, according to legend, the prominent Heizan and Ryū lineages within the island descended from Tametomo. In Yoron island, where Tametomo purportedly stayed for three months, there is a shrine to Ajinitchei, the purported offspring of Tametomo and a local woman.[4] Notice that the plot of Tametomo fathering a child with a local woman repeats itself all the way down the Ryukyu Arc to Okinawa.

There are also extensive Tametomo legends in both Higo and Satsuma. So we find a nearly continuous flow of Tametomo lore from Kumamoto south along the west coast of Kyushu all the way to Okinawa. This route covers a major portion of the sacred grove zone and most of the legendary route traveled by the founding deity Amamikyo/Amamiku—as well as many other aspects of culture common to the Ryukyu Islands, western Kyushu, and often areas farther afield.

It is worth noting that, implicitly or explicitly, the Tametomo legend appears in the household records of locally prominent lineages in

Amami-Ōshima.[5] The Shidama lineage, for example, traces its descent from Tametomo through (the legendary) King Gihon. The lineage founder, Taruyoshi, allegedly was Gihon's son, born in 1249, the year Gihon took the throne. Taruyoshi was "Prince Urasoe," and his lineage deity was Iwashimizu Hachiman in Kyoto, a shrine associated with the Minamoto family. Most lineage records were compiled during the early modern era, and the claim of a specific ancestor born in 1249 is purely legendary. The important point is that the Tametomo legend permeated many segments of Ryukyuan society, both in Okinawa and in the northern Ryukyu Islands. In a general way, these legends and their distribution reflect the migration south of people from Japan early in the Gusuku Era.

In the Satsunan and Tokara Islands as well as in Amami-Ōshima and Kikaijima, Tametomo legends coexisted with Heike (Taira family) legends. The basic idea of Heike legends is that Taira warriors defeated at the Battle of Dan-no-ura in 1185 made their way into these southern islands. Therefore, while some prominent island families claimed descent from Tametomo, others claimed descent from prominent Taira warriors. However, from Tokunoshima through Okinawa, there is little or no trace of Taira/Heike legends.[6] Interestingly, in the southern Ryukyu Islands, we find Taira legends but no Tametomo legends.

It is also worth noting that versions of the Yuriwaka legend spread to parts of the Ryukyu Islands. For example, according to *Yōsei kyūki* (1727) and *Irōsetsuden*, the Yuriwaka legend spread to islands in the Miyako group. Yuriwaka was a great archer and a powerful warrior. In these legends, he came into the Ryukyu Islands from Japan. Tales of heroes or antiheroes such as Tametomo, Taira warriors, or Yuriwaka probably had widespread appeal in the Ryukyu Islands during the Gusuku Era, especially later in the era. It was a time when recent arrivals from Japan were numerous and *wakō* activity was at its peak.

As waves of Japanese migrants arrived during the Gusuku Era, they spoke of Tametomo-like figures, nurturing images of rule by people from outside the islands. During the sixteenth century, Zen priests in Kyoto codified the tale. Both the Japanese Buddhist priest Gesshū Jukei, writing in the 1530s, and the priest Taichū, writing in the early seventeenth century, stressed that Tametomo became the ruler of Okinawa after subduing a demon deity. In other words, these men transposed the tale of Tametomo subduing "demon island" to Okinawa.

When we survey major early modern histories and compendiums from Japan like *Zoku-Honchō tsūgan* (1670), *Dai-Nihonshi* (started 1657), and *Wakan sansai zue* (1712), we find that they mention Tametomo sailing to Okinawa via Kikaijima as one far-fetched possibility or as one variant legend. Importantly, their main narrative has Tametomo killing himself in Izu-Ōshima. In other words, the legend of Tametomo sailing to Okinawa and briefly ruling over the island had not yet become mainstream in Japan during the eighteenth century.

That situation changed during the nineteenth century. For example, in 1818, Rai Sanyō wrote a "Chinzei Hachirō song" after being told by some Ryukyuans he encountered on a ship in Kagoshima that Tametomo was greatly venerated there. The song included a line stating that the mythical Okinawan king Tenson was Tametomo's son and another stating that Tametomo would be angry if he could know that Ryukyu maintains tributary relations with China. The song reflects a consciousness that the Ryukyu Islands were part of Japan and may also have promoted this idea.

Notice the main points. The arrival of the Tametomo legend in Okinawa and other Ryukyu Islands corresponded to the arrival of people from Japan during the Gusuku Era. Later, Ryukyu's official histories highlighted the Tametomo legend as well as creation myths that closely resembled those of Japan. Nevertheless, in the Japanese mainland during the seventeenth and eighteenth centuries, although the story of Tametomo sailing to the Ryukyu Islands was known, it tended to be regarded as an unlikely or fanciful tale. During the nineteenth century, however, this once fanciful version of the legend gradually entered the mainstream.

Shō Shōken's Revision of the Tametomo Legend

Although *Reflections on Chūzan* goes into the greatest detail, all the official histories state that Ryukyu's first king, Shunten, was the son of Chinzei Hachirō Minamoto-no-Tametomo and the sister of a local lord in southern Okinawa. Importantly, Shō Shōken's 1650 version of the tale in *Reflections* was new. Previously, the story was simply that Tametomo briefly ruled Okinawa, as if by the sheer force of his personality and skill as a warrior. Shō Shōken's making Tametomo the progenitor of a royal line was an innovation. That idea probably existed before 1650, but its first appearance in writing was in *Reflections*. Knowing of the waves of Japanese who came into the Ryukyu Islands during what we now consider the Gusuku Era, Shō Shōken took the Japanese Tametomo legend and reworked it to make Ryukyuan history appear to be older than it was and suggest a noble origin for Okinawa's kings.

In adapting the Tametomo legend to Ryukyu, Shō Shōken was skillful in dating the alleged events. He has Tametomo coming to Ryukyu in 1165 or 1166. He grafted this part of the story onto the narrative found in the *kokatsujibon Hōgen monogatari* (ca. sixteenth century), which has Tametomo crossing over to Onishima (demon island) in 1165 and killing himself in Izu in 1170. Shō Shōken fit Tametomo's Ryukyuan sojourn into this 1165–70 window of time. He fashioned a tale that was more finely grained than those that had been circulating in the writings of Buddhist priests since around the 1530s.

To understand Ryukyuan history, it is necessary set aside the simplistic Japan-versus-Ryukyu/Okinawa binary so common today. This mode of thinking has caused Shō Shōken's version of the Tametomo legend and the subtleties connected with it to be misunderstood.

By 1650, the territory of the Ryukyu Islands had gone from being an open frontier region of Japan to being a possession of the Shimazu lords of Satsuma. In that context, neither the Shimazu lords nor any intellectual in Satsuma promoted the Tametomo legend, although they were aware of it. Instead, they claimed that the Ryukyu Islands had been the territory of Satsuma since 1441. This claim rested on flimsy evidence, but Satsuma had been victorious in the 1609 war with Ryukyu. In the opening chapter of *Reflections*, Shō Shōken attempted to walk a fine line. He gently pushed back against Satsuma's claim to have possessed Ryukyu since 1441 by stressing the long history of Ryukyuan interactions with Japan as a whole, relations that began well before 1441. The enhanced Tametomo legend was part of this larger project of pushing back against Satsuma's claims. It reinforced the idea of ties between the Ryukyu Islands and Japan well before 1441 in addition to giving Ryukyuan kings a noble pedigree.

The Tametomo Legend as a Template for Royal Biographies

A common motif in Ryukyuan legends, either in oral traditions or in legends written down in the early modern era, begins with someone leaving his or her native place. The person relocates to an island, settles down with the local population, and takes a local spouse. Offspring typically become the local ruler and priestess of that place. There are many variations on this motif, but throughout the Ryukyu Islands founding legends are generally about the arrival of outsiders.

Popular myths or legends describe the origin of local male rulers (*aji*) and priestesses (*noro*). They do not explain the origins of kings (and recall that *king* was a Chinese title, not a local one). Only the stories in the official histories and other government-produced documents describe the origin of kings. This absence of royal legends probably reflects the late date (ca. 1520s–1530s) of formal state formation.

Shō Shōken created a new and improved version of the Tametomo legend from diverse elements. He took existing myths and legends about the origins of local rulers, priestesses, and common people and from them created royal and high-priestess origin stories, his basic formula being Shunten = powerful outsider Tametomo + local woman. In the process, he also created a template for the stories of all later kings. Nearly all the official biographies of kings and many unofficial folk tales involving kings or future kings closely resemble Shō Shōken's version of the Tametomo legend. Consider a few examples.

According to their official biographies, the founders of lines of kings prior to the second Shō dynasty (the lines started by Shunten, Eiso, and Shō Shishō) all had the qualities of outsiders. They were born after their father's arrival in Okinawa (Samekawa in the case of Shishō) and after his pairing with a woman from the household of a local ruler. Satto's story was slightly different, perhaps because of his likely Korean origins. He was born of a heavenly maiden and a lowly man. He was, in effect, an outsider who combined the qualities of heaven and earth within his person. He then married the daughter of a local ruler near Urasoe.

Shunten's case also follows a typical three-stage plot sequence by which someone becomes king. Tametomo came into Okinawa from Izu or Kyushu and married the sister of a local ruler, giving birth to Shunten (stage 1: exile and deportation). As a young man, Shunten conquered an unrighteous usurper named Riyū (stage 2: ordeal or battle). As a result, the people acclaimed him as their king (stage 3: take the throne). The story of Eiso is more complex, but it follows the same basic plot. That of Kanemaru/Shō En followed a similar pattern, although Shō En himself came in as an outsider, as opposed to being born in Okinawa to one outsider parent. Shō Shin's case also fits the template fairly well. Kanemaru/Shō En was the outsider, and his wife, Ogyaka, functioned like the sister or daughter of a local ruler. Considering all his wars and his struggle to keep the throne, Shō Shin certainly endured battles and ordeals, albeit technically *after* becoming king but *before* becoming de facto emperor.

Shō Shōken's version of the Tametomo legend also recapitulates the story of the Samekawa family, the group that included Shō Shishō and Shō Hashi, the founders of the first Shō dynasty in Okinawa. A common route from the islands of Iheya or Izena into Okinawa began with a landing at Unten Harbor near Nakijin. That is precisely the path Tametomo purportedly took according to *Reflections*. After landing at Nakijin, Tametomo made his way to southern Okinawa, where he married the sister of the ruler of Ōzato, which is very close to Sashiki.

According to *Origins of Lord Samekawa* (*Samekawa-ōnushi yuraiki*, ca.

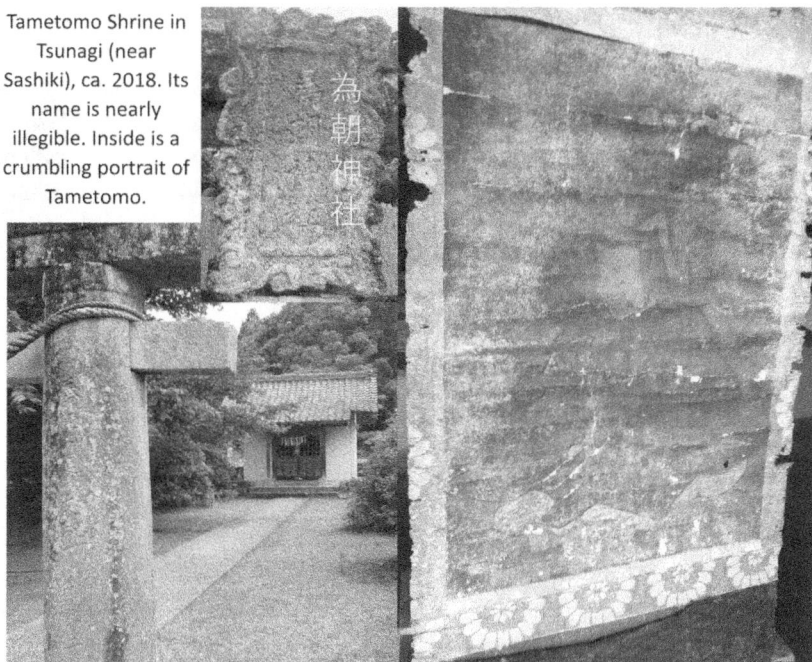

Tametomo Shrine in Tsunagi (near Sashiki), ca. 2018. Its name is nearly illegible. Inside is a crumbling portrait of Tametomo.

FIGURE 16.2. The Tametomo Shrine in Tsunagi, near Yatsushiro, Kumamoto Prefecture, ca. 2018 (photographs by the author)

eighteenth century), an early modern text of unknown provenance, Same-kawa followed the same route: Iheya/Izena to Nakijin to Sashiki. We also know from other sources that he came to Okinawa from Sashiki in Kyushu. There are at least two shrines to Tametomo in that area of Kyushu, one at Tsunagi (fig. 16.2) and the other in Minamata. However, we cannot know whether they existed during the time of Samekawa's migration, ca. 1390.[7]

What follows is a comparison of the two tales, first Tametomo, then Samekawa:

Izu to Kyushu to the northern Ryukyu Islands to Nakijin to southeast Okinawa: powerful outsider + local woman (local ruler's sister) = new king (Shunten).

Kyushu to islands north of Okinawa to Nakijin to southeast Okinawa: powerful outsider + local woman (local ruler's sister) = new king (Shō Shishō).

The two tales are almost perfectly congruent, and they closely resemble the official biographies of other kings. Moreover, the story of the father of

Nakama Mitsukeima Eigyoku, a powerful ruler in Ishigaki, also follows the plot of Shō Shōken's version of the Tametomo legend.

Versions of the Tametomo legend connect the Ryukyu Islands with Kyushu in various ways. According to the eighteenth-century *History of Higo Province* (*Higo kokushi*), the relevant shrine was originally called Yahachi-gū. According to one of the legends connected with it, Tametomo secretly made his way to Kyushu and enlisted a fisherman named Yahachi to take him to Okinawa. Before the fisherman returned to Kyushu, Tametomo gave him a piece of his sleeve. The fisherman realized that Tametomo was extraordinary, so he enshrined the piece of clothing. In the *Higo Province* version of the tale, fishermen in Okinawa obtained the clothing fragment, and Yahachi brought it from Okinawa to the shrine in Minamata. These versions of the Tametomo legend reveal the close maritime connections that existed between the Higo coast—especially the Shiranui Sea area of Yatsushiro—and the Ryukyu Islands.

Zooming out in our perspective, notice again that, from the Gusuku Era on, the Ryukyu Islands functioned as a frontier region of Japan and, to a lesser but important extent, Korea. People from all over the East China Sea region sometimes made their way into the Ryukyu Islands. In the 1450s, there were approximately one hundred Korean households in the vicinity of Naha. By the end of the sixteenth century, there was a vast population of Japanese merchants in the Naha area whose community featured frequent performances of Sarugaku *nō* drama for their entertainment. According to the 1712 *Jōsai hōshi den*, the Buddhist priest Kyori went to Okinawa and found several hundred Japanese households in Naha established by people from Kyushu, Chūgoku, Kinai, Osaka, Kantō, and Ōshū, that is, from all over Japan.

As we have seen, however, by 1712 Ryukyu's situation had changed dramatically. Those households may have been established by migrants from different parts of Japan, but their eighteenth-century descendants were no longer free to get on a ship and travel to Japan or any other country. From about the 1620s or 1630s on, the Ryukyu Islands became mostly closed off, both from Japan as a whole and from the broader region, except for small-scale, carefully orchestrated contacts.

The Modern Era

Moving ahead in time to the 1880s and later, after several centuries of relative isolation, the Ryukyu Islands had become fully part of Japan, at least in theory. Modern Japan was, however, a very different place from the Japan of the Gusuku Era or the sixteenth century. The late nineteenth century was a time when cultural ethnonationalism was intensifying all around the world, and Japan was no exception. The cultural nationalism that developed in modern Japan made assimilation difficult for residents of the Ryukyu Islands. This section discusses some manifestations of the Tametomo legend in the context of state-sponsored cultural assimilation.

That Tametomo had been the father of Ryukyu's first king was one of the sixteen specific points that Matsuda Michiyuki enumerated in justifying the formal annexation of the Ryukyu Islands in 1879. During the Meiji Era, a wide segment of Okinawa's population had come to regard the Tametomo legend as laid out by Shō Shōken in 1650 as historical fact. Iha Fuyū, Higashionna Kanjun, Majikina Ankō, and the other big names among the first generation of Okinawan studies scholars all agreed.

In 1914, the newspaper *Ryūkyū shinpō* sponsored a popular play adapted from Takizawa Bakin's *Chinsetsu yumiharizuki* (1807)[8] called *Ryukyu and Tametomo* (Ryūkyū to Tametomo). Soon thereafter, the monument Tametomo Making Landfall (Tametomo jōriku no hi) was erected at Unten Harbor near Nakijin. In 1926, the former royal palace in Shuri Castle became Okinawa Shrine (Okinawa jinja). Its principal deities were Shunten, Tametomo, and the last king, Shō Tai.

When the anthropologist Eguchi Tsukasa visited Unten Harbor around 2000 and asked some local people about Tametomo, one of them immediately sang this song (sometimes the English lines are reversed from the Japanese to make the syntax work):

> Chinzei Hachirō Tametomo kō
> with indefatigable ambition
> Setting sail across the great sea
> Arrived right here, in Unten Harbor!
>
> This tall monument
> at Matsukaze in Unten forest
> tells the story
> of Tametomo's coming ashore here
>
> A stone hut beyond the forest
> was Tametomo's temporary dwelling
> Asking about what he dreamed
> it is hidden way back in the past

Seven hundred years after the hero lived
the pounding waves of Urumagashima
unceasingly celebrate the lord's bravery
and tell of what he did in this place.

(Eguchi 2006, 106)

As this example shows, traces of the Tametomo legend have persisted even into the twenty-first century.

The Tametomo legend entered Okinawa and the northern Ryukyu Islands most likely from Higo in Kyushu or possibly Satsuma. Tales of against-the-grain heroes like Tametomo or Yuriwaka resonated with the *wakō*-dominated frontier society in the Ryukyu Islands of the fourteenth and fifteenth centuries. By the early sixteenth century, the basic idea that Tametomo had come to Okinawa and ruled the island for a while was in place among Zen Buddhist priests in Okinawa and in parts of Japan. Shō Shōken modified the story in 1650, although his version probably had been in circulation even earlier. We have also seen that some elite households in Amami-Ōshima traced their ancestors back to Tametomo. The flesh-and-blood Tametomo died in the Izu Islands, but the legendary Tametomo appeared all over Kyushu and the northern and central Ryukyu Islands.

Books like Shō Shōken's *Reflections on Chūzan* were accessible to only a small fraction of the Ryukyuan population, the vast majority of whom were illiterate. Over the centuries, however, the Tametomo legend spread into general society in Okinawa and other islands. So, too, did the idea that the Okinawan monarchy started with Shunten, someone who almost certainly did not exist. In Japan, during the seventeenth and eighteenth centuries, very few historians or literary scholars thought that Tametomo actually sailed to the Ryukyu Islands. However, that skepticism rapidly evaporated during the nineteenth century. By the time the Ryukyu Kingdom collapsed and was replaced by Okinawa Prefecture in 1879, the belief that Tametomo had been the father of Okinawa's first king had become widely accepted in Okinawa, in the other Ryukyu Islands, and in the rest of Japan. The tale had taken on a life of its own.

Notice that the Tametomo legend was not a case of people in Japan foisting a legend onto Okinawa for political purposes. Simplistic Japan-versus-Okinawa binaries are rarely, if ever, accurate. The legend did serve certain modern political purposes, but it had long been accepted in the Ryukyu Islands from Okinawa north. Notice the power of belief and the power of people to create new identities for themselves. Tametomo never set foot in the Ryukyu Islands, but, when enough people came to believe that he had, belief became de facto historical fact—until suddenly after 1945 it was not.

One reason for this strong-as-fact belief was repetition. When something is repeated often enough, especially by powerful people, we have a tendency to assume that it is accurate or at least mostly accurate. There is no shortage of examples of repetition being treated as fact in descriptions of Ryukyuan history and culture despite a lack of evidence, whether in the past or today.

PART FOUR

THE MODERN ERA,
1880–2024

The modern era in Okinawa is a complex, multifaceted topic, and the four chapters in this part of the book only scratch the surface of possible topics and analysis. There is plenty of room for a separate book devoted to this era. Not surprisingly, the modern era attracts the most scholarly attention. The quantity of Anglophone scholarship, especially, is overwhelmingly concentrated in the modern era.

Scholarship on modern Okinawa (Okinawa Prefecture) typically invokes the deeper Ryukyuan past, but often superficially, without a rigorous understanding of that past. One crucial point that I often stress is that, by the 1870s, the Ryukyu Kingdom was no longer viable. Although its governing institutions continued to function, its agricultural base had collapsed. At least economically, it had become a failed state. Moreover, the mature theatrical state iteration of the kingdom came to the end of its run at about the same time. For better or worse, modern conditions required the clarification of state boundaries. In that context, there was only one viable state affiliation for the Ryukyu Islands. While I am generally critical of the Meiji state's *kyūkan-onzon* policy—or at least cognizant of its contribution to human misery—it is also important to bear in mind the severe resource constraints of Japan's new government during the nineteenth century. Given the situation of the 1870s, I cannot conceive of any easy or smooth way forward for Shuri's former empire.

This era is awash in documentation, and the possible primary sources are too numerous to list. My suggestion for researchers is to make good use of web-based resources such as the Okinawa Migration Record Database, the Okinawa Prefectural Archives, the Okinawa Prefectural Library, the Okinawa Studies Research Guide, the Ryukyuan International Relations and Sources for Modern Okinawan History Digital Archives, the University of Hawai'i at Manoa Library, Okinawan Studies: Online Resources Links, and the University of the Ryukyus Repository. These sites provide access to photographs, films, posters, popular periodicals, personal accounts, and much other material in addition to the typical documents and records of interest to historians.

As for my past work, Smits (2001, 2002, 2006, 2010a, 2015a) are all directly relevant to the chapters in this part. A few sections of those chapters consist mainly of revised and condensed versions of earlier work. Individual research interests, of course, will guide reading in the secondary sources. Looking first at some of the English-language literature, the following works provide a good overview of Anglophone scholarship since the 1990s: Christy (1993), Clarke (1997), Figal (2012), Heinrich (2013), Hook and Siddle (2003), Iacobelli and Matsuda (2017), Ishida (2018), Kano (1993), Loo (2023), Matsuda (2019), Matsumura (2015), Molasky (2003), Molasky and Rabson (2000), Nakasone (2002), Nelson (2008), Oguma (2002, 2014), Rabson (2012), Røkkum (2006), Shimabuku (2019), Takahashi (2024), Tanji (2006), and Ziomek (2014, 2019). Some of this work differs substantially in tone and conclusions from the chapters offered here, and, were I to write a book only on the modern era, I would engage some of these authors critically. I would also note that the vast Japanese-language secondary literature on Okinawa includes a wider variety of approaches to the era's complexities than does the Anglophone literature.

Another feature of some of the Anglophone literature (with some counterparts in Japanese) is the extensive use of Marxist theory and other varieties of critical theory to frame modern Okinawan history. One representative example is Wendy Matsumura's *The Limits of Okinawa* (2015). Matsumura does a herculean job of fitting certain aspects of Okinawan history into a Marxist framework. If I were to state her overall argument concisely, it would be that many ordinary people actively rejected the versions of Okinawa created by public intellectuals such as Iha Fuyū and Ōta Chōfu. Indeed, *Okinawa*, however conceptualized, was inadequate to describe, contain, or label the diverse communities across Okinawa Prefecture. It is an important point, one with which I fully agree. Assuming that my characterization of Matsumura's main argument is accurate, I am not convinced that a Marxist framework is necessary or the best approach for advancing it.

We are fortunate to have very good scholarship on modern Okinawan literature, including translations of important work. For the basic lay of the land in this realm, see Bhowmik (2008, 2020), Bhowmik and Rabson (2016), Molasky (1999), and Rabson (1989, 1999a, 1999b). For a wide selection of literary works with academic commentary, see Okamoto, Takahashi, and Motohama (2015).

There are only a few works of military history and geopolitics in the bibliography, and the vast literature in this realm is beyond my expertise. Those interested in the Battle of Okinawa should see Yahara (1995) for an important, albeit often self-serving, Japanese perspective. For a remarkable collection of the experiences of ordinary people caught up in the battle, see Ryukyu Shimpo (2014). Otherwise, see the section "Okinawa Studies Research Guide: Battle of Okinawa" in George Washington University's Okinawa Studies Research Guide site, which is associated with the university's extensive Okinawa Collection (Gelman Library). That site also has sections on environmental issues and military base issues, among other things.

CHAPTER SEVENTEEN

The Early Decades of Okinawa Prefecture

Starting in the 1880s, the Ryukyu Islands emerged from several centuries of relative isolation and began a decades-long process of greater engagement with the broader world. I begin by revisiting the matter of personal identity. During the modern era, a variety of new identities arose in the Japanese islands and elsewhere in the world. This chapter begins by examining a process whereby fundamental power imbalances, formal education, other parts of the state apparatus, and trends in journalism combined to create the overdetermined, dual yet conflicting identities of Japanese and Okinawan/Ryukyuan among the denizens of Japan's newest prefecture. Next, it looks at the tragic life of Jahana Noboru (謝花昇, 1865–1908) as a window onto social tensions during the early decades of Okinawa Prefecture. Finally, it examines economic problems, the beginnings of the diaspora, and several specific manifestations of a growing obsession with culture. The time period is roughly the half century from the 1890s to about 1940.

Making Ryukyuans, Making Japanese

In 1861, a few years before Japan's Meiji Restoration, the Kingdom of Italy came into existence for the first time. That year, the statesman Massimo d'Azeglio (1798–1866) said: "We have made Italy. Now we must make Italians." Similar processes took place all over the word during the nineteenth century and the early twentieth. Germany, for example, came into existence in 1871 as a state, and one of its tasks was to create Germans out of the Bavarians, Saxons, Westphalians, and others living within its borders. In Japan at just about the same time, the new Meiji state cast about for ways to remake the people living in the Japanese islands into self-consciously Japanese subjects. Although many institutions played a role in this process, education proved to be especially effective. But this process was complex and fraught with tensions.

In the Ryukyu Islands, the process of identity formation was even more complex and fraught than it was elsewhere in Japan. Individual land ownership, military conscription, local and national elections, and many basic personal freedoms were implemented in Okinawa Prefecture much later than they were elsewhere. The rationale for the delays was that special circumstances prevailed in Okinawa Prefecture and that its people were not yet ready to shoulder the full burden of Japanese citizenship.

Okinawa Prefecture was created by the forced removal of the king and justified mainly on the basis of the 1609 war between Satsuma and Ryukyu and liberating ordinary Ryukyuans from oppressive rule by Shuri. The Ryukyu Islands had long been conquered territory, and other parts of Japan had been more recently conquered by the modern state. For example, many of the domains in northern Honshu militarily held out against the Meiji state into 1869, and we have briefly noted the Satsuma Rebellion of 1877. So Okinawa was not radically different in this respect. It was the legacy of the theatrical state that considerably slowed and complicated the smooth incorporation of Okinawa into the rest of Japan. That Okinawa had been a kingdom, albeit one acting under the authorization of Satsuma and the *bakufu*, highlighted its status as conquered territory compared with the other Japanese territory forcibly brought into the Meiji state. Moreover, the Sinification of many Ryukyuan elites, which had intensified from the end of the eighteenth century, helped promote the inaccurate notion that Ryukyuan culture was closer to that of China than to that of Japan. The theatrical state became so good at the optics of looking Chinese that many residents of newly created Okinawa Prefecture suffered as a result.

Cultural differences in Okinawa were real, and they existed at multiple social levels. Culture differed geographically, from island to island and even within different regions of the same island. It also differed as a function of education level or socioeconomic status. To take a simple example, most residents of Okinawa Prefecture would have had difficulty freely conversing with anyone outside their local districts owing to linguistic differences within the island. In this realm, too, the situation was not—or need not have been—radically different from that in many other parts of Japan. What came to be regarded as ideal Japanese culture was, for the most part, a variety of well-to-do Edo/Tokyo culture, and the new government imposed it on the rest of the country.

Consider that poorly educated farmers in the southern Satsuma Peninsula would have experienced great difficulty if, in 1880 or 1890, suddenly they were transported to Tokyo. Simple verbal communication would have been difficult, as would also have been the case for someone in rural Iwate Prefecture in the north. During this era, such people commonly encountered discrimination as "country bumpkins" (*inakamono* and other terms) when they relocated to large urban areas, but their membership in the national family was never in question. The situation was more precarious for people in Okinawa Prefecture. Although educated Japanese tended to regard such people as natural members of the national family, albeit in need of refinement, ordinary people were much more likely to hold in their minds early modern era woodblock print images of Ryukyuans in exotic costumes playing Chinese music.

In a classic article, "The Making of Imperial Subjects in Okinawa," Alan Christy describes the process of making Ryukyuans and Japanese simultaneously. The context here is the gap between Japanese academic studies, which emphasized the many linguistic and anthropological links between the Ryukyu Islands and the rest of Japan, and obvious differences in speech and day-to-day cultural habits. In this context, Christy notes: "The gap between the ideology of ethnic homogeneity and the heterogeneity of daily practices led the Meiji government to initiate a program of assimilation (*dōka*), signifying the imperative that Okinawans transform their speech, dress, work, and leisure activities from those labeled 'Okinawan' to those designated as 'Japanese.' ... [T]his involved, first, the construction of identities marked as 'Okinawan' and 'Japanese' in an overdetermined relationship to each other, and then interiorization of the latter by Okinawans" (Christy 1993, 610). The Okinawan case was an extreme example of a broader campaign of social and psychological engineering by the Meiji state. Other Japanese came under pressure to improve themselves in a myriad of ways supposedly befitting a proper imperial subject, but the process for them was comparatively more subtle. There was also a qualitative difference in that, for most people, this state pressure did not take the form of, for example, rejecting a Shinano (Nagano) identity in favor of Japanese one. People in Nagano Prefecture ca. 1900 could easily partake of real or imagined local Shinano culture without any sense that they were less Japanese for doing so.

Christy also notes the tendency in Okinawa during the early years of the twentieth century to portray economic problems caused by fundamental structural imbalances as cultural problems instead. Therefore, despite the existence of objective causes for Okinawan poverty, "many observers sought 'subjective' causes in some defect of the 'Okinawan character,' since it seemed perfectly clear to most of these critics that Okinawa was 'backward'": "This claim has frequently been used during the modern Okinawan-Japanese relationship, beginning with the reactions of the hawkish groups in the Japanese Popular Rights Movement (*jiyū minken undo*) to the dispute between Japan and Qing China over possession of the Ryūkyūs in the 1870s. Some *minken* writers, such as Takahashi Kiichi, for example, argued that Japanese control of the islands was necessary to save the common Ryūkyūans from the feudalistic governance of their ruling classes" (Christy 1993, 612). Notice the important point that some Japanese advocates of popular rights argued for Japanese annexation of the Ryukyu Islands to liberate ordinary Ryukyuans from the oppressive royal government. For reasons that should be clear from previous chapters, they had a good point. In practice, however, the Meiji state showed little or no concern for the personal well-being of individual Ryukyuans. Its overriding concern was to shore up its southern borders at minimal cost. The *kyūkan-onzon* policy may have been a successful expedient in the short term for both Okinawan elites and the Meiji state, but in the longer term it contributed to decades of suffering among the majority of the population that played out well beyond the formal end of the policy.

Nowhere Else to Go

At this point, it is worthwhile to pause for a thought experiment. What realistic option or options were there in the 1870s or 1880s with respect to the Ryukyu Islands? Perhaps the Meiji government could have granted them formal independence, which, of course, would also have ended the need for Shuri to send tax payments to Satsuma. Prominent people in Satsuma might have objected, saying that the Ryukyu Islands had been formally counted in Satsuma's net worth (*kokudaka*) since the seventeenth century, but suppose such protests were overruled. Would Ryukyu have been a viable state? The tribute trade with the Qing would have collapsed or been greatly curtailed because Satsuma's funding for it would have ended. Agriculture would have remained fundamentally unviable as the basis of the economy. Elites would have continued to squeeze ordinary people hard. It is possible that Ryukyu could have limped along for a while under these conditions, much as it did under the *kyūkan-onzon* policy. The islands' shaky economy, their militarily strategic position, and the intense imperialist pressures within the East China Sea region at this time would have made foreign intervention nearly certain.

What about military spending? In the early modern era, Satsuma provided the cannons and other weaponry necessary to protect tribute ships, which frequently encountered pirates. Had Ryukyu become an independent state, one option would have been to invest in modern military hardware and training, but that seems impossible given its economic state, even without the burden of a tax to Satsuma. Another option might have been to depend on an outside state for protection, but, in that case, what would

Ryukyu have been able to offer in return other than its territory? Although some people profess the belief that unarmed states will be left in peace by other states, regional and world history does not support this idea.

Another possible option would have been to continue the facade of the theatrical state, with the Meiji government filling in for Satsuma. During the early 1870s, some in the Meiji government advocated such a policy as a way to save on expenses or for other reasons (for details, see Oguma 2014, 16–21). It is difficult or impossible, however, to imagine that such an arrangement would have remained viable beyond the short term. The world was changing, and conditions that once made the theatrical state possible no longer prevailed. For precisely the same reason, the *bakuhan* state, which was also highly theatrical, was no longer viable.

Note that, even during the brief period in the sixteenth century when Ryukyu really was an independent state, the unique conditions that allowed it to thrive evaporated as the century went on. Even if the war of 1609 had not happened, it is still doubtful that the Shuri Empire could have survived long in its sixteenth-century form.

Even an assessment that sets aside the well-being of the Ryukyuan population as a consideration would probably conclude that an independent Ryukyu Kingdom would not have been viable in the 1870s or later. And, of course, if alleviating the suffering of most Ryukyuans were a consideration, as it was for Takahashi Kiichi, then preserving an oppressive kingdom with no popular support would have been unjust. Especially from the standpoint of ordinary people, therefore, Japan was the only viable way forward during the 1870s and later.

It is important to note that the vast majority of people who live in the Ryukyu Islands today unproblematically regard themselves as Japanese and with good reason. People who dream of a restored Ryukyu Kingdom are unlikely to be found in Okinawa Prefecture or any other part of Japan.[1] They are more likely to be found in certain diasporic communities and also include people with only a superficial knowledge of the region's history. One way to make the dream of a restored kingdom seem palatable is to imagine the former kingdom as a pacifist paradise filled with contented people, as some European sea captains did. We have seen, however, that the kingdom was neither pacifist nor benevolent nor (except in a limited sense) prosperous.

Another approach to palatability might be to imagine Okinawa and the southern Ryukyu Islands not as a kingdom but simply as a tiny modern state, perhaps a democratic republic. In that case, economic viability and security questions would still be vexing. Also relevant would be the nearly complete lack of interest in the idea among the people who currently live there. As an exercise, try typing "琉球独立" (Ryukyuan independence) into a search engine, and note the languages of the websites that appear. In late 2021, of the first fifty hits, forty-six were Chinese, three were Japanese (two of them booksellers), and one was English (also a bookseller). In other words, China is the place where the idea of an independent Ryukyu is especially popular today. I return to this topic in the final chapter.

Jahana Noboru and Social Conflict

In some respects, the life of the agronomist and political activist Jahana Noboru (1865–1908) resembles the plot of a tragic hero in Japanese literature. Jahana strove mightily against powerful forces that eventually crushed him. His career and legacy function as a window through which we can view the major lines of social conflict in Okinawa at the end of the nineteenth century.

Jahana was born a humble peasant in the waning years of the kingdom, and his adult career spanned the years of the *kyūkan-onzon* policy as Okinawa Prefecture moved toward integration with the Japanese mainland. At different points in his career, he interacted with Japan's new system of higher education, emigration, politically active peasants, new capitalist forces influencing Okinawan agriculture, differing responses to the problem of mainland discrimination, the power of the Meiji state, and different iterations of traditional Okinawan elites reasserting themselves. His struggles highlight some of the competing visions of Okinawa that emerged after the kingdom's formal demise.

The early governors of Okinawa Prefecture placed great emphasis on elementary education, and Jahana benefited by being selected in 1881 to attend Okinawa's newly minted teacher-training school. The following year, prefectural authorities selected him and four others to study in the mainland at government expense. Jahana's cohort included the *Ryūkyū shinpō* cofounder and social activist Ōta Chōfu and two future representatives from Okinawa to the lower house of the Diet, Takamine Chōkyō and Iwamoto Gashō. The other member was Nakijin Chōhan, who dropped out and was replaced by Yamaguchi Zenjutsu. Jahana was the only student of humble origins among the group.

Slotted into agricultural studies because of his peasant origins, Jahana excelled as a student. He graduated from Tokyo's Imperial College of Agricultural Science in 1891 with the approximate equivalent of a doctoral degree in agriculture. He researched sugar production in Sanuki Province (Kagawa Prefecture) and wrote his thesis about fertilizers and fertilizing methods, arguing among other things that efficient use of the by-products of agricultural processes could reduce production costs by reducing commercial fertilizer use. He later put this expertise to use in attempts to make sugar production in Okinawa more efficient and profitable. Returning to Okinawa, he joined the upper echelons of the prefectural administration. He was from the village of Kochinda (O. Kuchinda), today part of the town of Yaese, and his admirers often called him "Kuchinda Jahana" to highlight his modest origins.

Soon after Jahana's return to Okinawa, Narahara Shigeru (1834–1918) arrived from Kagoshima to become Okinawa's governor. Narahara was an especially influential governor, and he held the post for an unusually long sixteen years. Dubbed *king of Ryukyu* in part for his forceful approach, he brought with him a mandate to reform Okinawa. One problem that both Narahara and Jahana addressed was the severe impoverishment of low-ranking former nobles not supported by the *kyūkan-onzon* policy. The only viable way for most such people to make a living was to take up farming. The general idea was not new. Sai On, for example, encouraged impoverished nobles to farm specially designated lands (J. *yatori*, O. *yaadui*). By the 1890s, however, there was little or no excess land available that could be used for agriculture. The governor and Jahana decided to clear select forested land to create new farmland.

This move was potentially problematic. Sai On had created a system of land management that incentivized local peasants to oversee and manage forest resources near their villages. Of particular importance was land designated as *somayama* (forest land). Local peasants collected wood from these lands in a controlled manner and replanted trees as necessary. These forests became a crucial supplier of lumber and fuel. They also helped control erosion. Jahana argued that not all the land designed as *somayama* was genuinely suited for forests. Certain parcels were suitable for agriculture and would benefit everyone if they were brought into cultivation. Narahara appointed Jahana to implement this plan to turn some portions of *somayama* into farmland. Part of Jahana's job was to convince local peasants to cooperate.

Despite personal visits by Jahana to northern Okinawan villages, peasants living in the vicinity of the areas slated for clearing protested aggressively. Jahana repeatedly assured them that their livelihoods would not be affected, but to no avail. Indeed, local peasants organized, levied a small tax on themselves, and sent representatives to Naha directly to petition the prefectural government. This resistance was effective, and the governor removed Jahana from the project in 1894. Despite Narahara's reputation for decisive action, the prefectural government had limited resources with which to force unpopular change. For example, during the 1890s, Narahara attempted to reform the severe taxation system (often called the *poll tax*) in the southern Ryukyu Islands, but opposition by local elites delayed that reform until 1903. Resistance to Jahana's land-reclamation program is but one of several examples of peasants aggressively asserting their interests within a complex political arena.[2]

In telling the story of Jahana's life, there is a tendency to set him in opposition to Narahara. Jahana stood on the side of Okinawa's peasants, whereas Narahara represented business interests. This portrayal fits the latter part of Jahana's career, but, in 1894, Jahana and Narahara appear to have been aligned in terms of policy. The most likely reason Narahara removed Jahana from the land-reclamation project was because he failed to work amicably with local peasants. (It should be noted that historians of this era have proposed a variety of hypotheses.) Moreover, statistics for land clearance and sales while Jahana was in charge of land reclamation indicate a large proportion of sales to high-ranking former nobles and people outside the prefecture. In other words, the Jahana of 1894 does not obviously appear to have been a champion of peasant interests. Moreover, his dismissal from the land-reclamation board in 1894 did not end his career. He retained his title *prefectural engineer*, advanced in civil service rank, and even participated in other land-reclamation activities.

We should note that, during the late 1890s, after Taiwan became a Japanese colony and a de facto competitor with Okinawa as a sugar producer, many Okinawan elites became convinced that large-scale, mechanized sugar production was the only practical way to maintain Okinawa's agricultural sector. This vision clashed with the small-scale agriculture practiced at the village level. The generally poor state of Okinawan agriculture and an influx of capital from the mainland in the form of agricultural corporations exacerbated tensions between local customs and the perceived need for reform.

Jahana and Narahara were also on the same side in 1896 with respect to the Kōdōkai movement. Recall that the Kōdōkai proposed that Okinawa's unique circumstances required a special political arrangement. Among other things, the group called for a member of the Shō family to become a long-term governor of the prefecture. Kōdōkai rhetoric claimed that the people of Okinawa Prefecture would rally around the former royal family and thereby eventually be brought into better integration with the rest of Japan. In fact, this claim was self-serving. As we have seen, there was in the 1870s no popular loyalty to the kingdom. The real purpose of the Kōdōkai seems to have been to unite the former nobility and other Okinawan elites and provide them with a privileged position in society. If the movement had been successful, it would have been a de facto extension and intensification of the *kyūkan-onzon* policy.

A very small group of former Ryukyuan officials opposed the Kōdōkai because of its goal of integration with the mainland. The bulk of its opponents, however, regarded the group as anachronistic, unnecessary, and/or unhelpful. Jahana opposed it vigorously, which set him in opposition to Ōta Chōfu, one of the students sent to the mainland in Jahana's cohort. Ōta had been part of the progressive faction in the run-up to the Sino-Japanese War, and he was a vigorous proponent of Okinawan assimilation to mainland norms. Nevertheless, he and many other progressive intellectuals came to support the Kōdōkai. One reason was their realization that, no matter how thoroughly they internalized mainland norms, prejudice against Okinawans by mainlanders was unwavering. While Jahana was well aware of such prejudice, he regarded the Kōdōkai as making that situation worse. Moreover, as someone from a peasant background, he harbored no nostalgia for the former kingdom. After the central government refused even to consider the Kōdōkai's petition, the movement collapsed. Okinawan elites changed course in their ongoing effort to preserve their power and privileges.

The issue of land policy came up again in 1897, and this time Jahana and Narahara were at odds. The core problem was ownership of *somayama* land. For Narahara, the best way forward was for the prefectural government to take ownership of these forest lands. Nevertheless, peasants would be permitted to harvest forest resources without charge. This approach would be simple to implement, but there was no guarantee that local villages would retain control over forest lands going forward. Jahana advocated parceling them out to peasant households, which would then be the outright owners. This approach would incur significant administrative costs, but Jahana thought that government ownership of *somayama* carried with it too many possibilities for abuse.

At this point, Jahana does indeed seem to have become an advocate for Okinawa's peasants, or at least a substantial subset of them, in opposition to Narahara. The tension between the two increased, and Jahana resigned from the prefectural government in December 1898. In the meantime, Ōta and other former Kōdōkai supporters adopted perhaps the only strategy available to them. They became close allies of Narahara. By the end of 1898, Jahana was out of office and opposed by the majority of Okinawa's former nobility plus the powerful governor. He appears not to have appreciated the full power of this combination.

Jahana had amassed modest wealth during the 1890s, and he and a small group of like-minded colleagues created an organization called the Okinawa Club. They also created a trading company called Nan'yōsha as the economic foundation for publishing the political periodical *Okinawa jiron* (Timely issues in Okinawa). Its first issue appeared in 1899. Among other things, the editorial position of *Okinawa jiron* advocated broadening political participation in society and equitable resolutions to land problems. The periodical also functioned as a forum for criticizing the governor. The prefectural government pushed back.

The final blow to Jahana and his supporters came in connection with the Okinawa Agricultural Bank. A version of this bank was found in every prefecture, and its purpose was to promote agriculture by extending loans to small farmers otherwise unable to obtain financing. At the time Jahana resigned from the government, he was the majority shareholder in the bank and a member of its three-person board of directors. He soon came under pressure from other shareholders. At a stockholder's meeting on January 18, 1900, he proposed restructuring the bank to dilute the power of Shuri-Naha elites, that is, expanding the board from three to five members, one each from Shuri, Naha, Shimajiri (southern Okinawa), Nakagami (central Okinawa), and Kunigami (northern Okinawa). In other words, three of the five board members would come from rural areas.

Jahana's opponents and the governor saw the move as potentially dangerous. In their view, if Jahana and his Okinawa Club supporters could control the bank, they would be in a position to garner political support from Okinawa's farmers, a large proportion of the population. Narahara organized an opposition campaign and put the resources of the prefectural government at its disposal. Jahana's opponents allied with local leaders in rural areas, and this bloc purchased as many shares of bank stock as possible. Nahrahara even enlisted the police to influence the bank board election. The result was a resounding defeat for Jahana and his allies. Jahana declared the election void on the grounds of improprieties, the matter went to court, and Jahana lost. In addition to losing his position at the bank, he lost nearly all his assets in the process. He was insolvent and isolated, and the Okinawa Club soon disbanded.

Like many Okinawans in the early twentieth century, Jahana had to seek work in the mainland. He found a position in Yamaguchi Prefecture as an engineering assistant, a step down from his previous work. In 1901, he sailed to Kōbe to take a train to Yamaguchi, and it was on the station platform that he suffered a mental and physical breakdown. The final years of his life "were spent in a permanently crippled state, resembling that of a living corpse." He died at age forty-four muttering repeatedly: "Vermin devouring Okinawa have now arrived. Drive them out!" (Shinzato, Taminato, and Kinjō 1972/1983, 186).

Jahana's life and career shine a light on the turbulent, evolving society in

Okinawa around the turn of the twentieth century. With all its problems, agriculture continued as the economic basis of society in Okinawa Prefecture, and there was no ideal or obvious way to reform it. Both Jahana and his opponents tended to see sugar production as having the greatest potential for driving economic improvement, but any attempt significantly to reform agriculture was likely to be met with opposition by entrenched interests. More broadly, members of the kingdom's former elite tried repeatedly to reassert themselves. After the Kōdōkai failed, these elites had no choice but to align their interests with that of the prefectural government. Essentially, the late nineteenth century and the early twentieth was a time when competing concepts of Okinawa (or some similar notion) clashed. This clash produced turbulence but no clear resolution.

The Sago Palm Hell

The sago palm (*Cycas revoluta*) is a small tree, not a genuine palm tree, that produces a reddish-pink-orange fruit. In its natural state, the fruit is poisonous to humans. However, with proper processing and cooking, it can be rendered edible. The nutritional content is low, and most people find the taste unappealing. Sago palm fruit is a classic example of famine food.

In the modern era, the first large-scale use of sago palm fruit was during a seven-month drought-induced famine in 1904. In that context, improper preparation of the fruit caused or contributed to several fatalities. This famine underscored several weaknesses in Okinawan agriculture, including antiquated cultivation techniques, an increasing trend toward sugar or sweet potato monoculture, geographic barriers to efficient circulation of agricultural produce, and the persistence of older social practices such as agricultural serfs.

Okinawa's economy was fundamentally weak. About 40 percent of the gross economic output in 1912 was sugar production, and sweet potatoes plus sugar constituted about 60 percent. According to Mukai Kiyoshi, Okinawa's economy in the early twentieth century was "lost in a maze with no exit" (Mukai 1992, 196). While in general it might make sense for a region to leverage a relative advantage, such as sugar in the case of Okinawa Prefecture, a steady expansion of demand would be required for this approach to be viable in the longer term. However, there was no possibility of the demand for brown sugar steadily increasing. What enabled Okinawa's economy to prosper until about 1920 was the rise of sugar prices during World War I and for a few years thereafter. An additional factor was several successive poor cane harvests in Taiwan, Okinawa's main sugar competitor, during the early Taishō years. Toward the end of the Meiji Era, the price in Japanese markets for a one-hundred-*kin* unit of brown sugar was five or six yen. The First World War caused a rise in worldwide sugar prices, which peaked in 1920 in the form of a speculative bubble. By the start of 1920, brown sugar peaked at twenty yen. The price declined sharply thereafter as the bubble burst, never to recover. As sugar became cheaper, banks began to collapse, and Okinawa's economy entered a severe depression. By 1924, some commentators began to call this recession *sago palm hell* (*sotetsu jigoku*), and the depression lasted into the 1930s.

According to Mukai's analysis, a combination of specific characteristics of the economy of Okinawa Prefecture and instabilities in global capitalism caused the sago palm hell. The price of sugar stayed low from 1920 through the 1930s, exacerbated by higher production made possible by increasingly mechanized agriculture. While there was a sharp upturn in home sugar consumption in Japan from 1916, the demand for brown sugar—the type produced in Okinawan farming villages—shrunk from 1920 on. Compared with farming villages in the mainland, those in Okinawa Prefecture were especially sensitive to the consumer and market economy. Cash household expenses were also comparatively higher in Okinawa Prefecture.

To make matters worse, during the 1920s Japan's central government focused on developing agriculture in its colonies, Taiwan and Korea. The goal was to import food from such places, thus keeping prices for urban consumers low. One result was an agricultural crisis in Japan, and the plight of farmers became a mainstay of political rhetoric during the so-called Taishō democracy era of the 1920s. Colonial agricultural policies, Japan's ongoing agricultural crisis (especially severe in the Tōhoku region), the need to rebuild Tokyo after the massive 1923 Great Kantō earthquake, and depressed sugar prices worldwide created a perfect storm of economic misery for Okinawa Prefecture. One metric dramatically illustrates the rapid economic decline in Okinawa. In 1918, the rate of delinquency for national taxes in the prefecture was 0.2 percent. In 1922, it was 42.2 percent. In other words, nearly half the population had suddenly become unable to pay their taxes in full.

One way out of the depressed economy was literally to leave the prefecture. The rate of workers—mostly men—leaving the prefecture averaged two thousand a year from the late Meiji to 1920. Thereafter, the number briefly peaked at nearly ten thousand a year, dropping back during the late 1920s, and rebounding after 1935. The destinations for most people leaving the prefecture were foreign countries until about 1920, to the mainland until the late 1920s, and abroad thereafter.

The incentive structure for land use at this time is a complex topic beyond my scope here, but one key point is that large-scale industrial agriculture never became dominant in Okinawa Prefecture. During the 1920s, the typical quantity of farmland per household increased slightly to about 1 *chō* (2.45 acres), but there was no drastic change to the overall pattern of modest-scale cultivation. The only productivity variable that changed significantly was improved technology. Scientific techniques resulting from controlled experiments began to replace technology based on experience. In 1925, in response to the sago palm hell situation, the Diet passed a bill to assist Okinawan industry for five years, allocating ¥2.62 million in supplemental funding by 1930. Some of this funding went toward modernizing Okinawan agriculture.

A new large-stem variety of sweet potato accounted for only 0.2 percent of sweet potatoes in 1926, but by 1935 that figure was 93.8 percent. The new sweet potatoes were especially productive if well fertilized. Between 1926 and 1939, purchased fertilizer use increased 250 percent, and locally produced fertilizer increased 180 percent. By the late 1930s, sweet potato production had nearly doubled. Another change was the rapid replacement of *zairaitō* (red rice [an indica variety]) with the high-yielding hybrid Taizhong 65 rice from Taiwan. Row planting for sweet potatoes supplanted the hitherto common hole-planting method, which also influenced rice cultivation. Also importantly, large agricultural tools, both powered and unpowered, rapidly replaced the traditional small spades and sickles.

Powered machinery began to replace livestock in household- and village-level sugar production. In Okinawa, the most common device was a seven- to eight-horsepower oil-burning cane press, which was about four times more powerful than traditional presses and extracted about 10 percent more juice from the cane. This technology was introduced in the early Taishō Era, but it did not catch on at that time, except of course in factory settings. The depression of the 1920s reinvigorated the movement toward mechanization. Overall, one impact of the sago palm hell was a partial modernization of Okinawan agriculture.

Emigration to the Mainland and to the World

The sago palm hell accelerated emigration. Between 1899 and 1938, people from Okinawa Prefecture settled in the following places in the following (total) numbers:

Hawaii	19,507
US mainland	803
Canada	403

Mexico	764
Cuba	113
Peru	11,311
Brazil	14,829
Argentina	2,754
Bolivia	37
Philippines	16,426
Other places	5,187
Total	72,134

Given the 1940 census population for the prefecture, which was 574,579, first-generation emigrants constituted about 12 percent of the population.[3] How many descendants of these first-generation emigrants are there in the world today? A precise count (and definition) is impossible, but many estimates put the figure around 420,000.[4] In any case, Okinawans who settled abroad often prospered, and they contributed significantly to relief campaigns, especially in 1945 and the years immediately after the war.

The prominent scholar Iha Fuyū left Okinawa at the height of the sago palm hell, as did many of the members of his study circle. Iha's reason for leaving included personal problems, and he settled in Tokyo. There, his outlook changed. In Okinawa, he had been a public intellectual and a vigorous proponent of a complex, nuanced form of Okinawan cultural nationalism. His ideas frequently shifted, but the basic formula was that Okinawans were fully Japanese yet a distinctive and distinguished subgroup within the broader national family. As a corollary to this view, he promoted self-improvement campaigns throughout Okinawa. His vision of Okinawan self-improvement, however, collapsed in the face of the sago palm hell. After moving to Tokyo, Iha turned to formal academic research, producing an impressive body of work. In that context, he reassessed the Ryukyuan past with less romanticism than he had done previously. For example, while the young Iha once praised King Shō Shin as a great unifier, in his later thought he regarded Shō Shin as an exploitative imperialist, not much different from Satsuma's Shimazu rulers.

Culture Wars

The general obsession with culture in modern Japan had by the twentieth century spread to the Ryukyu Islands. Today it is relatively easy for people living in Okinawa Prefecture to combine local and national identities. Indeed, people throughout many parts of the Japanese islands typically combine multiple layers of culture to form personal identities, a process that rarely causes great anxiety. In Okinawa Prefecture during the early decades of the twentieth century, however, real and imagined layers of possible identity were often in conflict.

Many Okinawan intellectuals, journalists, politicians, and others sought to dissolve any disjuncture between the boundaries of the Japanese state and the (imagined) boundaries of the Japanese ethnos with the claim that Ryukyuans shared ancient cultural roots with Japanese and were, thus, essentially the same people. The basis of this claim was usually that Ryukyuan languages retain significant elements of ancient Japanese. Even with the knowledge available in the late nineteenth century, this case was easy to make, whether with respect to linguistic data or other forms of culture.

By the 1920s, however, it had become common for public intellectuals in mainland Japan to claim that what made Japanese people distinctive and superior was a combination of two components. On the one hand, Japan and its people were thoroughly steeped in all the great ancient traditions of Asia. On the other hand, they were fully modern, on a par with any other technologically advanced society in the world. In this rhetorical context, the claim of ancient common origins of Japanese and Ryukyuans covered only the ancient traditions part of the formulation, not the part about being modern. The stigma of Ryukyuans as rusticated relatives of contemporary Japanese remained.

A common approach among Okinawan scholars and journalists for explaining cultural differences was to blame Satsuma for any gaps between Okinawan and Japanese culture. The basic argument was that Satsuma forced the Ryukyu Kingdom into close political and cultural association with China. This unnatural Chinese interlude arrested the normal course of cultural development or progress that would otherwise have taken place in the Ryukyu Islands. Consider, for example, the following assertion by the historian Higashionna Kanjun as part of a 1914 address to an audience of mainland historians:

> Through its policies, Satsuma, vis-à-vis both the bakufu and China and other foreign countries, profited by preventing the Japanization of Ryukyu. This was the fundamental policy and remained unchanged over the course of three centuries. It was because of this policy that the Meiji government had such a difficult time [assimilating Ryukyu]. In other words, at the time of the abolition of the domains and creation of prefectures, breaking [Ryukyu's] ties with China proved terribly difficult—the result of three hundred years of well-established policy. My intent here today is that you kindly understand this policy [of Satsuma]. (quoted in Smits 2015a, 170)

Implicit in this line of argument was that, had the natural course of development been allowed to take place, Ryukyuans of ca. 1900 would have been much closer to the prevailing mainstream Japanese cultural ideal.

In a general sense, Higashionna had a point. However, the nearly two and a half centuries of isolation from Japan after 1609 was the more important factor, not the Sinicization of certain urban elites. At the time, however, Higashionna was reacting to the common stereotype that Ryukyuan culture contained many Chinese elements. Setting aside the accuracy of his claim, as persuasive speech there was little that he or other Okinawans could say about the apparent modernity gap other than to repeat the tragic tale of Satsuma's oppression by way of suggesting what might have been otherwise. Even in the eyes of sympathetic mainlanders, Okinawans were in need of modernizing changes to realize their potential of becoming Japanese in the fullest sense. Furthermore, in the view of many mainlanders and Okinawans alike, the state and its agents should impose these changes forcibly to ensure that they happened with maximum speed.

One motive behind renewed efforts in the twentieth century to promote cultural assimilation was the belief that embracing mainstream mainland Japanese culture would lead to economic improvement. In this context, Okinawan characteristics, real or imagined, were obstacles. Christy summarizes them as follows: "The communal land system (*jiwari seido*), supposed heavy alcohol consumption, walking barefoot, Ryūkyūan women's clothing, a preponderance of dialects (containing 'many ancient Japanese words'), 'lazy men and overworked women,' and Okinawan music were all taken together as the image of the 'loose Okinawan lifestyle' and visible signs of this backwardness" (Christy 1993, 613). Okinawa's poverty could have been explained fully in terms of structural conditions with respect to the regional and world economy, as we have seen. However, both mainland and Okinawan commentators frequently de-emphasized such reasons, instead alleging local cultural deficiencies. To illustrate some of the characteristics of this cultural discourse, consider three examples: the Hall of Peoples, debates over school uniforms, and the Dialect Dispute of 1940.

THE HALL OF PEOPLES

Expositions were immensely popular during the late nineteenth century and the early twentieth. One of the exhibits in a 1903 industrial exposition in Osaka was the Hall of Peoples (*Jinruikan*). In it, a man holding a whip presided over a display of Ainu, Koreans, and two Okinawan women depicted as prostitutes. As visitors came through, he pointed the whip at the people in question and explained some of the exotic items on display associated with them. It was a quasi-anthropological display of primitive peoples. The *Ryūkyū shinpō* editor Ōta Chōfu expressed his rage at the exhibit in a series of editorials, characterizing the display of Okinawans as being no different from the display of exotic animals. He did not, however, object to the display of primitive peoples in principle. His outrage was that Okinawans, "real Japanese," were on display along with Koreans and "barbaric Ainu."

Notice the discrepancy between official rhetoric at the highest levels of government, which declared that Okinawans were integral members of the national family, and widespread popular perception of Okinawans as exotic outsiders. The economic logic of such exhibitions was that, the more exotic the displays were, the more paying visitors they would attract. The display illustrates another common element in Japanese discourses on Okinawan backwardness: Okinawa was marked as female in contrast to the male mainland Japan, and it was submissive where Japan was dominant. The specific association of Okinawa with prostitution was also common in Japan at the time.[5]

NEW SCHOOL UNIFORMS

The issue of clothing and related aspects of self-presentation was in the forefront of the famous civilization and enlightenment (*bunmei kaika*) rhetoric of 1870s Japan. It remained a prominent social issue well into the 1930s, albeit with changing emphasis. During the 1920s and 1930s, for example, women's underwear (or the lack thereof) became a prominent issue in mainland Japanese discourse on social improvement and modernization. Typically, discussion of ideal dress focused on its utility in making people more productive, efficient, and modern. There was also a tendency to regard clothing as potentially didactic owing to its symbolic qualities. In Okinawa, concern with clothing took on similar contours.

A November 15, 1898, *Ryūkyū shinpō* article without a byline explained that there would soon be a change to Western-style school uniforms for girls at Shuri Elementary School. It then outlined four ideal principles that should guide selection of the new uniforms. The first two are straightforward: the uniforms should be suitable for Okinawa's climate and affordable. The third was that they should amplify the ideal female characteristics of gentleness (*nyūwa*) and grace (*yūbi*). Finally, they should help the wearer move from a primitive (*yabanteki*) to a refined (*bunmeiteki*) appearance, with *primitive* in this context defined as short skirts without collars in the manner of Taiwanese aborigines (for details, see Smits 2015a, 172–75).

Ryūkyū shinpō subsequently published two additional articles on the topic of the uniforms that gave voice to a wider range of viewpoints. The neat four-point scheme of the initial article became problematic in much of the subsequent discussion. For example, if clothing should accord with climate (notions of climate determinism were much in vogue at this time), then perhaps the Taiwanese aborigines are not necessarily deficient in their attire. Adopting Western-style clothing for the uniforms might conflict not only with the principle of climatic adaptation but also the principle of living within one's means. Indeed, the subject of disparities in wealth came up frequently in the follow-up articles. The assumption of a close connection between external appearance and one's spirit (*seishin*) came into question, and the issue of comparison with the rest of Japan, always implied, came explicitly to the surface.

Notice again the intertwining of economic, social, and cultural matters. Throughout Japan at this time, culture was often a proxy for debates over the proper approach to modernity and Japan's relationship with the rest of the world. In Okinawa, potential ambivalence vis-à-vis the rest of Japan added more complexity to cultural debates. Clothing—especially women's clothing—continued during the twentieth century to serve as a proxy for deeper social anxieties. The following excerpt is from a speech by the newly appointed governor Takahashi Takuya in 1913 at the opening of Okinawa's second middle school:

> Because from now on, things must change in accordance with the world's progress, we must reform what should be reformed and stop adhering stubbornly to outmoded ways. In this place [Okinawa], women do not fasten belts around their robes. . . . No matter where one might go around here, there are women without fastened belts as well as women who do not wear underpants. . . . Even in Korea, women wear underpants. . . . Try going to the mainland in your present state of dress. Not only will people laugh at you, they will hold you in contempt. However impressive and learned you may be, others will regard you as idiots. (quoted in Smits 2015a, 174–75)

In this view, peculiar or immodest clothing habits among women stand in the way of Okinawa's modern progress. Leveraging Okinawan anxieties about identity and status, the governor brought in the unfavorable comparison with Korea to enhance the rhetorical impact of his critique.

Such comparisons with colonial subjects of the Japanese Empire were a common ploy in the rhetoric of Okinawan cultural inferiority. Incidentally, the governor's claim about mainland women's attire was not accurate. Soon after the Great Kantō earthquake in 1923, public service posters encouraging women to wear underwear appeared in Japan's major cities. In any case, clothing functioned as a proxy for larger social issues in Taka-hashi's rhetoric.

THE DIALECT DISPUTE AND YANAGI MUNEYOSHI

In the context of Okinawan debates over culture, there was a tendency to assume a singular, idealized Japanese culture.[6] Nevertheless, as the nine-teenth century drew to a close, there remained substantial cultural diversity throughout the Japanese islands in such areas as language, religious prac-tices, clothing, social relationships, food habits, etc. The cultural differences between Kagoshima Prefecture, for example, and Tokyo were substantial, and Kagoshima Prefecture itself was home to several distinct cultural zones marked most prominently by different local dialects. In the context of the geographic sweep of the Japanese islands from Hokkaidō to Yonaguni, the various Ryukyuan cultures were at one end of a vast continuum of cultural variation. The main problem for Okinawans was, as we have seen, that, while the Ryukyu Islands had come to lie firmly within the state boundaries of Japan, they remained at the fuzzy edge of people's perceptual or psycho-logical boundaries of the Japanese cultural zone. The problematic notion of a unitary Japanese culture served further to exacerbate this disjuncture.

During the 1930s, in the wake of the sago palm hell, some bureaucrats and others tried to envision economic enterprises other than agriculture in the Ryukyu Islands. One idea was tourism and leisure. This entire realm was relatively new to Japan, but Okinawa's climate seemed well suited to it. Perhaps certain forms of local culture might also hold an exotic appeal to mainlanders, the thinking went. In this connection, a delegation from the mainland visited Okinawa at the start of 1940 to assess its potential as a tour-ist destination. On January 8, 1940, the major newspapers in Okinawa Pre-fecture reported on a panel discussion between local government officials and visiting folklorists, travel agents, journalists, and others from the main-land. The sponsors of the discussion had anticipated that it would function as a pep rally in support of tourism in the Ryukyu Islands.

The discussion unexpectedly turned into a heated dispute when the vis-iting folklorists, led by Yanagi Muneyoshi (柳宗悦), also known as Yanagi Sōetsu, criticized what they regarded as the heavy-handed policies of local officials in eliminating distinctive cultural practices of the Ryukyu Islands. Yanagi and his colleagues raised several points, but their sharpest criticism focused on a recent campaign to encourage the use of standard Japanese (*hyōjungo shōrei undō*). Officially, the campaign was phrased in positive terms, but the folklorists accused Okinawan officials of the more sinister goal of eliminating Ryukyuan languages altogether. As evidence, they cited

FIGURE 17.1. A "Welsh Not" (W.N.) tag to discourage the use of Welsh in the
United Kingdom, an Okinawan dialect tag, and the message "Speak French,
Be Clean" on the wall of a school in the Ayguatébia-Talau commune in the Catalan-
speaking part of southern France near the border with Spain. Schools in Brittany
(Bretagne) and other regions sometimes used tags (called *symbole* or *ar vuoc'h*)
to discourage students from speaking languages other than French. ("Welsh
Not," Wikimedia Commons, John Jones, CC BY-SA 4.0; dialect tag, Wikimedia
Commons, TeresaPikler; school wall, Wikimedia Commons, PimPamPoom)

such practices as forbidding students in the school system to speak local
languages and forcing them to wear shameful local-language tags (*hōgen
fuda*) around their necks when they were caught doing so. The only way to
get rid of the tag was to discover and expose someone else speaking a local
language. Shaming students who spoke local languages in school was not
unique to Okinawa Prefecture in the early twentieth century. It also took
place in Kagoshima Prefecture and the Tōhoku region of northeast Japan
in addition to locations in Europe and around the world as modern states
sought to impose language standardization in their territories (fig. 17.1).

Defending themselves, the Okinawan officials accused the folklorists of
meddling in affairs they did not understand. They pointed out—probably

accurately—that the prefecture's residents demanded and supported such policies. Thus began a rancorous debate about culture, politics, and identity that raged for months in the pages of various publications in Okinawa and the mainland, the Dialect Dispute (*hōgen ronsō*) or Language Dispute.

Informing this dispute, though often mentioned only obliquely by the participants, were the twin burdens of historical and contemporary circumstances. On the one hand, there was the traumatic recent history of Okinawa Prefecture. While declaring to the world that the Ryukyu Islands had always been an integral part of Japan, the central government in Tokyo often treated the newly created prefecture more like a conquered territory than a division of the homeland. The majority of local officials, including all those who participated in the panel discussion, were mainlanders serving tours of administrative duty away from their homes.

By 1940, Japan had become bogged down in de facto full-scale war in China with no end in sight. Criticism of Japan's involvement in China by the United States and other foreign powers was growing in intensity, and ordinary Japanese from all walks of life were beginning to feel the negative consequences of the war's human and financial costs. As Japan's leaders struggled to find an acceptable way out of the China quagmire, they urged the citizenry to embrace willingly whatever sacrifices the government might deem necessary.

Okinawa Prefecture's policy to promote the use of standard Japanese aggressively was in part an explicit response to calls for cooperation, sacrifice, spiritual mobilization, and unity from the central government. Lurking even deeper in the background of the policies designed to improve one or another aspect of Okinawan culture was the uncomfortable suspicion that Okinawans might not be sufficiently loyal to the nation in times of crisis. It is hardly surprising that the local officials criticized by the folklorists responded in part by saying that their accusers should focus their energies on more productive endeavors than useless arguments and unprofitable disputation during this time of national crisis.

By 1940, most Okinawans had become accustomed to the idea that they should speak standard Japanese. Public posters with messages like "Ikka sorotte hyōjungo" (The whole household speaking standard Japanese! 一家そろって標準語) and "Minna hakihaki hyōjungo" (Let's all speak standard Japanese crisply! みんなはきはき標準語) had been common fixtures of the public visual landscape since the early twentieth century. For many Okinawans, this message had become common sense.

The Dialect Dispute packed an emotional punch that attracted a wide range of participants. For example, one letter written in rambling style from a self-proclaimed "stupid, talkative woman" seethes with anger and sarcasm. Published in the newspaper *Okinawa nippō* under the title "O-erai katagata e" (To the great venerables)—a sarcastic reference to the folklorists—the letter berates the mainland folklorists for their arrogance: "We are not grateful for you who would praise our baby clothes. Instead, we are grateful for those who would scold us and push us quickly to stand on our own two feet" (Naha shiyakusho, Sōmubu, Shi-shi henshūshitsu 1970, 357). One wonders whether such a letter might have been forged by prefectural officials, but it undoubtedly reflects a strain of opinion held widely among Okinawans.[7]

A less emotional letter came from a teacher in northern Okinawa pointing out the "ten or twenty layers" to what people casually call *Okinawan dialect*. In other words, people in different islands cannot understand each other, nor can people from different parts—or social strata—of Okinawa do so. Not only was the promotion of standard Japanese immensely useful, but it also served to break down the old social class barriers from the days of the kingdom. In this context, "the 'Okinawa' which Yanagi understood as if it were a single presence was also something that involved complex struggle for the people who lived in it" (Oguma 2014, 119–20).

An entirely different view of the situation can be seen in the complex, nuanced essays of Yanagi, the most prominent of the folklorists. He argued that standard Japanese and Japanese culture were artificial social constructs. While necessary, they should never be confused with real, living cultures. By contrast, real, living cultures are necessarily local in scope. Collectively, these local cultures were the substantive basis from which the idea of a broader Japanese culture was derived. Therefore, Ryukyuan languages and other cultural practices were essential components of the broader national culture, and their suppression or elimination would impoverish all Japanese. Yanagi regarded Japanese culture as a compound or composite consisting of many local cultures.[8]

For all his nuance, Yanagi was a fervent cultural nationalist. For example, he regarded the standard Japanese of his day as having been corrupted by Western influences and in need of purification and correction. He argued that, because Ryukyuan languages are the closest living example of an archaic and pure Japanese language, they are an invaluable resource in this purifying task and that those officials who would seek to eliminate them act to becloud true Japanese identity and perpetuate unnecessary and undesirable foreign influences.

Yanagi made a distinction between the terms *kokugo* (lit. "national language") and *hyōjungo* (standard Japanese). For Yanagi, *kokugo* meant all the languages of Japan collectively. Ryukyuan languages, therefore, were an integral part of *kokugo*, that is, the national language writ large. *Hyōjungo*, on the other hand, was an artificial abstraction derived from *kokugo*. Yanagi argued that all Japanese had the duty to learn *hyōjungo*, but it was nothing more than a mechanical instrument of communication. Local languages, by contrast, were the living expressions of the vibrant cultures found throughout the Japanese islands. Therefore, they should be preserved and cherished, and their demise would lead to the impoverishment of Japanese culture as a whole, however it might be defined.

Yanagi liked to point out that the residents of Kagoshima Prefecture spoke local languages not understood in other areas of Japan. Yet nobody questioned their membership in the Japanese national family as a result. Why, therefore, should Okinawa be any different? Indeed, if one were to question the linguistic qualifications of the people in any particular locality to be considered Japanese, it should be the people of Tokyo, most of whose present residents, Yanagi included, grew up speaking only the sterile, artificial, foreign-influenced *hyōjungo*.

For their part, prefectural officials consistently claimed that they had no intention of suppressing local languages and bore no animosity toward them. However, the special circumstances of Okinawa Prefecture demanded additional efforts to promote standard Japanese. This recourse to Okinawa's vaguely defined special circumstances was a common rhetorical strategy among officials, often intended to shut down debate. In this context, outsiders like Yanagi could not really understand Okinawa and, thus, lacked credibility. Prefectural officials claimed to be agents of empowerment for Okinawans, whose alleged tendencies toward passivity and servility were the result of an inability to express themselves well. In a lengthy statement appearing in all the Okinawan daily newspapers, for example, the Prefectural Board of Education claimed: "We get letters from Okinawans who have entered the army or who are working abroad thanking us for our vigorous promotion of standard Japanese, which has enabled them to escape prejudice and discrimination. And military officials have noticed that soldiers from Okinawa no longer cluster together and that they can express themselves" (Naha shiyakusho, Sōmubu, Shi-shi henshūshitsu 1970, 356). In this way, education officials claimed that they and their policies were agents of Okinawan empowerment.

Yanagi's nuanced and sophisticated ideas were out of place in an emotional dispute such as this one. As we have seen, in social practice the categories *Japanese* and *Okinawan* had stood in opposition to each other since the 1880s. Although it is unlikely that they would ever admit to it, government officials and ordinary people who aggressively advocated standard

Japanese inevitably also advocated suppressing or even destroying local languages. In this sense, Yanagi's critique of the politics of culture in Okinawa was accurate and prescient.

The Dialect Dispute came to encompass a wide range of voices, not only those of the folklorists and the prefectural officials they criticized. Social critics and intellectuals in Tokyo and elsewhere also followed and commented on it. In its entirety, the dispute is a lens through which to view the contested nature of national identity (and other topics) at a time of tremendous state pressure on its citizens to conform to an official version of what it meant to be Japanese, an uncharacteristically frank exchange of opinion on a sensitive topic. It was part of a broader discourse on culture in the Ryukyu Islands and Japan as a whole that continues to some extent and in modified form to the present day.

CHAPTER EIGHTEEN

Midcentury Turbulence

By 1919, Okinawa Prefecture possessed the formal institutions and prac-tices of the other prefectures. That year was also the approximate peak of economic prosperity for an economy based on sugar. Japan's economy as a whole contracted between approximately 1927 and 1929, but it recovered during the early 1930s as much of the rest of the world experienced the Great Depression. In Okinawa Prefecture, however, economic woes con-tinued throughout the 1930s. As discussed in the previous chapter, there was some improvement owing to emigration and more productive agricul-tural practices, but low sugar prices and other structural problems carried over from the 1920s to the 1930s.

Increased central government spending between 1925 and 1930 was helpful, but the prefecture remained economically depressed. In 1930, Gov-ernor Ino Jirō commissioned a study of the causes of the prefecture's eco-nomic difficulties. He then drew up a fifteen-year plan for economic revival that the central government approved in 1933. However, by then Japan was well on its way down the path that would lead to the Pacific War. Even-tually, that conflict came directly to Okinawa and devastated the island. This chapter surveys education, scholarship, and literature from the 1920s through the 1940s. It then briefly examines the causes and course of the Pacific War as background for understanding the Battle of Okinawa during the spring of 1945.

Education, Scholarship, and Literature

The kingdom created institutions of formal education ca. 1800, but they mainly served urban elites. Formal education for ordinary people began almost as soon as the prefecture was created, although initially only in urban areas. The basic school system that emerged throughout Japan by the twentieth century consisted of elementary school (six years), middle school (five years), higher school (three years), and university (four years). There were other possibilities such as advanced elementary schools (usually for women) and normal schools to train teachers. In this system, middle schools roughly corresponded to high schools in today's United States or Japan, higher schools were roughly on a par with undergraduate college or university education, and university courses of study were similar to an advanced degree today. Middle school was the highest level of formal education available in Okinawa.

Of moderately well-off commoner background, Iha Fuyū benefited from formal schooling. While in middle school he participated in an 1895 student strike protesting the canceling of foreign language education. That matter caused him to relocate to Tokyo the next year to continue his education. Several other prominent Okinawan intellectuals of his generation were also products of the newly created formal schooling. The journalist and historian Majikina Ankō (真境名安興) was another leader in the 1895 student strike and was briefly forced out of school. Majikina began his journalism career after graduating from middle school in Okinawa. Higashionna Kanjun graduated from middle school in Okinawa in 1900, entered a higher school in Kumamoto Prefecture, and ultimately graduated from Tokyo Imperial University (Tokyo University) in 1908, a remarkable accomplishment.

In 1900, only about half the eligible residents of Okinawa Prefecture participated in formal education. By 1930, that figure had risen to nearly 100 percent. Moreover, although initially Okinawa lagged behind the rest of Japan in rates of formal education, this gap closed during the 1920s, at least for compulsory education.

Formal education in Okinawa Prefecture did not specifically encourage the study of local history, culture, or other Ryukyu-related topics. Nevertheless, the school system nurtured the minds of those who became the first modern generation of scholars and literary figures. Iha, Higashionna, and Majikina came to be known as *the three founders* (*gosanke*, 御三家) of Okinawan studies, rigorous academic research in realms such as linguistics, history, and anthropology as they related to the Ryukyu Islands.

Other prominent scholars who made significant contributions to Okinawan studies during the 1920s and 1930s came from mainland Japan, including the anthropologist Torii Ryūzō (鳥居龍蔵, 1870–1953) and the folklore scholars Yanagita Kunio (柳田國男, 1875–1962) and Orikuchi Shinobu (折口信夫, 1887–1953). They were especially interested in the Ryukyu Islands in connection with early and mid-twentieth-century debates over the deep origins of the Japanese people. Yanagita and Orikuchi, for example, proposed that the Japanese islands were populated mainly by people moving north through the Ryukyu Islands. This hypothesis is now thoroughly discredited, but it was influential into the 1970s. Iha argued the opposite, that the modern population of the Ryukyu Islands came from Japan. As we have seen, recent work in archaeology has proved Iha correct, at least in basic outline. In one way or another, all these figures saw the inhabitants of the Ryukyu Islands as culturally and anthropologically akin to the other inhabitants of the Japanese islands.

The diffusion of formal education in Okinawa Prefecture created a larger audience for art and literature, which began to flourish during the 1920s and 1930s. In 1936, Iba Nantetsu (伊波南哲) published a book-length epic poem, *Oyake Akahachi* (1964), about the leader of the Ishigaki forces who fought Shuri's invasion in 1500. *Oyake* was reprinted several times and also became a movie. Inspired by Ryukyuan history and culture, Iba went on to a brilliant literary career.

Another major literary figure of this era was the poet Yamanokuchi Baku (山之口貘 [Yamaguchi Jūsaburō, 山口重三郎], 1903–63). In one way or another, many of his poems deal with his Okinawan identity within the broader context of Japan. Yamanokuchi lived in Tokyo for roughly forty years. What follows is his recollection of a 1938 encounter in Tokyo in the context of stereotypes of Ryukyuan exoticness:

> In the coffee shop where I used to hang out, one of the regular customers showed up one day after a long absence, his face deeply tanned. He announced in a loud voice to the woman who ran the shop and her daughter that he had been on a business trip to Okinawa. I'd been talking to some other people at this time, but, being from Okinawa, I was slightly irritated to hear him mention it. Most Okinawans feel uncomfortable at such times. Still, I could not suppress a certain interest in this man's impressions of my homeland. But hearing him talk about how he was invited to the home of a "chieftain," how he drank *awamori* [Okinawa's distinctive rice liquor] from a soup bowl, and how "the natives" do this and that, I felt as though he was conjuring up visions of a place I'd never seen. (Rabson 1999b, 86)

Not only Yamanokuchi but also most Okinawan literary figures active ca. the 1930s addressed issues of identity in their work, often in sophisticated ways.

In 1932, for example, Kushi Fusako (久志芙沙子, 1903–1986) published the short story *Memoirs of a Declining Ryukyu Woman* (*Horobiyuku Ryūkyū onna no shuki*) (see Kushi 1932/2015). One of the major characters was the uncle of the narrator. The uncle lived in Tokyo and was a successful businessman. However, he did not tell anyone, even his wife, that he was from Okinawa. As he put it: "You have to understand that if people found out that I was Ryukyuan, it would cause me all kinds of trouble" (Rabson 1999b, 75).

As was common practice, Kushi's story was initially published in installments in the magazine *Women's Review* (*Fujin kōron*). In the midst of the process, however, the magazine abruptly stopped publishing the installments because of vehement protests from Okinawan students in Tokyo who claimed that the uncle who refused to acknowledge his roots was insulting and would invite discrimination against Okinawans. *Women's Review* allowed Kushi to publish a rebuttal in which she noted:

> These men [the current and former presidents of the Okinawa Student Association] . . . were particularly upset by one phrase I used in the story: "the Okinawan people" (*Okinawa minzoku*). It annoyed them, they said, to have Okinawans put in the same category as "the Ainu people" or "the Korean people," minorities with which this word is often associated in Japan. Yet are we not living in modern times? I have no sympathies for their efforts to construct racial hierarchies of Ainu, Korean, and so-called "pure Japanese," or their desire to feel some kind of superiority by placing themselves in the "highest" category. . . . Their outraged claims that what I wrote "demeans" and "discriminates against" Okinawans reveals, paradoxically, their own racial prejudices. . . . I certainly did not use the world "people" to insult the Okinawan people of whom I am one. (Rabson 1999b, 76)

Among other things, Kushi was arguing that someone could be both Okinawan and Japanese and that prevailing notions of ethnic or racial hierarchies were absurd.

Causes and Course of the Pacific War, 1931–45

The Pacific War (Taiheiyō sensō, 太平洋戦争) began as a conflict between Japan and China. This conflict eventually expanded, became linked with major warfare in Europe, and engulfed the island of Okinawa in the spring of 1945. The war also had a disastrous impact on several other Ryukyu Islands, an especially deadly and tragic reiteration of the historical phenomenon whereby political and military turbulence elsewhere in the region reverberated through the Ryukyu Islands.

The key to understanding the Pacific War, including US involvement, is to realize that it was ultimately a war about China. China was a major international concern in part because, from approximately 1917 to 1927, it had no effective central government. There was always some warlord or party controlling the capital, but rarely did his power extend beyond the capital suburbs. The rest of China was ruled mainly by a dozen or so warlords each of whom had his own territory. To the outside world and within China, the country appeared to be in danger of sinking into anarchy throughout much of the 1920s.

In 1931, Japanese forces seized all Manchuria (northeast China). Thereafter, they crept slowly toward Beijing. On July 7, 1937, fighting broke out between Japanese and Chinese soldiers near the Marco Polo Bridge in the northern suburbs of Beijing. The incident remained unsettled as of late July, and fighting between Chinese and Japanese forces broke out elsewhere in China. By August, both sides were engaged in full-scale warfare, although Japan's government never formally declared the China incident to be a war. Japanese forces won most of the battles, but China was too vast and Japanese forces too few for effective pacification of many conquered areas. Despite winning repeatedly in the battlefield, the Japanese invaders found themselves in a quagmire.

THE WAR EXPANDS

If Japan was bogged down in China, how could its leaders possibly have come to the conclusion that broadening the war was the way to make progress? At first glance, it may seem crazy, and, in hindsight, it was wishful thinking. Even at the time, Japan's war planners knew that attacking the United States was a risky move. By the late 1930s, the United States had adopted a position of opposing Japan's invasion of China and began to apply economic pressure in the form of increasingly severe sanctions. Japan's economy was sufficiently dependent on the United States that these sanctions caused great distress. Indeed, by mid-1941, the United States, with assistance from Britain and other countries, had isolated Japan economically.

In 1939, the United States abrogated its commercial treaty with Japan. In July 1940, the Export Control Act gave President Roosevelt the authority to regulate the export of essential war matériel. Using this authority, in October he imposed a de facto embargo on the shipment of scrap iron and steel to Japan. On July 26, 1941, commercial relations between Japan and the United States ended because he froze all Japanese assets, effectively cutting off US exports of oil and petroleum products to Japan. Roosevelt followed up the freeze with a formal embargo on all petroleum products, and he persuaded Britain and Holland (whose government in exile controlled the oil-rich Dutch East Indies) to join the embargo. Japan has no oil of its own.

By August 1941, virtually no crude oil or refined petroleum products were coming into Japan. Many civilian and military planners in the United States were confident that Japan would have no choice but to pull out of China in a year or two, when its fuel supply ran dry. This logic made sense, and, indeed, Japan's own military planners estimated that, at current levels of use, the country would run out of petroleum products in two years or less. In other words, by doing nothing under current conditions, Japan was sure to lose its war with China because its military machine literally would become immobile under the US-led embargo.

Leaving out many details, the course of action on which Japan's wartime leaders settled included an attack to immobilize the US Pacific Fleet, based in Pearl Harbor on the island of Oahu in Hawaii. Pearl Harbor was within reach of Japan's aircraft carriers, and it had a major structural flaw: the harbor mouth was so narrow that only one ship at a time could get through it. Thus, with careful planning and execution, it seemed possible that an attack might well catch most or all of the fleet bottled up. From Japan's perspective, the December 7, 1941, attack seemed successful, but it sowed the seeds of Japan's defeat.

THE MILITARY COURSE OF THE WAR FROM 1942

After the attack on Pearl Harbor, Japanese armies quickly overran most of the Philippines (a US colony at the time), Singapore (a British colony), the Dutch East Indies, and other Pacific islands. During 1942, Japan's empire reached its largest expanse. The US strategy was to overwhelm Japanese garrisons on key islands (ignoring those on unimportant islands), slowly but relentlessly island hopping through the central Pacific toward Japan itself. Part of the plan was to build air bases on some of the islands from which to bomb Japan. Because of the decision to give the war in Europe higher priority, it was not until late 1943 that US forces began to put this strategy into practice in a systematic way.

The main island-hopping campaign directly across the Pacific from Hawaii toward Japan began in November 1943 with assaults on Tarawa and other atolls in the Gilbert Islands. In this assault, as in most of the others that followed, Japanese defenders knew that they would receive no reinforcements. Moreover, Japan's military code forbade its military personal from surrendering (though, of course, some still did). Making the best of rugged terrain, Japanese defenders fought desperately and extracted a bloody price for the inevitable US victories. By mid-1944, Japan's prime minister, Tōjō Hideki, faced growing criticism of his handling of the war. He apparently still clung to the delusion that, if faced with sufficiently fierce opposition, the United States would agree to a negotiated settlement. In a desperate attempt to bring about that situation, Tōjō ordered his forces to go on the offensive in several theaters. The move was disastrous.

By the summer of 1944, it should have been clear to any reasonable person that the war was over and Japan had lost. Reasonableness of this kind, however, was in short supply by this point in the war, which lasted another full year. That summer, US invasions of Saipan, Tinian, and Guam in the Mariana Islands put the home islands of Japan within range of heavy bombers. More people, military and civilian, died during the final year of the war than in all the previous years of the conflict combined. Several major land battles remained, the most important and bloody of which were the invasions of Iwo Jima ("Sulfur Island") in February 1945 and Okinawa in April 1945. As US forces moved closer to Japan, military planners began to draft plans for an invasion of the main Japanese islands.

In the meantime, scientists working at a secret laboratory in Tennessee had perfected the means to harness the power of the atom for destructive purposes. On August 6, 1945, an atomic bomb destroyed the city of Hiroshima, and, on August 9, a second bomb destroyed much of Nagasaki. Although in retrospect some historians have criticized the use of atomic weapons for various reasons, there can be no doubt that it shortened the war. The bombings led to a high-level meeting of military and civilian officials, who remained evenly split regarding whether Japan should surrender. Therefore, the emperor made the final decision. On August 15, Japan's government announced its intention to surrender, and the signing of the official documents took place on September 2. By this point, Japan's people were thoroughly exhausted, and many of them had been reduced to living in primitive conditions.

THE BATTLE OF OKINAWA

The ultimate goal of island hopping was to create bases near the main Japanese islands from which to launch a massive invasion. In that context, Okinawa was an appealing target. It was home to a major air base at Kadena and a major port, Naha. Moreover, because it was formally part of the Japanese homeland, its conquest might inflict a blow to military and civilian morale. Throughout history, one appeal of the Ryukyu Islands was their strategic location.

The Battle of Okinawa (Okinawasen) officially lasted eighty-two days, from April 1 to June 22. However, small-scale fighting continued in some areas after June 22 because groups of Japanese forces remained in hiding. That nearly three months was required to conquer such a small territory indicates the severity of the fighting. The initial assault involved the largest

Hedo 4/13

(Note: U.S. forces
traveled along
coastal roads in
the north.)

Ieshima (4/16-4/21)

4/8

4/11

Nago

U.S. Forces

4/8

(Aguni Island 6/9-6/10)

4/4

Initial Landings 4/1

U.S. Forces

Tsuken Island (4/10)

(Kumejima 6/26-6/29)

4/4

Naha

"Shuri Line" 4/30

Region
of
most
intense
fighting

Itoman

(Kerama Islands 3/26)

6/14 (~6 weeks)

Kian Peninsula

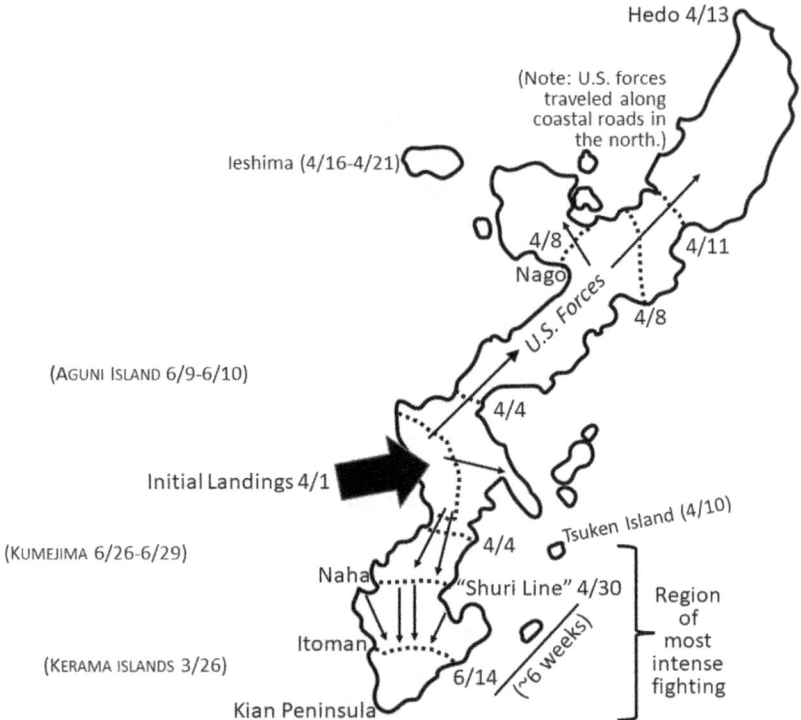

FIGURE 18.1. Basic map and timeline of the Battle of Okinawa

amphibious landing of the war, striking beaches in west central Okinawa in the Yomitan area (fig. 18.1). A feint toward southeast Okinawa was intended to confuse the defenders, although from Japanese accounts we know it did not make much of an impact.

US forces landed unopposed and rapidly occupied the Yomitan area, including Kadena airfield. One group of forces headed north from the beachhead. After about two weeks it had conquered all northern Okinawa and a week later the island of Ie. Fighting in the north was light. By contrast, Japanese forces in southern Okinawa had dug extensive networks of defenses, using networks of caves to good effect. The strongest concentration was in a line approximately from Naha across to the eastern coastline, the "Shuri Line." Japanese ground forces were motivated and had plenty of time to prepare. Their goal was not so much to win the battle as to slow down the US invaders and cause as many casualties as possible.

Leadership on both sides left something to be desired. The commander of the US forces was Lieutenant General Simon Buckner.[1] He was competent but unimaginative. Under his command, US forces attacked head-on and ground ever farther south. Taking heavy casualties all the while, they eventually pushed Japanese defenders to the edge of the Kyan (Kian) Peninsula. The Japanese commander was Lieutenant General Ushijima Mitsuru. Ushijima allowed his subordinates to plan and execute all operational details. The two key subordinates were Lieutenant General Chō Isamu and Colonel Yahara Hiromichi,[2] and their fundamental impulses were at odds. Chō tended to favor aggressive counterattacks, whereas the more cerebral Yahara favored carefully orchestrated defensive warfare. Initially, the higher-ranking Chō prevailed, but his counterattacks proved disastrous. Thereafter, Yahara dominated the Japanese leadership, but he had to alter his overall plans substantially because of losses that Chō's strategy had incurred.

US forces fought their way to the vicinity of the Shuri Line by the end of April. At that point, the battle came to a bloody standstill. Combat fatigue and related mental stress were especially severe during this phase of the fighting. Rain turned much of the terrain to mud, and the stench of decomposing bodies permeated the air. Japanese forces often used the civilian population as de facto human shields. The original plan, created by Yahara, was to fight to the end at the Shuri Line. Yahara had to modify the plan in late May because one flank of the Shuri Line was on the verge of collapse. On May 27, and for several days thereafter, nearly the entire Japanese force headed south to the Itoman area in an orderly retreat. In part because heavy rain interfered with reconnaissance flights, it took US forces several days to understand what had happened. By the end of May, the Japanese defenders had established themselves in a well-organized line across the Kyan Peninsula. Three more weeks of bloody fighting ensued. On June 23, Generals Ushijima and Chō killed themselves at the southern coastline of the Kyan Peninsula, and formal resistance ended. June 23 became Okinawa Memorial Day.

Meanwhile, local conditions in southern Okinawa were horrific for military personnel and civilians alike. Many Japanese soldiers and civilians sought shelter in the numerous caves that dotted the landscape. The damp conditions and limited supplies added to the suffering of wounded soldiers and the nurses who attended them, typically local teenagers. As one fifteen-year-old nurse recalled: "Disposing of urine and pus was not so bad. What I really hated was changing their bandages, which were crawling with maggots." Maggot-infested wounds were common throughout the battle area. According to another nurse: "The patients who waited to have their bandages changed had wounds full of maggots. . . . When we took the bandages off, the deeper part of the wound was always full of countless maggots." According to yet another nurse: "As soon as we removed a wounded soldier's bandage, the wound would erupt with enough maggots to fill a small bucket" (Ryukyu Shimpo 2014, 191, 303, 310). Owing to rampant infection, doctors in the caves often had to perform amputations, often without anesthesia.

LATE JUNE AND THE IMMEDIATE AFTERMATH

Mopping up after the main fighting ended in June took several more weeks. US forces used loudspeakers and other means of communication in attempts to convince both civilians and military personnel to surrender. In principle, Japanese soldiers were not supposed to surrender, preferring suicide when unable to fight. Okinawan civilians had also been thoroughly indoctrinated into a similar mentality. What follows is an account from one of the young nurses in the Himeyuri Student Corps who, along with some comrades, found herself stranded along the southern Okinawan coast:

> A small boat came toward us from a battleship. Then, for the first time, we heard the voice of the enemy. "Those who can swim, swim out! We'll save you. Those who can't swim, walk towards Minatogawa! Walk by day. Don't travel by night. We have food! We will rescue you!" They actually did! They took care of Okinawans really well, according to international law, but we only learned that later. We thought we were hearing the voices of demons. From the time we'd been children, we'd only been educated to hate them. They would strip the girls naked and do with them whatever they wanted, then run over them with tanks. We really believed that. Not only us girls. Mothers, grandfathers, grandmothers all were cowering at the voice of the devils. So what we had been taught robbed us of life. I can never forgive what education did to us! Had we known the truth, all of us would have survived. The Himeyuri Student Corps alone lost one hundred and some score students in the four or five days that followed the order to dissolve the unit [ca. June 18–23]. (Cook and Cook 1992, 360)

Several of this nurse's classmates killed themselves with the grenades that Japanese soldiers had distributed to civilians for that purpose.

Many other Okinawans took their own lives and even the lives of family members. US forces invaded the southern Ryukyu Kerama Islands in late March, ahead of the main attack on Okinawa. One sixteen-year-old boy there recalled the horror of mass civilian suicides without the benefit of grenades or other such tools. He described a man with a stick "striking his wife and children over and over again, bludgeoning them to death." As for

FIGURE 18.2. Aerial view of the nearly complete destruction of Naha in
the Battle of Okinawa (US Marines, National Archives, ID 532379)

his own family, he reported: "My memory tells me the first one we laid
hands on was Mother. Those who had blades, or scythes, cut their wrists
or severed arteries in their necks. But we didn't do it that way. We might
have used a string. When we raised our hands against the mother who bore
us, we wailed in our grief. I remember that. In the end we must have used
stones. To the head. We took care of mother that way. Then my brother and
I turned on our younger brother and younger sister. Hell engulfed us there"
(Cook and Cook, 365). Many of the civilians who survived such ordeals reported being astonished to see large numbers of Japanese military personnel who had voluntarily surrendered. The horrors connected with the battle
caused many survivors to remain quiet for decades afterward.

There are several ways in which to quantify the death and destruction
from the battle, but, to begin, approximately 90 percent of structures on
Okinawa were destroyed or damaged to the point of being unusable (for an
aerial photograph, see fig. 18.2). Most survivors of the battle lived in tents
and other makeshift shelters provided by the US military. Even after Japan's
formal surrender, the military leadership in Okinawa imposed a ban on anyone entering the island because there simply was no way to accommodate

"Iron and Blood" corps survivors   Himeyuri students prior to mobilization

FIGURE 18.3. Boys who survived service in the Blood and Iron Corps and some of the Himeyuri students who served as nurses. Ultimately, the majority of students and teachers perished among the Himeyuri group. (*Left*, Wikimedia Commons; *right*, Wikimedia Commons, Himeyuri Peace Museum, Okinawa)

them. Many Okinawans had settled in Taiwan and other Japanese colonies. Their repatriation became a complex operation that took several years fully to accomplish.

As for deaths due to the battle, perhaps the best approach is to use the statistics from the Cornerstone of Peace (Heiwa no ishiji) memorial park in southern Okinawa. The names of every person who died as a result of the battle, plus Okinawan casualties during the entire course of the war, are inscribed in the memorial park. The 241,281 names inscribed there by summer 2015 include 149,329 from Okinawa Prefecture, 77,380 Japanese from other prefectures, 14,009 from the United States, 365 from the Republic of Korea, 82 from North Korea, 82 from the United Kingdom, and 34 from Taiwan. Since then, more names have been added as they come to be known.

The Japanese forces included local schoolchildren, ages fourteen to seventeen. Ostensibly volunteers (but in fact coerced), about 1,780 boys formed the Iron and Blood Imperial Corps (Tekketsu kinnōtai). Similarly, 220 girls and eighteen teachers from two schools formed the Himeyuri Nursing Corps (fig. 18.3). Few from either group survived the battle.

More recently, the matter of mass group suicides has received considerable attention. The general term for such suicides is *shūdan jiketsu*, which emphasizes the resolve on the part of those killing themselves. As noted above, the civilian population in Okinawa came under considerable pressure to take their own lives rather than surrender to the invaders. One form of pressure was fear. Japanese propaganda emphasized that a horrible fate would befall anyone falling into US hands. Another powerful force was a desire on the part of many Okinawans to prove their steadfast devotion to their country. Suicide was a way to demonstrate loyalty and patriotism. Moreover, it has now been well-documented (in recent civil court cases among other venues) that Japanese soldiers supplied grenades to civilians for use in ending their lives. Authoritative voices conveyed to much of the civilian population that suicide was expected. Although the Japanese government then and now insists that these suicides were voluntary, many people have become convinced that many were coerced. Many who witnessed group suicides did not want to talk about them. It was not until the late 1980s that some elderly Okinawans began to tell their stories and journalists began to publish them. As a result, it is clear that, although some suicides may have been truly voluntary, many or most were coerced or coerced to a substantial degree.

OTHER ISLANDS

Many civilians suffered and died even in islands that did not experience military battles. A particularly notorious example is the island of Kumejima. There, a zealous junior naval officer named Kayama Tadashi was obsessed with the possibility of spies. During the Battle of Okinawa, US forces captured the sailor Nakandakari Meiyū, a native of Kumejima. When Nakandakari learned that they were planning to attack the island, he convinced commanders not to bombard it. He served as a guide and intermediary, convincing the island's population to cooperate with the 966 US troops who came to occupy it. As the US forces came ashore on June 26 without incident, the small contingent of Japanese naval personnel on Kumejima hid in the rugged mountains of the island. In the meantime, US forces distributed food to needy civilians.

The naval personnel remained in hiding throughout July and for most of the first half of August. On August 15, Japan's emperor announced his country's surrender. In Kumejima, the announcement was broadcast at the local elementary school. On August 18, Japanese forces in hiding bayonetted Nakandakari, his wife, and their infant child to death and set fire to their house. Two days later, they murdered Tanigawa Noboru, an ethnic Korean, and his family, including a baby. In all, the Japanese forces murdered twenty island residents, with some forty others on their kill list at the time they surrendered on September 7. According to Kayama, those killed were spies because they had accepted food from or otherwise interacted with US soldiers. Although several local governments passed resolutions calling for Kayama to be tried as a war criminal, neither he nor any of those who carried out the murders were ever brought to justice. In a 1972 newspaper interview, Kayama defiantly justified his actions as legitimate wartime acts.

Further south, in the Yaeyama Islands, there were no US invasions. Japanese forces there, however, pursued several polices under the guise of military readiness. One was to confiscate food from the civilian population. For example, people on the island of Hateruma raised cattle. Authorities confiscated local herds, slaughtered them, and distributed the meat to military forces. Their justification was that, because Americans are meat eaters, the cattle must be preemptively slaughtered. Elsewhere in the southern Ryukyu Islands, local residents suffered severe food shortages, in large part because of confiscation of supplies for the military. In some cases, local residents also faced relocation orders.

One result of these pressures on the civilian population was a surge in malaria. For example, people exposed themselves to malaria-infested areas as they foraged for food, and their semistarved condition made them more susceptible to disease. Moreover, the type of malaria prevalent in the southern Ryukyu Islands was especially severe compared with that in Okinawa. The total population of the southern Ryukyu Islands was just over thirty-one thousand, and approximately half contracted malaria. Roughly 20 percent of those infected died of the disease. In other words, even in areas where there was no military fighting and no US troops, many civilians suffered and perished.

CHAPTER NINETEEN

The Era of US Control, 1945–72

When the Pacific War ended in the late summer of 1945, the sprawling Japanese Empire collapsed. Japanese military and civilian personnel abroad, from Burma to various Pacific islands, faced expulsion from what had been their homes. Between 1945 and 1950, roughly 6.5 million Japanese nationals flowed into a war-ravaged country. Because so many residents of the Ryukyu Islands had settled in Japanese colonies, the influx of people from former colonies into the islands was proportionately even greater.

Immediate Postwar Era in Okinawa Prefecture

In 1944, the population of Okinawa Prefecture was 773,818. In 1950, it was 917,875, a substantial increase. A population of over 900,000 in 1950 is all the more remarkable considering a loss of some 100,000–150,000 people in 1945. How could the population have rebounded and even increased so quickly? The main answer was the inflow of people into Okinawa and the southern Ryukyu Islands from former Japanese colonies. Many estimates are that this inflow exceeded the number of those who perished in the battle. Among these incoming people were many who had never set foot in the Ryukyu Islands prior to their repatriation. When the Cold War began, roughly during 1948, the Ryukyu Islands came to the attention of the US government as a valuable location for military bases, much as the islands had been an ideal location for *wakō* bases centuries earlier.

During the roughly three years between the end of the Battle of Okinawa and the start of the Cold War, Okinawa and the other Ryukyu Islands were of relatively low priority in the eyes of the US government. Fighting had destroyed about 95 percent of housing and devastated agriculture. Local food production became a small fraction of what it had been before the battle. The vast majority of Okinawan civilians lived in spartan refugee camps operated by military personnel. During these years, therefore, the US officials in Okinawa prohibited most Okinawans who had been living in the Japanese mainland or in former Japanese colonies from entering Okinawa. There was no place for them to live in the island, and the food supplies and the basic infrastructure were inadequate. The southern Ryukyu Islands did, however, receive a large influx of returnees soon after the war ended. In most cases, they lodged with relatives. Residents of Okinawa Prefecture who found themselves in mainland Japan created the League of Okinawans (Okinawa-jin renmei), with Iha Fuyū as its president, to provide mutual assistance during the turbulent years just after the war.

In the aftermath of the battle, serious problems confronted the survivors. One example is unexploded ordnance, which remains a present and future danger. For example, on March 2, 1974, a construction crew was installing water mains in front of a kindergarten when a crane struck a bomb. According to an eyewitness:

> Sand flew everywhere. . . . The crane was blown to pieces and the man who had been operating the pile driver was killed instantly, along with three of his workmates. In the grounds of the kindergarten, a little girl about to turn three was playing in the sandpit and was buried in the sand, which the explosion had hurled in every direction. In all, the explosion left four people dead and thirty-two injured. . . . Uncontrollable anger wells up in the hearts of the Okinawan people at the realization that the war is still not over for them. (Ryukyu Shimpo 2014, 175)

This incident was one of eighteen accidental detonations resulting in casualties between 1948 and 2009, and there have been hundreds of discoveries of unexploded ordnance since 1945. By one estimate, twenty-two hundred tons of unexploded ordnance remained in Okinawa as of 2011. At current rates of clearance, it will take another seventy years or so to get rid of it all (Ryukyu Shimpo 2014, 181, 184–85).

The complex circumstances connected with Japan's defeat in war, the Battle of Okinawa, the US occupation of Japan, and the onset of the Cold War combined to cause considerable social upheaval at the level of individuals and families. By about 1950, this situation had stabilized, and the acute crisis had calmed. However, social unrest continued throughout the era of US occupation, flaring up from time to time depending on circumstances.

We can divide the twenty-seven years of US occupation of Okinawa and the southern Ryukyu Islands into four periods:

1. 1945–48: forgotten island
2. 1949–57: formation of a long-term governance structure; struggle over land
3. 1958–64: emergence of popular sentiment for return to Japan
4. 1965–72: base for the Vietnam War; merging of return-to-Japan movement with antiwar movement

The following sections explain the major developments in Okinawa during these periods.

In 1945, the northern Ryukyu Islands also came under US military administration. They joined the entity US officials called *the Ryukyus*. US policies in the northern Ryukyu Islands devastated the local economy, in part because the islands were cut off from the rest of Japan even though their economy was closely linked with that of Kagoshima. Opposition to US rule in these islands was particularly intense, especially after the general US occupation of Japan ended in 1952. Leaving out the many details of protests and negotiations, in late 1953, parties from all sides came to an agreement that the northern Ryukyu Islands would revert to Japanese control. The US occupation ended December 25, 1953; a development sometimes called *the Christmas gift*. The name *Ryūkyū* is especially unpopular in the northern Ryukyu Islands because it conjures up both conquest and oppression by Shuri and the relatively short but economically devastating US military occupation. Some politicians and economists have speculated that measurable economic damage from the military occupation lingers to the present day.

1945–48: Forgotten Island

Soon after Japan's surrender, US military officials in Okinawa created the Okinawa Advisory Committee (Okinawa shijunkai), consisting of fifteen locally prominent educators and journalists. They also divided Okinawa into twelve "cities" and carried out elections for a mayor and city council for each. In this election, for the first time anywhere in Japan, women voted as well as men. In 1946, the Advisory Committee transformed into the Okinawa Civilian Administration (Okinawa minseifu), with the chair of the Advisory Committee, Shikiya Kōshin, appointed as its governor. In response to complaints that the governor and legislators were appointed, not elected, US officials likened themselves to a cat and Okinawa to a mouse, bluntly stating that the mouse can act only within the limits set by the cat.

The message from US officials was that the scope of the civilian government would be narrow. Similar civilian governments were established in the other islands. The key point is that US officials kept the Ryukyu Islands outside and separate from Japan's civil government. For this reason, some residents began to speak of Okinawa as *the forgotten island*.

In 1947, political parties and other organizations developed organically from among Okinawa's residents. In general, they pressed the military authorities for a genuine voice in government via democratic elections. In response, US officials permitted local elections only and took measures to suppress the nascent political parties.

During the first two or three years after the war, many local leaders in Okinawa, in other islands, and among Okinawans in mainland Japan keenly felt the pain of the Battle of Okinawa and a sense of betrayal by Tokyo. Therefore, a variety of proposals emerged to the effect that the Ryukyu Islands would become a self-governing protectorate of the United States. In this context, Panama was often cited, naively, as a possible model.[1] Visions of a republic under US protection, however, quickly faded or soured. Many activists who sought such an arrangement became advocates of reversion to Japanese sovereignty.

Particularly influential in shaping events and policies was the onset of the Cold War in Europe and the ongoing civil war in China. In this context, the general US policy toward the Ryukyu Islands solidified. They would not be part of Japan administratively. Instead, they would remain under long-term US military control. In that context, the United States began enlarging its military bases on Okinawa and declared the island to be the "Keystone of the Pacific" (fig. 19.1). Okinawa became an important part of the US military posture in the region.

Not knowing much about either Japan as a whole or Okinawa Prefecture in particular, many US military and civilian officials relied on assessments of the Ryukyu Islands by anthropologists and historians, who, in reports drafted in the run-up to the Battle of Okinawa, stressed cultural and racial differences between Japanese and Okinawans. Initially, this focus on difference was in the context of preparing psychological warfare materials to influence the local population. It was a complete failure. In the context of the Cold War, US officials highlighted purported Japanese versus Okinawan differences to justify continued US occupation. On the whole, local populations in Okinawa and the other Ryukyu Islands did not find such rhetoric persuasive.

The local economy was in turmoil in 1945 and for years thereafter, and most local residents ate food provided by the US military. Over the years, military and popular US canned food influenced local cuisine. Today the

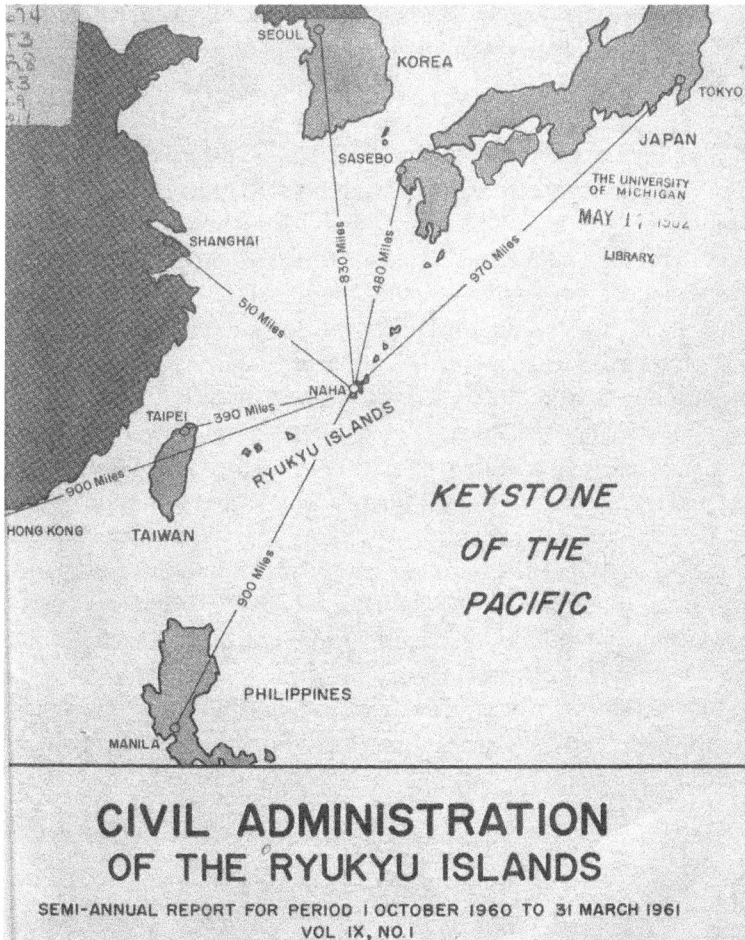

FIGURE 19.1. "Keystone of the Pacific" concept illustrated on the cover of a report by the US Civil Administration of the Ryukyu Islands (USCAR)

impact is minor, but root beer (generally disliked elsewhere in Japan), Spam, and a few other iconic US food items from the 1950s remain moderately popular. At the time, food distribution was uneven, and people suffered under chronic food shortages in remote areas. Food shortages led some residents to steal from distribution centers, and a black market for food and other items began to develop. Smuggling became widespread during the late 1940s and early 1950s. A major cause was inept, heavy-handed management of the local economy by US officials.

There was no official Okinawan currency until about mid-1946. After trying different approaches, military officials settled on a currency called *B-yen* in 1948. Military bases were the major employers, and local workers were paid in B-yen. However, their salaries were tied to the price of basic commodities, and those prices were fixed at artificially low levels. Therefore, most civilian employees received very low wages. This situation encouraged black markets, smuggling, and theft. Smuggling was especially common between the southern Ryukyu Islands and Taiwan. Many residents of the southern Ryukyu Islands had migrated to Taiwan starting in the 1920s. Most of them were back in the Ryukyu Islands by 1947, but many retained connections in Taiwan. Items entered the Ryukyu Islands from the Japanese mainland as well, along with ideas and news. People from the Ryukyu Islands became de facto (but illicit) merchants, trading goods and produce between various parts of Japan and places like Taiwan and Hong Kong.

Another social problem was sexual violence, typically perpetuated by US military personnel. In the early years of US administration, military policy and the attitude of local Okinawan officials vacillated. Very generally, top-down attempts to cordon off military personnel from contact with the local civilian population resulted in more sex crimes. Conversely, establishing de facto brothels (always called something else officially) reduced sex crime but introduced a host of other problems, including the spread of sexually transmitted diseases. Over time, de facto brothels became common. The broader issue of sexual violence and related problems remained vexing throughout the US occupation and remains an issue to this day.

1949–57: Formation of a Long-Term Governance Structure and Struggle over Land

In part reacting to the Korean War, the US Civil Administration of the Ryukyu Islands (USCAR) was formed in 1950 to take over most forms of governance from the military. USCAR was headed by a general with the title *high commissioner*, and its officers included US military personnel and civil bureaucrats. In 1962, the Kennedy administration added a civil administrator position to USCAR, but this person was always subordinate to the high commissioner.

In 1952, USCAR created the Government of the Ryukyu Islands (Ryūkyū seifu) as a vehicle whereby local personnel would provide many of the usual functions of government. It consisted of executive, legislative, and judicial branches. Members of the legislature were elected, and the legislature often passed laws that USCAR did not like. USCAR had veto power, which it often used, and it could even nullify local elections. The high commissioner could also issue ordinances on any matter that had the force of law. The head of the Government of the Ryukyu Islands was the chief executive (*Gyōsei shuseki*). This official was appointed by USCAR from 1952 to 1960,[2] selected by the majority party in the legislature from 1960 to 1966, elected by the legislature from 1966 to 1968, and elected by the voters at large from 1968 to 1972.

After the Battle of Okinawa, the vast majority of the island's inhabitants resided in refugee camps. During that time, vast areas of land were uninhabited. The US military constructed bases and other facilities as it saw fit, and it took over some preexisting Japanese military facilities. Therefore, as people gradually left the refugee camps, many found that their land was now the site of a US facility. Typical options for such people were to find jobs at the bases, find new lines of work, leave Okinawa, and/or simply subsist on rent if circumstances permitted.

The US government paid rent to the people whose land it appropriated. Because of differences in living standards, that rent was, at least initially, a fairly small cost for the United States. Even as more refugees left the camps and settled back into their family's land, the military continued to expand its bases. In 1953, a US law permitted the appropriation of any land in Okinawa, and US officials there acted on it aggressively. In some cases, bulldozers leveled people's homes while they made attempts to protest the seizure of their land. US military bases eventually came to occupy 14 percent of the land in Okinawa. This may not sound like much, but that figure was 43 percent of the island's arable land. In other words, nearly half of Okinawa's farmland became military bases.

Recall that the Ryukyu Islands are poorly suited to cereal-grain agriculture. Many people displaced from their ancestral lands resented their situation. However, replacing relatively unproductive agricultural land with military bases, which became major employers, benefited the overall economy. In this way, a contradiction developed whereby many Okinawans resented the military bases for a variety of reasons but the local economy became dependent on them. In addition to land appropriation, the bases came with a host of local problems such as crime, auto accidents, occasional plane crashes, noise pollution, and a general irritation vis-à-vis the presence of large numbers of young and often-rowdy foreigners. Some Okinawans also thought that such a concentrated military presence might make Okinawa a target in future conflicts. More recently, base-related environmental problems have become an issue.

In the realm of education, a curriculum closely resembling that used in mainland Japan became established in the lower grades by the 1950s.

Initially, local US officials insisted that English be required from elementary school on. However, as it became clear that Okinawans were never going to become US nationals, that requirement was dropped. The basic dynamic was that USCAR did not trust most teachers to promote a pro-US position, but US officials were in no position to monitor school activities, with the vast majority of US personnel unable to understand Japanese. Therefore, the general approach was to starve the school system of funds.[3] One effect was that the Okinawa Teachers' Association became an early and vigorous supporter of reversion to Japanese control.

The major change that US administrators made was establishing the University of the Ryukyus in 1951 as well as encouraging Okinawans to study at US universities. The plan was to discourage travel to the Japanese mainland for higher education and nurture a cadre of Okinawans familiar with and sympathetic to the United States to serve as partners in governing the islands.

In 1954, the US government announced that it would make onetime payments to compensate landowners. Such a policy amounted to de facto land purchase. Popular resentment exploded in protests and a demand that the US authorities adhere to the Four Principles of Land Preservation (Tochi o mamoru shigensoku):

1. No single payment for unlimited-term use
2. Rent paid yearly at market rates
3. Payment for any harm to people or property caused by US military forces
4. No further base expansion and the return of unused or unnecessary land

An appeal directly to the US Congress by a citizen group put the onetime payment plan on hold. Also in 1954, in response to this popular anger, for the first time USCAR provided funds for the rebuilding of schools that had been damaged in the Battle of Okinawa some nine years earlier.

Tensions boiled over again in 1956 in an outburst of protest called *the islandwide struggle (shimagurumi tōsō)*. Leaving out the details, the basic compromise that resulted was that the local civilian government agreed to support continued US control and bases in return for the military paying fair market rates to rent the land. The matter of compensating Okinawans harmed by military personnel remained unsettled, and it would continue to flare up as an issue.

One other important economic change took place in 1958. In that year, the currency in Okinawa changed from B-yen to US dollars. In 1958, and again in 1972, residents formed long lines to change over their money.

1958–64: Emergence of Popular Sentiment
for Japanese Sovereignty

In the peculiar society that developed under US military occupation, residents of the former Okinawa Prefecture lived in an ambivalent zone. In 1958, the poet Yamanokuchi Baku wrote:

> The words we use
> They are Japanese
> The money we use
> It is dollars
> It's like Japan
> But not so much like it
> It's like America
> But not so much like it
> [These] are elusive islands.

(quoted in Oguma 2014, 163)

With respect to many legal matters such as household registration and travel abroad, including travel to mainland Japan, Okinawans were neither Japanese nor Americans. If such ambiguity had come with the benefit of higher living standards, it might have been relatively easy to bear. By the end of the 1950s, however, the mainland began significantly to outpace Okinawa in terms of economic growth.

Arguably, through the 1950s, Okinawa and the other Ryukyu Islands recovered from the war at approximately the same pace as the mainland or even slightly faster. By the end of the decade, however, the rest of Japan began to pull ahead of Okinawa in terms of its standard of living, or at least its *perceived* standard of living. Closely connected with this matter was that, in the early years of the occupation, Okinawan media tended to portray the US presence as enhancing the local standard of living. Gradually, however, news of mainland economic growth became better known in Okinawa.[4]

Other issues influenced sentiment about reversion. For example, during the 1950s, Japan's military force—the so-called Japanese Self-Defense Forces—was still very small. Residents of Okinawa became increasingly weary of base-related crime, pollution, and other problems. In this context, many people began to look at Japan's "pacifist" constitution, which explicitly renounces war, through rose-colored glasses. For these and other reasons, anti-US sentiment began to build, and the residents of Okinawa Prefecture increasingly clamored for a return to Japanese sovereignty.

Many Okinawans were enamored of Article 9 in Japan's postwar constitution, the article prohibiting the maintenance of military forces, among other things. There was and remains an inherent contradiction in the embrace of Article 9 and the demand for a demilitarized Okinawa. Although probably not obvious to many local activists in the 1960s, in the minds of high-level strategists in Japan and the United States, a militarized Okinawa made Article 9 plausible. This idea goes back to the origins of Article 9. In March 1948, a high-level delegation of military and civilian officials from the US government visited General MacArthur in an attempt to persuade him to abandon support for Article 9 and begin establishing a small military force for Japan. MacArthur listed five reasons for rejecting their entreaties and maintaining Article 9. After those five reasons, he stated that US possession of Okinawa was the ultimate reason not to scrap Article 9 (Lummis 2023, 157–58). In other words, in MacArthur's view, Japan did require military force to remain a viable, sovereign country, and the air and naval bases on Okinawa provided that force. A similar logic informed the negotiations for Okinawa's reversion to Japan in the late 1960s and shaped the final agreement.

It is important to note that domestic political discourse in Okinawa and other Ryukyu Islands included a variety of viewpoints and that these viewpoints inevitably leveraged the past to craft arguments. In general, a focus on prewar discrimination against Ryukyuans by mainland Japanese was common among those who opposed reversion. Similarly, a focus on the horrific costs of the Battle of Okinawa usually came from reversion opponents. Some reversion opponents also glorified the days of the kingdom. By contrast, advocates of reversion stressed that Okinawa and Japan were a natural fit, ethnically, culturally, and economically. They stressed the suffering of ordinary people during the era of the kingdom, which was "built upon the blood and sweat of the commoner class," in the words of the future governor Nishime Junji (quoted in Oguma 2014, 179). Those favoring reversion also stressed the extent to which postwar Japan was a much different and better place than its militarist prewar iteration. Ultimately, it was growing dislike of the heavy hand of US military rule that turned the popular tide in favor of reversion to Japan.

Incidentally, advocates of the Ryukyu Islands becoming an independent or quasi-independent state were almost nonexistent during the 1950s and 1960s. The overwhelming tendency was to advocate either for a strong attachment to the United States or for a complete return to Japan. As we will see, even today, although many residents of Okinawa Prefecture favor

FIGURE 19.2. Public demonstrations during the 1960s for "Return to the Fatherland," that is, for Okinawan reversion to full Japanese sovereignty and administration (Okinawa Prefectural Archives)

greater administrative autonomy vis-à-vis Tokyo, only a tiny minority claim to favor complete independence from Japan.

On February 28, 1963, a middle school girl was struck and killed by a US military heavy truck while crossing the street in a marked crosswalk. The driver had run a red light. Local courts and police had no jurisdiction over the matter. The driver was tried in a US military court and found not guilty. He claimed that the evening sunlight prevented him from noticing that the traffic light was red. This case was a typical example of death and serious injury to local residents caused by military personnel. Vehicular accidents were most common, but rape and other forms of assault took place, as did property crime and disorderly conduct. In all cases, US military personnel were subject only to military courts, which often handed down light sentences. Even when the perpetrators were punished, victims or their families rarely received any compensation.

Also important in shaping popular sentiment was arrogance on the part of some military personnel and a dislike of being governed by foreigners on the part of Okinawans. The long US occupation reinforced a strong sense of Japanese identity in all segments of the population (fig. 19.2). In 1960, an organization called the Okinawa Prefecture Return to the Fatherland Council (Okinawa-ken sokoku fukki kyōgikai), along with several other civic organizations, provided formal outlets through which to demand a return to Japanese sovereignty. Demands by Okinawans for reversion to Japan or return to the fatherland (*sokoku fukki*) intensified throughout the 1960s.

1965–72: Merging of the Return-to-Japan Movement with Antiwar Sentiment

It was also in the 1960s that the Vietnam War intensified. The war increased US military activity and, thus, all the problems associated with the bases. Moreover, in Okinawa and throughout Japan, there was widespread opposition to the Vietnam War. In that context, ongoing Vietnamese resistance to US forces inspired many in Okinawa to protest the US military presence. In this way, antibase sentiment, antiwar sentiment, anti-imperialist sentiment merged with a desire to rejoin Japan, especially a Japan whose constitution renounced war explicitly. It is important to note that, during the 1950s and the early 1960s, most Okinawans who advocated reversion to Japan were not opposed to the presence of US military bases and assumed that those bases would remain even after a return to Japanese sovereignty. The Vietnam War worked to change that view. Intertwined with negative Okinawan views of the war in Vietnam was a rosy view of Japan's postwar pacifist constitution.

Sentiment against the Vietnam War had also built up in the United States. The 1968 Tet Offensive (Tet is the lunar new year) by North Vietnamese forces shattered the illusion that the United States and South Vietnam were on the verge of victory. From that point on, the war became increasingly unpopular. In Okinawan society during the 1960s, there were significant disagreements about military bases. Bases had become such a large part of the economy that those who worked at them or with them often favored their presence for obvious economic reasons. Many other Okinawans, however, resented them. In general, antibase sentiment grew during the 1960s and 1970s.

The majority of the population had been in favor of a return to Japanese sovereignty since the 1950s. During the 1960s, several factors intensified this sentiment, including the following:

1. People realized that genuine self-government was impossible under USCAR.
2. The standard of living in mainland Japan rose rapidly during the 1960s, and many in Okinawa began to perceive the gap.
3. For those who opposed bases and the Vietnam War, return to Japanese sovereignty promised a reduction in the military presence in Okinawa, or at least that is what many people assumed.

In addition to petitions and public demonstrations, the public found various ways to press this issue and irritate US officials. For example, it became common for members of the Communist Party to win local elections. The reason was not because most Okinawans at the time genuinely favored a Communist society. During the 1960s, anything considered Communist was anathema to US officials, so support for Communist Party candidates was a way to irritate the occupiers. Sometimes USCAR nullified the results of elections that brought avowed Communists to local offices. In such cases, Okinawan leaders highlighted US hypocrisy in nullifying the democratic will of the people.

As Okinawans clamored ever more stridently for a return to Japanese sovereignty, the public and politicians in mainland Japan took notice. It became impossible for Japan's central government to ignore the matter, and, by the mid-1960s, the return of Okinawa and the southern Ryukyu Islands became a major diplomatic issue between Japan and the United States. In 1965, Prime Minister Satō Eisaku visited Okinawa and declared that Japan's "postwar" would not end until Okinawa had been returned. Many Okinawans were delighted by Satō's strong statement but were filled with unrealistic expectations of a fast, unconditional return and an end to the military bases. In the midst of the Cold War, however, both Tokyo and Washington regarded Okinawa as the cornerstone of the Pacific. Their goal was to figure out a way to return Okinawan sovereignty to Japan without significantly disrupting the military situation.

As the return of Okinawa became a real possibility, opinion in Okinawa split regarding how to bring it about. In 1968, for the first time in eighteen years, there was an election for chief executive. Yara Chōbyō advocated an uncompromising position of rapid return to Japan with no conditions, no nuclear weapons, and no bases. His more cautious opponent, the future governor Nishime Junji, advocated a return to Japan that was more aligned with the policies of Washington and Tokyo. Yara won the election, prompting the US high commissioner to quip that, were the bases to be closed, Okinawa would quickly become a society of "potatoes and bare feet." Yara's political party also succeeded in making gains in the legislature.

Despite strong local sentiment for radical change, the Satō and Nixon administrations negotiated a plan that was more in line with the position of Nishime and the moderates. They summarized the plan as: "No nuclear weapons; on a par with the mainland; return in 1972." In other words, while agreeing to popular demand for the absence of nuclear weapons, the return to Japan would not happen quickly, nor would the bases be eliminated or reduced. The next few years were turbulent.

In late 1968, a B-52 bomber crashed near Kadena, close to an ammunition depot. The result could easily have been disastrous for people on the ground. This incident led to demands by Yara's administration for the removal of the B-52s, and he threatened a general strike. Tokyo and Washington replied that a general strike might delay the return of Okinawa. They also hinted that the B-52s might be removed in any case. So Yara called off the strike plans. Instead, there was a large demonstration. It was peaceful, but tensions vis-à-vis the US military were building.

In September 1970, a local couple was run over and killed in Itoman by a US soldier who was later found not guilty. On December 19, 1970, in the City of Koza (now called Okinawa City), an Okinawan military employee was hit at a traffic crossing by a soldier. When an MP came over to investigate, he was surrounded by an angry crowd demanding that he conduct an honest investigation. The context was anger about previous not-guilty judgments in Koza as well as the recent Itoman case. The MP fired a warning shot, and the crowd exploded in anger. They set fire to the MP's car and other foreign-owned vehicles. The crowd swelled to some five thousand people, and local police could not control it. The demonstrators pushed into the base and were met by armed soldiers who fired tear gas to repel them. The Koza Riot resulting in seventy-three vehicles and three structures on the base going up in flames, but there were no fatalities. Arakawa Sachio, a local business owner, recalled his sentiments at the time: "When I witnessed the Koza Riot, I thought it was only natural that the foreigners got what they deserved. . . . Rape someone? Not guilty. Run over and kill someone in a car accident? Not guilty. The civilians were tired of hearing about such incidents as they accumulated year after year. That's why their feelings about 'these assholes' suddenly exploded into the riot" (quoted in Shimabuku 2019, 121). Uprisings, strikes, and violence flared up in 1971 as well, with major clashes between rioters and police taking place on May 19 and November 10.

Okinawa Prefecture was reestablished on May 15, 1972, and many people rejoiced. However, the military bases continued on as before, and other problems remained unresolved. Governor Yara Chōbyō gave a lackluster speech on the occasion, noting that many problems persisted and that much work remained to be done. Local newspapers struck a similar tone. The long-anticipated reversion to Japanese sovereignty was anticlimactic. It was certainly an important event, but the reversion did not fundamentally change the situation in Okinawa.

[CHAPTER TWENTY]

From 1972 to the Twenty-First Century

In the years since reversion, some US military bases became joint US–Japanese Self-Defense Forces (JSDF) facilities. More recently, the JSDF has built additional bases of its own throughout the Ryukyu Islands to counter the threat of an increasingly aggressive Chinese posture in the region. For the prefecture's residents, the base issue has transformed somewhat, but it remains a major political and social issue. Overall, approximately 70 percent of the US military presence in Japan is located in Okinawa Prefecture (fig. 20.1). Although Japan's central government has become quick to condemn the actions of US military personnel when they commit serious crimes, the government has shown no interest in changing the fundamental structure of the US-JSDF military geographic deployment. Some Okinawan governors attempted to push back against the bases, but their efforts had no long-term impact. Others have sought to cooperate with the central government.

In the economic realm, the major story is the rise of tourism, both in Okinawa and in the southern Ryukyu Islands. According to prefectural government figures, the percentage of the base-related revenue in the Okinawan economy was 30 percent in 1965, 15.5 percent immediately after the reversion in 1972, and 5 percent in 2013 (Karube 2022). Tourism and related service industries account for approximately 80 percent of the current economic activity of Okinawa Prefecture, and agriculture (including fishing) is between roughly 2 and 9 percent, depending on how it is defined.

This chapter is a brief survey of selected topics in the recent history of Okinawa Prefecture, the situation in the prefecture today, and likely future challenges.

Some Survey Results

Japanese media companies frequently conduct surveys. What follows is a list of selected items from a 2017 survey of the residents of Okinawa

Dark areas indicate military facilities

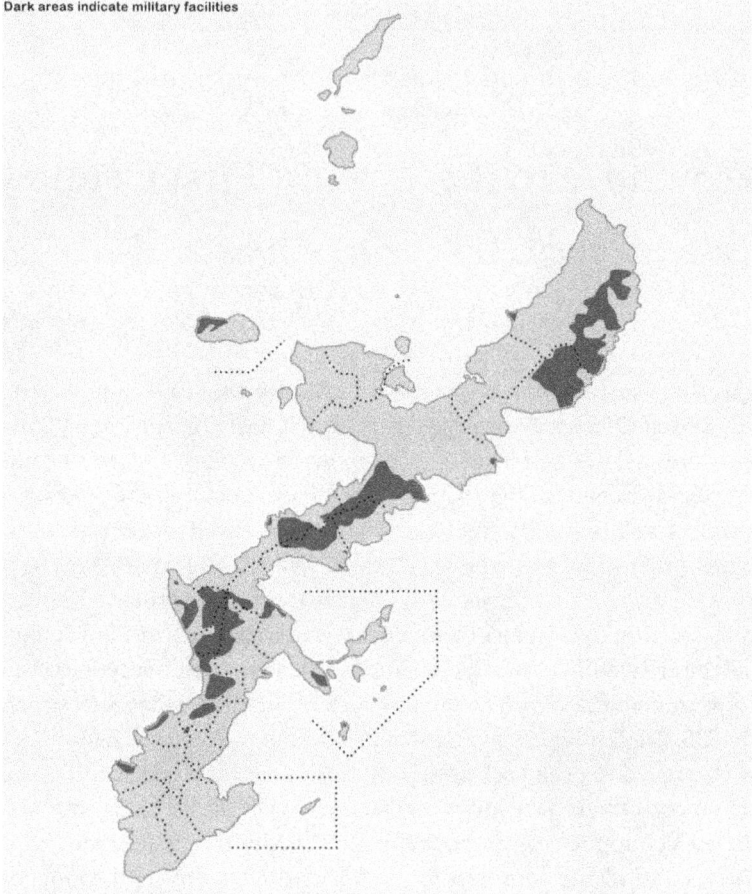

FIGURE 20.1. Military bases and facilities on Okinawa
(Wikimedia Commons, Misakubo, CC BY-SA 3.0)

Prefecture conducted by the newspaper *Asahi shinbun* over the period April 23–24, 2017, and reported on May 11, 2017:

Q: We would like to ask about the future of Okinawa Prefecture. What kind of autonomy do you think Okinawa Prefecture should aim for?

A: Status quo in Okinawa Prefecture, 35 percent; become a special municipality with stronger authority, 51 percent; independence from Japan, 4 percent.

Q: We are approaching the anniversary of Okinawa Prefecture returning

to Japan on May 15. Do you think it is good that Okinawa has returned to Japan? Do you think it is not good?

A: Is good, 82 percent; not good, 5 percent.

Qa: Do you think that [distinctive] "Okinawa-ness" remains? Or do you
  think much has been lost?

Aa: Still remains, 57 percent; much has been lost, 32 percent.

Qb: Of the 57 percent answering "still remains," what is it that remains?

Ab: Dialect, 8 percent; nature, 5 percent; traditional culture, 43 percent;
  spirit and mutual aid, 33 percent; lifestyle, 8 percent.

Qc: Of the 32 percent answering "much lost," what has been lost?

Ac: Dialect, 23 percent; nature, 21 percent; traditional culture, 12 percent; spirit and mutual aid, 20 percent; lifestyle, 23 percent.

Q: What is the most important issue in Okinawa now?

A: Economic growth, 19 percent; enhancement of education and
  welfare, 28 percent; base problem, 33 percent; perpetuation of
  Okinawa's unique culture, 6 percent; conservation of the natural
  environment, 12 percent.

Qa: There is a view that there are "various disparities" between Okinawa and the mainland. Do you think that is correct? Do you not
  think that is not correct?

Aa: Agree, 81 percent; disagree, 14 percent.

Qb: Of the 81 percent who agree, what is the most problematic
  disparity?

Ab: Income, 43 percent; employment, 8 percent; transportation
  network, 2 percent; education, 13 percent; base problem,
  33 percent.

Q: Regarding the US military base problem, there is the opinion that
  the concentration of bases and facilities in Okinawa compared with
  the mainland is discrimination against Okinawa by the mainland.
  Do you think that is right? Or do you disagree?

A: Agree, 54 percent; disagree, 38 percent.

Q: Do you think Okinawa's economy will improve if the US military
  bases shrink going forward? Do you think it will get worse? Or do
  you think there will be no change?

A: Improve, 36 percent; worsen, 18 percent; stay the same, 38 percent.

Notice that only 4 percent said that they favor independence from Japan, and only 5 percent thought reversion to Japan in 1972 was not good. However, a slight majority favored greater autonomy. Also, the vast majority agreed that there are significant discrepancies between Okinawa and other prefectures, and a slight majority agreed that the concentration of military bases constitutes discrimination against Okinawa Prefecture. Also notice that, overall, the base problem was a prominent issue. Indeed, the largest number of respondents, though not a majority, regarded military bases as Okinawa's most pressing issue, even more so than economic growth. However, when the question was worded slightly differently, a plurality highlighted the income discrepancy vis-à-vis the mainland, not the base issue. In terms of per capita income, Okinawa's is the lowest in Japan.

In 1978, NHK (Nihon hōsō kyōkai, the main television broadcaster) did an extensive survey of preferences, attitudes, moral issues, etc. for each prefecture (see NHK 1979). Araki Moriaki has analyzed the data from this survey as they pertain to Okinawa (see Araki 1981). The survey included 40 topics and 164 specific items. After completion, the results for each prefecture were compared. Okinawa was the most distinctive, coming in first or last on 43 items. Next was Tokyo at 35, followed by Kanagawa Prefecture (suburban Tokyo) at 15. To take some examples, Okinawa was lowest in interaction with neighbors, the idea that "it is inevitable that those who are not capable will be left behind," belief in Buddhism, belief that the emperor should be revered, and belief that Japan is currently a good society.

In a similar 1996 NHK survey (see NHK 1997a, 1997b), Okinawa was again the outlier, though there was some movement, a notch up or down for some categories. Okinawa was highest in the following: My prefecture is more distinctive than other prefectures; I like the local language. It was lowest in belief in Buddhism, belief in Shinto, belief that the emperor should be respected, belief that Japan is currently a good society, and support for the Jimintō (the dominant Liberal Democratic Party [actually a conservative party]). It was also lowest in agreement with the statement, "In today's world, people who don't care about others are numerous," and the statement, "It is inevitable that women will be discriminated against; men are superior to women." (For more details, see Asato 2010, 5–6.)

This distinctiveness makes sense given the history of the region. For example, although Buddhism was a prominent part of elite culture in the days of the kingdom, it never became as popular in the Ryukyu Islands as it did in mainland Japan. It follows, therefore, that the residents of Okinawa Prefecture would register the lowest degree of belief in Buddhism. Conversely, we have seen that women played a dominant role in Okinawan religion. This point may be part of the reason for disagreement with the statement about men being superior to women. The Liberal Democratic Party is the main entity in Japan supporting the large concentration of military bases in Okinawa. Therefore, it would be especially unpopular there.

On a question assessing the strength of local identity, although Okinawa Prefecture was the strongest, it clustered very close to several prefectures in northeast Japan's Tōhoku (northeast) region. The Tōhoku region has historically been the most impoverished area of the Japanese mainland, and it is home to local dialects that are difficult or impossible to understand for standard Japanese speakers. Not surprisingly, the prefectures around Tokyo, which constitute suburbs or exurbs of the city, have the lowest sense of local identity. Whereas the city itself harks back to a distinctive history and culture as the shogunal capital, suburbs and exurbs often lack cultural distinctiveness.

The Development of Tourism

Today, tourism dominates the economy of Okinawa Prefecture. Recall also that, ca. 1940, encouraging tourism began to be seriously discussed. The war ended such a possibility, and the Battle of Okinawa left the island devastated. Nearly a decade was required for a tourism industry to emerge, and the currently dominant form of tourism, with its emphasis on beaches and a colorful, exotic Ryukyu Kingdom, developed during the 1980s and especially the 1990s.

After the Battle of Okinawa, there were thousands of corpses strewn across southern Okinawa. As the months and years went by, the flesh rotted away, leaving only bones. Especially in southern Okinawa, human bones were to be found almost everywhere, and the identity of remains was typically unclear. Amid all the difficulties of the immediate postwar era, many people in Okinawa worked diligently to collect those bones and place them in memorial towers (*ireitō*).

Bone-collection campaigns took place during the late 1940s and early 1950s. Later, tree-planting campaigns mobilized local populations to help repair wartime damage to the physical environment. What follows is one person's account of bone collecting:

> Immediately after the end of war, soon after I had moved up to Naha High School, we students carried out bone collection work at Mabuni. With no bus or other transportation networks at the time I don't remember how we got there.... As far as the eye could see it was a treeless stretch of ruins, but the places where kaya and pampas grass were cut had become

FIGURE 20.2. Okinawa tourism in 1963 (Okinawa Prefectural Archives)

conspicuous small heaps of dry bones. After gathering these, we picked up shards of human bones that looked like coral. The buckets were filled in no time at all. (Figal 2012, 30)

During this era, approximately one hundred bone ossuaries of various shapes were constructed and filled in southern Okinawa. One of them, Konpaku-no-tō in Komesu, southern Okinawa, came to house the bones of approximately thirty-five thousand people. This ossuary, along with a memorial to the Himeyuri Corps and one to the Iron and Blood Imperial Corps, became the core of battle-related tourism during the 1950s and 1960s. Initially, tourists were mainly from Okinawa or were US military personnel. Gradually, more tourists from mainland Japan found their way to Okinawa (fig. 20.2).

Memorials for the Iron and Blood Imperial Corps and, separately, the Himeyuri Nursing Corps, each initially founded in 1946 (as was Konpaku-no-tō), became the major early tourist destinations. The Himeyuri memorial and the peace museum adjacent to it became especially well-known because of the poignancy of the tragedy of the nurses who suffered gruesome deaths in the caves at the site.

In addition to these three local memorials, Japan's government maintained an office in Naha from 1952 on. As new remains were found, those clearly identifiable as Japanese were sent to the mainland. Others found their way into the Japanese-government-funded Shikina Central Ossuary, which was formally established in 1957. (Shikina is a suburb of Naha.) In 1961, the Okinawan government established June 22 as the annual battle memorial day (the date was changed to June 23 in 1966). In this way, battle-related tourism gradually developed a seasonal rhythm and came to be centered on several specific sites in southern Okinawa. The general logic behind this is that, because tourism is a peaceful business, it can help heal the wounds of war and inculcate a culture of peace. In this context, the Okinawa Tourism Association, founded in 1954, created a Southern Battle Sites Tour.

Importantly, the existence of a formal tour circuit stimulated improvements to the road network connecting the various sites. As the roads improved, tours began incorporating sites of cultural interest and natural beauty in their circuits. Gradually, tourism took on a mixed quality. The same tour circuit would mix somber wartime sites with pleasant cultural and natural sites. In this context, the myth of Ryukyuan pacifism became especially useful. An emphasis on Okinawa as a place of peace not only in the present and the future but throughout its deeper past as well helped offset the gruesome image of a land soaked in blood and bones.

The major form of battle-site tourism was a bus tour narrated by a trained guide, always a young woman. Gerald Figal characterizes the tour narratives as follows: "Direct records of the actual content of early battlefield tour narratives no longer exist, but indirect accounts suggest that rather than providing nuanced and historically reflective content, they reinforced mainland Japanese expectations of a harrowing but patriotically redeemable story of loyal Okinawan sacrifice in which even schoolgirls from Japan's periphery willingly served and died for the fatherland" (Figal 2012, 44). Later, typically starting in the mid- to late 1980s, battle survivors began to speak out about their experiences and reject this type of narrative.

Mainland Japanese visitors often spoke favorably of the bus tours, but generally they complained about the lodging, the restaurants, and many other aspects of the tourism experience. This criticism, which dovetailed with older notions of Okinawan backwardness, became an impetus to improve all aspects of the island's infrastructure. Both the civilian local government and the USCAR looked favorably on tourism as a way to diversify the economy and reduce economic dependence on the US military presence. However, prior to reversion, a vigorous tourism industry remained out of reach.

One problem was the lack of investment. US investors were skeptical, and hardly anyone in Okinawa was in a position to help. Mainland Japanese investors were prohibited from funding projects in Okinawa by US regulations. Furthermore, tourism centered on battle sites and ossuaries inevitably generated controversy. For example, as some memorial sites improved their facilities, objections arose from those who favored a more solemn or austere approach to sacred sites. For example, one tourist offered the following critique of the practice of local women aggressively selling bouquets of flowers to tourists at the Himeyuri memorial: "First, in front of the Himeyuri-no-tō, when you alight from your vehicle several unsightly girls with flowers in their hands dart over shouting and putting on the hard sell. As friends, they quarrel and compete against each other. It is, you'd agree, a despicable sight. No doubt because it's the tourism business one can't help but to focus on money making, but I thought that rather than being so lewd and conspicuous one would like to do it nowadays in a way that's a little more sensitive to public relations" (Figal 2012, 54). There was no easy solution, however, because many memorial sites were maintained by local volunteers. It was not until 1983 that the Himeyuri memorial created booths for flower vendors and required them to sell only from those booths.

The next major tourism theme to develop was Okinawa as a tropical vacation paradise. Although the idea had long been out there, it was not until after reversion that suitable investment in hotels and other facilities became possible. By the mid-1970s, Okinawa was able to present itself as an easier and lower-cost alternative to Hawaii. Later, after Shuri Castle was rebuilt in the 1990s, and after the "Okinawan diet" became popular, themes like eco-tourism and health tourism merged with images of the Ryukyu Kingdom and tropical Okinawa.

All these things were modern creations, including the positive and colorful way in which the kingdom was presented. Genuine palm trees, for example, are *not* indigenous to Okinawa. It was not until 1962 that over fourteen thousand of them were planted as part of an effort to lay the groundwork for tourism. Palm trees and other tropical foliage is now ubiquitous in areas widely visited by tourists such as Kokusai Dōri (International Street). The introduction of these nonnative species, however, has caused a variety of environmental problems, and their upkeep is a significant expense.

The term *Ryukyu Kingdom* became popular mainly in the context of Okinawan tourism. In large part because the actual kingdom was so oppressive, *Ryukyu Kingdom* has never enjoyed modern popularity in Ryukyu Islands other than Okinawa. The rebuilding of Shuri Castle was done with meticulous attention to detail and, insofar as possible, historical accuracy. I experienced this attention to detail directly on a behind-the-scenes tour and detailed explanation of the site roughly a year before Shurijō Castle Park (as it came to be called) opened. Prior to the October 2019 fire, visitors to Shuri Castle were presented with all manner of historically accurate sights and explanations. What was lacking, however, was a broader context of what the Ryukyu Kingdom actually was: a maritime empire. The Shuri Castle that tourists saw was an idealized image of a happy, prosperous, and peaceful kingdom. Topics like conquest, warfare, taxation, and relations with other Ryukyu Islands were not mentioned. In a recent interview, the Canada-based writer and activist Shō Yamagusiku stated:

> When I hear this origin story about the Ryukyu Kingdom, I often wonder what exactly is a peaceful kingdom? Has there ever been a peaceful kingdom? I'm really curious how we could keep repeating the words peaceful kingdom. I don't know what it means. Perhaps if we were able to acknowledge the perilous lives of overtaxed workers from the Yanbaru, or from Miyako Island during the years of Ryukyu Kingdom into our field of vision, our narrative might change. Perhaps if we could peer into the bedrooms and intimate lives of the men who act as figureheads for the kingdom, this illusion of peace might explode. Until then, we're caught in a fantasy of trying to root ourselves in a narrative of a false, pristine past. (Ueunten 2004, 135)

Shuri Castle is not the only major tourist site connected with the Ryukyu Kingdom. Seifaa utaki, the kingdom's most important religious center, is a massive tourist site, and many tourists also visit Kudakajima, the sacred island across from Seifaa utaki. Throughout Okinawa and the other Ryukyu Islands can be found high-end resorts where well-to-do guests can indulge in tropical-themed relaxation, fine dining, golf, and so forth. Diving, fishing, and related forms of recreation are also a significant part of the tourist industry, especially in the southern Ryukyu Islands. In recent decades, tourists from other parts of Asia—especially China—have become a major presence in Okinawa, along with visitors from the Japanese mainland. The goal at the time of this writing was to have Shuri Castle rebuilt by 2026 (fig. 20.3).

Re/Discovering the Horror of the Battle of Okinawa

Survivors of the mass suicides occasioned by the Battle of Okinawa generally kept quiet about their experiences during the decades immediately after the battle. Without public discussion of such matters in the media, they tended to be isolated. This situation began to change during the mid-1980s, when some members of younger generations sought to find out details about the battle and the experiences of their relatives in it. Especially

Shuri Castle less than a year before it burnt down

FIGURE 20.3. Shuri Castle, December 2018 (photograph by the author)

important in this respect was a convenience store owner (now a Buddhist priest) named Chibana Shōichi (b. 1948).

Chibana began to unravel the story of Chibichirigama Cave, a place where dozens of civilians killed themselves and family members under pressure. The youngest victim was two years old. Chibana's family also owned a small piece of land that became part of a US military base. An avowed pacifist, Chibana became one of the earliest public voices stating that the mass suicides had not been voluntary and highlighting the murder and abuse of civilians by Japanese soldiers during the battle. Similarly, he vigorously opposed the military bases on Okinawa and the Japanese and US governments that kept them in operation. What catapulted him into the public eye in 1987 was his public burning of a Japanese flag during the opening ceremonies at a nationwide athletic event in Okinawa. Flag burning was not a crime per se, but Chibana was charged with destroying municipal property. He attracted considerable attention, much of it negative. For example, arsonists burned down his store. Following his trial for destroying government property, he received a suspended sentence.

Despite Chibana's notoriety in some circles, his activism inspired others to speak up. Moreover, over the years, it became increasingly easy for battle survivors to network. One result was that, starting in the 1990s, the matter of group mass suicide entered local politics. So much evidence has accumulated at this point that it is clear that many or most of the mass suicides were coerced and that the general environment in which they occurred was coercive. Nevertheless, Japan's government continues to maintain that the suicides were voluntary. Chibana and many others would argue that Okinawa has been the victim of both Japanese and US militarism, both in the 1940s and to this day. There are differences in the specific details of proposed remedies for this situation, but most peace activists seek the elimination or major reduction of military bases in Okinawa.

The Continuing Base Problem

Okinawa's reversion to Japanese sovereignty did not significantly change the situation regarding military bases. Protests against the bases continued, often flaring up whenever an aircraft crashed or military personnel committed a heinous crime. One example took place on September 4, 1995. One US sailor and two marines abducted and raped a twelve-year-old schoolgirl. Under the Status of Forces agreement between the United States and Japan, US authorities were not required to turn over the perpetrators to Japanese police. Massive public protests and worldwide media attention, however, did result in the three perpetrators being tried and convicted in a Japanese court and serving their sentences in Japanese prisons.

Despite attempts to rein in criminal behavior, sexual assault has continued as a problem in connection with US bases in Okinawa and elsewhere in East Asia. Periodically, especially severe crimes burst into the media. For example, in 2016, Kenneth Franklin Gadson (also known as Kenneth Shinzato), a former marine who was working as a civilian base employee, brutally murdered a twenty-year-old woman. In addition to widespread protests, Japan's prime minister issued a formal complaint, and President Obama issued an apology in response.

When US personnel commit serious crimes, the Japanese police and courts now typically handle their cases. Nevertheless, the concentration of military bases in Okinawa continues to pose crime, environmental, and other hazards to the island's residents. There have been many calls to redistribute the US military presence more evenly throughout Japan and to make greater use of territories like Guam as locations for military facilities. Creating new bases, closing existing ones, and moving military facilities and personnel around would be a costly and difficult undertaking. Moreover, it is unlikely that any locality in Japan would welcome a new military base. For these reasons, it is unlikely that those in power will try hard to change the status quo.

Moreover, China's increasingly aggressive posture vis-à-vis Japan in general and the Ryukyu Islands in particular has further complicated the base issue. While acknowledging base-related problems, increasing numbers of

Ryukyu Island residents have begun to look favorably on a strong military presence in the islands. The outbreak of war in Ukraine in February 2022, the increasing severity of Chinese threats vis-à-vis Taiwan, and claims by both China and Taiwan that the Ryukyu Islands are Chinese territory have been especially concerning to residents of the southern Ryukyu Islands.

Contemporary Misunderstandings Revisited

The Ryukyu Islands are of great strategic importance owing to their location. Just as the islands were an ideal abode for pirates in the fourteenth and fifteenth centuries, they would probably play a key role in likely future military scenarios within the region. The security of the Ryukyu Islands depends, for the most part, on decisions made in Tokyo. Nevertheless, attitudes in several other countries are relevant. Therefore, it is useful briefly to revisit the list of common misunderstandings about the Ryukyu Islands found in this book's introduction. By *misunderstandings*, I am referring not so much to questions of active academic debate (e.g., was the early Ryukyuan state built on agricultural surpluses?) as to matters about which there is widespread agreement among the relevant academic specialists. However, item 11 is a possible exception because the status of Okinawa within Japan's empire remains an actively debated question.

1. *The modern population of the Ryukyu Islands, people we could reasonably call "Ryukyuans," are descendants of a single, unbroken line of settlers who have resided in the islands since the Stone Age.* Even a cursory reading of the early chapters of this book indicates that the Ryukyu Islands were home to a variety of Paleolithic and Neolithic peoples who are no longer extant. The most important population changeover occurred during the eleventh and twelfth centuries, when Japonic peoples replaced the previous Jōmon population. Even after this time, there was a significant influx of people from Korea and newer groups from Japan as well as a few Mongols and Alans. This deeper history complicates the narrative of certain social activists who claim that there exists today a group of people that we could reasonably describe as *indigenous Ryukyuans*.

2. *The historical Ryukyu Islands constituted a natural, unified political community.* As noted in earlier chapters, the Ryukyu Islands are located within a continuum of Japonic cultures. Nevertheless, each major group of the

Ryukyu Islands—the northern tier islands, Okinawa and nearby islands, the Miyako Islands, and the Yaeyama Islands—is distinct from each other culturally and linguistically. Prior to conquest by Shuri in the early sixteenth century, these places were not part of the same political state. Much of the cultural distinctiveness within the Ryukyu Islands now survives only in museums or via other forms of preservation. Modern culture and media have exerted a strong homogenizing effect on the entire Japanese archipelago from Hokkaidō to Yonaguni.

3. *Throughout most of their history, the Ryukyu Islands were isolated.* As a result of Satsuma's policies following the 1609 war, the Ryukyu Islands became relatively isolated from about the 1620s through the 1880s. Otherwise, throughout most of their premodern history, they functioned as a frontier region, mainly vis-à-vis Japan, but also Korea and other parts of the East China Sea region.

4. *Ryukyuan culture and history started in Okinawa.* The history of the Japonic Ryukyu Islands began in Kikaijima at some point in the eleventh century and spread south. Before then, diverse groups of non-Japonic people lived in different islands at different times. Okinawa came to dominate the other islands during the thirteenth century, and, when the royal court began producing official histories in the seventeenth century, Okinawa dominated the narrative. Modern archaeology, however, has revealed a very different narrative of the deep past.

5. *Ryukyuan culture is, to a large extent, a blend of Chinese and Japanese elements.* An extreme version of this misconception is that Ryukyuan culture is mainly Sinitic. As we have seen, the various Ryukyuan cultures are Japonic, but there is some important Korean influence in the mix. Chinese cultural influences are much more recent in time and affected mainly a narrow segment of the population, mostly Kumemura elites. Because of geographic proximity, a few aspects of southeastern Chinese popular culture, mostly connected with popular religion, took root in the Ryukyu Islands.

6. *Participation in the Chinese tributary system during the Ming and Qing dynasties meant that the Ryukyu Islands were Chinese territory.* Recall that tributary states ritually acknowledged Chinese cultural superiority in return for

formal recognition and preferred trade status. None of them, however, were Chinese territory, and only in rare instances (e.g., Korea in the 1590s) did China ever intervene in their affairs. The common tendency among Anglophone writers to describe China as Ryukyu's *suzerain* is not historically accurate.[1] In the case of the Ryukyu Islands, participation in the tribute trade began as a policy to buy off pirates. During the early modern era, tributary relations were closely linked with Ryukyu as a theatrical state. Korea sent more tribute embassies to China than did any other country, but nobody seriously claims that Korea was Chinese territory as a result.

Of course, alleged historical claims on another country's territory are often facades for economic and military power. That is the case in the increasingly strident claims coming from China to the effect that, given their history, the Ryukyu Islands should be Chinese territory (see, e.g., McCurry 2013).[2]

7. *Prior to 1879, the Ryukyu Islands were an independent kingdom.* The precise start date for a Ryukyuan state is difficult to pin down, but Shuri's 1500 invasion of Yaeyama would be close. Shuri's thorough defeat by Satsuma in 1609 brought this state to an end as an independent entity. If one were to get into the weeds, a case could be made that the Ryukyuan Empire lost its independence during the 1570s, and we know that Toyotomi Hideyoshi regarded Ryukyu as his own territory. In any case, an independent Ryukyu Kingdom existed only relatively briefly. By 1609, if not earlier, that independence came to an end. The Ryukyu Islands became part of Satsuma's territory as per the surrender documents, *bakufu* recognition and policy, and Satsuma's governance and policies. One other important point to bear in mind is that the rise of an independent Ryukyuan state in the early sixteenth century occurred at the expense of the independence of various geopolitical communities throughout the Ryukyu Islands as Shuri conquered them.

Nevertheless, journalists and even some scholars frequently misunderstand this matter. For example, in an otherwise insightful piece, the historian A. A. Bastian states: "The independent Ryukyu Kingdom was taken over by Japan in the 19th century" (Bastian 2023). My point here is not so much to criticize specific individuals as to note the very shallow understanding of Ryukyuan history that often surrounds contemporary geopolitical discussions.

8. *The Ryukyu Kingdom developed independently of Japan.* Japonic Ryukyu and the state that eventually developed there were closely connected with Japan in almost every important respect.

9. *The Ryukyu Kingdom was a benevolent organization, and the Ryukyu Islands were a rare example in world history of a pacifist society without wars, weapons, or punitive coercion.* The myth of Ryukyuan pacifism remains potent today in some circles. It is an appealing notion, but there is no evidentiary basis for it.

10. *Most residents of the Ryukyu Islands opposed formal incorporation into Japan during the 1870s and 1880s.* By the 1870s, the Ryukyu Kingdom had become economically a de facto failed state with virtually no popular support. Those who opposed Tokyo's moves were officials of the kingdom trying to preserve their privileges and status. The success of the *kyūkan-onzon* policy in gaining their cooperation indicates the motives of these former royal officials. There was no popular resistance to the creation of Okinawa Prefecture.

11. *The Ryukyu Islands were a colony of Japan.* In the context of the 1880s and the *kyūkan-onzon* policy, I wrote in my first book: "Japanese actions within the new prefecture similarly indicate a de facto status more like a colony or conquered territory than an integral part of the motherland" (Smits 1999, 146). Looking only at the period from the 1880s to about 1903, such a view might be sustainable. Moreover, Tokyo's central government has at various points in the past regarded the Ryukyu Islands as expendable, for example, in the early 1950s, when the Shōwa emperor (Hirohito) agreed to continued US military administration of the islands in return for ending the occupation of the rest of Japan sooner. The Meiji state and subsequent iterations of Japan's central government can and should be criticized for policies (and inaction) that caused great suffering among residents of the Ryukyu Islands. Nevertheless, Okinawa Prefecture was fundamentally different from colonies such as Korea and Taiwan, and continuation of the kingdom was not a viable option ca. 1879. Without trying to coin a new word, I would say that, during the *kyūkan-onzon* era, the central government treated Okinawa Prefecture as a *quasi colony*, mainly owing to a lack of resources.

12. *Many or most contemporary residents of the Ryukyu Islands are conflicted about their identity.* Personal identity is typically a multifaceted construct, and people throughout the Japanese islands—indeed, throughout the world—combine local and national identities. While there will always be some individuals who experience identity conflicts, the vast majority of residents of the Ryukyu Islands unproblematically regard themselves as

Japanese, and many of those people also embrace local identities. Local and national identities existed in a severe state of tension during the late nineteenth century and the early twentieth, but that situation no longer obtains.

Present and Future Challenges

Okinawa Prefecture faces significant challenges going forward, perhaps most prominently with respect to the local economy, the geopolitical and military situation, and environmental degradation. In this section, I touch on each.

THE LOCAL ECONOMY

In the immediate postwar era, US military bases and related institutions constituted the majority of economic activity. Over time, base-related income has declined steadily to the present level of about 5 percent. Recently, there has been some downsizing of the bases, at least in terms of surface area. For example, the Aeon Mall Okinawa Rycom shopping center in Kitanakagusuku was built in 2015 on land that was formerly a golf course for the use of US personnel exclusively. Assuming that the current Futenma Air Station is returned to Okinawa as promised, some estimates are that it could be transformed into enterprises that will employ some thirty thousand people.

Public works and tourism are the foundations of Okinawa Prefecture's current economy. Tourism accounts for the vast majority of economic activity and about 26 percent of the prefecture's GDP. Public works account for about 13 percent of GDP. Defined broadly, agriculture is roughly 8–9 percent, with the major products being sugarcane, pineapples, orchids, cut flowers, and goya (*nigauri*, "bitter melon"). Manufacturing accounts for about 4 percent. Regarding tourism: "The number of visitors to Okinawa was only 440,000 per year at the time of reversion in 1972. However, visitor numbers grew steadily, passing 5 million in 2003, and then reached the 10 million mark in 2019. Naha's main street, Kokusai Dōri, overflowed with foreign tourists as more than 3 million people a year came from neighboring countries like China, Taiwan, and South Korea" (Karube 2022). COVID-19 dealt a severe blow to the tourist sector of the economy, but all estimates are that it will recover quickly. Despite an upsurge in visitors from nearby countries, approximately 70 percent of tourists are domestic.

Okinawa's tourism industry is robust, at least under normal conditions, but service work such as tourism is not the ideal basis for a thriving economy. Per capita income in Okinawa is the lowest of Japan's forty-seven prefectures. And the main reason is not unemployment, although unemployment in Okinawa is often slightly higher than the Japan-wide average. Underemployment and low wages are larger factors. Okinawan Prefecture also has the lowest rate of university enrollment in Japan. Recall that, in the 1920s and 1930s, the local economy was overly dependent on sugar. Today it is arguably overly dependent on domestic tourism and, therefore, would benefit from diversification.

The prefecture's website lists five strategies meant to spur future economic growth (as of this writing). In one way or another, they take advantage of Okinawa's location. One strategy is to make Okinawa a "world-class" tourist destination, that is, upgrading the tourist industry and attracting a wider array of international tourists. Another is to make the prefecture into an international logistics center "linking Asia." One concrete manifestation was the construction of a second runway at Naha airport, completed in March 2020. Similarly, a third strategy is to promote manufacturing industries that "connect Okinawa to Asia." Moreover, Okinawa could serve as an international telecommunications center.[3] These vaguely stated strategies have a sensible ring to them, but concrete implementation will be a challenge.

One other initiative involves the island of Iriomote in the Yaeyama Islands and the large Yanbaru region of northern Okinawa. Both these regions are in relatively pristine condition and constitute distinctive ecosystems with high levels of biodiversity. In coordination with Tokyo, these places, along with Amami-Ōshima and Tokunoshima in the northern Ryukyu Islands, were registered as UNESCO World Natural Heritage sites in July 2021.[4] Among other things, this move is likely to enhance ecotourism.

GEOPOLITICAL CONCERNS

The main geopolitical challenge for the Ryukyu Islands—and, therefore, for Japan as a whole—is dealing with an increasingly powerful and assertive China. During the twenty-first century, China has pursued an increasingly aggressive policy in several maritime regions. It has vigorously laid claim to the Senkaku Islands (Ch. Diàoyúdǎo), a group of small, uninhabited islands near the Ryukyus that are under Japanese administration. These islands, which are little more than large rocks, served historically as navigational aids. Therefore, they have long appeared in old maps from Japan, China, and the Ryukyu Islands. It is mainly these old maps that each side uses selectively to claim proof of ownership.

As we have seen, there is a strong consensus within China that the Ryukyu Islands were once Chinese territory and, therefore, should not be part of Japan. However, a more concrete or immediate danger is connected with Chinese strategic planning and execution. The details of this matter are potentially very complex. Simply stated, however, a major plank of Chinese maritime defense strategy is to use a blue water navy to hold off potential aggressors before they can reach or inflict serious damage on China. To accomplish such a defense would require China's navy to get beyond what it calls *the first island chain* (*dìyī dǎoliàn*): Borneo, the Philippines, Taiwan, the Ryukyu Islands, and the main Japanese islands.

Pursuant to this strategy, China has built a large blue water navy and has practiced sending flotillas of ships through the Miyako Straits (Kerama Gap), the relatively wide and deep expanse of ocean between Okinawa and the Miyako Islands. These straights are also a likely transit zone for submarines. Japan's response has been a somewhat belated effort to fortify the Ryukyu Islands in such a way that they could provide an early warning in the event of military conflict with China and deny the passage of ships using mobile batteries of antiship missiles, among other measures. In addition to already-existing facilities on Okinawa, Japanese forces have established a major presence in Amami-Ōshima and the southern Ryukyu Islands.

Reaction among island residents has been mixed. On the one hand, there is widespread agreement that the potential for conflict with China is a major issue, and impressions of China in Okinawa Prefecture are even less favorable than they are in Japan as a whole. According to 2013 survey data, 89 percent of the residents of Okinawa Prefecture viewed China unfavorably or somewhat unfavorably, compared with 84.3 percent nationwide. Conversely, only 9.1 percent of Okinawa Prefecture residents reported favorable or somewhat favorable views of China, compared with 15.6 percent nationwide (see Nagamoto 2013). The war in Ukraine and China's increasingly aggressive posture vis-à-vis Taiwan has had an especially strong impact on public opinion in the Ryukyu Islands. As of this writing, public opinion appears to be shifting toward supporting a stronger defense posture vis-à-vis China and reduced opposition to the presence of US and Japanese Self-Defense Force bases.

In response to the situation in Ukraine and Taiwan, Japan has embarked on an ambitious military buildup across the board, spelled out in detail in the white paper *Defense of Japan* (2024).[5] One phrase that comes up constantly is Japan's opposition to any "change in the status quo by coercion." Many residents of the Ryukyu Islands welcome the protection and deterrence that the new military facilities and capabilities will provide. Others see the situation more ominously—as making their islands prime targets in a future war. Tensions between Japan and China are unlikely to abate in the near future, especially if China continues to threaten Taiwan militarily.

ENVIRONMENTAL CHALLENGES

The biodiverse ecosystems of the Ryukyu Islands, including the extensive coral reefs, have come under threat from pollution, construction, tourism, the introduction of alien species, deforestation, and other sources. The massive tourist industry, which will become even larger if current plans are realized, is generally detrimental to the natural environment even though the natural environment is precisely the appeal to most tourists. Tourism-related environmental harms include the destruction of coral reefs by trampling or even poisoning the water via sunscreen products containing oxybenzone, the generation of trash, and the vastly increased per capita per capita use of fresh water, in addition to the construction of resort facilities. Because public transportation options are limited, tourists typically rent cars, thus contributing to traffic and pollution.

Although military bases have become a small component of the overall economy, they contribute massively to environmental degradation. Toxic spills are especially problematic, and there have been well over four hundred since 1998. Leaked agents include diesel fuel, untreated or poorly treated sewage, and even Vietnam War Era agent orange leaking from buried barrels. Perhaps the most well-known base-related environmental issue is the construction of a massive heliport in Henoko, along the coast of northeast Okinawa adjacent to Camp Schwab, to replace the air base at Futenma.

Henoko heliport construction has been beset by cost overruns, administrative problems, unexpected engineering challenges, and, most importantly, fierce opposition from local populations and many local governments. Constructing the heliport requires the dumping of large quantities of sand and gravel to reclaim land from the sea, construction of a massive seawall, and widespread destruction of coral reefs. Unforeseen negative consequences of this construction are likely. There is a mangrove ecosystem nearby that is home to dugongs, an endangered marine mammal. According to some reports, dugong sightings in the area have become rare since the seawall was constructed in 2015. Despite extensive, ongoing protests, the project slogs ahead, with an estimated completion date of 2040 as of this writing.

Some of the environmental threats to the Ryukyu Islands are the result of worldwide phenomena. Microplastics, for example, have worked their way into the local marine ecosystems, as they have throughout much of the world. This brief survey touches on only the major challenges concerning the natural environment that will have to be addressed if the Ryukyu Islands are to remain both a major tourist destination and a viable place to live for current and future residents.

Throughout their human history, the Ryukyu Islands have functioned as conduits through which people, culture, technologies, and products have passed. During much of this time, the islands functioned to connect states of the East China Sea—Korea, Japan, and China—plus parts of Southeast Asia. The volume of flow varied with time and circumstances. During the fourteenth and fifteenth centuries, for example, vigorous exchanges took place throughout the East China Sea region and beyond via the Ryukyu Islands. During the seventeenth and eighteenth centuries, by contrast, the islands were relatively isolated, although goods, technologies, and ideas continued to flow through them in exchanges between China and Japan. During the modern era, worldwide forces such as the fluctuating price of sugar or the tides of war had a profound impact on the islands. In recent decades, local governments in the islands have sought to reestablish to some degree the role of the Ryukyu Islands as a regional hub for the transmission of people, goods, and information.

Acknowledgments

It is a pleasure to thank the people who have contributed to this book. As with my previous books, I start by acknowledging Penn State University's superb interlibrary loan staff, who reached out all over the world to obtain material.

I spent spring semester 2022 at the University of Hawai'i at Manoa (UHM) as the Arthur Lynn Andrews Visiting Professor in Asian Studies. I thank Masato Ishida, then the director of the Center for Okinawan Studies, for bringing me to UHM and the faculty and staff of the Department of Asian Studies and Center for Okinawan Studies for making me welcome. This book benefited from access to UHM library resources and discussions with faculty and students. I used early drafts of some of the chapters as material for an undergraduate course on the Ryukyu Islands at UHM. In Honolulu, it was a pleasure to work with my longtime friend Shari Tamashiro, who has worked tirelessly to promote and preserve local culture. Shari also kindly provided one of the images for this book.

While in Honolulu, I discussed the general idea for this book with James Millward, the editor of the Silk Roads series at the University of Chicago Press. It has been a pleasure working with Jim and my acquiring editor, Dylan Montanari. Senior editorial assistant Fabiola Enríquez helped me with the preparation of the final manuscript and other logistics. Assistant managing editor Christine Schwab oversaw much of the production process, and Joseph Brown copyedited the manuscript.

I have benefited from comments and questions from and discussions with scholars in the aftermath of the publication of *Maritime Ryukyu* in 2019. These scholars include Fabian Drixler, Gerald Figal, Mark Hudson, Bob Huey, Thomas Monaghan, Scott O'Bryan, Morten Oxenboell, Len Schoppa, Timon Screech, Travis Seifman, Nozomi Tanaka, Marco Tinello, Watanabe Miki, and Yoshinari Naoki, among others. Two anonymous readers for the press provided a variety of useful ideas for improving the manuscript. Needless to say, any remaining shortcomings are entirely my own.

My early academic career, culminating in my first book, benefited tremendously from the published work of many Japanese scholars and, in some cases, from their active support and assistance. The list of such scholars is long, but I would especially like to thank Tomiyama Kazuyuki and Takara Kurayoshi. Moreover, the economist Kyan Shinichi, the bookstore owner and Yōju shorin publisher Takeishi Kazumi, the multidisciplinary scholar Josef Kreiner, and the historian Maeda Shūko have also provided extensive support and assistance at different times, for which I am grateful.

Although they are not direct contributors to this book, I am always grateful to my network of music friends for helping maintain well-being. Also, in recent years my wife, Akiko, became interested in the history and culture of the Ryukyu Islands. She has sent me useful video links and book references and read an earlier version of this manuscript.

Notes

CHAPTER TWO

1. Jōmon is also a concept that has undergone significant transformations in modern Japanese society. For a rigorous yet accessible analysis, see Hudson (2022b).

2. Other names include *ube, mizuimo, purple yam, water yam, violet yam,* and *greater yam.*

3. Dazaifu was a branch of the Japanese court located in Kyushu, slightly inland from Hakata. From the eighth century to the twelfth, it functioned as the formal government of Kyushu and some surrounding territory, including at times Kikaijima.

CHAPTER THREE

1. Citations indicate the chapter number followed by the song number, and there is no variation in the chapter and song numbers and the song content in the extant *Omoro.*

CHAPTER FIVE

1. https://www.merriam-webster.com/dictionary/king (accessed August 4, 2024).

2. There was no Japanese title at this time that is typically translated as *king* in an Okinawan context. The most common term in Japanese to refer to a local Ryukyuan ruler, warlord, or strongman during the fourteenth and fifteenth centuries was *yono-nushi* (ruler or lord).

3. They include Asato Susumu (2010), Yoshinari Naoki (2020, 49–72), Kurima Yasuo (2013, 2:235–49), and Tomiyama Kazuyuki (2003, 77–81).

4. The collection of trade-related documents known as *Rekidai hōan* includes some items from the fourteenth century, but Chinese merchant-officials residing in Naha produced those documents.

5. *Omoro sōshi*, 14-982, is about Janamoi ("the beloved one of Jana"), portraying him as a magnificent person who has opened up the storehouses of the many lords. Because the official histories claim that Satto was born in Jana, this Janamoi is conventionally regarded as Satto. It is possible that this passage is a reference to Satto initiating the tribute trade, but Jana and Satto may not have been the same person.

6. There are several possible Okinawan pronunciations of Eiso's name: "Iizu," "Izu," "Ueezu," "Eezu," and "Eesu." In the *Omoro*, *Eiso* appears as *Iizu* or, more often, as *Iizu-niya* (person of Iizu).

428 ‹ NOTES TO PAGES 108–121

7. In one repeated song, Iizu is described as a capable warrior who drinks different types of wine in both the summer and the winter (i.e., year-round). The wine reference emphasizes that Iizu is prosperous and wealthy. The second instance of the same song is immediately preceded by three *omoro* praising "Iizu gusuku," another indication that Iizu (Iso) Fortress, not Urasoe Castle, was Eiso/Iizu's base (*Omoro sōshi*, 12-671, 15-1066–69). According to legends in the Urasoe area, Eiso's father and other forebears were based at Iizu Fortress, and Eiso was born there.

8. The last known member of the group, Onsado, appears in *Joseon Veritable Royal Records* in an entry dated 1398. Some scholars regard Onsado as a variant spelling of Shōsatto. In any case, according to the story, Onsado had been the Sannan king, but he and fifteen members of his group fled to Korea. They received support from the Korean government, but Onsado died in the tenth month of that year. The key points for our purposes are the close connection that the Satto group had with Korea and the group's vanishing from Okinawa by 1398.

9. In 1405, e.g., four different tribute embassies arrived, one under the name of Han'anchi of Sanhoku, one under the name of Ōōso of Sannan, and two under the name of Bunei of Chūzan. The two from Bunei arrived only a month apart.

10. A tribute embassy in Satto's name was sent in 1403, but nearly all scholars of this era agree that, assuming that Satto was an actual person (unlikely in my view), then he died in 1398 at the latest (more likely in 1395). It was common practice to use the names of trade kings as long as a decade after their (apparent) death. For example, the last shipment sent under the name of Han'anchi of Sanhoku was in 1406. Afterward, almost a decade passed with no mention of Sanhoku or Han'anchi. Then, in 1415, Han'anchi appears in a terse entry as having sent an envoy to China along with Shō Shishō of Chūzan.

11. The relationship between Nakijin and other powers in northern Okinawa, if any, during the Sanzan Era is unclear. For example, after the fall of Nakijin, Nago gusuku, twelve kilometers away as the crow flies, does not appear to have undergone any change (Higa 2006, 150).

CHAPTER SIX

1. *Reflections on Chūzan* mentions Shishō only once, in the context of listing Hashi's father. The brief paragraph on Shishō in the 1701 *Genealogy* is mostly about Hashi and the envoys sent to China during Shishō's reign. The 1725 version of *Genealogy* contains a substantive chapter on Shishō. It identifies his father as Lord Samekawa but otherwise cribs from the Ming records regarding tribute embassies and other details about the various kings of that era as well as Hashi's activities. In other words, Shō Shishō functioned like his predecessors, as a banner under which Okinawan entities conducted the tribute trade. Otherwise, we have no indication of anything specific that he did.

2. Following a long line of scholars, I argue in *Maritime Ryukyu* that the Samekawa group was made up of seafarers or *wakō* who were associated the southern court in Kyushu migrated to Okinawa in the late fourteenth century (see Smits 2019, 107–10). For all the details, see Tanigawa and Orikuchi (2012). One indication of the close connections between Okinawa and the Yatsushiro area is the frequent mention of "Yashiro" in the *Omoro sōshi*, which I argue is Yatsushiro in Kyushu (Smits 2019, 31–32, 53, 73–74, 108, 258 n. 72).

3. In addition to the Yaeyama invasion of 1500, additional military action in the early sixteenth century eliminated Nakasone in Miyako and led to Shuri's conquest of Yonaguni.

4. The *hiki* system emerged during the reign of Shō Shin. It was meant to bring together groups of people to function as a military force and to perform public works.

5. For other examples, see Smits (2019, 97, 125–26).

CHAPTER SEVEN

1. In 1909 and 1943, the modern Japanese state attempted to make Ryukyuan groves into shrines. Although few full conversions took place, some groves were outfitted with shrine gateways (torii) as a result. Such groves are especially common in the southern Ryukyu Islands. There are eight major Shinto shrines in Okinawa, but they are unconnected with sacred groves.

2. For details about other cultural commonalities, see Smits (2019, esp. 25–59).

3. The *shigechi* groves of Tsushima are related to the shamanic trances of Tokara Islands priestesses. These trances are known as *shike*. Some *Omoro sōshi* songs describe Ryukyuan priestesses entering shamanic trances in "*shike* spaces."

4. During the Joseon Era (1392–1897), Confucian officials regarded worship at groves led by women as a debased form of religion. In 1702, e.g., the Korean court dispatched officials who destroyed sacred groves and Buddhist temples in 130 locations. Some four hundred priestesses and shamans were punished and forced to return to farming. The 1970 New Village Movement, infrastructure modernization, and the spread of Christianity also reduced the number of groves and, in many cases, altered their ostensible purpose.

5. Japan was, however, the source of a different type of Ryukyuan fortress (also called *gusuku*), one that featured earthworks and trenches for defense. Shō Hashi's fortress at Sashiki was of this type, as were many fortresses in northern Okinawa and the northern Ryukyu Islands.

6. "Archeologically, Chinese fortresses have several features. . . . (1) The cities were established on plains near rivers or streams. (2) The cities were virtually surrounded by walls. (3) The walls of the cities were made by the stamped earth method. (4) Almost all the cities were made in the shape of a square or rectangle, but a few of them did not have a regular shape. (5) Palaces and graves were built in the cities based on their belief of directions, considering the meridian line from north to south. (6) Earthen altars and great graves were politically or traditionally the most important constructions, so they were made to attract the eye. (7) Chinese people made special areas in the shape of a square in every city, which has not changed" (Korea Fortress Academy 2008a, 33). None of these characteristics apply to *gusuku* or to mountain fortresses.

7. These sites are Nakijin-jō, Zakimi-jō, Katsuren-jō, Nakagusuki-jō, and Shuri-jō (*-jō* is the Japanese suffix for *castle*).

8. The design of battlements, flanking towers (O. *azama*), and eyebrow-like overhanging stones in the walls of *gusuku* closely match the construction found in Korean castles. Many Korean fortresses are made of uncut naturally occurring stones. The same construction is found in much of Nakijin gusuku, Tamagusuku gusuku, and portions of the first enclosure wall of Nakagusuku gusuku. Other mountain fortress walls are made from well-fitted cut stones. Okinawan examples of the same include portions of the first

enclosure of Nakagusuku gusuku, portions of Itokazu gusuku, and Katsuren gusuku. Also common are walls from cut stone of similar shape, tightly stacked. Okinawan examples include the third enclosure wall of Nakagusuku gusuku and portions of Zakimi gusuku.

9. *Manyōshū* (Collection of ten thousand leaves) is the oldest extant collection of Japanese poetry in classical Japanese. Most of the poems in it were composed between 600 and 759. The entire collection, therefore, came together at some point after 759.

10. Iha's point is insightful, although we have no concrete evidence that the early modern government tried to suppress the *Omoro*. Also, it is quite possible that, by the eighteenth century, few government officials or other members of elite society would have understood most of its content.

11. Gosamaru's favorable portrayal in the official histories was probably the result of his early modern descendants working to rehabilitate his image.

12. The only inanimate objects the *Omoro* modifies with the adjective *kikoe* (re-sounding, acclaimed) are the sword Tsukushi-chara (regarded by many *Omoro* scholars as an alternative name for Teganemaru) and turbo shells, the source of the mother-of-pearl from which the ladle was made.

13. Silla's Ryeongchwisa, a Buddhist temple with shamanic origins. Among other functions, this temple symbolized royal authority and guarded sea-lanes.

14. In other contexts, glossed with different Chinese characters, *shikechi* can mean "*shike* space," i.e., the space in which a trance takes place.

CHAPTER EIGHT

1. Kimitezuri is a religious ritual, not a solar deity, but Shō Shōken was apparently confused about certain religious details.

2. *Omoro sōshi*, 22-1554, and part of 12-662. Both songs refer to the dancing of Shō En's daughter, so the point of the song in the context of this passage in *Reflections* is unclear.

3. Benzai is often depicted as a woman.

4. The male counterpart of the thirty-three great priestesses during Shō Shin's time was the *satonushi*, lit. "village lord." Despite the literal meaning of the title, initially these officials oversaw large territories such as harbors or districts. The *satonushi* of Shō Shin's era became the *jitō* (district-level administrators) of the early modern era. At least in terms of function, early *satonushi* overlapped with powerful local rulers (*aji*).

5. *Reflections on Chūzan* includes a dialogue in which Shō Sei declares that his older brother, Prince Urasoe (Shō Ikō), is blameless. In accord with heavenly principles, therefore, Prince Urasoe should become king. Shō Ikō responded by declaring himself morally corrupt and stating that following his father's orders is the way of the ancient sages. The virtuous Shō Sei must therefore become king. Throughout *Reflections*, Shō Shōken tended to overplay classical Chinese tropes concerning virtue. Sai On's 1725 *Genealogy of Chūzan* sensibly contains no such dialogue drawing attention to the royal rift.

6. The basic meaning of *Kawara* is "head" or "chief." It is a variety of what I have called *Gaara group names*, which, throughout the Ryukyu Islands, indicate *wakō* (see Smits 2019, 101–3, 125–26).

7. The language of the main record is classical Chinese, and the term for the monarch here is *tiānzǐ* (J. *tenshi*), "son of heaven." There are numerous ways that Amami-Ōshima household records refer to the king in Shuri, but it was not unusual for his title to be some variation of *emperor*.

CHAPTER NINE

1. These 1556 pirates were the latter-period *wakō*, who consisted mainly of Chinese and Japanese, with representatives of a few other ethnic groups in the mix.

2. Recall that this term appears erroneously in *Reflections on Chūzan* as the name of a deity in connection with Shō Sen'i's ill-fated enthronement ceremonies.

3. For details, see Smits (2019, 60–61, 67–69, 134–36).

4. For details on the complexities of maritime trade between China, Korea, certain powers in Japan such as the Ōuchi, and Ryukyu, see Conlan (2024).

5. Note that the members of Chinese investiture embassies were not paid wages for their trip to Okinawa. Their ability to turn a profit depended on the sale of the goods they brought along.

6. This section and the next are summaries of portions of the second half of Yoshinari (2018).

7. *Niraikanai* corresponds to Tokoyo-no-Kuni (常世の国) in ancient Japanese sources like *Kojiki* and *Nihonshoki*.

CHAPTER TEN

1. As of this writing, the most thorough discussion of European sources for sixteenth-century Ryukyuan history is Nakajima (2020).

2. Shō Shōken stressed this point in his introduction to *Reflections on Chūzan*, most likely as a way of pushing back against Satsuma's claim of its having had a long and close relationship with the Ryukyu Islands.

3. Ryukyuan officials stated in their defense that "everyone agreed" that this first mate deserved to be beheaded, but they offered no further details.

4. Amami-Ōshima possessed timber and certain valuable metals (mines operated into the twentieth century). Later, in the nineteenth century, it became a major producer of sugar, as we will see.

5. For his part, Jana Ueekata sent a secret message to the Ming court via Chinese in Nagasaki. The Ryukyuan official Ikegusuku Anrai heard of the matter and had the letter intercepted. Had he not done so, the letter probably would have inflamed Ming antagonism toward Japan and delayed the normalization of tribute relations.

CHAPTER ELEVEN

1. Elite Ryukyuans of this era might be known by their formal titles, their Chinese-style names, their local names, their pen names, their nicknames, etc. Moreover, different pronunciations of the same name are possible, and sometimes we do not know exactly how people of the past would have pronounced their names. Shō Shōken, for example, is sometimes rendered Shō Zōken or Shō Jōken. In some modern library catalogs, his name is rendered Kō Shōken. Why Kō? Because 向 is read *kō*, not *shō*, in the Japanese *on-yomi*. However, in this case, 向 is actually 尚 (Shō) with two strokes at the top removed. Prince Haneji was a member of the royal family but far enough removed from the main royal line that custom required removing the two strokes as a sign of humility.

2. In the variety of Okinawan spoken in the Shuri area, the most common term for Japan as a whole is *Ufu-Yamaatu* (J. *Ō-Yamato*), "great Yamato."

3. For more details, see "Parades and Processions of Edo, Japan," University of Hawai'i at Manoa Libraries, 2013, https://hdl.handle.net/10125/26736.

4. There is also an imbalance in the academic literature in English, with much of it focusing on Ryukyuan-Chinese relations (e.g., Akamine 2017; and Smits 1999). One reason is pragmatic. Documentary sources about relations between China and Ryukyu from the seventeenth century on are plentiful.

5. In the Ryukyu Islands and Japan, it was customary for children to go by one name until turning fifteen and becoming an adult and them receiving another. The childhood name might carry forward past age fifteen as a term of endearment.

6. For example, they might be tasked with reporting back on certain conditions in China or the details of Chinese weapons or with purchasing certain items that Satsuma's officials thought would sell well in Japan.

7. Tamagusuku Chōkun created *kumiodori*, a dramatic art form intended for the entertainment of Chinese investiture envoys and their entourage.

8. In traditional Ryukyuan lore, probably of Korean origin, noble bones attract rain. Therefore, it was common for people to construct tombs under the raised area where official prayers for rain took place. Sai On regarded such ideas and even the practice of praying for rain itself as baseless superstitions. Even among elites, however, such a degree of secular rationalism appears to have been uncommon.

9. For a detailed analysis of these matters, see Smits (2024, 137–55).

10. The construction of smaller dug-out boats, known as *sabani* and by other terms, never stopped.

11. Some scholars have convincingly argued that the term *Confucianism* is vague and overly used as an explanatory device. I find this argument persuasive in many contexts, but for simplicity I stick with typical terminology in these pages.

12. In his academic essays, Sai On denied that prayers for rain actually produce rain. Nevertheless, he justified the practice as "expedient means" (*ken*, 権) to set the minds of the common people at ease by a royal display of concern, i.e., the prayer ceremony, during a drought.

13. Zhèng Jīng was the son of and the successor to the relatively well-known Chinese pirate leader Zhèng Chénggōng (Koxinga).

14. Although obviously a cognate word, the Okinawan *sessei* should not be confused with the *sesshō* of *sesshō-kanpaku* (Fujiwara guardian/regent for an emperor, 摂政関白) of Japan's Heian period.

15. *Ukon* (鬱金), used as a dye, a spice, and a medicine.

16. For examples, see Gramlich-Oka and Smits (2010).

17. Examples include small dried fish, dried abalone, shark fin, kelp, dried squid, and agar-containing seaweed.

CHAPTER TWELVE

1. The situation was somewhat more complex in practice because it was not easy or even possible for Satsuma to sever the many cultural ties between the northern Ryukyu Islands and Okinawa. For example, the king in Shuri continued to preside over the appointment of priestesses for the northern islands into the eighteenth century.

2. The vertical threads (*tateito*, 縦糸) and the horizontal threads (*yokoito*, 横糸) of woven textiles, a typical tax imposed on women.

3. From *A Dialogue among Three Birds* (*Sanchō mondō* or *Sanchōron*), in which three birds discuss economic, social, and political matters. Although the author is not

known for sure, it was probably Matsunaga Peichin, the exiled ringleader of the riots in Kumemura in 1797.

4. Kurima (2022) does not provide hard evidence for this conclusion, relying only on impressionistic assertions that ostensibly harsh laws regarding taxation were *probably* not enforced. Similarly, he argues, unconvincingly, that, because taxation was assessed primarily at the level of districts or villages and labor taxes were usually group endeavors, individual tax burdens were unlikely to have been severe. Indeed, without much evidence, he tends to portray all the early modern Ryukyu Islands as a tranquil, self-sufficient collection of semiautonomous villages.

5. In Okinawa and nearby small islands, the typical tax system was for the government to assign a specific production quota to each village. Villages periodically redistributed farmland (through a variety of procedures) and allocated a portion of the total tax burden to each household. The village also determined penalties for households that came up short. The tax burden was quite heavy, but there was some room for flexibility, e.g., taking into consideration ability to produce and, thus, to pay. For example, larger households would be allocated more land, and the tax assessment was not identical for all households. Taxation in the southern Ryukyu Islands was similar, albeit generally more severe and less flexible.

6. Much of this section is based on Fumoto (2011, 63–99).

7. Replacing the previous (Shuri) *ōyako* (official, [首里]大屋子).

8. There was a saying, "Shimabuku sannen; Edo mikka" (島奉公三年、江戸三日). It meant that someone could work as an island official for three years and the quantity of wealth accumulated thereby would last only three days in Edo.

9. For a detailed analysis of agriculture and its limitations in early Ryukyu, see Smits (2024, 137–55).

CHAPTER THIRTEEN

1. A revised legal code, *Shinshū karitsu*, was completed in 1831. For the complete texts of these codes, see Sakihama (1986).

2. English translations of several plays are available in Komine (2008), and Edwards (2015) provides a rigorous academic analysis of *kumiodori* and its context.

3. For extensive excerpts from the crew members of these two ships, see Kerr (1958/2000, 249–60).

4. One excellent source regarding judicial proceedings and law codes is Higa and Sakihama (1965), a modern Japanese translation of *Okinawa no hankachō*, which details criminal cases before the Hirajo in the 1860s and 1870s. One case, e.g., involves the investigation into the actions of police officials who tortured a suspect excessively, thus causing his death. See Higa and Sakihama (1965, 85–94). See also Tomiyama (2004, 170–97). For a full text of the law codes, see Sakihama (1986).

CHAPTER FOURTEEN

1. These treaties were written in classical Chinese and the language of each of the countries. Modern and contemporary Chinese assertions that the Ryukyu Islands were Chinese territory commonly cite participation in the tribute system and the language of the treaties as evidence. However, classical Chinese was the common language of the

entire region for formal, written interstate communication. Korea, Vietnam and many other countries participated in the tribute system and used classical Chinese in formal written communication.

2. This claim was approximately half correct. The Ryukyu Islands had long been a frontier region of Japan. The idea that the islands had been a dependency of Japan is the peculiar part. It came from Satsuma's inaccurate claim that the islands had been part of Satsuma's territory since the 1440s, a notion embedded in the surrender documents after the 1609 war. The Meiji state's claiming Ryukyu as a dependency was a logical extension of the content of the surrender documents. Also relevant here is that the *bakufu* regarded the Ryukyu Islands as the territory of Satsuma and ultimately, therefore, under *bakufu* jurisdiction with respect to foreign affairs.

3. For a detailed study of these treaties and the correspondence between Japanese officials and foreign diplomats regarding Ryukyu in the years leading up to annexation, see Tinello (2022).

CHAPTER FIFTEEN

1. The discussion of Onna Nabe and Yoshiya Umitsuru is based mainly on Fuku (2010).

2. There were cases, however, of men discreetly watching and of dancers knowing that it was likely that they were being watched. Village life was subject to many subtleties.

3. Exactly who received the letter initially is unclear, but the point is that Satsuma's officials ended up with it. Also, some scholars have hypothesized that the letter was not a critique of Sai On per se but a petition for Satsuma fundamentally to alter its governance of Ryukyu. The letter is long gone, so there is probably endless room to speculate about it. Whether it was mainly a critique of Sai On or mainly a petition for Satsuma to alter its policies amounts to almost the same thing because Sai On and Satsuma were so closely aligned.

4. In light of the severe government suppression of Heshikiya and company and similar responses to other incidents such as the Kumemura Disturbance, it is worth noting the incongruity of the myth of Ryukyuan pacifism.

5. For an excellent, critical study of early modern and modern performing arts in English, see Edwards (2015).

6. In the front matter, Sai On stated that legends are empty words combined with clever rhetoric and that it is difficult to discern truth or falsity from such material. He argued against using legends for expedient purposes, saying that doing so would be "to try to make truth out of falsehood, dependability out of deceit."

7. Oshiro (1964) is a competent English translation of *Irōsetsuden*. Oshiro's literal rendering of the title is *Traditional Narratives Bequeathed by the Aged*.

8. This subsection is based largely on portions of Komine (1998) and Nagafuji (2000).

9. The major source for the material in this subsection is Tomiyama (2004).

CHAPTER SIXTEEN

1. Many parts of this chapter are based on Dana (2008), Harada (2017), and Tonaki (1992).

2. In vol. 5 of Kūkai's *Shōryōshū* (early ninth century), we find the description of Fujiwara Kanō and his party losing their courage when faced by ferocious Okinawans. In Miyoshi Kiyotsura's 902 account of travels to China in 852 (*Chishō-daishi den*), his

party drifted to the country of Ryukyu, a land of cannibals. This account also appears in *Konjaku monogatari shū* (twelfth century). In a 1244 account, *Hyōtō Ryūkyūkoku ki*, travelers who came ashore at an island found human bones roasting in an oven. Thereupon, they realized it was Okinawa and fled immediately.

3. Although today Hachiman is the most widespread deity in the Japanese islands, from the thirteenth through the sixteenth century, he was closely associated with *wakō*. He was also closely associated with the Seiwa Genji (Tametomo's branch of the Minamoto family).

4. Legends connected with Ajinitchei in Yoron also cast him as a local hero who resisted an invasion of the island by Okinawan forces.

5. Tameharu, e.g., is listed as the founder of the Kasari lineage, and the names of his successors all begin with the *tame-* of Tametomo.

6. The main exception is the claim in Okinoerabu that Guraru Magohachi was a descendant of Taira Arimori.

7. I was able to visit both shrines, which are very small. At the shrine in Tsunagi (Sashiki area; Sashiki no longer exists as a formal entity), I asked the person in charge about the shrine's age, but he did not know.

8. This novel is a fictional biography of Tametomo. It also has much to say about Ryukyuan history.

CHAPTER SEVENTEEN

1. Public opinion surveys of the residents of Okinawa Prefecture are routinely conducted by the major newspapers. One typical question is whether Okinawa should be independent of Japan. Responses tend to be consistent, and yes answers range between 2 and 4 percent. Moreover, saying in an anonymous survey that one favors independence is easy. How many of those respondents would actually go ahead with independence if it were in their power to do so is unclear, but it is unlikely that all of them would.

2. For more examples and analysis, see Matsumura (2015).

3. Okinawa Prefecture, https://www.pref.okinawa.jp/toukeika/so/topics/topics457.pdf (accessed August 12, 2024).

4. The Okinawan Migration Record Database is a valuable resource. See https://opl.okinawan-migration.com/main.php (accessed August 12, 2024).

5. For excellent studies of the Hall of Peoples and worldwide exhibitions, see Ziomek (2014, 2019).

6. This subsection is a revision of parts of Smits (2006). See also Clarke (1997), Henrich (2013), and Oguma (2014, 108–36).

7. For additional examples of criticism of Yanagi, see Oguma (2014, 115–22).

8. For a penetrating analysis of Yanagi's ideas, see Yakabi (1994). This paragraph and the three that follow summarize some of Yakabi's main points about Yanagi's thought.

CHAPTER EIGHTEEN

1. Buchner died on June 18, just before the battle ended, of wounds inflicted by an artillery shell. Joseph Stillwell subsequently took over command of the US forces.

2. Yahara was the only one of the three to survive the battle and the war. In 1973, he published a book-length account of the battle that was later translated into English (see Yahara 1995).

CHAPTER NINETEEN

1. Despite this momentary anti-Japanese sentiment, even as early as 1945 several prominent Okinawans petitioned the US authorities for speedy reversion of the Ryukyu Islands to Japan. Former Shuri mayor Nakayoshi Ryōkō, e.g., wrote in a 1946 petition to General MacArthur: "Just as blood is said to be thicker than water, all Okinawan residents have a powerful self-awareness of being ethnically Japanese, and no matter whatever circumstances befall them, their earnest desire is to share a destiny with their mainland compatriots prevails" (Oguma 2014, 172).

2. In 1950, prior to the creation of USCAR, there was an election for a civilian governor. In it, Taira Tatsuo, a prominent figure in the prewar system, overwhelmingly defeated the US-backed candidate, Matsuoka Seiho. Most likely this experience led USCAR to reject popular elections of civilian governors or their equivalents.

3. The central government in Tokyo provided funds to supplement the education budget in Okinawa. After Prime Minister Satō Eisaku visited Okinawa in 1965, these funds increased substantially. By the late 1960s, therefore, spending on education in Okinawa was roughly on a par with spending in mainland Japan.

4. As Oguma Eiji notes, "the reversion movement gained strength as information about the mainland's recovery and economic growth was conveyed [to Okinawans]; at the time when the only information obtainable was such that Okinawa was enjoying a better lifestyle than the mainland, the desire for reversion was accordingly weak" (Oguma 2014, 175).

CHAPTER TWENTY

1. For example, the modern Okinawan literature scholar Steve Rabson has written of "King Satto's 1372 treaty of suzerainty with China" (Rabson 1999a, 137). Similarly, Akamine Mamoru characterizes China as Ryukyu's "*sōshu* 宗主," which becomes *suzerain* in English translation (e.g., Akamine 2017, 153, 164).

2. Strictly speaking, the "return" of the Ryukyu Islands is not (yet) an official Chinese government demand vis-à-vis Japan. Nevertheless, the claim is widespread in journalistic and academic circles, and it is enforced in certain environments. For example, I have had to cancel talks on the Ryukyu Islands that I was scheduled to give in China because I would not agree that the Ryukyu Islands were once Chinese territory. In the context of rising tensions over Taiwan, on June 4, 2023, Chinese president Xi Jinping made public remarks about close historical ties between the Ryukyu Islands and China (Yoshinaga 2023). In September 2024, the newspaper *Sankei shinbun* reported that China's Dalian Maritime University will soon create a "Ryukyu Research Center" to advance Chinese claims to the Ryukyu Islands (*Sankei shinbun* 2024).

3. Okinawa Prefecture, https://www.pref.okinawa.jp/site/shoko/kigyoritchi/seibi /documents/gaiyou.pdf (accessed May 11, 2023).

4. UNESCO World Heritage Convention, 2021, https://whc.unesco.org/en/list /1574/, and Government of Japan Public Relations Office, November 2021, https:// www.gov-online.go.jp/eng/publicity/book/hlj/html/202111/202111_02_en.html (accessed May 12, 2023).

5. Yearly updates will be forthcoming.

Works Cited

This list includes all primary sources, secondary sources, and internet resources cited in the text or mentioned in the part introductions. The place of publication for Japanese books is Tokyo unless otherwise indicated.

Akamine, Mamoru. 2017. *The Ryukyu Kingdom: Cornerstone of East Asia.* Translated by Lina Terrell. Edited by Robert Huey. Honolulu: University of Hawai'i Press.

Akamine Seiki (赤嶺誠紀). 1988. *Daikōkai jidai no Ryūkyū* (大航海時代の琉球). Naha: Okinawa taimusu sha.

"Amami no rekishi" (奄美の歴史). 2016. In "Utsukushiki Amami, Ryūkyū himitsu no shimatabi e" (美しき奄美・琉球秘密の島旅へ), special issue (特別編集号), *Transit* (トランジット), Autumn, 20–21.

Arakawa Akira (新川明). 1981. *Ryūkyū shobun ikō* (琉球処分以降). 2 vols. Asahi shinbunsha.

Araki Moriaki (安良城盛昭). 1980. *Shin Okinawashi ron* (新・沖縄史論). Naha: Okinawa taimusu sha.

———. 1981. "Ryūkyūshi no tokushitsu ni tsuite" (琉球史の特質について). *Gekkan rekishi techō: Nihonshi, kōko, minzoku kenkyū no saishin jōhōshi* (日本史・考古・民俗研究の最新情報誌) 9, no. 4 (April): 4–11.

Asato Susumu (安里進). 2010. Sōron: "Ko-Ryūkyū" gainen no saikentō (総論:「古琉球」概念の再検討). In Okinawa-ken bunka shinkōkai (沖縄県文化振興会), ed. *Okinawa kenshi, kakuronhen dai-sankan (Ko-Ryūkyū)* (沖縄県史, 各論編第3巻 [古琉球]), 3–19. Naha: Okinawa-ken kyōiku iinkai.

Bastian, A. A. 2023. "Okinawa Is in the Crosshairs of China's Ambitions." *Foreign Affairs*, April 7. https://foreignpolicy.com/2023/04/07/okinawa-japan-china -us-bases-soft-power.

Bhowmik, Davinder. 2008. *Writing Okinawa: Narrative Acts of Identity and Resistance.* New York: Routledge.

———. 2020. "Unruly Subjects in Shun Medoruma's 'Walking a Street Named Peace' and Miri Yū's *Tokyo Ueno Station.*" *Wasafiri* 35, no. 2:60–66.

Bhowmik, Davinder, and Steve Rabson. 2016. *Islands of Protest: Japanese Literature from Okinawa.* Honolulu: University of Hawai'i Press.

Burbank, Jane, and Frederick Cooper. 2010. *Empires in World History: Power and the Politics of Difference.* Princeton, NJ: Princeton University Press.

Calhoun, Craig, ed. 2002. *Dictionary of the Social Sciences*. Oxford: Oxford University Press. Online edition. https://www.oxfordreference.com/view/10.1093/acref /9780195123715.001.0001/acref-9780195123715-e-559.

Chamberlain, Basil Hall. 1895. "The Luchu Islands and Their Inhabitants: 1. Introductory Remarks." *Geographical Journal* 5, no. 4:289–319.

Chén Kǎn (陳侃). 1534/1995. *Shi-Ryūkyū roku* (*Shǐ Liúqiú lù*, 使琉球録). Edited and Translated by Harada Nobuo (原田禹雄). Ginowan: Yōjusha.

China Teikan (知名定寛). 2008. *Ryūkyū Bukkyōshi no kenkyū* (琉球仏教史の研究). Ginowan: Yōju shorin.

Christy, Alan S. 1993. "The Making of Imperial Subjects in Okinawa." *positions: east asia cultures critique* 1, no. 13:607–39.

Churashima Okinawa. 2008. Okinawa Prefecture, March. https://www.pref.okinawa .jp/churahome/pdf/0803/14-15.pdf.

Clarke, Hugh. 1997. "The Great Dialect Debate: The State and Language Policy in Okinawa." In *Society and State in Interwar Japan*, ed. Elise K. Tipton, 193–217. New York: Routledge.

Comprehensive Database of Archaeological Site Reports in Japan. n.d. https://site reports.nabunken.go.jp/en. Accessed November 15, 2024.

Conlon, Thomas D. 2024. *Kings in All but Name: The Lost History of Ōuchi Rule in Japan, 1350–1569*. New York: Oxford University Press.

Cook, Haruko Taya, and Theodore F. Cook. 1992. *Japan at War: An Oral History*. New York: New Press.

Dana Masayuki (田名真之). 1984. "Shizoku, machikata mondai to Sai On" (士族・町方問題と蔡温). In *Sai On to Sono jidai: Kinseishi no shomondai shiriizu 1*, 49–59. Naha: Riuchūsha.

———. 1992. *Okinawa kinseishi no shosō* (沖縄近世史の諸相). Naha: Hirugisha.

———. 2008. "Ryūkyū ōken no keifu ishiki to Minamoto Tametomo torai denshō" (琉球王権の系譜意識と源為朝渡来伝承). In *Kyōkai no aidentiti* (境界のアイデンティティ), ed. Kyūshū shigaku kenkyūkai, 181–95. Iwata shoin.

Defense of Japan (Annual White Paper). 2024. https://www.mod.go.jp/en/publ/w _paper/index.html.

Doi Naomi (土肥直美). 1998. "Nansei shotō-jin kokkaku no keishitsu-jinruigakuteki na kōsatsu: Hone karamita Nanseishotō no hitobito" (南西諸島人骨格の形質人類学的な考察: 骨からみた南西諸島の人々). In *Okinawa no rekishi to iryōshi* (沖縄の歴史と医療史), ed. Ryūkyū daigaku igakubu fuzoku chiki iryō kenkyū sentā, 89–103. Fukuoka: Kyūshū daigaku shuppankai.

———. 2018. *Okinawa honegatari: Jinruigaku ga semaru Okinawajin no ruutsu* (沖縄骨語り: 人類学が迫る沖縄人のルーツ). Naha: Ryūkyū shinpōsha.

Doyle, Michael W. 1986. *Empires*. Ithaca, NY: Cornell University Press.

Edwards, James Rhys. 2015. "Between Two Worlds: A Social History of Okinawan Musical Drama." PhD diss., Department of Ethnomusicology, University of California, Los Angeles. https://escholarship.org/uc/item/9r74h4t8. Originally submitted January 2015, revised July 2015.

Eguchi Tsukasa (江口司). 2006. *Shiranuikai to Ryūkyūko* (不知火海と琉球弧). Fukuoka: Gen shobō.

Figal, Gerald. 2012. *Beachheads: War, Peace, and Tourism in Postwar Okinawa*. Lanham, MD: Rowman & Littlefield.

Fuku Hiromi (福寛美). 2008. *Kikaijima, oni no kaiiki: Kikaigashima kō* (喜界島・鬼の海域: キカイがシマの考). Shintensha.

———. 2010. *Ryūkyū no renka: "Onna Nabe" to "Yoshia Umitsuru"* (琉球の恋歌:「恩納なべ」と「よしや思鶴」). Shintensha.

———. 2013. *Omoro sōshi to gunyū no seiki: Sanzan jidai no ōtachi* (「おもろさうし」と群雄の世紀: 三山時代の王たち). Shinwasha.

Fuma Susumu (夫馬進). 1999. *Shi Ryūkyū roku kaidai oyobi kenkyū: Zōtei* (使琉球録解題及び研究: 増訂). Ginowan: Yōju shorin.

Fumoto Sumio (麓純雄). 2011. *Amami no rekishi nyūmon: Amamiko tachi ni okuru* (奄美の歴史入門: 奄美子たちに贈る). Kagoshima-shi: Nanpō shinsha.

Gi Tomihiro (義富弘). 2007. *Shimanuyu 1: 1609 Amami, Ryūkū shinryaku* (しまぬゆ1: 1609年、奄美・琉球侵略). Kagoshima: Nanpō shinsha.

Gramlich-Oka, Bettina, and Gregory Smits, eds. 2010. *Economic Thought in Early Modern Japan*. Leiden: Brill.

Guō Rǔlín (郭汝霖). 1561/2000. *Jūhen shi Ryūkyū roku* (*Zhòngbiān shǐ Liúqiú lù*, 重編使琉球録). Translated by Harada Nobuo (原田禹雄). Ginowan: Yōju shorin.

Harada Nobuo (原田禹雄). 2003a. *Ryūkyū o shugosuru kami* (琉球を守護する神). Ginowan: Yōju shorin.

———. 2003b. *Ryūkyū to Chūgoku: Wasurerareta sakuhōshi* (琉球と中国: 忘れられた冊封使). Yoshikawa kōbunkan.

———, ed. 2004. *Min-dai Ryūkyū shiryō shūsei* (明代琉球資料集成). Ginowan: Yōju shorin.

Harada Nobuo (原田信男). 2017. *Yoshitsune densetsu to Yoritomo densetsu: Nihonshi no kita to minami* (義経伝説と頼朝伝説: 日本史の北と南). Iwanami shoten.

Hashimoto Yū (橋本雄). 2005. *Chūsei Nihon no kokusai kankei: Higashi-Ajia tsūkōken to gishi mondai* (中世日本の国際関係: 東アジア通交圏と偽使問題). Yoshikawa kōbunkan.

———. 2008. "The Information Strategy of Imposter Envoys from Northern Kyūshū to Chosŏn Korea in the Fifteenth and Sixteenth Centuries." In *The East Asian "Mediterranean": Maritime Crossroads of Culture, Commerce and Human Migration*, ed. Angela Schottenhammer, 289–315. Wiesbaden: Harrassowitz.

Hateruma Eikichi (波照間永吉) et al., eds. 2022–. *Ryūkyū bungaku taikei* (琉球文学大系). 35 vols. Nago: Meio daigaku (distributed by Yumani shobō).

Heinrich, Patrick. 2013. "*Hōgen ronsō*: The Great Ryukyuan Languages Debate of 1940." *Contemporary Japan* 25, no. 2:167–87.

Higa Chōshin (比嘉朝進). 2006. *Okinawa sengoku jidai no nazo* (沖縄戦国時代の謎). Naha: Naha shuppansha.

Higa Shunchō (比嘉春潮) and Sakihama Shūmei (崎浜秀明). 1965. *Okinawa no hankachō* (沖縄の犯科帳). Heibonsha.

Hokama Shuzen (外間守善) and Tamaki Masami (玉城正美), eds. 1980. *Nantō kayō taisei 1: Okinawa-hen jō* (南島歌謡大成1: 沖縄編 上). Kadokawa shoten.

Hook, Glen D., and Richard Siddle. 2003. *Japan and Okinawa: Structure and Subjectivity*. London: Routledge.

Hucker, Charles O. 1985. *A Dictionary of Official Titles in Imperial China*. Stanford, CA: Stanford University Press. https://archive.org/details/dictionary-of-official-titles-in-imperial-china/mode/2up.

Hudson, Mark J. 2020. "Language Dispersals and the 'Secondary Peoples' Revolution."

In *The Oxford Guide to the Transeurasian Languages*, ed. Martine Robbeets and Alexander Savelyev. Oxford: Oxford University Press. https://academic.oup.com/book/41762/chapter/354243173.

———. 2022a. *Bronze Age Maritime and Warrior Dynamics in Island East Asia*. Elements in Ancient East Asia. New York: Cambridge University Press.

———. 2022b. "Re-Thinking Jōmon and Ainu in Japanese History." *Asia-Pacific Journal: Japan Focus*, vol. 20, issue 15, no. 2. https://apjjf.org/2022/15/hudson.

Iacobelli, Pedro, and Hiroko Matsuda, eds. 2017. *Rethinking Postwar Okinawa: Beyond American Occupation*. Lanham, MD: Lexington.

Iba Nantetsu (伊波南哲). 1964. *Oyake Akahachi: Chōhen jojishi* (オヤケ アカハチ: 長篇叙事詩). Miraisha.

Iha Fuyū (伊波普猷). 1974–76. *Iha Fuyū zenshū* (伊波普猷全集). 11 vols. Heibonsha.

Ijichi Sadaka. 1877. *Okinawa shi* (沖縄志). Ishikawa Jihei.

Ikeda Yoshifumi (池田榮史). 2012. "Ryūkyū rettō to Kan-hantō: Busshitsu bunka kōryū, kōeki shisutemu kaimei" (琉球列島と韓半島: 物質文化交流・交易システムの解明). In *Higashi Ajia no kanchihō kōryū no kako to genzai: Saishū to Okinawa, Amami o chūshin ni shite* (東アジアの間地方交流の過去と現在: 済州と沖縄・奄美を中心にして), ed. Tsuha Takashi (津波高志), 325–46. Sairyūsha.

———. 2019. "Ryūkyū rettōshi o horiokosu: Jūichi-jūyon seiki no ijū, kōeki to shakaiteki henyō" (琉球列島史を掘りおこす: 十一〜十四世紀の移住・交易と社会的変容). In *Ryūkyū no chūsei* (琉球の中世), ed. Chūseigaku kenkyūkai (中世学研究会), 13–44. Kōshi shoin.

Ikemiya Masaharu (池宮正治), ed. 2009. *Kian nikki* (喜安日記). Ginowan: Yōju shorin.

Ikuta Shigeru (生田滋). 1984a. "Ryūkyūkoku no 'Sanzan tōitsu'" (琉球国の「三山統一」). *Tōhō gakuhō* 65, nos. 3–4:175–206.

———. 1992. "Ryūkyū chūzanōkoku to kaijō bōeki" (琉球中山王国と海上貿易). In *Ryūkyūko no sekai* (琉球弧の世界), ed. Tanigawa Ken'ichi (谷川健一), 265–96. Shōgakkan.

Inamura Kenpu (稲村賢敷). 1957. *Ryūkyū shotō ni okeru wakō shiseki no kenkyū* (琉球諸島における倭寇史跡の研究). Yoshikawa kōbunkan.

Ishida, Masato. 2018. "Ifa Fuyū's Search for Okinawan-Japanese Identity." *Religions*, vol. 9, no. 6. https://doi.org/10.3390/rel9060188.

Ishigami Eiichi (石上英一). 2000. "Ryūkyū no Amami shotō tōchi no shodankai" (琉球の奄美諸島統治の諸段階). *Rekishi hyōron*, no. 603:2–15.

———, ed. 2014. *Amami shotō hennen shiryō: Ko-Ryūkyū ki hen (jō)* (奄美諸島編年史料: 古琉球期編 [上]). Yoshikawa kōbunkan.

———. 2018. *Amami shotō hennen shiryō: Ko-Ryūkyū ki hen (ge)* (奄美諸島編年史料: 古琉球期編 [下]). Yoshikawa kōbunkan.

Itaya Tōru (板谷徹). 2015. *Kinsei Ryūkyū no ōfu geinō to Tō, Yamato* (近世琉球の王府芸能と唐・大和). Iwata shoin.

Jarosz, Aleksandra, et al. 2022. "Demography, Trade and State Power: A Tripartite Model of Medieval Farming/Language Dispersals in the Ryukyu Islands." *Evolutionary Human Sciences*, vol. 4.

Johnson, Scott A. J. 2017. *Why Did Ancient Civilizations Fail?* New York: Routledge.

Joseon Veritable Royal Records (*Joseon wangjo sillok/Chōsen ōchō jitsuroku Ryūkyū shiryō shūsei, yakuchū hen*, 朝鮮王朝実録 琉球史料集成、訳注編). 2005. Translated and edited by Ikeya Machiko (池谷望子), Uchida Akiko (内田晶子), and Takase Kyōko

(高瀬恭子). Ginowan: Yōju shorin. This edition contains everything the editors considered relevant to Ryukyu.

Joseon Veritable Royal Records (*Joseon wangjo sillok/Chōsen ōchō jitsuroku Ryūkyū shiryō shūsei, yakuchū hen*, 朝鮮王朝實錄). n.d. Academia Sinica. http://hanchi.ihp.sinica .edu.tw/mql/login.html. Accessed June 27, 2025. This edition is complete.

Kamei Katsunobu (亀井勝信), ed. 1980. *Amami-Ōshima shoka keifu shū* (奄美大島諸家系譜集). Kokusho kankōkai.

Kamiya Nobuyuki (紙屋敦之). 1989. "Satsuma no Ryūkyū shinnyū" (薩摩の琉球侵入). In *Shin Ryūkyūshi, kinsei hen* (新琉球史、近世編), ed. Ryūkyū shinpōsha, 33–72. Naha: Ryūkyū shinpōsha.

Kano Masanao (鹿野正直). 1993. *Okinawa no fuchi: Iha Fuyū to sono jidai* (沖縄の淵: 伊波普猷とその時代). Iwanami shoten.

Karube Kensuke. 2022. "Okinawa's Continuing Economic Burden: Will Okinawa Ever Realize Equality with the Mainland?" May 20. https://www.nippon.com/en/in -depth/a08203.

Kerr, George H. 1958/2000. *Okinawa: The History of an Island People*. Rev. ed. Rutland, VT: Tuttle.

Kinjō Chōei (金城朝永), ed. 1903/1953. *Okinawa hōsei shi* (沖縄法制史). Rev. ed. Kanda shobō.

Kinjō Seitoku (金城正篤). 1969/1989. "Kinsei Okinawa no Keizai kōzō" (近世沖縄の経済構造). In *Okinawa kenshi 3, keizai* (沖縄県史3, 経済), ed. Okinawa Seifu, 51–117. Kokusho kankōkai.

Kinoshita Naoko (木下尚子). 1996. *Nantō kai bunka no kenkyū: Kai no michi no kōkogaku* (南島貝文化の研究貝の道の考古学). Hōsei daigaku shuppankyoku.

———. 2003. "Kai kōeki to kokka keisei: 9 seiki kara 13 seiki o taishō ni" (貝交易と国家形成: 9世紀から13世紀を対象に). In *Senshi Ryūkyū no seigyō to kōeki: Amami, Okinawa no hakkutsu chōsa kara* (先史琉球の生業と交易: 奄美・沖縄の発掘調査から), ed. Kinoshita Naoko, 117–44. Kumamoto: Kumamoto daigaku bungakubu.

Kishaba Chōken (喜舎場朝賢). 1980. *Tōtei zuihitsu* (東汀随筆). Edited by Naka Shōha-chirō and Gabe Masao. Perikansha.

Kobata, Atsushi, and Mitsugu Matsuda. 1969. *Ryukyuan Relations with Korea and South Sea Countries: An Annotated Translation of Documents from the Rekidai hōan*. Kyoto: Kawakita.

Kokuritsu rekishi minzoku hakubutsukan (National Museum of Japanese History, 国立歴史民俗博物館). 2021. *Umi no teikoku Ryūkyū: Yaeyama, Miyako, Amami kara mita chūsei* (海の帝国琉球: 八重山・宮古・奄美からみた中世). Nyūkaraa shashin insatsu.

Komine Kazuaki (小峰和明). 1998. "Irōden kara *Irōsetsuden* e: Ryūkyū no setsuwa to rekishi kijutsu" (<遺老伝>から『遺老説伝』へ: 琉球の説話と歴史記述). *Bungaku* (文学) 9, no. 3 (July): 26–37.

Komine, Naganori (小嶺長則). 2008. *Nufani: English Translation of Kumiodori and Okinawan Poetry*. Edited by Gustavo O. Fernández and José L. Rosado Santiago. Okinawa Book Service Co. Revised and extended 2nd ed. of *Okinawan Poetry* (1995).

Korea Fortress Academy. 2007. *A Basic Research on Mountain Fortresses in Central In-land Area of Korea*. Chungcheongbuk-do Province and the Korea Fortress Academy.

———. 2008a. *Mountain Fortresses of Central Inland Korea I: Samnyeon Sansong Moun-tain Fortresses*. Chungcheongbuk-do Province.

Kurima Yasuo (来間泰男). 2013. *Gusuku to aji: Nihon no chūsei zenki to Ryūkyū kodai* (グスクと按司 [上] 日本の中世と琉球古代). 2 vols. Nihon keizai hyōronsha.

———. 2015. *Jintōzei wa nakatta: Denshō, jijitsu, shinjitsu* (人頭税はなかった: 伝承・事実・真実). Ginowan: Yōju shorin.

———. 2022. *Ryūkyū kinsei no katachi* (琉球近世の社会のかたち). Nihon Keizai hyōronsha.

Kuroshima Satoru (黒島敏). 2016. *Ryūkyū ōkoku to Sengoku daimyo: Shimazi shinnyū made no han-seiki* (琉球王国と戦国大名: 島津侵入までの半世紀). Yoshikawa kōbunkan.

Kuroshima Satoru (黒嶋敏) and Yara Ken'ichirō (屋良健一郎), eds. 2017. *Ryūkyū shiryōgaku no funade: Ima, rekishi jōhō no nama e* (琉球史料学の船出: いま、歴史情報の生へ). Bensei shuppan.

Kushi Fusako (久志芙沙子). 1932/2015. *Memoirs of a Declining Ryukyu Woman* (*Horobiyuku Ryūkyū onna no shuki*, 滅びゆく琉球女の手記). In *Okinawa bungaku sen: Nihon bungaku no ejji kara no toi* (沖縄文学選: 日本文学のエッジからの問い), ed. Okamoto Keitoku (岡本恵徳), Takahashi Toshio (高橋敏夫), and Motohama Hidehiko (本浜秀彦), 54–60. Bensei shuppan.

Lebra, William P. 1966/1985. *Okinawan Religion: Belief, Ritual, and Social Structure.* Honolulu: University of Hawai'i Press.

Loo, Tze M. 2023. "Trapped in Text: The Changing Place of Female Ritualists in Taisho Okinawa." *Journal of Asian Studies* 82, no. 2 (May): 184–205.

Lummis, Charles Douglas. 2023. *War Is Hell: Studies in the Right of Legitimate Violence.* Lanham, MD: Rowman & Littlefield.

Makishi Yōko (真喜志瑶子). 2023. *Ko-Ryūkyū no ōgū girei to Omoro sōshi* (古琉球の王宮儀礼とおもろさうし). Heibonsha.

Mamiya Atsushi (間宮厚司). 2014. *Okinawa kogo no shinsō: Omorogo no tankyū* (沖縄古語の深層: オモロ語の探究). Rev. ed. Shinwasha.

Matsuda, Hiroko. 2019. *Liminality of the Japanese Empire: Border Crossings from Okinawa to Colonial Taiwan.* Honolulu: University of Hawai'i Press.

Matsumura, Wendy. 2015. *The Limits of Okinawa: Japanese Capitalism, Living Labor, and Theorizations of Community.* Durham, NC: Duke University Press.

Matsushita Shirō (松下志朗). 1983. *Kinsei Amami no shihai to shakai* (近世奄美の支配と社会). Daiichi shobō.

McCurry, Justin. 2013. "China Lays Claim to Okinawa as Territory Dispute with Japan Escalates." *The Guardian*, May 15.

Ming Veritable Records (*Min jitsuroku no Ryūkyū shiryō*, 「明実録」の琉球史料). 2001–6. Translated and edited by Wada Hisanori (和田久徳) et al. 3 vols. Haebaruchō: Okinawa-ken bunka shinkōkai, kōbunsho kanribu, shiryō henshūshitsu.

Molasky, Michael. 1999. *The American Occupation of Japan and Okinawa: Literature and Memory.* New York: Routledge.

———. 2003. "Arakawa Akira: The Thought and Poetry of an Iconoclast." In *Japan and Okinawa: Structure and Subjectivity*, ed. Glen D. Hook and Richard Siddle, 225–39. London: Routledge.

Molasky, Michael, and Steve Rabson. 2000. *Southern Exposure: Modern Japanese Literature from Okinawa.* Honolulu: University of Hawai'i Press.

Mukai Kiyoshi (向井清史). 1992. "Sotetsu jigoku" (「ソテツ地獄」). In *Shin Ryūkyūshi, Kindai, gendai hen* (新琉球史・近代・現代編), ed. Ryūkyū shinpōsha, 191–213. Naha: Ryūkyū shinpōsha.

Murai Shōsuke (村井章介). 2019. *Ko-Ryūkyū: Kaiyō Ajia no kagayakeru ōkoku* (古琉球: 海洋アジアの輝ける王国). Kadokawa.

Nagafuji Yasushi (永藤靖). 2000. *Ryūkyū shinwa to kodai Yamato bungaku* (琉球神話と古代ヤマト文学). Miyai shoten.

Nagamoto Tomohiro. 2013. "Who 'Owns' Okinawa?" Nippon.com, July 3. https://www.nippon.com/en/currents/d00086.

Nagoya Sagenta (名越左源太). 1855/1984. *Nantō zatsuwa: Bakumatusu Amami minzokushi* (南島雑話: 幕末奄美民俗誌). Edited by Kokubu Naoichi and Era Hiroshi. 2 vols. Heibonsha.

Naha shiyakusho, Sōmubu, Shi-shi henshūshitsu (那覇市役所総務部市史編集室). 1970. *Naha-shi shi, shiryōhen* (那覇市史資料篇). Pt. 2, vol. 3. Naha: Naha shiyakusho.

Naha-shi shiminbunka-bu rekishi shiryōshitsu (那覇市市民文化部歴史資料室), ed. 1966–2004. *Naha-shi shi, shiryōhen* (那覇市史資料篇). 29 vols. in 3 pts. Naha: Naha shiyakusho.

Naka Shōhachirō (名嘉正八郎). 1992. Gusuku no rekishi to kōkogaku (グスクの歴史と考古学). In *Ryūkyūko no sekai* (琉球弧の世界), ed. Tanigawa Ken'ichi (谷川健一), 130–58. Shōgakkan.

Nakagawa Masaharu (中川正晴). 2005. "Teigaku nintōzei fugata kōso seido to Miyako, Yaeyama hisan no yōin" (定額人頭税賦型貢租制度と宮古・八重山悲惨の要因). *Zeidai janaaru* (税大ジャーナル) 3 (December): 58–80.

Nakajima Gakusho (中島楽章). 2019. "The East Asian War and Trade between Kyushu and Southeast Asia in the Late Sixteenth Century: Centered on Katō Kiyomas's Trade with Luzon." *Chinese Studies in History* 52, no. 1:23–41.

———. 2020. *Daikōkai jidai no kaiiki-Ajia to Ryūkyū: Rekiosu o motomete* (Maritime Asia and Ryukyu in the age of commerce: In quest of the "Lequios," 大航海時代の海域アジアと琉球: レキオスを求めて). Shibunkaku shuppan.

Nakasone, Ronald Y. 2002. *Okinawan Diaspora*. Honolulu: University of Hawai'i Press.

Naze-shi (名瀬市). 1996. *Kaitei Naze-shi shi 1 kan, Rekishi-hen* (改定名瀬市誌1巻、歴史編). Edited by Kaitei Naze-shi shi hanesan iinkai (改定名瀬市誌編纂委員会). Naze-shi [Amami-shi]: Naze-shi yakusho.

Nelson, Christopher T. 2008. *Dancing with the Dead: Memory, Performance, and Everyday Life in Postwar Okinawa*. Durham, NC: Duke University Press.

NHK (Nihon hōsō kyōkai bunka kenkyūjo, 日本放送協会文研究所). 1979. *Nihon no kenminsei: Zenkoku kenmin ishiki chōsa* (日本の県民性: 全国県民意識調査), ed. NHK hōsō yoron chōsajo (NHK 放送世論調査所). NHK shuppan.

———. 1997a. Gendai no kenmin kishitsu: Zenkoku kenmin ishiki chōsa (現代の県民気質: 全国県民意識調査). NHK shuppan.

———. 1997b. *Zenkoku kenmin ishiki chōsa 1996: Deetabukku* (全国県民意識調査 1996: データブック). NHK shuppan.

Nishizato Kikō (西里喜行). 1969/1989. "Kyūkan-onzon ka no ken keizai dōkō" (旧慣温存化の県経済動向). In *Okinawa kenshi 3, Keizai* (沖縄県史3, 経済), ed. Okinawa Seifu, 121–292. Kokusho kankōkai.

———. 1992a. "Ryūkyū bunkatsu kōshō to sono shūhen" (琉球分割交渉とその周辺). In *Shin Ryūkyūshi, kindai, gendai hen* (新琉球史、近代・現代編). Naha: Ryūkyū shinpōsha.

———, ed. 1992b. *Ryūkyū kyūkoku seigansho shūsei* (琉球救国請願書集成). Hōsei daigaki Okinawa bunka kenkyūjo.

Oguma, Eiji. 2002. *A Genealogy of "Japanese" Self-Images*. Translated by David Askew. Melbourne: Trans Pacific.

———. 2014. *Okinawa, 1818–1972: Inclusion and Exclusion*. Translated by Leonie R. Strickland. Vol. 1 of *The Boundaries of "the Japanese."* Melbourne: Trans Pacific.

Ōhama Eisen (大濱永亘). 2005. *Oyake Akahachi, Honkawara no ran to San'yō-sei ichimon no hitobito* (オヤケアカハチ・ホンカワラの乱と山陽姓一門の人々). Ishigaki: Sakishima bunka kenkyūjo.

———. 2008. "Yaeyama shotō no kōeki: Suku bunka-ki o chūshin ni" (八重山諸島の交易: スク文化期を中心に). In *Nichi-Ryū kōeki no reimei: Yamato kara no shōgeki* (日琉交易の黎明: ヤマトからの衝撃), ed. Tanigawa Ken'ichi (谷川健一), 347–82. Shinwasha.

Ōhama Shinken (大浜信賢). 1971. *Yaeyama no nintōzei* (八重山の人頭税). San'ichi shobō.

Ōishi Naomasa (大石直正), Takara Kurayoshi (高良倉吉), and Takahashi Kimiaki (高橋公明). 2009. *Shūen kara mita chūsei Nihon* (周縁から見た中世日本). Kōdansha.

Okamoto, Hiromichi. 2008. "Foreign Policy and Maritime Trade in the Early Ming Period: Focusing on the Ryukyu Kingdom." *Acta Asiatica*, no. 95:35–55.

——— (岡本弘道). 2010. *Ryūkyū ōkoku kaijō kōshōshi kenkyū* (琉球王国海上交渉史研究). Ginowan: Yōju Shorin.

Okamoto Keitoku (岡本恵徳), Takahashi Toshio (高橋敏夫), and Motohama Hidehiko (本浜秀彦), comps. 2015. *Okinawa bungaku sen: Nihon bungaku no ejji kara no toi* (沖縄文学選: 日本文学のエッジからの問い). Bensei shuppan.

Okaya Kōji (岡谷公二). 2019. *Okinawa no seichi utaki* (沖縄の聖地 御嶽). Heibonsha.

Okinawa kenritsu toshokan shiryō henshūshitsu (沖縄県立図書館資料編集室). 1996. *Okinawa-ken shi, shiryō hen 2* (沖縄県史, 資料編2). Naha: San insatsu.

Okinawa kokusai daigaku, Nantō bunka kenkyūjo (沖縄国際大学南島文化研究所), eds. 2003. *Kinsei Ryūkyū no sozei seido to jintōzei* (近世琉球の租税制度と人頭税). Nihon keizai hyōronsha.

Okinawa Prefectural Archives (沖縄県公文書官). n.d. https://www.archives.pref .okinawa.jp. Accessed August 15, 2024.

Okinawa Prefectural Library (沖縄県立図書館). n.d. Ryūkyū, Okinawa kankei shiryō (琉球・沖縄関係資料). https://www.library.pref.okinawa.jp/about-okinawa /index.html. Accessed May 17, 2024.

Okinawa seifu (沖縄政府). 1969/1989. *Okinawa kenshi 3, Keizai* (沖縄県史3: 経済). Kokusho kankōkai.

Okinawa Studies Research Guide. n.d. George Washington University Libraries. https://libguides.gwu.edu/okinawa. Accessed June 5, 2024.

Okinawa-ken Okinawa shiryō henshūjo (沖縄県沖縄史料編集所) and Okinawa-ken Kyōiku iinkai (沖縄県教育委員会), eds. 1981–89. *Okinawa-ken shiryō, zenkindai* (沖縄県史料、 前近代). 7 vols. Naha: Okinawa-ken kyōiku iinkai.

Okinawan Migration Record Database. n.d. https://opl.okinawan-migration.com/main .php. Accessed May 17, 2024.

Okinawan Studies: Online Resources Links. n.d. University of Hawai'i at Manoa Library. https://guides.library.manoa.hawaii.edu/okinawa/onlineresources. Accessed May 17, 2024.

Omoro sōshi (おもろさうし). 1972. Edited by Hokama Shuzen (外間守善) and Saigō Nobutsuna (西郷信綱). Iwanami shoten.

Ōsato Tomoko (大里知子). 2003. "Okinawa kindaishi: 'Kyūkan-onzon' 'shoki kensei' kenkyū ni tsuite no ikkōsatsu" (沖縄近代史：「旧慣温存」「初期県政」研究についての一考察). *Okinawa bunka kenkyū* (沖縄文化研究) 29:287–322.

Oshiro, Sally Katsuko. 1964. "Kyūyō Gaikan Irōsetsuden ([Ryukyuan] Traditional Narratives Bequeathed by the Aged, Supplement to the Kyūyō): An Annotated Translation." MA thesis, University of Hawaiʻi.

Ōyama Ringorō (大山麟五郎). 1996. "Ryūkyū ōchō fukuzoku jidai" (琉球王朝服属時代). In *Kaitei Naze-shi shi 1 kan, Rekishi-hen,* ed. Kaitei Naze-shi shi hensan iinkai, 234–61. Naze [Amami]: Naze shiyakusho.

Pearson, Richard. 2013. *Ancient Ryukyu: An Archaeological Study of Island Communities.* Honolulu: University of Hawaiʻi Press.

Pellard, Thomas. 2015. "The Linguistic Archeology of the Ryukyu Islands." In *Handbook of the Ryukyuan Languages,* ed. Patrick Heinrich, Shinso Miyara, and Michinori Shimoji, 13–37. Berlin: De Gruyter Mouton.

Rabson, Steve, trans. 1989. *Okinawa: Two Postwar Novellas.* Berkeley, CA: Center for Japanese Studies.

———. 1999a. "Assimilation Policy in Okinawa: Promotion, Resistance, and 'Reconstruction.'" In *Okinawa: Cold War Island,* ed. Chalmers Johnson, 133–48. Cardiff, CA: Japan Policy Research Center.

———. 1999b. "Life on the Mainland: As Portrayed in Modern Okinawan Literature." In *Okinawa: Cold War Island,* ed. Chalmers Johnson, 71–91. Cardiff, CA: Japan Policy Research Center.

———. 2012. *The Okinawan Diaspora in Japan: Crossing the Borders Within.* Honolulu: University of Hawaiʻi Press.

Reich, David. 2018. *Who We Are and How We Got Here: Ancient DNA and the New Science of the Human Past.* New York: Pantheon.

Rekidai hōan yakuchūbon (歴代宝案訳注本). 1994–2022. Edited and translated by Wada Hisanori (和田久徳) et al. 15 vols. Naha: Okinawa-ken kyōiku iinkai.

Robbeets, Martine, et al. 2021. "Triangulation Supports Agricultural Spread of the Transeurasian Languages." *Nature* 599:616–21. https://doi.org/10.1038/s41586-021-04108-8.

Robinson, Kenneth R. 1997. "The Jiubian and Ezogachishima Embassies to Chosŏn, 1478–1482." *Chōsenshi kenkyūkai ronbunshū,* no. 35 (October 1997): 56–86.

———. 2000a. "Centering the King of Chosŏn: Aspects of Korean Maritime Diplomacy, 1392–1592." *Journal of Asian Studies* 59, no. 1 (February): 109–25.

———. 2000b. "The *Haedong Chegukki* (1471) and Korean-Ryukyuan Relations, 1389–1471: Part 1." *Acta Koreana* 3, no. 1:87–98.

———. 2001. "The *Haedong Chegukki* (1471) and Korean-Ryukyuan Relations, 1389–1471: Part 2." *Acta Koreana* 4, no. 1:115–42.

Røkkum, Arne. 2006. *Nature, Ritual, and Society in Japan's Ryukyu Islands.* New York: Routledge.

Ryūkyū ōkoku hyōjōsho monjo henshū iinkai (琉球王国評定所文書編集委員会), eds. 1988–2003. *Ryūkyū ōkoku hyōjōsho monjo* (琉球王国評定所文書). 20 vols. Urasoe: Urasoe-shi kyōiku iinkai.

Ryukyu Shimpo, ed. 2014. *Descent into Hell: Civilian Memories of the Battle of Okinawa.* Translated and with commentary by Mark Ealey and Alastair McLauchlan, with a foreword by Higa Tatsuro and an introduction by Ota Masahide. Portland, ME: Merwin Asia.

Ryūkyū shinpōsha, ed. 1989. *Shin Ryūkyūshi, kinsei hen* (新琉球史、近世編). Vol. 1. Naha: Ryūkyū shinpōsha.

———, ed. 1990. *Shin Ryūkyūshi, kinsei hen* (新琉球史、近世編). Vol. 2. Naha: Ryūkyū shinpōsha.

Ryukyuan International Relations and Sources for Modern Okinawan History Digital Archives (琉球王国交流史・近代沖縄史料デジタルアーカイブ). n.d. Okinawa-ken kyōiku iinkai. https://ryuoki-archive.jp/en. Accessed May 17, 2024.

Sai On (蔡温). 1984. *Sai On zenshū* (*Sai Onshū*, 蔡温全集). Edited by Sakihama Shūmei (崎浜秀明). Honpō shoseki.

Sakihama Shūmei (崎浜秀明), ed. 1986. *Ryūkyū karitsu, Shinshū karitsu, Kyūmei hōjō, Hirajo kiroku* (琉球科律・新集科律・糾明法条・平等所記録). Honpō shoseki.

Sankei shinbun (産経新聞). 2024. "Chūgoku no daigaku ga 'Ryūkyū kenkyū sentā' setsuritsu e Okinawa no Nihon kizoku mondai-ka de Nihon kensei nerau" (中国の大学が「琉球研究センター」設立へ沖縄の日本帰属問題化で日本牽制狙う). September 12.

Satō Ryō (佐藤亮). 2016. *Ryūkyū ōkoku o michibiita saishō Sai On no kotoba* (琉球王国を導いた宰相蔡温の言葉). Naha: Bōdaainku.

Scott, James C. 2017. *Against the Grain: A Deep History of the Earliest States.* New Haven, CT: Yale University Press.

Seto Tetsuya (瀬戸哲也). 2019. "Shūraku kara gusuku e: gusuku jidai ni okeru kōeki to nōkō no tenkai" (集落からグスクへ: グスク時代における交易と農耕の展開). In *Ryūkyū no chūsei* (琉球の中世), ed. Chūseigaku kenkyūkai (中世学研究会), 45–67. Kōshi shoin.

Shimabuku, Annmaria M. 2019. *Alegal: Biopolitics and the Unintelligibility of Okinawan Life.* New York: Fordham University Press.

Shimaura Kōichi (島村幸一), Okogi Toshiaki (小此木敏明), and Yara Ken'ichirō (屋良健一郎), eds. 2022. *Yakuchū Ryūkyū bungaku* (訳注琉球文学). Bensei shuppan.

Shimoji Kazuhiro (下地和宏). 2008. "Tōji kōeki to Miyako: Miyako-jin to Chūzan chōkō nitsuite" (陶磁交易と宮古: 密牙古人と中山朝貢について). In *Nichi-Ryū kōeki no reimei: Yamato kara no shōgeki* (日琉交易の黎明: ヤマトからの衝撃), ed. Tanigawa Ken'ichi (谷川健一), 327–46. Shinwasha.

Shinjō Chōkō (新城朝功). 1925. *Hinshi no Ryūkyū* (瀕死の琉球). Etsuzandō.

Shinzato Akito (新里亮人). 2018. *Ryūkyūkoku seiritsu zenya no kōkogaku* (琉球国成立前夜の考古学). Dōseisha.

Shinzato Keiji (新里恵二), Taminato Tomoaki (田港朝昭), and Kinjō Seitoku (金城正篤). 1972/1983. *Okinawa-ken no rekishi* (沖縄県の歴史). Yamakawa shuppansha.

Shinzato Takayuki (新里貴之). 2010. "Chūbu Ryūkyūken senshi jidai no hensen" (中部琉球圏先史時代の社会の変遷). *Kōkogaku jaanaru* (考古学ジャーナル), no. 597 (March): 9–11.

———. 2018. "Kaizuka jidaigo ikki no doki bunka" (貝塚時代後一期の土器文化). In *Amami, Okinawa shotō senshigaku no saizensen* (奄美・沖縄諸島先史学の最前線), ed. Takamiya Hiroto (高宮広土), 20–44. Kagoshima: Nanpō shinsha.

Shiroma Ari (城間有). 2020. "'Shuri-jō ni wa onnen o kanjiru' ritō kara mita Shuri no sugata ni kisha kunō: Naha chūshin no shiten toinaosu" (「首里城には怨念を感じる」離島から見た首里の姿に記者苦悩: 那覇中心の視点問い直す). *Okinawa taimusu* (沖縄タイムス), October 18.

Shō Shōken (向象賢). 1650/2011. *Chūzan seikan* (Reflections on *Chūzan*, 中山世鑑). Edited and translated by Moromi Tomoshige (諸見友重). Ginowan: Yōju shorin.

———. 1673/1981. *Haneji shioki* (羽地仕置). In *Okinawa-ken shiryō, zenkindai 1* (沖縄県史料、前近代1), ed. Okinawa-ken Okinawa shiryō henshūjo, 1–57. Naha: Okinawa-ken kyōiku iinkai.

Sin Sugju (申叔舟). 1471/1991. *Account of East Sea Countries* (*Haedong jegukgi*). In *Kaitō shokokuki: Chōsenjin no mita chūsei Nihon to Ryūkyū* (海東諸国紀朝鮮人の見た 中世日本と琉球), trans. and ed. Tanaka Takeo (田中健夫). Iwanami shoten.

Smits, Gregory. 1999. *Visions of Ryukyu: Identity and Ideology in Early-Modern Thought and Politics.* Honolulu: University of Hawai'i Press.

———. 2001. "The Ryūkyū Shobun in East Asian and World History." In *Ryūkyū in World History*, ed. Josef Kreiner, 279–304. Bonn: Bier'sche Verlagsanstalt.

———. 2002. "Jahana Noboru: Okinawa Activist and Scholar." In *The Human Tradition in Modern Japan*, ed. Anne Walthall, 99–113. Wilmington, DE: Scholarly Resources.

———. 2006. "The Politics of Culture in Early Twentieth Century Okinawa." In *Japanese-ness versus Ryūkyūanism*, ed. Josef Kreiner, 59–70. Bonn: Bier'sche Verlagsanstalt.

———. 2010a. "Examining the Myth of Ryukyuan Pacifism." *Asia-Pacific Journal: Japan Focus*, vol. 8, issue 37, no. 3 (September). https://apjjf.org/gregory-smits/3409 /article.

———. 2015a. "New Cultures, New Identities: Becoming Okinawan and Japanese in Nineteenth-Century Ryukyu." In *Values, Identity, and Equality in Eighteenth- and Nineteenth-Century Japan*, ed. Peter Nosco, James E. Ketelaar, and Yasunori Kojima, 159–78. Leiden: Brill.

———. 2019. *Maritime Ryukyu, 1050–1650.* Honolulu: University of Hawai'i Press.

———. 2024. *Early Ryukyuan History: A New Model.* Honolulu: University of Hawai'i Press.

Suíshū "Liúqiúguó" (隋書 "流求國"). 636. Chinese Text Project. https://ctext.org/wiki .pl?if=en&chapter=584840#流求國.

Taichū Jōnin (袋中上人). 1605/1988. *Zen'yaku Ryūkyū shintōki* (全訳琉球神道記). Translated and edited by Ginoza Shigō (宜野座嗣剛). Tōyō tosho shuppan.

Takahashi Ichirō (高橋一郎). 2008. "Umi no ko-Amami: Higashi-Ajia kaiiki no jūgo seiki o yomu" (海の古奄美: 東アジア海域の十五世紀を読む). In *Nichi-Ryū kōeki no reimei: Yamato kara no shōgeki* (日琉交易の黎明: ヤマトからの衝撃), ed. Tanigawa Ken'ichi (谷川健一), 151–81. Shinwasha.

Takahashi, Shinnosuke. 2024. *The Translocal Island of Okinawa: Anti-Base Activism and Grassroots Regionalism.* New York: Bloomsbury Academic.

Takamiya Hiroto (高宮広土). 2005. *Shima no senshigaku: Paradaisu de wa nakatta Okinawa shotō no senshigaku* (島の先史学: パラダイスではなかった沖縄諸島の 先史学). Naha: Bōdaainku.

———. 2018. *Amami, Okinawa shotō senshigaku no saizensen* (奄美・沖縄諸島先史学 の最前線). Kagoshima: Nanpō shinsha.

Takanashi Osamu (高梨修). 2008. "Gusuku isekigun to Kikaigashima: Ryūkyū-ko to Kikaijima seiryokuken" (城久遺跡群とキカイがシマ: 琉球弧と喜界島勢力圏). In *Nichi-Ryū kōeki no reimei: Yamato kara no shōgeki* (日琉交易の黎明: ヤマト からの衝撃), ed. Tanigawa Ken'ichi (谷川健一), 121–49. Shinwasha.

———. 2015. "Chūsei Amami no jōkaku iseki" (中世奄美の城郭遺跡). In *Ryūkyūshi o toinaosu: Ko-Ryūkyū jidai ron* (琉球史を問い直す: 古琉球時代論), ed. Yoshinari Naoki (吉成直樹), Takanashi Osamu (高梨修), and Ikeda Yoshifumi (池田榮史), 243–66. Shinwasha.

Takara Kurayoshi (高良倉吉). 1982. "Kinsei makki no Yaeyama tōji to jinkō mondai:

Onaga ueekata shioki to sono haikei" (近世末期の八重山統治と人口問題: 翁長親方仕置とその背景). *Okinawa shiryō henshūjo kiyō*, no. 7:1–45.

———. 1987. *Ryūkyū ōkoku no kōzō* (琉球王国の構造). Yoshikawa kōbunkan.

———. 1989. *Ryūkyū ōkokushi no kadai* (琉球王国史の課題). Naha: Hirugisha.

———. 2011. *Ryūkyū ōkokushi no tankyū* (琉球王国史の探求). Ginowan: Yōju shorin.

Takara Kurayoshi (高良倉吉) and Dana Masayuki (田名真之), eds. 1993. *Zusetsu Ryūkyū ōkoku* (図説琉球王国). Kawade shobō shinsha.

Takeuchi Yuzuru (竹内譲). 1933/1960. *Shumi no Kikaijimashi* (趣味の喜界島史). Rev. ed. Kuroshio bunka kai.

Tamura Hiroshi (田村浩). 1927/1977. *Ryūkyū kyōsan sonraku no kenkyū* (琉球共産村落の研究). Sōgensha.

Tanaka Takeo (田中健夫). 2012. *Wakō to kangō bōeki* (倭寇と勘合貿易). Edited by Murai Shōsuke. Expanded ed. Chikuma gakugei bunko.

Tanigawa Ken'ichi (谷川健一). 1986. *Okinawa, Amami to Yamato* (沖縄・奄美と日本). Dōseisha.

———. 2007. *Yomigaeru kaijō no michi, Nihon to Ryūkyū* (甦る海上の道・日本と琉球). Bungei shunjū.

———. 2008. "Jo: Nissō bōeki to Nichi-Ryū kōeki" (序: 日宋貿易と日琉交易). In *Nichi-Ryū kōeki no reimei: Yamato kara no shōgeki* (日琉交易の黎明: ヤマトからの衝撃), ed. Tanigawa Ken'ichi (谷川健一), 8–25. Shinwasha.

Tanigawa Ken'ichi (谷川健一) and Orikuchi Shinobu (折口信夫). 2012. *Ryūkyū ōken no genryū* (琉球王権の源流). Ginowan: Yōju shorin.

Tanji, Miyume. 2006. *Myth, Protest and Struggle in Okinawa*. New York: Routledge.

Tinello, Marco. 2018. "A New Interpretation of the Bakufu's Refusal to Open the Ryukyus to Commodore Perry." *Asia-Pacific Journal: Japan Focus*, vol. 16, issue 17, no. 3 (September 1). https://apjjf.org/2018/17/tinello.

———. 2022. "Islands between Empires: The Ryukyu Shobun in Japanese and American Expansion in the Pacific." *Critical Asian Studies* 54, no. 4:513–32.

Tōma Shiichi (當眞嗣一). 2012. *Ryūkyū gusuku kenkyū* (琉球グスク研究). Naha: Ryūkyū shobō.

Tomiyama Kazuyuki (富見山和行). 1991. "Tōitsu ōkoku keiseiki no taigai kankei" (統一王国形成期の対外関係). In *Shin Ryūkyūshi, Ko-Ryūkyū hen*, ed. Ryūkyū shinpōsha, 141–62. Naha: Ryūkyū shinpōsha.

———. 2002. "Minami no Ryūkyū" (南の琉球). In *Kita no Hiraizumi, Minami no Ryūkyū* (北の平泉、南の琉球), ed. Irumada Nobuo (入間田宣夫) and Tomiyama Kazuyuki (豊見山和行), 165–308. Chūō kōronsha.

———. 2003. "Kinsei Ryūkyū shakai no tokuchō to shoronten" (近世琉球社会の特徴と諸論点). In *Ryūkyū, Okinawashi no sekai* (琉球、沖縄史の世界), ed Tomiyama Kazuyuki (富見山和行), 67–81. Yoshikawa kōbunkan.

———. 2004. *Ryūkyū ōkoku no gaikō to ōken* (琉球王国の外交と王権). Yoshikawa kōbunkan.

Tonaki Akira (渡名喜明). 1992. "Aji, noro, ō: monogatari no kōzō to ronri" (アジ・ノロ・王: 物語の構造と論理). In *Ryūkyūko no sekai* (琉球弧の世界), ed. Tanigawa Ken'ichi (谷川健一), 159–92. Shōgakkan.

Uehara Kenzen (上原兼善). 1992. "Ryūkyū ōchō no rekishi: Daiichi, daini shōshi no seiritsu to tenkai" (琉球王朝の歴史: 第一第二尚氏の成立と展開). In *Ryūkyūko no sekai* (琉球弧の世界), ed. Tanigawa Ken'ichi (谷川健一), 195–264. Shōgakkan.

———. 2009. *Shimazu-shi no Ryūkyū shinryaku: Mō hitotsu no keichō no eki* (島津氏の
琉球侵略: もう一つの慶長の役). Ginowan: Yōju shorin.

———. 2016. *Kinsei Ryūkyū bōekishi no kenkyū* (近世琉球貿易史の研究). Iwata shoin.

Uema Atsushi (上間篤). 2018. *Chūsei no Nakijin to sono seiryoku no fūbō: Genchō ni
tsukaeta Aranjin to Han'anchi* (中世の今帰仁とその勢力の風貌: 元朝に仕えた
アラン人と攀安知). Naha: Bōdaainku.

Ueunten, Wesley I. 2024. "On Failure, Silence and the Kingdom: Interview of Shō
Yamagusiku." In *Okinawan Journal of Island Studies* 5 (November): 132–37.

Uezato Takashi (上里隆史). 2000. "Ryūkyū no kaki ni tsuite" (琉球の火器について).
Okinawa bunka 36, no. 91:73–92.

———. 2002. "Ko-Ryūkyū no guntai to sono rekishiteki tenkai" (古琉球の軍隊とその
歴史的展開). *Ryūkyū Ajia shakai bunka kenkyūkai kiyō*, no. 5 (October): 105–62.

———. 2009. *Ryū-Nichi sensō 1609: Shimazu-shi no Ryūkyū shinkō* (琉日戦争一六〇九:
島津氏の琉球侵攻). Naha: Bōdaainku, 2009.

———. 2010. "Bunken shiryō kara mita Ko-Ryūkyū no kinkōhin: Buki, bugu no bun-
seki o chūshin ni" (文献史料からみた古琉球の金工品: 武器・武具の分析を
中心に). In *Higashi-Ajia o meguru kinzoku kōgei: Chūsei, kokusai kōryū no shin-
shiten*, ed. Kubo Tomoyasu, 224–55. Bensei shuppan.

———. 2012. *Umi no ōkoku, Ryūkyū: "Kaiiki Ajia" kusshi no kōeki kokka no jitsuzō*
(海の王国・琉球:「海域アジア」屈指の交易国家の実像). Yōsensha.

Uezato Takashi (上里隆史) and Yamamoto Masaaki (山本正昭), eds. 2019. *Okinawa no
meijō o aruku* (沖縄の名城を歩く). Yoshikawa kōbunkan.

University of the Ryukyus Repository. n.d. https://roar.eprints.org/1436. Accessed
May 17, 2024.

Watanabe Hiroshi. 2012. *A History of Japanese Political Thought, 1600–1901*. Translated
by David Noble. International House of Japan.

Watanabe Miki (渡辺美季). 2011. "Nihonjin ni narisumasu Ryūkyūjin: Shin ni taisuru
Ryūnichi kankei no inpei to hyōryū, hyōchaku" (日本人になりすます琉球人: 清
に対する琉日関係の隠蔽と漂流・漂着). In *Satsuma shinkō 400-nen: Mirai e no
rashinban*, ed. Ryūkyū shinpōsha and Nankai Nichinichi shinbunsha, 111–21. Naha:
Ryūkyū shinpōsha.

———. 2012. *Kinsei Ryūkyū to Chū-Nichi kankei* (近世琉球と中日関係). Yoshikawa
kōbunkan.

———. n.d. "Ryūkyū-shi kenkyū rinku-shū" (琉球史研究リンク集). https://ryukyu
history.web.fc2.com/useful.html. Accessed May 17, 2024.

Xià Zǐyáng (夏子陽). 1606/2001. *Shi Ryūkyū roku* (Shǐ Liúqiú lù, 使琉球録). Translated
by Harada Nobuo. Ginowan: Yōju shorin.

Xú Bǎoguāng (徐葆光). 1721/1982. *Chūzan denshinroku* (Zhōngshān chuánxìn lù, 中山傳
信録). Translated by Harada Nobuo (原田禹雄). Gensōsha.

Yahara, Colonel Hiromichi. 1995. *The Battle for Okinawa*. Translated by Roger Pineau
and Masatoshi Uehara, with an introduction by Frank B. Gibney. New York: John
Wiley & Sons.

Yakabi Osamu (屋嘉比収). 1994. "Okinawa hōgen ronsō ni okeru Yanagi Muneyoshi
no shisō" (沖縄方言論争における柳宗悦の思想). *Okinawa bunka* (沖縄文化) 29,
nos. 1–2:12–52.

Yamashita Fumitake (山下文武). 2007. *Ryūkyū gunki, Satsu-Ryū gundan* (琉球軍記・
薩琉軍談). Kagoshima: Nanpō shinsha.

Yamazato Jun'ichi (山里純一). 2012. *Kodai Ryūkyūko to Higashi-ajia* (古代の琉球弧と東アジア). Yoshikawa kōbunkan.

Yanagita Kunio (柳田國男). 1925. *Kainan shōki* (海南小記). Ōokayama shoten.

Yano Misako (矢野美沙子). 2014. *Ko-Ryūkyūki Shuri ōfu no kenkyū* (古琉球期首里王府の研究). Kōsō shobō.

Yara Ken'ichirō (屋良健一郎). 2017. "Ryūkyū jiresisho no yōshiki henka ni kansuru kōsatsu" (琉球辞令書の様式変化に関する考察). In *Ryūkyū shiryōgaku no funade: Ima, rekishi jōhō no nama e* (琉球史料学の船出：いま、歴史情報の生へ), ed. Kuroshima Satoru (黒嶋敏) and Yara Ken'ichirō, 69–117. Bensei shuppan.

Yoshinaga, Akiko. 2023. "Xi Makes First Remarks on Ryukyus, Mentioning China's 'Deep Exchange' with Okinawa." *Yomiuri shimbun* (Japan news), June 11.

Yoshinari Naoki (吉成直樹). 2008. *Sake to shaaman: "Omoro sōshi" o yomu* (酒とシャーマン：「おもろさうし」を読む). Shintensha.

———. 2018. *Ryūkyū ōken to taiyō no ō* (琉球王権と太陽の王). Shichigatsusha.

———. 2020. *Ryūkyū ōkoku wa dare ga tsukutta no ka? Wakō to kōeki no jidai* (琉球王国は誰がつくったのか: 倭寇と交易の時代). Shichigatsusha.

Yoshinari Naoki (吉成直樹) and Fuku Hiromi (福寛美). 2006. *Ryūkyū ōkoku to wakō: Omoro no kataru rekishi* (琉球王国と倭寇：おもろの語る歴史). Shinwasha.

———. 2007. *Ryūkyū ōkoku tanjō: Amami shotōshi kara* (琉球王国誕生: 奄美諸島史から). Shinwasha.

Yoshinari Naoki (吉成直樹) with Takanashi Osamu (高梨修) and Ikeda Yoshifumi (池田栄史). 2015. *Ryūkyūshi o toinaosu: Ko-Ryūkyū jidai ron* (琉球史を問い直す: 古琉球時代論). Shinwasha.

Ziomek, Kirsten L. 2014. "The 1903 Human Pavilion: Colonial Realities and Subaltern Subjectivities in Twentieth-Century Japan." *Journal of Asian Studies* 73, no. 2 (May): 493–516.

———. 2019. *Lost Histories: Recovering the Lives of Japan's Colonial Peoples.* Cambridge, MA: Harvard University Asia Center.

Selected Additional Sources

This list consists of additional primary sources, internet resources, and secondary sources that are likely to be of interest to researchers. It includes only published works in English and Japanese, plus some primary sources in classical Chinese. Owing to space requirements, I have been especially selective regarding works in English, and I have omitted most local histories in Japanese. Also, I have tended to favor more recent work. For older items pertaining to early modern Ryukyu, see the bibliography in Smits (1999). Moreover, for topics with a large literature such as the Battle of Okinawa or migration, I have included only a few of the most important or representative works. The place of publication for Japanese books is Tokyo unless otherwise indicated.

Primary Sources

There are multiple editions of the major Ryukyu-related primary sources, so this list is not exhaustive. I have favored editions that include notes and/or modern Japanese translations.

Chūzan seifu (中山世譜). 1701/1998. *Sai Taku bon Chūzan seifu* (蔡鐸本中山世譜). Translated by Harada Nobuo (原田禹雄). Ginowan: Yōju shorin.

Chūzan seifu (中山世譜). 1725/1988. *Sai On bon Chūzan seifu* (蔡温本中山世譜). Vol. 4 of *Ryūkyū shiryō sōsho* (琉球史料叢書), ed. Yokoyama Shigeru (横山重). Hōbun shokan.

Goryeo History. 2005. *Kōraishi Nihonden* (高麗史日本伝) (Goryeosa, Ilbonjeon). Edited and translated by Takeda Yukio (武田幸男). 2 vols. Iwanami shoten.

Hokama Shuzen (外間守善) and Saigō Nobutsuna (西郷信綱), eds. 1972. *Omoro sōshi* (おもろさうし). Iwanami shoten.

Inamura Kenpu (稲村賢敷). 1977. *Miyakojima kyūki narabini shika shūkai* (宮古島旧記並史歌集解). Shigensha.

Isa Shin'ichi (伊佐眞一), ed. 1998. *Jahana Noboru shū* (謝花昇集). Misuzu shobō.

Kreiner, Josef. 1996. *Sources of Ryūkyūan History and Culture in European Collections.* Munich: Iudicium.

Kyūyō kenkyū kai (球陽研究會), ed. 1743–1876/1974/1978. *Kyūyō yomikudashi hen* (球陽 読み下し編). Kadokawa shoten.

Lǐ Dǐngyuán (李鼎元). 1802/1985. *Shi Ryūkyū ki* (*Shǐ Liúqiú jì*, 使琉球記). Translated by Harada Nobuo (原田禹雄). Gensōsha.

Matsuda Kiyoshi (松田清). 1981. *Kodai, chūsei Amami shiryō* (古代・中世奄美史料). JCA shuppan.

Matsushita Shirō (松下志朗), ed. 2006. *Amami shiryō shūsei* (奄美大島史料集成). Kagoshima: Nanpō shinsha.

Matsushita Shirō (松下志朗) and Yamashita Fumitake (山下文武), eds. 2007–12. *Nansei-shotō shiryōshū* (南西諸島史料集). 5 vols. Kagoshima: Nanpō shinsha.

Nagayoshi Takeshi (永吉毅), comp. 1968. *Okinoerabujima kyōdoshi shiryō* (沖永良部島郷土史資料). Wadomari-chō: Wadomari machiyakuba.

Nanpo Bunshi (南浦文之). 1649. *Nanpo bunshū* (南浦文集). Compiled by Nakano Michitomo. 3 vols. Edo [Tokyo]: Nakano Michitomo.

Okinawa kenritsu hakubutsukan (沖縄県立博物館). 1993. *Kizamareta rekishi: Okinawa no sekihi to takuhon* (刻まれた歴史: 沖縄の石碑と拓本), ed. Naha: Okinawa kenritsu hakubutsukan tomo no kai.

Okinawa seifu (沖縄政府). 1969/1989. *Okinawa kenshi 19: Shinbun shūsei (shakai, bunka)* (沖縄県史 19: 新聞集成 [社会 文化]). Kokusho kankōkai.

Origins of Ryukyu. 1713/1940/1988. *Ryūkyūkoku yuraiki* (琉球国由来記). Vols. 1–2 of *Ryūkyū shiryō sōsho* (琉球史料叢書), ed. Yokoyama Shigeru (横山重). Hōbun shokan.

Ōta Pēchin Chokushiki. 1778/2018. *Okinawan Samurai: The Instructions of a Royal Official to His Only Son.* Translated by Andreas Quast. Edited by Andreas Quast and Motobu Naoki. Waldbronn: Andreas Quast.

Sakita Mitsunobu, ed. (先田光演). 2012. *Yorontō no komonjo o yomu* (与論島の古文書を読む). Kagoshima: Nanpō shinsha.

Sasamori Gisuke (笹森儀助). 1894/1982/1983. *Nantō tanken* (南嶋探検). Edited by Azuma Yoshimochi (東喜望). 2 vols. Daiichi shobō.

Shimajiri Katsutarō (島尻勝太郎) and Uezato Ken'ichi (上里賢一). 1990. *Ryūkyū Kanshi sen* 琉球漢詩選. Naha: Hirugisha.

Torigoe Kenzaburō (鳥越憲三郎). 1968. *Omoro sōshi zenyaku* (おもろさうし全訳). 5 vols. Osaka: Seibundō shuppan.

Tsukuda Seisaku (塚田清策). 1970. *Ryūkyūkoku hibunki* (琉球國碑文記). 4 vols. Keigaku shuppan. This appeared in one main volume and three supplementary volumes.

Wāng Jí (汪楫). 1684/1997. *Sakuhō Ryūkyū shiroku sanpen* (*Cèfēng Liúqiú shǐlù sānpiān*, 册封琉球使錄三篇). Translated by Harada Nobuo (原田禹雄). Yōju shorin.

Xiāo Chóngyè (蕭崇業) and Xiè Jié (謝杰). 1579/2011. *Shi Ryūkyū roku* (*Shǐ Liúqiú lù*, 使琉球錄). Translated by Harada Nobuo (原田禹雄) and Muira Kunio (三浦國雄). Ginowan: Yōju shorin.

"Yaeyama utaki yuraiki" (八重山御嶽由来記). 1982. In *Shintō taikei, Jinja hen 52: Okinawa*, ed. Shintō taikei hensankai, 690–716. Seikōsha.

Yamaguchi Eitetsu (山口栄鉄) and Arakawa Yūkō (新川右好), eds. 2002. *The Demise of the Ryukyu Kingdom: Western Accounts and Controversy* (*Ryūkyū ōkoku no hōkai: Daidōranki no Nitchū gaikōsen, Eibun genshiryō hen*, 琉球王国の崩壊: 大働乱の日中外交戦: 英文原史料編). Ginowan: Yōju shorin.

Yokoyama Shigeru (横山重), ed. 1940/1998. *Ryūkyū shiryō sōsho* (琉球史料叢書).
5 vols. Hōbun shokan.
Yononushi yuisho sho (世乃主由緒書). 1850/1968. In *Okinoerabujima kyōdoshi shiryō*
(沖永良部島郷土史資料), comp. Nagayoshi Takeshi (永吉毅), 177–80. Wadomari-
chō: Wadomari chōyakuba, 1968.

Internet Resources and Archives

Chinese Text Project. n.d. https://ctext.org. Accessed May 17, 2024.
Tōma, Tsugumi (當眞嗣美). http://omorosaushi-original.o-ki-na-wa.com. n.d.
Accessed May 17, 2024. Untitled website containing *Omoro sōshi*, other primary
sources, and reference works, some portions with English translation.
Japan Soil Inventory (*Nihon dojō inbentorii*, 日本土壌インベントリー). n.d. https://
soil-inventory.rad.naro.go.jp. Accessed December 16, 2024.
Meiji University. Ryukyu Documents Database. n.d. https://www.isc.meiji.ac.jp
/~meikodai/obj_ryukyu-en.html. Accessed December 16, 2024.
Naha City Museum of History (*Naha-shi rekishi hakubutsukan*, 那覇市歴史博物館),
Digital Museum. n.d. http://www.rekishi-archive.city.naha.okinawa.jp/digital
-museum. Accessed December 16, 2024.
Omoro sōshi detabeesu (*Omoro sōshi* database, おもろさうし』テキストデータベース).
n.d. https://www.isc.meiji.ac.jp/~meikodai/datebasa/omorosaushi.txt. Accessed
May 17, 2024.

Secondary Sources

Amami-gaku kankō iinkai (奄美学刊行委員会), eds. 2005. *Amami-gaku: Sono chihei to
kanata* (奄美学: その地平と彼方). Kagoshima: Nanpō shinsha.
Asato Susumu (安里進). 1990–93. *Kōkogaku kara mita Ryūkyūshi* (考古学から見た琉
球史). 2 vols. Naha: Hirugisha.
———. 1998. *Gusuku, kyōdōtai, mura* (グスク・共同体・村). Ginowan: Yōju shorin.
———. 2006. *Ryūkyū ōken to gusuku* (琉球王権とグスク). Yamakawa shuppansha.
Asato Susumu (安里進) and Doi Naomi (土肥直美). 2011. *Okinawajin wa doko kara
kita ka: Ryūkyū-Okinawajin no kigen to seiritsu* (沖縄人はどこから来たか: 琉球＝
沖縄人の起源と成立). Rev. ed. Naha: Bōdaainku.
Azuma Yasuyuki (東靖晋). 2008. "Nissō kōeki no michi: Ojika, Hakata, Munakata"
(日宋交易の道: 小値賀・博多・宗像). In *Nichi-Ryū kōeki no reimei: Yamato
kara no shōgeki* (日琉交易の黎明: ヤマトからの衝撃), ed. Tanigawa Ken'ichi
(谷川健一), 27–52. Shinwasha.
Batten, Bruce L. 2006. *Gateway to Japan: Hakata in War and Peace, 500–1300*. Honolulu: University of Hawai'i Press.
Beillevaire, Patrick. 2000. *Ryukyu Studies to 1854: Western Encounter*. London:
Routledge-Curzon.
———. 2002. *Ryukyu Studies since 1854: Western Encounter: Part II*. London:
Routledge-Curzon.

Chang, Felix K. 2021. "The Ryukyu Defense Line: Japan's Response to China's Naval Push into the Pacific Ocean." Foreign Policy Research Institute, February. https://www.fpri.org/article/2021/02/the-ryukyu-defense-line-japans-response-to-chinas-naval-push-into-the-pacific-ocean.

Christy, Alan S. 1995. "A Fantasy of Ancient Japan: The Assimilation of Okinawa in Yanagita Kunio's Kainan Shoki." In *Select Papers of the East Asia Center: Productions of Culture in Japan* (no. 10), ed. Tetsuo Najita, 61–90. Chicago: East Asia Center, University of Chicago.

———. 2006. "Primitive Communists and Profiteering Women: Propriety and Scandal in Okinawan Studies." In *Orientalism: From Postcolonial Theory to World History*, ed. E. Burke and D. Prochaska, 414–36. Lincoln: University of Nebraska Press.

———. 2012. *A Discipline on Foot: Inventing Japanese Native Ethnology, 1910–1945*. Lanham, MD: Rowman & Littlefield.

Dana Masayuki (田名真之). 1983. "Kunigami Samanokami" (国頭佐馬頭). In *Okinawa daihyakka jiten* (沖縄大百科事典), ed. Okinawa daihyakka jiten kankō jimukyoku (沖縄大百科事典刊行事務局), 1:961. Naha: Okinawa taimusu sha.

David, Saul. 2020. *Crucible of Hell: The Heroism and Tragedy of Okinawa, 1945*. New York: Hachette.

Eguchi Tsukasa (江口司). 2008. "Nantō kōeki to yabusa: Shiranui-kai engan o chūshin ni" (南島交易とヤブサ: 不知火海沿岸を中心に). In *Nichi-Ryū kōeki no reimei: Yamato kara no shōgeki* (日琉交易の黎明: ヤマトからの衝撃), ed. Tanigawa Ken'ichi (谷川健一), 91–119. Shinwasha.

Fuku Hiromi (福寛美). 2018. *Amami guntō omoro no sekai* (奄美群島おもろの世界). Kagishima-shi: Nanpō shinsha.

———. 2021. *Kazan to take no megami: Kiki, Manyō, Omoro* (火山と竹の女神: 記紀, 万葉, おもろ). Shichigatsusha.

Fukunaga, Fumio. 2021. *The Occupation of Japan, 1945–1952: Tokyo, Washington, and Okinawa*. Japan Publishing Industry Foundation for Culture.

Gotō Akira (後藤明). 2010. *Umi kara mita Nihonjin: Kaijin de yomu Nihon no rekishi* (海から見た日本人: 海人で読む日本の歴史). Kōdansha.

———. 2016. "Solar Kingdom of Ryukyu: The Formation of a Cosmovision in the Southern Islands of the Japanese Archipelago." *Journal of Astronomy in Culture* 1, no. 1:77–88.

Hamashita, Takeshi. 2011. "The *Lidai Baoan* and the Ryukyu Maritime Tributary Trade Network with China and Southeast Asia, the Fourteenth to Seventeenth Centuries." In *Chinese Circulations: Capital, Commodities, and Networks in Southeast Asia*, ed. Eric Tagliacozzo and Wen-Chin Chang, 107–29. Durham, NC: Duke University Press.

Hanihara, Kazuro. 1991. "Dual Structure Model for the Population History of the Japanese." *Japan Review*, no. 2:1–33.

Hateruma Eikichi (波照間永吉), ed. 2007. *Ryūkyū no rekishi to bunka: Omoro sōshi no sekai* (琉球の歴史と文化:『おもろさうし』の世界). Kadokawa kakugei shuppan.

Hein, Ina, and Isabelle Prochaska-Meyer, eds. 2015. *40 Years since Reversion: Negotiating the Okinawan Difference in Japan Today*. Vienna: Department of East Asian Studies/Japanese Studies, University of Vienna.

Higa Minoru (比嘉実). 1991. *Ko-Ryūkyū no shisō* (古琉球の思想). Naha: Okinawa taimusu sha.

Higashionna Kanjun (東恩納寛惇). 1978–82. *Higashionna Kanjun zenshū* (東恩納寛惇全集). Edited by Ryūkyū shinpōsha. 10 vols. Dai'ichi shobō.

Hisaoka Manabu (久岡学). 2011. "Uta ga tsutaeta waboku kōshō" (唄が伝えた和睦交渉). In *Satsuma shinkō 400-nen: Mirai e no rashinban* (薩摩侵攻400年未来への羅針盤), ed. Ryūkyū shinpōsha and Nankai nichinichi shinbunsha, 47–52. Naha: Ryūkyū shinpōsha.

Hong-Schunka, S. M. 2005. "An Aspect of East Asian maritime trade: The exchange of commodities between Korea and Ryūkyū (1389–1638)." In *Trade and Transfer Across the East Asian "Mediterranean,"* ed. Angela Schottenhammer, 125–61. Wiesbaden, Germany: Harrassowitz.

Hudson, Mark J. 1999. *Ruins of Identity: Ethnogenesis in the Japanese Islands.* Honolulu: University of Hawai'i Press.

Ikehata Kōichi (池畑耕一). 1990. "Kai no michi: Kai no bunka to Hirota iseki" (貝の道: 貝の文化と広田遺跡). In *Hayato sekai no shimajima* (隼人世界の島々), ed. Ōbayashi Taryō (大林大良) et al., 111–38. Shōgakkan.

Ikemiya Masaharu (池宮正治). 2015. *Ikemiya Masaharu chosaku senshū 2: Ryūkyū geinō sōron* (池宮正治著作選集2: 琉球芸能総論), ed. Shimamura Kōichi (島村幸一). Kasama shoin.

Ikeno Shigeru (池野茂). 1994. *Ryūkyū Yanbarusen: Suiun no tenkai* (琉球山原船: 水運の展開). Ginowan: Roman shobō honten.

Ikuta Shigeru (生田滋). 1984b. "Taigai kankei kara mita Ryūkyū kodaishi: Nantō inasakushi no rikai no tame ni" (対外関係からみた琉球古代史: 南島稲作史の理解のために). In *Nantō inasaku bunka: Yonagunijima o chūshin ni* (南島稲作文化: 与那国島を中心に), ed. Watanabe Tadayo and Ikuta Shigeru, 94–125. Hōsei daigaku shuppankyoku.

Inafuku Seiki (稲福盛輝). 1995. *Okinawa shippeishi* (沖縄疾病史). Daiichi shobō.

Inamura Kenpu (稲村賢敷). 1969. *Okinawa no kodai buraku makyo no kenkyū* (沖縄の古代部落マキョの研究). Naha: Shirono insatsu.

Ishihara Masaie (石原昌家), Kishi Masahiko (岸政彦), and Okinawa taimusu sha (沖縄タイムス社), eds. 2023. *Okinawa no seikatsu shi* (沖縄の生活史). Misuzu shobō.

Jinam, Timothy, et al. 2012. "The History of Human Populations in the Japanese Archipelago Inferred from Genome-Wide SNP Data with a Special Reference to the Ainu and Ryukyuan Populations." *Journal of Human Genetics* 57:787–95.

Kamakura Yoshitarō (鎌倉芳太郎). 1982. *Okinawa bunka no ihō* (沖縄文化の遺宝). 2 vols. Iwanami shoten.

Kamei Meitoku (亀井明徳). 1993. "Nansei shotō ni okeru bōeki tōjiki no ryūtsū keiro" (南西諸島における貿易陶磁器の流通経路). *Jōchi Ajia-gaku* 11:11–45.

Kanehisa Tadashi (金久正). 1978. *Amami ni ikiru Nihon kodai bunka* (奄美に生きる日本古代文化). Rev. ed. Shigensha.

Katsukata-Inafuku Keiko (勝方＝稲福恵子) and Maetakenishi Kazuma (前嵩西一馬), eds. 2010. *Okinawagaku nyūmon: Kūfuku no sahō* (沖縄学入門: 空腹の作法). Shōwadō.

Kawamura Minato (川村湊). 2011. *Gendai Okinawa bungaku sakuhinsen* (現代沖縄文学作品選). Kōdansha.

Kim Talsu (金達寿). 1989. *Nihon no naka no Chōsen bunka* (日本の中の朝鮮文化). Vol. 11. Kōdansha.

Kinjō Seitoku (金城正篤). 1978. *Ryūkyū shobun ron* (琉球処分論). Naha: Okinawa taimusu sha.

Kinoshita, Naoko. 2019. "Prehistoric Ryūkyūan Seafaring: A Cultural and Environ-mental Perspective." In *Prehistoric Maritime Cultures and Seafaring in East Asia*, ed. Chunming Wu and Barry Vladimir Rolett, 315–32. Singapore: Springer.

Kitami Toshio (北見俊夫). 1986. *Nihon kaijō kōtsūshi no kenkyū: Minzoku bunkashi-teki kōsatsu* (日本海上交通史の研究: 民族文化史的考察). Hōsei daigaku shuppankyoku.

Kondō Ken'ichirō (近藤健一郎). 2008. *Hōgen fuda: Kotoba to shintai* (方言札: ことばと身体). Shakai hyōronsha.

Korea Fortress Academy. 2008b. *Mountain Fortresses of Inland Korea II: Sangdang Sansong Mountain Fortresses*. Chungcheongbuk-do Province.

Kreiner, Josef, ed. 2001. *Ryūkyū in World History*. Bonn: Bier'sche.

Kubo Noritada, ed. (窪徳忠). 1990. *Okinawa no fūsui* (沖縄の風水). Hirakawa shuppansha.

Kurima Yasuo (来間泰男). 1990. *Okinawa no keizairon hihan* (沖縄の経済論批判). Nihon Keizai hyōronsha.

Linke, Michael. 2023. *The Korean Castle: Understanding Korean Castles through Photo-graphs*. Linklandiya.

Loo, Tze May. 2014. *Heritage Politics: Shuri Castle and Okinawa's Incorporation into Modern Japan, 1879–2000*. Lanham, MD: Lexington.

Maehira Fusaaki (真栄平房昭). 2019. *Tabi suru Ryūkyū, Okinawa shi* (旅する琉球・沖縄史). Naha: Bōdaainku.

McCormack, Gavin, and Satoko Oka Norimatsu. 2012. *Resistant Islands: Okinawa Con-fronts Japan and the United States*. Lanham, MD: Rowman & Littlefield.

Miyagi Eishō (宮城栄昌) and Takamiya Hiroe (高宮廣衛), eds. 1983. *Okinawa rekishi chizu, rekishi hen* (沖縄歴史地図＜歴史編＞). Kashiwa shobō.

Miyanaga Masamori (宮良當壮). 1924. "Waga kodaigo to Ryūkyūgo to no hikaku" (我が古代語と琉球語との比較). *Shigaku* (史学) 3, no. 3:51–89 (394–432).

Miyara Angen (宮良安彦). 2002. "Yaeyama shotō no Heike densetsu to wakō no kōseki" (八重山諸島の平家伝説と倭寇の行跡). *Okinawa bunka kenkyū*, no. 28:259–89.

Miyazato Chōkō (宮里朝光), ed. 2001. *Okinawa monchū daijiten* (沖縄門中大辞典). Haebaru-chō: Naha shuppansha.

Morimoto Isao (盛本勲). 2008. "Gusuku jidai no makuake: Bunbutsu to nōkō o me-gutte" (グスク時代と幕開け: 文物と農耕をめぐって). In *Nichi-Ryū kōeki no re-imei: Yamato kara no shōgeki* (日琉交易の黎明: ヤマトからの衝撃), ed. Tanigawa Ken'ichi (谷川健一), 263–84. Shinwasha.

Mukai Kiyoshi (向井清史). 1988. *Okinawa kindai keizaishi* (沖縄近代経済史). Nihon Keizai hyōronsha.

Murai Shōsuke (村井章介). 1988. *Ajia no naka no chūsei Nihon* (アジアの中の中世日本). Kōsō shobō.

———. 2008. "Chūsei Nihon to ko-Ryūkyū no Hazama" (中世日本と古琉球の狭間). In *Kodai chūsei no ryōkai: Kikaigashima no sekai*, ed. Ikeda Yoshifumi, 97–122. Kōshi shoin.

———. 2013. *Zōho, Chūsei Nihon no uchi to soto* (増補, 中世日本の内と外). Chikuma gakugei bunko.

Murayama, Hina, and Temo Dias. 2018. "Invasive Bases and Tourist Hordes Threaten Okinawa's Environment." *Asia Times*, September 1.

Naka Shōhachirō (名嘉正八郎) et al., eds. 1980. *Nihon jōkaku taikei 1: Hokkaidō, Oki-nawa* (日本城郭体系1: 北海道・沖縄). Shinjinbutsu ōraisha.

Nakamura Kazumi (中村和美). 2008. "Manosegawa ryūiki no iseki: Ibutsu karamiru kōeki no kanōsei" (万之瀬川流域の遺跡: 遺物からみる交易の可能性). In *Nichi-Ryū kōeki no reimei: Yamato kara no shōgeki* (日琉交易の黎明: ヤマトからの衝撃), ed. Tanigawa Ken'ichi (谷川健一), 73–90. Shinwasha.

Nakamura Satoru (中村覚). 2018. *Kore dake wa shitteokitai Okinawa no shinjitsu: Dare ga Okinawa o Mamoru ka?* (これだけは知っておきたい沖縄の真実: 誰が沖縄を守るのか). Meiseisha.

Nakasone Masaji (仲宗根將二). 1990. "Sakishima ni okeru shūken katei kara mita ōken" (先島における集権過程からみた王権). *Okinawa bungaku*, no. 85 (Autumn): 97–103.

———. 1992. "Miyako no rekishi to shinkō" (宮古の歴史と信仰). In *Ryūkyūko no sekai* (琉球弧の世界), ed. Tanigawa Ken'ichi (谷川健一), 503–31. Shōgakkan.

Nakayama Tarō (中山太郎). 1929/2012. *Nihon fujoshi* (日本巫女史). Kokusho kankōkai.

Nakazawa, Katsuji. 2023. "Analysis: Xi throws Okinawa into East Asia Geopolitical Cocktail." *Nikkei Asia*, June 15.

Nakijin kyōiku iinkai, eds. 2004. *Gusuku bunka o kangaeru: Sekai isan kokusai shinpojiumu "Higashi Ajia no jōkaku o hikakushite" no kiroku Gusuku bunka o kangaeruu* (グスク文化お考える: 世界遺産国際シンポジウム「東アジアの城郭を比較して」の記録グスク文化を考える), 133–46. Naha: Okinawa kōsoku insatsu kabushiki kaisha.

Nelson, Thomas. 2006. "Japan in the Life of Early Ryukyu." *Journal of Japanese Studies* 32, no. 2 (Summer): 367–92.

Nishizato Kikō (西里喜行). 1996. "Ryūkyū—Okinawashi ni okeru 'minzoku' no mondai: Ryūkyū ishiki no keisei, kakudai, jizoki ni tsuite" (琉球＝沖縄史における「民族」の問題: 琉球意識の形成・拡大・持続について). In *Atarashii Ryūkyū shizō: Araki Moriaki sensei tsuitō ronshū* (新しい琉球史像: 安良城盛昭先生追悼論集), ed. Takara Kurayoshi (高良倉吉), Tomiyama Kazuyuki (豊見山和行), and Maehira Fusaaki (真栄平房昭), 173–99. Ginowan: Yōjusha.

Nobori Shomu (昇曙夢). 1949/2009. *Fukkoku Dai-Amami shi* (復刻、大奄美史). Kagoshima: Nanpō shinsha.

Ōbayashi Taryō (大林太良). 1984. *Higashi Ajia no ōken shinwa: Nihon, Chōsen, Ryūkyū* (東アジアの王権神話: 日本・朝鮮・琉球). Kōbundō.

Ochiai Sadao (落合貞夫). 2022. *Gendai Okinawa bungakushi* (現代沖縄文学史). Naha: Bōdaainku.

Okinawa kogo daijiten henshū iinkai (沖縄古語大辞典編集委員会), ed. 1995. *Okinawa kogo daijiten* (沖縄古語大辞典). Kadokawa shoten.

Okinawa kōkogakkai (沖縄考古学会), eds. 2018. *Nantō kōko nyūmon: Horidasareta Okinawa no rekishi, bunka* (南島考古入門: 掘り出された沖縄の歴史・文化). Naha: Bōdaainku.

Okinawa kokusai daigaku kōkai kōza iinkai (沖縄国際大学公開講座委員会), eds. 1997. *Ryūkyū ōkoku no jidai* (琉球王国の時代). Naha: Bōdaainku.

Okinawa-ken kyōikuchō bunkaka (沖縄県教育庁文化課), eds. 1983. *Gusuku: Gusuku bunpu chōsa hōkoku (1): Okinawa hontō oyobi shūhen ritō* (ぐすく: グスク分布調査報告 [1]: 沖縄本島及び周辺離島). Okinawa kyōiku iinkai.

———. 1986. *Kadokawa Nihon chimei daijiten 47: Okinawa-ken* (角川日本地名大辞典47: 沖縄県). Edited by Kadokawa Nihon chimei daijiten hannsan iinkai (「角川日本地名大辞典」編纂委員会). Kadokawa shoten.

Orikuchi-hakase kinen kodai kenkyūjo (折口博士記念古代研究所), ed. 1976. *Orikuchi Shinobu zenshū* (折口信夫全集). Vol. 16. Chūō kōronsha.

Ōsato Kōei (大里康永). 1971. *Jahana Noboru den: Okinawa kaihō no senkusha* (謝花昇伝: 沖縄解放の先駆者). Taihei shuppansha.

Ōshiro Itsurō (大城逸郎). 1992. "Ryūkyūko no chishitsugaku: Ryūkyū rettō no seiritsu to tokushoku" (琉球弧の地質学: 琉球列島の成立と特色). In *Ryūkyūko no sekai* (琉球弧の世界), ed. Tanigawa Ken'ichi (谷川健一), 69–87. Shōgakkan.

Ōshiro Kei (大城慧). 1983. "Okinawa no tetsu" (沖縄の鉄). In *Ine to tetsu: Samazamana ōken no kiban* (稲と鉄: さまざまな王権の基盤), ed. Mori Kōichi (森浩一) et al., 282–300. Shōgakkan.

Ōshita Eiji (大下英治). 2019. *Uchinaa: San daiteikōsha no densetsu: Tōyama Kyūzō, Jahana Noboru, Taira Shinsuke* (ウチナー: 三大抵抗者の伝説: 当山久三・謝花昇・平良新助). Kawade shobō.

Ōtsuru Masamitsu (大鶴正満). 1998. "Okinawa no mararia" (沖縄のマラリア). In *Okinawa no rekishi to iryōshi* (沖縄の歴史と医療史), ed. Ryūkyū daigaku igakubu fuzoku chiiki iryō kenkyū sentā (琉球大学医学部付属地域医療研究センター), 149–55. Fukuoka: Kyūshū daigaku shuppankai.

Ouwehand, [Cornelius]. 1985. *Hateruma: Socio-Religious Aspects of a South-Ryukyuan Island Culture*. Leiden: Brill.

Ōyama Ringorō (大山麟五郎). 1980. "Amami ni okeru jinshin baibai, yanchu no kenkyū" (奄美における人身売買・ヤンチュの研究). *Okinawa bunka kenkyū*, no. 7:159–78.

———. 1996. "Shimazu-shi no Ryūkyū iri to Amami" (島津氏の琉球入りと奄美). In *Kaitei Naze-shi shi 1 kan, Rekishi-hen*, ed. Kaitei Naze-shi shi hensan iinkai, 265–89. Naze [Amami]: Naze shiyakusho.

Ptak, Roderich. 2005. "The Image of Fujian and Ryūkyū in the Letters of Cristóvão Vieira and Vasco Calvo." In *Trade and Transfer Across the East Asian "Mediterranean,"* ed. Angela Schottenhammer, 303–19. Wiesbaden: Harrassowitz.

Ryall, Julian. 2013. "Japan Angered by China's Claim to All of Okinawa." *Deutsche Welle*, October 5.

Sakihara, Mitsugu. 1987. *A Brief History of Early Okinawa Based on the Omoro Sōshi*. Honpō shoseki.

Sato, Takeshiro, et al. 2014. "Genome-Wide SNP Analysis Reveals Population Structure and Demographic History of the Ryukyu Islanders in the Southern Part of the Japanese Archipelago." *Modern Biological Evolution* 31, no. 11:2929–40.

Schottenhammer, Angela, ed. 2005. *Trade and Transfer Across the East Asian "Mediterranean."* Wiesbaden: Harrassowitz.

Serafim, Leon A., and Rumiko Shinzato. 2021. *The Language of the Old-Okinawan Omoro Sōshi: Reference Grammar, with Textual Selections*. Leiden: Brill.

Seyock, Barbara. 2005. "Pirates and Traders on Tsushima Island during the Late 14th to Early 16th Century: As Seen from Historical and Archaeological Perspectives." In *Trade and Transfer Across the East Asian "Mediterranean,"* ed. Angela Schottenhammer, 91–124. Wiesbaden: Harrassowitz.

Shimamura Kōichi (島村幸一). 2010. *Omoro sōshi to Ryūkyū bungaku* (『おもろさうし』と琉球文学). Kasama shoin.

Shimizu Nobuyuki (清水信行). 1998. "Kankoku Ronsangun Kaitaiji shutsdo meibum kawara ni tsuite no ikkōsatsu" (韓国論山郡開泰寺出土銘文瓦についての一考察). *Nihon kōkogaku* (日本考古学) 5, no. 5:19–46.

Shimono Toshimi (下野敏見). 1999. *Minzokugaku kara gen Nihon o miru* (民俗学から原日本を見る). Yoshikawa kōbunkan.

———. 2005. *Amami, Tokara no dentō bunka: Matsuri to noro, seikatsu* (奄美、吐噶喇の伝統文化: 祭りとノロ、生活). Kagoshima: Nanpō shinsha.

———. 2013. *Amami shotō no minzoku bunkashi* (奄美諸島の民族文化誌). Kagoshima: Nanpō shinsha.

Shinoda Ken'ichi (篠田謙一). 2018. "DNA kara mita Nansei shotō shūdan no seiritsu" (DNAから見た南西諸島集団の成立). In *Amami, Okinawa shotō senshigaku no saizensen* (奄美・沖縄諸島先史学の最前線), ed. Takamiya Hiroto (高宮広土), 69–84. Kagoshima: Nanpō shinsha.

Shinoda, Ken-ichi, and Naomi Doi. 2008. "Mitochondria DNA Analysis of Human Skeletal Remains Obtained from the Old Tomb of Suubaru: Genetic Characteristics of the Westernmost Island Japan." *Bulletin of the National Museum of Nature and Science: Series D, Anthropology* 34:11–18.

Shinoda, Ken-ichi, Tsuneo Kakuda, and Naomi Doi. 2012. "Mitochondrial DNA Polymorphisms in Late Shell Midden Period Skeletal Remains Excavated from Two Archaeological Sites in Okinawa." *Bulletin of the National Museum of Nature and Science: Series D, Anthropology* 38:51–61.

Shirakihara Kazumi (白木原和美). 1992. "Ryūkyūko no kōkogaku: Amami to Okinawa o chūshin ni" (琉球弧の考古学: 奄美と沖縄を中心に). In *Ryūkyūko no sekai* (琉球弧の世界), ed. Tanigawa Ken'ichi (谷川健一), 88–129. Shōgakkan.

"60% of Locals Say US Base Burden on Okinawa 'Unfair,' but Figure Lower Nationwide: Poll." 2022. *The Mainichi*, May 12.

Smits, Gregory. 1996. "The Intersection of Politics and Thought in Ryukyuan Confucianism: Sai On's Uses of Quan." *Harvard Journal of Asiatic Studies* 56, no. 2 (December): 443–77.

———. 1997a. "Sai On no gakutō to shisō: toku ni bukkyō/shaka ron o chūshin to shite" (蔡温の学統と思想: 特に仏教・釈迦論を中心として). *Okinawa bunka kenkyū*, no. 23 (March): 1–38.

———. 1997b. "Unspeakable Things: Ryukyuan Confucian Sai On's Ambivalent Critique of Language and Buddhism." *Japanese Journal of Religious Studies* 24, nos. 1–2 (Spring): 163–78.

———. 2010a. "Guiding Horses with Rotten Reins: Economic Thought in the Eighteenth-Century Kingdom of Ryukyu." In *Economic Thought in Early Modern Japan*, ed. Bettina Gramlich-Oka and Gregory Smits, 67–88. Leiden: Brill.

———. 2010b. "Sai On no jugakuteki shakai no kōchiku" (蔡温の儒学的社会の構築). *Higashi-Ajia kaiiki kōryūshi, genchi chōsa kenkyū: Chiiki, kankyō, shinsei* (東アジア海域交流史、現地調査研究: 地域・環境・心性), no. 4:94–102.

———. 2011. *Ryūkyū ōkoku no jigazō: Kinsei Okinawa shisōshi* (琉球王国の自画像: 近世沖縄思想史). Translated by Watanabe Miki. Perikansha. A Japanese translation of Gregory Smits, *Visions of Ryukyu: Identity and Ideology in Early-Modern Thought and Politics* (Honolulu: University of Hawai'i Press, 1999).

———. 2015b. "Rethinking Ryukyu." *International Journal of Okinawa Studies* 6, no. 10 (December): 1–19.

Sūn Wěi (孫薇). 2016. *Chūgoku kara mita ko-Ryūkyū no sekai* (中国から見た古琉球の世界). Naha: Ryūkyū shinpōsha.

Suzuki Mitsuo (鈴木満男). 1994. *Kan Higashi-shinakai no kodai girei: Kyoju tōkai jōdo,*

soshite mizu no rei to no seikon (環東シナ海の古代儀礼: 巨樹, 東海浄土, そして水
の霊との聖婚). Dai'ichi shobō.

Takahashi Ichirō (高橋一郎). 1998. *Unabara no Heike denshō: Amami setsuwa no genzō*
(海原の平家伝承: 奄美説話の原像). Miyai shoten.

Takamiya Hiroto (高宮広土). 2021. *Kiseki no shimajima no shenshigaku: Ryūkyū rettō
senshi, genshi jidai no tōsho bunmei* (奇跡の島々の先史学: 琉球列島先史・
原史時代の島嶼文明). Naha: Bōdaainku.

Takanashi Osamu (高梨修). 2005. *Yakōgai no kōkogaku* (ヤコウガイの考古学).
Dōseisha.

Takara Kurayoshi (高良倉吉). 1980. *Ryūkyū no jidai: Ōinaru rekishizō o megutte*
(琉球の時代: 大いなる歴史像をめぐって). Chikuma shobō.

Tanaka Fumio (田中史男). 2008. "Kodai no Amami, Okinawa shotō to kokusai shakai"
(古代の奄美・沖縄諸島と国際社会). In *Kodai chūsei no ryōkai: Kikaigashima no
sekai* (古代中世の境界領域: キカイガシマの世界), ed. Ikeda Yoshifumi (池田
栄史), 49–70. Kōshi shoin.

Tanaka Takeo (田中健夫). 1997. *Higashi Ajia tsūkōken to kokusai ninshiki* (東アジア
通交圏と国際認識). Yoshikawa kōbunkan.

———. 2012/2015. *Wakō: Umi no rekishi* (倭寇: 海の歴史). Kōdansha gakujutsu bunko.

Tanigawa Ken'ichi (谷川健一). 1992. "'Ko-Ryūkyū' izen no sekai: Nantō no fūdo to
seikatsu bunka" (「古琉球」以前の世界: 南島の風土と生活文化). In *Ryūkyūko
no sekai* (琉球弧の世界), ed. Tanigawa Ken'ichi (谷川健一), 9–66. Shōgakkan.

———, ed. 1995. *Nihon minzoku bunka shiryō shūsei, dai nijūichi kan: Mori no kami no
minzokushi* (日本民族文化資料集成、第二十一巻: 森の神の民族誌). San'ichi
shobō.

———. 2006. *Tanigawa Ken'ichi zenshū*. Vol. 5, *Okinawa 1: Nantō bungaku hassei ron*
(谷川健一全集5沖縄1: 南島文学発生論). Fuzanbō intaanashonaru.

———. 2007. *Tanigawa Ken'ichi zenshū*. Vol. 6, *Okinawa 2: Nantō bungaku hassei ron*
(谷川健一全集6沖縄2: 南島文学発生論). Fuzanbō intaanashonaru.

———. 2010. *Rettō jūdan, chimei shōyō* (列島縦断、地名逍遥). Fuzanbō
intaanashonaru.

Uehara Shizuka (上原静). 2003. "Buki, bugu no yōsō" (武器・武具の様相). In *Okinawa kenshi, kakuronhen*, vol. 2, *Kōko* (沖縄県史、各論篇 2 : 考古), ed. Okinawa-
ken bunka shinkōkai kōmonjo kanribu shiryō henshūshitsu (沖縄県文化振興会公
文書管理部、史料編集室), 315–23. Naha: Okinawa-ken kyōiku iinkai.

Ueunten, Wesley. 2010. "Rising up from a Sea of Discontent: The 1970 Koza Uprising
in U.S.-Occupied Okinawa." In *Militarized Currents: Toward a Decolonized Future
in Asia and the Pacific*, ed. Setsu Shigematsu and Keith Camacho, 91–124. St. Paul:
University of Minnesota Press.

Uezato Takashi (上里隆史). 2008. "The Formation of the Port City of Naha in Ryukyu
and the World of Maritime Asia: From the Perspective of a Japanese Network." In
"Studies of Medieval Ryukyu within Asia's Maritime Network," special issue, *Acta
Asiatica*, no. 95:57–77.

Wada Hisanori (和田久徳). 2006. *Ryūkyū ōkoku no keisei: Sanzan tōitsu to sono zengo*
(琉球王国の形成: 三山統一とその前後). Ginowan: Yōju shorin.

Wheelan, Joseph. 2020. *Bloody Okinawa: The Last Great Battle of World War II*. New
York: Hachette.

World Heritage: Gusuku Sites and Related Properties of the Kingdom of the Ryukyus
(*Sekai isan: Ryūkyū ōkoku no gusuku oyobi kanren isangun*, 世界遺産: 琉球王国

のグスク及び関連遺産群). Edited by Culture Department, Okinawa Prefectural Education Bureau, Executive Committee for Commemoration Registration. Naha: Muramasa.

Yakabi Osamu (屋嘉比収). 2010. *Kindai Okinawa no chishikijin: Shimabukuro Zenpatsu no kiseki* (近代沖縄の知識人島袋全発の軌跡). Yoshikawa kōbunkan.

Yamamoto Hirofumi (山本弘文). 1999. *Nantō keizaishi no kenkyū* (南島経済史の研究). Hōsei daigaku shuppankyoku.

Yamashita Kin'ichi (山下欣一). 2003. *Nantō minkan shinwa no kenkyū* (南島民間神話の研究). Dai'ichi shobō.

Yoshinari Naoki (吉成直樹). 2009. "Gusuku jidai izen no Ryūkyū no zaichi shūdan: Gengo, shinwa, DNA" (グスク時代以前の琉球の在地集団: 言語・神話・DNA). In *Okinawa bunka wa dokokara kita ka: Gusuku jidai toiu kakki* (沖縄文化はどこから来たか: グスク時代という画期), by Takanashi Osamu (高梨修), Abe Minako (阿部美奈子), Nakamoto ken (中本謙), and Yoshinari Nakoki (吉成直樹). Shinwasha.

———. 2022. *Ryūkyū kenkoku shi no nazo o otte: Kōeki shakai to wakō* (琉球建国史の謎を追って: 交易社会と倭寇). Shichigatsusha.

Index

www.ingramcontent.com/pod-product-compliance
Lightning Source LLC
Chambersburg PA
CBHW022129020426
42334CB00015B/823